A Summary of Christian History

ROBERT A. BAKER

A SUMMARY OF

CHRISTIAN HISTORY

BROADMAN PRESS • Nashville, Tennessee

Dedicated with love

to

the REVEREND FRED A. and
MRS. ONA HARRIS MCCAULLEY,
faithful witnesses of Jesus

© 1959 • BROADMAN PRESS
Nashville, Tennessee

All rights reserved
International copyright secured

270

ISBN: 0-8054-6502-2

4265-02

Library of Congress catalog card number: 59-5852

Printed in the United States of America

Preface

For sixteen years a part of my work has involved the teaching of a rapid survey of church history to a group who has had little previous background in the field. While it was in print, W. J. Mc-Glothlin's book *The Course of Christian History* was used. The present summary was begun a decade ago as a temporary make-shift until a suitable text could be located. The fine one-volume texts that have appeared in the meantime have been too encyclo-pedic and full for this group.

I have tried to tell this story as briefly as possible. Brevity, in fact, is at the same time the merit and the weakness of the sum-mary. It has been most difficult to distinguish between the neces-sary and the desirable. Here the main stream of Christian history is greatly telescoped, and many important fringe areas are omitted altogether. It may be that my surgery was too radical, but, if so, perhaps the bibliographies will provide the remedy.

The material in this work is the common stock of all church his-torians. I am indebted to everyone for it. An effort has been made to incorporate as far as possible the results of the latest research in the various periods, but generally speaking, this same story in more detail and larger sweep is found in every standard history. For that reason documentation would be superfluous, although the interpretations have an undeniable evangelical bias. The bib-liography following each period will provide additional help for the student desiring to secure more knowledge of that section. These works in turn have detailed bibliographies for additional study, if desired. From this general summary, then, a student may step through additional doors to specialized study of almost unlimited extent. On the other hand, if the reader is the average "man in the street" who simply wants a glimpse of the general stream of Christian history, this work may be useful to him.

One change has been introduced in the general outline. Usually the Reformation period is dated from 1517 when Luther prepared his Ninety-five Theses, but one cannot properly understand the Reformation without a great deal of background before 1517. This background has been inserted into the Reformation section. Since the radical collapse of papal prestige in the Avignon visit and papal schism, along with the almost universal clamor for reform, followed nearly immediately the achievement by the Roman Church of its highest pre-eminence as exemplified in the Fourth Lateran Council of 1215, that date has been chosen as the dividing line between the height of Roman Catholic domination and the antecedents of reform. It makes the picture clearer.

Contents

List of Maps

I. PERIOD OF CHRISTIAN BEGINNINGS (4 B.C. to A.D. 100)

Introduction to the Period

Jesus Christ was born between 6 and 4 B.C. The error in dating his birth occurred because time was not calculated according to Christ's birth until the sixth century. A mistake of several years was made during the process of numbering back. The Mediterranean world was ruled by the Roman Empire at the time of Jesus Christ's birth. Their armies had overrun Palestine about sixty years before. For most of that time the ruler of Palestine was Herod the Great. When Herod died in 4 B.C., Palestine was divided so that his three sons might share authority. Philip ruled over the extreme northeastern area east of Jordan; Herod Antipas ruled in Galilee and Perea. Both of these men were in office during Christ's ministry and are referred to in the Scriptures. Archelaus, the third son of Herod, received the large central section of Palestine (Judea, Idumea, and Samaria), but was removed from office by the Roman emperor in A.D. 6. Roman governors or procurators were appointed to rule this portion of Palestine. During the entire ministry of Christ the procurator was Pontius Pilate (A.D. 26–36), also mentioned in the Scriptures.

Christianity spread rapidly during the first century. The end of the period (A.D. 100) finds it growing, pure in doctrine, and relatively unaffected by the destruction of what had been its home base.

Points of Special Interest

The student should notice the divine preparation for the revelation in Christ, not alone in Judaism but in other great races also. He should also keep in mind the New Testament pattern of a functioning church, its local character, its officers, its organization, and its autonomy. It is in these matters, as well as in doctrine, that later developments turn away from the original pattern.

1

1

The Beginnings of Historical Christianity

ANY THOUGHTFUL PERSON will look with real curiosity at the description of the apostle Paul in Acts 21:37–40. Paul had stirred up his customary riot, this time in the Temple at Jerusalem, and was only saved from severe injury at the hands of the Jewish mob by the intervention of the Roman soldiers patrolling the city. As Paul endeavors to speak to the people from the stairs of the prison castle, four aspects of his life are presented in quick succession: (1) He spoke the Greek language and was a citizen of a city noted for its Greek culture. (2) He was a Roman citizen (notice Acts 22:25–29, along with 21:39). (3) He was a Jew and was fluent in the Hebrew tongue. (4) He was a Christian, bearing testimony of the Master to his own race.

The diverse racial, linguistic, and religious elements reflected here are intelligible only as the background of Paul is understood. Here is the function of church history—to explain *why* and *how*. It is impossible to interpret Paul or any part of Christianity without an understanding of the historical background. For the New Testament period this includes Greek, Roman, and Jewish influences. Customs, parties, traditions, and allusions that are meaningless unless they are explained in historical terms constantly crop up in the New Testament.

Greek Influence on Christianity

The Greek elements in the world into which Christianity came may be traced to the conquest of Palestine (and almost all of the known world) by Alexander the Great in the last half of the fourth century before Christ. This Macedonian soldier scattered into almost every part of the known world the tremendous culture and spirit of the Greeks. After Alexander's death his military generals and their successors ruled Palestine for over a century and a half. Without attempting to relate the remarkable history of Greek life and development, the outstanding contributions of that race to the Christian movement may be summed up under three heads.

First, Greek philosophy, some good and some bad, was scattered everywhere. Strangely enough, God used both the good and the bad to prepare for the coming of Christ. The atheistic and skeptical philosophy of the Greeks turned many in the Gentile world away from the superstitious worship of false gods and intensified their heart-hunger for the true God. The good Greek philosophy, on the other hand, prepared the world for the coming of Christ by magnifying the worth of the human spirit and by placing high value upon spiritual and moral truth.

In the second place, the Greek language became the common tongue throughout the whole Mediterranean world. Even in Palestine good Jews were forced to learn the Greek language in order to carry on trade in the markets. The fact is of more importance than might appear at first glance. For one thing, the missionaries of Christ could begin their work immediately without waiting to learn a new language. Furthermore, the presence of a common language brought a sense of unity to the various races. Compare the present-day slang expression "he speaks my language," suggesting a basic unity. Finally, the language itself was marvelously adequate. The Greeks had developed a language that made it possible to express clearly and precisely the great truths of the Christian revelation. Greek was the language of most (if not all) of the New Testament.

Third, the Greek spirit made its contribution to the Christian movement. It is difficult to put this spirit into words, but it included an intense love for truth, vision that encompassed large sweep, and initiative that was bold and daring.

3

Roman Influence on Christianity

The constant protection afforded Paul because he was a Roman citizen suggests the contribution of the Roman Empire to the Christian movement. Historically, Greek rule in Palestine ended about 167 B.C. when the Jewish patriots under Judas Maccabeus defeated the Greeks. In 63 B.C., after Jewish independence of about a century, the soldiers of Rome took possession of Palestine. A glance at the New Testament reveals evidence of Roman rule. It speaks of Roman centurions, Roman guards, Roman jailers, Roman castles, Roman governors. One of the questions which the Pharisees asked Jesus concerned whether a good Jew could serve God under Roman rule. The unpopularity of Matthew, the publican, grew out of the fact that he was collecting taxes for Rome.

Roman rule in the world when Jesus was born was not altogether good nor completely bad in its effect upon Christianity. The strong centralized government of Rome provided a measure of peace and protection. Rome would not permit any sort of violence to take place within the borders of her empire, lest the uproar should serve as a cloak for political revolt. This made it possible for Christian missionaries to move among the various races of the Mediterranean world with a minimum of political friction. Roman citizens like Paul were protected from unjust treatment by local officers. The network of Roman roads and ship routes made travel less hazardous and more convenient. Two hundred years later the language of the Romans would be adopted as the principal medium for religious expression.

On the other hand, the world government of Rome became the great enemy of Christianity before the end of the first century. It will be noted that the Roman mind had little conception of the value of an individual soul, choosing, rather, to exhaust religious devotion in the service of the state. The Roman armies adopted the false gods of every nation whom they conquered, only requiring that in return the subjugated nation accept Roman gods, including the Roman emperor. When Christians refused to worship the Roman emperor, severe persecution was inflicted.

Jewish Influence on Christianity

The third racial influence upon the Christian movement was the most significant. The Jewish nation provided the immediate background of Christ and all of his early disciples. The history of the Jews as related in the Old Testament is too well known to be repeated in detail. God chose a family of faith which, under divine care, developed into a nation. Several factors combined to bring political division about 975 B.C. The Northern Kingdom was carried into Assyrian captivity about 722 B.C. The Southern Kingdom stood until about 587 B.C. when it officially fell to the Babylonians. After about seventy years, remnants of the Southern Kingdom were permitted by the Persian empire to return to Palestine. They remained subject to the Persians until about 334 B.C., when Alexander the Great conquered them. The Greek period (334–167 B.C.), the century of Jewish independence (167–63 B.C.), and the beginning of Roman rule (63 B.C.) bring the history of the Jewish people to the New Testament era.

During this long history the Jewish people were, to some extent unconsciously, making preparation for the coming of Christ. They carefully preserved the revelation which God had given them. Through adversity and captivity two great truths were burned into their souls: first, that there is only one God for men; and second, that the relationship of God to men is personal, not national. Before the Babylonian captivity the Jews had often fallen into idolatry and polytheism, but after their return to Palestine they became zealous teachers of the truth that God is one (monotheism). While residents of Palestine, the Jews had sometimes conceived of God in national terms, but in captivity their isolation from every material reminder of a national deity brought them to realize that the *individual* must commune with God through the spirit. It was worth the experiences of the Babylonian captivity to learn this lesson.

Although some, like Jonah, were reluctant to witness to Gentiles, the entire world became familiar with the beliefs and practices of the Jews. Early in the Greek period a movement known as the

Dispersion began. This was the voluntary movement of great numbers of Jews from Palestine to almost every part of the Mediterranean world. Wherever they went the Jews made numerous proselytes to their religion, establishing synagogues for teaching God's revelation, witnessing to the sovereignty of one God, and looking into the heavens for the Messiah. This leaven prepared the world for Christ's coming.

The Jewish institutions and parties that form so much a part of the New Testament story have their background in these historical experiences. The synagogue was developed as a place of teaching and worship during the Babylonian captivity when there was no temple available. The prominent place that it held after the return of the Jews from the exile brought into existence the groups known as scribes and lawyers. Their chief duty at first was to copy Scriptures; because they became experts in what the Scriptures said, their duties were enlarged to include scriptural interpretation and instruction.

Perhaps the contact between the Jews and the Persian religious ideas helped to produce the party known as the Essenes, which probably arose about 150 B.C. This group numbered about four thousand at the time of Christ and was characterized by rigorous orthodoxy, celibacy, communal ownership, and the elimination of animal sacrifices in worship. The Pharisees doubtless grew out of the separatist tendency when the overtures of the Samaritans were rejected during the days of Ezra and Nehemiah (about 500 B.C.). During the Maccabean struggle (beginning about 167 B.C.), this party took distinct form. In the New Testament they are pictured as narrow, bigoted, and to some extent hypocritical. They were numerous and popular in the time of Jesus, rallying to traditional supernaturalism and ceremonial exactness. The Sadducees probably arose during the second century before Christ. Friendly to Roman and Greek culture, they represented religious and political liberalism. Their rationalism led them to deny the resurrection and divine providence, to refuse all tradition, and to magnify the freedom of the human will.

The Samaritans arose through the intermarriage of Jews who

had been left in Palestine after the beginning of the Babylonian captivity with Gentiles who had been brought into the land. The Herodians were the Jewish political patriots who supported the Herod family against Rome. The Zealots were probably the heirs of the Maccabean tradition of fervent zeal to throw off the yoke of foreigners.

Jesus Christ (4 B.C.–A.D. 30)

Into this sort of world Jesus Christ was born. Practically all that is known of his earthly life may be found in the Synoptic Gospels (Matthew, Mark, and Luke) and in John. John's Gospel describes Jesus' eternal nature and preincarnate existence; Matthew and Luke record his human genealogy. It is likely that Matthew gives the genealogy of Joseph while Luke deals with the genealogy of Mary. Matthew and Luke alone recount the birth and childhood of Jesus and of John the Baptist, the forerunner of Jesus. All of the Gospels speak of John's ministry and look from different points of view at the life of Christ.

The birth of Jesus Christ occurred about 4 B.C. This means that Christ actually began his public ministry about A.D. 27 and was crucified about A.D. 30. The Lord's ministry may be conveniently divided into seven sections. (1) His early Judean ministry, described principally in John's Gospel, includes the calling of the first disciples and the first cleansing of the Temple. (2) The great Galilean ministry covers the principal period of Christ's work and lasted about a year and a half. During this time the Lord was rejected at Nazareth, moved to Capernaum, chose the twelve apostles, set forth the Sermon on the Mount, and toured Galilee three times. (3) His several withdrawals from the press of the crowds gave opportunity for special instruction to the disciples, for securing the great confession at Caesarea Philippi, and for the transfiguration experience. (4) His later Judean ministry continued for about three months and is described by Luke and John. It centered on the attendance of Jesus and his disciples at the Feasts of Tabernacles and Dedication in Jerusalem. (5) His brief Perean ministry is spoken of by all four of the Gospels and

7

is characterized by final miracles, parables, and prophecies of his resurrection. (6) The last week in Jerusalem is treated in great detail by John's Gospel. It begins with the triumphal entry and closes with the crucifixion. (7) The postresurrection ministry of Jesus for about forty days before his ascension marks the close of the Gospel accounts.

The teachings of Jesus are remarkable both in their method and content. He drove home truth through parables, questions, discourses, and debates. God's person and purpose were revealed in Christ's life and teachings. Love is to be the dominant theme of the Christian's life. Because God loved men, Christ died on the cross for man's sins; by personal trust in Christ, men could receive a birth from above and assurance of eternal life. The conquering power of the cross and the ultimate triumph of the kingdom of God were central in Christ's teachings. He established his church, a local autonomous body where two or three gathering together in prayer could find his presence and power.

After the death and ascension of Christ, the disciples whom he had chosen and instructed set out on the seemingly impossible task contained in the Great Commission. Despite efforts of many other religions to attract men, Christianity began growing like a mustard seed. From a human standpoint, many reasons may be advanced for this tremendous development. (1) Heathenism was bankrupt and could not answer the call of hungry hearts. (2) The great welter of religions of every description clamoring for devotees could not compete with God's revelation in Christ. (3) Every Christian became a missionary; the sacred fire leaped from friend to friend. (4) The Christians had a burning conviction that Christ alone could save the lost world about them and that since the return of Christ was imminent, there was no time to be lost.

The seventy years of Christian growth from Christ's death to that of the last apostle may be divided into three periods.

Period of Local Witnessing (A.D. 30–45)

The first twelve chapters of Acts describe the history of the Christian movement during the first fifteen years after Christ's death and resurrection. The Holy Spirit was given in accordance with the promise of Christ, providing power for witnessing in a hostile world, bringing the presence of Christ for fellowship and strength, and giving leadership from Christ in the initiation of important movements. At Pentecost men from every part of the world were saved and doubtless went back to their own cities to establish Christian churches. Persecution, want, and internal bickering were only temporary hurdles (see Acts 3–6).

The martyrdom of Stephen marks a turning point in two respects: it began the persecution that drove the Christians out of Jerusalem into all Judea and Samaria in their witness; and it profoundly moved Saul the persecutor in the direction of personal conversion to Christ. The local witness was expanded by the preaching of Peter to a Gentile (for which he was required to give explanation to the church at Jerusalem), the founding of the Gentile church at Antioch, and the martyrdom of James, son of Zebedee. The conversion of Saul, his preparation for service, and his ministry at Antioch provide the background for the second stage of Christian development.

Period of Missionary Expansion (A.D. 45–68)

Under the leadership of the Holy Spirit a new direction of witnessing was begun with the inauguration of the missionary tours of Paul and Barnabas. Paul is the central figure in at least three great missionary tours between the years 45 and 58, when he was seized in the Temple at Jerusalem. During these thirteen years he wrote two letters to the church at Thessalonica, two to the Corinthians, one to the Galatians, and one to the Romans. After his imprisonment in Rome about A.D. 61 he wrote the letters known as Philemon, Colossians, Ephesians, and Philippians. He probably was released for four or five years, but the extent of his travel during this time is not known. His two letters known as 1 Timothy and Titus were prepared in this interim. Tradition suggests that he may have gone as far west as Spain on one journey. He was imprisoned again about 67 at Rome. Just before his death at the hands of Nero he wrote 2 Timothy.

It is quite possible that tradition is correct in speaking of extensive missionary activity by other apostles, but such accounts are too meager and too far removed from the occasion to be of much value. It is known that Paul's missionary activity accounts for the rise of practically all of the important Christian centers of the first century. Churches were established through his efforts in some of the strongest cities of the empire.

Between the first and second missionary journeys, Paul and Silas attended a conference at Jerusalem (about 50). James presided at the meeting, and several discussed the question of whether a man needs to become a Jew first in order to become a Christian. After some, including the apostle Peter, had spoken, James gave his decision that any Gentile could find salvation by simple faith in Christ without going through Judaism.

During this period, which closes with the death of the apostle Paul at Rome in A.D. 68, nine other books that form the New Testament were written. These were James, Mark, Matthew, Luke, Acts, 1 Peter, Jude, 2 Peter, and Hebrews, perhaps in that order.

Period of Westward Growth (A.D. 68–100)

After Paul's death the center of Christian strength moved toward the western section of the Mediterranean area. Although the material for this period is scarce, it is not difficult to find reasons to substantiate the tradition of the westward move. About the year 66 the Jewish War broke out in Palestine, resulting in the complete destruction of Jerusalem in 70 at the hands of the Roman Titus. This catastrophe marked the end of Herod's Temple and the sacrifices of the Jews; at the same time it uprooted the Christian church in Jerusalem and scattered the people abroad. In which direction should Christianity move? Tradition reports that the apostle John went to Ephesus about the time Jerusalem was destroyed. This is plausible, since the most logical move would be toward the great church centers in the West established by the apostle Paul. Here and there in later literature are hints that Christians may have gone to every part of the western Mediterranean. The tradition of Christianity in Britain is very early; perhaps one of the soldiers chained to the apostle Paul was won by him to Christ and then transferred to the British garrison, there to witness and organize a Christian church. Possibly a similar situation sent the good news to central Europe, North Africa, and elsewhere to the fringes of the Roman Empire.

Conservative scholars assign five books by the apostle John to this period. Written by a "son of thunder," these books contain warnings against diluting Christianity and minimizing either the humanity or the deity of Christ. The advocates of such heretical views cannot be identified, but their presence is significant in view of the rise of these very doctrinal aberrations in the next century. Apparently John was exiled to the Isle of Patmos from Ephesus during the course of a severe persecution by the Roman Emperor Domitian (81–96). The book of Revelation, defying the effort of the Roman Empire to require Christians to worship the Roman emperor, was written in the closing decade of the apostolic period.

Concluding Summary

The literature that became the New Testament canon had not as yet been brought together into one book. The various churches used the Old Testament, together with such Christian writings as they might possess. The evidence shows that at the close of the century the Christian movement was pure in doctrine and growing in numbers. It is true that there were efforts on every hand to dilute the nature of Christianity, but apostolic leadership helped to maintain a strong internal unity.

The functioning New Testament church showed no signs of developing into an ecclesiastical hierarchy or spiritual despotism. It was a local autonomous body with two officers and two ordinances. The two officers were pastor (sometimes called bishop, presbyter or elder, minister, shepherd) and deacon. These leaders usually worked with their hands for their material needs. There was no artificial distinction between clergy and laity. The pastors had no more authority in offering salvation through Christ than

11

did any other member of their body. Their distinguishing marks were the gifts of leadership given them through the Spirit and their willingness to be used of God. In view of the later pretensions of the Roman pastor or bishop, it should be mentioned that each church was completely independent of external control. There is no indication anywhere in the literature of this period that the apostle Peter ever served as pastor in Rome; nor, for that matter, is there any basis for believing that the church at Rome was founded by any apostle. Doubtless it was organized by men converted at Pentecost.

The two ordinances were baptism and the Lord's Supper. These were simply symbolical memorials. Salvation or spiritual gifts did not come through either one. The transference of spiritual regeneration and spiritual merit to these ordinances is a development that comes through later corruptions. Worship was simple, consisting of the singing of hymns, praying, reading of Scriptures, and exhortations.

BIBLIOGRAPHY

ANGUS, SAMUEL. *The Environment of Early Christianity*. New York: Charles Scribner's Sons, 1920.

BETTENSON, HENRY (ed.). *Documents of the Christian Church*. New York: Oxford University Press, 1947.

BOUQUET, A. C. *Everyday Life in New Testament Times*. London: B. T. Batsford, Ltd., 1953.

GRANT, CHARLES M. *Between the Testaments*. New York: Fleming H. Revell Co., n.d.

HESTER, H. I. *The Heart of the New Testament*. Liberty, Missouri: William Jewell Publishers, 1950.

LATOURETTE, K. S. *A History of Christianity*. New York: Harper & Brothers, 1953.

NEWMAN, A. H. *A Manual of Church History*, I. Philadelphia: American Baptist Publication Society, 1953.

STEVENSON, J. (ed.). *A New Eusebius*. New York: The Macmillan Co., 1957.

II. PERIOD OF PAGAN DOMINATION
(A.D. 100–325)

Introduction to the Period

The story of Christianity between 100 and 325 reveals a period of extreme peril to the movement. Two dangers confronted it: (1) hostility and violence from the pagan government; (2) corruption and division within.

From the outside the principal danger came from the Roman Empire. After the close of the apostolic era (A.D. 100), Roman emperors viewed Christianity as an outlaw. It meant death to bear the name Christian. On two occasions during the period determined efforts were made to exterminate Christianity throughout the world. Relief came when Constantine espoused the Christian cause—perhaps from political motives—and fought his way to the place of sole emperor in 323. This period closes with the first world council of Christians at Nicea in 325, when Christianity began to develop in a new direction.

Within Christianity the danger of corruption and division grew out of its close relationship with Jewish and pagan movements. Christianity was influenced internally by its environment. Sometimes the reaction from fighting heresy was as harmful as the corruption.

This period is discussed in three chapters—one describing the struggle against outside forces, one describing the struggle against internal corruptions, and one summarizing the condition of Christianity in 325.

Points of Special Interest

Several matters should claim the student's attention and interest in the study of this period. He should notice the sort of response that was made by the Christians when they were persecuted—no military action like that of the Jews, no general compromise of principle to the pagan state, but the development of an effective literature to enlighten the persecutors, and the display of Christian fortitude and constant testimony. He should notice also the gradual infiltration of error, as displayed in the writings of the second century. No violent change can be dated, but the Christian vocabulary began to take on new meanings

WHY NOT TODAY ?

13

and to be enlarged rapidly, marking radical changes from the New Testament pattern and innovations in all Christian areas. He should carefully weigh the influence of the various parties in the pagan environment of Christianity, noticing the transferring of ideas.

2

Pagan Opposition to Christianity

THE PRINCIPAL OPPONENTS of Christ in the New Testament were
Jews. His followers during the next several centuries found their
most formidable foes to be Romans. It may be noticed that the
writings of Paul do not speak unfavorably of the Roman government. This does not mean that Rome was friendly to Christianity.
It is doubtful that Rome at first even recognized that Christianity
would develop into a movement separate from Judaism. The
Jewish War of 66–70 accentuated the difference between the two,
however, for the Christians refused to join in the Jewish insurrec-
tion. Christians were never in doubt about the fact that their
worship of Christ was completely incompatible with the demands
of the Roman government for all faithful citizens to worship the
Roman emperor.

The death of Paul was occasioned more by the caprice of the
Emperor Nero than any policy of persecuting Christians. Nero
(54–68) had set fire to Rome. In order to shift blame from himself,
he accused Christians of burning the city and brutally slaughtered
them. The second pagan persecution, under Domitian (81–96),
was not a universal movement against Christianity as such but was
directed against anyone who would not worship the emperor,
which, of course, included the Christians. The last book of the
New Testament, written in the closing decade of the first century,
names the Roman Empire with its emperor worship as the very
opponent of God.

After the first century the opposition to Christianity took three
general forms—popular antagonism, intellectual assaults, and
physical persecution.

15

Popular Antagonism

Despite its remarkable growth, Christianity was not a popular movement in the second century. Its character, so altogether different from anything known by the people of the Roman Empire, made it an object of suspicion and hate. It offended the people religiously, ethically, and economically. The religious aspect of Christian unpopularity took strange forms. During the second century an unusual number of floods, earthquakes, and other natural catastrophes occurred. Immediately the populace cursed the Christians. The old gods are displeased with us and are punishing us, they said, because of this new religion. Either wilfully or ignorantly, the pagans twisted the vocabulary of the Christians to involve atheism (no idols), cannibalism (eating the Lord's body and drinking his blood), immorality (growing out of a sensual conception of the word "love"), and magic and sorcery (in the Supper and baptism).

The large gulf between the ethical ideas of the Christian and those of the pagans constantly exposed Christianity to the ire of the people. Christians refused to attend the immoral and brutal shows and contests, refused to murder their young children by abandoning them in a lonely place, refused to live by standards which magnified lust and material possessions.

The exclusiveness of Christianity caused it to become an offense economically. Christians refused to recognize any other gods. In so doing they struck at several well-established types of business in the communities where they lived. Those who manufactured pagan idols or raised animals for pagan sacrifices found that Christianity was hurting their business. Like Demetrius the silversmith (Acts 19:24), they opposed vehemently the movement that touched them at such a sensitive point.

Intellectual Assaults

The intellectual assaults on Christianity represent one of its severest struggles and greatest victories. Pagan writers, skilled in logical argumentation and trained in the best scholarship of the revived classical era, leveled against Christianity every criticism that modern infidels and agnostics have used. With ridicule and sarcasm they scornfully attacked Christian beliefs about the person of Christ and his miracles and resurrection, the truth and authority of the Christian Scriptures, grace, regeneration, heaven and hell, and immortality. The principal names in the attack were Celsus and Porphyro, Greek philosophers of the second and third centuries respectively.

In a sense these literary attacks were disguised blessings to Christianity. They stirred up the Christians to produce literary monuments to second-century Christianity. Christians had already produced some literature. The edificatory writings of the second century will be discussed in the next chapter. The external attacks upon Christianity called forth a group of writings known as apologies; the internal struggle for purity resulted in writings known as polemics; while both the external and internal struggles helped to bring forth the systematic expositions of Christian beliefs. In this chapter the apologetical writings only will be discussed.

The Apologists.—The group of trained writers in the second and third centuries who endeavored to justify the doctrines of Christianity against the attacks of the pagan philosophers were called "apologists." In general, the apologists defended Christianity from charges of atheism, licentiousness, and cannibalism; they linked Christianity with the prophetic Scriptures of the Old Testament to show that the movement was no innovation but was very ancient and respectable.

The principal apologist of the second century was Justin. He was slain as a marytr in 166. Justin was a Samaritan philosopher who was converted to Christianity in his maturity. He retained his philosopher's garb and traveled as an evangelist to the educated class. His great *Apology* was addressed to Emperor Antoninus Pius and adopted son Marcus Aurelius and was prepared about 150. In its first section the *Apology* argues that Christians should not be condemned without a hearing, for they are innocent; they are not atheists, but true worshipers of the true God; they are not dangerous to the political safety of the Roman Empire,

17

but with a wonderful ethic constitute its strength, and their doctrine of the resurrection is most reasonable and glorious. In the second section Justin asserts that Christianity alone has full truth; that in Jesus Christ the Son of God actually became incarnate; and that paganism consists of fables invented by demons. The final section of the *Apology* describes the religious practices of Christianity.

In his imaginary *Dialogue with Trypho the Jew* Justin defends Christianity against Jewish attacks, especially attacks upon the person and work of Christ.

Other prominent apologists of the second century were Quadratus, of Athens, who addressed Emperor Hadrian; Aristides, who addressed the same emperor; Athenagoras, of Athens, who addressed Emperor Marcus Aurelius and the emperor's son Commodus; and Melito, of Sardis, and Apollinaris, of Hierapolis, who addressed Marcus Aurelius.

Although not generally considered apologists, Tertullian (160–220) prepared apologies against paganism and Judaism in behalf of Christianity, and Origen (185–254) wrote his apologetical work *Against Celsus,* probably the ablest production of early Christianity against paganism.

Other results of intellectual assaults.—There were other results from the intellectual assaults against Christianity. For one thing, Christianity became intellectually respectable in a world in which that was very important. Again, these assaults, together with the internal controversies described in the next chapter, helped to show the necessity for an authoritatively recognized canon or collection of inspired writings. For generations the churches had been testing the writings which now comprise the New Testament. Through the leadership of the Holy Spirit and in the crucible of Christian experience they had already indicated their conviction that these writings were inspired of God. It took many decades for the external ecclesiastical machinery to place its official stamp of approval upon the books so collected, but it would seem that this action constituted simply a formality anyway.

Physical Persecution

Jesus had warned his disciples that the world would treat them as it had treated him. If tradition can be trusted, most of the disciples experienced martyrdom. Unnumbered thousands of Christians were slain at the hands of the imperial soldiers during the second and third centuries. The popular hatred of Christianity can be understood in the light of religious, social, and economic tensions. The intellectual assaults on Christianity are understandable, since pagan philosophers attacked any system that differed from their own. But why, it may be asked, should the government of Rome engage in the destruction of its own citizens simply because they were Christians?

The answer is found in the Roman conception of religion. As suggested in the first chapter, Romans practiced religion mainly for political reasons. The religious department was one of the branches of government. Through it attempts were made to appease known and unknown gods and to foretell the future. Christian ideas of morality and personal immortality had no counterpart in the Roman view of religion. Gods were numerous, the Roman state itself claiming deity in the person of the emperor. Conquered nations were required to worship Roman gods, including the emperor. At the same time Rome "legalized" any local gods in these nations so long as the local worship did not interfere with loyalty to the Roman state.

The Jews had been excepted from this general rule because of their spirited refusal to worship any god but Jehovah and because of respect for their great antiquity. When, therefore, Christianity separated itself from Judaism and refused to worship Roman deities, it was officially entitled "an illegal religion." As such, the laws of the Roman Empire demanded prosecution, even though the action seemed to the Christians to be persecution. When the Christians, fearing violence, met secretly for worship, they were accused of the worst crime a Roman could imagine— plotting the overthrow of the government.

Before the close of the apostolic period the Roman government had moved against the Christians. The caprice of Nero brought the persecution in 67–68, which included Paul among its victims. The persecution by Domitian in the last decade of the first century did not constitute a general policy against Christianity but was an attempt to make them conform to the ancient laws. After the close of the apostolic period two types of physical persecution may be identified.

Local and intermittent persecution.—The period from 96 to 180 was one of outward prosperity in the Roman Empire. The five "good" emperors (Nerva, Trajan, Hadrian, Antoninus Pius, and Marcus Aurelius) were comparatively diligent in government and had considerable success in meeting contemporary problems within and without the empire. During the reign of Emperor Trajan (98–117) the imperial pattern for the persecution of Christianity was developed. In 112 Pliny, the Roman governor in the Asia Minor province of Bithynia-Pontus, wrote Trajan a description of how he was handling the superstition known as Christianity. By the use of torture he had learned that the movement was rather harmless, involving mainly the worship of Jesus Christ as God and a resolution to live nobly. Pliny's method had been to demand that Christians deny Christ and leave the sect. Should they refuse after three such requests, they were executed because of their "obstinacy." If they should agree, they were released without further punishment. Trajan's reply commended Pliny's conduct, suggesting that no effort be made to search out the Christians but that if responsible men brought charges, the death penalty should be pronounced upon those who refused to deny the Christian faith. This comparatively lenient pattern was followed in the empire generally for over a century.

The kind of persecution that could have been leveled against Christianity may be glimpsed in the imperial persecution of the Jews. By specific law the Jews were forbidden to practice their religion, including such vital features as the observance of the sabbath and circumcision. As a direct blow at the Jews, the site of Jerusalem was to be made into a Roman city with pagan temples. Enraged beyond reason, the Jews proclaimed a messiah about 132 in the person of Bar Cochba (Son of the Star), and making the destroyed city of Jerusalem their rallying point, they attempted to throw off the Roman yoke. It took the Romans three years to crush the movement, during which about half a million Jews were slaughtered.

So far as the Christians were concerned, however, the policy of the Emperor Trajan was continued under Hadrian (117–38), Antoninus Pius (138–61), and Marcus Aurelius (161–80). Under each of these emperors Christians were slain, in particular under Marcus Aurelius, but there was not yet a worldwide effort to exterminate the Christian movement as such.

Universal attempt at extermination.—Political conditions played a large part in the two efforts by the Roman government to destroy Christianity. The severest persecutions ever directed against the Christians grew out of attempts to restore the ancient glory of the Roman Empire. The "golden age" of the empire was experienced under Augustus (31 B.C.–A.D. 14). Various relatives succeeded him in the office but could not match his accomplishments, and this method of securing an emperor was discontinued with the death of Nero in 68. Vespasian seized the throne as the strongest military commander in 69, and his two sons ruled after him until 96. The Roman senator Nerva was elected by his fellow senators and introduced a new method of imperial succession, not of blood or election but personal selection. Each of the five emperors following Nerva selected his own successor. Following the death of Commodus in 192, the Roman armies named his successor and continued to name the emperors for about a century.

Although all of the reasons for the striking decline of the Roman Empire after the death of Marcus Aurelius (161–80) are not clear, one very important contributing factor was the breakdown at the top—the weakness of imperial leadership. Almost all of the "barracks emperors" secured the throne by violence and were themselves the victims of violence. Internal decay and external aggressors combined to tear away the foundations of the empire.

Christianity entered into this picture because it was conceived as an innovation that in some way had contributed to the general decline of the glory of Rome. Religious pagans attributed all of their ills—natural calamities, heavy taxation, invading barbarians —to the anger of the pagan gods because Christianity was allowed to continue. Some political thinkers, influenced by these attitudes, wondered if the extermination of Christianity would help restore the glory of Rome that had existed before the Christian movement began. These ideas were discussed widely in 248 when the Roman Empire celebrated the one-thousandth anniversary of the founding of the city of Rome. The new emperor, Decius (249–51), decided to attempt a revival of the empire's ancient glory and, among other things, determined to destroy Christianity and restore the worship of the spirit of the Roman state. In 250 an edict was prepared requiring every Christian to deny the faith or be subject to extreme penalties, including death. His successor Valerian (253–60) continued the effort. Many Christians were slain, many were tortured, many compromised. The continued decline of the empire, despite the effort to exterminate Christianity, contributed to the cessation of active persecution after the death of Valerian.

A similar persecuting effort was made under Emperor Diocletian (284–305). Desiring to stop the evident decay of the Roman state and conceiving that a restoration of the ancient state worship would bring unity and political strength, Diocletian issued a series of edicts, beginning in 305, which ordered Christian churches destroyed, all bishops and presbyters imprisoned, and all Christians to choose between denying Christ or suffering death. Again the fires of persecution took the lives of many Christians and forced others to compromise.

Results of physical persecution.—In general, the periods of persecution greatly affected the nature of Christianity. Abnormalities developed which are common to repressed minorities or underground movements. On the one hand, the situation caused many to center their religious devotion in relics of former martyrs and to magnify the magical efficacy of the vehicles of worship; on the other hand, some became fanatical in their desire for martyrdom and ascetic sufferings. A serious problem arose after each persecution concerning what to do with those who had denied Christ or had in some other way compromised with the Roman power. Furthermore, the person of the bishop acquired an unusual prestige and sanctity during this experience. The bishops had become to the Roman state the symbol of the Christian movement and were sought out for special persecution. The many courageous bishops who died for the faith enhanced the office of bishop as a rallying point for Christian faithfulness.

The Decline of Imperial Opposition

Political factors finally brought an end to the long struggle of Christianity against the Roman state. Emperor Diocletian determined to set up a system of imperial succession that would insure capable leadership for the empire and at the same time prevent revolution from occurring whenever the emperor's throne became vacant. Consequently, he appointed Maximianus as co-emperor and, in addition, appointed two subordinate rulers with the title "caesar"—Constantine Chlorus in the West and Galerius in the East. His theory proposed that whenever an emperor died, the co-emperor would immediately become the sovereign, thus preventing an effort to seize the office by violence. One of the subordinate caesars would then theoretically be elevated to the co-emperor's place and a new caesar would be appointed. The system appeared to be foolproof. However, in 305, when Diocletian retired, the various armies nominated their caesars to be not only co-emperors but sole emperor. Military considerations again determined who should rule as emperor.

The rise of Constantine.—The soldier who finally conquered all his rivals and became also the sole ruler of the empire was Constantine, son of Caesar Constantine Chlorus in the West. Constantine's mother had been a Christian and his father had looked tolerantly upon Christians, refusing to enforce the edict of Diocletian for their persecution. Copying his father's attitude, Constantine, upon succeeding his father as ruler in the West, gladly united with the eastern rulers Galerius and Licinius in an edict in 311 which provided limited toleration for Christians. In the following year Constantine fought a crucial battle with Maxentius and claimed that he had seen a vision in the heavens which caused him to adopt Christianity and win the victory. In 313 Constantine and the eastern Emperor Licinius issued the Edict of Milan, granting full toleration to Christianity. In 323 Constantine defeated Licinius in battle and became the sole ruler.

Constantine and Christianity.—Constantine's adoption of Christianity was more of a political than a religious decision. The Roman Empire was fast declining. Its greatest need was a strong, internal unity that could both engender loyalty within and beat off attacks from without. Constantine proposed to attain this unity by making Christianity the cement of the empire. This would supply a double bond for the citizenry—political loyalty supplemented and strengthened by religious unity. At the same time Constantine did not divorce himself from religious support of the pagan devotees; he retained the title of chief priest of their system and became one of their deities after his death in 337. It is hardly conceivable that Constantine really became a Christian. His considerable crimes, including murder, long after his alleged vision, could hardly be the acts of a Christian. Thinking that baptism washed away sins, he delayed receiving this rite until he was at the point of death.

He did shower favors upon Christianity. Almost without help he secured the cessation of persecution. He destroyed pagan temples and filled official positions with Christians. Christians were exempted from military service, their churches were allowed to hold property without taxation, their day of worship was made a civil holiday, and their growth was encouraged. In 325 Constantine issued a general exhortation to his subjects to become Christians.

The effect of Constantine's adoption of Christianity upon the movement itself has been widely debated. It led directly to the official declaration that Christianity was the state religion at the time of Emperor Theodosius (378–95). Constantine was not responsible for all of the corruptions of Christianity from the New Testament pattern, for these had developed long before his day.

He did, however, introduce many new elements of corruption and greatly contributed to the rise of the Roman Catholic Church. It is impossible to know how Christianity would have developed had it not been adopted by the imperial authority, but doubtless it would have escaped many of the most hurtful evils which now beset it.

Concluding Summary

The Christian movement developed during its most crucial period in the midst of an unfriendly environment. The literary attacks upon Christianity during the period were not an unmixed evil, for they made it clear to Christian leaders that an authoritative canon and a definition of beliefs were necessary. Physical persecution by the Roman Empire was local and intermittent until the middle of the third century when two worldwide efforts were made to exterminate Christianity. The opening years of the fourth century witnessed the rise of Constantine, a friendly emperor, who turned the Christian movement in a new direction by providing secular support.

3

The Struggle for Purity

AT THE SAME time that Christianity was meeting its severest test from the outside it was also struggling to retain its original purity of doctrine and practice. Of the two battles the second was more important; yet, while the first was won, the second, though not entirely lost, inflicted great and terrible wounds upon Christianity.

Early Purity

The earliest Christian writings outside of the New Testament are of interest because they reveal the internal condition of Christianity and indicate the direction of thinking. Six early writings (apart from several fragments) have been preserved. (1) A letter written about A.D. 96 by Clement, pastor at Rome, in reply to one addressed to him by the church at Corinth, is probably typical of a great many such letters written by the various influential bishops over the empire. It appears that the Corinthian church had deposed some presbyters who had been appointed by the apostles. Clement urges the church to return these men to office and comments at length upon the evils of jealousy and faction. (2) A letter entitled the "Epistle of Barnabas" (but probably not written by Barnabas, the fellow laborer of Paul) has been preserved. Its main emphasis is upon the superiority of Christianity over Judaism. This writing may be dated between 70 and 135. (3) A great deal of controversy has arisen over the epistles of Ignatius. Scholars disagree about how many epistles Ignatius wrote, about the genuineness of many references within the epistles, and about the correct text of the letters. Some assign twelve epistles to him, some seven, and some follow a Syriac version which allows only three epistles. If authentic, these letters would appear to have been written about 115 after Ignatius had been condemned to death by the Emperor Trajan. These letters contain many exhortations to the churches to be faithful to the bishops, presbyters, and deacons whom God had given them. The letter to the church at Rome, in particular, constantly reiterates the desire of Ignatius to be devoured by the wild animals in the arena as a martyr for Christ. (4) A religious allegory called the *Shepherd of Hermas,* written about 140, was quite influential in the second century. It is made up of five visions, twelve commands, and ten similitudes, endeavoring to promote purity and faithfulness. (5) The Epistle of Polycarp dates from about 116. Polycarp was pastor at Smyrna; he was quite important in that he was an intimate disciple of the apostle John and the teacher of Irenaeus, a prominent writer of the second century. Polycarp's epistle consists mainly of scriptural quotations designed to inculcate purity in doctrine and steadfastness in service. (6) The *Didache* or *Teaching of the Twelve Apostles* was not discovered until 1883, but many have accepted it as being a genuine writing of the first or second century. It seems to have been a manual prepared by a Jewish Christian for use in a Jewish Christian community. The most controversial section is its seventh chapter, which describes baptism as trine immersion but allows pouring if there is not sufficient water to immerse.

These early Christian writings reflect a healthy and pure Christianity. The strong emphasis upon obedience to the church officers in Ignatius (if these are actually the letters of Ignatius in 115 and do not contain interpolations by a later hand) shows a tendency that later became an actual corruption of the New Testament pattern. Other later writings than those ascribed to Ignatius, however, show no evidence of that tendency. In the main, these writings show the extensive use of the Scriptures as authoritative, give a great deal of good advice, and aim at producing purity of life and faithfulness in service.

Later in the second and in the third century Christianity was faced with several internal struggles, which may be outlined under four heads, as follows: the struggle against diluting Christianity; the struggle against inadequate views of Christ and the Trinity; the struggle against pagan corruptions; and the struggle against lowering Christian standards.

The Struggle Against Diluting Christianity

Christianity would have been destroyed had it, like the Roman religious system, incorporated other religions within it. There were several efforts to alter the character of Christianity by attempting to add other religious systems in part or in whole.

Attempt to dilute with legalism.—The first of these efforts attempted to combine Judaism with Christianity. Such a move began during the life of Jesus Christ, and he emphasized the impossibility of putting new wine into old wineskins. The Judaizers who hounded Paul endeavored to mingle the legalism of the Jews with the spiritual Christian movement. How does a person become a Christian? The Judaizer would answer that he must first become a Jew, meeting certain legal requirements, then move on out into the realm of what Jesus had added to Judaism. This perversion, which Paul answered in the book of Galatians, was the occasion of the first church council in Jerusalem in the year 50. At this council Paul boldly asserted that a person need not become a Jew before becoming a Christian and produced Titus, one of his converts, as proof. The council agreed that Paul was correct, and a decree to that effect was prepared by James, who presided at the council. The Judaizers paid no attention to the council. A number of parties sprang up, taking such names as Ebionites, Nazarenes, and Elkesaites. They insisted upon regarding Christ as simply a Jewish prophet and Christianity as an extension of Judaism. Because Judaism had been badly scattered in the destruction of Jerusalem (70) and in the Jewish War (132–35), and because Gentiles soon dominated Christianity, these various Jewish-Christian sects died out within the first few centuries. The influence of their legalistic thinking, involving the merit of obedience and works, has not yet died out.

Attempt to dilute with philosophy.—A second effort to dilute Christianity had its source in Jewish speculation, although it was adopted by Gentile philosophers and in its developed state actually became anti-Jewish in its teachings. This movement took the name Gnosticism, which means knowledge, because its followers claimed to have a special knowledge about God and the world which the remainder of mankind did not possess. Its roots may be found in Jewish writings like those of Philo of Alexandria (20 B.C. to A.D. 40). As a fully developed system by Gentile philosophers, Gnosticism laid stress on the nature of evil, the nature of God and his relation to the world, and on the meaning of the present order of existence. The definition of the nature of evil forms a central idea in Gnosticism. An effort was made to isolate evil by affirming that it resided in matter or material things. If a thing had mass, it was evil; goodness was found in spirit. Thus it followed that a chair is evil, a house is evil, the physical world is evil, the physical body of man is evil.

Some far-reaching inferences, decidedly anti-Jewish in nature, followed this definition of evil. If the physical world was evil and the Jewish Old Testament taught that in the beginning God had created this physical world, then the nature of God was compromised, for how could a perfect God create an evil world? In reply the Gnostics took the position that the Jehovah of the Old Testament was not the true God but was a lower creation of the true God.

At this point the many Gnostic systems offered various explanations of the creation. Most of them taught that evil broke into the completely spiritual existence before the creation of the world, growing out of envy and spiritual pride and resulting in the imprisonment of men's pure souls in evil bodies. The good God, they continued, was too holy to create an evil world, but in order to provide a place for human habitation, this good God formed a divine being a little less holy than himself, this process continuing until finally, after a series of descending gods or aeons, the Jehovah of the Old Testament was created. He was so much less holy at this stage that he found no difficulty in creating

29

an evil world. In this way the Gnostics magnified the complete holiness of God and yet accounted for the creation of an evil world by the ultimate authority of the true God.

Applied to Christianity, this system affirmed that Christ was the highest of the aeons—the divine being which the true God himself had created. Christ did not have a real body in the incarnation, they said, since he was too holy to be attached to an evil substance; rather, Christ was just a spirit who appeared to be in human form. The Gnostics twisted the idea of Christian redemption in accordance with their peculiar idea of sin as residing in all material substances. Salvation, they said, consisted of freeing the spirit from the evil body in which it resided. Christ's redemptive work was to come from the true world of spirit into a material, and thus evil, world in order to teach men this true knowledge. Of course, Gnosticism denied the fundamental Christian doctrines of an actual incarnation, an actual physical ministry, and an actual death on the cross. Any idea of the resurrection of the body was in their thinking ridiculous, since every material body was completely sinful. This conception of the sinfulness of the body resulted in a twofold attitude toward morality. Some Gnostics said that since the body was sinful anyway and would be cast away at the time of death, it was not wrong to live in a most licentious way; the soul would remain pure in the midst of any physical debaucheries. Others said that since the body was sinful, it should be starved, neglected, and mistreated. Thus licentiousness and asceticism branched out from the same tree.

Evidences of the struggle by Christianity to keep this philosophical system from swallowing up the Christian message are found in the New Testament itself. Tradition has it that John the apostle had this group in mind when writing his Gospel and first epistle. His Gospel graphically describes the actual physical ministry of Jesus, particularly emphasizing the story of the cross. His epistle speaks of Christ as the One whom the disciples had "seen with our eyes, which we have looked upon, and our hands have handled" (1 John 1:1), and he identifies the Spirit of God as the one that "confesseth that Jesus Christ is come in the flesh"

(4:2). The book of Colossians combats the doctrines of the Gnostics, and the Nicolaitanes condemned in Revelation were probably Gnostics (2:6, 15).

During the several centuries after the apostolic era Christian writers fought savagely against this system which would deny the true deity as well as the true humanity of Christ. The principal writers against it were Irenaeus (about 130–202) and Tertullian (160–220). Irenaeus had been a disciple of Polycarp in Asia Minor, who in turn had sat at the feet of the apostle John. Perhaps some of the fire which burned against the Gnostics in the heart of Irenaeus had been kindled secondhand by John. Irenaeus moved from Asia Minor to France and in 177 became the bishop at Lyons. In 185, out of wide experience and painstaking scholarship, he wrote his principal work entitled *Five Books Against Heresies,* directed almost wholly against the Gnostics. His refutation of the Gnostic system was thorough and effective. Tertullian was a hotblooded Roman lawyer in North Africa before his conversion to Christianity about 180. He became a Montanist about 200. His writings are pungent and thought provoking. He attacked practically every opponent of Christianity—the pagans for their idolatry, persecution, and bloodshed; the heretics for holding inadequate views of the Trinity; the Jews for not coming to Christ; and the Gnostic systems described above.

The influence of Gnosticism upon Christianity was tremendous. On the surface the very fact that Christians answered the attacks of Gnosticism provided a valuable source of literature which mirrored the condition of Christianity in the second and third centuries. Beyond this literary interest, Gnosticism required that Christianity define itself. If, said the Gnostics in effect, Christianity is not what *we* say it is, then what is it? Thus it became necessary for Christianity to define its essential elements. This was done in several ways.

In the first place, under the leadership of the Holy Spirit the various churches gathered together the writings of the apostles and primitive Christians and formed the canon (rule), or the inspired writings. These writings had been tested in the crucible of daily living. It is true that a council of churches did not recognize this collection officially until some time later, but from the writings of the various Christian leaders it is apparent that Christians of this period recognized as inspired the books that are now included in the New Testament.

In the second place, Christians began preparing short statements of faith which could be memorized easily. One of the earliest creeds or statements of faith dates back to about the second century, and it reads as follows:

> I believe in God the Almighty Father,
> And in Christ Jesus his Son,
> Who was born of the virgin Mary,
> Crucified under Pontius Pilate and buried,
> Who arose from the dead on the third day,
> Ascended into the heavens,
> Sits at the right hand of the Father,
> From whence he shall come to judge
>   living and dead,
> And I believe in the Holy Spirit,
>   [and] the resurrection of the flesh.

It may be observed that this statement is a direct answer to the claims of the Gnostics, in that it emphasizes the actual earthly body of Christ, his crucifixion, and the resurrection of the body of the Christians—all of which were completely antagonistic to Gnostic doctrine.

In the third place, Christians began formulating the entire Christian teaching into systematic form as a means of answering Gnostic thinkers and began establishing Christian schools for teaching Christian doctrine. Clement of Alexandria (born about 160) was one of the first systematizers of Christian doctrine. He was trained in a Christian school formed by Pantaenus at Alexandria and succeeded his teacher as head of the school when Pantaenus was forced to flee from persecution in 190. Clement's principal writings illustrate the importance of this type of literature. He prepared an elementary book of Christian instruction for children or new converts; on a higher level he addressed an eloquent work to the Greeks in an effort to win them to the gospel; and, finally, he prepared some speculative discussions of the profound truths of Christianity as a challenge for philosophers to accept the Christian faith.

The other important systematizer of Christian doctrine was Origen (about 185–254), who succeeded Clement as head of the Alexandrian school. Origen gathered texts of the Scriptures in various languages, wrote commentaries on almost the whole Bible, fought literary battles with paganism, set forth devotional and practical exhortations on many aspects of Christian life, and prepared the first systematic theology. His work abounds in speculation, some of which is quite unsound. In particular he went astray in teaching the eternity of matter, in advocating a sort of human pre-existence of each individual soul, in supposing that everyone (including rebellious men and the devils themselves) would finally be restored to divine favor, and in holding several Gnostic ideas concerning man and creation. Origen's two disciples, Gregory Thaumaturgus and Dionysius of Alexandria, did much to popularize Origen's theology.

In addition to causing Christianity to define itself, the Gnostic movement set in motion ideas and methods of argument that greatly influenced Christianity. Philosophy and religion were wed. Intermediary beings between God and man were suggested. The authority of the Gnostic came, they said, from a secret knowledge, not written but brought down from primitive times by tradition. In answering this allegation, Irenaeus replied that true Christianity also had a tradition given by the Lord through the apostles and preserved by many churches which could trace their history back to apostolic days. Thus the Gnostic movement led to a veneration of tradition and antiquity; succession, more than conformity to the revealed Word of God, became the ultimate proof of authority and orthodoxy.

Finally, the Gnostic movement, along with other heresies, so emphasized the worthlessness of the material body that it paved the way for asceticism and monasticism. Asceticism refers to the view that the soul may be purified and merit gained by punishing the body through neglect, isolation, or some positive discomfort. Monasticism, in effect, organized ascetical tendencies so that the individual might cut himself off from all social intercourse with the outside world and systematically discipline his body for the benefit of his soul. This movement will be discussed in a succeeding chapter.

Attempt to dilute with other religions.—The third effort to dilute Christianity is known as Manichaeanism. Christianity had been preached in Persia quite early in the Christian era. In the middle of the third century a Mesopotamian known as Mani felt the influence of the many religious movements about him, and from them he compounded a composite religion which took his name. It included elements from the older pagan religions of Persia, from Judaism, and from Christianity. The vocabulary of Christianity and a few of its teachings were incorporated into the movement. Many of the Gnostic interpretations of Christianity were adopted. This religion did not have a great deal of influence upon orthodox Christianity as a whole.

The Struggle Against Inadequate Views of Christ and the Trinity

The question of Jesus to the disciples at Caesarea Philippi, "Who do men say that I the Son of man am?" was not answered in such a way as to preclude a similar question during the succeeding several centuries. The shibboleth of Judaism for over a millennium had been their Shema, "Hear, O Israel, the Lord thy God is one God." The New Testament describes Christ as God and the Holy Spirit as God. Second-century Christianity pondered a good deal over the question of how the incarnate Christ could be God without affecting the oneness of God. Five principal views that attempted to answer this question may be briefly summed up.

One view solved the problem by denying the eternal sonship of Christ. This group was known as the *alogoi* (which means literally "not the Word"—referring to John 1:1). As their name suggests, they denied that Christ was the Word, the expression of God, insisting that there was no Trinity since God was one. Christ, they said, was a great teacher, but not divine.

A second view asserted that Christ was born simply as a man but that God adopted him. The principal tenet accounts for the name "adoptionism" given to this theory. Although agreeing in the idea that Jesus was adopted of God in a special way, the followers of this view differed at various points from one another. A popular viewpoint asserted that Jesus was adopted at his baptism when the dove descended from heaven and God's voice announced, "This is my beloved Son, in whom I am well pleased." At this time divine power descended upon Jesus—for that reason the view is sometimes referred to as "dynamism," meaning "empowered"—and remained with him as a teacher and healer until the experience of the cross. His cry, "Why hast thou forsaken me?" was interpreted as indicating that at this time the divine power had departed from him. After all, it was argued, God could not die on a cross, so whatever deity Jesus received at his baptism was taken from him at the cross before his death. In this sense, then, Christ became the adopted Son of God only for a brief season of earthly ministry, and no doctrine of the Trinity was necessary.

A third view said that Christ was divine but subordinate to the Father. Such a view would eliminate the necessity for a doctrine of the Trinity, for while Christ was divine, he was less than God the Father and thus could not be one with the Father in essence.

One group advanced the idea that Christ was just another name for God. This school of thought argued that when Christ was born into the world in the incarnation experience, it was God the Father being born; there was no Father left in heaven. When Christ ascended again into heaven, he became God the Father. And when the Holy Spirit was given in power at Pentecost, heaven was emptied again. In other words, this view said that the Son and the Holy Spirit were simply God the Father in another mode or function; from this idea the movement was known as "modalism."

Many followed the orthodox view that Christ is of one essence with God and that the identification of the three persons in the

Godhead in no sense affected the basic monotheism of the Old Testament.

These several views relative to Christ and his relation to the Trinity were gathered up in the Arian controversy which will be discussed later.

The Struggle Against Pagan Corruptions

The principal converts to Christianity after the first century were Gentiles or pagans, most of whom were won to Christianity from other religious backgrounds. It is not surprising then that many of the corrupting ideas of these contemporary religious systems were reproduced to some extent in the Christian movement. Several of these pagan tendencies are as follows:

Fetishism.—All forms of paganism magnified the vast importance of religious externals, things and acts. The early Christians were scornfully referred to as atheists because they had no material evidences of their religious zeal. Such externalities began to be added to Christianity in the second and third centuries. Bones of saints began to possess a sanctity; religious possessions and the sign of the cross began to give outward evidence of piety. True religion began to be judged by participation in religious acts and possession of sacred relics.

Sacramentalism.—Closely akin to this development was a new attitude toward the ordinances. The two symbolical ordinances of the New Testament were baptism and the Lord's Supper. These were given the name "sacrament" (from the Latin military oath of loyalty), which carried with it the idea that the physical elements themselves were judged to possess salvation and spiritual grace. The water of baptism began to have a saving efficacy. According to Justin Martyr (about 165), baptism completes salvation; Irenaeus (about 185) boldly asserted that baptism is the new birth and brings regeneration. In Irenaeus' writings is the first hint that perhaps infants were now subjects of baptism, which would confirm the conception that water baptism without reference to repentance brings redemption. The bread and wine of the Lord's Supper were called the "medicine of immortality" by

36

Ignatius (about 115)—perhaps in symbolical language, but by the time of Irenaeus the assertion is flatly made that after the bread has been consecrated it is no longer common bread. In some sense it has been given a new character that enables it to convey spiritual grace to men.

Sacerdotalism.—This word means "priestism." Not only the Jewish system but all of the ancient pagan cults required priests and ritual as a part of their religious worship. The introduction of pagan ideas of external magical efficacy into the rites of baptism and the Supper demanded that such "magic" must be preserved by securing men who were trained and qualified to administer them. The view became current that only the bishop or those trained and authorized by him could effectively call forth the grace resident in these rites. Thus salvation became identified with the rites of baptism and the Supper, and these were effective only under the supervision of the bishop.

A female deity.—Every pagan religion in the ancient world had its female deity. Even Gnosticism posited a female counterpart to their deity. Converts from these systems quickly magnified the place of the virgin Mary until she became an object of adoration and worship.

Professionalism.—Jesus said that the kings of Gentiles exercise lordship over them, but that among Christians service and humility were to characterize the leaders. This Scripture was forgotten as bishops began to seek lordship and authority in the ecclesiastical sphere. Copying from practically every pagan religion, the Christian leaders began to make a distinction between the sacred character of the inner group who dispensed religion and the rest of the mortals. The very names adopted in Christianity show the official attitude of superiority, for clergy means "those who have been called of God," while laity means "the people."

The Struggle Against Lowering Christian Standards

There were three movements during the first several centuries which, although separate and distinct, yet overlapped and to some extent included one another. All of them accepted the contemporary corruption that viewed baptism as a saving ordinance, but all protested against allowing the unworthy—whether these had denied Christ in the persecution or had surrendered sacred Scripture to be destroyed—to receive or administer the benefits of a saving church and saving sacraments.

Montanism.—The first of these was known as Montanism. Between 135 and 160 Montanus, apparently a recent convert from the heathen priesthood, suddenly began to upbraid the Christians in Asia Minor where he lived, charging them with accepting Gnostic ideas, with following human leadership instead of the Holy Spirit in church life and organization, and with becoming criminally lax in Christian discipline. With two female helpers, Priscilla and Maximilla, he denounced the bishops in his area for their unspirituality and asserted that they were not qualified for office since they lacked the proper gifts of the Holy Spirit. Montanus magnified two distinctive doctrines. The first was an emphasis upon the Holy Spirit. At times the preaching of Montanus suggests that he himself was the Holy Spirit promised by Christ. He claimed an immediate inspiration for himself and his assistants so that their words were authoritative, even beyond the written Scriptures.

An emphasis upon Christian discipline was the second of the doctrines. Montanus predicted that Christ was coming shortly to begin the millennial reign in the little Phrygian village where Montanus was preaching. Because this was true, Christians ought to be completely separate from the world and ready for Christ's kingdom. He drew up a list distinguishing between mortal sins (which bring condemnation) and venial sins (which are forgivable). The clergy, in particular, must follow a stricter ethic than the ordinary Christian. At a time when Christians were being persecuted to the death, Montanus warned that if a Christian fled from suffering or denied the faith, it would bring total and final condemnation. Physical suffering and similar hardships for Christ purified and strengthened the spirit. Such a rigid screening of worldliness, punctuated by the example of Montanus, had great influence in forwarding the monastic movement a little later. The outstanding convert of Montanus was Tertullian, the great writer of North Africa, about 200. Tertullian did not accept all of the doctrines of Montanus but saw the inroads of worldliness and laxity on the Christian movement as most perilous.

Novatianism.—In many respects Novatianism was the reappearance of Montanism. When Emperor Decius (249–51) attempted to root out all Christianity from the world, there were two ideas about the treatment of those who had fled from persecution, surrendered sacred Scriptures, or denied the faith. One party allowed these people to return into the bosom of the saving church after certain conditions had been met; the other party said that these should never be allowed to return. Since it was conceived that salvation outside of the church was impossible, this question was of more than academic importance. In 251 Cornelius, the leader of the lenient party, was chosen bishop at Rome after considerable controversy; whereupon, Novatian, leader of the strict party, withdrew from fellowship with the lenient party on the ground that they were no longer the true church. He was elected bishop by his followers. Churches following his leadership sprang up in various parts of the empire, particularly in North Africa and Asia Minor. Many Montanists saw in this movement the revival of their own ideas and flocked to Novatian. There are evidences that this movement persisted until almost the fifth century.

Donatism.—The severe persecution by Diocletian brought the same problem to the fore in the opening years of the fourth century. During the crisis Bishop Mensurius of Carthage and his deacon Caecilian made themselves quite unpopular by attempting to discourage overzealous Christians from seeking martyrdom. After the death of Mensurius in 311, Caecilian was ordained bishop of Carthage by Bishop Felix of Aptunga, who was accused by the strict party of having surrendered Christian Scriptures during the persecution. The strict party objected to this ordination on the ground that Felix was a heretic and asserted that a heretic's ordination did not transmit power to perform saving baptism or other episcopal act. In 312 a council of about seventy bishops of the strict party assembled at Carthage and elected Majorinus bishop, causing a schism quite similar to that of Novatian. The name of this controversy was that of Donatus, who was ordained bishop of the strict party after the death of Majorinus in 313. The doctrinal position of both sides was about the same, save that the strict party insisted that when a bishop is personally unworthy (having denied the faith under persecution or surrendered Christian Scriptures) or has been consecrated by an unworthy bishop, any ecclesiastical acts of that bishop are invalid. In other words, he is unable to administer saving baptism. The Donatists, on the other hand, claimed that they represented the true line of episcopal succession and thus were qualified to administer such saving baptism and perform other episcopal rites.

The Donatists attempted to consolidate their position by requesting an ecclesiastical hearing before disinterested bishops. In 313 before six bishops (including the bishop of Rome) the case was heard, but the decision favored Caecilian. The next year the Donatists appealed the case to a council, but again the decision favored Caecilian. The Donatists then appealed to the Roman emperor who had become sole ruler in the West. Constantine, however, in 316 decided against them and threatened them with banishment if they did not cease this schism. Only after the Donatists had appealed to the secular power and been spurned did they finally come to the position that there ought to be no civil interference with religion. This movement gathered strength and continued until about the fifth century.

Concluding Summary

During the period from 100 to 325, the Christian movement faced various internal forces that threatened to move it away from the New Testament pattern. Some of these internal problems were caused by the external forces of persecutions and corruptions. Christianity was affected in some instances by the very machinery it set up to deal with these problems. The next chapter will discuss some of the changes in character that came to Christianity because of the struggle against external and internal forces.

4

The Close of an Era

THE SECOND PERIOD of church history (A.D. 100–325) closes with the meeting of the first universal council. The occasion for this council was a doctrinal struggle over the person of Christ. That story will be told in the next chapter since it inaugurates a new direction on the part of Christianity—the beginnings of the Roman Catholic Church. The close of this very crucial period offers an opportunity to examine Christianity in 325 and to compare it with the kind of Christianity taught in the New Testament.

New Testament Christianity taught that salvation came through simple faith in Jesus Christ. Nothing is required for salvation, declared Paul, but the regenerating work of the Holy Spirit that comes when one confesses Jesus as Lord and acknowledges Jesus' resurrection from the dead. Saving faith is an immediate experience with Christ, and all men are capable of coming directly to Christ. No external institution, good work, human priest, or religious rite is required to qualify a man for coming to Christ and receiving the free gift of salvation. New Testament Christianity also taught that a New Testament church is a body of persons who have been born again, baptized, and possess the Spirit of Christ. The officers of the local body were two—pastors and deacons. The pastor has various names in the New Testament; he is called the bishop, the shepherd, the presbyter or elder, and the minister. The ordinances were two—baptism and the Lord's Supper. All churches were on the same level, and each one possessed authority to govern its own affairs without outside interference.

By the close of this period (325) it is difficult to look at the general state of Christianity and recognize a picture such as the one drawn from the New Testament. No longer were the people the church; now the pastor or bishop, given a new office, is viewed as constituting the church. The word "church" had come to mean not a local body or a local institution, but the totality of bishops. Salvation was viewed as coming through the bishop as the custodian of the saving sacraments of the church. He alone is qualified, it was believed, to administer or authorize saving baptism and to serve the "medicine of immortality," the Lord's Supper. No longer were all churches and pastors equal under God and before men. Territorial divisions had been marked off to show the boundaries of the authority of various strong bishops.

By 325, then, the very nature of Christianity had been corrupted. Changes had come in several overlapping areas.

Change in the Nature of Faith

By 325 faith had lost its personal character as being the whole dependence of a person immediately upon the person and work of Jesus Christ. Rather, while Christ was a part of the system, faith was to be directed toward the institution called the Church; and salvation did not result from the immediate regenerating power of the Holy Spirit but was mediated by the sacraments of baptism and the Lord's Supper. Since the sacraments were under control of the Church and since salvation came through them only, it followed that a person must join the Church in order to be saved. That is exactly what Bishop Cyprian meant in 250 when he said that no man can have God for his Father who does not have the Church for his mother. No wonder those who denied the faith in the time of persecution were so extremely anxious to be forgiven by the Church, for they believed that salvation outside of this institution was impossible.

During this period personal faith was eliminated entirely in some instances. In the writings of Irenaeus (about 200) there is a hint that perhaps in his generation infants were baptized in order to save them. Under these circumstances individual faith becomes unnecessary. With someone to act as proxy for the infant in order to make pretense of faith, the "saving water of baptism" was applied. Furthermore, there is evidence that the first instance of pouring for baptism took place about this time. Novatian, leader of the strict ecclesiastical party at Rome, became quite ill, and it was feared that death was near. He had never been baptized. Since he was not strong enough to permit immersion in water, it was decided to pour a quantity of water upon his body. This was done and marked the beginning of a change in the form of baptism. Sprinkling soon developed, for if the water does the saving, a little water can be as effective as a great deal. It was more convenient also.

With this view of church and sacraments, it is evident that complete dependence upon Christ, clearly the only requirement for salvation in the New Testament, was modified to require obedience to the institution and reception of the sacramentals. Thus faith alone, without church and sacraments, cannot save; church and sacraments alone, as in the case of the infant, can save without faith by the individual.

Change in the Nature of the New Testament Church

Sacramentalism made a vast difference in the conception of a New Testament church. In the New Testament period the church consisted of the people in a local body; the leaders were on the same level with the people but served because they had been given special gifts by the Spirit. The ordinances were not magical but symbolical. Now, however, this view was entirely changed. For one thing, the original equality among the several pastors, bishops, or presbyters serving in a church began to disappear. In the New Testament church there was no difference in office between a bishop and a presbyter, the two names simply describing functions of the one office (see Acts 20:17-35). But quite early in the second century it became common for one of the ministers to assume leadership, sometimes because of unusual scholarship, strong personality, or maturity.

As early as 150 one of the writers speaks of a president of the ministers in a single church. There were several reasons why such an officer should develop rapidly. The earliest bishops or presbyters engaged in secular labor to make their living and performed the duties of their church office when not at work. As Christians increased in number and financial ability, one man, the best qualified, was asked to resign his secular labor and give full time to the religious task. It became his business to "oversee" (the word which means "bishop") the work of the Christian community. He received the title of bishop in a special sense and finally claimed the name as a unique dignity. The other ministers were now called "presbyters" in distinguishing them from the overseeing minister, the bishop. Early in the second century the churches at Antioch and in Asia had developed such a leader over all other presbyters, although this had not yet manifested itself in Rome, Philippi, or Corinth.

Another factor that brought authority and prestige to the new officer known alone as the bishop was the development of local councils for advice and discussion. Leaders of the several churches in a given geographical area began to hold such councils or synods, and because of his place in the local congregation, the new bishop acted as spokesman for his church. It was he who brought word back to the congregation concerning the united action of all Christians in fighting heresy, in exercising discipline, and in other matters of common action. By the end of the second century, generally speaking, the office of bishop had become a third church office. This meant that in each local church, or diocese, there were three grades of ministers: one bishop to oversee all and exercise total authority, many presbyters, many deacons.

The office of bishop soon developed beyond the confines of a single congregation. When Christians were comparatively few, one church could serve an entire city. As new congregations were organized in different sections of cities where a bishop was already serving, a significant departure from the New Testament conception occurred. The New Testament plan called for each congregation to have its own leadership and to be independent of any authority from another congregation. What actually happened was that in these cities the bishops already serving were influential enough simply to extend their jurisdiction to include new con-

44

gregations. New presbyters were ordained to provide workers for the new congregation, all under the authority of the bishop of that city. In Rome, for example, by the end of the third century there were forty congregations; each congregation or parish had its own presbyter or—as he came to be known—priest. And over the entire city was a single administrative officer who bore the title of bishop. Influential city bishops soon extended their authority in this fashion to include villages around the large cities.

Although, therefore, there are late writings that identify the bishop with a local congregation, by the fourth century the separation of the office of bishop from that of the presbyters and the development of a territorial authority over a large area was the normal situation. The strongest bishops (assuming additional titles such as archbishop—ruling bishop, or patriarch—ruling father, or pope—papa) presided at large councils attended by bishops and presbyters from adjacent territory and began looking toward extending their jurisdiction even further. The extent of such development is indicated by the sixth canon of the first universal council at Nicea in 325, which asserted that according to custom the bishop of Alexandria shall exercise authority over Egypt, Alexandria, and Pentapolis; the bishop of Antioch shall have similar authority in the area adjacent to his city; and the bishop of Rome shall exercise a dominant influence over the territory around his city.

The influence of the bishop developed in other directions also. The church was conceived now as a saving institution because it possessed the saving sacraments of baptism and the Lord's Supper. But who within the church controlled these sacraments? The bishop, of course. The view became current that only the bishop could authorize or perform the sacraments; thus the bishop personally possessed the essential power of the church. Such a view was greatly forwarded during the persecutions and the heretical movements. The bishop had been thrust into the position of embodying the Christian faith. The strongest Christians had been placed in that office. During the persecutions the bishops bore the brunt of the attacks; during the conflicts with heresy they had been looked to as the bulwark of orthodoxy. As a result, the bishop became the church both in popular conception and in authority to wield her sacramental powers. Bishop Cyprian of Carthage could say in about 250 that where the bishop is, there is the church, and there is no church where there is no bishop.

Thus it may be seen that the original nature of a New Testament church was completely corrupted. It no longer consisted of the congregation, for the bishop was the church. It was no longer a fellowship; it had become a saving institution. Its ordinances had become saving sacraments, not symbolical reminders of Christ. Its ministry was no longer in two offices but in three. It was no more a democracy in government but a hierarchy.

Change in the Nature of Ecclesiastical Authority

Conforming to the historical developments described in the previous section, the literary remains of ancient Christianity show clearly a shift from the New Testament conception of the final authority of a local church to the idea that the final word of authority in all matters religious was the bishop. It has been pointed out that Christianity produced four general types of literature in the two centuries following the apostolic period.

The earliest chronologically was primarily *edificatory* in nature. In none of the writers of this early type of literature is there any evidence that the New Testament pattern for ecclesiastical authority has been altered. The letter of Clement of Rome to the Corinthians urges the church to restore some officers who had been disciplined, even though they had originally been appointed by the apostles. This means that the Corinthian church exercised authority even beyond apostolic appointment. Clement's letter gives advice but shows no authority to require the Corinthian church to follow it. The writings of Ignatius (about 115) place great emphasis upon the necessity for obedience to the pastor and the deacons and are morbidly ascetical. Because of the emphasis upon these two ideas, there is considerable suspicion that interpolations by later hands have endeavored to give early authority to matters developed later. However, at this early period the bishop was simply one of the pastors of a local body. Although later than

46

the writings of Ignatius, the Epistle of Polycarp and the *Shepherd of Hermas* reveal no episcopal development.

The second type of Christian literature was *apologetic* in nature. Its main purpose was to defend Christianity against such charges as atheism, licentiousness, and cannibalism, leveled against it by the pagans. In the doctrinal discussions of this literature the ground of authority was the Scriptures, primarily the Old Testament. There was no appeal to episcopal authority.

The third type of Christian literature was *polemical.* Its purpose was to fight heresy that threatened to break out within the Christian ranks. Two important writers in this field were Irenaeus (about 130–202) and Cyprian (195–258). In the course of his arguments to discredit Gnosticism around 185, Irenaeus first refutes their doctrines from the Christian Scriptures. He then proceeds to say that the continuous existence of the various churches from the days of the apostles proves that they have not erred in the interpretation of the apostolic teachings. Referring to Rome as an example of one of such churches, Irenaeus names its bishops in succession back to apostolic days (but his list poses problems in its disagreement with other lists). In other words, Irenaeus makes historical succession of the bishops the basis for confidence that orthodox Christianity was true Christianity while Gnosticism was a false perversion. Basically, then, the authority cited by Irenaeus was the Scriptures; the correct interpretation of the Scriptures he attempted to prove through succession.

The other important polemical writer was Bishop Cyprian of Carthage (195–258), who did more than any other individual to forward the office of bishop as the ultimate Christian authority. Cyprian's theory grew out of practical problems in administrating his diocese. In his struggle over what to do with those who had denied Christ or surrendered Scriptures under persecution, he finally rested his argument on the fact that he as the bishop had authority over all churches and individuals in his diocese because he was the successor of the apostles. He conceived of one universal (Catholic) church in the world, composed of many bishops, the successors of the apostles. The unity of all the various bishops

47

constitutes the unity of the catholic (universal) Church. Only those who are in fellowship with this universal episcopal unity (the Catholic Church) are saved. Thus if any person in any diocese anywhere refuses to be obedient to his bishop, that person forfeits his salvation.

The interesting paradox about Cyprian is that while he firmly taught that all bishops were of equal rank (and practiced it when he fought the Roman bishops and told them to quit meddling in his diocese), yet he called the Roman church the "mother and root of the catholic church." When the Roman bishop attempted to instruct Cyprian on the validity of heretical baptism and to exercise whatever authority was involved in the title Cyprian had applied to the Roman church, Cyprian vigorously denied the right of any bishop, even the Roman bishop, to exercise jurisdiction in the diocese of another bishop.

It was Cyprian, then, who corrupted the New Testament pattern of authority. Instead of the local church, the territorial bishop became the final word of authority. The universal (Catholic) church rested upon the sole sovereignty of the bishops as successors of the apostles. Local churches lost every vestige of authority.

The fourth type of Christian literature—*systematic* development of doctrine—does not concern episcopal development.

Change in the Nature of Worship

In the New Testament the pattern of worship consisted principally of singing, Scriptures, prayer, and preaching. The service required no altar or ritual, for God was recognized as spirit and could be reached through spirit. But a change had occurred by 325. The idea that the sacraments were magical brought a change to the nature of worship. Instead of magnifying his prophetic or preaching ministry, the local presbyter began to function as a priest. In fact, after the fourth century the very name "presbyter" began to drop out, and the title of this office became "priest." This development could be expected when the sacraments became magical; it required a priestly qualification to administer this sort of rite. Consequently, the center of worship became the observance of the Lord's Supper, which was already being called "mass" (from the Latin word meaning "dismissal," when those not qualified to partake of the Supper were asked to leave the church).

The magical nature of the sacraments also brought emphasis upon the proper form, words, and materials used in administering them. In the Roman religion great stress was laid upon pronouncing the ritual exactly as a means of making the service effective. If a word was mispronounced or omitted, the magical nature of the religious service could not be appropriated. This spirit began to prevail in Roman Christianity; the ritual must be repeated exactly according to formula in order to be efficacious. Furthermore, this corruption in the nature of the worship services contributed greatly to the development of the catechetical means of instruction in religious doctrine. Since the worship service was dedicated to a priestly ritual, it became necessary to instruct children and new converts in the proper ritual as well as in the rudiments of Christian doctrine on some other occasion than in the church services. Summaries of the ritual and of the doctrines were prepared, and newcomers were required to memorize these as a prerequisite to admission.

Finally, the purely spiritual nature of religious services was changed. Magnificent processions and external splendor, after the manner of pagan parades, became popular. Places identified with early Christianity became holy and were accorded unusual reverence. Bones of martyrs and other material remains were sought and attributed magical power. Holy days were named and observed. Easter had been set apart from the time of the apostles, but new days were added. Both the baptism and the birth of Jesus had been celebrated in January during this period; but in an effort to win the pagans, the celebration of Christ's birth was changed shortly after the close of the period to December 25, a Roman and Scandinavian feast day.

Reasons for Extensive Corruption of Christianity

It is impossible, of course, to plumb entirely the various interacting factors that moved Christian development in the direction

49

that it took. The several suggestions that follow simply mention the most obvious of the elements that turned Christianity away from its original purity.

The tremendous growth of the Christian movement.—The growth of Christianity in the three centuries following the death of Christ was phenomenal. Figures cannot be given with any accuracy, but some think that Christians numbered from five to ten millions by the time of Constantine (323). From a human standpoint this tremendous growth may be explained by three general factors.

First, heathenism had failed as an answer to the needs of man. Greek rationalism had emptied the pagan heavens. Men thoroughly disbelieved the superstitious legends that had power neither to affect their daily lives nor promise good things to come. In the dizzy maelstrom of social, economic, and political foment which threatened men in the early Christian centuries, pagan religious systems were silent.

Second, the Christian message was positive and effective. The content of Christ's teachings tugged at the hungry hearts of men everywhere. The pagans could see what Christianity meant by observing the lives of the Christians. Love was the theme of their living. When called upon to die during the various periods of severe persecution, the Christians responded with faith and courage. Such a spirit the pagans could account for only in terms of the power of God.

Finally, the zeal of the Christians in witnessing for Christ was overpowering. Unlike the pagans about him, the Christian insisted that all religions were not of equal value; either accept Christ as Saviour or be lost was the conviction of the Christian. Every Christian was a missionary, every crossroad a pulpit, every person a prospect. There was a sense of urgency in the Christian witness. Conscious of Christ's injunction to be watchful and busy, the Christians worked with a feeling that the Lord might return at any time. As a consequence they pleaded with unction and personal conviction.

The remarkable growth that followed was one of the factors that helped corrupt the original purity of the Christian movement. Without question it promoted the development of the power of the bishop. His prestige was enhanced when large numbers of converts made Christianity the religion of a majority of the people in many areas. These converts were not drawn entirely from the lower class of people. Education, wealth, and civil rule soon were enlisted in the Christian cause, bringing to the overseeing bishop powerful new weapons and influential friends.

This growth also enhanced the danger of sacramentalism. Large numbers of pagans flocked to the doors of the Christian church and were admitted through the use of magical sacraments. Great masses of unregenerated pagans were brought into the churches in this way. Thoughtful Christians watched uneasily as these pagans introduced ideas from the background of their early religious training. With other factors, this situation led to monasticism, as Christians fled from the paganized churches to find purity and spirituality in the caves of the desert.

Finally, the influx of large numbers into the Christian churches furthered the institutional development of Christianity. Young children and uninitiated pagans required extensive instruction in ritual and doctrine. The sprinkling of water upon them could not bring a new heart; it was hoped that extensive instruction would make them good Christians.

Pagan persecution.—The external opposition to Christianity described in the second chapter was also a contributing factor in the changes that occurred in Christianity. What should be the attitude of a church toward a member who, when brought to physical torture by secular authorities, denies Christ and surrenders precious Christian Scriptures to be destroyed? This happened many times in periods of severe persecution during the first three centuries. The two severest trials came about 250 and about 300 during the Decian and Diocletian persecutions. Many nominal Christians defaulted during these periods. In general, after each period of persecution five rather distinct groups could be named. (1) There were *martyrs,* who had refused to put a pinch of incense upon the altar of the Roman emperor and to deny Christ and were slain.

(2) There were *confessors,* who were true to Christ but because of local influence or leniency were not put to death. Sometimes they were blinded or maimed. (3) There were *apostates,* who denied Christ and offered incense upon the altar of the emperor. (4) There were *falsifiers,* who by bribes or passive compromise received certificates from the imperial officers stating that they had offered pagan incense and had cursed Christ, although this was not actually the fact. (5) There were the *unfaithful,* who surrendered true Christian Scriptures to the officers.

The early leaders divided over how to treat the apostates, falsifiers, and unfaithful. Some, like Montanus, Novatian, and Donatus, wanted to bar them forever from the church; others, like Caecillian and Callixtus, wanted to let them return to the church after evidence of repentance. Various plans were suggested for bringing such offenders back. One system permitted them to kneel outside the church and give evidence of grief for a full year—these were called *weepers;* the next year they were allowed to come into the church and hear the service, hence were called *hearers;* the next year they could kneel during the service until the time for the Lord's Supper, when they must leave—these were called *kneelers;* the fourth year they were allowed to stand during the service— they were called *co-standers;* and finally, they were admitted to the Supper and restored to fellowship.

It can easily be seen how such a system would magnify the nature of the church as a saving institution; else such strenuous efforts to get back into its fellowship would hardly be worth the protracted ceremonies. The persecution also fostered other elements that contributed to the corruption of Christianity, such as the deterioration that always comes from literary warfare, the centralizing of ecclesiastical authority in the bishop to meet the threats of the persecutors, and the development of the attitude that physical coercion was the best means of dealing with dissenters.

Internal conflicts.—One of the most important factors in the corruption of Christianity was the series of internal controversies described in the previous chapter. While officially condemning many of the heretical perversions, Christianity unconsciously imbibed some of the teachings that were so widely propagated through these controversies. The doctrine of mortal and venial sins was lifted from Montanism, as well as ascetic and monastic emphases. Gnosticism had taught that there was a series of mediating persons between man and God; the idea of mediating saints for invoking the blessings of God grew up in Christianity. The magical power of the ordinances that changed them to sacraments came unrefined from paganism. Jewish ideas hastened the development of the priestly system. The secular Roman government provided a pattern for organization that was duplicated by the ecclesiastical monarchy which grew up in later centuries. The expression of Christian truth in philosophical terminology was inevitable in the course of the various controversies, but it served to glaze over spirituality with argumentation. The various internal struggles played a large part in enlarging the stature of the bishop, since he was called upon to be the champion of orthodoxy.

Ecclesiastical rivalry.—It will be remembered that the office of bishop had been separated from that of the presbyter or priest and had successively become the governing power in a local church, the ecclesiastical head of a diocese (a city) and the spiritual prince of a territory, sometimes an entire province. The development of councils or synods for mutual help and advice had introduced the bishops to one another and encouraged the opportunity of larger leadership by the more gifted bishops. One of the common practices during the controversies was for one of the parties to secure favorable response from one or more of the strong bishops before the outbreak of the conflict. This insured allies. But it also enhanced the prestige and influence of the bishops to whom appeal had been made, for it gave them opportunity to act as judge. By 325 the three most influential bishops in the Mediterranean world were those in Rome, Antioch, and Alexandria. Already these bishops were sparring for the chief place, and other bishops were striving to elevate themselves to the place occupied by these bishops. This intense rivalry fanned the flames of ambition that normally did not lack fuel. Recrimination, condemnation, and outrageous forgery of official documents in an effort to attain first place characterized this struggle between bishops. What a contrast with the teachings of the humble Galilean!

Concluding Summary

By 325, then, tremendous changes in the nature of Christianity had taken place. The developments brought a new movement that did not greatly resemble Christianity except in terminology. There was no Roman Catholic Church as yet, for the bishop of Rome was only one of several powerful bishops; but the direction had been taken. The church had become a saving institution centering in the bishops. A small group of strong bishops had been elevated into world leadership. One of them was already claiming first place and was working feverishly to secure it.

BIBLIOGRAPHY

BAKER, G. P. *Constantine the Great and the Christian Revolution.* New York: Dodd, Mead & Company, Inc., 1930.

BETTENSON, HENRY (ed.). *Documents of the Christian Church.* New York: Oxford University Press, 1947.

CADOUX, C. J. *The Early Church and the World.* Edinburgh: T. & T. Clark, 1925.

GWATKIN, H. M. *Arian Controversy.* London: Longmans, Green & Co., Inc., 1896.

HARDY, E. G. *Christianity and the Roman Government.* New York: The Macmillan Co., 1925.

LATOURETTE, K. S. *A History of Christianity.* New York: Harper & Brothers, 1953.

NEWMAN, A. H. *A Manual of Church History,* I. Philadelphia: American Baptist Publication Society, 1953.

RAMSAY, WILLIAM M. *The Church in the Roman Empire Before 170 A. D.* Grand Rapids: Baker Book House, 1954.

ROBINSON, JAMES HARVEY. *Readings in European History,* I. Boston: Ginn & Co., 1904.

STEVENSON, J. (ed.). *A New Eusebius.* New York: The Macmillan Co., 1957.

UHLHORN, GERHARD. *The Conflict of Christianity with Heathenism.* New York: Charles Scribner's Sons, 1891.

WORKMAN, HERBERT BROOK. *Persecution in the Early Church.* Cincinnati: Jennings and Graham, 1906.

III. PERIOD OF PAPAL DEVELOPMENT (A.D. 325–1215)

Introduction to the Period

From 325 to 1215 the Roman Catholic Church, under the headship of the pope, developed and reached its height. The opening date is that of the first world council, which initiated a new direction; the closing date of the period marks the meeting of still another council— the Fourth Lateran Council (also called the Twelfth Ecumenical Council by the Roman Church). The Fourth Lateran Council represents the highest pinnacle attained by the Roman Catholic Church. Thus between the Nicene Council of 325, when the new direction was taken, and the Fourth Lateran Council of 1215, the Roman Catholic Church developed, expanded, and reached its height.

The large historical movements of this period were political and military. In the fourth and fifth centuries the German barbarians from the north and northeast overran the Western world, bringing what has been called the Middle Ages. The old Graeco-Roman culture and economy were overwhelmed, but the tribes in general were either won from paganism or indoctrinated away from Arian Christianity through efforts of the Roman Church. One of the tribes, the Franks, became the dominant military power, and with them the Roman Church made alliance. One of the Frankish kings, Charlemagne, was crowned in 800 as the Holy Roman Emperor. The Holy Roman Church and the Holy Roman Empire struggled for mastery—the "spiritual" against the secular—throughout the remainder of the period.

The Eastern world was not invaded by the Germanic hordes but was overwhelmed by an even worse fate. The Mohammedans of Arabia began their conquest for world domination in the middle of the seventh century. Almost the entire eastern section around the Mediterranean fell to the Saracens in little over a half century; by 732 they had conquered all of North Africa and Spain and were menacing France. In that year Charles Martel defeated them at Tours. The threat which these Mohammedans and their successors offered to western Europe played a large part in the movement of history.

The next seven chapters will describe this period from the viewpoint of ecclesiastical history. The first chapter in this section will introduce the student to the new direction which was begun in 325, and the last one will review the ecclesiastical development of the nine centuries. The five chapters within this framework describe the laying of Roman Catholic foundations between 325 and 451; the expansion of the Roman Catholic Church between 451 and 1050; the religious and secular opposition to this Roman Catholic expansion between 451 and 1050; and the attainment of complete supremacy, both secular and religious, by the Roman Catholic system between 1050 and 1215.

Points of Special Interest

The student will notice several significant matters during this period. (1) The Roman Catholic development was gradual and slow, but effective. Two groups opposed autocratic power: those within the church who rejected Roman pretensions and the secular governments without the church which resented Roman domination. These two elements of opposition were never completely overcome. A special chapter has been devoted to each; although overlapping somewhat, they present in unified and topical form the struggle against the expansion of Roman power. (2) The records of dissenting movements are very meager. The nature of the religious spirit would demand dissent. Laxity always develops asceticism of some kind; rigor and repression always breed disobedience or dissent. (3) The long-range program of the Roman Church represents its greatest strength. The ups and downs of Roman ecclesiastical power sometimes made it seem doubtful that world domination would ever come. The historic policy of the papacy never to retract one of the claims made in earlier centuries, however preposterous and arrogant it may be, and to assert that claim when the occasion is favorable, contributed directly to the world domination of the twelfth and thirteenth centuries.

5

A New Direction

THE DEVELOPMENTS SKETCHED in the previous chapters represent more than a departure from the New Testament pattern; they also constitute a preparation for further significant changes. Church government no longer proceeds from the people but from the officers; the two sacraments, endowed now with magical efficacy, have made the church a saving institution; salvation now comes through admission into this saving institution, not from the power of a message by the institution; the bishop has been separated from other local church officers and now rules as a monarch, not only in the local church, but in large areas contiguous to his own. The new direction of the development that begins with the first world council at Nicea in 325 leads directly to the Roman Catholic Church. Such a development would have been impossible without the friendly attitude and strong arm of the secular power. These elements were secured when Constantine chose to link up his future with the growing, dynamic movement called Christianity.

Constantine's Purpose

Constantine was a political genius. From his comparatively meager understanding of Christianity and his brief contact with it he concluded two things: that Christianity would become the dominant religious system of the world, and that the dying Roman Empire could be saved, or at least prolonged, by a union with this dynamic religion. Constantine wanted Christianity to become the cement of the Empire; he wanted religion to act as a unifying factor in the political system. This was not an altogether new idea, for religion had been a part of the Roman system of government through the centuries. The innovation consisted in the kind of religion that was not a state-projected syncretism that invited all who would to join, but a widespread and powerful movement which was exclusive in its view of God and its requirements for admission.

Such a union of forces was something new, both for the Empire and for Christianity. Each developed differently because of their alliance. Christianity was not able to save the Roman Empire—it was too far gone; and Constantine was wrong, also, in supposing that Christianity would act as cement for the Empire. How could Christianity bring unity to the political world when Christianity itself did not possess unity? Already three schools of thought had developed and displayed antagonism to one another.

Alexandria formed the center of the earliest of these schools. A converted philosopher, Pantaenus, organized a school for instructing Christian converts. He was succeeded by Clement, and Clement by Origen—both of whom have been mentioned in connection with the literary monuments of the second period of church history. These men looked upon philosophy as the means of interpreting Christianity. In the best philosophical tradition, the Bible was read allegorically. Great emphasis was placed upon redemption as a mystical union with God through Christ.

Antioch was the second center. This school was founded by Lucian in the closing quarter of the third century. Representing the tradition of the apostle John, this school of thought magnified the Scriptures as their own best interpreter. Because of the intensive struggle with the Gnostics, philosophy was mistrusted. The literal meaning of a text, as understood in the light of its grammatical and historical background, was sought.

The Western school of thought claimed writers from both the Continent and North Africa. Like the Antiochian center, it also mistrusted philosophy and placed its principal emphasis upon the practical application of Christianity.

The controversies that begin to arise in Christianity will follow the pattern of thought represented in the various schools; that is, with the same facts and Scriptures the followers of the Alexandrian school, using the philosophical approach, reached different conclusions from the Antiochian school and the Western school. Many times the search for truth was simply a secondary stimulus to the controversy; the intellectual rivalry spurred on the adherents of each type of thought far beyond the limits of Christian charity.

With this sort of disunity in the Christian movement, there was considerable doubt that it would bring unity to the Roman Empire when they formed the alliance. It was not long before this fact rudely awakened Constantine. Gathering up historic schismatic movements like Montanism and Novatianism, the Donatist split in North Africa thrust itself upon Constantine at almost the time he had decided to make Christianity the cement of the Empire. Constantine's treatment of Donatism was, of course, motivated by political factors. He did his best by appeal, argument, threat, and finally, physical persecution to close the ranks of Christianity, all without success. This problem for Constantine was just a taste of what was yet to come. The cry of the Donatists later on, "What has the emperor to do with the church?" was one that symbolized the greatest dilemma of the new alliance between church and state. What should an emperor do in order to maintain political control when his Christian citizens insisted upon forming hostile theological camps on the basis of their scriptural interpretations? Whether it was his original intention to relate himself in such fashion or not, Constantine was forced to become "bishop of the bishops" in an attempt to restore unity. This position was accorded him by the ecclesiastical princes of the Empire.

The controversy that brought Constantine into this place of doctrinal and ecclesiastical leadership was called the Arian controversy and concerned the interpretation of the person of Christ in relation to God.

The Beginning of the Arian Controversy

It will be remembered that one of the earliest doctrinal discussions in Christianity centered in the nature of Christ and his relation to God the Father. Was Jesus Christ completely God or was he less than God? This question had never been adequately answered. Many outstanding Christian writers had wrestled with the problem. If Jesus were completely God, it was asked, then do Christians have three Gods (including the Holy Spirit) ? But, came the response, could Jesus bring salvation to men if he were not God, as he had claimed? Origen of Alexandria had probed deeply into this question in the third century. His writings contain two different views. In one place Origen affirmed that Christ is subordinate to God, is less than true God. In another he asserts that Christ was the eternally generated Son of God; Christ had always existed as the divine Son, both before time and since the temporal creation. Strange as it may seem, these two positions in Origen form the center of the Arian struggle, the first view precipitating the controversy and the second view finally resolving the conflict.

Arius, the man responsible for beginning the controversy, was a presbyter under Bishop Alexander of Alexandria but had been trained at Antioch to interpret the Scriptures in a literalistic sense. About 318 Arius decided that it would compromise the dignity and honor of God the Father to say that Jesus Christ was of the same divine, eternal essence as God. Consequently, he worked out a system which declared that Christ was a being who had been created before time and that through Christ God had created all other things. His theory made Christ greater than man and less than God—somewhere between the two, but fully neither.

The controversy spread rapidly beyond Alexandria and soon gripped the entire Eastern world. The Antiochian school of thought could see nothing wrong with the interpretation and added intellectual rivalry to the issue. Arius was a popular and able preacher and gained much support through his personal charm. As the controversy grew, Constantine acknowledged that some sort of action would have to be taken. After becoming the sole emperor in 323, following the experience he had gained in dealing with the Donatists, he directed that a meeting of all Christian leaders be convened to settle the issue. This universal (the meaning of the Greek word for catholic) council met at Ni-

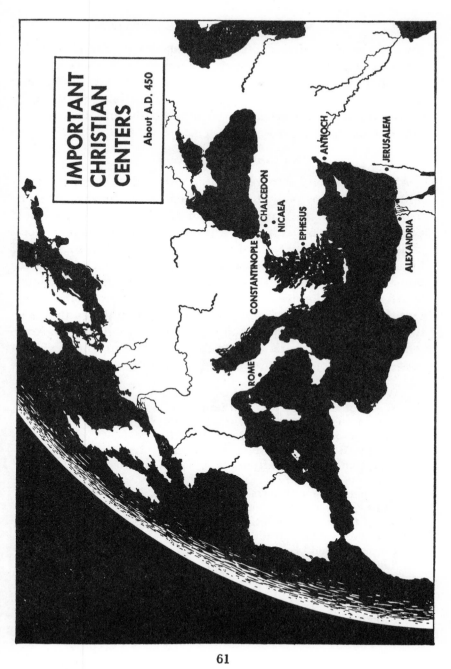

IMPORTANT CHRISTIAN CENTERS

About A.D. 450

ROME

CONSTANTINOPLE

CHALCEDON

NICAEA

EPHESUS

ANTIOCH

JERUSALEM

ALEXANDRIA

cea and consisted of over three hundred bishops. Since the bishops were considered to be the church and since this was a world gathering of the bishops, in reality this meeting gave visible expression to the catholic (universal) church. Constantine dominated the council, addressing it when he desired and determining the doctrinal position to be adopted.

The Council of Nicea (325)

After preliminary matters had been attended to, a confession of faith by Arius was presented. It defined the nature of Christ as being different from that of God and viewed Christ as a created being, greater than man and worthy of worship, but less than God. This creed was promptly and vehemently rejected. Bishop Eusebius of Caesarea then offered a creed which he said had been used previously in his church. The wording of this creed was ambiguous. When the orthodox party saw that the Arians were willing to accept the creed, they led a movement to reject it on the ground that it was not explicit enough. Then Athanasius, a young deacon from the church in Alexandria and the champion of the orthodox view, presented the following creed to the council:

> We believe in one God, Almighty Father,
> Maker of all things seen and unseen,
> And in one Lord Jesus Christ, the Son of God,
> Begotten of the Father and only begotten
> That is, from the essence of the Father,
> God from God, Light from Light, True God from True God,
> Begotten, not made,
> Of one essence with the Father.
> Through whom all things were made, both the things in heaven
>   and the things upon the earth,
> Who for us men and for our salvation,
> Descended and became flesh and became man,
> Suffered and arose on the third day, and ascended into the heavens,
> And is coming to judge living and dead.
> We believe also in the Holy Spirit.

Following this creed was the condemnation of anyone denying its doctrine, mentioning specifically the assertion by the Arians that Christ did not exist in all eternity. It should be noticed that this creed emphasizes the oneness of Christ with God the Father. The key words were "of one essence with the Father." Constantine decided that this creed would bring political and religious peace, doubtless at the advice of Bishop Hosius of Cordova, his ecclesiastical adviser. Therefore, with his approval the creed was adopted, and a decree of banishment was issued against Arius and those who followed his view. Christians who had been victims of imperial power just a few years before now utilized imperial power to persecute one another. Constantine later changed his mind and recalled Arius, banishing Athanasius. The complete doctrinal reversal meant nothing to his political mind. It is likely that Constantine had little grasp of Christian principles of doctrines. His deferred baptism, moral and ethical standards, and retention of the pagan office that guaranteed his place as a Roman god after death were in themselves evidence of his spiritual character.

Later History of Arianism

There was much dissatisfaction within Christianity after the decision of the Nicene council. The language of the creed led some to fear tritheism (three gods) and others to fear modalism (the loss of individual personality). By political maneuvering and playing upon the fears of sincere thinkers in the religious realm, Arianism gained the upper hand for a generation. A semi-Arian school developed which took a position halfway between that of Athanasius and the Arian view and asserted that while Christ was not of one essence with God, yet he was similar to God. This drew many followers from the strict Athanasian party. Athanasius himself was repeatedly banished for holding to the views of the Nicene Creed.

The political scene aided in bringing temporary Arian triumph. When Constantine died in 337, his three sons, Constantine II, Constans, and Constantius, divided up the Roman Empire. However, Constantine II was slain in 340 in a battle with Constans, and Constans committed suicide in 350. These two men favored the Nicene view. The third son, Constantius, was an Arian. His reign from 337–61, as sole ruler after 350, provided opportunity for Arianism to develop with the blessing of imperial authority.

In addition to banishing Athanasius, Constantius dealt severely with pagan and Jewish adherents. The death penalty was enacted for offering pagan sacrifices and for becoming a Jewish proselyte. Partly because of this severity, a pagan reaction took place. Constantine had slaughtered his relatives, other than the three sons, in order to insure proper succession. He missed two intended victims. One of them, Julian, the son of a brother whom Constantine had slain, secretly embraced paganism and in 361 wrested control of the Empire from Constantius. He did everything he could to increase divisions in Christianity. Athanasius was brought out of banishment, and the other dissenters were encouraged. Julian also endeavored to introduce a reformed and refined paganism— adopting many Christian elements—as a rival to Christianity. After his death in 363, however, the succeeding emperors favored Christianity of the Nicene type. Arianism slowly receded in influence through the succeeding centuries. The second universal council of 381 at Constantinople reaffirmed the position of the first council relative to the person of Christ.

Results of Arianism

One important result of the Arian movement was the spread of its doctrine of Christ through missionary activity. In 340 while Arianism enjoyed imperial favor, a young missionary called Ulfilas, trained in the Arian doctrine, was sent to the Visigoths. He served until his death in 383, apparently receiving much assistance that cannot now be determined. Ulfilas himself labored diligently, but the conversion to Arian Christianity of great masses of Visigoths and neighboring tribes could hardly have been the work of one man. Ulfilas is best remembered for reducing the Gothic tongue to writing through the translation of the Scriptures. As a result of his work and that of others, when the Roman Empire was finally overrun by these German tribes in the late fourth and fifth centuries, the task of Roman Catholic Christianity was made easier. A remarkable number of the invaders had already embraced Arian Christianity and required only indoctrination into Nicene formulation.

Another result of the Arian movement was the adoption by Constantine of the general policy of physical persecution against ecclesiastical dissenters. It is true that the Donatists had suffered physical persecution at the hands of Constantine in 316, following their refusal to accept the decision of the Council of Arles. After five years Constantine ceased closing Donatist churches and banishing their bishops, feeling that the results of this use of force were unsatisfactory. With this experience there was some question of whether Constantine as sole emperor would continue such a policy. His determination to continue it suggests his deep desire to secure at least external conformity.

Furthermore, the Council of Nicea provided a precedent and pattern for future councils of this sort. Everyone knew that the decision of the council had been arbitrary. Constantine had determined what the council should decide. Yet at the same time decrees of the council were recognized as authoritative Christian pronouncements. Thoughtful leaders pondered this new development. Christian motives and conduct were secondary; decisions were the authoritative matters and the goal to be attained. Apparently the lesson was learned. Many of the later universal councils reached their decisions through physical coercion and rough-and-tumble tactics. It is difficult to see what part genuine Christianity had in some of them.

Finally, the Council of Nicea gave visible form to the catholic church. It will be remembered that in the writings of Cyprian in the previous century it was asserted that the church existed in the bishops. The catholic church (universal Christianity), then, could become visible when all the bishops gathered in council. This was effected at Nicea. It completed the ecclesiastical machinery for universal domination by a spiritual monarch.

The New Relationship

The beginning of an alliance between Christianity and the Roman Empire under Constantine profoundly influenced the history and development, both of the religion and of the state. Christianity was officially decreed the religion of the Roman state under Emperor Theodosius (378–95).

A new area of controversy.—Before Nicea Christianity had really had no occasion to ponder what its relations to the state should be. Centuries of secular persecution had followed the original antagonism of the Empire against an "illegal" religion. The attempt to adjust the relations between Christianity and the secular power forms a large part of the history of Christianity in the centuries to come. Some felt that the state should control the church. Roman history recommended this view, for religion had been a department of the government long before Christianity had been established. Constantine assumed this attitude, as did his sons. The emperor was the "bishop of bishops." Such a relationship became known as caesaropapacy—state domination of the church. Others felt that the church should be above the state. This became the ideal of the developing Roman Catholic system. Still others looked upon each institution as having a peculiar stewardship from God and believed that the two should work alongside one another without undue interference. It should be said that this problem has never been settled to the satisfaction of all. A new direction, tremendously significant in the history and development of Christianity from Nicea to the present, was begun.

The increase of secular influence.—It is difficult to conceive how much secular influence was exerted upon Christianity through the alliance between church and state under Constantine. In the area of organization, for example, Christianity made use of the imperial pattern. In the terminology of American geography, Christianity organized on the basis of city, county, state, sectional, and national political divisions. After the development of the office of pope in the next century, the imperial organization and that of Christianity were strikingly similar.

The very motives of Constantine in adopting Christianity indicate the direction to be taken. He wanted to use Christianity as a political and social factor in building the state. This meant the use of secular power, as has been seen, in establishing uniformity.

Dissent must be stamped out. It meant imperial settlement of doctrinal and ecclesiastical disputes. The administrative officers of state found themselves advising ways to increase efficiency in Christian administration; Christian officers under Constantine began to use methods and ideas in church life that they had learned in government service.

SOUNDS LIKE U

Nicea also brought with it the problem of secular authority in the filling of important ecclesiastical offices. The Christian movement was too important politically to allow radicals of any kind to hold high office. A bishop must now be pleasing to state as well as to God. In this sphere secular influence was widely exercised.

The influx of the unregenerate.—All historians speak of the mass movement into Christianity after it had come into imperial favor. While Christianity was not officially termed the religion of the state for about half a century, yet Constantine's appeal to his subjects to become Christian, his generous gifts to those who were Christians, and the ease with which Christianity could be embraced aided many to make their decision. The similarity between the magical sacraments of Christianity and parallel rites in paganism gave the prospective members a feeling of familiarity in their initiation. In the army, especially, the influence of some sagacious leader might result in the winning of all his loyal followers within a short time.

An example of the ease with which this could be accomplished may be seen in the conversion of one of the Frankish chieftains in the next century. Clovis faced a crucial battle on the following day. He made a solemn vow that if the Christian God of his wife would give victory in battle, then he would become a Christian. Having won the victory, he kept his vow. When his army learned what was happening, they also wanted to join. It was accomplished rather easily. The soldiers marched alongside a river where priests stood with branches from trees. As the soldiers went by, the priest dipped the branches into the river and flung baptismal water upon them, all the while repeating the proper formula. As soon as the water touched the soldiers, of course, they supposedly were made Christians. It is not surprising that when these sprinkled pagans entered the membership of the Christian churches, they brought pagan ideas with them. Consequently, Christianity was more and more infected with pagan corruptions as it became a popular movement.

Impetus to the rise of monasticism.—The gorging of Christian churches with sprinkled pagans was responsible in part for the rapid development of asceticism. Laxity in Christian life and ethics has always brought reactionary movements. Sometimes these did not develop into parties or schisms but brought expression in individual remorse that led to ascetical practices. Remaining within the regular churches, conscientious Christians found relief of soul through fasting, long hours of prayer, and rigorous spiritual discipline. Others, however, chose a more radical method. In the East, where the climate was inviting during most of the year, men left the churches and their homes and became religious hermits. They took literally the injunction of Jesus to the rich young ruler to "leave all and follow me." They felt that by burying themselves in a cave away from men and engaging in prayer and spiritual contemplation they could "lose their lives in order to save them."

One of the most famous of these hermits was Anthony of Thebes in the middle of the third century. Fleeing from men at about the age of twenty, he spent the next eighty-six years in a cave. He was venerated as a very holy man, and his cave became a place for blessing. Others began leaving their homes and following his example. Before long there were so many hermits in the desert that the caves were all taken. Soon there came the formation of community or cenobitic groups. A number of hermits banded together under a common rule of organization. The earliest known movement of this kind was that of Pachomius which took place about 335 in Egypt.

From the East this movement spread into Asia Minor. The Western practical mind and the rigorous climate discouraged those who would flee to caves, but by the sixth century an orderly and effective movement was begun in Italy by Benedict of Nursia. This will be discussed in a succeeding chapter.

68

Concluding Summary

A new direction had come. The problem of imperial persecution had been replaced with the problem of imperial favor. The Christian ideal was greatly influenced by the pattern and patronage of the Roman government. The development of the universal council as an authoritative legislative body for all Christianity, coupled with the intense desire of Constantine for universal conformity to a single Christian pattern of doctrine and practice, was a large stride in the direction of a monarchial government in Christianity. Christians had learned to persecute fellow believers in an effort to secure uniformity.

The succeeding chapters will tell the story of the rise of the Roman Catholic Church. All of the ingredients necessary to make up such a system were now assembled—sacramentalism, sacerdotalism, episcopal government, Roman ambition, ecclesiastical rivalry, an authoritative world gathering, and the pattern and power of the secular state. All of these elements were utilized fully by the Roman bishop in the next period.

6

Roman Catholic Foundations

By 325 WHEN THE first catholic (universal) council met, Christianity had assumed several characteristics that were distinctively nonscriptural and may be called by the name "Catholic." These include the idea of a visible universal church composed of the bishops, the belief that the sacraments (as they will now be called) carried with them a magical kind of transforming grace, the employment of a special priesthood (the clergy) which alone was qualified by ordination to act in the administration of those sacramentals, and the recognition of the bishops as the ruling officers (episcopal government). All of these characteristics may be seen at the present time in the Christian groups which call themselves Catholic—Roman Catholic, Greek Catholic, and Anglican Catholic.

After 325 came the foundations for a new advance in hierarchal development. The oligarchy, the rule of many bishops, began to change into a monarchy, the rule of one bishop—the bishop of Rome. This does not mean that the Roman bishops were not among the outstanding bishops of all Christianity before 325; for as early as 58 the apostle Paul had complimented the church at Rome for her excellent reputation through the whole world. The earliest noncanonical writings tell of the great influence of the large, wealthy, and generous body of Christians at Rome. The church had benefited from the illustrious name and history of the city in which it was located, for Rome had been the center of the world for centuries. It was customary, furthermore, for churches having problems to write larger and more experienced churches for advice in matters of discipline and doctrine; it is known that the Roman Church received many such appeals for help. A good example is the letter which the church at Corinth addressed to Rome in the last decade of the first century. The Corinthian church, exercising her prerogatives as an autonomous body, had removed several presbyters who had been appointed by the apostles, and in the controversy someone had written to the church at Rome for advice. The reply by Clement, a pastor or bishop at Rome, is probably typical of letters written by many bishops to churches asking for advice in such matters. The Roman Church was later than some of the others in setting forth a single bishop above the remainder of its officers, apparently Bishop Anicetus (154–65), being the first monarchical head of the Roman congregation.

The reference of Bishop Irenaeus of Lyons to the apostolic tradition of the Roman bishop carried with it an emphasis on the doctrinal rightness of Rome rather than the ecclesiastical authority of Rome. Irenaeus, like Cyprian, could write more eloquently about the eminence of the bishop of Rome than he could act out. In the middle of the second century a quarrel broke out between Rome and certain of the leaders in Asia Minor involving the proper date for observing Easter. The Eastern practice was to celebrate it according to the moon, regardless of what day of the week the celebration came on, while the Roman practice was to wait until the following Sunday. Bishop Polycarp (a disciple of the apostle John), representing the East, and Bishop Anicetus, representing the West, could not agree, and each continued to observe Easter according to his own practice. The controversy was taken up in every church and threatened the peace of the Christian world. Synods (or councils) were called at Rome and in Palestine, in particular, which debated the merits of each side, and the practice of observing Easter on Sunday was generally favored. When the Ephesian bishop and many churches in Asia Minor refused to change their ancient practice, synods or no synods, Bishop Victor of Rome (189–98) declared them excommunicated. Promptly Irenaeus rebuked Victor for this action, raising a doubt as to what Irenaeus actually believed relative to the orthodoxy and authority of the Roman bishop.

Tertullian, the Carthaginian presbyter who has been called the father of Latin Catholic theology, had no sympathy with claims by the Roman bishop and in 207 broke with him and joined the Montanist movement. His pupil Cyprian also could write eloquently about the unique place of the Roman bishop, but about 250 he vigorously told the bishop to quit meddling outside of the Roman diocese. The only superiority he would allow to the Roman bishop was in dignity. It is significant that the fourth-century Donatists addressed their appeal to a council, then to the emperor, not to the Roman bishop.

By 325, then, the Roman bishop, although undoubtedly considered to be one of the strongest bishops and viewed by some as possessing an unusual dignity among bishops, yet was but one of many bishops, all of whom, according to Cyprian, possessed equal and apostolic authority. The sixth canon of the Council of Nicea (325) recognized the Roman bishop as being on a par with the Alexandrian and Antiochian bishops. It is significant that a forgery was inserted into the copy of this canon in the possession of the Roman bishop, which alleged that Rome had always held the primacy. This pious fraud was later discovered when the Roman copy was compared with other copies of the Nicene records. It suggests the mind of those in Rome as they sought by every means, fair or otherwise, to claim pre-eminence. It is no wonder that many scholars today doubt the texts of some of the older writings which have been preserved by Rome; forged insertions and false decretals appear throughout the history of the Roman Church in an effort to forward their position.

Between the first universal council of 325 and the fourth held at Chalcedon in 451, however, the Roman bishop laid the foundations for the ecclesiastical monarchy now known by his title. There were many outstanding factors that entered into this development.

Able Men

One of the most important reasons for the rise of the Roman bishop is the type of men who held the office. They recognized the dignity of their position and sought in every way to forward it. As evidenced by the forgery mentioned heretofore, they wanted first place and actively sought it. Their immediate territory was well organized so as to consolidate their holdings. The marvelous organizational skill of the Romans was turned into ecclesiastical channels. A whole series of subordinate officers guaranteed discipline and uniformity.

Two of these men were quite vocal in their claims. Innocent I (402–17) was the first bishop of Rome to claim universal jurisdiction by the Roman bishop on the basis of the Petrine tradition. Leo I (440–61), who may be rightly called the first pope, asserted scriptural authority for Innocent's claims, secured imperial recognition of his claims to primacy, and by a confluence of political and ecclesiastical interests was able to dictate the doctrinal statement of the Council of Chalcedon, the fourth universal council in 451. "Peter has spoken," cried the bishops when Leo's *Tome* was read; and such recognition, imperial and ecclesiastical, laid the foundations for the papal system.

Geographical Position

The bishop of Rome had no rival in the Western world. Rome had been the ecclesiastical mistress of the West long before the rise of strong bishoprics in North Africa and Europe. This was not true in the East. Ancient and powerful bishops in cities like Alexandria, Jerusalem, Antioch, and Ephesus disputed constantly. Rather than choose an umpire among themselves, these bishops regularly appealed to the sole Western bishop. By so doing they unconsciously increased the Roman bishop's stature. Furthermore, the movement of history was westward. The eastern Mediterranean was surrendering its place in the sun. With the stirring of the German tribes in central and northeastern Europe and the westward surge of empire, Rome was in the center of advance.

Move of the Imperial Capital

In 330 the Emperor Constantine moved the capital of the Roman Empire from Rome to Byzantium, which became known as

73

Constantinople. Instead of weakening the position of the Roman bishop in so doing, the emperor unknowingly aided the growth of the bishop's prestige. As long as the emperor resided in Rome, the bishop must take second place. As "bishop of bishops," the emperor could overshadow his political subject and dominate the ecclesiastical policies of the bishop. The removal of the emperor to a new city in the East emancipated the Roman bishop from the secular influence and allowed him to develop without restraint. As a matter of fact, with the move of the emperor the bishop became both ecclesiastical and secular sovereign. The Roman bishops became administrators of the secular affairs of the city, defending it against military aggressors, maintaining internal order, supplying its physical needs, and initiating its foreign policy.

Political Prestige

Rome had been the center of the political world for several centuries when the last of the apostles died. How much prestige this political situation brought to the church of the city cannot be estimated. The importance of such political centrality is seen in the fact that Constantinople, location of the new capital, had no other claim to ecclesiastical prestige than that it was the seat of the emperor; yet in a little over a century it was Rome's greatest ecclesiastical rival because of its political importance.

History and Tradition

It has been pointed out that the church at Rome had a long and honorable history. It is impossible to find evidence of the present Roman claim that Peter was bishop of Rome for twenty-five years. The Scriptures connect Paul, not Peter, with the church at Rome. The tradition that Peter was pastor at Rome for a quarter of a century is very late, and outstanding Roman Catholic writers admit that it can never be proved. Furthermore, Roman claims of authority based upon this tradition were not made until the fifth century. That is, after the Roman bishop had become powerful, the right to wield such power was claimed in terms of the Petrine succession.

The whole theory was given scriptural basis by Bishop Leo I (440–61). He claimed that Peter had been the first bishop of Rome and then interpreted three Scriptures to prove that Peter was given the authority to rule all Christendom. The first passage is found in Matthew 16:18–19. This was interpreted to mean that Christ would build his church upon Peter personally and that Peter was given authority to bind and loose souls in a spiritual monarchy. The second scripture is John 21:15–17, which was interpreted to mean that Peter was to be the chief shepherd and have the task of feeding, tending, and caring for all of Christ's sheep in the world. The third scripture is Luke 22:31–32, which was construed as meaning that Peter, after having been turned from his errors by Christ, would become the chief teacher of Christendom. The theory alleged that Peter wielded this authority over the other apostles; that he passed this same authority down to his successors in the office of bishop of Rome; and that other bishops, like other apostles, were subject to the authority of the Roman bishop.

Doctrinal Wisdom

The bishop at Rome was able to strengthen his position as leader of other bishops by his ability to handle himself well during the doctrinal scuffles between 325 and 451. There were three controversies in the East (Apollinarian, Nestorian, and Eutychian) and one in the West (Pelagian) during this period. The speculative nature of the Eastern mind and the practical nature of the Western mind may be glimpsed in these controversies.

Was Christ human?—Apollinaris was bishop of Laodicea in the middle of the fourth century. In his effort to understand how Christ's nature could be viewed as both divine and human, he eliminated a rational human spirit in Christ and substituted the divine Word, taking literally John 1:14, "And the Word was made flesh." This protected the deity of Christ but eliminated his true humanity. Bishop Damasus of Rome condemned this view in 377 and gained added prestige when the second universal council at Constantinople took similar action in 381.

75

Was Christ's human nature separate from his divine nature?—The Nestorian controversy grew as much out of the ecclesiastical rivalry between the bishops of Rome, Alexandria, and Constantinople as it did from an effort to find the truth. Nestorius became bishop of Constantinople in 428. Shortly thereafter he strenuously objected to the name given to the virgin Mary—the mother of God. He asserted that Mary might be called the mother of Jesus' human nature but certainly should not be viewed as the mother of Christ's divine nature, as the term might suggest. Bishops Cyril of Alexandria and Celestine of Rome promptly condemned Nestorius. Their doctrinal objections were based upon the feeling that the view of Nestorius disrupted the unity of Christ's person and so separated Christ's nature into human and divine as to deny the deity of Christ. By physical and political force Bishop Cyril controlled the third universal council (at Ephesus in 431), which pronounced Nestorius guilty of heresy and deposed him. His followers fled to Persia and established a separate church which has continued through the centuries.

Did Christ have one nature or two?—The Eutychian controversy followed as a reaction to the Nestorian controversy. Eutyches, a zealous monk near Constantinople, profoundly moved by the differences between Bishop Cyril of Alexandria and the Nestorians, took the position that after the incarnation Christ had only one nature and that it was divine. Bishop Leo I of Rome sided with Bishop Flavianus of Constantinople in condemning Eutyches. In a long letter to Flavianus, Leo insisted upon two natures in Christ. In 449 Bishop Dioscurus, who had succeeded Cyril at Alexandria, caused a synod to be assembled at Ephesus in which by threat and violence the theory of Eutyches was approved. Leo of Rome called this the "robber synod" and refused to accept its findings, but because Emperor Theodosius supported Eutyches, the Roman bishop was powerless to act. In 450, however, Theodosius died, and his sister was favorable to the Roman view.

With her approval another council was summoned (recognized as the fourth universal council) and met at Chalcedon in 451. During the meeting the letter of Leo to Flavianus was read, and the assembled clerics cried out, "God has spoken through Peter; the fisherman has spoken." Leo's view was followed in the doctrinal definition of Christ's nature. The nature of Christ, said the council, was the same as that of God as to his deity and the same as man as to his humanity; Christ is one person in two natures united "unconfusedly, unchangeably, indivisibly, inseparably." The feeling of superiority over even a universal council was revealed by Bishop Leo of Rome. In deference to the political power of Constantinople, the bishop of that city, although without apostolic tradition, had been recognized as a patriarch by the council of 381 in Constantinople, and the Chalcedonian council of 451 asserted in its twenty-eighth canon that the bishop of Constantinople had authority equal to that of the Roman bishop. Leo refused to accept this decision by the ecumenical council, declaring that he would not recognize the bishop of Constantinople as his peer. He preferred to rule alone.

How is man saved?—The one Western controversy of this period centered in a very practical question and one which influenced the machinery of the church. The Western world did not argue over speculative matters, but when it came to a practical question that affected their program, they promptly and effectively dealt with it.

Could man have been saved without the special revelation in the Bible and through Christ, and does it require a special divine grace working upon the soul in regeneration to attain salvation? The controversy raising these questions began when Pelagius, a British monk, and his disciple Coelestius fled from Britain to Italy, then to North Africa about 411. Their teachings quickly came into conflict with the beliefs and practices of the churches in North Africa, for the Pelagians taught that it was not necessary that a child be baptized, since he had no original sin to be washed away. Such a direct denial of one of the important tenets of the Catholic churches brought prompt bickering. The Pelagian group said that every man could either choose to sin or choose to be righteous. They considered all of man's environment to be God's revelation, including creation, friends, circumstances, and insisted that no special regenerating grace was necessary for salvation. It was quite possible to be saved without the Scriptures and Christ's revelation, although these should not be minimized since they provided inspiration and guidance. There was no such thing as original sin for, they said, God creates each soul at the time of birth and endows it with purity and freedom. After the child is able to make his own choice, God expects him to use his environment, friends, education, and intellect to choose righteousness; and the child is capable of doing it.

Because of these views Coelestius was excluded from the church at Carthage in 412 and fled to Palestine to rejoin Pelagius. Here in 415 an interesting incident occurred which illustrates the general attitude toward the Roman bishop by Eastern bishops. Bishop John of Jerusalem and his presbyters were assembled to hear charges against Pelagius. After the evidence had been presented, John gave the decision that since Pelagius was from the West, he came under the authority of the bishop of Rome. That is, all *Latin* Christianity was viewed as coming under the sway of the Roman bishop.

The Roman bishops intermittently took both sides of the controversy. In 416, Bishop Innocent condemned the movement. After his death, in that year Bishop Zosimus publicly approved the teachings of Pelagius and Coelestius. In the following year, not accepting the idea that the Roman bishop might be infallible, the North African bishops condemned the Pelagian movement. Even the Roman Emperor Honorius in Constantinople issued an edict condemning the Roman bishop and any others holding to this heresy. Finally, Bishop Zosimos of Rome changed his position and approved the African view, ordering all Western bishops to make the shift in doctrine at the same time. Many eminent bishops refused to condemn entirely the views of Pelagius. At the universal council in 431 at Ephesus the Pelagian view was officially condemned, along with the Nestorians with whom the Pelagians had been friendly. A semi-Pelagian position was maintained by many of the bishops, laying emphasis upon man's good works and initiative in salvation. This position was taken in opposition to the alternative theory by the great opponent of Pelagius, Augustine of Hippo.

Augustine was the great theologian of the fourth and fifth centuries. He was born in North Africa in 354. Turning successively from philosophy to Manicheanism to skepticism to Neoplatonism to Christianity, he became the dominating figure in Christian thinking for a millennium. His profound experience of finding God and his deep devotion to God gave richness to his theological ideas. His *Confessions,* deeply personal and mystical, explain his doctrinal point of view.

In the Pelagian controversy Augustine asserted that Adam had been created faultless and with freedom, but that in Adam's fall all mankind had lost its purity and freedom. Augustine felt that the baptism of babies or adults washed away the guilt of original sin but not sin itself, and he taught that the sacraments of the Church were necessary to preserve the individual from additional guilt and penalty of this sin. He insisted that men cannot work for salvation, that even the ability to accept salvation is a gift of God. The helpless condition of man requires that God do everything. God both chooses those who should be saved (predestination) and enables them to be saved. Augustine's inconsistency may be glimpsed at this point. In his emphasis upon God's sovereignty Augustine left nothing for man to do in salvation; yet he demanded that infants be baptized in order to be saved from inherited guilt. If God predestinated a child to be saved, it would appear that baptism would have little effect in attempting to accomplish the same thing. Augustine's strong emphasis upon God's total sovereignty repelled some of his contemporaries as much as Pelagius' doctrine of man's ability to co-operate with God in attaining salvation, thus giving rise to the semi-Pelagian and semi-Augustinian views mentioned before.

In addition to his *Confessions* and his opposition to Pelagius, Augustine made two other distinct contributions. He established the official doctrine of the Roman Catholic Church relative to the Donatist controversy. The Donatists had said that when a bishop's character is unchristian or unrighteous, all the sacramental acts of that bishop are invalid. Thus, they had said, Bishop Felix could not properly ordain Caecillian and Caecillian could not administer saving baptism, because these two men were heretics; they had delivered up Scriptures to be destroyed during the time of persecution. Augustine reinterpreted the issue by teaching that a bishop's character made absolutely no difference in the validity of his acts, since the authority or insignia of the church guaranteed the validity of any official acts that a bishop might perform. This marked a great advance in the idea of an authoritative Church.

Augustine also put into written form the ideal toward which the Roman Catholic Church was struggling. Although unfinished, his twenty-two books entitled *City of God* sketched the conflict between earthly rule and the heavenly rule. It should be remembered that Augustine was writing at the time when the Germanic barbarians were overrunning the Western world. In the very year that he died these pagans were pounding at the gates of Hippo, his own city. Augustine described the earthly city, maintained through war, hate, and evil; in contrast he pictured God's city, slowly but surely growing to cover the earth and overcome the secular rule of the earthly city. This idea of a conflict between the spiritual—identified with the ecclesiastical system—and the secular was a prophecy of events to come and did much to fashion the thinking of Augustine's era and the Medieval period.

Concluding Summary

Thus from 325 to 451 the foundations for the Roman Catholic Church were laid. The world councils had provided an arena where the Roman bishop was able to exert growing authority. Arguing on the same grounds that had proved so effective against the Gnostics, the Roman bishops said that their tradition of succession to the apostle Peter endowed them with a continuing authority, and they quoted Scripture texts to prove that Peter had such authority. When wrong doctrinally, and even when snubbed by an ecumenical council, the Roman bishop showed his tremendous prestige and sagacity by shifting his position or standing firm, as circumstances warranted, and in it all maintaining his powerful place. The recognition by imperial and ecclesiastical authorities of Bishop Leo's pretensions to primacy, based upon the Petrine tradition, provides grounds for believing that Leo was the first of the Roman Catholic popes.

7

Roman Catholic Expansion

BETWEEN 325 AND 451 THE FOUNDATIONS of Roman papal control of the Catholic Church were laid. Roman claims were given a scriptural tone through the alleged primacy of Peter and the alleged apostolic succession through the Roman bishop. The period from 451 to 1050 was one of confusion and violence, but the very historical movement that brought the crisis to Roman Christianity—the barbarian invasions—also provided the opportunity for the papacy to expand its claims to include authority over secular powers and to widen the geographical extent of papal control.

Invasion by the Germanic Tribes

Even while Bishop Leo I of Rome (440–61) was securing recognition of some of his claims at the Council of Chalcedon (451), great racial migrations were taking place. During the second century it had been necessary for the Roman government to maintain large garrisons across central Europe to keep the German tribes from spilling over into the Roman Empire. As other tribes wandered south and west from the broad steppes of what is now Russia, additional pressure was put upon the tribes facing the Roman garrisons to move on into the empire. Throughout the third and fourth centuries of the Christian era the Roman rulers fought continuously to stem the invasion of the various tribes known as Goths, Visigoths (western Goths), Ostrogoths (eastern Goths), Vandals, Franks, Burgundians, Lombards, etc. The tribes began moving in during the fourth century. The date when the Ostrogoths finally overthrew Rome is usually given as 476, but Rome had fallen as early as 410 to Alaric the Goth. Attila (452) and Geisric (455) were subdued only by the sagacity of Pope Leo I.

Some of these tribes were already nominal Christians. Ulfilas and his movement had reached many of them with Arian Christianity. As these Germanic tribes overran the old Roman Empire, it is true that they broke down the old Graeco-Roman civilization. But it is also true that they provided an opportunity for the Roman Catholic Church to mold a new civilization and to be elevated by it. These tribes did not destroy and slay as they advanced into Roman territory. Rather, they adopted whatever elements of the old culture appealed to them and intermarried with the population. Because of these factors, the power of the Roman Catholic system was not harmed permanently by the invasions.

Lasting benefits were secured. At least five of these benefits stand out. (1) The Germanic tribes provided new and numerous subjects for Roman Catholic control. They were awed by the beautiful and solemn services in the orthodox churches and were delighted with the magical sacramental system that provided for all of their needs. The Arian Christians among the tribes were unskilled in doctrinal matters, and it was not difficult to win all of them to the orthodox point of view on the person of Christ. (2) The tribes gave an opportunity to enlarge and tighten the machinery of the Roman Church. New churches were established, new priests trained, new catechisms provided. The untutored Germans brought no new doctrinal problems to complicate this tremendous expansion. (3) The Germanic tribes were rulers over the domains which they had conquered but became subjects of the religious training of the Roman system. This meant that the Roman hierarchy quickly attained great prestige and extensive influence. In addition, it gave the point of view suggested by Augustine's *City of God:* that the heavenly city was superior to the secular and would one day become dominant. (4) The Western world was cut off from the influence of the Roman emperor in Constantinople. Except for a brief period, the entrance of the Germanic tribes made it impossible for the emperor to exercise secular or ecclesiastical power over the Roman Church. Before

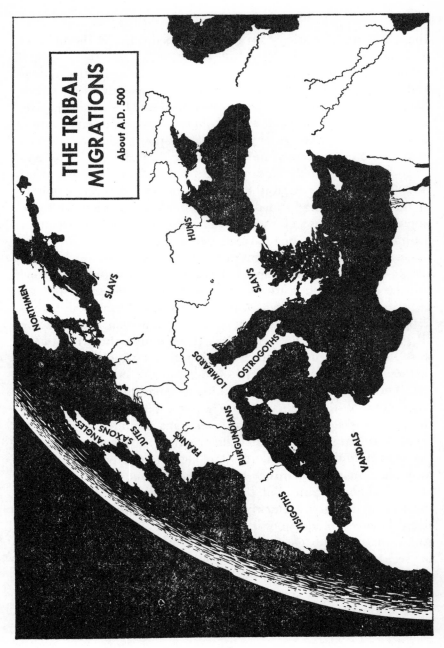

THE TRIBAL
MIGRATIONS
About A.D. 500

NORTHMEN

SLAVS

HUNS

SLAVS

OSTROGOTHS

LOMBARDS

ANGLES
SAXONS
JUTES

FRANKS

BURGUNDIANS

VANDALS

VISIGOTHS

the invasion the emperor had still viewed himself as bishop over all bishops and with his army had held a threat over the Western world. But with the barbarian wall surrounding the West, the emperor was helpless to interfere. (5) The winning of these barbarians to a recognition of the spiritual sovereignty of the Roman Church was a deathblow to the ambitions of any other Western bishop and brought gifts of territory and military protection.

Monasticism in the West

The barbarian invasions probably gave impetus to the monastic ideal in the West. It will be remembered that in the Eastern world Anthony and Pachomius had begun hermit life and cenobitic organization. In the West the movement developed more slowly but became more influential. The example of the East doubtless offered incentive to Western leaders to emphasize ascetical life. Men like Athanasius, Jerome, Ambrose, Augustine of Hippo, Martin of Tours, and Eusebius of Vercelli strove to convince many of the superior virtue of losing their lives monastically that they might save them. The cessation of persecution by the state also helped to popularize the monastic movement. Martyrdom was now rarely possible; the most rigorous means of self-denial and suffering for Christ came now through monasticism. The triumph of the "lax" party over the "strict" party in dealing with those who had been untrue to Christ caused many to look askance at the regular means of worship and service and to betake themselves to the caves or to monastic seclusion. Some viewed the Germanic invasions as the wrath of God upon Christianity for leaving its early purity and passion and determined to flee for safety into the rigorous movement that was developing in the West. Still others were dismayed by the pagan corruptions which were introduced into the thinking and practice of the churches. Another group bewailed the formalism in worship that now characterized Western Christianity and sought in monasticism a more personal communion with God. These and other factors help to explain the growth of the movement in the West.

Historically, the Western movement modified the character of monasticism. Although monasticism had originally been a layman's movement, Western monasticism made priests of all those taking the monkish vows. Furthermore, the Western movement magnified monasticism as an instrument to advance the very church system against which it was in part a protest. Monks became the missionaries and front-line soldiers of Christianity. As a matter of fact, monastic orders have been at the forefront of every victory achieved by the Roman Church since the Middle Ages.

The outstanding name of Western monasticism was that of Benedict of Nursia. About 500 Benedict became a hermit and in 529 founded a monastery at Monte Cassino, south of Rome. His system emphasized worship, manual labor, and study. In less than three hundred years monastic houses following his rule covered the European continent. More than any other man, Benedict was responsible for molding the monastic movement into practical lines and reconciling its ideals with those of the Church.

The most important monastic reform occurred in the opening years of the tenth century. Duke William of Aquitaine provided for the founding of a new monastery at Cluny in eastern France in 910. In an effort to free this monastery from corruptions which had entered into many others because of secular control and ecclesiastical interference, William provided that this house should look immediately to the pope for protection. Heretofore, under the Benedictine system, the various monasteries were controlled by the bishop in whose diocese they were located. Now a new type of monasticism was begun as a reform movement, which brought the institution into direct loyalty and obedience to the pope. The rule of this monastery was that of Benedict, interpreted strictly. This type of reform became popular and spread rapidly.

A development of the next century transformed even more the new type of monasticism. The abbots of Cluny began to assume jurisdiction over the new monasteries founded by Cluniac followers, as well as those embracing reform after Cluniac principles; consequently, the abbot of Cluny became the head of an extensive network of monasteries whose aims he could dictate and whose abbots he could appoint. Such an organization, whose head swore allegiance immediately to the pope, was greatly influential in undermining episcopal and secular authority opposing the papacy.

Missionary Expansion

Rome did not foster missions to any extent until the sixth century. Reference has been made to the work of Ulfilas in the fourth century under the auspices of Eastern Christianity. Bishop Martin of Tours vigorously assailed paganism in his country during the fourth century. Missionary work had been carried on in the British Isles. A Scotchman named Patrick, whose Christianity was not of the Roman Catholic type, evangelized Ireland in the early part of the fifth century, and an Irishman named Columba preached extensively in Scotland in the latter part of the same century. Another Irishman, Columbanus (543–615), began to preach in south Germany but was diverted into France, thence again into south Germany, to Switzerland, and finally to Italy, where he died.

The work of these missionaries, while not under the direction of Rome, prepared the way for Roman Catholic domination. In 596 at the direction of Pope Gregory I (590–604), a Benedictine monk named Augustine and forty companions went to England as missionaries. After a struggle with the different type of Christianity from Ireland and Scotland already there, the Roman Catholic type of organization and worship prevailed. At the Synod of Whitby (664), it was decreed that Roman Christianity should be practiced in all of England. The older type of Christianity was dispersed.

From England, Roman Catholic missionaries moved to the Continent. Wilfrid, a Benedictine monk who had been influential in establishing Roman Christianity in England, began mission work in what is now Holland about 678. He was followed there by Willibrord about 690. The greatest of the Roman Catholic missionaries from England was Boniface. During the first half of the eighth century Boniface worked tirelessly in northwestern

Europe to bring existing churches under Roman Catholic authority and to win the pagans. Other Roman Catholic missionaries pushed toward the north and east. Early in the ninth century Ansgar reached Denmark and Sweden. Cyril and Methodius, sent out by the Greek Church but voluntarily transferring to the Roman Church, worked extensively in the Balkans in the same century.

As a result of this missionary activity the Roman Catholic Church brought vast areas of population under its tutelage, instilling in them a loyalty that knew no ecclesiastical rivals.

Military and Political Aid

In the long run the barbarian invasions of the West brought new and important allies to the Roman Catholic Church. It is true that for a period the various marauding tribes caused considerable trouble, fighting with one another and with the Romans. By skilful and armed opposition, the popes at Rome were able to maintain some semblance of order during the death of one culture and the molding of another. As secular rulers of the city of Rome, they gained prestige and power. Many of the barbarians were won quickly. When Clovis, the great Frankish chieftain, decided to cast his lot with the Christian God in the closing years of the fifth century, his entire army made the same decision, although hardly on religious grounds. Furthermore, several of the popes, such as Gregory I (590–604), made alliances with tribal leaders nearby and secured a measure of political freedom.

The story of the alliance of the papacy with the Frankish kingdom will be told in more detail later. It should be noticed here, however, that papal alliance in the eighth century with the strongest military power in Europe aided greatly in the expansion and the development of authority by the Roman Church. First, the immediate crisis was met when the Frankish kings defeated the Lombards who were threatening Rome. Second, the Frankish leaders gave to the papacy a large territorial domain in the vicinity of Rome, marking the beginning of what is known as the "papal states" during Medieval history. And in 751 the pope crowned Pippin, the strong military leader of the Franks, to be king instead of one of the hereditary line. What Pippin had asked for was simply the moral support of the papacy to forestall revolution in the Frankish kingdom during the change of the ruling house, but the prestige of a pope who could dispense, or at least insure, kingdoms was greatly exalted. When the pope crowned Charlemagne as Holy Roman Emperor in 800, there was a feeling that the papal office had the authority to make or unmake emperors.

Charlemagne

The greatest of the Frankish rulers was Charles the Great (771–814). As a military and political leader he had no peer in the Medieval era. He doubled the geographical extent of his empire. More than that, the empire was consolidated and well administered during his reign. His contribution to the expansion of the Roman Church was greater than that of any of the popes. As he pushed his secular military conquests, Charlemagne carried Roman Christianity with him. By 777 he had utterly destroyed the kingdom of the Lombards in northern Italy, replacing it with inhabitants who recognized the authority of the pope. He forcibly required the Saxons in northwestern Germany to accept Christianity. When he moved against countries already nominally Christian, he required them to come into the orbit of the Roman pope, as in the case of the war against Bavaria.

One of Charlemagne's important contributions came in the fields of education and literature. He combed Europe to secure scholars who would found schools and produce literature. Priests were encouraged to widen their learning, in some cases to begin it. From Charlemagne's hand the Roman Church received many gifts and great prestige.

It is clear that Charlemagne viewed his relation to the Church much as Constantine had. Even in matters of controversial theology he felt free to summon synods and issue authoritative decrees. At the Synod of Frankfurt in 794 Charlemagne took a position opposite to that of a general council—that of Nicea in 787—

and also to that of the pope by forbidding image reverence and worship.

In all, however, the secular support of Charlemagne probably did more to advance the papal cause than any other single factor in this period.

Forged Documents

Two important forgeries were effectively used by the Roman popes during this period. The first was known as the *Donation of Constantine.* This spurious document asserted that when the Emperor Constantine had moved his capital to Constantinople in 330, he had donated to the bishop of Rome sovereignty over the Western world and had ordered all Christian clergy to be obedient to the Roman bishop. The forgery was a crude one, for it had literary and historical reflections of the eighth century. It probably was produced about 754 in an effort to induce Pippin the Short and his successors to recognize the secular claims of the papacy in the West. It was a successful forgery, for not only did Pippin give to the papacy the land in Italy conquered from the Lombards, but his successors recognized the *Donation* as genuine and based their conduct upon it. The forgery was not discovered until the fifteenth century, after the document had served well its purpose.

The other documents involved in the same forgery were known as the "Pseudo-Isidorian Decretals." Isidore of Seville had collected genuine ecclesiastical laws and decretals in the seventh century and published them as a guide for future action. The forgery of some additional decretals took place about a century later. Its effort was to magnify the office of the pope against the claims of the archbishops and metropolitans by quoting the primitive documents in papal favor. It was officially used by the popes after the middle of the ninth century. By the time that it had been proved to be a forgery in the eighteenth century, this pious fraud also had been effective in establishing the power of the pope over the Church.

Feudalism

Charlemagne's son and three grandsons continued his kingdom, but decay had begun to undermine it. The rule of the Carlovingian line (the line of Charles) broke down in the closing years of the ninth century. With the decline of a strong central government, the movement known as feudalism developed. It was a simple and natural process. When there was no central king, local strong leaders organized themselves and those whom they could control into small armies and small kingdoms. The size of the kingdom depended upon the strength of the leader. Sometimes it consisted simply of a city; sometimes it included large areas. Each kingdom became a complete monarchy. The sovereign or ruler required that all in the area of his kingdom swear personal fealty to him.

The lowest class in this system was that of the *serfs*. These men and women were the slave laborers and were treated as chattel, bound to the soil. Above them in dignity were the *freedmen*, who were not slaves but had no privileges and very little liberty. The *leudes* were holders of land by the favor of the sovereign, administering sometimes small tracts and sometimes vast areas. It was they who exercised complete supervision over the freedmen and the serfs beneath them. The more important of the leudes served as a sort of advisory council to the sovereign and assisted in community functions, such as administration of justice and community enterprises. When enemies threatened, all of these vassals took up arms to protect the rights of the sovereign.

At first glance it might appear that feudalism would greatly harm the interests of the Roman Catholic system. Some of the petty sovereigns might be unfriendly to the pretensions of the pope. As a matter of fact, the immediate result of feudalism was the decline in authority and prestige of the papal office. Bishops were leudes in many of these small kingdoms and were forced to take the oath of allegiance to the secular sovereign. Religious work was neglected in the press of secular duties.

However, when measured in terms of centuries, the papal system was not permanently injured by feudalism. Bishops sometimes became sovereigns in small kingdoms or as vassals were sometimes given large grants of land by the sovereign. Subsequently, much of this land fell into the hands of the Roman Church. In addition, a popular reaction against secular authority resulted in a zealous devotion to spiritual things on the part of the bishops. Furthermore, the kindly treatment accorded to vassals by bishops in places of authority, contrasting considerably with the treatment accorded by secular sovereigns in many cases, resulted in a feeling of affection and loyalty among the lower classes for the religious leadership. All of these factors in feudalism worked to the advantage of the Roman system, even while papal prestige and authority were at a low ebb.

Internal Developments

Worship.—During the period from 451 to 1050 the Roman Catholic method of worship began to be copied throughout the West. Variations in language, order, and liturgy were eliminated as much as possible. Worship was centered in the observance of Mass (the Supper) which, as described previously, had become more than a sacrament to bring grace to the one partaking; it was now looked upon as the "unbloody" sacrifice of Christ again, the shedding of his blood and the breaking of his body. The symbolism had become completely literal. The wine was not yet withheld from the people. Although not defined, it was generally conceived that something happens to the bread in the Mass to change it into the body of Christ. An extensive system of mediating saints had grown up. Martyrs were invoked by name to ask their intercession. The worship of the virgin Mary also increased considerably during this period. The story was spread that she had been taken immediately into heaven at her death. Prayer was offered to Mary for help and intercession. Relics became an increasingly important part of the religious life. The number of sacraments was not yet fixed; some theologians argued for simply two (baptism and the Supper), some insisted upon five, while some would have a dozen. Auricular confession had been well established, and the idea of merit from external works became widespread. Monasticism of the Benedictine type covered Europe.

Doctrinal controversies.—The doctrinal controversies in which the Roman popes engaged had their source, as might be supposed, primarily in the speculations of the East. These controversies were influential, however, in establishing ecclesiastical and secular relationships. In this period the papacy moved directly to assert its authority, not only over ecclesiastical rivals, but over secular powers as well.

[handwritten margin note: CONTROVERSY GOOD IN SOME SENSES - KEEPS LEADERS ON TOES AND HONEST AND TEACHING PEOPLE]

One of the first disputes occurred when the patriarch of Constantinople refused to banish a heretic. Pope Felix III (483–92) attempted to excommunicate the patriarch, dismissing him from the priesthood, cutting him off from Catholic communion and from the faithful. Felix asserted that his authority as the successor of Peter enabled him to do so. However, even the Eastern bishops who had been loyal to the papacy informed Felix that he had no power of this kind, and they chose communion with Constantinople rather than with Rome. For thirty-five years this schism continued. Through political sagacity, a succeeding pope healed the schism with no loss of dignity.

A very important doctrinal controversy was brought over from the previous era—the question of the nature of Christ. The Council of Chalcedon (451) had defined the nature of Christ as being twofold—completely divine and completely human. Conciliar action did not convince many in the East. The opponents of this decision took the name of Monophysites (one nature). Practically all of Egypt and Abyssinia, part of Syria, and most of Armenia took up Monophysitism and have retained it to the present. In an effort to mollify this large section of the Eastern World, Emperor Zeno (474–91) at Constantinople issued a decree that practically annulled the definition of Chalcedon, but the only result was to alienate the West.

In another effort to placate the Monophysites, Emperor Justinian (527–65) issued a series of edicts in 544 which also compromised the Chalcedonian definition in favor of the Alexandrian interpretation so as to mean that the human nature of Christ was subordinate to the divine. Pope Vigilius (538–55), who owed his office to imperial influence, at first refused to accept the action of Justinian, but imperial pressure in 548 induced him to consent. Two years later he changed his mind and refused to attend a council to discuss the question. At the conclusion of the council in 553, Pope Vigilius was excommunicated and Justinian's edicts were given conciliar authority. The pope then apologized and accepted the council's action, and the excommunication was lifted.

Still another attempt was made to conciliate the Monophysites. Through the influence of Patriarch Sergius of Constantinople, Emperor Heraclius set forth a doctrinal interpretation which in 633 brought favorable response from the Monophysites. This interpretation shifted the area of discussion from the *nature* to the *will* or *energy,* asserting that Christ had one divine-human energy or will. Pope Honorius (625–38) was consulted and replied that Christ had one will but that the expression "energy" should not be used since it was unscriptural. Succeeding popes took the other side of the question. One of them, Pope Martin I (649–55), defied the order of Emperor Constans II (642–68) not to discuss the question and assembled a Roman synod in 649 which, among other things, condemned the emperor's order. The emperor promptly seized the pope and sent him into exile to die. However, the Monophysites meanwhile had been overcome by the Mohammedan invasion; so to please Rome and restore unity, Emperor Constantine IV (668–85) summoned the sixth universal council at Constantinople in 680–81, which asserted that Christ had two wills. Interestingly enough, this council condemned the so-called infallible Pope Honorius as a heretic.

Probably the bitterest of the doctrinal controversies began in the eighth century and is known as the "iconoclastic [image-destroying] controversy." The use of images in worship had become quite popular in both Eastern and Western Christianity since the time of Constantine, who had died in 337. The primitive Christians had refused to keep any kind of idol or image either in the home or at church and for that reason were called atheists by the pagans of the second century. However, the influence of paganism brought the extensive use of images, ostensibly at first for the sole purpose of teaching through pictures and statues. These images soon began to be looked upon as possessing divine qualities. They were venerated, kissed, and, in some cases, worshiped by enthusiastic supporters. The Mohammedans objected strenuously to this idolatry and, partly as a political move to conciliate the Mohammedan Caliph, Emperor Leo the Isaurian (717–41) issued an edict in 730 against the use of images. Despite the fanatical opposition of the monks, the images were removed from Eastern churches.

When the emperor commanded the churches in the West to remove images, he met further opposition. He argued with the pope that image worship is prohibited by both the Old and New Testament and by the early fathers, that it is heathenish in its art and heretical in its doctrinal ideas. In reply Pope Gregory II (715–31) said that God had commanded the cherubim and seraphim (images) to be made; that images preserve for the future the pictures of Christ and the saints; that the commandment against images was necessary to prevent the Israelites from heathenish idolatry, but this danger no longer existed; and that adoration and prostration before the images do not constitute worship, simply veneration. The controversy continued for more than a century.

Through political maneuvering by the regent Irene, the seventh universal Council of Nicea in 787 upheld the right of image worship. Charlemagne, emperor in the West, flatly opposed the decree of this council and the position of the popes, insisting that images were for ornaments, not worship. During the controversy Pope Gregory III (731–41) pronounced the sentence of excommunication against anyone removing, destroying, or injuring images of Mary, Christ, and the saints. This attitude was continued by the popes, despite the opposition of Charlemagne. Emperor Leo the Armenian (813–20) voided the decrees of the Second Nicene Council of 787 as soon as he had taken office, but image worship achieved final victory when the regent Theodora

(842–67) ordered the images restored and the iconoclasts persecuted. A limitation was placed upon images in the East, permitting only paintings and mosaics in the churches. Statues project-
ing beyond the plane surface were forbidden. No limitation of this
kind was made in the West. Images were even more venerated
and widely used there as a result of the controversy.

Strong popes.—The expansion of papal authority during this
long period (451–1050) rested, in the final analysis, upon the able
men who occupied the chair at Rome. The work of Leo I
(440–61) has been mentioned. During the last years of his pontificate he showed his growing power by humiliating Archbishop
Hiliary of Arles through restoring a bishop whom Hiliary had
deposed legally and by having Hiliary imprisoned for disobedience. He meddled with ecclesiastical rivalries in Greece and
North Africa and claimed final authority in everything Christian.

Gelasius (492–96) asserted the primacy of the Roman pope in
every church in the world; Symmachus (498–514) claimed that
no tribunal on earth could try a pope. Gregory I (590–604) was
probably the ablest pope of the Medieval period. By careful diplomacy he wooed imperial support. He established the practice
of bestowing the pallium upon every bishop, making the pope's
consent necessary to a valid ordination or consecration. A part of
his program emphasized the need for a celibate (unmarried)
clergy. His theology summed up the sacramental system of the
Medieval period and was notable especially for its emphasis upon
good works and purgatory. His missionary interest in England
caused him to send Augustine the monk in 596. He revised church
music and ritual and worked toward making Rome's pattern uni-
form throughout the world. His encounter with the patriarch of
Constantinople was not entirely successful (as will be seen in succeeding pages), but he did not allow this to diminish his exalted
view of his office. Nicholas I (858–67) was the last outstanding
pope before the deluge of anarchy. He magnified the missionary
program, excommunicated the patriarch of Constantinople during a brief schism, required the Holy Roman Emperor, Lo-
thair II, to take back a divorced wife, and humiliated those

archbishops who were tardy in obeying his instructions to the letter.

Anarchy and Confusion

The closing two centuries of this period provided a crucial test for the papacy. The events of this era will be discussed in more detail in chapter 9. It may be sufficient to note that Europe was in anarchy after about 880. The turmoil in Italy turned the papal office into a petty political prize. Between 896 and 904 there were ten popes, murder and treachery disposing of most of them. The period from 904 to 962 is known as the "pornocracy," connoting lewdness and immorality, because the papal office was controlled by unscrupulous and wicked men and women. From 962 to about 1050 the popes were named and controlled by the German emperors of the re-established empire. The papacy had reached its lowest point in prestige and authority, but a new day was dawning. Through an effective internal reform, the rise of orderly central governments, and the ability to use ecclesiastical weapons, the papacy soon reached new heights of power in both ecclesiastical and secular realms.

Concluding Summary

Between 451 and 1050 the Roman Catholic Church and the papacy which directed it made remarkable advances. The barbarian invasions were disguised blessings. Monasticism provided militant and trained soldiers. Missions expanded Roman Catholic influences even beyond the widely extended boundary of the new Holy Roman Empire under Charlemagne. The doctrinal controversies generally worked to the benefit of the papacy, although Honorius was condemned as a heretic and Vigilius was humiliated by Eastern councils. The alliance of Rome with the Franks during the eighth and ninth centuries brought it land, prestige, and authority. The breakdown of that central government brought loss and humiliation to the papacy. The Church had become so dependent upon the military and political strength of the state that it could not stand without them.

The struggle of the papacy to dominate both ecclesiastical and secular authorities has been described in this chapter in terms of papal expansion. There was another side that should also be noticed. The succeeding two chapters will deal with opposition from ecclesiastical rivals and from secular powers. The overlapping in the story will be justified by the different point of view which will be presented in these two chapters.

8

Religious Opposition to Roman Authority

THE ROMAN CATHOLIC Church did not attain its dominant position without encountering strong opposition from other Christians. This would be expected. The dignity of the Roman see had
always been recognized, but to create an ecclesiastical monarchy
with the Roman bishop as its head was hardly in accord with the
thinking of early Christian leaders. The earliest Roman bishops
about whom there is direct historical information were rebuked
by neighboring bishops for breaches in ecclesiastical and doctrinal matters. Before the close of the second century Roman bishops were condemned because they followed the Montanist heresy
and were excommunicated for ecclesiastical laxity. Men familiar
with this history could hardly be expected to accept at face value
the arrogant claims that later developed.

Weakness in Rome's Claims

There were several definite weaknesses in the claims for primacy by the Roman Church. Some of these may be noted.

Relative to apostolic succession.—Rome was not the only
church with a strong tradition. Both Irenaeus (185) and Tertullian (200) point out that many churches were founded by the
apostles and had apostolic writings. Corinth, Philippi, and Ephesus were mentioned in particular. More than that, Gregory I
(590–604), one of the greatest of the Roman popes, admitted that
the churches at Alexandria and Antioch had the same apostolic
background as Rome. His letter said, "Like myself, you who are

at Alexandria and at Antioch are successors of Peter, seeing that Peter before coming to Rome held the see of Antioch, and sent Mark his spiritual son to Alexandria. So, do not permit the see of Constantinople to eclipse your sees which are the sees of Peter." In other words, if the basis of Roman authority, as claimed, is succession from Peter, then Antioch and Alexandria should have a claim prior to that of Rome. As a matter of fact, if tradition constitutes the basis of authority, then Jerusalem, where Jesus established the first church, should have the primacy.

Relative to Peter.—It should be noted in particular that the claims of the Roman Church to universal dominion because of the alleged primacy of Peter were made very late. Innocent I (402–17) was the first Roman bishop to base his authority on the Petrine tradition. By that time, due to the influence of many other factors, Rome was already recognized as one of the principal bishoprics in Christianity. Leo I (440–61) prepared the first scriptural exposition of later papal claims about the primacy of Peter, basing them, as previously discussed, on Matthew 16:18–19, Luke 22:31–32, and John 21:15–17.

In the first passage the important words are "upon this rock," since the promise of binding and loosing is repeated to all the disciples on other occasions (see Matthew 18:18 and John 20:23). What is the rock upon which Jesus would build his church? The greatest theologians of the first four centuries did not agree with the Roman view. Chrysostom (345–407) said that the rock was the faith of the confession; Ambrose (337–97) said that the rock was the confession of the universal faith; Jerome (340–420) and Augustine (354–430) interpreted the rock as Christ. If one desires to be literal in the interpretation of this passage, he should continue his literal view to verse 23 where Jesus names Peter as Satan. The passages in Luke and John must be utterly twisted out of their meaning to buttress universal papal domination.

Furthermore, a reading of the New Testament fails to give the impression of any primacy on Peter's part. Apparently Peter did not recognize it; he gave a labored explanation to the Jerusalem church for baptizing Cornelius. The other disciples apparently were ignorant of it, for James, not Peter, presided at the Jerusalem conference. Paul's sharp rebuke to Peter and Peter's admission of error suggest that Paul had not been informed of Peter's primacy.

The Roman Catholic claim that Peter was the first bishop of Rome and served in that capacity for twenty-five years is completely unsupported by Scripture or primitive tradition. It is most difficult to see how this position can be sustained in view of Paul's letter to the Romans (about 58), which makes no mention of Peter, and the account of Paul's residence in Rome in the Acts of the Apostles. An agreement was made at the Jerusalem conference that Peter should limit his ministry to the Jews and Jewish Christians. It seems probable that the Roman church was predominantly Gentile, and it would be quite unlikely that Paul's letter to the Romans could have contained some expressions that are there had Peter founded the Roman church and been serving as bishop.

Relative to primacy of the Roman bishop.—If antiquity and tradition possess any authority, the principle of the equality of all bishops should claim a primary place. This was a very ancient and universal belief. The New Testament shows that even the apostles themselves respected the authority of the churches which they had established. Antioch did not ask Jerusalem for permission to begin the missionary movement, and Paul did not first consult Peter before preaching salvation to the Gentiles throughout the Roman Empire.

In the second century the same principle was followed. Bishop Irenaeus of Lyons condemned Bishop Eleutherius of Rome (174–89) for following after heresy and rebuked Bishop Victor of Rome (189–98) for intolerance, but still recognized their ultimate right to hold their own opinions. Origen (182–251) denied that the Christian church was built upon Peter and his successors; all the successors of the apostles, said he, are equally heirs of this promise. Cyprian (200–258) emphatically asserted the equality of all bishops, stating that each bishop holds the episcopacy in its entirety. Even Jerome (340–420), famous as a papal proponent and translator of the Greek and Hebrew Scriptures into the Vulgate (the official Latin version of the Bible), acidly remarked that whenever a bishop is found, whether at Rome, Constantinople, Eugubium, or Rhegium, that bishop has equality as a successor of the apostles with all other bishops. Pope Gregory I could use such an argument when protesting against the ecclesiastical pretensions of his rivals. If the patriarch of Constantinople is the universal bishop above all others, then bishops are not really bishops but priests, wrote Gregory. In other words, Gregory based his argument on the fact that all bishops are equal, and if one is exalted above the others, then the others cease in reality to have the episcopal office.

The victory of Leo I at Chalcedon in 451—which, in the thinking of many, established him as the first Roman pope—grew out of the recognition of Leo's claims concerning Peter's primacy and the transference of that primacy to the Roman bishops through historic succession. Even this achievement did not break down the ancient belief that one bishop is equal to another. Had it not been for the political and military support of the secular powers, the Roman bishop could never have asserted his claims, even in the West. Bishop Hiliary of Arles fought strenuously to maintain this principle, but Leo humiliated him through political power. The same thing was true with Bishop Hincmar of Rheims in his struggle with Pope Nicholas in the ninth century.

Opposition to Roman Pretensions

Since Rome was the earliest and strongest bishopric in the West, opposition in that section of the Mediterranean world was nominal. It is true that Tertullian and Cyprian, bishop of Carthage, defied the Roman bishop, and through the Medieval era many efforts were made by various bishops to resist the encroachments of papal power. Invasions by the Germanic tribes in the third and fourth centuries provided the opportunity for Roman Christianity to gain great multitudes of new followers who knew no rival loyalty; the Mohammedan seizure of North Africa in the seventh and eighth centuries eliminated any rivals from that area.

102

In the East the situation was different. Two outstanding religious centers vied for supremacy: Antioch, famous for its Pauline tradition, and Alexandria, viewed as Petrine in origin since it was thought that Peter had sent John Mark to that city as leader. Even before the founding of Constantinople in 330 as the capital of the Roman Empire and before the bishop of Jerusalem was strong enough to be recognized as a patriarch, these two cities had been ecclesiastical rivals. Mention has been made of the varying points of view in the doctrinal interpretation between the two cities. One of the causes for the influence of the bishop of Rome was that each of these rivals sought Roman support for his position against the other side. Consequently, appeals to the Roman bishop came frequently.

The Council of Nicea (325) recognized the equality of the bishops of Rome, Antioch, and Alexandria. The Council of Constantinople in 381 raised the bishop of Constantinople to the dignity of a patriarch, and the Council of Chalcedon in 451 gave that position also to the bishop of Jerusalem. Thus there were five strong bishops who were potentially rivals for first place. The Roman bishop had the great advantage. He was the only candidate from the West; sharp and ancient rivalry kept the Eastern patriarchs constantly vigilant lest one should gain some favored place; constant controversy and schism prevented careful organization and ecclesiastical consolidation in the East. The principal opposition to Rome came from Constantinople for two reasons: first, the political situation of Constantinople insured its prestige and power; and second, all of the rivals except Constantinople were overwhelmed by the Mohammedan invasion of the seventh century. These two elements deserve a brief discussion.

The rise of Constantinople.—The move of the imperial capital from Rome to Constantinople in 330 brought it important ecclesiastical influence promptly. Within a half century after the establishment of the city as capital, Constantinople was elevated to the place of chief rival of Rome, mainly through the work of Emperor Theodosius (378–95), who made Christianity the official state religion. The Council of Chalcedon in 451 reasserted the dignity of Constantinople and naïvely remarked that such eminence was due because of the *political* importance of the city. Evidently it took neither apostolic tradition nor religious orthodoxy to attain such a high place. By this time the bishop of Constantinople was simply a tool of the emperor in most respects. This situation is known as caesaropapacy, the domination of the church by the emperor. The several controversies of the Eastern world made Christianity a potential political danger. So it became necessary, in order to preserve unity in the political sphere, for the emperor to keep his finger constantly upon the Church. Doctrinally, Eastern Christianity developed the same sort of sacramentalism and sacerdotalism as Western Catholicism, although it practiced trine immersion for baptism.

Despite the inevitable clash between the strongest power of the East and that of the West, the day of reckoning was delayed because of invasions in each area. The Germanic invasion of the West and its far-reaching consequences have been described in chapter 7. The Mohammedan invasion of the East did not begin until the seventh century. Even before the Eastern collapse, it became apparent that the bishops in Alexandria, Antioch, and Jerusalem would not be able to stand in ecclesiastical conflict with Rome and Constantinople. Civilization was moving westward, and these cities lived in the glory of the past.

The bishop of Constantinople, however, challenged the pretensions of the Roman bishop, particularly after the Council of Chalcedon (451) had spoken in such exalted terms about the place of the Constantinopolitan office. Reference was made in the previous chapter to the effort by Pope Felix III to excommunicate Patriarch Acacius of Constantinople in 484 and to the refusal of the Eastern world to accept such authority on the part of the pope. The story of Pope Vigilius and his humiliation by the East (through imperial power) in the Council of 553 has been told. The claims of the patriarch at Constantinople became more extravagant when Emperor Justinian (527–65) recaptured Italy from the barbarians in about 536 and began to control the pope. The ambitions of Constantinople were not different from those

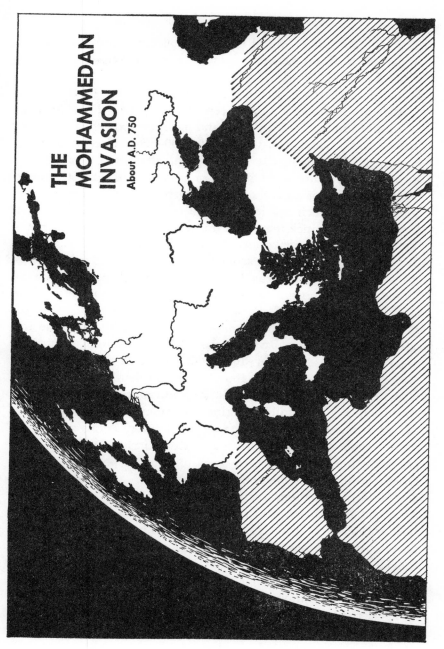

THE
MOHAMMEDAN
INVASION

About A.D. 750

of Rome. No longer would Constantinople, the imperial capital, be second to Rome or even equal with Rome, but it would supplant Rome.

In the last decade of the sixth century Bishop John of Constantinople claimed the title "ecumenical patriarch." The pope at Rome, unaided by military and political power, could only protest and scheme. He, Gregory I (590–604), circulated letters among the bishops of the East, arguing that there could be no such thing as a universal bishop or pope, basing his statements on the equality of all bishops. He begged the patriarchs at Alexandria and Antioch not to recognize the claims of the bishop of Constantinople since they, like himself, were successors of Peter. The pope did not make any demands because of his succession from Peter, nor did he excommunicate anyone. The battle of titles was temporarily won by the bishop of Constantinople, although Gregory assumed a new one—"servant of servants of God."

The Mohammedan invasion.—The opening years of the seventh century produced a religious and national movement that was destined to affect Christianity in both East and West for almost a thousand years. Its founder was Mohammed (570–632), who in his youth was a camel driver and merchant of Mecca in Arabia. In his trips into Palestine Mohammed had ample opportunity to observe the Jewish and Christian religions and to see the influence of Greek culture and Roman rule. In 610 he proclaimed a new religion which was a mixture of Jewish, Christian, Greek, and Roman elements, together with Arabian ideas and emphases. His system included prophets from Judaism (like Abraham and Moses) and Christianity (Christ) and outstanding military leaders from pagan history. The last and greatest prophet of God, however, was Mohammed, who supposedly was the Holy Spirit promised by Christ.

The Mohammedan system was completely fatalistic—all things are already determined. An individual's good works prove that he is elected to a paradise of sensual and fleshly enjoyment. These good works include prayer, fasting, almsgiving, and war against the unbeliever. After Mohammed's death in 632, his followers planned a conquest of the world. Striking westward, the Saracens overran Palestine and practically all of the East except Constantinople. Within a hundred years they had conquered all of North Africa, had crossed the Straits of Gibraltar into Spain, and were arrayed for battle near Tours, France. In 732 Charles Martel engaged them here in battle and defeated them in a crucial encounter that determined the culture of Europe. Again, seven years later, Charles inflicted a severe defeat upon them to save continental Europe from their devastations.

As a result of this movement, all of the Eastern rivals to Rome were swept away except Constantinople, which was under constant threat of capture. Wherever the Mohammedans ruled, Christianity became stagnant through rigorous repression. Priceless Christian manuscripts and books were destroyed by the invaders in Palestine and Alexandria.

Renewed Controversy Between East and West

The several doctrinal controversies of this period were discussed in the previous chapter. The bitterness of these struggles served to accentuate the ecclesiastical rivalry between Constantinople and Rome. Added to these factors were racial differences, political distrust (especially after Charlemagne was crowned in Rome in 800), and doctrinal and ceremonial variations. It appeared that a permanent schism would occur in the ninth century. Patriarch Photius of Constantinople (858–67 and 878–86—twice in the office) rejected the claims of the Roman popes and instituted a vigorous program to win the bordering Slavic states to Greek Christianity. Photius charged that the Roman Church was heretical in doctrine and practice, particularly in amending one of the ancient creeds without calling a universal council to discuss the matter. Pope Nichols I (858–67), however, was one of the ablest of the Medieval popes and maintained the Roman prestige. The issue was temporarily straddled by the Synod of Constantinople in 869.

The controversy was renewed in the eleventh century, resulting in a permanent schism between Latin and Greek Christianity. Patriarch Michael Cerularius (1043–58) of Constantinople deliberately provided the occasion for the schism. He was ambitious to forward the office which he held and felt that a break with the West would offer the greatest opportunity for advancement. Without too much difficulty he was able to stir up the wrath of Pope Leo IX (1049–54).

In the conferences to discuss the situation, the ancient differences between Eastern and Western worship were debated. Rome used unleavened bread; Constantinople, leavened bread. Rome had added a word to the Nicene Creed which taught that the Holy Spirit proceeded from Father and Son; Constantinople denied that additions could be made to the creed without an ecumenical council. Rome required clerical celibacy; Constantinople allowed the lower clergy to marry. Rome allowed only bishops to anoint in confirmation; Constantinople allowed priests to do so. Rome allowed the use of milk, butter, and cheese during Lent; Constantinople said no. These differences, however, were not the cause of the schism which came. By deliberate design the Roman representatives were irritated to the breaking point, and on July 16, 1054, the schism was begun. East and West formally excommunicated one another. Such is the situation at the present time, although efforts have been made to heal the break.

Dissent from Catholicism

Reference has been made in the previous period to dissenters from the general movement toward Catholic and Roman Catholic Christianity. Montanism, Novatianism, and Donatism maintained themselves through several centuries of struggle. Nestorian, Monophysite, and Monothelite parties, denouncing both Roman and Greek Catholicism, have continued to the present time in considerable strength.

Jovinianus and Vigilantius.—Two distinctly antipapal movements appeared within the Roman Church in the fourth and fifth centuries. One was headed by Jovinianus of Rome (about 378), who bitterly denounced the movement toward asceticism and

108

righteousness by works. His main tenet asserted that a saved man does not need merits from fasting, withdrawal from the world, and celibacy. A similar movement was begun by Vigilantius (about 395), who protested strongly against the honoring of relics, asceticism, and image worship. The first of these movements was condemned by Bishop Siricius of Rome (384-98) in a local synod, while the second was swallowed up in the barbarian invasions of the fifth century.

Paulicians.—One of the important dissenting minorities during the Medieval period was called the Paulicians. The origins of this group are obscure. Its general doctrinal position suggests that it grew out of primitive Armenian Christianity. Its name came either from veneration for Paul the apostle or from Paul of Samosata, bishop of Antioch until about 272. It is generally admitted that in the seventh century Constantine introduced a reform to a much older movement and was not the founder. The Paulicians bitterly opposed the Roman, Greek, and Armenian churches as "satanic." They viewed Christ as the adopted Son of God. Their emphasis upon the power of Satan has brought charges of dualism. It is uncertain whether they observed the ordinances or viewed them as completely spiritual elements. The apostle Paul was greatly venerated, and his ethical and moral teachings were emphasized and practiced. Their history has been a tragic one. Except under emperors Leo the Isaurian (717-41) and Constantine Copronymus (741-75), they were rigorously persecuted. In their zeal against images they took the side of the Saracens and assisted in destroying and pillaging. In the eighth and ninth centuries many Paulicians emigrated to Thrace and Bulgaria, thence on to the lower Danubian regions. It is thought that the Bogomiles of the Balkans and the Cathari of southern France gathered up their teachings and continued their movement. Some think that the Anabaptists were a product of these influences.

Concluding Summary

Ecclesiastical opposition to Roman pretensions had Scriptures and primitive principles in their favor. Apostolic and even Petrine succession were not confined to Rome. The scriptural evidences of Rome's primacy were developed late and are unconvincing. The ancient principle of equality of bishops was overcome by Rome only through severe struggle and the use of military and political coercion.

Constantinople, the principal opponent of Rome, made a determined bid for first place. After numerous and bitter controversies, a permanent schism was effected in 1054. Other ecclesiastical rivals of Rome were overwhelmed by the Mohammedan invasion of the seventh century. The Mohammedans succeeded in pushing into southern France before their defeat by Charles Martel in 732.

The record of ecclesiastical opposition to papal authority is very sketchy. Those within the hierarchical system who might oppose the domination of Rome would think twice before making outward protest or recording literary dissent. The only records were kept by those who looked upon the dissenters as heretical schismatics. There must have been much dissent that had no voice, for during the centuries immediately following the eleventh, opposition to papal authority sprang up in every part of Western Christianity.

9

Secular Opposition to Roman Authority

WHEN CONSTANTINE ASSUMED a friendly attitude toward Christianity and became sole emperor in 323, it was hoped that tension between the secular state and Christianity was a thing of the past. It is true that Constantine passed imperial edicts making it possible for Christianity to develop in a favorable atmosphere. One reason for the removal of the capital of the empire to Constantinople was that Rome was crowded with pagan temples and memorials. At the Council of Nicea (325) Constantine displayed a paternal attitude and until his death in 337, whatever his motives may have been, maintained a singularly constant devotion to the Christian movement. After Constantine's death some segment of Catholic Christianity was conscious of the antagonistic or repressive aspect of secular power throughout the remainder of the period. Before discussing specific instances of this, it is well to give a résumé of why secular opposition arose.

Reasons for Secular Opposition

Various reasons caused secular powers to struggle against Christianity. (1) *Religious antagonism* motivated a man like Emperor Julian (361–63) in his opposition to the Christian movement. It will be recalled that his family was slain by the order of his uncle, the Christian emperor. His personal resentment was transferred to the religion which his uncle professed, although Julian was enamored with paganism while a student. Upon becoming emperor, Julian attempted to reintroduce a refined paganism, but the attempt failed. (2) *A desire to control* Christianity for political or selfish purposes led many secular rulers, both East and West, to impose severe restrictions upon Christian leaders. As has been mentioned, this condition was known as Caesaropapism. (3) *Material possessions* in the hands of Christian bishops provided an excuse for attempts by some of the Germanic tribes to seize the land and goods of the Church. (4) *Rivalry with secular powers* constituted another reason for secular opposition. By the fifth century the Roman popes were beginning to assert their right to rule not only the spiritual world but the secular world as well. Such assertions, supported later on by ecclesiastical weapons, kept the papacy in constant struggle with secular powers. (5) *Internal controversies* added another reason for secular restriction and repression. Religious controversy, particularly in the East, could be very dangerous politically. Secular rulers felt that it was a political necessity to maintain control over Christianity. (6) *Corruption and decay* in Western Christianity brought the strong arm of imperial rule. Sometimes for religious reasons and sometimes for political considerations the late Medieval emperors appointed the occupants of the papal office and dictated their policies.

A brief summary of relations between the various secular powers and the developing Roman Church will provide historical examples of these several reasons for secular opposition.

Opposition from the Roman Empire Before 476

The three sons of Constantine succeeded him in 337. One was killed in battle, one committed suicide, and the third, Constantius, ruled until 361. Constantius was an Arian Christian, and his long rule brought repressions and antagonism to Nicene Christianity, which included Rome. It is significant that Athanasius, not the Roman bishop, was singled out as the target in the persecution of Nicene Christianity.

Emperor Julian (361–63) was anti-Christian in his attitude and actions. Had Constantine been a consistent Christian (or even a Christian at all), Julian might well have been reared to respect

Christianity and to embrace it. Julian's brief reign and the fundamental weakness of the refined paganism which he tried to introduce blunted the force of his antagonism.

The basic rivalry between church authority and secular authority was made clear in this period. Augustine's very influential writing, the *City of God,* set secular and religious authority over against one another and magnified their incompatibility. Fifth-century popes grasped the ideal, soon beginning to describe the relationship between the two powers as two swords—the *spiritual* sword as greater than the *secular* sword.

Struggle with the Germanic Tribes (476–800)

It is difficult to describe in a few words the complex story of the barbarian invasions of the West. Perhaps as a summary the movement can be divided into six general periods.

The breakdown of old Roman authority (about 392).—It has already been mentioned that since primitive times the Germanic tribes north and east of the Empire had only been restrained from overrunning the southern area through the establishment of strong garrisons across the northern frontier. In the third century the Gothic tribes almost succeeded in invading the Empire on two occasions. Finally, because of the increasing pressure of less civilized and stronger tribes pushing south and west from central Asia, the Visigoths were allowed to cross the Danube and secure refuge within the Empire proper. Aroused in 378 by alleged mistreatment, the Visigoths met the Roman army in the Battle of Adrianople and inflicted a severe defeat. Emperor Theodosius (379–95) was able to control them, but at his death the deluge began. The Visigoths were beaten away from Constantinople but moved westward to capture Rome in 410, Gaul two years later, and then settle down to rule in what is now France and Spain. The dikes had been breached, and barbaric tribes of every sort flowed into the Western empire. Vandals, Alans, and Suevi entered Gaul and Spain; the Franks and Burgundians settled in Germany; the Angles, Saxons, and Jutes occupied England; the Spanish Vandals conquered North Africa.

The rule of the army (until about 493).—The century after the barbarian invasions was one of confusion and conflict. Army chieftains became rulers. In 476 a mutiny by the Germanic tribes within the army resulted in the overthrow of the nominal Roman government and the elevation of a German general to the kingship, but this event was of no special significance.

The rule of Theodoric the Ostrogoth (493–526).—In 493 a new wave of barbarians invaded Italy—the Ostrogoths, the eastern Goths from Russia. Their chief, Theodoric, ruled from Ravenna in northern Italy and was successful in maintaining order.

The re-establishment of imperial control (535–72).—Justinian the Great secured the emperorship in Constantinople in 527 and immediately made plans for reconquering the West. By 534 the Vandals of North Africa had been defeated and the Ostrogoth kingdom in Italy had been attacked. During the lifetime of Justinian, imperial control of the West was maintained.

The kingdom of the Lombards (572–754).—More barbarians bearing the name Lombards swept south into Italy and captured the northern section. Although they did not take Rome, their strong military power prevented any other tribes from doing so. They were a constant threat to Rome's security, but on the other hand, their presence guaranteed a certain amount of freedom from Constantinople to the bishops of Rome.

The rise of the Franks (754–800).—The tribe known as the Franks was destined to become the dominating power in all Europe. The Romans had fought to hold this tribe, along with the others, from crossing the Rhine in northern Germany as early as the second century. With the breakthrough of the Visigoths in the fourth century, the Franks had fought their way into southern Germany and eastern France. An event of great significance for Christianity occurred in 496. Influenced by his wife, who was an orthodox Christian, and his great victory over the Alemanni at Strassburg in 496, the Frankish chieftain Clovis (481–511) adopted Christianity and with his army was baptized. Succeeding kings enlarged the Frankish kingdom until it included most of what is now France.

When the Lombards in northern Italy threatened the capture of Rome itself in 739, Pope Gregory III appealed for help to Charles Martel, the military dictator (although not the king nor of the kingly line) of the Franks, without success. Charles' son, Pepin the Short, on the other hand, entered into friendly relations with the papacy after the death of his father. His plan was to seize the kingship from one of the weak descendents of Clovis who had succeeded to that office by right of inheritance. In order to forestall serious opposition and perhaps revolution, Pepin desired to secure ecclesiastical approval, along with the good will of the Frankish nobility. In return, Pepin could offer ample protection against the Lombards. Gladly the papacy entered into this trade and Pope Zacharias (741–52) arranged for the anointing of Pepin as king of the Franks in 751. The new line was known as the Carolingians, after either Charles Martel or Charles the Great.

Pepin kept his part of the bargain. By 756 he had forced the Lombards to recognize the pope as the sovereign over a large area of land in central and northern Italy. This was the beginning of the papal states which the Roman Church held until 1870. Perhaps the desire to secure those lands motivated the forgery at Rome known as the *Donation of Constantine* just at this time, by which it was asserted that the emperor Constantine in 330 had given to the Roman bishop all of the western lands. At any rate, Pepin and his successors were greatly influenced by this forgery.

Holy Roman Empire versus Holy Roman Church (800 on)

Pepin's son was Charles the Great (Charlemagne). His aid to the Roman Catholic Church has been described in the last chapter. He dominated the Western world ecclesiastically, in addition to ruling it as sovereign. The climax, not only to his rule but to the Middle Ages, came in 800 when Pope Leo III (795–816) crowned him as Holy Roman Emperor. This act, apparently by the initiative of the pope, shaped ideas and history for a millennium. For one thing, it was popularly looked upon as the reestablishment of the old Roman Empire in the West, an office unfilled since Constantine moved the capital to Constantinople in

115

330. Racial and sectional patriotism immediately hailed the beginning of a day that would restore the ancient glory to Rome and the West. In the second place, this restoration was viewed as proceeding from divine purpose. The title "Holy" called attention to the fact that God now had provided a secular power that was the counterpart to the spiritual power in the Roman Church. In the third place, papal prestige was lifted to new heights. Following up the antecedents laid in the crowning of Pepin the Short, the bestowal of the imperial title marked the pope as the giver of the greatest secular blessings of the earth. This prestige was enhanced when the Eastern Emperor Leo V (813–20) later recognized the validity of the transaction. Finally, unknowingly the papacy had given birth to its greatest rival throughout the remainder of the Medieval period. Perhaps Pope Leo had in mind the ideal described in Augustine's *City of God,* but, if so, the results must have been most disappointing. The earthly ruler controlled the heavenly; Charlemagne dominated the Church, appointing bishops at will and for the most part dictating papal policy.

After the death of Charlemagne, his weak son Louis ruled until 840; his three grandsons divided the empire in 843. The three divisions that were carved out at this time became roughly the states of Germany and France and the intervening strip.

Anarchy and Papal Degradation

The Carolingian line collapsed about 880. Strong nobles ruled feudal kingdoms and the Church as well. After the pontificate of Nicholas I (858–67), the papal office sank to indescribably low depths. Violence, murder, and mutilation were practiced on its occupants as various political factions intermittently seized control. New invasions terrified and devastated the population. Northmen and Hungarians swept the northern plains. The Mohammedans in North Africa and Spain were on the verge of winning the victory which they had been unable to accomplish because of Charles Martel in 732. From bases in Africa, Egypt, and Spain, these raiders captured Corsica, Sardinia, and Sicily, then Palermo and Messina in Italy proper. Rome was sacked in 841.

The German Re-establishment of the Empire

A new direction was taken in the middle of the tenth century when Pope John XII (955–64) appealed to the German king Otto I (936–73) for aid against the military attacks of Berengar II, an Italian noble seeking the imperial title. Otto had already invaded Italy in 951 with considerable success; ten years later, complying with the pope's request, Otto completed the task. In 962 Otto was crowned Holy Roman Emperor by John XII. He and his successors exercised complete control of the papacy for a century. Otto III (983–1002) appointed the first German pope in 996 and the first French pope in 999.

Before the middle of the eleventh century even the emperors were looking longingly for a church reform. Henry III (1039–56) attempted to introduce such reform by brusquely ending a papal schism involving three claimants and appointing German popes who agreed to reform measures. His last nomination was his cousin, a zealous reforming bishop, who became Leo IX (1049–54).

Thus at the close of this period the papacy was under the complete domination of the secular authority. However, this situation was about to be remedied. The reforming work of Leo IX and the rise of Hildebrand, who became Pope Gregory VII (1073–85), began the movement to rid the Roman Church of secular control.

Concluding Summary

In its relations with secular power the Roman Catholic Church came out second best during this period. Even when such power was friendly, as in the case of Charlemagne, it reserved the right to handle Christianity as a part of imperial administration. The various popes strongly asserted the ideal introduced by Augustine —namely, that the spiritual power in the world is superior to secular power and one day will completely overcome it. This ideal was not attained during the period from 325 to 1050.

The papacy made significant advances, however, despite many

117

hardships. The forgeries of the eighth century greatly increased papal prestige. The *Donation of Constantine* was doubtless influential in causing Pepin to make his donation of large areas of land in central and northern Italy to the pope. The forged decretals which bore the name of Isidore of Seville had their bearing upon the relations of the papacy to the secular power in that they established Rome as the focal point of the Christian movement.

The papacy was undergoing one of its greatest humiliations during the immediate centuries preceding the close of this period. However, the end of this situation was near. Within a century the papal office had regained its dominant place in ecclesiastical life and was well along toward dominating secular authority.

10

Roman Catholic Domination

THE AUTHORITY AND prestige of the Roman Catholic pope reached their height in the period from 1050 to 1215. Building upon the claims made before the deluge of anarchy and feudalism and the domination of the two empires (800 and 962), the Roman Church not only regained its power but was victorious in new and greater conquests. There were many contributing factors that made this possible. One principal factor was the attitude of the people everywhere. Tired of war and violence, men were ready to follow any leader that promised peace and justice—the key words of the papal promise. There was universal rejoicing when the spiritual weapons of the papacy began to overpower the familiar swords and spears. Secular unity had been destroyed in feudalism, and the hope of one universal spiritual government, resting upon sure and eternal foundations, provided an almost irresistible appeal.

The Roman Catholic revival began from the inside with a thorough reform and regrouping of papal forces; the revived papal monarchy then achieved domination of the Western world, both secular and spiritual. The most important movements contributing to this revitalization of the papacy and the Roman Church will be briefly discussed.

Monastic Reform

The Benedictine monks had been one of the foremost factors in the expansion of the papacy and the Roman system. They were skilled both as missionaries to carry the gospel and farmers to till the soil. The success of Augustine the monk in winning England is more spectacular than the work of many of his brethren who formed small bands and conquered nature in large sections of the European wilderness, but the accomplishments of the latter were almost as important. Monasteries sprang up all over Central Europe, providing large tracts of land under the control of the Roman Church, as well as a place of refuge for the needy, a retreat for the scholars, and a conservatory of learning through the period of the Dark Ages. These monasteries, however, did not escape the secular spirit of their times. Even though a monk must take an oath of poverty, for example, nothing was said about the material possessions of a monastery. Through valiant community of effort, through gifts of admirers, through special religious offerings for services, and by other means, monasteries became extremely wealthy. The monks could not *own* possessions but they could *use* them, and this distinction made it possible to circumvent entirely the idea of personal poverty. Other abuses crept into the system. Feudal lords sometimes lavished goods upon the monasteries, demanding (and securing) in return the right to name the abbots and direct their policies. Monasteries became the places of pleasant and leisurely service by the closing years of the ninth century.

A reform was needed and soon came. Under the leadership of its strong abbot, the monastery at Cluny began such a reform in the opening years of the tenth century. Strict ascetical living again was magnified. Complete separation from secular favors and control took place. The pope became the immediate superior rather than the local bishop. Several monastic communities banded together under the leadership of the Cluniac abbot to forward this reform. The religious sincerity and fervor of such a movement was bound to induce support and admiration. Even the secular rulers in Germany, the emperors themselves, encouraged the reform after 962. It is a revealing commentary upon the decayed condition of the papacy in these centuries to notice that the popes in Rome opposed this movement, even though a main purpose, through spiritual reform, was to magnify the papacy. Emperor Henry III (1039–56) would allow no Roman opposition to the Cluniac movement to blunt the reform, however, and in 1049 appointed his cousin, one of the Cluniac reformers, as Pope Leo IX. Without delay Pope Leo began reform in Rome along the lines of the Cluniac movement, choosing as one of his assistants a young and zealous reformer named Hildebrand. These men brought the reform into the papacy and made possible the tremendous upsurge of the Roman Church during the succeeding centuries.

The Crusades

Another factor that greatly aided in the rapid rise of the papacy is known as the Crusades. This movement began as an effort to capture Jerusalem from the hands of the infidels. The Roman Church had for centuries laid great emphasis upon pilgrimages as a means of securing forgiveness for postbaptismal sins. A pilgrimage to Jerusalem was considered the great satisfaction for sin. In the seventh century the Mohammedans captured the Holy Land but allowed pilgrims to visit Jerusalem for religious purposes. In the eleventh century the land was overcome by the Seljuk Turks, a new Saracenic power from Asia Minor. These Turks were completely unsympathetic to any pilgrimages by Christians. For centuries Western Europe had played with the idea of a vast attack upon the Mohammedans to rescue the Holy Land. Great impetus had come from the conversion of the Normans in 911, a warlike people who enjoyed nothing more than fierce fighting. They had conquered areas of France, England, and southern Italy. They had been particularly effective in driving the Mohammedans out of Sicily, Sardinia, and Corsica. Because they were seafaring people, the Normans were especially equipped to attack the Holy Land; they could sail the Mediterranean almost to within striking distance of Jerusalem. Furthermore, the conversion of Hungary had provided a point of departure at the very edge of the Turkish empire and had shortened the distance through hostile territory by thousands of miles.

The popes had hinted at the idea long before it was carried out. Pope Silvester II (999–1003) had spoken of such a grand crusade against the Turks; Gregory VII (1073–85) had actively planned

121

the attack but because of his struggle with Emperor Henry IV was unable to secure the secular support necessary for such an undertaking. In 1095 the Greek emperor Alexius appealed to the West not to delay such a crusade any longer. The Turks were threatening to take Constantinople. In that year Pope Urban II (1088–99) called upon secular powers to devote themselves to this divine crusade, promising forgiveness of sin to those dying in the effort. Europe was swept with the passion of slaughtering for the cross (the word "Crusades" comes from the word "cross").

In 1096 the first crusade began. About half a million soldiers moved toward Jerusalem. As this enormous and undisciplined army moved eastward, it lived on the countryside, completely devastating the areas through which it moved as though it were a hostile army. About forty thousand finally reached Jerusalem and captured it. There were about eight other crusades, including a children's crusade in 1212—a tragic, evil thing in every respect.

The results of the Crusades were manifold. In a sense they worked toward the immediate strengthening of the papacy. They brought an immediate prestige to the papacy which could give orders to princes everywhere and assume such international leadership. The papacy profited enormously from a financial standpoint. The people lavishly bestowed gifts upon the Roman Church and arranged to give their possessions to the Church in the event they did not return. The papacy used the Crusades as an excuse to levy a new ecclesiastical tax, which continued to be sought long after the crusading movement had ceased.

Papal methods were both aided and shaped by the Crusades. The idea soon became widespread that the pope could call upon all faithful secular rulers to march against heretics anywhere, including minority religious dissenters in Europe and secular princes who refused to be obedient to papal orders. A new and powerful weapon for coercion had been formed.

The Crusades were based upon the idea that had brought relics and fetishism into popularity. Extreme reverence for, and even actual worship of, physical remains followed the struggle to recapture the greatest of all relics, Jerusalem. During the period of the Crusades almost every sort of relic was allegedly brought back from Jerusalem. When Jerusalem was recaptured by the Turks, the market value of relics went out of sight; cutting off the source of relics brought inflation. Fraud and misrepresentation were the rule in trafficking in these items. The use of the Rosary increased considerably in the Roman Catholic system during this period.

On the other hand, from the long look of history the Roman Catholic Church was harmed by the Crusades. The popes weakened their prestige by continuing to press for new crusades after the fad had gone out of style. The continuance of the crusade tax did not increase papal popularity either.

The Crusades opened the eyes of many to a new world. New literature, new interests, and new ideas crowded upon those who had invaded the Eastern world, and they brought these things back with them. Even some of the popes became enamored with the ancient literary remains and forms and emphasized culture more than Christianity. The Renaissance was not far when the minds and hearts of the people were stirred and enlightened. Such general diffusion of enlightenment could not fail to undermine an institution which was based upon superstition and fear.

The Crusades introduced new economic and social reforms. Commerce and trade were fostered, and new items for manufacture called for industry. The middle class—neither peasant nor prince—developed. Those returning from the wars flooded the cities and changed social and economic forms.

Politically the papacy was not permanently forwarded. The breakdown of feudalism resulted in the rise of the nations, a potential threat to papal power. As the strong nobles were slain in the struggle, the monarchs in the various states increased in power. Even the opposite situation in the German states did not work out to papal advantage. The German knights refused to go on the Crusades. The tardy decline of feudalism in the German states may have been an immediate help to the papacy in its effort to divide and conquer; but this situation brought general unrest among the Germans, and when the struggle came, the papacy had to fight individual battles in scores of small feudal areas instead of simply winning over the monarch in a large domain.

Scholasticism

The third movement that made a distinct contribution to the rapid recovery of the Roman Church has been called "scholasticism." The term refers to the teaching of the schoolmen. It will be remembered that Charlemagne had encouraged the education of the clergy and the upper class. Perhaps from this inspiration the universities of the twelfth century arose, principally in order to teach civil and ecclesiastical law. These institutions of learning became small, self-governing cities within cities. Every European city ardently longed for its own university during the thirteenth and fourteenth centuries. Two types of universities developed: in Italy, growing out of considerable political freedom, the students organized their own schools and administered them; in France, following the monastic system, the faculty constituted both the teachers and the administrators of the school. The curriculum included theology, medicine, canon and civil law, and the liberal arts (grammar, logic, rhetoric, music, arithmetic, geometry, and astronomy).

The religious scholars of these schools developed the system known as "scholasticism." It was based upon a method of thought (deductive reasoning) and a preconceived conclusion (the intellectual proof of papal doctrine). Deductive reasoning begins with a general truth that is authoritative and develops subsidiary refinements through the application of valid principles. The important factor, then, is the starting point. Scholasticism, magnifying the thought forms and philosophy of Aristotle and Plato, started with the Bible, the decrees of popes, the canons of councils, and tradition as authoritative; from these it reasoned out the doctrines of the Roman Church. Although the various schools of thought differed in their viewpoint relative to the place of reason and revelation, the total result of scholasticism was to undergird with philosophy the Roman Catholic system. Bible and tradition are so inter-

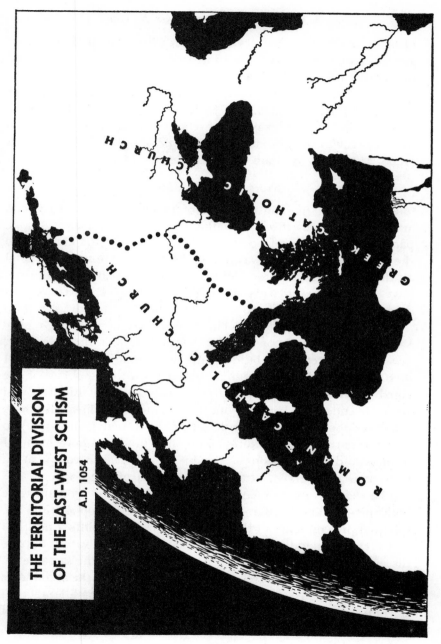

THE TERRITORIAL DIVISION
OF THE EAST-WEST SCHISM

A.D. 1054

GREEK CATHOLIC CHURCH

ROMAN CATHOLIC CHURCH

125

mingled in the doctrinal development of the Roman Church that any attempt to eliminate tradition would require a complete re-definition of every doctrine.

Some of the leading scholastics were Johannes Scotus Erigena (about 800), Anselm (1033–1109), Roscellinus (about 1090), Abé-lard (1079–1142), Alexander of Hales (about 1245), Albertus Magnus (1206–80), Thomas Aquinas (1225–74), John Duns Scotus (1265–1308), and William of Occam (about 1349).

Strong Papal Leadership

Even beyond the contributions of monasticism, the Crusades, and Scholasticism, the spectacular rise of the Roman Catholic papacy to the height of power in the period from the eleventh to the thirteenth centuries was the work of three strong popes. Had all the contributory factors existed, the Roman Church could not have attained the place that it did without the initiative and determination of the strong men who headed it.

Gregory VII (1073–85).—The first of these popes was Gregory VII, who is better known as Hildebrand. Under the reforming program of Leo IX, Hildebrand was appointed a cardinal in 1049. Before long he assumed leadership in the policies of the papal government and did not relinquish it until his death in 1085. He endeavored to carry out three principles: (1) to eliminate internal opposition to papal rule within the Roman Church; (2) to free the papacy from external influence in the appointment of bishops and the election of popes; (3) to secure co-operation from secular rulers in attaining the ideals of the papacy.

The weapons used by Gregory to accomplish his program were both spiritual and secular. In dealing with secular opposition, the spiritual pre-eminence of the papacy was fashioned into a political club. It was generally accepted that there was no salvation outside the external Church, that salvation came through the sacraments, and that no Western church could properly observe the sacraments unless it was in communion with Rome. Thus for all practical purposes, the pope controlled salvation. The manipulation of this power formed the basis of papal coercion. When any person, for example, refused to obey the Roman pontiff, an edict of excommunication was prepared and published. This officially cut off the person from the Church; this separation would include salvation. A total excommunication was a fearful thing. Not only was the individual deprived of salvation, but he infected those about him. Mass could not be held in his presence; those giving him refuge of any kind were subject to severe discipline by the Church. If the one excommunicated was a ruler, it was within the power of the Church to release his subjects from all loyalty to him, thus opening the way for general political revolt. Loyal Catholic rulers were invited to crusade against the heretic and seize his kingdom for themselves, which gave double incentive.

A second weapon based upon control of the sacramental vehicles of salvation was called the "interdict." In a sense, the interdict was excommunication applied to a community, whether a small town or a large kingdom. An interdict closed the churches, which were viewed as the only means of salvation for the people. The only ministry that was carried on provided baptism (to bring babies into the Church and salvation) and extreme unction (the sacrament at death to prepare the individual for judgment). It will be noted that the giving of these two sacraments during the period of interdict was a means of maintaining the strength of the Church if the interdict was applied for a long period.

By these weapons—excommunication and interdict—papal power could be applied quickly in a practical and political way. Furthermore, when civil rulers were friendly, the popes used their influence to secure still another coercive weapon. This was known as the "ban," by which the civil rulers made an outlaw of the person involved in ecclesiastical disobedience. The machinery of secular punishment could then be applied to the heretics.

Freely using these weapons, reasserting the claims of the pseudo-Isidorian decretals and the *Donation of Constantine,* and invoking the authority of the apostle Peter, Gregory VII quickly brought an effective internal reform of the papal government and soon began speaking with an authoritative accent to all secular rulers.

Under his leadership Roman synods took the right of nominating or appointing popes completely out of secular hands and placed it in the power of the cardinal bishops and cardinal clergy. In addition, kings and secular princes were denied the power of appointing or installing any bishop. These measures looked to the elimination of all secular power in the appointing of church officials and placed that power directly in the hands of the papal government.

Furthermore, under Gregory an edict requiring clerical celibacy was ratified. This meant that deacons, priests, and bishops could not take wives. It eliminated the financial burden upon the Church of providing for the families of its officers; it enlarged the distinction between the clergy and the laity; it made the clergy more mobile, for without wife and family the priest or bishop could move quickly to whatever place he might be sent; it insured the right of the Church to appoint a bishop's successor without family influence in case the bishop's son should be an ecclesiastic and desire the post; and it made the Church heir to the possessions of most of its clergy, for they had no one else to whom they might leave their worldly goods when they died.

Pope Gregory used the interdict freely in an effort to establish papal power. He sent legates (or representatives) to every civil government in order to guard papal interests in the various countries. Perhaps the greatest triumph came in his enforcement of the synodical decrees relating to the appointing and installing of a bishop by secular powers. In this struggle the pope fought against an ancient and popular practice. In feudalism, it will be recalled, the sovereign, or lord of the manor, was the sole ruler in his own domain. If a bishop happened to serve in that domain, the bishop must swear allegiance to this secular ruler. Should the bishop die, the sovereign usually appointed someone else to that office from his own domain. Since papal power was greatly compromised during the several centuries of anarchy and feudalism following the breakdown of the Carolingian line, no protest was voiced over this situation for generations. But now Pope Gregory refused to allow the bishop to be appointed, installed, or controlled by the secular power. The Roman synod of 1075 reiterated this principle, denying the right of the emperor himself to appoint and invest bishops.

A test quickly came. Henry IV (1056–1106), the German emperor, could not discern the changed situation. Had not his predecessors appointed even the popes less than a century before? Had not the popes agreed solemnly that the emperor should forever have the right to appoint even the bishop of Rome? So when a bishopric became vacant in the northern part of Italy, the emperor immediately appointed a successor and installed him in office. When Pope Gregory denied the validity of the action, the emperor declared the papal office empty. But a century had made a great difference. Now the pope, prestige restored, hurled the dreaded weapon of excommunication against the emperor, freeing that sovereign's subjects from allegiance. More from a political than a religious standpoint, the emperor made a pilgrimage southward to ask the pope's forgiveness and secure restoration to the Church. Meanwhile, the pope had started northward toward Germany to carry on the struggle. They met at Canossa, where the emperor *short run victory + long run establishment of power pope* stood outside the castle in the snow, barefooted, for three days, begging the privilege of asking the pope's forgiveness. Upon being admitted, he made promises to be obedient and was restored to fellowship.

The emperor's humiliation strengthened his influence with his *his own long run victory* people; despite his reinstatement, the emperor declared war on the pope and succeeded in driving him into exile to die in 1085. The successors of the emperor and the pope continued the battle. In 1122 an agreement was reached known as the Concordat of Worms. This provided that the Church should have control of the election of bishops and abbots but that the emperor should exercise supervision over the elections. In case of a dispute the emperor would have the deciding vote. The pope should invest every bishop or abbot with the spiritual symbols of office—the ring and the staff—while the emperor should be allowed to touch the candidate with sceptre to indicate imperial approval. Neither popes nor emperors were true to this compromise.

Alexander III (1159–81).—The second of the strong popes who were responsible for bringing the papacy to the height of its power was Alexander III. He entered into the papal office under fire. The cardinals elected him by a small majority. The minority of the cardinals, with the support of the Roman clergy and of the imperial authority, elected a rival pope called Victor IV. The emperor, Frederick Barbarossa (1152–90), disliked Alexander and supported Victor, even going so far as to summon a church council, which obediently voted in favor of Victor. Alexander was supported by England, France, Spain, Hungary, and Sicily, however. For almost twenty years Emperor Frederick tried to force his way to Rome in order to set up Victor as pope, without success. In 1177 he submitted to Alexander.

Meanwhile, Alexander had continued the work and spirit of Gregory VII. Typical of his efforts to advance the power and prestige of the papacy were his dealings with England. In 1163, after the death of the archbishop of Canterbury, King Henry II of England (1154–89) forced the appointment of Thomas à Becket, one of his cronies. To the king's dismay, Becket became a champion of the pope against the king. In 1164 the king called a national council in an effort to eliminate papal influence in England. This council passed all of the king's measures, known as the Constitutions of Clarendon. Ecclesiastical courts were shorn of extensive jurisdiction; no appeal could be made to Rome without the king's permission; the king could appoint abbots and bishops in England; the revenues from vacant episcopal offices in England would revert to the king. Because of strong opposition to King Henry over this program, the archbishop was assassinated. Popular feeling was so aroused by this act that Henry was forced to submit to the pope and renounce the Constitutions in 1172.

The Third Lateran Council was convened by Pope Alexander in 1179, and decreed that the cardinals alone should elect the pope, that Roman Catholics should take arms against heresy with the promise of full forgiveness of all sins if death should result, and that secular authorities may not meddle with internal affairs of the Church.

130

Innocent III (1198–1216).—The third and greatest of the popes of this period was Innocent III. Gregory VII had made exalted claims concerning the dignity of the pope and the Roman Church: God alone had founded the Roman Church; the pope's feet shall be kissed by all princes; emperors may be deposed by the pope; the pope may be judged by no man; and the Roman Church has never erred, nor will it err in all eternity. But Innocent III magnified these pretensions to make the pope alone God's authoritative representative upon the earth. With the work of Gregory VII and Alexander III to prepare the way, with the continuing spirit of the Crusades to foment religious passion and fanatical loyalty, and with doctrine and organization perfected, Innocent was able to dominate the entire world, secular and ecclesiastical.

Through his influence he deposed emperors, forced heads of states such as Spain and France to submit to his authority, required states to pay annual tributes of money, and most spectacular of all, humiliated King John of England. The English king had tried to defy Innocent and found himself excommunicated and his kingdom under interdict. Without papal support, King John was captured by his nobles in 1215 and was forced to grant the Magna Charta, a bill of rights for protection against oppression by the crown. The pope refused to admit the validity of the document because, he said, it was secured under duress. Meanwhile, by interdict and other coercive measures, Innocent brought every secular government into his orbit. He put into practical operation the claim that he was the immediate instrument of God for world rule.

The Fourth Lateran Council of 1215 marks the height of official Roman Catholic domination. This council is unrivaled as a picture of universal subjection to the pope by every ecclesiastical and secular power. The bishop of Constantinople, once a strong rival, was there to bow his knee. The spectacle of this tremendous pageant was more important than what was done. A new crusade was discussed, union with the Greek church was looked into, the punishment of heretics by the state was arranged, and a number of canons were enacted providing for ecclesiastical discipline. The

131

doctrine of transubstantiation, which affirms that the bread and wine of the Mass lose their character and become actually the body and blood of a newly crucified Christ, was officially defined.

The universal dominion of the papacy was an accomplished fact. Between the Council of Nicea of 325 and the Fourth Lateran Council of 1215 the Roman bishop had become master of the world, spiritual and secular. The structure was complete. Its builders thought that it was eternal. In less than a century it began to crumble.

Concluding Summary

The papacy accomplished a spectacular revival of authority and prestige in the eleventh and twelfth centuries. An internal reform through the agency of monasticism began the recovery. Papal prestige skyrocketed as a result of the Crusades under their leadership, but the long-range results were not favorable. Scholasticism provided intellectual justification for papal doctrines. Three outstanding popes, using the ecclesiastical weapons of excommunication, interdict, and crusade, humbled every secular power.

11

Retrospect and Prospects

THE ROMAN CATHOLIC papacy had now reached its height. Secular and ecclesiastical princes bowed to its authority. Until the closing years of the thirteenth century it appeared that a new and permanent world order had been created. It is instructive to compare the Christianity of this golden age of Roman Catholicism with the Christianity of the New Testament. Even beyond the strange externals of glittering wealth, false pride symbolized in the kissing of feet and the holding of stirrups by earthly princes, and the kneeling of men to men, a vast difference in character between the movement described in the New Testament and that in the Roman Catholic Church of the thirteenth century had developed.

Roman Catholic Domination

The New Testament picture of ministers (bishops) serving in an autonomous local church, theoretically equal with all other bishops everywhere, has disappeared. Out of the circumstances which have been sketched in previous chapters a few important bishops began to shape the policies of all Christianity. One of these bishops, that of Rome, was able to impress upon all other Western bishops not only his example but his authority. In addition, the Roman bishop, through spiritual and political coercion, had managed to assume control over secular kings. Sometimes retreating, sometimes compromising, sometimes demanding, the Roman bishops constantly kept in mind their ultimate aim of universal rule, both ecclesiastical and secular, and attained it after about a millennium of struggle.

133

Roman Catholic Organization

The simple local church government of the New Testament days was gone. In its place was the Roman hierarchy. The Roman bishop headed a vast network of ecclesiastical organization that manipulated the sacramental vehicles commonly supposed to bring salvation. Such a widespread function demanded a strong central organization. In the fourth century Rome was divided by the bishop into twenty-five parts, each headed by a presbyter or priest. Each of the twenty-five divisions was called a parish or *titulus*. Furthermore, in order to provide for the administration of charity, seven deacons were appointed for the city of Rome, each with a specific geographical section under his responsibility. This scriptural number of deacons was later augmented by seven subdeacons.

In the eleventh century these twenty-five priests, the seven deacons, and several bishops from the area about Rome formed the basis of what is known as the College of Cardinals. The name "cardinal" developed from a Latin word which means a hinge, and although the play on words has nothing to do with the original application of the word, it is true that the Roman system hinges on cardinals. Since the time of Gregory VII (1073–85), the cardinals have been entrusted with the most important organizational tasks of the Roman Church. At the present time it is their duty to elect and advise popes and to determine administrative policy through committee functions. Because of the historical developments related above, there are three types of cardinals: the cardinal bishops, the cardinal priests, and the cardinal deacons. The original names of these three types are now without meaning, for cardinal priests are usually strong bishops from various parts of the world, while cardinal deacons are usually priests. The total number of cardinals has varied from about thirteen to seventy-six. At the present time the maximum is seventy—fourteen cardinal deacons (the original seven plus the seven subdeacons who were elevated), fifty cardinal priests (doubling the original number), and six cardinal bishops who are still the bishops of dioceses in the immediate vicinity of Rome. The cardinals are appointed by the pope, and he could depose them, although that would be quite unusual.

The committee work of the cardinals developed rapidly after the thirteenth century. Probably the most important committees, or congregations (in their terminology), are the Sacred Consistory, a rather full cabinet meeting to consider matters of policy and those of high importance; the Congregation of the Inquisition, that watches for heresy and deals with it; the Congregation of Rites, that deals with liturgy and ceremonies; and the Propagation of the Faith, the missionary organization. In addition, the cardinals also constitute the principal members of ecclesiastical tribunals. Ecclesiastical appeals are handled by seven tribunals, each with jurisdiction over certain classes of litigation. The supreme court of appeal is the Rota Romana, consisting of twelve members.

All of these committees and tribunals—the central core of Roman Catholic organization—are termed the Roman Curia.

Roman Catholic Doctrine

Attention has already been directed to the corruption of New Testament teachings in the developing Roman Catholic system. The New Testament pattern of salvation emphasized faith in Jesus Christ without the mediation of any person or institution. The ordinances of baptism and the Supper were symbolical, not magical. In the Roman system the ordinances became sacraments, vehicles of grace. Salvation was conceived as coming from the Catholic Church alone through the administration of the sacraments. The question of the number of sacraments, argued by Catholic theologians for centuries, was finally resolved. Chief credit for establishing the official position should probably be given to Peter Lombard in the twelfth century. About 1150 he prepared his *Four Books of Sentences,* the last division of which discussed sacraments. Over against earlier theologians like Augustine (who died in 430), who felt that all ministries of the Church were sacraments, and later theologians like Hugo of St. Victor and Abélard (contemporaries with Peter Lombard), who emphasized five sacraments, the *Sentences* named seven sacraments. Peter Lombard's *Sentences* were taught in practically all of the schools for theological training during the succeeding several centuries. It is likely that Thomas Aquinas (1225–74), who provided the most influential synthesis of Catholic doctrine for the modern period, followed Peter Lombard in asserting that the Church has seven sacraments.

As developed by Peter Lombard and Thomas Aquinas, the seven sacraments were baptism, confirmation, penance, the Lord's Supper (Mass), extreme unction, ordination, and matrimony. A word of description about each will suffice.

The sacrament of baptism is the initiatory rite. By it, the Church taught, original sin and all acts of sin committed up to the time of baptism are forgiven. Sprinkling became the general mode of baptism in the West after about the ninth century, and infants began to be subjects of baptism in the second or third centuries. In order to maintain the appearance of baptism as profession of faith, the use of sponsors developed quite early after the adoption of infant baptism. The priest administering baptism asked the infant if he were willing to renounce Satan, if he believed the various points of the creed, and if he were willing to be baptized. The sponsor, or godparent, answered all such questions for the undiscerning infant. The catechism says that this ceremony makes the child a Christian, a child of God, and an heir of heaven.

The sacrament of confirmation claims to impart the Holy Spirit. Its scriptural basis is usually given as Acts 8:17 and 19:6. In the Western world this sacrament could be administered only by a bishop. Until about the thirteenth century it was conferred shortly after baptism; then the time was changed to allow the subject to reach his twelfth or thirteenth year. The age does not matter, since a sponsor is required and the sacrament works without reference to any understanding by the subject. In this sacrament, which in a sense inducts the child into the duties and responsibilities of church life, the bishop anoints the subject with oil which has been blessed.

The sacrament of penance provides forgiveness of sins committed after baptism. Scriptures like 1 John 1:9 are used to buttress this doctrine. The earliest confessions of sin were made to the congregation, but such a practice manifestly could not continue. The very volume of such confessions would make it difficult to have any other type of service. The intense persecutions of Christianity under Emperors Decius (249–51) and Diocletian (284–305) caused many nominal Christians to deny the faith. To meet this need, as well as the normal demand, a division of functions was required. Through successive developments, auricular confession (confession in the ear of the priest) became the custom. Not until the Fourth Lateran Council in 1215 was confession to the priest made a Church law.

Under the theory developed by Aquinas and now generally accepted, the subject of this sacrament must first be moved by contrition, sorrow for sin, or attrition, a fear of the punishment of sin. With this motive, confession is made to the priest who in turn requires that the subject must give "satisfaction." This idea probably also grew out of the rigorous persecutions of the early period. The original purpose of satisfaction was to give evidence that the subject was really contrite and willing to do what he could to show this spirit. In a sense this satisfaction originally had a twofold function: it provided a basis for the forgiveness of eternal and deadly sins, and it displayed contrition for sin in the temporal order. In other words, sin was viewed as having eternal consequences and temporal disabilities.

This distinction became very important in view of the development of various methods of making satisfaction and the exceptional extent of the effectiveness of such satisfaction. The method of making satisfaction before the tenth and eleventh centuries had been primarily through making religious pilgrimages to some shrine or through other channels of revealing personal piety. In the eleventh century, however, the temporal penalties could be remitted in whole or in part by the use of indulgences. "Indulgence" was the name given to the remission of punishment due to temporal sins. After the eleventh century, instead of taking pilgrimage as a part of penance, it was possible to purchase an indulgence in order to give satisfaction for temporal sins.

In addition, the interpretation of the large area in which temporal sins brought hurt increased the importance of the distinction between temporal sins and eternal. Temporal sins, it was taught, must be paid for in purgatory after death, if they were not completely expunged through satisfaction. The Church, it was further taught, could issue these indulgences for temporal sins because of the possession of a treasury of merits bequeathed to it by the good works of Christ and the saints. This development was reflected in the order of the elements of penance. Earlier the order consisted of contrition, confession, satisfaction, and then absolution or forgiveness by the priest. That is, satisfaction was given before the priest pronounced absolution or forgiveness. The developed order was changed somewhat; contrition and confession formed the first part, but absolution came after confession, and satisfaction was placed last. Thus after confession the priest, in his authority of the keys granted him by the Roman bishop, would forgive the eternal sins of the subject; then there was imposed upon the subject the necessity of giving satisfaction for the temporal guilt which, if not expiated, required suffering in purgatory. It should be said that the doctrine of purgatory was first taught as a matter essential to the faith by Gregory I (590–604).

The sacrament of the Lord's Supper, or Mass, is described as the unbloody sacrifice of the body and blood of Christ. According to Roman Catholic catechism, Christ is slain again in every church each time Mass is performed. By this means Christ's soul and divinity are reproduced in both bread and wine. This is the theological reason why the Roman Church refuses to allow the people to partake of the wine; they get all they need in the bread. The Mass has become the central feature of Roman Catholic worship services, for through partaking of the bread, which allegedly has been changed into the broken body of Christ, and witnessing the transubstantiation of the wine into the blood of Christ, the subject actually partakes of Christ's body, which gives spiritual merit.

The sacrament of extreme unction is, as the name indicates, the last anointing. Its practice is based upon James 5:14. In the administration of this sacrament the priest anoints the eyes, ears, nose, lips, palms of the hands, and feet to expiate sins contracted through any of these organs. A plenary, or full, indulgence is granted but does not take effect until the time of death.

The sacrament of orders applies only to those entering upon the service of the Roman Catholic Church. It sets them apart and qualifies them for the task which they have assumed.

The sacrament of matrimony consists of the union of a man and woman in marriage. Of course, ordinarily the sacraments of orders and matrimony mutually exclude one another.

Thus the Roman Catholic sacramental system, which had developed its present features by the thirteenth century, aimed to control the life of the subject. It touched the individual at birth, in childhood and adolescence, and at death. It required regular confession of sin and absolution at the hands of the priest as a means of escaping the purgatorial sufferings which the earthly Church could remit. The Roman Church utilized every means of influence; an appeal was made through beauty to the eyes, through melody to the ears, through incense to the nose, through participation to the hands and knees. Solemn rites and incantations brought a sense of belonging and initiation, and a common language spoke of unity.

Roman Catholic Monasticism

Throughout the Medieval period the monastic movement retained its great popularity. It was universally felt that the perfect life could only be found in monasticism. The monks were viewed as men who had lost their lives to save them again, who had given all to follow Christ. Papal advance insured great encouragement for monasticism, for the monks were the strongest supporters of papal supremacy. Particularly after the new type of monasticism inaugurated by the Cluniac reform had developed, the pope was able to undermine the power of any antagonistic bishop. Since these monks were no longer under the control of the local bishop, the pope could send them into any diocese to hear confessions, forgive sins, baptize and bury, bless or condemn. As a consequence, the bishop of that diocese would find himself bypassed and his functions taken over by the monks.

Furthermore, the monasteries provided a place of refuge for many—for the scholar who desired peace and quiet for study, for the pious who wanted a haven from worldliness, for the fearful who would flee from the misery and disorder of society. In a sense, monasteries also provided a place for minor dissent. Some might disagree with the papal program, yet desire to remain within the ecclesiastical structure from either conviction or fear. The various monastic orders, magnifying different emphases in doctrine and practice, offered a choice of minor variations from the normal pattern. Many a monk doubtless found himself in a congenial atmosphere for ideas which would not have been generally acceptable outside his haven.

From the eleventh to the thirteenth centuries several new monastic orders arose. The Cistercians were one of the reform movements and became famous because Bernard of Clairvaux, maker of popes, joined it in 1113. The Augustinian canons represented an effort to bring monastic discipline into the parish clergy. In 1119 an order known as the Premonstrants was founded, providing for communal living in a monastic house by the several priests of a particular parish. Another type of monasticism grew out of the Crusades. Three outstanding military orders developed. The Knights of St. John, or the Hospitallers, were organized in the twelfth century to aid sick and helpless pilgrims on their way to Jerusalem; the Knights Templars were a lay order organized in 1119 to protect Jerusalem pilgrims; and the Teutonic Knights, with a similar mission, date from 1190. The two most important orders of these centuries were the Dominicans and the Franciscans. Dominic (1170–1221) organized an order for the purpose of winning heretics back to the Roman Church through preaching. Recognition was obtained in 1216 from the pope, and the movement spread rapidly. Before Dominic's death, his order numbered sixty houses, situated in every part of Europe. Doubtless copying the Franciscan movement, the Dominicans became mendicants, or beggars. Because of their emphasis upon education and preaching, the Dominicans have produced some of the greatest theologians and scholars of the Roman Church.

Francis of Assisi was born about 1182. At about the age of twenty-five his military and business pursuits were changed by a conversion experience, and two years later he determined to form an order which would endeavor to reproduce the spirit and work of Christ. This order was approved by Pope Innocent III in 1216. The inclinations of Francis himself turned away from formal and effective organization, but through able friends, especially Pope Gregory IX (1227–41), the Franciscan movement developed and spread rapidly. After Francis' death in 1226 his followers divided over the interpretation of his teachings.

Both the Dominicans and the Franciscans included provision for nunneries, where women might serve the cause. These two mendicant orders have been a tremendous force in the development of the Roman Catholic system.

The Inquisition

The several elements of Roman Catholic strength which have been mentioned—prestige, organization, doctrine, and passionate defenders—seemed to give promise of the continued domination of the world by the papacy. But the picture would not be complete without a word concerning factors which threatened and finally overthrew universal papal domination. One of these factors was the extraordinary spread of religious dissent. In a succeeding chapter, specific instances of dissent will be described. It is significant that the very pope who symbolized the complete domination of Roman Catholic power should find it necessary to institute special ecclesiastical machinery for the suppression of dissent.

The inquisition of heresy had at first been under the supervision of the local bishop. With the rise of the Roman bishop to power, it became his prerogative to ferret out those who refused to follow the pattern. The founding of the Dominican order followed directly the discovery of the strength of the Albigenses in southern France and constituted an effort to win these dissenters back to the faith. The Fourth Lateran Council of 1215 passed new decrees designed to compel the various bishops to seek out heretics in their own dioceses. A new direction was taken in the thirteenth century. Emperor Frederick II (1215–50) offered the services of the civil government to the papacy for the suppression of heresy, and in 1252 a papal bull directed that civil magistrates be utilized in the detection and punishment of heresy. After 1233 the Dominicans were given the task of searching out dissenters and handling them. In 1262 the office of inquisitor general was set up at Rome to spearhead the fight against heresy.

The inquisitorial methods have been publicized. Despite lurid descriptions, it is doubtful that any of the stories exceeded the horrors of the actual movement, particularly in the Spanish Inquisition. Christians were very adept in devising ways to torture Christians. Informers were secured by promising them a part of the estate of the condemned. Torture was the principal method of securing evidence. No person was safe. Simply the accusation of heresy by anyone, whether through personal hatred, greed, or other motive, was sufficient to start the machinery of torture, under the pains of which almost anyone would confess almost anything. Cynicism and bitterness filtered into all parts of the Continent. Things were not well with the dominating ecclesiastical system.

Political Developments

A new set of strong rulers was arising, supported by the zeal of nationalism. Drawing new strength by the destruction of many of the nobility in the Crusades and enriched by the increase of trade and the development of industry following the Crusades, these new secular sovereigns prepared to challenge the supremacy of the pope over civil government. That story will be told in a succeeding chapter.

The Diffusion of Light

The Roman Catholic system reached its height through coercion because it allegedly controlled the only font of salvation. Superstition and fear played a large part in this sort of Christianity. The entrance of light of any kind constituted a threat to the system.

And the light was growing. The movement called the Renaissance was not far. Here and there in the thirteenth century were signs of spiritual awakenings and intellectual advance. When once men learned that God was a Saviour as well as a Judge, that they could find his love and blessings apart from the ecclesiastical organization known as the Church, and that the service of God was not bound up with merits and penance, then the great sacramental system of the papacy was undermined.

Concluding Summary

The difference between the New Testament pattern and that of the Roman Catholic Church in the thirteenth century was great. The Roman bishop had become dominant. His authority was recognized in spiritual and secular areas. His organization was strong and well disciplined. The doctrinal definition of Rome's principal tenets was almost complete. New monkish orders provided recruits for every kind of special service. The future seemed bright. But there were elements that would have disturbed an observant onlooker. Dissent was widespread. The methods that were adopted to combat dissent only scattered the spirit across the Continent. New secular rulers were developing who were not afraid of the papal excommunication and interdict. The foregleams of the dawn were casting light against which the Roman system could not continue to dominate the minds and hearts of men.

BIBLIOGRAPHY

BETHUNE-BAKER, J. *An Introduction to the Early History of Christian Doctrine to the Time of the Council of Chalcedon.* London: Methuen & Co., Ltd., 1951.

BETTENSON, HENRY (ed.). *Documents of the Christian Church.* New York: Oxford University Press, 1947.

FOAKES-JACKSON, F. J. *An Introduction to the History of Christianity A.D. 590–1314.* New York: The Macmillan Co., 1921.

LATOURETTE, K. S. *A History of Christianity.* New York: Harper & Brothers, 1953.

NEWMAN, A. H. *A Manual of Church History,* I. Philadelphia: American Baptist Publication Society, 1953.

ROBINSON, JAMES HARVEY. *Readings in European History,* I. Boston: Ginn & Co., 1904.

STEVENSON, J. (ed.). *A New Eusebius.* New York: The Macmillan Co., 1957.

SULLIVAN, JOHN F. *The Visible Church.* New York: P. J. Kenedy & Son, 1920.

WORKMAN, HERBERT BROOK. *The Evolution of the Monastic Ideal.* London: The Epworth Press, 1927.

IV. PERIOD OF WESTERN REFORM
(A.D. 1215–1648)

Introduction to the Period

The papacy could attain no higher prestige than it displayed in the Fourth Lateran Council of 1215. For a comparatively brief period it seemed that the papacy would be able to maintain its imposing position indefinitely. The claims of the popes who succeeded Innocent III (1198–1216) sounded like him, but there developed a difference in the ability to enforce these claims. The removal of the papal throne to France from 1305 to 1378 made it a tool of national interests; the papal schism from 1378 to 1409 (with two popes) and from 1409 to 1415 (three popes) stripped the office of much of its prestige and authority. Strong attempts were made to reform the Church in "head and members," but these failed. From the Council of Constance (1414–18) to the theses of Luther (1517), papal abuses became even more flagrant.

The various types of revolt against the Roman Church occurred between 1517 and 1534. The Council of Trent (1545–64) represented the Roman Catholic reform. The Reformation period closes with the Thirty Years' War (1618–48), which in a measure brought mutual toleration between the Roman Catholics and their opponents.

Points of Special Interest

The student should notice that the roots of reform were imbedded deeply in medieval Christianity. For that reason it has been thought wise to push back the traditional date of 1517 to the date at which the Roman Church reached its highest peak—the Fourth Lateran Council of 1215. Widespread dissent, the Avignon papacy, schism and confusion, and attempts to reform in the three centuries before Luther's theses justify the inclusion of that period.

The student should notice carefully the interaction of all factors in the Reformation—political circumstances, for example.

It should not be overlooked, also, that the Roman Catholic reform looked primarily toward modernizing its machinery to meet the threats of the schismatics. There was no attempt to continue the radical reforming measures taken by the councils of the fifteenth century.

145

12

Collapse of Papal Prestige

I<small>T</small> IS SIGNIFICANT that the factors which helped to establish the prestige of the Roman papacy also co-operated in bringing its downfall. The very height which the papal monarchy attained for a few centuries was a guarantee that a decline must take place. Secular rulers could not fail to see that the papacy was an institution of this world, not of the next. Papal policies were ofttimes greedy and vicious. Despite assertions that the Roman leadership could not err, civil sovereigns saw many examples of mistakes in doctrines and in policies. Papal avowal of the Crusades and the Inquisition were examples. The tragic slaughter of untold hundreds of thousands of men, women, and children in the fruitless march toward Jerusalem brought many to their senses. What could the will of God have to do with this sort of political undertaking?

The German nobles bluntly refused to go, papal promises of complete forgiveness of sins notwithstanding. The popes were slow to see that the aroused passion had died down, and their continued pleadings for new crusades and their collections of gifts and taxes, ostensibly for such crusades, disgusted thoughtful and spiritual people. Furthermore, the Roman slaughter of the Albigenses and their appropriation of the crudest tortures in the Inquisition were a shocking disclosure of the character of the papacy. As the Inquisition spread into all parts of Europe, the tyranny of the Roman system became more and more visible. Fear had always been a major part of the hold upon the people by the Roman Church; and now to the fear of purgatory, excommunication, interdict, ban, and zealous crusaders the night-

146

mare of accusation of heresy, against which there was no defense, was added. The brutality of the whole movement prophesied the downfall of such tyrannical monarchs, whether in the ecclesiastical or the secular sphere.

Financial Exploitation by the Roman Catholic Church

An important area of rising resentment against the papacy was their financial demands. The tremendous expansion of the central organization demanded immense revenues. One example will suggest the picture. When Rome set up the Rota Romana in 1234, constituting the supreme ecclesiastical court in Christendom, sufficient personnel was required to handle appeals from every part of the world. Subsidiary courts for special appeals were necessary. An army of clerks was required to maintain the records. Worst of all, flagrant abuses characterized every step of the legal proceedings. Official records show that in some cases simply securing the briefs cost approximately forty times the legitimate amount. Furthermore, litigants from all over the world were encouraged to appeal their cases directly to Rome, and it was well understood that the highest bidder won the case.

The financial gain secured by this fashion was not sufficient to care for the vast expenditures, legitimate and otherwise, of the papacy. Especially during the fourteenth century the papacy utilized every possible means for increasing its revenue. Some of these methods were through annates, collations, reservations, expectancies, dispensations, indulgences, simony, commendations, the *jus spoliorum,* tithing, and special assessments.

Annates refer to the gift by a newly appointed bishop or abbot of his first year's income in the office to which he was appointed. Collations refer to the practice of shifting several bishops or abbots in order to secure annates from each one. For example, if the archbishop of Cologne were to die, the pope would not appoint simply one person but would shift, let us say, the archbishop of Mainz to the open place, then appoint the bishop of Trier to the Mainz office, another bishop of Trier, and so on. An effort would be made, of course, to give each man a better situation, which would be possible when a strong prelate died. Before exhausting his possibilities the pope could have a dozen annates paid in through one vacancy.

Reservations refer to the practice of reserving the best and richest offices for papal use. The pope himself did not, of course, serve the particular bishopric or archbishopric but would send a priest to minister to the needs of the people while the revenue was sent to Rome. Expectancies mean the practice by papal authorities of selling to the highest bidder the right of nomination to an unusually desirable benefice before the person filling the office had yet vacated it. It became the practice of ambitious men to keep a watchful eye on the health of the incumbents of the various desirable offices, and when there was any encouragement that one might not continue long, the bidding began. Occasionally some embarrassment was experienced when it was found that several men had paid huge sums in anticipation of securing the same office. In reality, then, expectancies became almost a bid for the right to bid again when the incumbent of the desired office actually did die.

Dispensations has reference to the papal practice of excusing ecclesiastical violations upon the payment of the proper amount of money. In one of his outbursts against the Roman Curia, Luther wrote that it was a place where vows could be annulled, monks could get permission to leave their orders, priests could buy a dispensation to get married, the illegitimate might be legitimatized, and where evil and disgrace were knighted and ennobled. His closing sentence, in typical impetuous language, declares that at the Roman Curia there is "a buying and a selling, a changing, blustering and bargaining, cheating and lying, robbing and stealing, debauchery and villainy and all kinds of contempt of God that Antichrist could not reign worse." Even allowing for Luther's usual enthusiasm, it is evident that considerable income was secured by allowing dispensations for breaking canonical restrictions.

Indulgences have been described before. They were the pardons for temporal sins. Individuals might buy them instead of taking a pilgrimage or showing some other evidence of contrition. The revenue from this one source alone was considerable because of the widespread fear of spending a season in purgatory.

Simony refers to the sale of a church office. It takes its name from Simon Magus (see Acts 8:9 ff.) , who tried to buy the power of the Holy Spirit with money. Closely associated with simony was the practice of nepotism. This word refers to the installing of relatives in lucrative church offices.

Commendations has reference to the practice of paying an annual tax to the papacy in return for a provisional appointment year by year to a desirable benefice. The *jus spoliorum* was the name applied to the papal practice of demanding that any property secured by a bishop or other officer during the tenure of office should, upon the death of the person, become the property of the Church, since such property was judged to come to the deceased individual in consequence of holding the office.

Tithing applies to a levy against church property, the value of which formed the basis for the amount demanded. Special assessments were made under any pretext. The Crusades opened the way for an annual tax. Unusual blessings, unusual sins, or any other situation might call for such assessments.

Even beyond these various methods of raising money, gifts of every kind were solicited. Gifts for approving relics, for permission to view the papal rooms, for jubilees, for charities, etc., swelled the revenue of the Roman Church almost beyond computation.

There were other factors that brought resentment. The Roman system was reasoned out carefully and made a distinct appeal to philosophical minds, but it was not meeting the needs of the people's hearts. Dissent was spreading. There was disaffection in the monastic system, as well as among the clergy. Some were openly skeptical. The enforcement of celibacy upon the clergy brought immorality and concubinage. The doctrinal teaching that the character of a priest or bishop was of secondary importance and did not affect his ability to forgive sins and administer valid sacraments played havoc with the morals of many.

It was the political aspect, however, that brought an end to the

149

universal sway of the papacy. As on previous occasions, it became evident that papal prestige and authority could not yet be divorced from secular power.

The Beginning of Papal Humiliation

Pope Innocent III died in 1216, one year after the spectacular Fourth Lateran Council which marked the height of papal pretensions. For about seventy-five years no direct challenge was made to papal domination in both ecclesiastical and secular spheres. But with the election of Pope Boniface VIII (1294–1303), the new order of things began to appear. Not that Boniface was less vocal in his claims for the papacy nor less aggressive in his demands upon secular and ecclesiastical princes; if anything, he was more vociferous and more arrogant than previous popes. But his claims and demands were not heeded in the way that those of his predecessors had been. In his meddling with the political affairs of the Italian states he was less than successful. He attempted to force an end to the Hundred Years' War between France and England but was ignored by both nations. Enraged, he threatened both England and France with interdict and excommunication should they continue to levy war taxes upon the Roman Church in their realms. King Edward of England simply disregarded the pope; his parliament voted the taxes. King Philip of France, on the other hand, was not so kind. He promptly forbade the exporting of any revenues from France to the papacy. Hurt at a sensitive point and with morale shaken, Boniface canonized Philip's grandfather in an effort to placate the French king. But the war had begun. In 1302, after a preliminary skirmish, Boniface issued his bull entitled *Unam Sanctam*—named, as usual, after the first two words of the bull—excommunicating Philip and placing France under interdict. This famous bull plainly states that every man must obey the pope or forfeit his salvation. Philip was undisturbed, however; the weapons that had brought Gregory VII and Innocent III to power had lost their sting. Philip had the pope seized and imprisoned. The death of Boniface occurred in the following year.

The Babylonian Captivity and Papal Schism

The successor to Boniface, Benedict XI (1303–4), lived only nine months after his election to the office. Benedict's successor, Clement V (1305–14), was appointed through the influence of King Philip of France. In his pontificate papal headquarters were moved from Rome to Avignon, France, in 1309. During the next seventy years seven French popes filled the office. Because the papacy was absent from Rome for about seventy years (just as the Southern Kingdom was in Babylonian captivity for about that length of time), this period of papal residence in France has been called "the Babylonian captivity of the Church."   *SET UP THE GREAT SCHISM*

Clement showed his subservience to Philip of France by acquiescing in the destruction of the Knights Templars. There can be little doubt that this action was dictated by the French king. The Templars had constantly opposed Philip, and he was fearful lest the order should become a military rival. Through promises and torture, enough evidence was secured to convince Pope Clement. In October, 1311, he convoked an ecumenical council (the fifteenth in Roman records), which voted to suppress the order because of corrupt and immoral practices and other crimes, including blasphemy.

The events of the next seventy years convinced the states of Europe that the papacy had become a French institution. French cardinals were appointed in sufficient number to constitute a majority. Many new methods of raising money were fashioned, particularly by John XXII (1316–34).

The return of the papacy to Rome became an issue in each papal election. It was recognized that identification of the papacy with French interests was a serious blunder, particularly in view of the rising tides of nationalism on every hand. Finally, in 1377 Gregory XI ended the fiasco by returning to Rome to die. Urban VI (1378–89) was elected to succeed Gregory upon a promise to return to Avignon, but after his election Urban decided to remain in Rome. The cardinals met again and elected another pope, Clement VI (1378–94), who returned to France. Now there were two popes, each claiming to be validly elected—and each was. For

*GREAT SCHISM
OR
SPLITING OF CHURCH*

a quarter of a century rival popes at Avignon and Rome anathematized one another and sought to undermine the work of the other. Of course, there had been antipopes before. In 251 Novatian had been elected bishop of Rome by a rival party. Other rival popes include Felix II (355–65), Boniface VII (974), and John XVI (997–98).

Probably the strangest papal schism had occurred in the middle of the eleventh century. Benedict IX had been placed on the papal throne in 1032. In 1044 he was driven out of Rome and certain of the local nobles placed Silvester III in the papal chair. Benedict returned to Rome, however, and sold the papal office for about a thousand pounds of silver to an archpriest in Rome, who took the name of Gregory VI. Benedict refused to abide by the bargain, and as a result there were three popes, each with enough strength to resist his opponents but not enough to conquer them. The situation was finally cleared up by Emperor Henry III.

The presence of two popes in the fourteenth century over a long period of time created a number of problems. The validity of almost every ecclesiastical act was brought into question. Which one should bestow the pallium upon newly consecrated bishops? To which should the monastic orders swear their solemn vows? Which should be recognized by the various states? From an organizational standpoint, the situation was almost intolerable. Theoretically each pope, if he were the correct one, should oversee the appointment of bishops in every diocese, fill the numerous vacancies in the archbishoprics, maintain the number of cardinals, appoint administrative heads in the Curia, and carry on the other multitudinous duties required in the operation of a widespread ecclesiastical monarchy. With two popes there were likely to be two appointments to the various positions, rivalry in ecclesiastical law cases, and overlapping in jurisdiction. The Christian world was aghast. Protests came from everywhere.

In 1409 an ecumenical council was called by cardinals of the two popes to meet at Pisa. This council in a rather hasty fashion declared the papal office vacant and elected a new pope, who took the name Alexander V (1409–10). To the dismay of all, the two incumbents refused to recognize the authority of the council, and now there were three popes. By political maneuvering and liberal bribery, the several strong states were induced to support a new council, called this time by one of the popes. The Council of Constance (1414–18) deposed all three of the popes and elected another, who took the name of Martin V (1417–31). This time, however, by political means the task was accomplished. Once again the secular sword controlled the spiritual. The schism was ended, but the prestige of the Roman papacy had been brought low. Voices everywhere were calling for a drastic reform of the whole system. The next chapter will discuss in some detail this clamor for reform.

Concluding Summary

The Roman papacy had exercised world domination through the imposing ecclesiastical structure built up between 1050 and 1215; but the building could not stand. Its essentially tyrannical and non-Christian character was seen in its initiation of movements like the Crusades and the Inquisition. The great increase in central organization, together with the squandering proclivities of the papal court, demanded vast revenues. Every papal policy appeared to be designed to raise money. Religious disaffection was widespread. The popes could not read the signs of the times, and endeavored to speak arrogantly to the strong monarchs of the developing states. Nationalism, however, had blunted the force of the ecclesiastical weapons wielded by Gregory VII and Innocent III, and the states paid little attention to papal demands.

King Philip of France gained control of the papal office, and for over seventy years papal headquarters were at Avignon. During this time the papacy was completely subservient to French interests, causing the alienation of the political rivals and enemies of France. The attempt to return the papacy to Rome in 1378 brought schism, which continued until 1417, when it was finally healed by conciliar action.

13

Clamor for Reform

THE LONG "BABYLONIAN captivity" of the Church and the disas-
trous papal schism of about forty years dramatically symbolized
the need for papal reform. Many recognized that these tragic
events were symptoms of the trouble, not its cause. Certainly the
financial, political, and moral abuses by the papacy did not help
the situation, but the basic problem was not the abuse of the system but the system itself. The clamor for reform did not refer
simply to the immediate problem but challenged conceptions
advocated by the popes for centuries. Some calls for reform had a
distinctly biblical basis. The doctrinal and ecclesiastical tenets
built up by the Roman Church over a long period were compared
with the Scriptures and criticized from that viewpoint. Patriotic
motives impelled some to demand reform. The rising nationalism
of the late Medieval period brought conflicting loyalties into the
hearts of men everywhere. Not a few of the protests against Roman
domination grew out of the resentment against French control of
the papacy during the "Babylonian captivity." Wretched economic
and social conditions and the poised Turk on the very border of
the Empire in the Balkans led many to think that God was punishing the world because of the misdeeds of the papacy. Finally,
spiritual men in all countries were sincerely grieved to see the low
state to which Christianity had come. Mysticism and dissent increased as men sought to find communion with God apart from
the prevailing ecclesiastical system. *TODAY TOO! REBELING + WANTING TO GET BACK TO THE B*

One of the greatest antecedents of reform was the movement
known as the Renaissance. The throbbing of new intellectual life
and the discovery of new worlds profoundly prepared the way for

reformation. The resulting movement known as "humanism" brought the refocusing of men's eyes, and their new vision discerned many of the superstitions that characterized the Medieval Roman Catholic system. Some writers have minimized the scope of the Renaissance, insisting that Western culture required no rebirth. However, the very theological system of the Roman Catholic Church was partly responsible for the slow recovery from the barbarian invasions and the Dark Ages that followed. Because Medieval theology rested upon the extensive unraveling of established propositions through the use of deductive reasoning, it follows that the sources of Roman Catholic doctrine were completely authoritative and traditional. There was very little new grist for the mill but a constant regrinding of the old. For this reason, truth and progress were actually impeded by the scholastic systems of Roman Catholic theology.

But the Renaissance came. The Arabic scholars who followed the Mohammedan invasion of Spain in the eighth century helped to pry open the doors of learning in the West. Classical culture and the study of antiquity became the vogue. The Crusades helped to introduce a new world. The fall of Constantinople (1453) gave impetus to the movement when Greek scholars fled to the West for haven. A score of other factors—Italian nostalgia for the ancient glory of Rome, the appearance of genius in artistic and literary forms, economic developments, geographical discoveries, revolutionary inventions—made up what has been called the "rebirth" (Renaissance) of the West.

This awakening touched Christianity at many points. The movement known as "humanism," which will be discussed in the next pages, sprang directly from these elements. Humanism was greatly influential in preparing the way for reform. The excellence of the ancient literary forms brought contempt for scholastic writings. The revival of interest in the ancients also brought the study of Hebrew and Greek texts making up the Christian Scriptures, as well as the careful perusal of the ancient Christian writings. The eyes of men, so long focused only on the heavens, began to turn toward the world about them and upon themselves. The very foundations of Roman Catholic authority were undermined by the new thought forms.

The centuries just before the sixteenth resounded with calls for reform. Perhaps the best picture of this clamor for reform can be secured by discussing it from a geographical standpoint.

Italy

The strongest protests from Italy against the papal system were based upon the intellectual revival and the resulting humanism. Humanism was the name arbitrarily given to the classical and literary revival which began in Italy about the fourteenth century. It was largely patriotic as well as cultural. It was hoped that the glorious history of past days, spread before the eyes and minds of the present generation, might bring inspiration to attain a new unification of Italy and secure again Roman supremacy in the secular sphere. No little part in creating this longing was due to the removal of the papal chair from Rome to Avignon, France.

The humanists collected manuscripts of classical writers of antiquity, learned to criticize ancient texts through internal study, reveled in imitating the literary style and social manners of the ancients, and viewed the world in which they lived from a rich historical and literary background. Societies were organized to study the Greek language, to read Plato and Cicero, and to gather libraries of the ancient authors. The movement spread from Italy rapidly into northern Europe through religious, intellectual, social, and even economic ties. The development of the printing press helped to spread the gospel of humanism, just as half a century later it reproduced the writings of the Christian reformers for transmission to every part of the world.

It should be noted, however, that the emphasis of humanism took a different turn in northern Europe. In Italy the interest was primarily cultural and patriotic, resulting in disdain for religious ideas and activity. It bred actual cynicism in many cases. Northern humanism, on the other hand, channeled its literary and cultural interest into religious antiquities. The study of Hebrew and Greek looked to better interpretation of the Scriptures; the recovery of the best text of the Scriptures encouraged the critical examination of ancient manuscripts; while those interested in historical investigation republished the ancient Christian writings with critical interpretations. That is, the northern emphasis looked toward uncovering the ancient origins of the Christian faith and restoring the primitive purity of the movement.

So far as reform was concerned, then, the influence of humanism in Italy and in the northern areas performed different services. In Italy its contribution was mainly negative; in the remainder of Europe it was more nearly positive. The negative factors of humanism in Italy that encouraged the reforming spirit were twofold. First, humanism brought a widespread neglect of Christianity and enthroned ancient vices as well as virtues. Even the papacy was infected after its return from Avignon. In 1447 an out-and-out humanist scholar was elected pope and took the name of Nicholas V (1447–55). Religious matters became secondary; libraries, poems, and classics became the foremost items of business. Pius II (1458–64) was an outstanding versifier before his election as pope.

Humanism also encouraged the application to Christian documents of the critical methods used on ancient classical manuscripts. Under Nicholas V, Lorenzo Valla, a young humanist scholar, was brought to the papal court to assist in the translation of Greek classics. While in and out of papal service he wrote a great deal about Christianity from the humanist viewpoint. His study of the Greek text of the New Testament was of great value to the reformers half a century later. He scoffed at the monastic movement and handled roughly the Vulgate translation, which is the inspired Latin version for the Roman Catholics. One of his most spectacular feats was his convincing proof of the spurious nature of the *Donation of Constantine* by the application of internal criticism.

A product of this Italian patriotic revival was the celebrated poet Dante. Exiled to Ravenna in North Italy in the fourteenth century, Dante longed for the restoration of the glory of ancient Rome. His work entitled *On Monarchy* discusses the proper relations between the papacy and the empire. God has given each a sword, said Dante, and neither should control the other. The papacy should not control the empire or meddle in secular matters. While this idea was not new, its application would move the papacy back to an earlier stage of development. The fact that it was suggested by a thoroughly orthodox Catholic, in opposition to papal claims of several preceding centuries, together with the fact that Dante used biblical exegesis to controvert the papal interpretations, made the ideas of Dante quite significant.

The Empire

The loose collection of German states known as the Empire added their protest. Humanism played some part as the background for reform demands. The work of men like Rudolph Agricola, teacher of Greek at the University of Heidelberg, Sebastian Brant of Basel, Johann Reuchlin, and others was mainly negative. Their writings helped to undermine the Roman system with both the populace and the thinkers. Satirical verse and scholarly research joined hands in the protest. Some of the German humanists like Ulrich von Hutten, Franz von Sickingen, and Pirkheimer of Nuremberg actively supported the reform movement when it came. Philip Melanchthon, nephew of Reuchlin and himself an accomplished humanist, became Luther's right-hand man.

The political situation provided the principal protest against papal power, however. In 1314 Duke Louis of Bavaria became emperor following his military victory over a rival candidate. Louis became embroiled in a dispute with Pope John XXII at Avignon over the right of the pope to sanction the election of every emperor. Among other things, French control of the papacy made it quite distasteful for Louis to submit. In 1324 the pope excommunicated Louis. Two scholars, Marsiglio of Padua and John of Janduno, collaborated to prepare one of the most unusual treatises of the day. It was known as the *Defensor Pacis* (Defender of Peace).

This document asserted that the people are the final authority in all things, whether secular or ecclesiastical. Thus in ecclesiastical matters the whole body of Christians, following the principles of the New Testament, constitute the highest power. This remarkable document undermined the papal theory of government. Arguing from the New Testament, it denied that the pope had superior power over any bishop and remarked that there was no scriptural evidence that Peter was ever in Rome. All spiritual power rests in the body of Christian believers, not in priests, bishops, or popes. Furthermore, in a Christian state, reflecting the character and will of the people, the civil ruler has the right to control ecclesiastical affairs, including the calling of ecumenical councils and the appointment of bishops. The ultimate authority resides in a general ecclesiastical council of the people, not simply the bishops.

Another powerful voice that supported Emperor Louis was that of William of Occam, the great English theologian, who took refuge with the emperor. Occam also insisted that the true church did not reside in the bishops but in the believers. He denied the infallibility of the pope and magnified the Bible. The papacy should never deal in secular matters and should be subordinate to a general council of all Christians.

France

French humanism made a distinct contribution in the protest against the unreformed papacy. The movement was late in its beginnings in France but quickly gained strength. Through it the upper class in particular received considerable enlightenment as to the abuses of the Roman system. Jacques Lefèvre Étaples (1455–1536) became an accomplished biblical scholar and antedated Luther in his advocacy of salvation by faith alone, without sacraments, and his emphasis upon the authority of the Scriptures.

The University of Paris provided the early center calling for reform. William of Occam had taught there and expressed his views. John Gerson (1363–1429) and the chancellor of Notre Dame, Pierre d'Ailly (1350–1420), inheritors of Occam's attitude and outlook, headed a scholarly group of men in the university who desired earnestly to reform the papacy in head and members. This group finally succeeded in ending the papal schism through the use of general councils.

England

Resentment against papal claims had deep roots in England. William Rufus, successor to William the Conqueror, notified the pope that he was unwilling to bow the knee, since his predecessors had not done so. The humiliation of England by Innocent III in 1215 produced a reaction against papal absolutism. One of the great reforming churchmen of England was Robert Grosseteste, who became bishop of Lincoln in 1235. Besides reforming his own diocese, Grosseteste addressed Pope Innocent IV about 1250 relative to the corruptions of the Roman Curia and of the Roman Church in general; eight years later Grosseteste refused to accept Innocent's appointment of a relative to the Lincoln diocese. In the struggle between Boniface VIII and King Edward I in 1299, the English Parliament upheld their king and defied the pope. The "Babylonian captivity," which brought the papacy under French domination, occurred just at the time France and England were engaged in war. King Edward III (1327–77) secured the passage of two legislative blows against the papacy. In 1350 the Statute against Provisors was enacted, which provided English free elections of archbishops and bishops—an attempt to eliminate foreign influence in the filling of high church offices. Two years later the Statute of Premunire was enacted, which made it treason for any English subject to accept jurisdiction of papal courts outside of England or to appeal cases to them.

John Wycliffe and the Lollards.—One of the outstanding opponents of the papacy in the latter years of his life was the patriot and preacher, John Wycliffe (1320–84) . Before about 1376 Wycliffe withheld his attacks against the papacy, but the disreputable conditions surrounding the closing years of the Avignon papacy and the beginning of the papal schism in 1378 touched off his violent protests. Wycliffe urged that both of the popes be deposed. In his lectures at Oxford he advanced the idea that if any secular or ecclesiastical prince were not faithful to his task, his right to hold the office was forfeited. If bishop or even pope proved unworthy, civil rulers, as agents of God's will, had the right to despoil him of

160

his temporal property. Probably encouraged by the protection given him by powerful English patriots, Wycliffe boldly continued his criticism of the papacy. Using the Bible—which he helped translate into English about 1382—as final authority, he vigorously attacked the Roman Catholic sacramental system, particularly the doctrine of transubstantiation. He also asserted that the New Testament made no distinction between the bishop and the presbyter (priest) and that consequently the Roman bishop had wrongfully usurped power which was not his. Wycliffe's views were greatly colored by his patriotism—he objected to papal extortion of English funds, to papal appointments of foreigners to English benefices, and to papal encouragement of mendicant monks in England who, said he, robbed the poor.

To give scriptural instruction, Wycliffe organized a group known as the "poor priests" who wandered about two by two (following scriptural injunctions), preaching and teaching. They were received joyfully by the people. Wycliffe was condemned by the pope in 1377 but was protected until his death in 1384 by political influence. The Lollards, as his poor priests were called, continued to increase in number and influence until 1399. In 1395 they delivered a bold memorial to Parliament denouncing Romanism. However, the accession of King Henry IV (1399–1413), an ardent papist, was the signal for persecution. Scores of Lollards were burned at the stake and their churches suppressed. Lollard followers went underground after 1431 and doubtless provided a fertile soil for the reform movement which came about a century later.

English humanism.—English humanism also played a part in increasing antipapal sentiment. John Colet (1467–1519), dean of St. Paul's Cathedral in London, was an outstanding humanist. With William Grocyn and Thomas Linacre he formed a nucleus for the school of thought that despised the scholastic methods and theology. Colet, a deeply spiritual and capable leader, was especially skilled in biblical interpretation. His eloquent voice constantly called for reform. He greatly influenced Erasmus, the outstanding continental humanist, between about 1498 and 1514.

161

Bohemia

The clamor for reform in Bohemia was partly religious and partly patriotic. Bohemia was under German domination. Her Christianity had originally been received from the Greek Church, but the great Magyar invasion of the thirteenth century had forced the nation into a German alliance, and through the Germans the Roman type of Christianity had been introduced. The University of Prague was the center of religious and patriotic opposition. A number of eloquent preachers and teachers advocated stringent religious reforms. Among these were Conrad of Waldhausen, who openly denounced the Roman monks and clergy; Milicz of Kremsier; Matthias of Janow, a remarkably able teacher and writer; and Thomas of Stitny, a very popular preacher. Two events brought great impetus to the reform movement. One was the marriage of Ann of Bohemia to King Richard II of England in 1382; the other was the exchange of scholars and correspondence between the universities of Prague and Oxford, resulting from the closer ties between the two nations because of the marriage. The exchange of scholars and correspondence between the universities brought Bohemia into familiarity with the writings of John Wycliffe.

The man who inherited these factors and headed up the reform movement in Bohemia was John Huss (1369–1415). Huss was a native of Bohemia, educated at the University of Prague. A careful student of the Scriptures and of Wycliffe, he filled some of the highest offices in the University of Prague. By his struggle against the Germans in the university he was able to secure from the king a change in the constitution of the school in January, 1409, which brought the native Czechs into a favored position over the German majority. As a consequence the German teachers and students withdrew.

Huss became increasingly bolder in his attacks against foreign and papal usurpations. In 1410 he was excommunicated and his teachings were condemned. Huss then published his treatise *Concerning the Church,* in which he repeated the views of Wycliffe,

162

sometimes copying page after page from Wycliffe's writings. His preaching was directed against papal abuses and demanded reform. He was summoned to the Council of Constance in 1415 to discuss his views and was promised his safety if he would attend. *NIAVE!* The Roman bishop violated the promise, however, remarking that the Church did not need to keep its word with heretics. Huss was condemned by the Council and was burned at the stake in 1415. A follower, Jerome of Prague, suffered the same fate months later.

The burning of Huss and Jerome aroused Bohemia to open revolt. The Hussite wars, both political and religious in nature, lasted only until about 1435, but the influence of the strict party, the Taborites, led to the formation of the Bohemian Brethren.

The Netherlands

Probably the greatest continental humanist was Desiderius Erasmus of Rotterdam (1465–1536). The son of a priest and gifted in many ways, his life was profoundly affected by the death of his parents when he was but thirteen. For a brief time he attended the school of the Brethren of the Common Life at Deventer but was shunted to a monastic school when his guardians squandered the money left for him. After splendid training at Paris and Cologne, he took his place as the outstanding humanist of his day, making his living by dedicating his works to the patrons who supported him. He had little inclination to break with the Roman system, but his writings are filled with ridicule of the abuses and superstitions that prevailed in the papal Church. His publication in 1516 of a critical edition of the Greek text of the New Testament was of double value—the text itself was quite helpful to reformation scholarship, and the Preface spelled out the need for reform. His hope for reform was through the process of education and infiltration. If men simply knew the gospel of primitive Christianity, the prevalent ills and abuses would be corrected.

Mysticism

A number of groups not specifically confined to one geographical area provided great impetus toward the reform movement. The mystics were one of the most important. Mysticism viewed man as having within him an affinity with God that does not require ecclesiastical machinery to make the contact. God's presence could be felt in the heart and soul without reference to sacraments. It may be observed that this attitude could completely bypass all of the machinery of the Roman Church, for if one could have an immediate and intuitive vision of God, it would be unnecessary to use the services of the priest and the Church. Most of the mystics, however, did not actively oppose the external spiritual exercises of the Roman Church. They were willing to utilize these as aids to supplement their own consciousness of the nearness of God. They had a real concern over the corruptions and schisms in the visible institution.

The principal leaders of this group were Meister Eckhart (1260–1327) in Germany and Jan van Ruysbroeck (1293–1381) and Gerhard Groote (1340–84) in the Netherlands. Eckhart's theology was simple: men should allow God to fill them until they are actually absorbed into God and become Godlike. The modification of this central idea into orthodox harmony with the sacramental system of the Roman Church accounts for differences in the thinking of Eckhart's successors, such as Johann Tauler (1290–1361) and Henry Suso (died 1366). The influence of these men and many other mystics went far beyond simply producing additional mystics. In fundamental conceptions their thinking modified the crass sacramentalism and formalism of many continental theologians. One anonymous writer produced a work which Martin Luther, the great German reformer, later published and prized highly and which Luther termed "German theology," as over against scholastic theology of the Roman Church. This writing was deeply influenced by German mysticism and scriptural theology.

The system of Ruysbroeck in the Netherlands magnified the study of the New Testament and was quite influential in preparing the way for the reform movement that broke out later. Gerhardt Groote, a layman mystic of the Netherlands, led in the formation of the organization called the Brethren of the Common Life, whose purpose was to forward the mystical and pious conceptions of

Ruysbroeck and make them available to others. They established several schools in the Netherlands and Germany. Erasmus attended one of these schools for a period, and Luther himself did likewise. Thomas à Kempis is credited with writing a devotional guide that is still valuable, the *Imitation of Christ*.

Many of the mystics were found in the monasteries. Meister Eckhart was a Dominican monk. Doubtless the long hours of reflection and contemplation gave ample opportunity for the development of mystical tendencies or, as a matter of fact, for the rise of extreme ideas for ceremonialism. The tendency would be to reach either extreme—to attain a passionate love for excessive sacramentalism or a genuine attachment to God apart from any externals. One large party from the Franciscans broke with the majority in an effort to follow more closely the simple ethic of their founder. Their mystical and scriptural simplicity abhorred the luxurious and schismatic Christianity of the papacy. They joined so zealously in the clamor for reform that they were condemned as heretics and many were martyred.

Popular Calls for Reform

The papal schism, extending as it did into every diocese and raising serious questions in the mind of every Roman Catholic concerning which pope (and which bishop) was the valid one, stirred up on every side a popular desire for reform. The immediate motive was to secure the unity of the papacy. Since the rival popes anathematized one another and all supporters of one another—which really negated the effectiveness of any sacraments and official acts of the false pope and his followers—and since no one knew which was the correct pope, utmost confusion and widespread fear prevailed among the masses. Lay organizations sprang up, and orders of women arose whose main emphasis was upon the necessity of reform.

Concluding Summary

The desire to reform the Roman Church sprang from various motives. The study of the Bible, intellectual awakening, patriotism, economic and social conditions, military considerations, and religious hunger combined to seek reform. Voices could be heard from practically all of the principal countries. Mysticism and dissent increased considerably.

The next chapter will discuss the effort to bring reform, primarily by the conciliar method. This did at least heal the papal schism, although no progress was made toward reforming the papacy itself.

14

Efforts at Reform

THE DOMINATION OF the papacy by French interests from 1309 to 1378 and the scandalous schism for almost forty years after the attempt to return the papacy to Rome emphasized the necessity of reform. But circumstances and traditional beliefs seemed to make any sort of reform completely impossible. In the first place, there was no way to determine just who was the proper occupant of the papal chair. Each of the popes was supported by a legitimately appointed and properly consecrated group of cardinals. Each had declared himself the rightful pope and had anathematized his opponent. Even worse, each had sufficient political backing to maintain himself in office. In the second place, what could be done against a pope, assuming that one of the two or three was the proper one? As early as the fifth century, Pope Symmachus had set forth the theory of papal irresponsibility. By 503 this idea had received dogmatic approval. As enlarged through the centuries, this doctrine taught that even if the pope were in complete error, he could not be tried by any but God; no tribunal on earth could challenge the doctrines, morals, motives, or decrees of a pope. How, then, could there be any action taken to heal the schism?

Individual Protests

In the previous chapter some of the protests from every part of the Roman Church were sketched. Plans of reform were urged; severe criticism was directed against the papal government and papal doctrines. But in view of the traditional notion that no one may correct a pope and the doubt concerning which claimant actually was the true pope, no practical move was taken.

167

The Opinions of Scholars

Despite repeated appeals to both popes after 1378, neither would take the initiative to restore papal unity. The scholars in the various theological schools, whose views had often borne great weight in doctrinal controversies, were consulted about the best way to end the schism. It was inevitable that the idea of Marsiglio of Padua, written in 1324 into his *Defensor Pacis,* should be asserted, namely, that a general council possesses supreme authority in Christianity. This same suggestion was made by two other scholars, Conrad of Gelshausen in 1379 and Heinrich of Langenstein in 1381. By 1408 most of the scholars in the great universities of the Continent agreed that the only method of healing the schism was through a general council. The scholars could not agree as to the makeup of the council. Some thought that all true Christians should constitute the membership; others would favor the precedent of the earlier general councils and limit the membership simply to the bishops who, they said, constituted the visible Church. But there were other problems. Who should call the council? The emperors had called some of the early councils, but the popes had claimed that prerogative for many centuries. Neither of the popes was willing to call the council; however, the cardinals of the rival popes were convinced that a general council was necessary to restore peace and unity.

The Council of Pisa (1409)

At the call of the cardinals a general council was assembled at Pisa in March, 1409. The council attempted to solve three problems: the papal schism, reform, and heresy. The first of these problems was viewed as the principal purpose of the council. It was well attended and took definite action by declaring the papal throne vacant. Cardinals representing both popes united to elect a new one, who took the name Alexander V. Since neither of the two existing popes, Gregory XII and Benedict XIII, recognized the council as validly assembled or authoritative, the net result was simply the addition of another pope.

The Council of Constance (1414–18)

The mistakes of the Council of Pisa were evident. For one thing, many of the bishops desired more information about the authority of a council, particularly in deposing a pope. Others felt that the council should have been summoned by a pope, not by the cardinals or by a secular power. Furthermore, it was apparent that political factors would determine whether or not any action of a future council would be effective. As it was, each of the three popes had enough political and military support to maintain himself in office. The new pope, Alexander V, was recognized by England, France, Hungary, and parts of Italy; Benedict XIII was called pope by Spain and Scotland; while Gregory XII had most of the Italian support and that of Germany.

Two men remedied these defects. John Gerson, one of the champions of the conciliar idea after 1408, determined to clothe a future council with express authority to take action in dealing with schism, reform, and heresy. The other, the German emperor Sigismund (1410–37), determined to provide political support sufficient to make the decrees of the council effective. Sigismund had the first task, and he worked diligently at it. He induced Pope John XXIII (successor to Alexander V) to call a general council to convene at Constance. By clever political tactics he secured the support of the Spanish, English, and Burgundian rulers for the council. He had chosen Constance in Germany as the place of meeting in order to neutralize the influence of the Italian clergy, practically all of whom favored John XXIII. In addition, arrangements were made for the council to vote by nations rather than by individuals, in this way circumventing plans by some of the incumbent popes to "pack" the meeting. Thus each of the five nations—England, France, Spain, Germany, and Italy—had one vote and must vote as a unit.

Gerson and his supporters did their part. Through Gerson's influence the council passed a decree in April, 1415, defining its own authority. It claimed to represent Jesus Christ and asserted that its decisions on all religious matters were binding upon every

169

Christian, including the pope or popes. This decree, of course, cut directly across papal claims for centuries. Passed unanimously by the ecumenical council, it challenged ancient dogmas of the Roman Church which were alleged to be incapable of change and provided an example of an alleged infallible council and infallible papacy in conflict. Acting upon this decree, the council forcibly seized Pope John XXIII and deposed him in May, 1415; Gregory XII then resigned; Benedict XIII was twice deposed, although he refused to accept this action.

Another innovation occurred. Instead of having a new pope elected by the cardinals, it was agreed by the council that those cardinals present at the council, supplemented by thirty members of the council, should elect a new pope, with only a two-thirds majority required for election. They chose one who took the name Martin V. He took office immediately, possessing sufficient political support to guarantee his universal acceptance. The schism was almost over. Benedict XIII had refused to resign, but after his death in 1424, his successor was recognized only by Aragon and Sicily; and in 1429 the schism was completely ended.

The second problem of the Council of Constance was reform. After the election of Martin V the council passed another decree which denied papal claims of almost a millennium. This decree provided that general councils would meet again in five years and in seven years, and that thereafter such councils would meet every ten years. Future popes would be subject to instructions from these councils. The ancient papal claims of superiority to councils seemed doomed. However, the attitude of the new pope should have warned the conciliar leaders. Martin V had supported the conciliar idea until his election as pope; then he immediately became anticonciliar. When the council endeavored to bring reform, the new pope worked feverishly to prevent the adoption of antipapal measures. This he was able to do.

The problem of heresy also occupied the attention of the council. The burning of John Huss and Jerome has already been mentioned. The outbreak of the Hussite wars shows that the council was not only religiously suspect but was also politically unwise.

Council of Pavia and Siena (1423)

The papal schism had been healed, but reform still was not begun. Martin V (1417–31) asserted traditional papal claims in an effort to neutralize the decrees of the Council of Constance, which claimed to be the supreme authority in Christendom. However, the pope felt it necessary to carry out the decree of Constance providing for the calling of a general council in five years, especially since the Bohemians were still threatening and the Ottoman Turks were winning new military victories. The plague at Pavia caused the removal of the council to Siena. The pope dismissed the council soon, however, alleging poor attendance as the reason.

Council of Basel (1431–49)

It had been planned at the Council of Constance to call another general council seven years after the Council of Pavia. Pope Martin V had agreed to call this council but died before it assembled. His successor, Eugenius IV (1431–47), had promised to support the conciliar program as a condition of election but violated his promise. When the council met and showed the spirit of the Council of Constance, Eugenius tried to dissolve the assembly before any action was taken. Political pressure dissuaded him. Three problems faced this council: how to deal with the warring Hussites; what to do about a reform of the Church; and how to effect a reunion of Eastern and Western Christianity, desired by some of the Eastern leaders as a means of driving away the Ottoman Turks who were threatening to capture Constantinople.

The council was partially successful in dealing with the Bohemians. By appeasing the moderate party (the Utraquists or Calixtines), a division was caused between them and the more radical Taborites. The result was another civil war in Bohemia, but the Catholics were able to defeat the Taborites and repress the spread of their ideas.

For a brief period it seemed that some effective ecclesiastical reforms might result from the deliberations of the council. However, as soon as the council touched the person of the pope and his authority, papal influence blocked further progress. Eugenius decided to deal with the council as the council had dealt with the Bohemians—to divide and conquer. The question of union between East and West was pressed upon the council. When sharp differences appeared, the pope denounced the council and in 1437 removed it by papal bull to Ferrara, thence to Florence in 1439. A substantial party refused to abide by the papal edict and continued to meet at Basel. They voted to depose Eugenius as pope and selected another who took the name of Felix V (1439–49). Now there were two popes again, but Felix had no political support, and there was widespread revulsion at the thought of another papal schism. Consequently, the Basel council was discredited and in 1449 surrendered to Nicholas V (1447–55), who had succeeded Eugenius. The conciliar efforts to reform the papacy had failed.

Council of Ferrara and Florence (1437–39)

The principal reason of Pope Eugenius for moving the council from Basel to Ferrara and then to Florence was to discredit the Basel reforming party. The pope was determined that there would be no reform by a council. Because of this fact, considerable responsibility for the schismatic movement known as the Reformation must be laid at his door. The Council of Basel was eager to make reforms and doubtless would have done so along the lines of the Pragmatic Sanctions of France, which will be mentioned hereafter.

It is true that the representatives from the Greek Church preferred to meet in an Italian city, but this was of small moment. As a matter of fact, the question of uniting East and West was doomed before the Greek delegation arrived at Ferrara in 1438. A majority of the East definitely opposed the union under any circumstances. The minority desired union simply to secure military and political assistance against the Turks. In the council the pope agreed to organize a new crusade against the Turks, in return for which the East would recognize the universal supremacy of the pope. This agreement, however, was promptly repudiated by the Eastern clergy.

Reasons for Failure of Conciliar Efforts

The collapse of the Council of Basel in 1449 brought to an end the movement begun about forty years before in the Council of Pisa. Some reasons for the failure of this effort to reform the Church in head and members are apparent. For one thing, there was a lack of unity in motives for reform. Some were interested in reform only from a political standpoint, some were seeking to fish in troubled waters in the hope of personal advancement, while some were willing to go along with the movement so long as it was popular.

A partial solution of the immediate problem at hand, the papal schism, blunted the desire for thorough reform. When the Council of Constance solved the most pressing problem facing it in 1417, even the brave statement of the authority of the council did not hide the fact that in the minds of many the council had gone as far as it should. With a single pope to deal with, leadership in a stringent reform brought danger of effective reprisals.

The active antagonism of the popes predestined to failure any attempts at reform. The several popes of the first half of the fifteenth century agreed in principle with the efforts of the conciliar reformers until they had been elected to the high office. Their sympathy for reform and their recognition of the authority of a council then vanished immediately. The comparatively long period of time between the meetings of the reforming councils gave the papacy an opportunity to recoup much of its strength and prestige.

After the Reforming Councils

Although an effective program of reform was not accomplished, the battle had not been lost entirely. The various nations represented in the councils had seen at first hand the need for reform and the attitude of the papacy toward reform. They had also caught a glimpse of the authority that political and military strength carried. Consequently, England, Spain, and France, already strong and unified, were able to secure important concessions from the papacy with reference to the control of the Church within their boundaries. France, in fact, shortly after the failure of the Council of Basel assembled a meeting of the clergy and enacted the Pragmatic Sanctions of 1438, which accomplished the very thing for France that the conciliar proponents had hoped would come for all of Christianity from the general council. These Sanctions asserted that a general council was the supreme authority in Christendom and, among other things, claimed French autonomy in filling its ecclesiastical vacancies. It is just as significant that the loosely organized German states, where the reform movement subsequently broke forth, were unable to secure any such concessions and consequently felt even more heavily the burdens of papal financial and ecclesiastical tyranny.

The failure of the conciliar movement seemed to increase the arrogance of the Roman popes. The religious and moral tone of the papacy from the close of the Council of Basel until the Lutheran Reformation was indescribably low. Two of the popes were out-and-out humanists (Nicholas V, 1447–55, and Pius II, 1458–64); one of them a second-rate despot (Sixtus IV, 1471–84); two were shameless in their immorality and vice (Innocent VIII, 1484–92, who openly acknowledged and promoted his seven illegitimate children, and Alexander VI, 1492–1503, noted for his immorality, vice, and violence); one should have been an army officer (Julius II, 1503–13); while the pope of the Reformation, Leo X (1513–21), reportedly called Christianity a profitable fable and spent his time in his hunting lodge. Had there been wise and upright popes in this period, it is very likely that the next effort at reform would have been different in its direction and consequences. The succession of men of this calibre guaranteed the certainty of the deluge to come.

Concluding Summary

The ticklish problem of ending a papal schism was finally accomplished by the authority of a general council, buttressed by political and military support. Such action marks the council as superior to popes, a fact which was subsequently denied by succeeding popes but which established them in their office and succession. To deny the authority of a council to depose popes would appear to deny the validity of their own succession.

The thorough reform of the Roman Catholic Church in head and members, however, could not be accomplished by reforming councils, despite many efforts during forty years. The occupants of the papal office in the half century immediately before the Reformation constitute ample evidence of the need for reform.

15

Ecclesiastical Dissent

ONE FACTOR OF great importance relating to the papal decline and the clamor for reform was the presence everywhere of anti-papal dissent. It is difficult to lump together into one descriptive term all of the extensive movements which existed just prior to the Reformation. The only record of so many of them comes from their persecution in the Inquisition. Some of the movements were distinctly medieval in their religious conceptions. Others held evangelical tenets. It is hard today to interpret contemporary religious movements correctly despite the possession of extensive literature by their own adherents. The problem of attempting to give a true picture of movements whose only records are those of one man, an enemy to the cause and one unversed in differentiating objectively between evangelicalism and heresy, is far greater.

The same situation renders most difficult the matter of determining the relations and history of any such movement. Were these antipapal dissenters isolated and separate in their several movements, or was there correspondence among them? Did they represent the fruits of earlier movements, or did they spring *de novo* from the earth? Such questions have passionate defenders at both extremes and cannot be settled completely. Conclusions, therefore, in many cases are a matter of personal attitude and judgment.

Evidences of Unity and Continuity

Literary remains of concerted opposition to the Roman Church would naturally be quite scarce. There is indisputable evidence, however, that many of the movements which were at one time thought to be isolated and separate were, in reality, in close fellowship and correspondence. For example, evangelical parties in Germany, Austria, and Italy assembled in convention as early as 1218 to discuss points of mutual belief. Constant correspondence had taken place also long before the Reformation between evangelical dissenters throughout Germany and those in Bohemia. In the thirteenth century Pope Innocent III denounced the translation of the Scriptures into the language of the people, and the possession of Scriptures in the vernacular tongue was looked upon as heresy. Even before Wycliffe's version in English in the late fourteenth century, dissenters were translating the Bible into the language of the people. Dozens of German translations existed in the fifteenth century, some showing evidence of independent work while others, betraying a common source, turned up among widely separated groups. Long after the Reformation had begun, the Anabaptists of Germany used these ancient translations rather than the translation of Luther. An interesting reflection of connections among the dissenters is seen in the fact that the Waldenses of Italy and France, the Brethren of the Common Life in the Netherlands and Germany, and the United Brethren of Bohemia used the same catechism for the instruction of the children in their movements. Editions of the identical catechism are found in French, Italian, German, and Bohemian.

It is not difficult to find convincing evidence that many of the dissenting movements of the thirteenth and fourteenth centuries were the successors of more primitive groups. Peculiar doctrines, noticeable in the system of the Eastern Paulicians of the early Middle Ages, for example, are reproduced in the Bogomiles of the Balkans and the Cathari of France and Germany. The Western dispersion of the Paulicians is a historical fact. The name of the Cathari (Greek both in form and in spirit) marks them as an Eastern movement transplanted to the West, probably a reappearance of the Paulician and Bogomile dissenters. There are evidences of the persistence of the older Christianity of Britain (discountenanced by the Synod of Whitby in 664), as well as older Christianity upon the Continent proper. The rapid spread of Luther's reform and the sudden appearance of organized Ana-

177

baptist congregations all over the Continent in the sixteenth century testify to a widespread evangelical background.

Handicaps to Historical Certainty

It is impossible to be dogmatic about the history of dissent in this period. The sparsity of historical material would forbid it. Most of the literary remains were prepared by the enemies of dissent, secured through the most excruciating torture by the inquisitors. Before the suppression of dissent through the central organization of the Roman Curia, this work was carried on locally by bishops or crusading preachers like Bernard, the Cistercian monk. Under these circumstances even inquisitorial records are lacking, and there is practically no evidence of any kind about the dissenters and their beliefs.

For example, although the Bogomiles of the twelfth century may have numbered as many as two million, one of the principal records of their beliefs comes from a Byzantine monk named Euthymius who died in 1118. He gave an account of how, among other things, they rejected the Lord's Supper as the sacrifice of demons, called the churches the dwelling places of demons and the worship of images in them idolatry, and termed the "Fathers of the Church" false prophets against whom Jesus warned. Such charges doubtless were similar to the charges brought against the early Christians: they were called atheists because they had no idols, cannibals because they partook of the body and blood of Christ, and immoral because they spoke of Christian love. Perhaps the Bogomiles did reject the Mass, reject the orthodox churches, and oppose idolatry. From the entire description given, the Bogomiles seem to have been the product of missionary work by the Paulicians among the Bulgarians. At least, their alleged doctrines reflect some of the peculiarities of the Paulicians, modified by dualistic and Manichean tendencies.

Another example of the sparsity of records is seen in the story of the Petrobrusians and Henricians. These movements were begun separately but coalesced. Much of what is known about the Petrobrusians comes from the pen of a Roman Catholic enemy.

Peter de Bruys was a priest of the Roman Church in the twelfth century. He had been a student of Abélard, the great freethinker. About 1104 he began a career as a reformer in southern France and was widely influential until his martyrdom about 1126. Henry of Lausanne was a Roman Catholic monk who associated himself with Peter as a reformer. After a long and active ministry he died as a martyr in 1148. The evangelical nature of the things these men taught is evident in spite of the denunciation of their doctrines by their enemy biographer. (1) They denied that the christening of infants was baptism and said that only an intelligent profession of faith by a person for himself (without proxy) brought salvation. (2) They vehemently rejected crosses in worship, since Christ was slain upon one. Even temples and churches were unnecessary for the worship of God. (3) They denied the doctrine of transubstantiation and perhaps refused to observe the Supper at all. (4) They recognized the Scriptures alone as authoritative, denying the authority of the early Fathers and of tradition.

Innocent III and Dissent

The pope who both closed the previous period and opened the present one (Innocent III, 1198–1216) had contact with two dissenting groups, the Waldenses and the Cathari. Both of these movements had a long history before that time. The origin of the Waldenses is disputed. Even the source of their name is in doubt. Perhaps it was begun by Peter Waldo of Lyons, France, in the closing years of the twelfth century. He headed a movement in which laymen wandered about teaching and singing Scriptures. The group was excommunicated in 1184 but continued to spread rapidly through southern France, Italy, Spain, and the Rhine Valley.

The inquisitors who sought out information on the beliefs of the Waldenses testify that they had about the same doctrines as the Petrobrusians: the sole authority of the Scriptures, the necessity for believer's baptism, the denial of the authority of the Roman Church, the denial of purgatory and the merit of praying to the saints, and refusal to believe that the bread and wine are changed into the body and blood of Christ by the priest. In addition, it was alleged that the Waldenses permitted men to preach without proper ordination, vilified the pope, refused to make canonical confession, and rejected oaths and war. About 1212 Innocent III was approached by some of this group for permission to assemble and read the Scriptures. The pope gave this permission but three years later initiated a decree of condemnation against all Waldenses. In an effort to cripple the movement, two successive Catholic synods forbade the reading of the Bible in the language of the people, either by laymen or clergy. Although severely persecuted, the Waldenses continue to the present time.

The group known as the Cathari came to light in France in the eleventh century. Their doctrines were quite similar to those of the Bogomiles. As a matter of fact, the Cathari of France looked toward Bulgaria as their source and recognized a Bogomile leader as their spiritual head. Their dualistic view of God and Docetic Christology suggest a strong Manichean influence, another indication that perhaps their doctrinal system originated in the East where Manicheanism was strongest.

The dissenters known as the Albigenses (because they lived near Albi in southern France) were Cathari. Innocent III (1198–1216) decided, in view of the great strength of the movement, that strong means must be taken to root it out. Accordingly, Innocent sent two legates to France to begin the effort. They were persuaded by the bishop of Osma and by Dominic to try religious measures first. Assuming the garb of beggars, the legates and others wandered about barefooted and presented an example of humility and poverty. Few Albigenses were convinced. Violent measures soon followed.

Count Raymond of Toulouse was the nominal ruler over the area where the heretics lived but was indifferent to their religious views so long as they were good subjects. One of the legates was murdered in 1208, and Raymond was suspected of complicity or at least accused of it. Innocent III proclaimed a crusade against Raymond and the Albigenses. Whoever conquered them should have both territory and spoils from the war. For twenty years the war raged. As cities were captured, their inhabitants were either slaughtered or sold into slavery. The Albigenses fled throughout Europe, and others of the Cathari followed their example. Pope Innocent pushed through the Fourth Lateran Council in 1215 three canons relating to heretics: secular rulers must not tolerate heretics in their domain; secular rulers refusing to uproot heretics must themselves be driven out, either by their subjects or by crusaders from the outside; crusading against heretics at home brings all the sacramental privileges and indulgences which accrue from crusading against the Turks in Jerusalem.

The Extent of Ecclesiastical Dissent

One method of noting the wide extent of dissent against the Roman Catholic system is geographical. Between 1215 and the theses of Luther in 1517 it is possible to find sizable groups of dissenters in almost every section of the Western world. Dissent was also strong in the East, but that area was not involved in the domination of the papacy after 1054 and did not share in the Reformation.

England.—In England the Lollards (the name given to the "poor priests" of Wycliffe) constituted a large and aggressive dissenting movement. A Roman Catholic writer of the late fourteenth century said that one out of every two men seemed to be a follower of Wycliffe. The Lollards were strong enough in 1395 to present a memorial to Parliament attacking the Roman Church and its doctrines, in particular condemning the Roman priesthood, Roman celibacy, Roman transubstantiation, Roman liturgies and prayers for the dead, auricular confession, and Roman crusades. Four years later, with the accession of Henry IV who was under the influence of Archbishop Thomas Arundel of Canterbury, persecution of the Lollards began. After 1417 they were driven underground, but their influence and doctrines were not destroyed.

France and Spain.—Reference has already been made to the dissenting movements of Peter de Bruys and Henry of Lausanne and to the Cathari. Some historians believe that through these

181

groups almost the whole of southern France was antipapal during the twelfth century. When the Albigensian persecution came in the thirteenth century, many of the Cathari fled into Spain and became victims of the Spanish Inquisition. One of the letters of Bernard, the outstanding preacher of the twelfth century, remarks that the churches were without congregations because of the heretical movement.

Italy.—Reformers were not unknown at the very door of the papal see. One of the outstanding reforming figures was Arnold of Brescia in northern Italy. His strictures against the papacy were aimed mainly at the secular and financial activities of the clergy which, he said, should not occupy their attention. Freewill offerings alone should provide for the support of all religious leaders. He fled from Italy in 1139 to escape charges of heresy but in 1145 assumed leadership of a popular movement which expelled the pope and looked to the restoration of the ancient Roman republic. Ten years later, overwhelmed through the military alliance of Pope Alexander III, Arnold was martyred.

It is likely that Arnold was the founder of the group known as Arnoldists and the inspiration of the movement developing later known as the Poor Men of Lombardy. Not a great deal is known about these two sects, except that they are frequently mentioned as heretics in the Roman Catholic writings of the thirteenth and fourteenth centuries. They seem to have opposed vigorously the Roman Catholic system, to have denied that water in baptism brings forgiveness, and to have excoriated the Roman clergy for secularization and corruption.

Another Italian group known as the Humiliati arose in the twelfth century; about them little is known, except that they were classed as heretics and mentioned in such fashion that they seem to have been associated with the Waldenses.

The influence of these dissenters was extensive in northern Italy. In a document written about 1260, an anonymous author remarked that in northern Italy the Waldenses had more schools than the orthodox Church and also had more hearers. He further asserted that because of their large numbers, these heretics held public disputes against Catholicism and services in the market place or the open field.

The Germanic states.—The Waldensian movement also infected many areas in the Germanic states. The same author who describes the large number of Waldenses in Italy speaks of the extensive spread of the Waldenses around Passau on the Danube River. He named forty-two places in the Catholic diocese of Passau which were affected by the heresy. In twelve of these places the Waldenses had schools and in one of them a bishop. Roman Catholic documents a century and a half later (1389) describe ninety-two points of papal doctrine and practice rejected by the Waldenses and provide evidence that this movement had become thoroughly evangelical in its doctrinal views.

In the fourteenth century two theologians in German schools openly taught doctrines at variance with the teachings of the Roman system. One was John of Wesel. He placed the Scriptures alone as the final authority in Christianity. He rejected the priestly pretensions of controlling salvation and denied the doctrine of transubstantiation. Imprisoned by the Roman authorities at Mainz, he died in 1482. The other theologian was Wessel Gansfort, who died in 1489. He proclaimed the doctrine of justification by faith and attacked the doctrine of indulgences. Luther later confessed that his entire Reformation doctrine was so evident in the writings of Wessel Gansfort that had Luther been acquainted with these writings, his enemies might have charged him with securing material from that source.

Netherlands and the Rhine Valley.—The records speak of heretical movements in the twelfth century in northern Europe also. In the Netherlands, Tanchelm (1115–24) strongly denounced Roman Catholic churches and sacraments as pollutions and in general followed the teachings of Peter de Bruys, with whom he was a contemporary. At about the same time Eudo de Stella carried on a similar ministry in the Rhine Valley. His followers were so aroused by his preaching that they destroyed Roman Churches and monasteries. He was seized by the Roman Church and died as a martyr about 1148. Other dissenters, quite evangelical and antipapal, left a record of their work along the Rhine Valley. They clearly denied the Roman doctrines of transubstantiation and infant baptism.

Bohemia.—Perhaps of all the areas of Europe, Bohemia had been most completely infected with dissent. Historically, of course, Bohemia had looked to the Eastern world for her religious pattern and had only accepted the Latin Church because it was brought by the Germans who protected Bohemia against the Magyar invasions of the eleventh century. Resentment against foreigners politically and religiously formed a background of Bohemian dissent. It is known that the Waldenses were quite strong in southern Bohemia—so strong, in fact, that in about 1340 they threatened to destroy their Catholic foes should an attempt be made to coerce them religiously. Out of the Hussite wars, following the burning of John Huss in 1415, came the two parties, the strict one (the Taborites) holding views much like those of the evangelical Waldenses. They fiercely opposed the Roman Catholic Church in every point save one, the retention of infant baptism. One of the outstanding leaders of Bohemian dissent in the fifteenth century was Peter Chelicky, a native Bohemian, born about 1385. He, too, followed closely the doctrines of the evangelical Waldenses; he would allow infant baptism in practice, although denying its validity in principle.

The Bohemian Brethren constituted the evangelical wing of the Hussite reform. It was organized in an effort to bring a general reform within the national church so as to restore to Christianity the original purity which had been lost. In its practical aspect this movement formed a community which endeavored to live according to the law of Christ. Specific organization was effected about 1457. Before the Reformation crisis of 1517 this movement had spread throughout Bohemia and Moravia and had become a considerable force for reform. Through extensive use of the newly invented printing press, the organization of schools, and the wide dissemination of their doctrines through Austria and Germany, the Brethren played a large part in preparing for the events of the sixteenth century.

Concluding Summary

It may be seen, then, that dissent of some sort appeared in almost every section of Europe in this period. The sparsity of records makes it difficult to judge accurately either the doctrines or the extent of the movements. It should be remembered that this description of these movements is not exhaustive. The myriad of reformers who lingered just below the surface of recorded history can never be known. But they were there. The rapidity with which the Reformation developed in the sixteenth century provides evidence of this. How else is it possible to explain how a large part of the Continent and England embraced the reforming movements so rapidly between 1517 and 1534? Such widespread defection from the Roman Church demanded widespread dissent as an antecedent.

16

The Fulness of Time

THE WORD "REFORMATION" describing the revolution of the sixteenth century is, in a sense, a misnomer. The principal events did not center in reform but in schism. Certainly those who participated in the organization of new ecclesiastical bodies conceived of their movements as true Christianity moving into, or toward, its primitive channel. In that sense there was a reformation of Christianity, not of the Roman Curia, for the Curia refused to be reformed.

In the latter months of 1517 a monk named Martin Luther, incensed by the recent sale of indulgences in a nearby German town, gave public notice on the door of the church at Wittenberg that he desired to debate what the Catholic Church actually taught about indulgences. In this rather ordinary fashion the Lutheran Reformation began. What was it that brought comparative success to Luther's efforts when so many previous efforts had failed? Was it in the monk, in his environment, in the circumstances of his life, in his inheritance from previous generations? It was in all of these.

Political Factors That Aided the Reformation

Practically every political body in Europe contributed in some way to the progress of the reform movement. In most cases it was done unwittingly. The strongest state in Europe during this period was Spain. The peninsula had been unified politically by the marriage in 1469 between Ferdinand of Aragon and Isabella of Castile and by the subsequent conquest of contiguous areas. The grandson of this couple, Charles I, became king in 1516 and in

1519 was elected Holy Roman Emperor of the German nation. The latter succession titled him Charles V, by which he is best known. He inherited a strongly Catholic nation, made so by the work of Cardinal Ximenes, principal adviser of Queen Isabella. Ximenes had instituted a reform of the Catholic Church in Spain which abolished papal abuses and much papal control; consequently, neither Charles nor his people were sympathetic with the continental reform movements. Emperor Charles V was the principal enemy of the Lutheran Reformation and was more powerful and apparently more interested in suppressing it than were the popes. Only nineteen when elected emperor, his youthfulness was not marked by frivolity but by a zeal to restore to pre-eminence the ancient Catholic faith which his forebears had followed.

The principal rival of Spain during the Reformation period was France. This nation had achieved a strong centralized government through a succession of able kings. The rivalry between Spain and France flared up before the outbreak of the reform. Both King Ferdinand of Spain and Charles VIII of France had claims in the Kingdom of Naples in southern Italy. In 1495 Charles VIII was crowned king of Naples after leading a French army through the center of Italy and defeating the Aragonese claimant. King Ferdinand of Spain decided to assert his claim in Naples and in 1504 drove Louis XII (1498–1515), successor to Charles VIII, out of Naples and eight years later drove him completely out of Italy. This marked the beginning of a series of wars between France and Spain, which in a sense saved the Lutheran Reformation. The chief opponent of Luther, Emperor Charles V of Spain, became so busy fighting France and the Turks that he could not devote himself to smothering out the religious revolt until it had become strong enough politically to offer formidable opposition. The king of France during most of the Reformation was Francis I (1515–47), who did not favor the reform movement as such but helped it considerably by his political and military feuds with Spain.

The third of the centralized monarchies of this period was Eng-

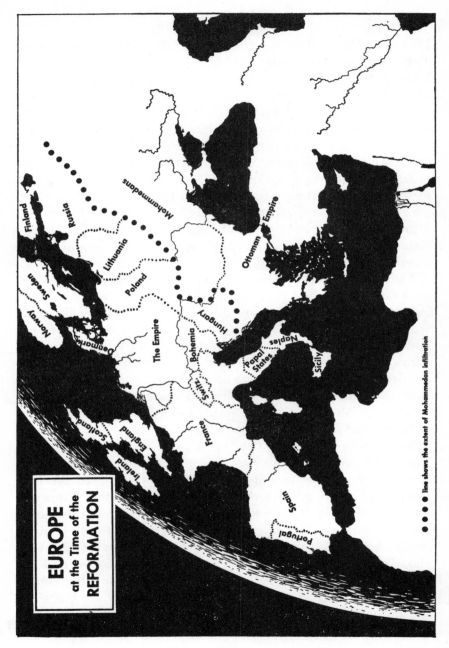

EUROPE
at the Time of the
REFORMATION

Finland

Russia

Mohammedans

Norway

Sweden

Lithuania

Poland

Denmark

The Empire

Ottoman Empire

Hungary

Bohemia

Switz.

Scotland

England

Ireland

France

Naples

Papal States

Sicily

Spain

Portugal

●●●● line shows the extent of Mohammedan infiltration

land. A military struggle among the nobles for royal succession almost eliminated them as a political factor, allowing the new king, Henry VII (1485–1509), to rule with a free hand. His son, Henry VIII (1509–47), was the sovereign during the principal portion of the continental movement. Henry VIII was a bitter opponent of the Lutheran reform during its early stage. He inaugurated a schism with the Roman Church in 1534 which was primarily external and governmental. He did not depart from most of the doctrines of Rome.

The fourth political power in Europe during the reform movement was the Empire. It will be remembered that the Western Empire was restored under Charlemagne in 800 and again under Otto the Great in 962. After about the middle of the thirteenth century the Empire began to decay again. A literary struggle over the right to bestow the imperial dignity (pope versus German electors) led to the *Defensor Pacis* of Marsiglio of Padua. The elective system won out. Although there were scores of small German states, seven strong sovereigns (three ecclesiastical and four secular) had named the emperor since 1356. The ecclesiastical electors were the archbishops of Mainz, Trier, and Cologne; the secular electors were the king of Bohemia, the elector of Saxony, the elector of Brandenburg, and the count palatine on the Rhine.

For generations the emperor had been chosen from the family of Hapsburgs. In the opening years of the Reformation the emperor was Maximilian I (1493–1519). Maximilian's son Philip was married to Joanna, the daughter of Ferdinand and Isabella of Spain. Through the efforts of Maximilian, his two grandsons, Charles and Ferdinand, controlled practically all of central Europe and Spain, excepting only France. Charles became king of Spain through his mother's succession and from his father inherited the Netherlands and large portions of northern and eastern Europe. Ferdinand was married to Anne of Bohemia, by which the Hapsburgs acquired rule over Bohemia and Hungary. In a strong shuffling of political interests both the popes and the king of France, through their efforts to undermine the Hapsburg power heading up in Emperor Charles V, were enemies of their own religious cause. It should be pointed out that the actual authority of the emperor over this loose confederation of German states was quite limited. The strong princes within the Empire ruled their own states as completely sovereign, many times circumventing the desires of the emperor through political sagacity. Such a situation allowed the elector of Saxony, for example, to protect Luther from the anger both of popes and of the emperor.

Another political and military power that played a large part in affecting the progress of Western reform was the group known as the Turks. After the capture of Constantinople in 1453, the Turks drove north and westward through the Balkans with an avowed purpose of overrunning all of Europe. During the Reformation the emperor's desire to stamp out Lutheranism was greatly affected by the Turkish menace. He could hardly afford to start a civil war when the Turks appeared to be on the verge of breaking into central Europe.

Italy had little political significance during the Reformation. Russia was rapidly becoming a strong political power but played no part in the Western reform. Christianity from the East had begun work in Russia, and later on Russia formed her own national church, loosely in fellowship with Constantinople. The Eastern world from Palestine to the Balkans had been overrun by the Mohammedans in the Medieval period, and it neither influenced nor was affected by the Western reform. Although not directly related to the movement, the states of Transylvania on the southeast of the Empire and Poland on the northeast were involved indirectly, since these areas, lying outside of the boundary of the Empire, were havens for dissenting leaders.

Economic and Social Factors That Aided the Reformation

New economic and social patterns were greatly influential in fostering the reform movement. The German states entered into a period of economic and social transition in the fourteenth and fifteenth centuries. The merchant or capitalist class had arisen because of trade and commerce in the Mediterranean area. Geographical discoveries of the period opened a new world economically. The Portuguese discovery of a new route to India and the development of colonies provided new opportunity for the profitable investment of capital.

Furthermore, the discovery and development of German mineral resources threatened to supplant the agrarian interests, pyramiding economic and social problems. With the withdrawal of many peasants from agricultural labor and the increase of mineral production, the natural economic consequence of inflationary prices for food followed. Worse yet, harvest failure over Germany occurred for almost thirteen successive years, beginning about 1490, bringing starvation and malnutrition on every hand. There was universal discontent. Because of the necessity for harder work on the part of the peasants still working the land, resentment by the middle and upper classes at the sudden skyrocketing of food prices which nobody could explain or control, and the devaluation of wages incident to the economic inflation, the entire social and economic attitude was antagonistic. Peasant revolts became common, particularly after the attempt to supplant the old German legal customs by principles of Roman law. It is no wonder that the inordinate avarice of the Roman Church in demanding annates, tithes, indulgences, etc., was looked upon as tyranny.

Intellectual Factors That Aided the Reformation

One reason for failure of earlier reform movements was the general lack of intelligence. Fear and superstition were obstacles too great for any antipapal movement to hurdle. The intellectual renascence that followed the Crusades gave a great deal of impetus to popular enlightenment. The development of the printing press in the middle of the fifteenth century made it possible to reproduce the spoken message for thousands of audiences. Luther's reform could not have been so effective had there not been widespread information and interest through the use of pamphlets and books. Furthermore, the movement known as "humanism," while not always religious in its emphasis, provided enlightenment and leadership that contributed greatly to Luther's reform.

Finally, the attitude of the common man toward the papacy had undergone a profound transformation. It is quite doubtful that Luther or anyone else would have dared to take the steps which might sever them from the visible Roman Catholic Church if it had been believed that such a schism would result in the loss of salvation. Foreign to philosophical realism and the claims of the Roman Church, there had developed a widespread conception that salvation could be attained apart from the Roman system.

It is true that some followers of Luther forsook him when he deliberately turned away from the Roman Church; but the very fact that the German multitudes followed him in a schismatic movement, sharing with him the anathematizing by the Church, speaks of a new point of view. The principal events that inculcated such a conception may only be guessed, but it is likely that the recollection of the papal schism had shaken the implicit faith of many in a visible and unrent body of Christ. The defiance of papal excommunication by the secular states both revealed the popular mind and strengthened the idea that salvation did not rest only with the Roman system; the presence for centuries of strong movements of dissenters like the Waldenses and Bohemian Brethren discounted Roman claims; and the constant conflict between the Church and the Empire, each conceived as a divine institution, brought confusion and doubt concerning the claims of the former. Whatever the reasons may have been, it is evident that millions were willing to leave the body which claimed to be the only font of salvation. They were convinced that salvation could be found elsewhere.

Religious Factors That Aided the Reformation

Almost inseparable from the intellectual factors described were the religious elements that moved the multitudes toward reform. Some of the dissenting movements have been described in the previous chapter. It is impossible to measure the influence exerted by these groups, but it must have been tremendous. Whether judged from the meager records that are available or from the attempt to explain the sudden widespread support of the reforms of Luther

192

and others, it must be plain that either a great historical phenomenon occurred without sufficient antecedents or that the masses of people were extensively prepared for a break with the dominant Church before Luther and others called them out. Negative factors undoubtedly aided, such as the extremely low tone of religion and morality in the popes just before the Reformation and the unspeakable abuses of the entire Roman Catholic system as epitomized by the selling of pseudoindulgences. That these alone account for the tremendous revolution of the sixteenth century is difficult to believe.

Luther the Man

Without all of the factors that have been mentioned, even a Luther could not have accomplished what he did. He would have suffered the same fate that had befallen John Huss a century before. Yet a Luther was required to complete or weld together all of the factors which have been mentioned. In a real sense Luther combined all of the motives for reform that had previously been exhibited. Some had wanted reform on the basis of their devotion to the Bible; Luther was their man, for he was an outstanding Bible scholar and attempted to fashion his reform around the Bible. Patriotism had been a motive for reform; and Luther's Reformation gathered up all the love that a German could have for his race and exploited it to the utmost. Many mystics desired reform that would emphasize the ability to approach God without human priests and institutions; Luther read and published their literature and spoke in language that they understood. Humanism clamored for reform on the basis of a new intellectual approach; Luther sympathized with their general point of view.

Beyond these unifying elements in Luther's life, he symbolized a German peasant who had been aggrieved by papal tyranny for half a millennium. Long-standing demands found in him a champion who could speak the language of the people. His personal experience in moving slowly step by step from protest to disputation to condemnation and schism probably formed a mirror of the experience of the average German who followed him. They understood him because they were so much like him. Without the very kind of man that Luther was, reform in the Germanic states would have been handicapped or perhaps impossible at the time. Somewhat similar historical and personal factors thrust forth Zwingli and Calvin in their particular areas. The time was ripe for reform.

Concluding Summary

The fulness of time had come. Reform was in the minds of many and on the lips of a few. A pioneer was required to inaugurate a successful revolt against the Roman Catholic system. Luther was that pioneer. Zwingli and Calvin were not far behind.

17

The Lutheran Reform

AFTER CENTURIES OF preparation began the movement which led to the shattering of the Medieval Roman Catholic system and the formation of some of the principal branches of the Christian movement that exist today. The first of these reforms was that of Martin Luther.

Luther's Early Life (1483–1517)

Martin Luther was born in Eisleben, Saxony, a small Germanic state, on November 10, 1483. It is not surprising that the one who was to break through the heavy crust of the Medieval ecclesiastical tyranny should spring from this geographical area, for the German people were suffering much from papal avarice. Nor is it surprising that he came from peasant stock. This class of people above all others bore the brunt of oppression and mistreatment from both secular and religious authorities.

Luther's parents were like most other peasants—poor and religious to the point of superstition. Luther himself never got away from some of their primitive ideas about witches and goblins. Shortly after Luther's birth his parents moved to Mansfeld, a nearby village, where his father engaged in the new mining industry. The boy attended elementary school here and further prepared for the university by enrolling at Magdeburg in the spring of 1497 and at Eisenach in the following year. In 1501 he entered the University of Erfurt, where he received the bachelor of arts degree in 1502 and the master's degree in 1505.

Up to this point Luther's life had not varied greatly from that of any other young man preparing for a professional career in the field of law. He did not continue in this direction as the result of a tremendous religious crisis. The religious tensions deliberately induced by the Medieval Catholic system worked in Luther, as in every typical man of his day, a constant religious unrest. The Roman Church demanded obedience to the earthly institution as the price of salvation. When man became careless, the pains of purgatory were magnified to bring dread and subservience. The sacramental wealth of the Church was then offered as a means of limiting the sufferings of the nether world. God was pictured as completely inaccessible; Christ was portrayed as a dread judge. Only the benefits sold by the Roman Catholic Church could avail for the trembling sinner. Even the most obedient Catholic must suffer the pangs of purgatory. The best opportunity of escaping divine wrath was to be found in the monasteries.

How long Luther had been pondering these things cannot be determined. By the time he received his second degree at Erfurt, he had an overwhelming feeling that he must get right with God. He had experienced several frightening incidents that caused him to think about eternal things. The climax came on July 2, 1505. While Luther was walking near Stotternheim, he became unnerved when a bolt of lightning struck near him and vowed that if spared from death, he would become a monk. This was the first step of Luther in an effort to find peace with God. Against the wishes of his father he kept his vow and fifteen days later entered the Augustinian monastery at Erfurt.

To his dismay Luther found no lasting peace in this surrender. When he attempted to perform his first Mass in May, 1507, his fear of God almost prostrated him. Following the precepts of the Medieval Church, he sought relief through performing good works. His reputation for self-denial spread across the land, but still he found no peace. Obediently, he opened every door prescribed by the Roman Catholic Church. He sought the merits of the saints; he engaged in almost fantastic confession of every type of sin, whether in thought, word, or deed; he performed regular religious duties feverishly; he even walked to Rome, the center of the Catholic religious world, where the greatest sins of every

196

sort could be forgiven with the least effort—all to no avail. The merits of the saints reminded him of his own need; confession only spoke of unremembered sins not yet forgiven; his work as a priest increased his trepidation at approaching God; and his trip to Rome brought him into contact with cynical and greedy leaders. Through all of these tumultuous experiences Luther was approaching the object of his search.

Luther does not relate exactly when his burden was lifted, but he does indicate how it happened. The human agency was John Von Staupitz, the vicar of the Augustinian monasteries, who counseled with Luther and pointed him to the study of the New Testament. Equally important was the theological study which he found in a new occupation assigned him by Staupitz—that of teaching in the University of Wittenberg. He received the doctorate of theology degree in October, 1512. His lectures during the next five years on Psalms, Romans, and Galatians worked within his heart that which the entire sacramental system of the Roman Church could not accomplish. He discovered the true scriptural insight that salvation is a gift. Heretofore he had tried to deserve salvation; now he learned to accept it by faith without deserving it. He seized upon the text, "The just shall live by faith," believed it, and found the peace for which he had so long sought.

Luther's Reform Movement (1517–46)

Manifestly such a discovery by Luther apart from the religious system that environed him constituted a threat that he would urge others to find peace in the same way. Apparently Luther did not at first recognize the logical conclusion to which he must surely go—to challenge the validity of the system which could not bring him peace. Step by step his experience led him away from the obedience which he had exercised formerly. Luther did not always know when he took these steps and perhaps was not fully aware of the tremendous strides he had taken until he paused to look around. The first of these steps centered in his opposition to the Roman doctrine of indulgences.

Luther's question about indulgences.—It will be remembered that the Roman Church taught that all sins before baptism were washed away in that rite. The sacrament of penance was provided to care for postbaptismal sins. Should a man sin, he must present himself to the priest with sorrow in his heart for the sin, confess his sin to the priest, receive absolution (in which the priest on behalf of God forgives the eternal guilt of this sin), and then perform some good work or satisfaction to take care of the earthly penalty. That is, every sin gave offense in two directions: it brought guilt before God and it wronged the earthly Church. The priest pronounced God's forgiveness; the hurt to the earthly institution must be atoned for by specific prayers, gifts of money, a religious pilgrimage, or some similar act of devotion. To neglect the earthly penalty, it was taught, brought additional suffering in purgatory after death.

The most popular way of paying this earthly debt in Luther's day was through the purchase of writs of indulgence from papal representatives. These indulgences were written statements announcing a specified remission of penalty to the purchaser. They were sought by those who wished themselves to escape extensive residence in purgatory after death, as well as by those who had loved ones supposedly in purgatory already and wished to apply this credit to the account of the one already suffering.

As early as 1516 Luther had questioned the doctrine of indulgences. His own ruler, Frederick, the elector of Saxony, had a vast collection of relics. Should a person view these relics and make the proper offering, a writ of indulgence granting remission of specified canonical penalty was given. The genuineness of Luther's spiritual change was verified as in 1516 he endangered his own livelihood to question the correctness of the doctrine of indulgences, because a part of his own salary came from the proceeds of indulgence sales. In 1517 Luther had reached the point of exasperation. Pope Leo X had sold the archbishopric of Mainz to Albert of Brandenburg. In order to allow Albert to repay the money borrowed for the purchase of this office, and also in order to gain money allegedly for the building of the Cathedral of St. Peter at Rome, Leo declared a special sale on indulgences. To attract buyers the older Catholic doctrine of indulgences was perverted, and it appears that some claimed that pardon for sin could be obtained through them. The Dominican monk Tetzel was given the task of hawking these indulgences.

The thing that infuriated Luther was the suggestion that both guilt against God and the penalty against the earthly Church could be taken care of by the indulgences. Since Frederick, Luther's prince, was also engaged in selling ecclesiastical indulgences to the people, Tetzel was forbidden to enter electoral Saxony for the purpose of selling these new indulgences. However, Tetzel crowded the very borders of electoral Saxony in order that those who might be interested could cross over and buy the indulgences. Whereupon, on October 31, 1517, Luther prepared ninety-five statements for debate and, according to university custom, tacked them on the door of the church at Wittenberg, which was in a sense the university chapel. These statements (or theses) invited debate on three general subjects: (1) the traffic in indulgences, which Luther avowed was unscriptural, ineffective, and dangerous; (2) the power of the pope in the forgiveness of guilt and noncanonical penalties, which Luther denied; and (3) the character of the treasury of the Church, alleged to consist of the merits donated by Christ and the saints. Luther denied that the merits of Christ and the saints constituted such a treasury to be used by the Church.

The widespread storm following this protest seems to have been a surprise to Luther. Printing presses, a new method of intellectual warfare, reproduced Luther's protest, translated from Latin into German, for the eyes of all Germany. Luther's language was plain and direct, written in the vocabulary and spirit of a typical German. From various angles the protest gathered up popular antagonism against the papacy from many classes— biblicists, patriots, mystics, humanists. The pope, Leo X, was not at first alarmed by the protest. When he did take notice specifically, his first direct action was to appoint a new general of the Augustinian order with instructions to discipline Luther. However, at a meeting of Luther's chapter in April of 1518 at Heidelberg, Luther found some support. Thereafter, he began to assume a bolder attitude. He soon began to question the continuous historical primacy of the papacy and then completely denied the power of the pope over purgatory.

In July, 1518, Silvester Prierias, a Dominican official in Rome, attacked Luther as a heretic. Luther's reply went even further toward the evangelical position. He asserted that both the pope and the ecumenical council could err and had done so, and that only the Scriptures are an infallible authority. Luther was ordered to report at Rome to answer for heresy, but through the influence of his prince, Frederick, the consultation was referred to Cardinal Cajetan in Augsburg. This interview in October, 1518, drew from Luther the direct denial of the authority of a papal bull, for Luther asserted that the voice of the Scriptures outweighed the voice of the pope.

In November Luther appealed to a general council as the ultimate earthly authority in Christianity to pass on his views. This constituted a direct act of hostility to the person of the pope, since previous popes had for a century described such an appeal as open heresy. Luther's precarious position, however, was greatly aided by the influence of Frederick. The Holy Roman Emperor died on January 12, 1519, and Frederick was one of the seven men who would elect a new one. The pope earnestly desired to dictate who should be elected and consequently was quite deferential to Frederick. This probably accounts for a reversal of the antagonistic papal policy.

Karl von Miltitz, a German, was sent to conciliate Luther until after a new emperor had been chosen. Miltitz only asked Luther to refrain from debating the question. Luther agreed on the condition that his opponents would do likewise. However, Professor Johann Eck of the University of Ingolstadt did not keep this truce and attacked Luther without calling him by name. Through Eck's influence a debate was arranged and took place in Leipzig in early July of 1519. Here Luther was driven to approve doctrines of John Huss, who had been condemned and burned by the Council of Constance a century before. On July 15, 1520, a bull of excommunication against Luther was issued, commanding him to recant within sixty days. Luther later burned it publicly.

During the remainder of that summer and fall Luther wrote the principal tracts describing his beliefs. In August the *Address to the German Nobility* was published. In this tract Luther urged a reform of the Church by the Christian magistrate. He attacked the claims of the papacy that the spiritual power is above the temporal, that the pope alone can interpret the Scriptures, and that ecumenical councils can be assembled only by a pope. His proposals for reform would strike off the material wealth and possessions of the pope and magnify a spiritual ministry. Luther also attacked monasticism and celibacy. Abuses and corruptions within the Church must be corrected.

[margin: ✶ 1 POLITICAL ADDRESSED TO LEADERS FOR SUPPORT TO PITCH IN TO REFORM CHURC]

In October Luther's tract *On the Babylonian Captivity of the Church* was printed. In this tract Luther denied the efficacy of indulgences and boldly attacked the sacramental system of Rome. He insisted that both the wine and bread of the Supper should be served to the people and dwelt on the necessity of faith by the partaker in order to assure its efficacy. In his discussion of baptism, he created a continuous tension in his theological system by eliminating the necessity for personal expression of faith as a prerequisite to baptism. That is, he demanded personal faith for the Supper but made no provision for such faith before baptism. He continued with a critical discussion of penance, confirmation, matrimony, orders, and extreme unction. He would eliminate all sacraments except the Supper and baptism but praised parts of the sacrament of penance. In the following month his tract on *The Freedom of the Christian Man* appeared. This writing magnified the freedom and priesthood of every believer, whether layman, priest, bishop, or pope.

[margin: ✶ 2 DOCTRINAL TREATY ATTACK ON SACRAMENTAL SYSTEM of CHURCH]

[margin: ✶ 3]

These writings and others in a similar vein, progressively becoming bolder in their attacks upon the central doctrines supporting the papacy, completely alienated Luther from the Roman Church and made compromise impossible. On April 17, 1521, following a summons by Emperor Charles V, Luther appeared before the Diet of the Empire, meeting at Worms. After two hearings in which Luther boldly defended his views, he was kidnapped by his friends (perhaps under secret orders from Frederick) and on May 4 arrived in disguise at Wartburg. Meanwhile, at Worms on May 26, after Luther's supporters had returned home, the papal forces were able to secure an edict banning Luther as an outlaw. Thus by the middle of 1521 Luther had been excommunicated by the Roman Church and banned by the Empire.

Delay in suppressing Lutheranism (1521–29).—It appeared that the cause of reform was again lost, and history seemed destined to add the name of Martin Luther to the long list of victims of ecclesiastical intolerance. However, the kidnapping of Luther by his friends removed him from possible physical danger for about a year. In addition, Emperor Charles V became engaged in war with King Francis I of France shortly after the close of the Diet of Worms in 1521. This war continued intermittently for the next eight years. Furthermore, the hands of the emperor, the chief opponent of Luther, were withheld from Luther because of the menacing Turks who were driving through the Balkans with the intention of overthrowing the Empire. It is rather interesting that Emperor Charles was also delayed from suppressing the Lutherans by the political maneuvering of the pope himself, who was afraid of the amount of power in the hands of Charles.

During this time, with the aid of Melanchthon and others, Luther prepared a great deal of literature, including an excellent German translation of the Scriptures. Luther also revealed the character of his movement. In 1522 at Zwickau several religious radicals attempted to carry out what seemed to be the implications of Luther's ideas. The Roman Catholic priestly system of conducting the Supper was altered; the common people were given both elements—bread and wine; and Roman liturgy, chanting, and altars were eliminated. The city was in an uproar. Luther voluntarily left his haven at Wartburg to take personal command in fighting these radicals. Thenceforth Luther may be described as a conservative reformer; that is, he retained those elements of Roman Catholic tradition which in his judgment were not specifically prohibited by the Scriptures. Thus infant baptism, robes, candles, and similar Roman Catholic characteristics appear in Lutheranism.

In 1525, the year of Luther's marriage, a great peasant's revolt occurred. For half a century there had been increasing tension between the nobility and the peasants who tilled the soil. The attempt to apply Roman law in the place of the ancient Germanic law, the breakdown of feudal estates with the resultant suffering and confusion, and economic turmoil incident to the rise of the third estate—commercial and financial princes—fanned the flames of dissatisfaction and revolt among the peasants. In addition, Thomas Müntzer, a radical millennarian, accelerated the outbreak of violence by injecting a religious note. "God will not let you fail; on to slaughter!" was his cry. Unnumbered thousands of peasants were mercilessly put to death in the revolt of 1525. Luther lost his faith in the common man and thereafter looked to the nobility as the hope of the reform movement.

Because of the preoccupation of the emperor, the annual meetings of the German diet had practically left the task of adjusting the religious situation in the hands of each prince or ruler for his own hand. By 1529, however, the situation was changed. The Lutherans faced a new crisis. By that time the emperor had soundly defeated King Francis of France, had seen the Turks driven back from Vienna, and had permitted the pope to be imprisoned for a period. The diet met at Speyer in that year. Ferdinand, brother of the emperor and a strenuous opponent of the reform movement, presided. By his direction the diet passed an edict which looked to the complete annihilation of the Lutheran reform and the recatholicizing of Lutheran areas. A minority protested this action, receiving thereafter the name "Protestant." This is the first occurrence of the name in ecclesiastical history. The Lutherans were required to answer the edict within one year.

The crisis (1530).—At the meeting of the diet in 1530 at Augsburg the Lutherans were fearful concerning events to come. In the previous year Philip of Hesse, one of the Lutheran princes, had endeavored to secure a military alliance between the Lutherans of Germany and the Zwinglians of Switzerland. At a meeting in Marburg in 1529, however, Luther refused to have any sort of connection with Zwingli, despite the fact that the only point of disagreement in their theology centered in the interpretation of Jesus' words, "This is my body." Luther, of course, being under the ban of the Empire, could not appear at the diet in Augsburg. He aided Melanchthon in the preparation of the confession which was presented to the diet. The confession and a subsequent defense were rejected by the diet, and the Lutherans were given one year to forsake their heresies or feel the edge of the sword. The Lutheran princes formed a military alliance known as the Schmalkaldic League. The Catholic princes had also joined together for military action. Again Emperor Charles did not find it expedient to attack the Lutherans. The Turks were threatening, the Lutherans were fairly strong, and King Francis I of France was ready to fight again.

Luther's death.—This uneasy truce between Protestants and Catholics was still in effect in February, 1546, when Luther died. The death of Luther was not a great blow to his movement. Other hands had taken up the torch.

The Schmalkaldic War and the Peace of Augsburg (1555)

The Schmalkaldic War broke out in 1546 when Pope Paul III declared a crusade against the Protestant princes. Within a year the Protestants had been utterly defeated. Jealousy between Emperor Charles and the pope prevented the immediate destruction of Protestants, however, and in 1552 after a period of political maneuvering the war erupted again and in a few months the Protestants regained all that they had lost.

The Peace of Augsburg admitted the right of the Lutheran religion to exist within the Empire. Each prince was to determine the religion of his state, and should any of the subjects desire a different faith, the right of emigration without loss of honor or goods was guaranteed. In case a Catholic prelate desired to become a Lutheran he must resign his ecclesiastical position so that it might be filled from Rome. In the free cities where both faiths had adherents, each should be permitted to continue.

The Spread of Lutheranism

Before 1540 most of northern Germany was officially Lutheran. In the border states, such as Bohemia and Poland, and in the earlier years of reform in Hungary, Lutheranism was very strong. Denmark adopted the reformation by 1536 through its rulers and the preaching of Hans Tausen. By the preaching of Olaf and Lars Petersen and Lars Andersen and the work of King Gustavus Vasa, Sweden adopted Lutheranism in 1527. Finland, a Swedish satellite, adopted Lutheranism principally through political action, the most important preacher being Michael Agricola.

Concluding Summary

Martin Luther, then, was the pioneer reformer that broke the power of the Roman Catholic system. He secured sufficient political influence among the Germans to maintain his system despite coercion.

It must not be forgotten that during the latter years of Luther's life, other reform movements were also in progress. Ulrich Zwingli at Zurich, John Calvin at Geneva, the radicals and Anabaptists in various parts of the Continent, and Henry VIII in England present other instances of reform. These will be considered in the following chapters.

18

The Zwinglian and Calvinistic
Reforms

THE SECOND OF the attempted general reforms of the Roman
Catholic Church during this period began in two Swiss cities but
spread extensively and soon was a rival of the Lutheran movement.
The Swiss republic offered unusual opportunity for the reform
movement, while at the same time it presented unusual obstacles.
Almost three hundred years before, the several independent cantons, as the small county-like states were termed, had entered into
a confederation, each canton, regardless of size, having one vote
in the diet or congress. This made it possible for a minority of the
people (in the less populated cantons) to prevent the majority of
the people (in the cantons made up of larger cities) from embracing the Reformation movement by political vote. The struggle between the country cantons and the city cantons characterizes the
course of the early Reformation efforts.

The country cantons had good reasons for opposing the reform.
The Roman Catholic Church had for centuries employed strong
young men from the Swiss rural cantons to be used as mercenaries
in the papal army. Papal abuses were not burdensome. The rural
cantons possessed considerable independence of spirit and little
money and so were hardly aware of papal exploitation. The more
wealthy city cantons, on the other hand, had long fought papal
financial exploitation and political domination. Humanism had
made vast inroads into the larger cities, particularly Basel, where
educational and printing facilities provided instruments of wide
propagation to agitate reform.

The two cities of Switzerland which became leaders in the reform were Zurich and Geneva. Ulrich Zwingli was the principal figure in beginning the reform at Zurich, while John Calvin played the chief role in Geneva. Calvin's movement swallowed up the Zwinglian reform in one generation, so the two will be discussed as one movement.

The Zwinglian Reform in Zurich

Ulrich Zwingli was born in 1484 at Wildhaus in Switzerland. His uncle, a priest in the Roman communion, supervised his education in some of the outstanding schools of the Continent. From 1502 to 1506 Zwingli taught school at Basel while finishing his education. In this active humanist center he was greatly influenced toward enlightened views and was brought to the study of theology. The lectures of the humanist Thomas Wyttenbach, in particular, gave the young teacher a passion to eliminate the superstitious elements in Christianity and to restore the ancient authority—the Scriptures.

Through the influence of his uncle, in 1506 Zwingli was appointed parish priest at Glarus, where he served for ten years. From 1516 to 1519 he was priest at Einsiedeln. Here his pungent preaching and reforming tendencies attracted widespread attention. In 1519 he was appointed the chief preacher at the great cathedral church in Zurich. He had been moving already toward the application of scriptural principles. While at Einsiedeln in 1518, with the approval of his bishop he had opposed the sale of indulgences by Bernard Sampson. Upon beginning his work at Zurich, Zwingli caused a sensation by preaching an exposition of the Gospels in the language of the people, scorning the traditional lessons assigned and the Latin tongue of the Roman Church.

Several experiences apparently kindled his reforming zeal. By 1520 he had become familiar with the reformatory works of Luther. Zwingli always insisted that he was not indebted to Luther for the principles of reform in Zurich. An analysis of the reforms instituted by the two men partly bears out Zwingli's contention. Zwingli's reform was intellectual, biblical, and political. He ap-

207

proached religion as a humanist seeking truth. Luther, on the other hand, was moved by a great experience which convinced him that the Roman system could not bring peace to the soul of a man. So while Zwingli through reform sought to satisfy his *mind* with respect to the truth of Christianity, Luther aimed at satisfying his *heart* through the appropriation of true Christianity. Thus while Luther's writings doubtless gave encouragement to Zwingli, it is possible that Zwingli's reform developed somewhat independently.

In addition to the writings of Luther, other factors turned Zwingli more zealously toward an active reform. The dreaded plague struck Zurich, and Zwingli was laid low. At the very door of death he had a mystical experience in which he was conscious of the strengthening presence of God. From this and the bereavement in the loss of a brother, Zwingli seemed to deepen considerably in his spiritual life. For years he had been receiving a pension from the pope, a retainer for encouraging young men to engage in mercenary military service. In 1520, consistent with his new insights, he resigned this pension and took a more positive stand against the hiring of Swiss lads as mercenaries.

His preaching began to emphasize the authority of the Scriptures alone. Acting upon this principle, some of his followers in Zurich in 1522 refused to fast during Lent on the ground that the Bible did not forbid eating. Zwingli defended them against the strictures of their bishop and wrote a tract *On Choice and Freedom in Eating.*

In July, 1522, Zwingli attacked clerical celibacy. He knew firsthand the terrible evils involved in this system, openly admitting in his writings that he was unmarried but not chaste. In 1524 he announced his marriage to the woman with whom he had been living in common-law relations for some years.

Exercising great influence over the city government at Zurich, Zwingli was able to develop his program of reform. The city council adjudged him to be victorious in two public disputations with Roman Catholic representatives in January and October, 1523. Zwingli presented sixty-seven brief articles of faith, which went beyond Luther toward the evangelical position. In these Zwingli magnified the scriptural position in contrast with the teachings of the Roman Church. Salvation is by faith. Roman sacraments, intercession of saints, and purgatorial sufferings are unscriptural. All believers are priests. Clerical celibacy must be abolished.

At one point Zwingli had disagreement within his own ranks. It has been pointed out that his movement was partly political because he had to work through the government of the Zurich canton. When the question of baptism arose, the political aspect weighed considerably. Zwingli knew that if he denied the validity of infant baptism he would "unchurch" the Zurich city council, for all of them were sprinkled as babies. Apparently this factor caused him, after considerable hesitation, to retain infant baptism. He did not teach that infant baptism brought salvation, after the fashion of the Roman Church; rather, said he, infant baptism simply identifies the child with the Christian covenant, much as the rite of circumcision identified the Jewish child with the Israelitish covenant. He viewed the Lord's Supper as a symbol of the body and blood of Christ. Zwingli was able to justify to the Zurich government the elimination of images, relics, monasteries, and the traditional observance of Mass.

By 1524–25, however, because of the retention of infant baptism, Zwingli was obliged to defend his movement against the attacks of a group which had stood with him in the early days of reform. Conrad Grebel, Felix Manz, and others among his early supporters insisted that Zwingli must abolish infant baptism if he wanted to be consistent in his main principle—to restore the scriptural pattern. Even political circumstances, they said, should not prevent steadfast allegiance to scriptural injunctions. At first it appeared that Zwingli might move in this direction, but soon he vigorously resisted the movement.

Zwingli's reform transformed Zurich by 1525. His influence also aided in the reform of other Swiss and south German cities like St. Gall, Basel, Bern, and Strassburg. The rural cantons of Uri, Schwyz, Unterwalden, and Zug, however, completely satisfied with the old Roman Catholic relationship, formed with Lucerne a league to withstand the reform. Most of the other Swiss cantons and some of the southern German cities confederated in a reform league. Both groups sought outside alliances. In 1529 a civil war seemed imminent, but by negotiation hostilities were postponed in a peace favorable to the Zwinglians.

In the fall of 1529 at Marburg there occurred an important meeting between the Lutherans and the Zwinglians. The second Diet of Speyer had recently condemned all dissent from the Roman Catholic Church. Conformity within one year was demanded. Philip of Hesse, an influential Lutheran, desired to secure a political and military alliance between Lutheran and Zwinglian forces in order to withstand the Catholics. Luther insisted that there must first be agreement in doctrine. On fourteen articles of faith Luther and Zwingli were in general agreement, but in a part of one article Luther rejected Zwingli. The point of difference lay in the interpretation of the presence of Christ in the Supper. Luther contended that Christ's physical body was present for the faithful in the true observance of the Supper; Zwingli objected that a physical body could not be everywhere at the same time. Zwingli said that the bread symbolizes or represents Christ's body. This single point of disagreement outweighed all else. The dream of an alliance was shattered.

Zwingli returned to his task of endeavoring to secure acceptance of his reform throughout all of the thirteen cantons of Switzerland. The five Catholic cantons, however, alert for an opportunity to retrieve the initiative, raised an army in 1531, and in the ensuing battle Zwingli was slain. His successor in Zurich, Henry Bullinger, respected the treaty signed with the Catholics and limited his work to his own canton. In less than a generation the Zwinglian movement was swallowed up by the larger and more influential movement of John Calvin.

The Calvinistic Reform at Geneva

The city of Geneva first felt reform as an indirect result of the Zwinglian movement. The winning of Bern to reform in 1528 brought additional impetus through the increased evangelical interests of this, the strongest Swiss city in the south. It was through the encouragement of Bern that William Farel, impetuous reformer from France, made his way to Geneva in 1533. Geneva had felt already the political pressure of Bern to accept the evangelical reform. Political factors, as a matter of fact, played the most important role in winning Geneva to the reform movement. The city was ruled by a bishop and an administrator, both of whom were controlled by the duke of Savoy, monarch over an adjacent kingdom. The citizens shared in local government through a general assembly and an elected committee known as the Little Council. Larger committees were appointed by the Little Council to resolve questions involving fundamental principles. Beginning about 1527, the ancient hostility between the citizens of Geneva and the duke of Savoy erupted into open war. The citizens were able to beat off the duke's attacks through the aid of Bern and a Catholic neighbor, Freiburg, and establish Geneva's freedom. With the encouragement of Bern, William Farel and Antoine Froment, two French preachers, infiltrated Geneva in the interest of the evangelical cause. About 1535 the reform movement took a strong foothold, and Geneva entered the evangelical fold. In July, 1536, John Calvin paused in the city en route to Strassburg, and Farel enlisted him in the task of making Geneva a strong Protestant city.

The work of John Calvin.—John Calvin was born in Noyon, France, on July 10, 1509. His father was an influential ecclesiastical functionary and secretary of the bishopric. As a result, Calvin's education was provided through benefices in the Roman Catholic Church. In 1528 he received the master of arts degree from the University of Paris. At the request of his father Calvin entered into the study of law at Orleans and Bourges and received the doctorate in law from the former institution in 1532. His first love was literary, not legal, however, and after the death of his father Calvin was free to forsake the practice of law.

Calvin was familiar with reforming ideas. Jacques Lefèvre Étaples, a French scholar living in Paris, had magnified evangelical ideas as early as 1512 in a commentary on Paul's epistles. He also translated the New Testament a decade later. The writings of Luther were circulated freely in France, and Calvin became familiar with them. Calvin's conversion to evangelical views was sudden, his own testimony asserts. Perhaps the complete explanation will never be known, but a number of factors were involved. His father and brother had been excommunicated by the Roman Church, which may have loosened the hold of that system upon Calvin. His cousin, Robert Olivétan, was already a full-fledged reformer. The humanistic atmosphere of Calvin's university training and teachers doubtless moved him toward evangelical convictions. In May, 1534, he resigned his benefices and for some reason was imprisoned for a brief period. This is the first definite indication that Calvin had now entered the evangelical fold. With the outbreak of widespread and severe persecution in France in 1534, Calvin fled here and there in France, thence to Strassburg and Basel. While at Basel in 1536 Calvin published the first edition of his outstanding work, *The Institutes of the Christian Religion*, which brought immediate fame. His dedication of the *Institutes* to King Francis I of France is a masterpiece of argumentation from Scriptures and history. Calvin visited for a short time in Italy and Paris and on the journey to Strassburg passed through Geneva, Switzerland. Here William Farel convinced him that it was God's will for them to set up the evangelical standard in Geneva.

For the next two years Calvin labored in this important city. In January, 1537, he presented to the Little Council of Geneva a series of articles relative to the reform. The Lord's Supper was made central in church discipline. Moral lapses and the neglect of divine services without excuse brought exclusion from participation in the Supper. A confession of faith was submitted to the council for their approval, after which all citizens were required to assent to it. The purpose was to require total conformity to evangelical doctrines. The next step logically was to train the growing children in the doctrine. Calvin provided a catechism for their use. A system of lay inspectors to observe the conduct of the citizens was felt to be necessary. Immediate opposition to Calvin's program came from both political and religious dissenters. Calvin was attacked as a foreigner and a meddler. The annual city election in 1537 favored the Calvinistic supporters, but a year later the opposition succeeded in taking over the reins of government, and in April Calvin and Farel were banished from Geneva.

Calvin went to Strassburg, a city already strongly evangelical, and became pastor of the French refugees. He had a remarkably free hand in his preaching and administration of the church. He was called upon after January, 1539, to lecture to the advanced classes in the schools. He laid the groundwork for his famous expositions of biblical books, which subsequently were printed in commentary form. He also had opportunity to prepare a greatly enlarged edition of the *Institutes*.

While Calvin was absent from Geneva, Cardinal Sadoleto appealed to the city to return to the Catholic fold. Since no one in Geneva felt qualified to answer this appeal, it was finally handed to Calvin in Strassburg. His *Reply to Sadoleto* in 1539, justifying the evangelical position, added to his reputation.

At Strassburg Calvin was married in August, 1540, to Idelette de Bure, widow of an Anabaptist convert. Calvin spoke in highest terms of his wife and their happiness. She died in 1549. Their only child, born in 1542, lived but a few days.

In 1541, after considerable persuasion by his friends, Calvin returned to Geneva. He faced a difficult task. The party which had ousted Calvin had been overthrown in the elections of 1540 but still were formidable. The relations of Geneva with Bern were threatening, and the internal situation was bad. It appeared that rioting and disorder would soon break out within Geneva. Calvin returned with the assurance that he would be allowed to institute his reforms. A committee from the Little Council aided Calvin in the preparation of his *Ecclesiastical Ordinances*. Provision was made for four officers in Genevan church life—pastors, teachers, elders, and deacons. The most distinctive aspect of this program was the office of elder or presbyter, from which the name

"Presbyterian" is derived. Twelve laymen were chosen by the Little Council to serve as ruling elders in the Genevan church. This was a departure from the general idea that presbyters were to be ordained and should preach rather than govern. These twelve presbyters were combined with the regular ministry (at first numbering but six ministers) to form the Consistory, which had supervision over all ecclesiastical discipline. Calvin apparently had desired that the Genevan church exercise her own discipline apart from the secular authorities but was forced into the compromise that allowed the Little Council to take a large hand in this sphere. The Consistory exercised detailed and extensive authority over Genevan ecclesiastical life.

Calvin's system of doctrine, as set out in the *Institutes,* began with the sovereignty of God and, following the general order of the creeds, discussed Christ, the Holy Spirit, and the Church. His emphasis upon the predestination of God was attacked by several, and his retention of infant baptism reflected the importance he placed upon the sociological aspect of the sacramentals. His view of baptism was quite similar to that of Zwingli, and he taught the real spiritual presence of Christ in the Supper.

Despite the entreaties of the Genevan authorities in 1541 for the return of Calvin, many opponents had remained. By 1553 it appeared that Calvin's supporters might be defeated in the popular vote and that another banishment might result. However, in that year Michael Servetus, an exasperating and unorthodox Spaniard, made his way to Geneva. An old opponent of Calvin, Servetus already was under condemnation by Romanists and evangelicals alike for his attacks upon the doctrines of the Trinity and the person of Christ. Calvin vigorously prosecuted Servetus, and the opposition party unwisely gave indications of favoring Servetus. Consequently, when Servetus was condemned and burned in October, 1553, Calvin's victory was complete. The elections of the following year gave him a resounding triumph. From 1555 until his death in 1564 Calvin ruled Geneva with little opposition.

The spread of Calvinism.—It will be remembered that after the death of Zwingli in 1531 his reform spread no farther. The aggressive system of Calvin and his thorough training of preachers soon began to bear fruit in the Zwinglian cantons. By 1566 Calvin's doctrines were acceptable to most of the Zwinglian cantons, and thereafter these became identified with the Calvinistic system.

The government of France was centralized under the control of the king. King Francis I (1515–47) had a working agreement with the papacy whereby each would profit by the maintenance of the Roman Catholic system. In co-operation with the pope, France had warred against Spain intermittently from 1521 to 1529, and for purely political reasons France and Spain had continued the struggle in 1536–38 and 1542–44. These wars required Francis to adopt a policy which would best serve his immediate plans. As a result, a considerable foundation for reform in France was laid without extended persecution.

Reference has been made to Jacques Lefèvre Étaples who spread evangelical views long before Luther. A number of his pupils continued to propagate evangelical views. Reform ideas appeared among the faculty of the University of Paris, long a Catholic stronghold. Calvin fled from France in the latter part of 1534, just as the full weight of royal persecution was beginning. Despite the frequent martyrdoms that occurred, French preachers by the score attended Calvin's school at Geneva and returned to their homeland to preach what was known as the Huguenot gospel. By 1559 there were forty-nine congregations of Calvinists in France, and in that year a synod was held in Paris which formed a national organization and adopted a Calvinistic confession of faith. Within two years the number of congregations had increased to 2,150. Between 1562 and 1598 a series of wars between the Huguenots and the Catholics took place, and on the latter date through the efforts of King Henry IV (who had become a Roman Catholic in order to secure the French crown) the Edict of Nantes was enacted, providing certain "perpetual" liberties for French Calvinists. However, as a result of continued struggle in the seventeenth century these liberties were eliminated in 1685.

The Netherlands consisted of about seventeen provinces in

what is now Belgium and Holland. They had long been known as the center of opposition to Roman Catholic doctrine. The Waldenses, the Brethren of the Common Life, mysticism, and humanism were represented in this section. Between 1517 and 1529 Lutheranism spread rapidly in the Low Countries. The Mennonites made great progress until about 1540, when Calvinism began to become influential. One reason why many left the Mennonite ranks to become Calvinists was that the former demanded pacifism. In this period Spain was waging a determined war against the Netherlands for both political and religious reasons. Consequently, a great number of the inhabitants embraced the militant Calvinistic movement in preference to the pacifistic Mennonite belief. By 1550 the Calvinists began organizing churches in the homes. In 1559 a national synod was held, the Dutch Reformed Church (Calvinistic) was organized, and a Calvinistic confession adopted. From 1566 to 1578 the patriots under William the Silent (1553–84) fought the Spanish overlords and in 1581 the northern provinces declared their independence.

Scotland had been evangelized very early by British missionaries. The Roman Catholic system gained control of Scotland in the eleventh century. The fight with England in the thirteenth and fourteenth centuries, which resulted in Scottish independence under Robert Bruce, brought Scotland into close alliance with France. Reform movements had begun in Scotland under the inspiration of the work of Luther, Tyndale, and others. Patrick Hamilton, trained in the University of Paris, voiced evangelical doctrines and was burned in 1528. As a result many noblemen, both from political and ecclesiastical motives, turned toward Protestantism. In 1546 George Wishart was also burned. His martyrdom inflamed John Knox. Subsequently, Knox attended Calvin's school in Geneva in 1554 and served as pastor there after 1555. In 1559 Knox returned to Scotland and was victorious in establishing the Presbyterian system.

Calvinism did not attain its large influence in the German states in this period. It was excluded from toleration in the Treaty of Augsburg in 1555. Melanchthon became increasingly sympathetic toward Calvinistic doctrine, particularly after 1546, when Luther died.

Neither was England greatly affected by Calvinism in this period, although the regents of Edward VI (1547–53) were familiar with its tenets. Its greatest influence in England came in the next period.

Concluding Summary

Reform erupted in Switzerland under the leadership of Ulrich Zwingli and John Calvin. The untimely death of Zwingli radically turned his reform into different channels. His movement was later swallowed up by that of John Calvin.

Both of the Swiss reformers condemned and persecuted the radicals and Anabaptists. By the time of Calvin's death in 1564, his movement was known in every part of Europe and England and was very influential in Scotland and Switzerland.

19

Anabaptists and the Radical Reformation

FOR CENTURIES THE principal historians either ignored or grossly misunderstood what is now recognized as one of the important movements of the Reformation period. This movement was for centuries called Anabaptism, although with some reservations by those most familiar with it. A. H. Newman, for example, recognized—as scholars of other denominations now agree—that the name "Anabaptist" was an epithet of reprobation or condemnation. It was long identified with fanaticism, schism, and lawlessness. As early as the fifth century the Theodosian Code named the death penalty for any who rebaptized another. This law was aimed at the Donatists, who sometimes were referred to as Anabaptists because they insisted upon performing the rite of baptism upon anyone coming from the corrupted Catholic churches, which, said the Donatists, had lost the power to administer saving baptism. With this sort of background, the name "Anabaptist" came to be applied to any religious iconoclast or fanatic.

It is now generally recognized that to find someone referred to as an Anabaptist in the sixteenth century does not necessarily mean that such a person rebaptized; it may simply mean that his views were considered radical. For this reason, the name "Anabaptist"—emphasizing the single doctrine of believers' baptism—can hardly be applied properly to all religious radicals who were threatened or condemned by being classed in this category.

A better classification to describe more accurately the various types of radical thinkers has been attempted recently by many historians. Perhaps, as some have suggested, the word "radical" is the best generic term for all of them, for these groups were radical both in relation to the practices of contemporary religious reformers and in the opinions of both the Roman Catholics and the Protestants of that day. The various groups, then, will be discussed under four categories: radical biblicists, radical chiliastics, radical mystics, and radical rationalists. Before discussing each of these groups, a word should be said about the possible origins of these movements.

Origins of the Radical Reformers

In general, there are two points of view concerning the origin of these reformers and their extensive constituency. One is that they were called forth by the immediate historical situation and the renewed study of the Scriptures. This view would deny that there were any antecedents before the sixteenth century.

It would appear to be more consistent to hold that the sudden appearance of these reformers over such a large area and embodying such varying doctrinal emphases cannot be explained in terms of a single or localized factor. History does not turn corners suddenly or reveal multiform expressions without antecedents. A movement as complex and widespread as this one would seem to demand a multiplicity of factors—the lingering of medieval ideas, the immediate economic and religious commotion of the sixteenth century, the restudy of the New Testament in terms of contemporary interpretations, and perhaps other elements which cannot be classified.

Types of Radical Reformers

It should be recognized that these classifications of the various types of radicals are totally arbitrary. Often one man could be put into several categories and another man would fit into none. There is value, however, in pressing some sort of outline upon the material in order to provide a better context.

Radical biblicists.—This group has recently been termed the "Anabaptists proper" by one author, with good reason, for they demanded personal faith before baptism as a basic element of their belief. They were radical in the sense that they eliminated all traditions in favor of biblical authority, which they counted the source of their ideas about believers' baptism, separation of church and state, the elimination of sacramental and sacerdotal grace, the centrality of the gathered church, the restoration of the primitive Christian spirit of love and the New Testament pattern of organization, and holy living as the result of an experience of regeneration through God's Spirit.

It will be recalled that in his reform at Zurich, Ulrich Zwingli advocated the view that the Scriptures alone must constitute the basis for faith and practice. In 1523 in conferences with Zwingli, Balthasar Hübmaier (then pastor at Waldshut, Austria), Felix Manz, and others discussed with him the necessity of rejecting infant baptism. Zwingli at first seemed to look favorably upon the doctrine of believers' baptism, since it followed his avowed principle of following only scriptural injunctions and since already his elaboration of his Sixty-Seven Articles had pointed to the primitive practice of baptizing only after faith and confession.

His theory of Christianity's relation to society, however, finally drew him away from this position. Zwingli felt that he must have the support of the civil authorities in Zurich in order to carry out his reform. The denial of infant baptism would have forfeited that civil support, for the city council itself, upon whom he depended for aid, would have been unchurched. Consequently, on January 17, 1525, in a disputation at Zurich, Zwingli denied the principle of believers' baptism. He was opposed by many of his former associates, stalwart men like the able and respected Conrad Grebel. The city council, acting as judge, decreed Zwingli victorious in the debate and gave orders that all babies must be baptized. The Anabaptists were to be banished or imprisoned. A second disputation in November ended similarly. In March, 1526, Anabaptists were ordered to be drowned if they persisted in their heresy, and Felix Manz, Jacob Faulk, and Henry Riemon were early victims of this sentence.

The Anabaptist movement gained multitudes of adherents in

Switzerland between 1525 and 1529. Upon being banished from Zurich, Anabaptist leaders like George Blaurock, William Reublin, Hans Brötli, and Andreas Castleberg went everywhere preaching. Great numbers were baptized in Schaffhausen, St. Gallen, Appenzell, Basel, Bern, and Grunigen. Not only were numerous Anabaptist churches formed, but the movement aided in purging from other groups unworthy ministers, whose evil lives were rigorously attacked by the Anabaptist preachers.

By 1529 the Swiss Anabaptist movement had greatly declined but did not die out. Men like Pilgrim Marbeck worked extensively in Switzerland and south Germany thereafter. Particularly at Bern the Anabaptist congregations continued their struggle. Like other persecuted movements, Anabaptism went underground, and its influence cannot be judged.

One reason for the decline of Anabaptist activity in Switzerland was the beckoning of an adjacent country. Anabaptism had spilled over into contiguous areas like Austria and Moravia. It was to the latter country that many Anabaptist leaders made their way. Moravia had been sown with radical seed by the Hussite and Taborite revolts. In June, 1526, Balthasar Hübmaier fled to Nickolsburg, Moravia, after being persecuted in Austria and Switzerland. Here he had instant success, within a year baptizing between six and twelve thousand. He was also able to publish several excellent apologetical works in defense of the Anabaptist position. His work in Nickolsburg, however, was undermined by Jacob Wiedemann and others who advocated a strong pacifism (not only refusing to engage in war but declining to pay taxes to support those so engaged) and a communistic sharing of personal goods. Perhaps the bitterness of this controversy may have stripped Hübmaier of friends sufficiently that the Austrian authorities were able to seize and burn him in March, 1528. So died one of the greatest and wisest of the Anabaptists.

The pacifistic and communistic party grew rapidly in Moravia. Leadership was assumed by Jacob Huter, and a large community practicing communal economy became an Anabaptist haven for refugees from all Europe. Despite almost continuous persecution in the succeeding two centuries, Moravian Anabaptists increased and prospered. Their church government was quite similar to that of the earlier Waldenses of this area. The growth of the group in nearby Tyrol and Austria was at first rapid, but because of severe persecution the movement there was drastically curtailed.

The third principal group to advocate a rigid biblicism were the Mennonites, who took their name from Menno Simons (1496–1561). Menno was born and reared in the Low Countries, received a good education, and was ordained a priest in the Roman Catholic Church in 1524. The atmosphere of reform sent him to a careful study of the Bible, especially after the execution of an Anabaptist near his home. The radical fanatics at Münster between 1533 and 1535 repelled him, but also impelled him to leave the Roman Church under the pressure of conviction. In 1536 he received the new baptism and became an Anabaptist minister. With Obbe and Dietrich Philips, Menno gathered and organized the biblicists of the scattered Anabaptist flock. He spent the remainder of his life as a fugitive from Catholics and Protestants alike. Traveling and writing extensively, Menno preserved the heritage of the biblical Anabaptists.

It is noteworthy that Menno Simons, doubtless because of his intense repugnance to the fanatics of Münster, disclaimed any historical connection with early Anabaptism but traced a succession of his movement through the Waldenses back to apostolic days. He also followed the Waldensian pattern in several key doctrines.

Radical chiliastics.—The chiliastic wing of the radical movement turned their faces away from the ideal of restoring the primitive pattern in gathered congregations. Instead, taking their text from apocalyptic writings, securing training and inspiration from earlier fanatical fires still burning in Bohemia, and counting themselves chief actors in God's drama of restoring a millennial kingdom, these men sought to bring heaven to earth by means of sword and coercion.

The Waldensian and Taborite ideas that covered Bohemia were reproduced in many details in the work of Nicholas Storch. Influenced by his early contacts in Bohemia, Storch displayed a fierce, denunciatory spirit toward those dissenting with him. He aligned himself in 1520 with Thomas Müntzer, a highly educated Lutheran pastor at Zwickau, who like Luther was attacking the monastic and priestly establishment of the Roman system. Storch set up a distinctive type of church organization after the model of the Taborite churches which he had known in Bohemia. In the following year Müntzer himself turned up at Prague; apparently the indoctrination he received here put him into the party of irrecoverable radicals.

Storch, meanwhile, who seems to have influenced Müntzer toward Bohemian polity and principles, remained at Zwickau, where he almost made radicals out of several of the Wittenberg faculty, despite the fact that he was holding "Bohemian" errors. Carlstadt, Cellarius, and even Melanchthon were greatly impressed with Storch. The latter confessed himself to be greatly perplexed about how to answer Storch's arguments against infant baptism. After returning from Bohemia, Müntzer settled as pastor at Alstedt. Here his revolutionary preaching against religious and social inequalities did much to prepare the way for the Peasant Revolt. Driven from Alstedt in 1524 by the authorities, he hastened to Mühlhausen, where his doctrine of social revolution, mingled with apocalyptic and fanatical rabble-rousing, hastened the Peasants' War. Here was a radical who was never an Anabaptist. Although Müntzer was put to death shortly, his influence did not die with him. Two other leaders, Hans Hut and Melchior Rinck, attracted by Müntzer's chiliastic ideas, preached millennial ideas far and wide across the German states.

The successor to the spirit of Müntzer, and a man who resembled him in many respects, was Melchior Hofmann (*ca.* 1490–1543). It is quite possible that some of Hoffman's chiliastic ideas were gained at Strassburg from Nicholas Storch, the teacher of Müntzer. After the disaster of the Peasants' War, many of the radicals made their way to Strassburg in south Germany where a measure of toleration prevailed. Leaders like Storch, Jacob Gross, Hans Denk, and Michael Sattler had given chiliastic coloring to Strassburg radicals. In 1529, after a riotous ministry in

Sweden and Denmark, Hofmann turned to Strassburg and perhaps was baptized there in 1530. Hofmann now boldly set the year 1533 as the date of the beginning of Christ's millennial reign and named the city of Strassburg as the "new Jerusalem." He ordered that baptism be suspended for two years to prepare for the event. For most of the two years he traveled in the Netherlands, meanwhile gaining a disciple in Jan Matthys, who would outdo his master in chiliastic fanaticism. Hofmann was thrown into jail in May, 1533, at Strassburg, where he died ten years later. Matthys announced in 1533 that he was the prophet Enoch who had been promised by Hofmann, and he assumed leadership of the fanatical party.

It was Matthys who set the stage for the Münster fiasco. The people in Münster, a city of northern Germany, had reacted favorably to the evangelical preaching of Bernhard Rothmann between 1529 and 1532. Many radicals flooded the city, and in 1534 John of Leyden and Gert tom Closter, representing Matthys, arrived to take charge. Matthys himself then announced that Münster, not Strassburg, was to be the "new Jerusalem." The seizure of the city by the radicals brought the troops of the Roman Catholic bishop. In the siege and war that followed, John of Leyden, who became leader when Matthys was slain, introduced polygamy and required baptism or banishment. The city held out for almost a year. The few leaders that were captured were tortured and then hoisted in a cage to the tower of the principal church of Münster. Their bones remained there for centuries, a constant reminder of the dire effects of the radical movement.

Radical mystics.—The extreme emphasis upon sacramental observances and the cold, strictly intellectual scholastic theology brought a reaction from those who looked within themselves for the witness and illumination of the Spirit. Moving in an atmosphere that scorned both Roman Catholic and Protestant sacramental systems, these mystics ofttimes found themselves attracted by nonsacramental Anabaptist and radical doctrines.

One of these was Hans Denk (1495–1527), a humanistic scholar and reformer associated with Zwingli for a period. In 1525 he organized an Anabaptist church in Augsburg but was successively driven to Strassburg, Worms, and Basel, where he died of the plague in 1527. His writings link him with earlier mystics. His friend, Ludwig Hetzer (1500–29), had a somewhat similar experience with his persecutors before his execution in 1529. Sebastian Franck (1499–1542) moved from Romanism to Calvinism and was accused of turning to Anabaptism. His pronounced mysticism and defiant admiration of heretics who had dared to follow the truth make it difficult to classify him under any single category. He doubtless influenced Kaspar Schwenkfeld (1487–1541), who moved similarly out of Lutheranism, although Schwenkfeld's doctrines remained closer to orthodoxy than did those of Franck.

Jacob Kautz and John Bunderlin should be classed among these mystics; perhaps even Heinrich Niclaes (*ca.* 1501–60), the founder of the "House of Love" or the "Familists," should be included. Niclaes passed from Roman Catholicism to Lutheranism, finding in neither what he desired. His mystical nature was stirred by David Joris (1501–56), and he seems to have felt that he had been given a special divine revelation beyond anything man had yet known. He spent much time in England, and the influence of his movement was found there during the next century.

Radical rationalists.—Both Catholicism and Protestantism in the Reformation period abhorred the radical rationalists, whose reasoning not only led them out of orthodox churches but also developed doctrinal aberrations that put them "out of bounds." As a matter of fact, all types of radicals (biblical, chiliastic, mystical, and rationalistic) were averse to orthodox symbols and creeds. The mystics in particular often followed recognizable heresy in their doctrines of the church, of salvation, and of Christ. Men like Franck, Hetzer, Denk, Kautz, and Bunderlin approached the views of rationalists, and in some cases went beyond them in their radicalism, but their methods and course of travel were different. One well-known rationalist was John Campanus (*ca.* 1495–1575). Influenced by Erasmus and the atmosphere of the radicals in the duchy of Julich, Campanus moved away from Catholic and Lutheran views and finally fell into anti-Trinitarianism. His influence was widespread in Julich, and many followed his antipedobaptistic ideas. He was jailed about 1555 and died there about twenty years later.

The best known of the radical rationalists was Michael Servetus (1509–53), a brilliant but erratic Spaniard. In 1534 he met John Calvin at the University of Paris, beginning a long relationship of mutual distrust and dislike. From 1546 until his death, Servetus greatly irritated Calvin through provocative correspondence and ill-tempered criticisms. In the year of his death Servetus published his *Christianismi Restitutio,* which asserted anti-Trinitarian and other doctrines abhorrent to Calvin and the rest of the orthodox world. He was seized in Geneva by Calvin and after an ecclesiastical trial was burned.

His influence may have survived in the work of Laelius Socinus (1525–62) and Faustus Socinus (1539–1604). The former was an Italian lawyer whose extensive skepticism about contemporary orthodoxy was not fully known until after his death. In 1547 he left Italy, already being suspected of heresy. He traveled widely and was an attentive observer at the trial of Servetus in Geneva in 1553. At his death in 1562 he left his manuscripts and his skepticism to his nephew Faustus, who became an outstanding propagator of anti-Trinitarian doctrines. In 1579 Faustus moved to Poland, a haven for liberal thinkers, where he met men of similar views like Peter Gonesius, George Biandrata, and Gregory Paulus. Here he founded a college and disseminated rationalistic views over a wide area until his death in 1604.

Some mention should be made of the strong anti-Trinitarian movement in Italy which was snuffed out by the Roman Catholic Inquisition. Such figures as Renato and Tiziano characterize these radicals, who seem to have grasped evangelical ideas in general but held to an adoptionist Christology, with its consequent weak notions of sin and the atonement.

Other radicals.—The principal effort in this discussion has been to furnish a workable outline of the radicals and to name some principal figures. There are many other radicals of this period who have not been mentioned and some important leaders that can hardly be classified. For example, Sebastian Castellio (1515–63), Pierre Paolo Vergerio (d. 1565), and Bernardino Ochino (1487–1564) are typical of those who found themselves out of step in their day. Some continued their seeking pilgrimages all of their lives.

The Significance of These Reformers

Some sober historians believe that twentieth-century Christianity reflects more of the ideas of the Anabaptists and the radicals than of any of the other reforms. In a sense this is true, because in their efforts to restore the primitive New Testament order these radical movements, unfettered by political and social commitments that tied the hands of Luther, Zwingli, and Calvin, simply without inhibition tossed aside hoary and respectable ideas on the ground that the New Testament did not specifically contain them.

From one point of view, most of the struggle between the radicals and the traditionalists, both Catholic and Protestant, centered in the relationship between the Christian and the world or community about him. The true Anabaptists and many of the radicals insisted that the world or community cannot make Christians. This basically was the significance of rejecting infant baptism. Traditional Christianity, including the Protestant reformers, used proxy or community faith—spelled out in terms of "godfather" and "godmother"—to induct the newborn child into the Christian fold. Both Luther and Zwingli faced problems at this point. Luther's theme of "faith alone" was compromised by his final solution. Unwilling to divorce his movement from the traditional community tie of infant baptism, he made laborious efforts to justify it in terms of proxy faith for the infant or subconscious faith in the infant. His final result was to introduce a basic tension into his system by demanding personal faith for the Lord's Supper but eliminating personal faith for the induction of the person into the Christian life.

Furthermore, the world or community cannot constitute a true

227

church. There must be a gathered church in the sense that only believers, those with a faith baptism, may participate. At this point, also, Luther struggled heroically. He earnestly desired in the early days of his reform to separate the church from the world. His theme of "faith alone" demanded it. He finally turned away from this ideal in order to retain the church-community solidarity. In thus turning away from a gathered church, Luther destroyed the possibility of attaining another of his ideals— separation of church and state. A gathered church cannot be a part of the secular state. Abandonment of infant baptism drew a sharp line between world and church. Even heresy was not punishable by the state, because a man is accountable only to God for his spiritual response. Religious liberty could not be simply a privilege but must be a right and a duty. Pope and emperor could no longer rule all mankind in different spheres. A gathered church eliminated the pope as completely as the rising national states eliminated the emperor; a gathered church also eliminated church-community solidarity and brought separation of church and state.

In addition, the world cannot determine the ethics and attitude of Christians. These must come from God alone but are more demanding than secular laws. The concepts of a disciplined community, an ethic of love, and a spiritual brotherhood were common ideas among the radical groups.

Finally, the world cannot satisfy the longings and impulses of the spirit. All of the radicals were to some extent mystics. For them God was near, and his demands were personal. God's purposes seem to have been misinterpreted ofttimes, and eschatological schemes of frightful magnitude were developed. This is partly understandable in the light of the disorderly and violent world faced by these radicals. Withal, however, was the sense of personal participation in the eternal plans of a watchful and omnipotent Lord.

In the large sweep of history these radical ideas, designed to restore the primitive Christian pattern, have come to be understood and appreciated more than they were when they were voiced.

Concluding Summary

The radicals and Anabaptists were the most hated religious groups on the Continent in the sixteenth century. Roman Catholics and Protestants alike persecuted them. They present a complex picture of uninhibited men who in some groups endeavored to reproduce primitive Christianity, in others sought to find God's presence in the temporal order, and in still others tried to bring in the millennial kingdom. Their contributions have been varied and significant.

20

The Anglican Reform

THE LAST OF the great reform movements occurred in England. This large island off the coast of continental Europe proper received Christianity at a very early period, perhaps from the lips of soldiers who had been chained to the apostle Paul in Rome and who, after their conversion to Christianity, had been stationed in the island. The Romans had first invaded the British Isles in 55 B.C. under Julius Caesar. After the withdrawal of Roman troops in the fifth century because tribal invasions threatened Rome, the island was overrun by the Angles, the Saxons, and the Jutes. Seven principal states evolved (the Heptarchy), until they were united under Egbert in 827 into one kingdom—Angle-land, or England.

Meanwhile, the Roman Catholic Church had sent Augustine the monk as a missionary in A.D. 596, and by 664 the Roman type of Christianity became dominant. After a period of struggle in which English and Danish kings intermittently ruled, the island was invaded in 1066 by William I of Normandy, who attained the kingship by defeating King Harold at the Battle of Hastings. William set the pattern for the attitude England would in general have toward papal supremacy. In a letter to Pope Gregory VII he refused to render fealty to the pope, although he agreed to send financial gifts. He carefully limited the influence of Rome upon the English church, almost to the point of denying the ecclesiastical authority of the pope. Between William (d. 1087) and Henry VII (d. 1509), English kings alternately obeyed and defied the popes. During the Hundred Years' War, when the popes were living in France and under the influence of the enemy of England, King

Edward III and Parliament passed the statutes of provisors and praemunire in 1351 and 1353, respectively, limiting papal influence in England. In the same century John Wycliffe and his Lollards actively opposed the Roman papacy. In 1450 the War of the Roses erupted—a civil war among the nobles to determine who should succeed to the throne. The victor in 1485 was Henry Tudor, who attained considerable royal power because the strong nobles had been slain in the civil war and because he married the heiress of the House of York, his principal rival. He became Henry VII and the head of the English line which gave direction to the reform in that land.

Roots of Reform

The reform in England was not caused by the divorce of Henry VIII, as some suggest. That provided the occasion, but as mentioned in the previous paragraph, England had for centuries tugged at the strings binding her to the papal see. The outbreak of reform in England cannot be described as coming from doctrinal conviction. The leaven of the teachings of Wycliffe and the Lollards and the oblique attacks on Rome by the English humanists assisted in the preparation of the people for a non-Roman Catholicism. The strong nationalistic spirit that enveloped England played an important part in preventing strong opposition to the ecclesiastical changes which Henry VIII introduced.

The Occasion for Reform

The principal mover in the English revolt against papal control was the sovereign himself—Henry VIII. Despite his later fondness for changing wives, there were other factors than the flashing eyes of Anne Boleyn that pushed Henry toward a break with the papal see. The trouble began when Henry's father arranged for a marriage between Arthur (Henry VIII's older brother) and Catharine, youngest daughter of Ferdinand and Isabella of Spain. Such a union would strengthen the hold of the Tudor line upon the English throne and was felt to be necessary. The wedding occurred on November 14, 1501, but Arthur died on April 2, 1502. A union between the two nations was still desired, so it was arranged that young Henry should marry Catharine. The pope, Julius II, under pressure from England and Spain, granted a dispensation with serious doubts, and the wedding was celebrated on June 11, 1509. It should be said that Catharine herself later in solemn oath asserted that she had never in fact been Arthur's wife.

Apparently Henry VIII never got away from the feeling that the marriage was a sin, since canon law and the Old Testament forbade one to marry his brother's widow. The only child to survive the marriage was Mary, born in 1516; four children before her birth and several thereafter either were stillborn or died in early infancy. This meant that Henry had no male heir. Since the Tudor line had just won the throne and since England might resent a female sovereign, it was feared that the lack of a male heir would bring revolution. Henry determined to have the pope declare the marriage to Catharine invalid and thus permit another marriage in an effort to secure a male heir. The pope delayed accommodating Henry, since Catharine's nephew was Emperor Charles V of Spain, who refused to permit the pope to take that action. When in 1529 the papal representative gave clear evidence of the papal refusal, Henry moved deliberately to break England away from Roman ecclesiastical control. By false accusation and coercion Henry secured legislation from Parliament in 1534 which separated England from papal control and declared Henry the supreme head of the Church of England. Meanwhile, in January, 1533, Henry had married Anne Boleyn, and as soon as Thomas Cranmer was consecrated as archbishop of Canterbury, the marriage to Catharine was declared invalid.

In addition to Anne Boleyn, between 1533 and his death in 1547 Henry married Jane Seymour (1536), Anne of Cleves (1540), Catherine Howard (1540), and Catherine Parr (1543). The principal events during the closing years of Henry's reform were: the confiscation of monastic property; the publication of Tyndale's Bible and later, through the influence of Thomas Cranmer and Thomas Cromwell, the wide circulation of an English translation of the Bible based upon the works of Tyndale and Miles Coverdale; the preparation by Henry of the Ten Articles, which attempted to wean the people away from Roman superstitions; and the issuance of the Six Articles, which identified the Church of England as entirely Roman Catholic in doctrine although in all things (save ordination) under the headship of the sovereign of England. Such was the condition of the reform when Henry died on January 28, 1547.

The Continuing Reform Under the Tudors (1534–1603)

It will be remembered that Henry VII began the Tudor line in England. The children of his son (Henry VIII) completed that line. These were Edward VI (Henry's son by Jane Seymour), who reigned from 1547 to 1553; Mary Tudor (Henry's daughter by Catharine), who reigned from 1553 to 1558; and Elizabeth (Henry's daughter by Anne Boleyn), who reigned from 1558 to 1603. The beginning of the reform under Henry VIII has been sketched above.

Reform Under Edward VI (1547–53).—Henry VIII apparently looked toward further ecclesiastical reform, for the Council of Regency which he provided in his will for the nine-year-old king, Edward VI, was composed of men known for their reforming views. The new Duke of Somerset was made Lord Protector and moved cautiously in the direction of continued reform. The clergy was instructed to preach against the usurpations of the Roman bishops, and visitation showed a deplorable religious illiteracy among the established clergy, which made it impossible for them to carry on an effective preaching ministry. The Six Articles of Henry VIII were repealed, along with most of the other heresy laws. Clerical marriage was permitted; royal control over the Church in England was tightened. In 1549 the first prayer book of King Edward VI, along with an Act of Uniformity prescribing its use, was prepared and circulated, reflecting Roman Catholic doctrine and ritual. After the replacing of Somerset by the Duke of Northumberland (although without the official title of Protector), a revision of the prayer book was made (1552) which reflected Protestant thinking. In the next month a creed known as the Forty-two Articles was prepared, which was even more Protestant than the prayer book. On July 6, 1553, Edward died and despite plotting by Northumberland, Mary, oldest daughter of Henry VIII, succeeded to the throne as England's queen.

Reform Under Mary (1553–58).—Mary came to the throne determined to take vengeance upon those who had declared her mother's marriage to Henry invalid, to return England to the bosom of the Roman Catholic Church, and to inflict God's judgment upon those heretics who loved England more than Rome. In 1553 Cardinal Pole was sent by the pope to act as legate to England, and under his guidance every vestige of ecclesiastical reform set in motion by Henry VIII and Edward VI was expunged from the law books. England was restored to the Roman Catholic Church on November 30, 1554; suffering and death had already begun. A few months later, Bishops Ridley and Latimer were burned for heresy, and soon thereafter Archbishop Thomas Cranmer suffered the same fate. Historians judge that the burning of these three leaders, along with approximately three hundred others during the five-year reign of Mary, made England a Protestant nation. In July, 1554, Mary married Philip II of Spain, soon to become the Spanish king, but she died without heir.

Reform Under Elizabeth (1558–1603).—Elizabeth, daughter of Henry by Anne Boleyn, was the last of the Tudor line. It is surprising that she remained alive to secure the throne. The reason for sparing her was purely political. Philip of Spain recognized that if anything happened to Elizabeth, then Mary, Queen of Scots, and wife of Francis II of France, would be the successor to the English crown. This would have meant that England, Scotland, and France would unite under one crown, an overbalancing of continental power that Philip feared greatly. His father, the emperor, felt that Elizabeth should be slain regardless of possible succession; and too late to accomplish it, Philip came to the same conclusion. It was a foregone conclusion that Elizabeth would be anti-Roman, since the pope had declared that her mother was not properly the wife of Henry VIII. She was trained under Bishop Hooper, who was strongly Calvinistic in his doctrinal ideas.

Elizabeth moved slowly at first, but in 1559 with considerable opposition Parliament passed legislation acknowledging Elizabeth as supreme governor of the church and possessing even more ecclesiastical power than her father had known. She worked carefully to finish demolishing the entire pro-Roman structure which Mary had built. In 1559, by an Act of Uniformity, Elizabeth required again the use of the second prayer book of Edward VI with a few revisions.

Less than two hundred of the nine hundred Roman Catholic clergy refused to take the oath of allegiance to Elizabeth, but all of the Marian bishops were included in the minority. Cardinal Pole had died shortly after Mary, so for a non-Roman succession Elizabeth secured four bishops who had been consecrated under Henry VIII and Edward VI to lay hands on Matthew Parker and consecrate him as archbishop of Canterbury. The Church of England claims that this continuance of succession was valid under church law, while the pope has officially ruled that this succession is invalid. In 1563 the Forty-two Articles of Edward were revised and issued as the Thirty-nine Articles (although the twenty-ninth article was suppressed until 1571 for political considerations), and these articles have become the official doctrinal statement. They show a tendency toward Calvinism.

In 1570 Elizabeth was excommunicated and deposed by the Roman Church, who declared her kingdom a proper target for crusades by the faithful. In 1587 Mary, Queen of Scots, was executed for alleged complicity in a plot to overthrow Elizabeth. As a result of these events, Philip II, now sovereign of Spain, assembled a fleet of ships, and on July 12, 1588, the Spanish Armada set sail to capture England. They were defeated by the superior seamanship and equipment of the English navy, although storms later assisted in the destruction of many of the invading vessels.

By the time Elizabeth died in 1603, England had a strong Protestant government. This did not mean, however, that dissent would be permitted, for religious dissent could not be differentiated from civil rebellion in a realm where church and state were united in one sovereign.

Rise of the Puritans

With the rapid oscillation of the royal religious ideas, it is not surprising that the people did not quickly change their religious convictions to match. This was particularly true in the case of those who had been exposed to continental reform movements where convictions were much deeper and more influential than they were on the English isle.

As early as 1550, Bishops Hooper and Ridley (both later burned by Mary Tudor) revealed their repugnance to popish superstitions and unscriptural practices. The reversal of royal religious demands under the Catholic rule of Mary Tudor (1553–58) sent scores of Protestant leaders fleeing to the Continent for safety. Many of them came into contact with Calvin's system in Switzerland. From this doctrine they were convinced that worship should contain only those elements that were distinctly enunciated by the Scriptures. Such a principle would undercut the many Roman Catholic practices that rested simply upon tradition and would in many cases dispense with some Lutheran retentions, for Luther chose to leave traditional practices and regalia in worship unless they were expressly prohibited by the scriptures. Thus when a Protestant sovereign ascended the English throne in 1558, many of these exiles returned to their own country favoring a more radical Protestantism than the "middle-of-the-road" English reform.

They demanded the elimination of popish elements in worship, such as the adoration of the wafer in the Supper through kneeling, the retention of the priest as over against the minister, and other such barnacles which tradition had added to the scriptural teachings. By 1564 these reformers were known as Puritans in popular vocabulary, because of their desire to purify the English reform. They were encouraged by several of the archbishops of Canterbury who were Puritans in fact, if not in name. One of the Cambridge teachers, Thomas Cartwright, became outspoken in asserting that Calvin's system was of divine origin and authority and, although ejected from his post by Archbishop Whitgift, was quite influential after about 1572 in converting men to Puritan views and in rallying them to the standard.

From this time until many of them were gathered up in the Wesleyan movement of the eighteenth century, the Puritans played a large part in English religious life. They, along with the Separatists and the Baptists, are introduced here because references to them will be made in the reign of the first Stuart king, beginning in 1603.

The Development of Separatism

It was inevitable that some would not be satisfied with efforts simply to purify the established church. Across the channel on the Continent Lutherans had separated from the Roman Church and by the treaty of Augsburg in 1555 were officially recognized in their separation. The radicals, the Zwinglians, the Calvinists, and many others across the Continent had denied the claims of authority by the Roman Church and had appealed to the Scriptures as their sole guide. Already the Scriptures had been provided in the English tongue. In 1525–26 William Tyndale, from his exile on the Continent, made an English translation of the New Testament and smuggled it into England. Apprehended and slain in 1535 by the Roman Catholic Church for this translation, his last words prayed God to open the eyes of the king of England.

The prayer was answered in the next year. Henry had now broken with the Roman Church and permitted Miles Coverdale to translate the entire Bible into English. Matthew's Bible was published in 1537 and the Great Bible in 1539. Fittingly, these last three English translations almost reproduced Tyndale's. Perhaps God had opened the eyes of the king to permit the extensive circulation. The reading of the Scriptures in the English tongue by the common people sowed seeds for what amounted to a second reformation in England.

As early as 1567, after Archbishop Matthew Parker had demanded conformity to the symbols of the established church in England, the authorities apprehended a group of London Separatists under the leadership of Richard Fitz; they were of the congregational type, although it is difficult to estimate how far their organization had progressed. About 1580 an outspoken Puritan minister, Robert Browne, adopted separatist principles and with Robert Harrison founded an independent church in Norwich in the next year. Browne fled from persecution to the Netherlands and published three treatises which have remained an exposition of the basic views of the Congregationalists, although Browne returned to the established church. In 1587 Henry Barrowe and John Greenwood were imprisoned for separatism, and through their tracts Francis Johnson, a Puritan and an enemy of separatism, was won to their principles. In 1592 Johnson became pastor of an organized Congregational church in London, but in the following year, because of increasing persecution that brought death to Barrowe and Greenwood, Johnson was forced to flee to Amsterdam where he became pastor of a congregation.

Soon a second Separatist church came to Amsterdam. A group of Separatists in Gainsborough, England, among the leaders of which were Thomas Helwys and John Murton and later John Smyth, fled about 1607 to Amsterdam and formed another independent church in that city. Out of this group there came a new type of biblicism, which will be discussed shortly under the heading of English Baptists. A third independent congregation to flee from England about 1607 settled at Leyden, after first stopping in Amsterdam. This group had come from Scrooby Manor, not far from Gainsborough, and was led by men with familiar names —William Bradford, William Brewster, and John Robinson. From them came the Pilgrims who emigrated to New England in 1620.

English Baptists

The pastor of the second Separatist church in Amsterdam was John Smyth, who had been a pupil of the pastor of the first Separatist church in the same city—Francis Johnson. Smyth had been reared in the Church of England under Elizabeth and in 1600 had been appointed preacher in the city of Lincoln. After serious study of the Scriptures he decided in 1606 to leave the established church and join the Separatists.

It was a dangerous time to decide that. James I had determined to harry the nonconformists out of the land. Smyth joined the Gainsborough group and with them fled to Amsterdam about 1607. Here Smyth came to the conviction that the Scriptures must be the sole guide for faith and practice and that the Scriptures demanded the baptism of believers only. This, of course, went far beyond what the other Amsterdam independent church believed and helped bring alienation between the two churches. About 1609 Smyth baptized himself (by pouring) and thirty-six others and formed the first English church holding to believers' baptism. Smyth and a small following soon seem to have doubted his authority to baptize, so they appealed for admission to the Mennonite church nearby. Smyth died before being admitted to their communion, but eventually some were received.

On the other hand, Thomas Helwys and John Murton with the minority returned to England to form the first Baptist church on English soil about 1611–12. Here Helwys published his famous plea for liberty of conscience in a little book, *A Short Declaration of the Mystery of Iniquity.* He addressed his dedication to King James I, boldly asserting that the king was a man and not God, and that while political fealty was due him by his subjects, every man was responsible only to God in spiritual things. Helwys was imprisoned at Newgate and probably died there. Murton became the pastor and leader of this first English Baptist church. By the time James I died in 1625 there were six or seven of these early Baptist churches, and by the close of the period (1648) about fifty churches containing perhaps ten to fifteen thousand members. Because of the influence of their environment in Holland they held to what is known as a "general atonement," that is, the doctrine that Christ died for all men, not for just a particular few. For this reason they have been known as General Baptists. They were at first called Anabaptists because of their rejection of infant baptism, but they rejected the name. They were the first English group to champion complete religious liberty. After 1644 they were called Baptists.

English Calvinistic or Particular Baptists generally are dated

239

from 1638. A Separatist or independent church was organized in London by Henry Jacob in 1616. Several schisms came under succeeding pastors. In 1638 a group separated because of their conviction that only believers should be baptized. With others these formed the first Calvinistic Baptist church in England in 1638 under the pastoral leadership of John Spilsbury. They were later called Particular Baptists because of their belief in a limited atonement—Christ died only for the elect. By the close of the period there were more than seven Particular Baptist churches in England. Some of their outstanding leaders were William Kiffin, Hanserd Knollys, and John Bunyan.

Reform Under the Stuarts

James I (1603-25).—Elizabeth reigned for a long time, but it was evident when she died in 1603 that she had not lived long enough to stabilize the religious settlement which she had provided for England. The succession to the crown of England went to King James VI of Scotland, the great-great-grandson of Henry VII of England. Both the restless Roman Catholics and the vocal Puritans were heartened by the prospects of the Scottish king's accession as James I of England. He was the son of Mary, Queen of Scots, and had displayed his rancor toward the dominant Presbyterianism of his native land. Since he had married a Roman Catholic wife, and since his mother was executed by Elizabeth, the Catholics reasoned that their cause would be close to the new king's heart. The Puritans, on the other hand, felt that James' experience with Scottish Presbyterianism had conditioned him to favor them in the new realm. Meanwhile, leaders of the Church of England felt that the subservient character of their church to royal supremacy would recommend them to the new king. The Church of England won the tug of war. The other contenders for royal favor were spurned.

Two plots against the king's life were attributed to the Roman Catholics and led to a demand that papalists conform. The Puritans met James in 1603 with a petition to purify English Christianity from papist superstitions (by adopting Calvinistic doctrines), but James curtly refused. In the following year at the Hampton Court Conference, James again spurned Calvinism but did grant a request for additions to the catechism and a revision of the English Bible. From the latter permission came the famous King James Version of the English Bible in 1611. By 1604 the king had rejected all Puritan bids and made it his policy to harass them constantly. An example is seen in the Declaration of Sports of 1618. James knew that the Puritans were quite careful to keep Sunday as the holy day of God. As a repressive measure, he required every clergyman to announce from the pulpit the sports program for the entertainment of the people on Sunday. This was a severe trial for any conscientious Puritan.

Charles I (1625-49).—Upon James' death in 1625, his son Charles, inferior to his father in ability and diplomacy, succeeded to the throne. He was suspect to the Protestants when he was installed, since his mother was a Roman Catholic and he had married a Roman Catholic princess. He tried to continue his father's policies, but the mounting resentment carried over to him from his father's reign was ominous. The situation was not eased by the persecuting tactics of Archbishop William Laud who through spies, the Star Chamber, and the Court of High Commission endeavored to suppress all dissent. The Declaration of Sports was again pressed.

Because they resented his rigorous tactics, Charles dismissed the Parliament in 1629 and ruled without their aid until 1640. He called them into session then only because of a crisis which he was unable to handle without the co-operation of the people themselves. The crisis sprang from Scotland. The Scots resented royal interference with their Presbyterianism. Since 1603 (when James became sovereign of both countries) the Church of England and the crown had desired to extend the establishment of episcopacy into Scotland. By wily diplomacy James had been able to make considerable progress in that direction. In 1637, however, Archbishop Laud attempted to force upon Scotland a replica of the English establishment, including a drastic revision of the liturgy. Opposition was immediate. The struggle of the Scots to

241

maintain Presbyterianism against royal policy became rebellion, but the king had insufficient funds and men to wage war against the Scots. Thus in April, 1640, Charles was forced to call Parliament into session. But these Englishmen were in no mood to acquiesce in the face of royal flaunting of English law and equity. When Parliament demanded political and religious reform, Charles dissolved the body. It had met for just three weeks and is known as the Short Parliament. Then Charles completely alienated his people by illegally holding convocation (the assembly of the clerical leadership) after the dissolution of Parliament. Under Archbishop Laud's direction a number of canons were adopted, declaring that the king had unlimited power over the persons and possessions of his subjects by divine right, without respect to their consent. The clergy were required to sign an oath never to change the government of the English church, and in describing their submission the canon ended a list of surrendered privileges with the words "et cetera" (and so forth), which could be interpreted in almost any sense. This legislation aroused such feeling that Charles suspended it. It showed the people what they might expect from their king.

Meanwhile, the Scots had invaded England, and Charles had no other choice than to call Parliament to secure funds and men. In November, 1640, Parliament assembled and quickly showed that Puritanism was in the majority. Religious and political reforms were begun. When Charles attempted to seize several members of the House of Commons in January, 1642, civil war broke out between the king and Parliament. Drastic alterations then took place. The episcopal and liturgical (prayer book) forms were abolished, and an assembly (the Westminster Assembly), made up principally of Puritans, was summoned to advise Parliament on the creed and government of the new English church. Parliament badly needed Scottish aid in their fight with Charles and agreed to work for uniformity in ecclesiastical organization and doctrine in England, Scotland, and Ireland, and to oppose episcopacy. This Westminster Assembly, primarily Puritan, recommended a Presbyterian type of church government, which was established in 1646 and provided a Presbyterian liturgy for public worship in place of the prayer book. The famous Westminster Confession was adopted by Scotland in 1647 and by England in 1648.

Meanwhile, Parliament's armies were winning substantial victories, bringing into prominence a new leader in Oliver Cromwell. The new Presbyterian establishment and intolerance were no more attractive to Cromwell than the episcopal intolerance. Cromwell and most of his leaders were independents and favored no intolerant government, whether Presbyterian or episcopal. In December, 1648, dissatisfied with the Presbyterian Parliament, the army purged Parliament of those members who refused to carry out the army's wishes. King Charles, meanwhile, had been defeated in the field and had surrendered to the Scots. He convinced them that if they would take his side, he in turn would favor Presbyterianism in England. The Scottish leaders, noting that the army of Cromwell was opposed to the Presbyterian Parliament and fearing that Cromwell would overthrow the Presbyterian reforms which had been made, agreed to support Charles.

However, in August, 1648, the Scottish army, endeavoring to invade England, was soundly defeated by Cromwell. After the purge of Parliament, under the influence of the army Charles was tried for treason and beheaded. The period closes with the temporary defeat of royal power in England; with the Tudor reforms, the work of the early Stuarts, and the Presbyterian revolution swept away through the military power of Oliver Cromwell and his army of independents; and with considerable uncertainty as to the outcome of the struggle in both political and ecclesiastical life in England.

The impact of the events in England was considerable in her American colonies. That story is a succeeding chapter.

Concluding Summary

The occasion of the English reforms was the caprice of Henry VIII (1509–47), but the causes were much deeper. In 1534 the Church of England was established. It maintained Roman

Catholic doctrine in most respects, although denying the headship of the pope. The regents of Edward VI moved toward Protestant doctrine, but Mary returned the English church to the bosom of Rome in 1554. Five years later Elizabeth permanently wrenched it away. James VI of Scotland became James I of England (1603–25) to institute the Stuart line. His son, Charles I (1625–49), was beheaded for treason at the close of the period. The decade before his death was a stormy one. A civil war took place. Episcopacy and Presbyterianism were disestablished successively, and scores of tracts advocating religious liberty and toleration of dissent appeared. Oliver Cromwell and the army assumed control of the government at the close of this period.

21

The Roman Catholic Revival

THE TERM "COUNTER REFORMATION," sometimes applied to the activity of the Roman Catholic Church during this period, is not entirely accurate. It is better simply to call it the Roman Catholic revival. It is true, of course, that the direction taken by the Roman Catholic Church both responded to, and reacted against, the reform movements by Luther and others. As a matter of fact, it is difficult to judge whether the Roman Catholic Church was hurt or blessed by the movement known as the Reformation. The events of this period may have saved the Roman Catholic Church from complete inner decay and provincialism at a time when the world was expanding rapidly. Certainly, without the stimulation and redefinition that grew out of conflict with the reformers, the Roman Church would have been ill prepared to face what lay in store for it in a new and larger world.

Background of Roman Catholic Revival

National reform movements.—It has been noted that the reforming councils which were aimed at the Roman Church in the fifteenth century failed because of papal opposition. The popes never again have had to deal with antagonistic reforming councils like those of Pisa and Constance. By manipulation of the constituency, the agenda, and the method of voting, the popes have been able to control succeeding councils and their decisions.

A new world was being born in the fifteenth century. Heretofore the principal struggles of the Roman Catholic Church had been with her counterpart in the political sphere, the Holy Roman Empire. The ideal of a universal political empire was dying, however, and in its place came the rise of a strong nationalistic spirit. The papacy was now forced to reckon with sovereign states. The French king during the Reformation, Francis I (1515–47), was able to a large degree to control both church and state in his country. It will be remembered that after the breakdown of the Council of Basel, Charles VII of France, together with the nobles and clergy, had in 1438 enacted the Pragmatic Sanction of Bourges, which provided state control sufficient to offset some papal abuses. England under Henry VIII (1509–47) exercised considerable state control over the Church before her break with Rome in 1534. The German states, honeycombed by ecclesiastical princes and retarded by papal divide-and-conquer tactics, possessed no national political unity and continued to suffer under the papal abuses, all the while observing the more fortunate states about them. No wonder the reform spread like wildfire in this atmosphere.

Perhaps the most significant area in the rise of the national states was that of Spain. It developed rapidly. In 1469 it was united by the marriage between Ferdinand of Aragon and Isabella of Castile and enlarged through their subsequent conquests. Repressing all dissident forces within the peninsula and moving with boldness and firmness in European politics, Ferdinand and Isabella aided in leaving to their grandson, Charles I, the strongest government on the Continent. Although there was no hint of revolt in Spain against papal control, the dual sovereigns recognized the necessity of maintaining the integrity of the state in dealing with the Roman Church. In assuming control of the Roman Church in their state, Ferdinand and Isabella directed their efforts toward purifying and strengthening the clergy and maintaining as far as possible the medieval conception of papal suzerainty. The Spanish king (Charles) became the Holy Roman Emperor in 1519 and declared himself at the Diet of Worms as being determined to maintain the medieval standards of Roman Catholicism which his forefathers had known. The history of the Roman Church during this period was greatly colored by the conflicts between the emperor, determined to protect the ancient Roman

Catholic Church and its pure doctrine, and practically every other power, including the popes.

Preparing the way for Charles, and in many respects constituting the inspiration of the Spanish type of reform, was Ximénes de Cisneros (1436–1517). Trained in Spain and Rome, Ximénes was talented, dedicated, tireless, and ruthless. Picked by Queen Isabella as her confessor, Ximénes, despite seemingly sincere protests against holding high office, was appointed archbishop of Toledo and chancellor of Castile. Uniting ecclesiastical and royal authority, Ximénes founded the University of Alcala (Complutum) and arranged for the production of the Complutensian Polyglot, in which the Old Testament was printed in Hebrew, Greek, and Latin, and the Targum on the first five books of the Bible, while the New Testament had the text in Greek and Latin. Erasmus published his Greek New Testament in 1516, but Ximénes had printed his text by 1515, although papal permission for publication delayed its appearance until 1520.

Ximénes demanded that all of the Mohammedans in Spain— who had settled there after Charles Martel had thrown them back from France in 732—either become Christians or be banished. In addition, Ximénes' rigid discipline is said to have driven over a thousand monks out of Spain before his death in 1517. His zeal inspired a theological revival and complemented the work of Torquemada in the enforcement of the Inquisition, which the crown had begun in 1480. Thus Spain had already instituted a type of reform of the Roman Church in the closing years of the fifteenth century, but it was primarily a nationalistic movement, strongly medieval and intolerant. No Protestant reform movement either began or survived in this realm during the Reformation period.

Humanism and the Roman Church.—Another factor that affected the Roman Catholic Church in its relation to the reform movement was the work of the humanists. Delving as they did into the ancient writings, Christian as well as classical, these men saw the wide differences between the early Christian movement and the contemporary Roman Church. There can be little doubt that humanists in every country helped prepare the way for the Protestant reform. Some of them joined it; more stayed within the framework of the Roman Catholic Church and endeavored to coax it in the direction of eliminating abuses and superstitions. Desiderius Erasmus of Rotterdam (1466–1536), doubtless the outstanding humanist of the Continent, actually suggested a plan for the proper kind of reform. For years he had been assailing the superstitious legends of contemporary Roman Catholicism, and his writings sounded so much like those of Luther that he was later forced to disclaim authorship of some of Luther's tracts. Erasmus wanted a reform without violence or ill feeling. He suggested that the priests simply be trained in the right way and then teach the people a pure type of Christianity. His efforts did not succeed. For the most part, humanism was unwilling to plunge into revolution to attain reform, and apparently revolution was required.

Roman Catholic piety and reform.—Within the top echelon of the Roman Church there was a genuine concern for the strengthening of the spiritual life of that body. In the very year that Luther posted his theses, a group of Italian Catholics formed the Oratory of Divine Love, a devotional type of society designed to deepen spiritual life and eliminate abuses. Among its members were Caraffa (who subsequently became Pope Paul IV) and Sadoleto (who attempted to woo Geneva back into the Catholic fold when Calvin was exiled to Strassburg). This piety, it should be noted, was channeled into loyalty to the ancient institution.

Papal Response to Reform Efforts Before 1540

The strong but unsuccessful efforts to reform the papacy through councils were apparently wasted. The succeeding popes seemed to consider the failure of the councils as a vote of confidence in the unscrupulous methods and careless lives of the previous popes, as well as an evidence that widespread abuses in doctrine and practice were of minor concern. The looseness of Pius II (1458–64), Sixtus IV (1471–84), and Alexander VI (1492–1503) has already been mentioned. Julius II (1503–13) found it necessary to call a general council as a means of defeating a reforming council of the king of France and the emperor in 1510. The council met in Rome in 1513 shortly before the death of Julius. It had happy results for the papacy. The French cardinals who had sharply criticized papal corruptions were pacified. More important, in 1516 a new understanding was reached between Pope Leo X (1513–21) and Francis I of France, by which the Pragmatic Sanction of 1438 was abrogated and king and pope agreed to share the ecclesiastical spoils of France. After approving this agreement, the general council dissolved in March, 1517; in October of that year the Lutheran reform erupted.

Although tardy in appearing, a papal bull on November 9, 1518, corrected some of the worst abuses. It will be remembered that the marrow of Luther's early protest consisted of his denial that indulgences could forgive guilt without repentance. This pivotal point was conceded by the papal bull. It also fixed papal authority as immediate on the earth only, although allowing considerable influence to the petitions of the pope for souls in purgatory, because of the merits of Christ and the saints. This bull did not represent a concession to Luther or a revision of official Roman Catholic doctrine. The reverse was true. The pope had now made explicit declarations of Roman Catholic orthodoxy, and unless he conformed, Luther could be condemned for ecclesiastical anarchy as well as doctrinal defection. Lines began to form for each side in the controversy. A considerable body of literature appeared, some attacking and some defending Roman Catholic government and doctrine. Even Henry VIII of England and, later on, Erasmus wrote as defenders of the faith.

The brief pontificate of Hadrian VI (1522–23) accomplished little but lip service toward reform. Clement VII (1523–34) attempted the time-honored customs of crushing ecclesiastical dissenters by branding them as heretics fit to be burned and of countering Protestant princes by resort to political alignment. His judgment was often poor. His support of King Francis I of France actually tied the hands of Emperor Charles V of Spain, when Charles was willing and able to kill the young and weak

Lutheran movement. Clement's "balance of power" politics directed against the growing Hapsburg influence during the critical period of reform may have saved the Protestant Reformation. In 1527, angered by the tactics of Clement, Charles allowed an army to invade Italy and take the pope prisoner, the hardships from which probably hastened Clement's death.

His successor, Paul III (1534–49), worked carefully. From the ranks of the Oratory of Divine Love and others known to favor limited reform to suppress abuses, he appointed several new cardinals—Caraffa, Sadoleto, Pole, and Contarini—and set up a commission under their leadership to investigate and report on the need for reform. Although their report in 1538 was not immediately effective in obtaining action, yet the preparation of it and the training given these men who soon would have the highest places of leadership in the Roman Church made it significant. Many of the ideas in this report were included in the action taken by the Council of Trent.

Final Roman Catholic Decision on Reform

The Roman Church hesitated briefly. Should it attempt to conciliate the Lutherans or condemn them unequivocally? Some, like Contarini, remembering the effort made by Philip Melanchthon at Augsburg to minimize the differences between the Lutheran and Roman Catholic viewpoints and the abortive plan of Philip of Hesse to unite all reform movements against the Roman Church, desired to see if it were possible to work out an understanding that would be satisfactory to Lutheran leaders and still would not compromise the traditional Catholic dogma. Others, like Caraffa (who had been trained in the Spanish reformation), desired simply to condemn the schismatics and organize to meet the challenge of the evangelicals. Besides, argued this party, what could be done with the Zwinglians, the Calvinists, the Anglicans, and others? Conciliation would lead quite far from the historic position of the Roman Church. However, under pressure from Emperor Charles, a series of conferences was held—one at Hagenau in 1540, one in Worms in the same year, and one in Regensburg in

1541. Despite some strong efforts at compromise, these conferences failed to reach common ground for agreement.

After the conference at Regensburg (Ratisbon) in 1541, the Roman Church set its face like flint toward the Protestants and has never swerved from a position of open and complete hostility toward them. This decision made, Roman Church leadership now began to bend all efforts toward halting the inroads of Protestantism and toward getting its own house in order so that it could best wage its war. Again the quarrels between the pope and Emperor Charles V saved the Lutherans. The Schmalkaldic War, begun in 1546, resulted in the early defeat of the Lutherans. The pope then had a vigorous controversy with Charles over the place of meeting for a proposed general council. Perhaps the quarrel was necessary, for the pope might not have been able to control a council under the shadow of Charles. Perhaps the papacy came out as well as it would have otherwise in the "calculated risk" taken by Paul III. At any rate, the Lutherans fought again and were successful.

Two movements greatly aided the struggle of the Roman Church with the reformers: the rise of the Society of Jesus (known more familiarly as the Jesuits) and the Council of Trent.

The Society of Jesus

Ignatius Loyola, founder of the Society of Jesus, was born in 1491 in Spain. At the battle of Pampeluna with the French in 1521, he was so severely wounded that he could no longer pursue military service. While convalescing he read legends about Francis and Dominic, who were described as Christ's soldiers. Loyola determined to become a knight of the virgin Mary. After his recovery he entered the Dominican monastery at Manresa. His deep devotion drove him as a pilgrim to Jerusalem in 1523. Unable to carry on mission work there as he desired, he sought an education and returned to a school at Barcelona at the age of thirty-six to sit in class with boys ten years old. He made rapid progress and in 1528 entered the University of Paris. Here he gathered a small group of like-minded followers, chief among whom was Francis Xavier,

251

and in 1534 the group took solemn vows to work in Jerusalem or anywhere the pope might direct.

Three years later the expedition to Jerusalem began, but because of the Turkish War they were stopped at Venice. Here Loyola met Caraffa and attracted the attention of Contarini. Pope Paul III (1534–49) was impressed by the ability of Loyola and his devotion to the Roman Church, and on September 27, 1540, the Society of Jesus was authorized. A membership of but sixty was permitted originally. Two years later this limitation was removed. Loyola was chosen as the first general of the order and held that position until his death in 1556.

Organization and doctrines.—The tremendous impact of this new order may be seen in the fact that when the Council of Trent met, only five years after the authorizing of the Society, it was Jesuits who played a leading part in this important council. This Society has been at the forefront of some of the Roman Catholic Church's greatest achievements. The organization bore a military simplicity—a general at the head, provincials over geographical districts, and a careful system of recruitment and training. As early as 1522–23 Loyola had begun preparing a series of spiritual exercises for Christian soldiers. The manual outlined a four week's course—twenty-eight general divisions with five hourly meditations covering the entire redemptive drama. Novitiates were to be tested by difficult service for a two-year period, then were promoted to be scholars trained in both ecclesiastical and secular learning. The next step was the coadjutor. This office was given those who were chosen and carefully trained for particular service. It included teachers, priests, missionaries, authors, consultants, and advisers. After long and faithful service, a few coadjutors could be admitted to the inner circle of the Society—the professed, from which the general officers would be chosen.

The thorough training and ethical standards of the Jesuits quickly brought them into places of leadership throughout Europe. As confessors and ecclesiastical lawyers they greatly influenced the Catholic princes in their affairs of state; their schools, their compromising nature at the confessional, their crafty preaching, and their missionary zeal gave them a wide following. Perhaps the word "obedience" is the largest word in Jesuitism. Loyola wrote in his *Spiritual Exercises:*

That we may be altogether of the same mind and in conformity with the Church herself, if she shall have defined anything to be black which to our eyes appears to be white, we ought in like manner to pronounce it to be black. For we must undoubtingly believe, that the Spirit of our Lord Jesus Christ, and the Spirit of the Orthodox Church His Spouse, by which Spirit we are governed and directed to Salvation is the same. . . .

And again, in the Constitution, the statement is made:

And let each one persuade himself that they that live under obedience ought to allow themselves to be borne and ruled by divine providence working through their Superiors exactly as if they were a corpse which suffers itself to be borne and handled in any way whatsoever; or just as an old man's stick which serves him who holds it in his hand wherever and for whatever purpose he wishes to use it. . . .

This blind obedience demanded renunciation of individual conscience. Other unacceptable moral standards of the Jesuits are the doctrine of probabilism (any course may be justified if one authority can be found in its favor), intentionalism (if the intention is good, other considerations may be overlooked), and mental reservation (the whole truth does not necessarily have to be told, even under oath). Two other doctrines have been ascribed to the Jesuits but have been denied by some of their responsible leaders. One is that the end justifies the means; if the result is for the greater glory of God, then any means used to accomplish it are permitted. The other is the assassination of tryants. Despite Jesuit protests, there is evidence that these last two principles were acceptable at an earlier period of the Society's history and, as a matter of fact, are implicit in the first three of these moral standards.

The progress of the Society.—The Society made rapid progress in Italy, Portugal, Belgium, and Poland. Its greatest victories were won in Germany and Austria where, coupled with the Lutheran controversies, the Roman Catholic Church won back almost all of the territory in south Germany which the Reformation had alienated. The Society's activities were only partly successful in France until after the death of Henry IV (1589–1610), but thereafter the Jesuits controlled France until the French Revolution. In Venice, England, and Sweden their program was not at all successful during this period. True to the original purpose for which the Society was founded, the Jesuits entered wholeheartedly into missionary work. Although it was not possible to go to Jerusalem, in 1542 Francis Xavier (1506–52) was sent to India and Japan, where for ten years he labored sacrificially and heroically; in 1581 Matteo Ricci (1552–1610) went to China; in 1606 Robert de Nobili (d. 1656) sailed to India; and in 1685 Jesuits began work in Paraguay.

Council of Trent (1545–64)

Background.—The second great weapon of the Roman Church against the Protestant movement was fashioned in a well-controlled general council. It will be recalled that when Luther was condemned by Pope Leo X, he appealed from the pope to a general council. Such an appeal infuriated the supporters of the pope. The reforming councils of the fifteenth century had only been suppressed by the boldest action and good fortune; and Pope Martin V, after his election by the Council of Constance in 1417 ending the terrifying papal schism, had promulgated a bull condemning any person that appealed from the decision of a pope to a general council. However, Leo X (1513–21) had dealt with an ecumenical council and was confident that the best method of suppressing Luther would be to call such a council and let it under his control repress him. His death in the opening years of Luther's reform prevented this action, and despite clamor for a general council from all sides—Lutheran, Catholic princes, and even the emperor Charles—the popes and their advisers had not felt it to be a propitious time to summon a general council. Paul III (1534–49), familiar with the demands of all groups and confident that he could control a general council, began preliminary negotiations soon after assuming the pontificate. At this stage he still had hopes of conciliating the Protestants, so his legates conferred with both Catholics and Protestants about attending such a council. Neither desired to have a council in Italy where the pope could dictate to it. Twice Pope Paul issued a call for a council to assemble in Italy, and twice he was ignored. Finally, in conference with Emperor Charles, it was agreed that the council should meet in Trent, a small Austrian city, and after a delay caused by another Spanish-French war, the council was set for March, 1545. The emperor was hoping that this council would unite Europe religiously and politically, not through suppressing Protestantism but through conciliation; the pope, on the other hand, had determined by 1545 to have no part in conciliation of the Protestants and looked to the council to define and declare Catholic doctrine for the purpose of confuting and condemning the Protestants.

The sessions.—Seven sessions of the council were held at Trent during the first two years (1545–47). When pestilence threatened at Trent, Pope Paul ordered the council to meet in Bologna, Italy, which aroused the hostility of the emperor. The council met in Trent again in 1551 with some Protestant princes attending by invitation from the emperor, but they saw that papal control of the agenda and committees robbed the council of any autonomous action, so they soon withdrew. Another outbreak of the Schmalkaldic War ended this meeting of the council. Finally, after the death of several popes and a number of Protestant gains, Pope Pius IV (1559–65) negotiated for the reopening of the council as a weapon against Protestantism. In 1561 the council again assembled at Trent and remained until 1564 when its work was finished, mainly under Jesuit leadership.

The results.—The results of the council show that the papal party was in control most of the time. Occasionally uninhibited dissenters raised their voices relating to some of the more fundamental problems, but for the most part it was a complete victory for the ultramontane party. The emperor's hopes for religious and political unification of Europe were shattered. He soon retired from his office. The only elements of reform included in the coun-

255

cil's recommendations were aimed at meeting the challenge of Protestantism. Priests must know their Bibles and be able to preach; stronger episcopal control in the parishes was ordered; arrangements were made for better education of clergy and for more care in making appointments; and morality and discipline were emphasized. All of these items were an attempt to gird the Roman Church to fight back at Protestantism.

The doctrinal decrees of the council were aimed in the same direction. Doctrines of Lutherans, Zwinglians, Calvinists, Anabaptists, and other dissenters were specifically anathematized. An authorized canon of Scriptures was announced, which included the Old Testament Apocrypha, and the Latin Vulgate was pronounced inspired in all its parts. The seven sacraments were defined; Scriptures and tradition were combined for authority; good works were judged to aid in justification; and it was reaffirmed that the Church alone can interpret doctrine. These were strengthening measures taken by the Church.

Inquisition and Piety

Two other factors, looking in opposite directions, completed the Roman Catholic response to the challenge of Protestantism. The first was the establishment in 1542 of the Roman Inquisition. This intensive ferreting out of heresy was not effective except in Italy where Caraffa and Loyola, who had charge of the inquisitorial reorganization, strongly enforced it. By driving out or destroying evangelicals like Bernardino Ochino, Pietro Martire Vermigli, Galeazzo Caraccioli, Vergerio, and Aonio Paleario, the Inquisition gave the Roman Church in Italy more freedom from dissent than it had ever known there.

At the same time, there was a revival of a medieval type of piety within the Roman Catholic Church in Spain and Italy. Mysticism and asceticism combined to popularize a sort of oriental "union with God" experience of exaltation in Spain. New monkish orders arose; stringent reform occurred in some of the older orders. Earnestness and zeal were added to the weapons of the Roman Church in her effort to face Protestantism.

256

Concluding Summary

The sixteenth century brought an active revival of the Roman Catholic Church. Unquestionably the Protestant Reformation provided the stimulus to much of this revival. The Roman doctrine was clarified and standardized. A powerful new order, the Jesuits, became the assault troops against Protestantism. A strong missionary program was launched. Most of the territory wrenched away from the Roman Catholic Church by the Protestant Reformation now became a new ecclesiastical battleground because of revived Catholic strength. As a matter of fact, before 1648 the Roman Catholic Church had won back most of the territory in southern Europe. Generally speaking, that area which had once been the old Roman Empire in Europe was retained or won back by the Roman Church. This struggle by the Roman Church, with other factors, led directly to the wars over religion which will be discussed in the next chapter.

22

The Continuing Conflict

NOTHING COULD ILLUSTRATE better the secularized condition of Christianity in the sixteenth century than the fact that efforts to reform the Roman Catholic system brought two centuries of the bloodiest fighting men had yet known. The antecedents to the use of military force for suppressing religious dissent were many and ancient. There was no support for it in the teachings of the New Testament or in the example of the early Christians. The adopting of Christianity by Constantine in 312, however, brought the use of political methods and weapons for the suppression of religious dissent. On this ground alone the alleged beneficent rule of Constantine proved to be a more deadly blow to true Christianity than the severest persecutions by his predecessors on the Roman throne.

Wherever it could control secular rulers, the developing Roman Catholic Church followed Constantine's example of suppressing dissent with the sword. During the Medieval period it is likely that the secular sword did more for the growth of Roman power than all of Rome's missionaries combined. The Crusades represented on a large scale the foul spirit of military coercion in the name of religion. Heresy-hunting by torture and punishment by burning occupied the attention of most orthodox bishops in the Roman Catholic system until 1243, when special inquisitorial machinery was set up by the papacy for locating and forcibly suppressing religious dissent.

The Hussite Wars of the fifteenth century brought a foreglimpse of the horrors to come in the next century. Julius II (1503–13), the warrior pope who boasted of his prowess with the sword, is a typical figure in an age when might made right—even in religion. In the sixteenth century the attempts to reform the Roman Church brought repressive wars in four countries—Switzerland (against Zwingli), Germany (against Luther), France (against the Huguenots), and the Netherlands (against Calvinism)—while the Thirty Years' War of the seventeenth century ravaged most of the Continent.

Causes of the Thirty Years' War (1618–48)

The first phase of the reform movement was completed by 1555 when the Peace of Augsburg closed the struggle between the Roman Catholics and the Lutherans (now called Protestants). The immediate result was a victory for Lutheranism. The secular empire now recognized the legal right of Lutheranism to exist and expand. This was in marked contrast with the picture two decades before, when the Lutheran movement, its leader officially judged a heretic and an outlaw, continued to exist only because Emperor Charles V was too busy fighting France, the pope, and the Turks to suppress it. Despite vehement protests by the pope, Lutheranism could propagate its faith boldly. It seemed that the use of the sword as a means of settling religious jurisdiction had come to an end.

Glancing back at this period from the present vantage point, however, it can be seen that all factors pointed to another war. In general, the following matters led to the outbreak of a new war between Roman Catholics and Protestants.

Lutheran disunity.—Even while Lutheranism was being threatened with extinction in the Schmalkaldic Wars that began in 1546, the Lutheran theologians were fighting vigorously among themselves in the area of doctrine. It is not surprising that doctrinal controversies occurred among the followers of Luther. The break with the Roman Church led Luther to push out into new directions of thought. Sometimes his impetuous nature prompted him to emphasize certain aspects of theology to an extreme; at other times he might express himself in terms that seemed to contradict what he had previously said. He hardly had time to meditate upon a

259

complete and consistent scheme of theology but was forced to produce it piecemeal in various writings. Furthermore, as he developed and matured in his reforming ideas, he ofttimes changed his views expressed just a few years or even months before.

In addition, the diverse backgrounds and ideas of his prominent followers sometimes did not actually represent Luther. Philip Melanchthon, for example, after Luther's death in 1546 introduced new elements and attitudes into the movement which represented a divergence from Luther's general position. As a result, violent internal controversy rocked Lutheranism in the sixteenth century after Luther's death, various secular princes supporting this or that theologian in his doctrinal views. These Lutheran princes were not adverse to the use of force in suppressing what they believed to be erroneous Lutheran doctrines. No wonder the Romanists were encouraged.

The Roman Catholic resurgence.—Meanwhile, the Roman Catholic Church was busy also. Unified and strengthened by the internal readjustments of the sixteenth century, the Roman Church steadily won back territory and followers. The Society of Jesus provided trained and zealous soldiers who infiltrated into Protestant lands and schools with subversive effect. In addition, the Catholic princes soon began to persecute the Protestants in their lands. This was particularly true in Bavaria, Austria, Bohemia, and Hungary. Not only was the defection of Roman Catholic princes and ecclesiastics to Protestantism halted, but extensive and important gains were made by the Roman Church.

The challenge of Calvinism.—The Peace of Augsburg (1555) had granted recognition to Lutheranism as a legal religion, but no recognition was given to the followers of John Calvin, who were becoming numerous and powerful. Calvinism became a rival not only of Catholicism but also of Lutheranism. While the Roman Catholics were strengthening their forces in the closing years of the sixteenth century, Lutheranism became engaged in a bitter struggle with the Reformed Church (Calvinism). In many instances Calvinism partly supplanted the Lutheran movement, as in Poland, Hungary, Bohemia, and the Palatinate. Perhaps one explanation why Calvinism made such vast inroads was that Lutheranism retained so much of the medieval Roman system. While Calvinism was strongly anti-Roman, it had no Melanchthon to seek areas of compromise with the Roman Catholic system. Rather, Calvin rejected all tradition and insisted upon a fresh start from the direct teachings of the Scriptures. In addition, the Calvinistic system was more nearly self-consistent in its teachings and its methods. Its emphasis upon God's predestination in human experience put iron into the souls of men as they fought the Roman system.

Violations of the Augsburg Treaty.—The pope had never agreed to the Treaty of Augsburg in 1555. Quite naturally his followers were not at all scrupulous to observe the legal right of the Lutherans. Nor was the papacy alone at fault. The Lutherans also were guilty. The union of church and state, practiced through the centuries by the Roman Catholic Church and adopted in Lutheranism, Zwinglianism, Calvinism, and Anglicanism, made it imperative for them that military and political weapons be used in the advancement of any movement which was a part of national interest. Under this philosophy, religious differences were viewed as political and military threats. Flagrant violations of the Augsburg Treaty were excused on the ground of national interest. They led unerringly toward war.

Political rivalry.—When the war finally came, it presented a confusing scene. Ofttimes political interests took precedence over religious beliefs. Catholic France and Catholic Spain could not fight on the same side because of political rivalry. Protestant princes looked first to political factors before taking up arms and choosing sides. Consequently, although the struggle was basically between Roman Catholics and Protestants, the Thirty Years' War brought strange alliances and questionable motives.

Outbreak of War

The immediate occasion for the war occurred in Bohemia. The emperor Matthias (1612–19) forbade Protestants to erect certain churches, despite his initial oath that he would tolerate the numerous Protestant subjects of Bohemia. To add fuel, the dyspeptic Matthias arranged for his cousin Ferdinand, a militant Roman Catholic, to succeed him as the king of Bohemia. The Protestant reform flared into violence in Prague in May, 1618, and war was made certain when the Bohemian Protestants rejected Ferdinand as their king in the following year, choosing instead a Protestant.

The war that followed had four distinct phases.

Struggle in Germany (1618–23).—The Roman Catholic policy of continued preparation was quickly rewarded. By 1620 the Bohemian Protestants were crushed. All Protestant schools and churches were closed in Bohemia, Moravia, and Austria. Their pastors were driven into exile. The Romanists were not generous in victory, taking immediate steps to re-Catholicize the conquered lands. The Calvinistic government of the Palatinate was over-whelmed in 1623, and Protestants were required to conform or leave. This victory was significant in that the prince of the Palatinate was one of the seven electors of the emperor, and with the Catholic victory in the Palatinate the pope controlled the majority of the electors, guaranteeing emperors subservient to the Roman Catholic Church.

The European phase (1623–29).—Thoroughly alarmed by the rigorous repression of Protestantism by the Catholics in the newly won lands, Lutheran princes of north Germany prepared themselves for conflict, seeking aid from Denmark, England, and Holland, nominally Protestant states. The Roman Catholics, however, defeated the new foes. The Edict of Restitution of March, 1629, continued the severe terms by the victorious Roman Catholics. All Protestants were to be banished from Catholic lands, and it appeared that all of the gains of the Protestant Reformation would be wiped out under the Roman program.

Gustavus Adolphus (1629–32).—In this dark hour for the Protestants, two developments changed the picture. The first was the quarrel among the various Catholic leaders, secular and ecclesiastical, over the division of the spoils. The second was the intervention of Gustavus Adolphus, the sagacious and brilliant Swede. In 1630 he began his invasion of Europe. At first other Protestants paid him scant attention, but within two years he had defeated all of the Roman Catholic armies and was master of the Continent. In his moment of victory at Lützen in 1632, however, he fell in battle.

Indecisive fighting (1632–48).—The next sixteen years brought terrible slaughter and great destruction of property, but neither side could secure victory. Germany, in particular, served as the battleground and suffered greatly. Despite the vocal opposition of Pope Innocent X, the exhausted armies on each side agreed to terminate the war.

Results of the War

The Peace of Westphalia in 1648 is a landmark in religious history. It closed the last of the general wars over religion and usually is considered as the beginning of the modern era. By the terms of the treaty, Lutherans, Calvinists, and Roman Catholics were recognized as equally entitled to civil and religious rights. The year 1624 was designated as the normal year; that is, each state or territory would revert to its religious status as of that date.

There can be little question that France won the war. The long battle between that nation and the Hapsburg line was finally resolved. The German states would not recover from devastation of the land for over a generation, and many of her finest leaders were slain. The emperor continued to exist in name only. The pope protested the cessation of hostilities and, in fact, paid little attention to the terms of Westphalia. He continued actively his efforts to re-Catholicize through subversion and diplomacy. Generally speaking, south Europe remained Roman Catholic, north Europe remained Protestant. The German states and Switzerland included both groups. It is ironic that the Protestants in Bohemia and Austria, who had begun the great battle thirty years before, received no relief in the final terms. This exhausting war apparently convinced the Roman Catholic Church that Protestantism could not be defeated with arms.

Other Conflicts

Arminianism in the Netherlands.—The theological system of John Calvin magnified God's predestination. There was widespread objection to this system, because it was felt that it involved human fatalism and compromise of God's character. Jacob Arminius (1560–1609) was the leader of the group opposing Calvin's doctrine. He denied an unconditional election, asserted a universal atonement for all believers, taught that man could cooperate with God in achieving regeneration, insisted that God's grace was not irresistible, and believed that men could fall from grace. These views were condemned in the Synod of Dort in 1618, and dissent was dealt with vigorously.

England and Scotland.—During this period occurred the fierce struggle in England and Scotland over the religious establishment. Although that story is told in connection with the English reformation, it is referred to here to complete the picture of the confused and violent situation during the first half of the seventeenth century.

Concluding Summary

The Peace of Augsburg (1555) did not end the struggle between Roman Catholics and Protestants. Strife continued for half a century. In 1618 war erupted in Bohemia and spread across the continents. The Peace of Westphalia in 1648 marks the close of the last great Roman Catholic-Protestant conflict on the Continent. Legal recognition was accorded to the two most extensive continental reform movements—Lutheranism and Calvinism. Political motivations began to outweigh religious differences, although religious persecution was by no means a thing of the past.

23

American Christianity

AMERICAN CHRISTIANITY WILL be discussed in three sections. The first covers the period from the discovery of America in 1492 to the year 1648—an arbitrary date in American history but quite significant in the English homeland and on the Continent. The second section covers the remainder of the American Colonial period, while the third section begins with the founding of the American Republic (1789) and continues to the present. This chapter will cover the first of these sections.

Importance of American Christianity

There are several reasons why American Christianity deserves extended treatment. (1) In a comparatively short time—by the standard of continental Christianity—American Christianity developed rapidly into an area of great vitality and influence. The United States is now the strength of the Roman Catholic Church as well as of the Reformation groups. (2) In the twentieth century American Christianity has become the principal base for world missionary efforts. (3) The gradual deterioration of vitality in Christianity on the European continent has accentuated the extraordinary progress made on the North American continent. (4) Christianity in the United States has assumed forms diverging from the historic pattern. Even the physical characteristics of the earth and rivers in what became the United States have tended to unify the nation, minimizing the sharp demarcations that characterized European states and racial groups. This basic unity, along with the tremendous resources of the great expanse of land, providing an economy of plenty, produced a new type of man. Self-reliant, independent, suspicious of coercion, and conscious of the opportunities afforded by personal worth and industrious application, the colonial American was a new factor in the complex religious picture of the world.

Significance of the Time

The discovery and settlement of America came at a peculiarly opportune time. The reformations in Europe and England were working their purifying effects to provide an evangelical base for gospel extension. There was great improvement in the Roman Catholic Christianity that was transplanted, in that many of the medieval abuses of doctrine and morals had been repressed. Most of the Roman Catholic immigrants in the formative years came from the British Isles, where they had been tempered by their minority position and their contact with other persecuted minorities. Roman Catholicism in the United States has not known the harsh and vindictive spirit which it has shown elsewhere. The tremendous growth of Roman Catholicism in the United States (with its different spirit in many respects) into a dominant power in the entire Roman movement gives hope that some day Roman Catholicism everywhere may cease its persecuting and coercive tactics.

Not only the Roman Catholics but all Christian groups in early colonial America had contact with the sweeping religious currents of seventeenth-century England. Thousands had fled to America to escape the intolerable policies of Archbishop William Laud. The avalanche of tracts and books in the last years of Charles I advocating religious toleration and even religious liberty were known in colonial America. The harshness of the reactionary legislation of the restoration Parliament conditioned Englishmen in the colonies for the exultant national and anti-Roman surge that brought William and Mary to the throne and gave homeland and colonies alike the Act of Toleration in 1689.

With this background and the comparative isolation of the American colonies from English interference, the men and women who fled to a new world planted a new sort of Christianity that

266

could not have been understood or tolerated a century or two before.

Characteristics of American Christianity

This new kind of Christianity flowed to a considerable extent from the activity and efforts of the religious dissenters, aided at some points by philosophical and humanistic idealism. A strong democratic spirit and the principle of separation of church and state greatly influenced, and gave direction to, the religious life of the United States. These distinctives encouraged the rise of religious individualism, of denominationalism, of religion by conviction rather than coercion, of competition in religion, of a sharpened sense of lay obligation, of zealous and extensive missionary activity, of the organization of nonecclesiastical ethical and philanthropic bodies or societies, and of the secularization of public benevolences and institutions.

Early Struggle for Domination

The discovery of America was not mere chance. The explorers did not just happen to stumble upon it. Solid financial reasons sent ships from various maritime nations scurrying westward in the closing decades of the fifteenth century. A very profitable trade with the Far East had been funneled through the eastern Mediterranean countries, but in 1453 the Turks seized Constantinople, and their conquests successively swallowed up all of the former points of trade. The development of the compass, astrolabe, and maps, making possible navigation when both stars and land were obscured, provided stimulation for adventurous voyages. In addition, with the increasing conviction by many that the world was round and that the vast ocean bordering China, described by Marco Polo almost two centuries before, was probably the western terminus of the same ocean that washed the shores of Spain, hardy men sailed westward. That there might be lands within that ocean between Spain and China was not at first commonly considered.

Portuguese explorers began poking into inlets and harbors in west Africa, thence southwestward as far as the Cape Verde Is-

267

lands. Christopher Columbus was possessed with the great dream that he could reach the profitable markets of the East by a voyage, not too hazardous or distant, due west. He sailed on August 3, 1492, arriving on October 11 at what is probably one of the Bahama Islands. This began a number of explorations, laying the basis for Spain, Portugal, France, and England to claim large sections of the Western Hemisphere. The Spanish led the way, a series of explorers touching land from North Carolina south to the Straits of Magellan. Portuguese explorers visited Labrador, Newfoundland, and Brazil. England paid scant heed at first to the explorations of the east coast of the United States by John Cabot (perhaps accompanied by his son) but a century later made them the basis for claims in the New World. France entered the field late, touching the northern section of the continent through the work of Verrazano and Cartier.

Spain first began efforts at colonization. Within half a century after Columbus by their explorations Cortez, Balboa, Ponce de Leon, de Soto, and Coronado made claims for Spain in Florida, Mexico, and what is now the southern United States. Priests and monks accompanied these men and set up the Spanish type of Catholicism; but as soon as the Spanish sword was withdrawn, the movement deteriorated.

It seems providential that France did not capture the entire American continent and institute a zealous type of Jesuit Christianity. Her magnificent plan was conceived by the explorers themselves. It involved no less than the complete control of America by straddling "the core of the continent"—the Saint Lawrence, the Lakes, and the Mississippi to the Gulf. For a century and a half it appeared that this grand scheme would certainly be successfully consummated, since by 1754 the French flag floated unchallenged in the very areas of the grand design. Major diplomatic and military struggles on the Continent in what is called the Seven Years' War (1756–63) blasted this great dream when France surrendered to Great Britain all of her American possessions. There were subsidiary reasons, but the main one was military supremacy on the Continent.

Other Christian Colonies in America (1607-48)

Apart from the Roman Catholic movements established by the Spanish and French, American Christianity during this period may be divided into six groups. As far as possible, as a means of emphasizing the continuity of Reformation movements despite geographical and racial influences, the outline of American Christianity will follow the general pattern of Reformation groups. At times, of course, extensive modifications in a denomination or the dilution of the original influence of one of the Reformation movements may bring a denomination that must be treated as a different group. A denomination in America like Congregationalism, for example, although greatly indebted to Calvinism, is not put under the reformed group but is treated as a separate body.

The six denominations involved in early American colonization were the Church of England (1607), Congregationalists (1620), Calvinists (1623), Lutherans (1623), Roman Catholics (1634), and Baptists (1638).

Church of England in Virginia (1607-48).—English attempts to colonize the American continent began during the long reign of Queen Elizabeth (1558-1603). Adventurous sea captains had discovered a profitable venture in preying on Spanish ships sailing to and from colonial areas with valuable cargos. Meanwhile, the English seafarers explored the lands along the southern coast of the North American continent and published glowing accounts. Sir Humphrey Gilbert and his half-brother, Sir Walter Raleigh, secured patents from Queen Elizabeth to enable them to colonize new lands. After Gilbert's untimely death, Raleigh endeavored to plant a colony on Roanoke Island in Virginia in 1587, without success. Profiting considerably from his experiences, in 1607 the first permanent settlement was established at Jamestown, Virginia. Despite great hardships, the colony survived. Its religious background was the Church of England, and a church was established. It was handicapped, however, by the lack of a resident bishop.

Congregationalism in Massachusetts (1620-48).—The English independents, or Brownists, who had fled to Holland in 1607 under the leadership of John Robinson, William Brewster, and others, determined in 1620 to sail for Virginia in the New World. The ship of these Pilgrim fathers, the *Mayflower*, was driven northward by the elements and landed instead in November, 1620, in what is now Massachusetts. A large colony of Puritans under John Endicott entered the area in 1629, causing misgivings among these Pilgrim Separatists, but through the medical skill and gracious spirit of Dr. Samuel Fuller of the Separatist colony, hostility and misunderstanding between the Separatists and Puritans were removed. From a common council the group united into a single church system in which the authority lay in the congregation, banded together by covenant, guided and instructed by the ministers whom they set apart, and supported as a part of a theocratic government. In 1631 the colony enacted a regulation that only members of the established Congregational churches could be freemen. Thus the ministers in the local congregations were able to regulate suffrage on the basis of religious orthodoxy. By 1648 this colony had increased considerably, swelled by the Puritan exodus from England between 1630 and 1640.

The Massachusetts Bay Colony was completely intolerant of Separatism. The reasons were both religious and political. For one thing, the colony was born with a "divine right" sense which transformed them from the category of dissenters in England to the established church in America (and curiously enough made dissenters out of Church of England followers in the colony). Those dissenting in the American colony were viewed as abhorring God's revealed will and rebelling against God's appointed order. This was to be an ideal theocracy. Furthermore, the colony was schismatic from the Church of England. Noisy strife, particularly any that might seem to favor a radical Separatism in the colony, could have brought the ire of Archbishop Laud and Charles I and had serious consequences. Thus when Roger Williams arrived in 1631 and immediately denounced the Massachusetts Bay theocratic system, every effort was made to silence him. He was banished in 1636 and in 1638 organized Providence plantations. Similarly, when in 1637 Mrs. Anne Hutchinson introduced variant ideas, she too was banished. By the end of this period the Massachusetts Bay Colony was engaged in a struggle to maintain her theocratic nature and political independence.

Calvinism.—The Dutch Republic also made explorations along the North American coast and made subsequent claims of territory. In 1609 Henry Hudson inspected the North American coast from Newfoundland to Virginia in an effort to locate a passage to the Far East. Although he failed in this, he explored the river which bears his name and secured the adjacent area for the settlement in 1623 of New Amsterdam, later to become New York. The Dutch Reformed Church (Calvinistic) was organized here in 1628, although many other different religious groups found a foothold also. Until the close of the period there was little religious persecution. Peter Stuyvesant became governor in 1647 and changed this policy.

English and Scotch-Irish Presbyterianism also began to infiltrate the colonies during the latter part of this period. It is sometimes difficult to distinguish between the Presbyterians, the Puritans from the Church of England, and the Congregationalists, all of whom were greatly influenced by John Calvin's doctrines and organization. Between 1637 and 1639, in fact, there was considerable correspondence between English Presbyterian leaders and leaders of Massachusetts Bay Congregationalism respecting the new type of Calvinistic modification in the American colonies. Sometimes, as in Connecticut generally, Presbyterianism was integrated without friction, and even Massachusetts Bay Congregationalism absorbed some Ulster Presbyterian immigration. Other Presbyterians had considerable trouble over doctrine with Congregational neighbors early in the 1640's but were well received by the Dutch Reformed leaders in New Amsterdam. The large Calvinistic immigration came after the close of this period.

Lutheranism.—The movement of continental Lutheranism to the American colonies came about 1623 when Dutch Lutherans were included among the early colonists in New Amsterdam. In addition, Swedish Lutherans began colonizing New Wilmington, Delaware, in 1638 and established the first Lutheran congregation

271

in America in that year. Lutheran immigration was small during this period.

Roman Catholicism.—The first permanent English Roman Catholic colony was established in Maryland in 1634. Sir George Calvert, a secretary of state under James I (1603–25), embraced Roman Catholicism in 1623. Long interested in colonization and desirous of founding a state for personal affluence and religious refuge for Roman Catholics, Calvert secured grants to Newfoundland in 1622 (under James I) and to what now includes Maryland and adjacent areas in 1632, although he died before the transaction was completed. His son Cecil proceeded with the plan, and in March, 1634, the colony was founded near the Potomac River. Jesuit priests worked actively in settling the colony and in converting the inhabitants to Catholicism. Indeed, Lord Baltimore (Cecil Calvert) became uneasy at the zeal of the Jesuits and their ability to secure land and special immunities; he issued surprisingly repressive orders to them, doubtless because he feared the effect on public opinion in Protestant England should it be learned that the new American colony was dominated by the feared and disliked Jesuits.

A considerable improvement in the treatment of Roman Catholicism in England after the death of James I forestalled the expected immigration to the new Catholic colony. Consequently, Cecil, anxious to guarantee the success of the colony, welcomed settlers of all faiths and refused to establish the Roman Church with civil support. An admirable toleration was provided. However, it was not religious liberty, for the famous Act of Toleration of 1649 at the very close of this period enacted the punishment of death for speaking against the Trinity and assessed heavy penalties for not believing in Jesus Christ, for breaking the sabbath by swearing and disorderly recreation, and for similar offenses.

Baptists.—American Baptists trace most of their early ancestry to England. During the reign of Charles I (1625–49) large numbers of dissenters of every sort fled from the stringent persecuting measures of Archbishop William Laud. One of these was Roger Williams, a highly educated and talented "godly minister," according to the first description of him by Governor Winthrop in Massachusetts Bay Colony. He arrived in February, 1631, about six months after Boston was settled and named. Williams is significant not only as the organizer of perhaps the first Baptist church in America but because of his advanced views. Religious liberty, separation of church and state, and democracy were condemned almost universally on both sides of the Atlantic in 1631, save by a few General Baptists in England and Williams in America. It took a decade more of time and a political and constitutional revolution in England before dissenters there of any sort, apart from the Baptists, championed such ideas.

Where did Williams get such notions? Perhaps a clue is found in his writings. He preserves a story about the second pastor of the first Baptist church in London, John Murton, an early contemporary of Williams. This tale speaks of how Murton wrote Baptist tracts from prison by using milk and paper bottle stoppers for writing paper. A confederate outside browned the dried milk to rescue the writings of Murton. Murton died in London about 1626 when Williams was about twenty-seven years of age. Perhaps there is a larger context for this anecdote which Williams alone remembers from Murton, for some of the ideas of Williams were those of Thomas Helwys, first pastor of the church, and John Murton.

At any rate, Williams was banished in 1636 from Massachusetts Bay Colony for holding such opinions. His critics in America thought that he had "windmills" in his head. In 1638 he founded a colony at Providence based upon his advanced concepts of democracy and religious liberty, and in the following year he organized what was perhaps the first Baptist church in America. He began to doubt the validity of his baptism before long—a question that plagued others of the Baptists in England—and became a Seeker.

No such doubts assailed Dr. John Clarke, founder of the Baptist church at Newport, Rhode Island, perhaps in 1644 or before. His warmhearted and unselfish spirit, expressing itself in extensive and sacrificial labors in behalf of the gospel, religious liberty, and separation of church and state, marks him as the outstanding Baptist of this period.

Baptists appeared during this period in New Hampshire and Connecticut and perhaps elsewhere, in addition to Massachusetts Bay Colony and Rhode Island, but their numbers were few.

Concluding Summary

From the beginning the religious forms and tensions of the Old World were projected into the tiny English colonies scattered along the eastern seaboard of America. Before the Peace of Westphalia (1648) American Christianity was already providing a foreglimpse of the rich and complex development of denominations that was to characterize her later history. In half a dozen colonies there were that many different religious groups. Already a wide ocean and a seemingly limitless frontier were shaping a new sort of man in America.

BIBLIOGRAPHY

BAINTON, ROLAND. *Here I Stand.* New York: Abingdon-Cokesbury Press, 1950.

BETTENSON, HENRY (ed.). *Documents of the Christian Church.* New York: Oxford University Press, 1947.

BINNS, ELLIOTT. *The Reformation in England.* London: Gerald Duckworth & Co., Ltd., 1937.

GEE, H., AND HARDY, W. J. *Documents Illustrative of English Church History Compiled from Original Sources.* London: Macmillan & Co., 1896.

LATOURETTE, K. S. *A History of Christianity.* New York: Harper & Brothers, 1953.

LINDSAY, THOMAS M. *A History of the Reformation.* 2 vols. New York: Charles Scribner's Sons, 1941.

LITTELL, FRANKLIN H. *The Anabaptist View of the Church.* Philadelphia: American Society of Church History, 1952.

MCNEILL, JOHN T. *The History and Character of Calvinism.* New York: Oxford University Press, 1957.

NEWMAN, A. H. *A Manual of Church History.* 2 vols. Philadelphia: American Baptist Publication Society, 1953.

ROBINSON, JAMES HARVEY. *Readings in European History,* II. Boston: Ginn & Co., 1904.

SWEET, WILLIAM W. *The Story of Religion in America.* New York: Harper & Brothers, 1950.

V. PERIOD OF ENCROACHING
RATIONALISM (A.D. 1648–1789)

Introduction to the Period

At the beginning of this period the world was badly disorganized. The Thirty Years' War on the Continent had ravaged most of the German states, and the continuation of sporadic struggle projected the misery of the earlier catastrophe. In England the fratricidal war between the people and the house of Stuart ended dramatically in 1649 with the beheading of Charles I and the assumption of power by Oliver Cromwell. Throughout this entire period the Continent was dominated by France, although the political and religious repression of the people laid the foundations for the great revolution at the end of the period which was to sweep France out of her high place among the nations. England, meanwhile, moved toward the democratization of her monarchy. Parliament increasingly assumed more responsibility for government and policy. The Wesleyan revival doubtless saved England from a revolution similar to the one in France.

During this period the intellectual world threw off traditional restraints in its theological and philosophical systems. It will be recalled that the formulations of Francis Bacon (1561–1626) and René Descartes (1596–1650) brought a new emphasis on rationalism in interpreting the world. This emphasis was continued in Spinoza and Leibnitz. The empiricism of John Locke (1632–1704) turned in a different direction, giving inspiration for the idealism of Berkeley and the skepticism of Hume. In this period Immanuel Kant (1724–1804) brought the age of reason to its height. By making man's mind the dominant factor in categorizing the world of experience, Kant demolished older rationalism but introduced a new type. He laid the foundations for later systems of thought that developed more fully the truth that man is not simply a thinking creature but has other facets in his nature.

Points of Special Interest

In this period the student can see the successive thrusts of Christianity against militant rationalism and skepticism. On the Continent this took the form of pietism. This movement was quite important in

275

its immediate contributions, as well as in its influence upon the revival both in America and England in the following century. The dominating theme in English Christianity in this period was the Wesleyan revival. Every part of English life was blessed by it, and the rise of England to a dominant place in world affairs in the next century stems in large part from the saving character of this revival, both in social and political life. The Great Awakening in the American colonies, evidently sparked by Pietistic antecedents, did much to lay the foundations in religious and political life for the rise of the new nation.

24

Continental European
Christianity

THE PEACE OF WESTPHALIA of 1648 marked the close of the period known as the Protestant Reformation. The principal European nations during the Reformation were England, Spain, France, and Sweden, with the loosely confederated Holy Roman Empire and the threatening Turks in southeastern Europe completing the picture. New nations were now beginning to develop—Austria, Brandenburg-Prussia, the Dutch, and Russia. It will be the purpose of this chapter to trace Christianity on the Continent from the close of the Reformation to the French Revolution. England will be considered in a separate chapter.

Political Background

It will be remembered that Francis I of France and Charles V of Spain battled intermittently during the Reformation and, unintentionally, greatly aided the success of the Protestants. These wars were not incidental. National aspirations rose sharply in the sixteenth century. The old order was changing. The empire was decadent, and as though sensing their destiny, each of the several states endeavored vigorously to secure the advantage in the new order. Although Spain, through colonial discovery and early centralization, was the dominant power in the Reformation period, the leadership soon passed to France. A century of exhausting wars, a fatal weakness in maintaining a strong succession to her throne, and the inability to exploit her colonial empire toppled Spain from her high place. On the other hand, King Louis XIV of

France (1643–1715) was a shrewd, heavy-handed man who ruled long enough to carry out an extensive and energetic program of aggression and expansion. The Holy Roman Empire, so potent a factor during the Reformation, was rapidly declining. Political decay and economic stagnation combined to pull down this imposing medieval edifice and deliver its opportunities and duties to the individual German states, principally Bavaria, Saxony, Hanover, Austria, and Brandenburg-Prussia. Italy remained divided into small states.

The Turks, too, soon moved off the principal stage of events. Once more in the latter half of the seventeenth century the armies of the Turks threatened Vienna, as they did during Reformation years, but thereafter the tide subsided. Sweden also, after a brief period of glory through the work of Gustaphus Adolphus (1611–32), was defeated by a coalition of her enemies in 1709.

This was the golden age of the Dutch Republic, for a time undisputed mistress of the seas. In this period also the Russian giant began to bestir itself. Peter the Great (1689–1725) made a start toward westernizing the nation, and under Anna (1730–40) and Catherine the Great (1762–96) Russia added considerable territory and moved toward assuming a larger place in the European family of nations.

Roman Catholic Church

The new nationalistic spirit sweeping the world demanded complete control by the state. The Roman Catholic Church, on the other hand, claimed the immediate allegiance of clergy and people. The replacing of the power of the medieval empire by that of the individual states meant the weary repetition of conflict between overlapping powers. The strife between universal empire and universal church was replaced by the battle between many strong national states and the militant Roman church. Particularly in France and Austria on the Continent was this true. In France Louis XIV (1643–1715) attained absolute authority, while later on Marie Theresa (1740–80) in Austria sought the same ideal.

The principal story of the Roman Church between 1648 and

1789 is the interaction between the ecclesiastical and diplomatic ✗ aims of France and Rome. The religious attitude of Louis XIV was governed by his nationalistic aims at the particular time, for he apparently had little religious conviction. In 1682 he forced the Roman Catholic clergy in France to issue what are known as the Gallican Articles, a direct strengthening of national interests by limiting the pope to spiritual things only and by putting all ultimate spiritual authority into the hands of ecumenical councils. The pope, Innocent XI (1676–89), was one of the ablest and most conscientious pontiffs of the entire period, but he saw instantly the subversive nature of this legislation and fought it bitterly. In fact, so great was his hatred of Louis XIV of France that he may have consented to the overthrow of Catholic King James II of England partly because of James' friendship with Louis XIV. Innocent's successor, Alexander VIII (1689–91), tried to work out a compromise with Louis but did not quite succeed. However, the next pope, Innocent XII (1691–1700), found Louis in a trading mood, and in return for favors from the pope the French king allowed his bishops to disapprove the Gallican Articles.

Persecution of the Huguenots.—It will be remembered that the Huguenots (French Calvinists) had received the "perpetual and irrevocable" promise of certain liberties in the Edict of Nantes ✗ (1598). The Roman Church regarded this toleration as deplorable and worked continually and effectively to undermine it. The Catholic sovereigns of France during most of the seventeenth century were bitterly hostile to the Huguenots and waited only for the opportunity to smite them. In the arena of practical politics the Huguenots improved their situation by standing firm for the government amidst popular uprising and received in turn the commendations of Louis XIV. In 1656 the Catholic clergy remonstrated with Louis XIV about the privileges granted the Huguenots. The king showed his true distrust of the Huguenots by moving against them, particularly after 1659. Persecution began. It was as vicious as the combined shrewdness of Bourbon absolutism and vindictiveness of Jesuit bigotry could contrive.

In October, 1685, the original charter of French Protestant

liberty, the Edict of Nantes, was revoked by the same meaningless words that brought it into being—a "perpetual and irrevocable edict." All Protestant houses of worship were to be destroyed and schools abolished, all Protestant religious services halted, and all Protestant ministers must leave France within fifteen days. If Protestant ministers would become Catholics, they could continue with a substantial raise in salary and other specific rewards. Torture, prisons, and galleys now became the rule. Over a quarter of a million Huguenots fled from France, despite border guards posted to halt them. As a result, France lost perhaps one fourth of her best citizens; those who remained defiled their consciences, and their children were reared as skeptics or actual unbelievers; the established Roman Catholic Church shamelessly exploited state and people in such fashion that the first strong blows of the French Revolution a century later were aimed at the Church; and the monarchy became so impervious to the rights of the people that the foundations were laid for the great deluge.

Persecution of the Jansenists.—The Jansenists received their name from the founder, the French bishop Cornelius Jansen (1585–1638), who revered the theological system of Augustine. Augustine, it will be remembered, magnified the sovereignty of God in all areas of grace and salvation. The Jesuits, on the other hand, were for the most part strongly Pelagian, emphasizing the ability of man to aid in the redemptive transaction.

After the death of Jansen in 1638, his friends published his theological masterpiece lauding the Augustinian system. Naturally the Jesuits did their best to get this work condemned by the pope. The whole matter came to be a test between the Jesuits and their enemies. In 1653 the pope condemned five propositions which apparently contained the marrow of Jansen's views on grace. Prominent leaders like Blaise Pascal and Antoine Arnauld were arrayed on the Jansenist side. Pope Alexander VII and Louis XIV joined hands to require the Jansenists to conform. Persecution and coercion continued for over half a century, finally virtually overthrowing French Jansenism, although it survived in the Netherlands. The significance of this controversy rests in the fact that it represents the Roman Catholic condemnation of the teaching of Augustine, one of its early fathers, and a victory for the Pelagian ideas of the Jesuits. The synergism of the Roman Catholic system is more favorable to Pelagianism than to Augustinianism.

Persecution of the Salzburgers.—In the mountainous areas of upper Austria the people, unaccessible for regimentation, had long been followers of evangelical doctrines. The Waldenses, the Hussites, the Lutherans, and the Anabaptists had disciples there. Outwardly, most of the people conformed to the Roman Catholic Church but met secretly for evangelical worship. By the time of the Peace of Westphalia (1648) many of these had become staunch Lutherans. Since the Westphalian treaty provided that Lutherans in the territory of a Catholic prince had the right of peaceable emigration, the Protestants of Europe were shocked when Lutheran congregations in the territory of the Bishop of Salzburg were harshly imprisoned for their faith. The archbishop conveniently died and stopped both the persecution and the furor. In 1728, however, a new archbishop was appointed who vowed that he would destroy the heretics. Persecution began again, and in 1731 about twenty thousand Lutherans were driven from the country in the midst of winter. Most of them went to Prussia, where they were gladly received.

Suppression of the Jesuits.—The Jesuit order was probably the most influential party in the Roman Church during the first century after Loyola founded the society. Its tightly knit organization, clear-cut objectives, oscillating ethics, and overwhelming zeal brought it to the front rapidly, but these same characteristics also incurred enmity from many quarters.

In the opening years of the eighteenth century the Dominicans charged that the Jesuits in China were allowing the Chinese to continue worshiping pagan idols with a thin veneer of Christian vocabulary. In 1721 one of the men whom the Jesuits had driven from his assignment in Portugal was elected pope and took the name of Innocent XIII (1721–24). He promptly withdrew from the Jesuits the right to conduct mission work in China and nearly abolished the order entirely. Benedict XIV (1740–58) also condemned the heathenish practices of the Jesuits on the mission fields. Clement XIII (1758–69), a staunch supporter of the Jesuits, brought the final blow by the issuance of two bulls praising the Jesuit order. Portugal had already expelled the Jesuits in 1759; France had done likewise in 1764; and in 1767 Spain and Sicily took similar action.

The storm of protest against papal support of the Jesuits resulted in the election in 1769 of an anti-Jesuit pope, Clement XIV (1769–74). France, Spain, and Naples demanded suppression of the Jesuits as a condition of their continued relations with the papacy. After several preliminary steps, Clement abolished the Jesuit society in 1773 in vitriolic language. No Protestant has ever condemned them more unequivocally. Frederick of Prussia, a Lutheran, and Catherine of Russia, a Greek Catholic, gave the Jesuits haven in the hope of profiting by Jesuit resentment. Restoration came forty-one years later.

The approaching storm.—A glance at the history of the popes during this period shows that in the eighteenth century they faced a hostile world. Bitter rivalry with nationalism and the trading of blows with Protestantism account for only part of their struggle; the other part came from what has been called the Enlightenment. The first enthusiasm of discovering an orderly world—one operated on the basis of fixed and determinable laws—was almost uncontrollable. In the minds of many authority was shifted from a sovereign God to a thinking man, who was the measure of all things. In the eruption of the revolution in France, the Roman Catholic Church and Christianity in general were looked on as enemies of human rights and opponents of the highest achievements of mankind.

The Lutheran Church

The Lutheran lands bore the brunt of the war that closed in 1648. The frightful results of this war impoverished these German states for a century. The male population was decimated, and the constant march of armies which lived off the land brought devastation from enemy and ally alike.

Doctrinal controversies.—The harsh controversies among the Lutherans following the death of their founder barely subsided before the outbreak of the Thirty Years' War in 1618. War partially stopped most theological disputation, but the torrent of angry words soon erupted again. This time it began with Georg Calixtus (1586–1655), a spiritual descendant of the party of Philip Melanchthon. The training and experience of Calixtus fitted him to play his role. Through extensive traveling and diversified study he learned to appreciate other Christian groups. About 1630 he began to minimize distinctively Lutheran doctrines and to suggest plans for Christian union. His opponent was Abraham Calovius (1612–86), whose temperament and training inspired a strong loyalty to Lutheran confessionalism and made him abhor all that Calixtus advocated. This controversy, foreshadowing a similar but less bitter division among American Lutherans, engaged much of the vitality and attention of continental Lutheranism in this period.

Pietism.—Within Lutheranism one fruit of the depressed economic and religious conditions following Westphalia was an attempt to bring a vital renewal of practical Christianity. Pietism represents a reaction against rigid intellectual scholasticism and an effort to return to biblical principles. It was not an isolated movement. England had somewhat of a counterpart in her Puritan and Wesleyan revivals. The leaders of Pietism among the Lutherans were Philipp Jakob Spener (1635–1705) and August Hermann Francke (1663–1727). Spener was the pioneer, while Francke carried the movement to its greatest success. Neither of these men desired to separate from the Lutheran church but wanted to reform it from within. As a pastor in Frankfort in 1666, Spener saw the difference between the true Christianity of the heart and the rather formal and intellectual acceptance of doctrine that characterized church life about him. He introduced Bible and prayer classes into his church in an effort to revitalize Christian living. In 1675 he published a little work entitled *Pious Wishes,* which urged that Christianity should be more personal, scriptural, practical, and loving. Fellow Lutherans accused Spener

283

of leaning toward Calvinistic doctrines and turning away from the Lutheran faith.

Francke carried forward the work. He had a conversion experience in 1688 and became strongly evangelical and pietistic. His great work was done at the University of Halle. While there he translated Christianity into practical living, founding an orphanage and providing educational opportunities for thousands of boys from grade school through university. From this center came the early gleams of the modern mission movement when in 1705 it supplied the first missionaries for the Danish mission in India. Likewise, Henry M. Muhlenberg, probably the outstanding early American Lutheran, came from Halle in 1742.

In addition, the work of Spener and Francke resulted in the founding of the Moravian Brethren. Count Nikolaus Ludwig von Zinzendorf (1700–60) was reared by his Pietistic grandmother and received his schooling at Francke's institution in Halle. He permitted two families of Bohemian Brethren to settle on his estate in Saxony. Becoming interested, he joined their group and assumed leadership. It is interesting to note that he secured episcopal succession through both Lutheran and Reformed sources. Zinzendorf desired to establish a Christian association of all true Christians of all churches. He was banished from Saxony in 1736 by the state authorities and used the occasion to visit Moravian Brethren, as his group was called, in England and America. In 1742, much to his displeasure, his community in Saxony in his absence organized into a separate church. He was allowed to return to his home in 1749. The zeal and missionary activity of the Moravian Brethren were quite pronounced during the eighteenth century.

Beyond its own organizational life, Pietism had a considerable influence. It gave a renewed emphasis to study of the Scriptures and magnified the place of the conversion experience. In a reaction against its views, some of its opponents prepared the way for rationalism.

Rationalism.—During the Medieval period Christian philosophers had struggled with the question of the relationship between

284

human reason and divine revelation. Particularly when reason seemed to conflict with some area of revelation did this problem become acute. Many Christians looked upon the synthesis of Thomas Aquinas as setting forth the proper relationship. Aquinas took the position that reason should go as far as it could, forming a base for knowledge, and that revelation should then complete the structure, thus providing in a sense a capstone or completion for the whole. Other forces, however, continued to raise the original problem. For one thing, the Renaissance opened up new worlds of knowledge and understanding to men. Furthermore, during the late fifteenth and sixteenth centuries the movement known as humanism turned men increasingly toward faith in their rational powers. In a sense the Protestant Reformation itself, by fighting superstition and appealing to the reasoning of men as well as by formulating rational confessions and debating over doctrine, aided the swing toward reason. Some leaders of the Reformation magnified human reason and drastically attenuated the field of the supernatural, but generally the struggle was in bounds with respect to basic supernaturalism.

In this period, however, the onslaught against supernaturalism in favor of radical rationalism became critical. Strangely enough, the severest blow was doubtless delivered by one who was endeavoring to protect Christianity against the deism of England and the skepticism of France. Christian Wolff (1679–1754) was reared in the tradition of the philosophers Descartes and Leibnitz, who emphasized that all truth is capable of clear demonstration and is basically harmonious. Wolff tried to bring all philosophical concepts into self-evident and incontrovertible clarity and then turned to theology with the same purpose. Believing that he could do so, he asserted that Christian doctrines must be capable of demonstration with as much clarity as a mathematical proposition. This left revelation completely under the sway of human reasoning. Unless revealed doctrines were completely demonstrable to the satisfaction of the mind, they were unworthy of belief.

Because of his views Wolff was driven from his professorship of philosophy in the University of Halle but was restored by the Prussian ruler, Frederick the Great. Liberalism and skepticism were widely scattered throughout Germany. The Illumination— as the movement was called—ruled almost supremely in Germany throughout this period. Revelation became almost meaningless. Rational demonstration only was acceptable in teaching Christian doctrines. The curious religious system of Emanuel Swedenborg (1688–1772) and his New Jerusalem church was a direct result of this background, as he attempted to justify the spiritual world by showing its correspondence with the natural order.

This rational movement reached its height in Immanuel Kant (1724–1804). While often called the father of German rational- ism, he introduced some elements that turned away from a strict and final intellectual interpretation of all life. He demol- ished Wolff's idea that all truths must be demonstrable by clear ideas, and while insisting that the existence of God could not be proved objectively, yet in his *Practical Reason* he introduced a moral imperative into life that suggested a moral governor of the universe. His entire system, however, discarded supernatural rev- elation and made man's reason the ultimate criterion of truth. This period in Lutheran life closes with rationalism strong and religious skepticism widespread throughout the German states.

Calvinism

Calvin's system of theology was more self-consistent than that of Luther, and as a consequence, there were fewer internal con- troversies in the century after the death of Calvin. The contro- versies that did develop were in the nature of radical revolt against the entire system rather than disagreement with one facet. A brief survey of Calvinism in this period can be made in a geo- graphical outline.

Switzerland.—It will be remembered that Calvin began his movement in Geneva about 1534. After Calvin's death in 1564 his emphasis on predestination was taught even more rigidly by his disciple, Theodorus Beza. The movement was not greatly af- fected by the Thirty Years' War. However, the development of theological liberalism, along with German and French skepticism surrounding the area, greatly undermined the faith of Swiss Calvinists after 1750.

The Netherlands.—The Arminian controversy of the previous period gradually diminished. The dissenters were for the most part permitted to return and propagate their views. Two outstanding theologians lived in this period. Hugo Grotius (1583–1645), ofttimes called the founder of international law, felt the persecuting hand of the extreme Calvinists. He is remembered for his theory of the atonement of Christ in terms of the vindication of the majesty of God's government. The other leader was John Cocceius (1603–69), probably the outstanding biblical scholar of his area. Cocceius popularized the idea of the covenants: the covenant of works in Adam having failed, God gave a new covenant of grace in Christ. In the middle of the eighteenth century, Dutch Calvinism was also adversely affected by deism, skepticism, and rationalism. The Dutch Reformed Church was carried to America in 1628.

The German states.—The Peace of Westphalia recognized Calvinism as having equal civil and ecclesiastical rights with Roman Catholicism and Lutheranism. As suggested previously, however, the Roman Catholic Church vigorously attempted to re-Catholicize as many of the German states as they could reach and were successful in replacing Calvinism in some areas. The German Reformed Church also was greatly affected by materialism and skepticism in the eighteenth century. Some of its members emigrated to America in 1746.

France.—France had been fighting constantly (usually with Spain and the Hapsburgs) since the early days of the Reformation. The Thirty Years' War brought victory almost beyond the dreams of the earlier kings. France became the principal power of the Continent. During the long reign of Louis XIV (1643–1715), his chief aim was to establish royal absolutism on the basis of divine appointment. He developed a thorough organization, a strong army, and a meticulously loyal court. His extravagances brought great burdens to the people. He had a lofty conception of his office that brooked no rivalry. He made every effort to destroy Calvinism. After the revocation of the Edict of Nantes in 1685, the Calvinists fled to the Cevennes Mountains and waged guerrilla warfare against the Catholics. For a century the persecution of the Calvinists continued intermittently. The outstanding names that are preserved from this period are those of Antoine Court, the restorer of the Reformed Church of France, and Paul Rabaut, the apostle of the desert. The closing years of this period brought some toleration through the efforts of Robert Turgot.

Concluding Summary

During this period the controversy over Pietism and syncretism divided the Lutherans and encouraged rationalism. The resultant skepticism adversely affected both Lutheran and Reformed (Calvinistic) movements in every part of Europe. Roman Catholic persecution added to the miseries of the period and drove many toward skepticism and revolution.

The hierarchical organization in the Roman Catholic Church forestalled much of the radical rationalistic influence that blighted Protestantism. Internal conflicts brought the suppression of the Jansenists and Jesuits, and persecution of Protestants was widespread and vicious. Politically, the Roman Church made peace with the various states, in particular with France, the strongest power on the Continent.

Other small groups, such as the Mennonites, carried on in this period, but that story cannot be told here.

25

English Christianity

THE STORY OF English Christianity in this period is closely related to the political history because of the union of church and state. At the close of the previous period Charles I (1625–49) had been beheaded by Cromwell to institute what has been called the Commonwealth period (1649–60). A Presbyterian Parliament had become so intolerant that Cromwell purged its membership and sponsored his own parliamentary reorganization.

Church of England

During the Commonwealth (1649–60).—After the beheading of Charles I, Cromwell was faced with armed opposition from Scotland and Ireland who recognized Charles II as the rightful king of England. With his well-trained armies, however, Cromwell overcame the portions of the nation favoring Charles II and in 1653, after dissolving Parliament, declared himself Lord Protector of England. The Presbyterian Parliament had disestablished the Church of England from the support of the government in 1641 and subsequently had put Presbyterianism in that favored position. Cromwell altered this situation by providing that all acceptable ministers should be supported by the state. As a means of determining which ministers were acceptable, he instituted a Board of Triers to test those ministers applying for state support. Views on doctrine and polity were never to be questioned in determining who was fit for employment; only one's character as a godly man and his ability to communicate religious truths were considered. For the most part, religious toleration was provided for all except Roman Catholics and anti-Trinitarians.

Charles II (1660–85) and James II (1685–88).—After the death of Oliver Cromwell in 1658, there was a reaction in favor of restoring the royal house of Stuart to the throne of England. The traditionally poor memories of the people had forgotten the unspeakable tyranny of Charles I but remembered the harshness of the Presbyterians and the highhanded authority of Cromwell. Perhaps also the promise by Charles II of religious liberty for tender consciences caused many to turn toward him. Upon his restoration to the throne Charles found that he had promised more than he could give. The Church of England party was still entrenched in a powerful position and lost no time in taking the new king in hand. In addition, almost before Charles was settled as king, Thomas Venner and a group of millennial-minded fanatics known as the Fifth Monarchy Men staged an uprising in an effort to seize the throne from Charles and set up a kingdom for the return of Christ. They were repelled without great difficulty but certainly influenced the king against all dissenters.

The Church of England (the episcopacy) was established again in 1660, and in that year persecution against all dissenters began. Five acts were passed. *a.* The Corporation Act of 1661 excluded all dissenters from taking part in local government in England by requiring them to partake of the Supper in the established church, to repudiate the Solemn League and Covenant oath, and to swear not to take up arms against the king. *b.* The Act of Uniformity of 1662 required every minister to believe and follow the Book of Common Prayer in his services. Out of approximately ten thousand pastors in the Church of England at this time, two thousand were driven from the pulpits because they were unwilling to subscribe. The same requirements were prescribed for all teachers in public or private schools. *c.* The Conventicle Act of 1664, aimed especially at the Baptists, forbade all religious meetings by dissenters. *d.* The Five Mile Act of 1665 prohibited dissenting ministers from coming within five miles of any city or town or of any parish in which they had ministered. *e.* The Test Act of 1673 was aimed particularly at the Roman Catholics. Charles had issued a Declaration of Indulgence in 1672 in an ef-

290

fort to spare the Catholics from the effect of some of these acts, but in direct defiance of the crown, Parliament passed the Test Act, which excluded Catholics from all civil and military positions by requiring as a prerequisite for such offices the condemnation of the doctrine of transubstantiation and the partaking of the Supper in the established church.

Although some of these acts were aimed at specific groups, all of them brought great trial to Presbyterians, Congregationalists, Baptists, Quakers, and Roman Catholics.

On his deathbed Charles II was received into the Roman Catholic Church and his brother James II (1685–88), an active Roman Catholic, succeeded him on the throne despite an Exclusion Bill which Parliament had earlier passed in an effort to prevent a Roman Catholic from assuming the crown. Without delay James attempted to aid the Roman Catholics. In 1687, without parliamentary approval, he published a Declaration of Indulgence, granting liberty of conscience and freedom of worship to all his subjects. James also released Catholics from the obligations of the Test Act of 1673. Early in 1688 James again published his Declaration of Indulgence, ordering it to be read in all the churches of England. Seven bishops refused to do so and were tried for sedition. They were acquitted amidst general rejoicing.

The birth of a male child in the home of James meanwhile brought universal fear that Catholicism would be firmly planted on the English throne. On the very day that the seven bishops were acquitted—June 29, 1688—seven leading members of Parliament invited William of Orange, ruler in the Netherlands and a Protestant, son-in-law of James II, to take the throne of England. Partly because William felt that his wife was properly the sovereign of England and partly as a means of circumventing Roman Catholic continental power, William agreed to accept the throne and in November, 1688, with little resistance, invaded England and secured the crown. Parliament regularized his equality on the throne with his wife Mary. Coincident with this, Parliament declared Roman Catholics and those married to Roman Catholics to be forever incapable of wearing the English crown;

all Catholics were deprived of whatever ecclesiastical holdings they might have; and no Catholic was allowed to approach within ten miles of London.

William and Mary (1688–1702) and Anne (1702–14).—One of the first moves of the new sovereigns was to pass the Act of Toleration (1689). This relieved dissenters from most of the persecuting acts of Charles II, although it still left many disabilities to pass away through the influence of public feeling. Catholics and Socinians were still proscribed. Dissenters had few political rights and still were forced to support the Anglican clergy.

Some of the bishops were unwilling to take the oath of allegiance to William and Mary, protesting that the Stuart line (James II) was divinely instituted on the English throne. Nine bishops and other clergy refused to sign the oath and were called the Nonjuring clergy. They fled to Scotland and kept up an independent succession until 1805.

Queen Anne (1702–14) entered into office at a time when Parliament was dealing tolerantly with dissenters, but an event in the fifth year of her reign aroused her ire against dissent. In 1707 Scotland was united with England officially by the admission of fifteen Scots (Presbyterians) into the House of Lords and forty-five into the House of Commons. This, with other acts designed by a tolerant Parliament to conciliate dissenters, led to a violent reaction among the leaders of the established church. In 1709 Henry Sacheverell preached a fiery sermon against toleration. Parliament promptly tried him and punished him for libel. Anglicans were incensed, and through their influence a reactionary Parliament was elected in 1710. Queen Anne favored the repression of dissent, and by 1714 severe laws were prepared against dissenters. Her death ended this movement.

The Hanover line (1714 to end of period).—Through legislation by Parliament, George I (1714–27) was brought from one of the German states as the nearest Protestant relative of Queen Anne. He and his successors, George II (1727–60) and George III (1760–1820), followed the general policy of toleration set out by William and Mary. It was under the last of the three that the

English colony in America protested against taxation without representation and won independence. The Church of England was greatly influenced by the Wesleyan revival during this period, a movement that will be discussed in succeeding pages.

The Roman Catholic Church in England

It will be recalled that Charles I (1625–49) favored Romanism and married a Roman Catholic. His overthrow and execution ushered in a period of stringent persecution for Roman Catholics. Cromwell was tolerant toward most groups but specifically excepted the Roman Catholics from this favor. Charles II (1660–85) was personally favorable to the Roman Catholics but was unable to aid them because of the universal feeling against them in England. He joined the Roman Church on his deathbed. James II (1685–88) vigorously pursued a pro-Roman Catholic policy, which was the cause of his expulsion from the English throne and the declaration that no Roman Catholic should ever wear the English crown. Roman Catholics were excepted from the Act of Toleration of 1689, and their movement was rigorously persecuted. Throughout the entire period Catholicism was also vigorously repressed in Ireland. The rule of the Hanovers brought no relief to the Catholics in England, although prejudice against them was dying out by the time of the French Revolution.

Lutheranism in England

Lutheranism did not gain a foothold in England.

Calvinism in England

Calvinism, appearing in England under the various forms of Presbyterianism, Congregationalism, Independency, or simply Puritanism within the established church, was in control in England at the close of the previous period. A church assembly from Scotland and England, made up principally of Calvinists, was preparing what has become known as the Westminster Confession of Faith, one of the most influential of modern Christian confessions, not only in its relationship to Presbyterians, but in its modification into the basic formulations of Congregationalist and some Baptist confessions of faith as well.

Presbyterian intolerance, however, became insufferable. Their severe laws, developed in the comparatively brief period of parliamentary control, provided the death penalty for errors in doctrine. In 1648 Cromwell purged the Parliament, wresting it from Presbyterian control. Many Presbyterians became pastors of state churches under Cromwell's regime. Like all dissenters from the episcopal establishment, they suffered considerably from the persecuting legislation under Charles II and rejoiced in the coming of toleration in 1689. Unitarianism, however, made large inroads into English Presbyterianism in the eighteenth century.

Presbyterians in Scotland meanwhile were forced to disestablish their church under the restoration policy of Charles II in 1661. The episcopal type of church government used by the Church of England was re-established. Scottish Presbyterians chafed under the whip of persecution. A small group gathered and signed a covenant to continue the fight against episcopacy. From a leader, Richard Cameron, they secured one of their names —the Cameronians. They are also known as the Covenanters and the Reformed Presbyterians. Although comparatively few in number, they were able to survive the vicious persecution that followed. Under William and Mary's Act of Toleration (1689), Presbyterianism was restored to state support.

In the first half of the eighteenth century two struggles took place in Scotland. One was against the inroads of Socinianism and deism, both of which made great gains from Scottish Presbyterianism. The other was against lay patronage. In 1711 Queen Anne restored the principle of lay patronage for Scotland, which permitted influential parishioners to control the appointment of the ministers. Opposing both theological laxity and lay patronage, Ebenezer Erskine (1680–1754) was expelled from the church of Scotland in 1733 and organized the Secession Church. In 1752 Thomas Gillespie was expelled from the state church because of lay patronage and formed in 1761 the Relief Presbytery. These two groups united in the next period.

A very significant movement occurred in Ireland. Even before the stirring events surrounding the seizure of the throne of William and Mary, some Scottish Presbyterians had settled in north Ireland. After the defeat of the Irish in 1691 in the struggle over the accession of William and Mary to the English throne, the English government appropriated a large tract of land in the province of Ulster and invited Scottish Presbyterians to settle there. Thousands came and began a vigorous Presbyterian movement in Ireland. In the first part of the eighteenth century many of these Scotch-Irish Presbyterians were driven to America because of the failure of the potato crop and the raising of rents by English landlords. These Ulster Presbyterians were never an established church and for that reason were much more democratic in spirit than English Presbyterians. From them came some of the outstanding leaders of American Presbyterianism in the early years, principally Francis Makemie.

The Congregational movement in England was greatly aided under Cromwell, who encouraged the calling of a Congregational assembly for the adoption of a confession of faith. The assembly was not convened until after Cromwell's death in 1658. A declaration of faith was adopted, following quite closely the Westminster Confession of Faith of 1648 by the Presbyterians. The Congregationalists suffered with other dissenters during the reigns of Charles II and James II and welcomed toleration under William and Mary.

Other Denominations in English Christianity

Baptists.—English Baptists became vocal during the parliamentary struggles taking place in the fifth decade of the seventeenth century. Their convictions regarding religious liberty had been expressed a generation before in England, and they took the opportunity to urge their point of view. While in England in 1644 Roger Williams published his *Bloody Tenet of Persecution*, detailing the melancholy story of persecution in New England and pleading for liberty of conscience. English Baptists were prominent in the army of Cromwell and at the same time were probably the strongest deterrent to Cromwell's ambition to head a new line of kings in England. Perhaps beguiled by the promise of Charles II that he would allow liberty of conscience, Baptists joined in laboring for the restoration of the Stuart line. With other dissenters they suffered severely in the period between 1662 and 1688.

Strangely enough, after toleration was legislated in 1689, Baptists did not grow rapidly, as would be expected. They seem to have exhausted their strength during the harsh days of persecution. Particular Baptists framed a confession of faith in 1677 on the pattern of the Westminster Confession. A larger assembly adopted this confession in 1689, and it has become the principal English Baptist confession. It was the model for the Philadelphia Confession of Faith adopted in America in the next century. General Baptists were overwhelmed by the Socinian currents in the opening years of the eighteenth century, and many of their churches became Unitarian. Particular Baptists fell under the blight of hyper-Calvinism, hemmed in on every side by what they believed was God's elective limitation.

Quakers.—The Quakers were a product of the mystical experience of George Fox (1624–91). He became opposed to organized Christianity when as a young man he could find no help from the churchmen for a personal problem. Mystical in nature, although trained in Presbyterian background, he had what he felt was an inner revelation from God in 1646. His emphasis upon the inner light, and his defiance of organized Christianity brought much persecution. The movement grew rapidly. The size of his group is illustrated by the fact that in 1661, under the persecuting acts of the Restoration, there were more than 4,200 Quakers in prison. Quaker missionaries went everywhere. In 1681 William Penn founded his colony in America as a haven for the persecuted of his group and others. The central doctrine of the Quakers was the "inner light" from God. Formal worship, singing, the ordinances of baptism and the Supper, ministers and special theological training were rejected—perhaps a reflection of Fox's intense opposition to all that constituted organized Christianity in his day. Pacifism and philanthropy have characterized the Quakers from the beginning, although the movement has lost the radical and condemnatory spirit it first knew.

The Evangelical Revival

One of the most influential movements in the modern period was the evangelical revival of the first half of the eighteenth century. In England it was known as the Wesleyan Revival; in America, the Great Awakening. The Continent, with its Pietistic movement and with historical connections between Augustus G. Spangenberg and John Wesley, deserves some share for the background of the Awakening, although the unwillingness of the Pietists to organize for the perpetuation of their ideals prevented them from the possibility of spreading extensively like the Methodists.

The strong rationalism that brought skepticism in Germany and France, along with the widespread destruction of property and ideals by the Thirty Years' War and its projection, turned the thoughts of men on the Continent away from the things of God. In England this rationalism took the form of deism or naturalism and in its influence upon continental Christianity, particularly in France, was probably more hurtful than a philosophical skepticism. Deism was an effort to minimize special revelation. There is no need for a supernatural revelation, the deists argued; religion is not mysterious and mystical, but the natural expression of man's need for God and virtue. In this sense, all religions of the world have equal worth insofar as they are rational. These ideas were slowly developed from the early skepticism of Lord Herbert of Cherbury (1583–1648) to their more complete description in John Toland (1670–1722) and Matthew Tindal (1653–1733). Along with deism, various other types of philosophical skepticism grew out of English rationalism in the eighteenth century. William Law (1686–1761) and Joseph Butler (1692–1752) were the noteworthy opponents of English deism.

Other elements in English life brought Christianity into general disrepute in the opening years of the eighteenth century.

The low state of morals and indifference to religion by earlier sovereigns (especially the later Stuarts), who were supposed to exemplify some Christian ideals as supreme governors of the Church of England, gradually filtered down to the man on the street. Social unrest and economic stringency were everywhere. The rapid industrialization of England, accelerated by continental events, crammed new and old cities with submerged masses of bewildered and frustrated people. Wealth began to concentrate, abject poverty to spread. Reacting equally against Roman ritualism and mystical enthusiasm, the Church of England became even less than lukewarm. Most of the dissenting groups, racked with rationalism or hyperorthodoxy, had little to say to the needy people. Morals and religion alike were at their lowest ebb.

Into this arid country flowed the refreshing streams of the Wesleyan revival. The leaders were John and Charles Wesley, bred in the parsonage of a High-Church rector, and George Whitefield, son of a saloonkeeper. Both Wesleys spent a brief but important period in missionary service for the Church of England in Georgia. There they came into contact with the Moravian leader Spangenberg, from whom they learned the need for a personal experience of faith in Jesus Christ. Both returned to England and in 1738 professed conversion and regeneration. Whitefield, too, had experienced a rebirth, and the three formed the triumvirate of the new Methodist movement.

Of the three, doubtless Whitefield was the ablest preacher, Charles Wesley was the great hymn writer, while John Wesley was the methodical organizer who gave structure and endurance to the movement. It is noteworthy that Whitefield was a Calvinist, while the two Wesleys were Arminian. As a result, two types of Methodists were developed, although the great majority followed the Wesleyan type. These three Methodist leaders preached and sang throughout all of Britain, Wales, and Scotland, while Whitefield made extensive preaching tours in the American colonies. In some instances these men built upon the foundation others had laid. In Wales a layman, Howel Harris, had begun a Welsh revival two years before the Methodist leaders arrived to kindle fresh fire. In America Whitefield built upon the efforts of Frelinghuysen, the Tennents, and Jonathan Edwards.

The Wesleys did not desire to break with the Church of England and between 1738 and 1784 organized Methodist "societies" like those of the Moravians. The rapid growth of these societies and the acquisition of property required additional organization and supervision. In 1744 the first annual conference of preachers was held in London, and two years later England was divided into circuits for preaching. Finally, in 1784, because of the need for preachers in America, Wesley made a radical departure from his former plan. For the first time Methodist preachers were ordained and given the authority to baptize and celebrate the Supper. In addition, Wesley gave form to the annual conference of preachers and transferred to it much of the authority that he had personally exercised over the movement through the years. In 1784, because of the separation of the American colonies from England, the Methodist Episcopal Church in America was organized.

The results of this evangelical movement both in England and in America were phenomenal. Within the Church of England a whole generation of evangelical-minded leaders profoundly breathed new life into the old Anglican forms—men like James Harvey, William Romaine, Isaac Milner, Charles Simeon, and William Wilberforce. In addition, there sprang forth missionary, Bible, and tract societies and other aids to the spread of the gospel. Many historians believe that the Wesleyan revival so thoroughly regenerated English life that it warded off a catastrophe similar to the French Revolution. A permanent evangelical party arose within the Anglican Church. Later on a new and significant phase of Methodism was the Salvation Army.

Among other English groups the revival had profound effects. Its emphasis upon personal experience validated religion for many in the face of skepticism and rationalism. It renewed the zeal of English Baptists, resulting indirectly in the beginning through them of the modern mission movement. Other denominations were similarly blessed. In America the movement heightened the revival already begun, and the whole is known as the first Great Awakening. Practically every religious movement in America felt the surge of the revival fires. A new church—the Methodists—was founded, and other groups that magnified a crisis experience in conversion, such as the Baptists, benefited greatly.

Concluding Summary

England was ruled as a commonwealth from the death of Charles in 1649 until the restoration of the monarchy in 1660. Oliver Cromwell served as protector from 1653 to 1658. This was a period of comparative religious toleration. However, after the restoration of Charles II in 1660, persecution began against all but the established Church of England (the episcopacy). The "bloodless revolution" of 1688 brought the Protestants William and Mary to the throne, and in the next year an Act of Toleration was enacted. Strangely enough, the end of active persecution in 1689 seemed to bring lethargy to all Christian groups in England. The Wesleyan revival, which began about 1738, profoundly affected all England and beyond.

26

American Christianity

THE PRINCIPAL STORY in the Americas during this period concerns the area now forming the eastern part of the United States. The western area was still a wilderness. Latin America and Canada were being colonized slowly. Because of lack of space, most of the story in the Americas during succeeding periods will be devoted to Christianity in the United States.

Rapid growth characterized the Colonial period in the principal area to be discussed. From less than fifty thousand colonists hugging the Atlantic seaboard in the opening years, the population increased to almost four million by the time the first census was taken in 1790. Able now to provide for their own needs, the colonies began a brisk trade. New England exported grain, livestock, cloth, fish, rum, and lumber products; the Middle Atlantic states shipped rice, tobacco, and lumber products; the South provided rice, indigo, tobacco, lumber products, and cotton.

General Survey of the Period

Political background.—It should be kept in mind that the American settlements of England were simply colonies during the main portion of this period, and each was more directly related to the crown than to corporate life with one another. That they would become an independent nation was a thought that was comparatively late in finding popular support. France and England were strong rivals for control of the North American continent. For a long while it appeared that the French might be victorious. However, the English won the last battle, this time in

Europe. England and France had ranged themselves on opposite sides in a series of conflicts in Europe during the eighteenth century. Particularly in the War of Austrian Succession (1740–48), known as King George's War in America (1744–48), the English colonies in the New World played a significant role. After a valiant expedition from New England captured Louisburg, the strong French fortress on Cape Breton Island, the European treaty between England and France in 1748 returned the fortress to France. Americans resented this move after they had risked so much to capture it.

The Seven Years' War on the Continent—known in the American phase as the French and Indian War (1756–63)—prepared the way for American independence. In it France was forced to surrender her claims in America. This eliminated a possible rival in America for a new nation and provided an important ally against England when war for independence came. In addition, the important part played by the colonials in this war brought to them a feeling of self-consciousness and unity. The unwise policies of King George III brought rebellion in America; the European nations defeated by Britain in the Seven Years' War—France, Spain, and others—combined against Britain to help bring about victory for the Americans by 1783.

Colonization by other Christian groups.—During this period several additional Christian groups emigrated to the new land.

The Quaker movement that began in England in 1647 soon had adherents in the American colonies. They were roughly handled. Massachusetts executed four in 1659, while Virginia and New York enacted rigorous laws against them. Quaker zeal and courage, despite erratic behavior at times, carried the day, however, and they continued as a part of the wonderfully rich and complex religious heritage of America. The haven of the American Quakers became Pennsylvania, founded in 1681 by William Penn, although already in New Jersey the Quakers had developed their characteristic type of worship. Penn had been granted a large tract of land by Charles II of England, and he specifically appealed to those suffering from religious persecution, both in

England and on the Continent, to flee to "Penn's woods" in the New World. Large numbers of dissenters responded, particularly the Quakers, with whom Penn had identified himself.

Mennonites from Germany also sought Penn's colony and settled at Germantown in 1683. This constituted the first organized congregation of the group, although occasional Mennonite emigrants (Dutch, Swiss, and German) had appeared in America almost fifty years before. A substantial number of Mennonites from the several parts of Europe flowed into Pennsylvania during this period.

The Moravians found Pennsylvania a welcome haven. They had first entered Georgia in 1735, but in five years most of them had moved to Pennsylvania. The founder of their movement, Nikolaus Ludwig von Zinzendorf, spent about a year in the colonies in 1741 when exiled from Saxony and visited Moravian settlements in Pennsylvania and in North Carolina.

American Methodism took its start about 1766 from the work of Philip Embury, Barbara Heck, and Captain Thomas Webb in New York, and Robert Strawbridge in Maryland. Growth was slow at first. The first American conference of 1773 reported a few over a thousand members; by 1775 there were about three thousand; and by 1783, about fourteen thousand. It will be remembered that John Wesley desired to keep Methodism within the framework of the Church of England and that Methodist organization was first effected so that none of the prerogatives of the Anglican Church would be assumed. Consequently, in both England and America during the first half century Methodism had no ordained preachers. All baptizing, marrying, communion, and other acts requiring ordination were administered by Church of England priests. American Methodists followed the English pattern for forming local classes of about a dozen members who would meet to pray and worship under the supervision of a class leader. Several of these classes constituted a "society," which subsequently became the local Methodist church. Each of the early American preachers had a circuit of societies which he would visit regularly for preaching. This simple type of organization was both thorough and productive of great zeal and personal enlistment.

Since the Methodist movement was a part of the Church of England prior to the Revolutionary War, it was looked upon by American patriots with considerable suspicion. The situation was not improved when Wesley himself urged his followers to be faithful to the crown. Practically all of his preachers returned to England during the Revolution, the notable exception being Francis Asbury. After the war Wesley was convinced that Methodist preachers must have ordination. He first approached the Church of England with a request that they ordain Methodist preachers for America. When they declined, Wesley, himself a presbyter in the Church of England, ordained Richard Whatcoat and Thomas Vasey as presbyters on September 2, 1784, while Dr. Thomas Coke was ordained as superintendent for America. Francis Asbury, already in America, was to be ordained as joint superintendent with Coke. Upon their arrival, Asbury insisted that he would take office only if elected by the Conference of American Methodist preachers. He was so elected and was ordained. In December, 1784, at Baltimore the Methodist Episcopal Church was organized and continued to grow rapidly during the remainder of the period.

Other less numerous groups settled in America during this period, such as the German River Brethren and the Shakers. At the very close of the period the first Protestant Episcopal church in New England became the first Unitarian church in America.

The first Great Awakening (1726 on).—One of the formative factors in American Christianity was the great revival of the early eighteenth century which swept across the colonies. The roots of this revival seem to have sprung from Europe. The warmhearted evangelistic movement there known as Pietism had prepared the hearts of many of those emigrating to America. Several groups of Germans in Pennsylvania who had come under its influence were among the first to experience revival. By 1726 the preaching of Theodore J. Frelinghuysen, a deeply spiritual minister of the Dutch Reformed Church in New York, became peculiarly effective in winning men to Christ and moving his hearers toward God. He inspired others during the next several years, one of the most important of whom was the Presbyterian minister, Gilbert Tennent, who became a zealous (and not always wise) promoter of the revival.

By 1734, in what seems to have been a separate movement, Jonathan Edwards, Congregationalist pastor of Northampton, Massachusetts, found a deepened spiritual sensitiveness in his congregation and in the whole community, so that (he wrote) the town seemed to be full of the presence of God. A great revival followed. The entire revival movement was characterized by the conversion experience of those seeking God for themselves. It spread rapidly to every part of the colonies. Even John Wesley in England, as yet unturned, learned about it in 1738 and marveled.

Another great name associated with this awakening was that of George Whitefield, colaborer of Wesley in England, who had a conversion experience in 1735 and in 1738 arrived in Georgia to take up the work the Wesleys had left. Returning to England to raise money for his orphanage in Georgia and for ordination in the Church of England, he was delayed because of military operations but spent his time in evangelistic preaching throughout Britain. After the ship embargo was lifted, Whitefield sailed for Philadelphia en route to Georgia. His fame had spread, and multitudes flocked to his ministry. In all of the American colonies he trumpeted the gospel message. Utilizing the fires of religious revival already evident in the work of Frelinghuysen, Tennent, and Edwards, he led the revival movement to its highest point.

The results of the revival were many. They will be seen more particularly in the survey of the important American denominations in this period. In general, the results normally to be expected from a widespread spiritual awakening were present—many conversions, strengthening of churches, ethical gains in the personal lives of the people, and moral and benevolent institutions founded or strengthened. Christian education was advanced. Two rather unexpected results also were important. (1) The great strengthening of the minority groups and the interdenominational character of the spiritual visitation combined to lay the groundwork for religious liberty in the New World. (2) A sense of spiritual unity was engendered among the colonists in America at the very time the political relations with the mother country were being strained to the utmost. The tours of Whitefield from Maine to Georgia tied the colonies together; his converts were found in every colony; his preaching was a common bond that united diverse groups. In their struggle toward the great destiny which they knew not, the colonies were being unified in a most fundamental way.

Skepticism and religious decline.—In some parts of the South the Great Awakening continued almost unabated until the close of this period. In general, however, the Revolutionary War marked the beginning of a rapid religious decline. In addition to the loss of church property and the difficulties confronting the holding of religious services, the war brought the customary callousing of spiritual sensibilities and encouraged moral looseness. Along with these factors, the entire intellectual and theological atmosphere was discolored by the deistic speculations from England, the atheistic assertions of France, and the rationalistic systems of the German thinkers. Many of the outstanding leaders and patriots during the Revolutionary War were infected by such currents. Skeptical and atheistic literature circulated extensively. Even the church-fostered schools became hotbeds for infidelity. Less than 10 per cent of the population were professing Christians just before the close of this period in 1789. A new revival was greatly needed, and it came shortly after the opening of the next period.

The Older Denominations (1648–1789)

The Church of England.—The Church of England had accompanied the English settlements in Virginia (1607) and the Carolinas (after 1665). It was also established in Maryland in 1692, after that colony, founded by the Roman Catholics, was

306

assumed by the English crown following the accession of William and Mary in England. New York was captured by the English from the Dutch in 1664, and in 1693 the Church of England was at least partially established there. The Society for Propagating the Gospel in Foreign Parts (established by the Church of England in 1701) was instrumental in planting missions and churches in New England after 1702.

The progress of the established church in the colonies was slow. It faced many foes. The quality of ministers sent from England was generally low, with notable exceptions. The lack of an American bishop made discipline next to impossible. The increasing number of dissenters and the aversion to ecclesiastical authoritarianism which had driven many to America militated against the popularity of the leaders. In Virginia in 1619—when the Church of England was established—there were only five clergymen, two of whom were deacons. A century later the number had increased only to about two dozen, although there were forty-four parishes in the colony. The constant political and religious turmoil in England during the seventeenth century was bound to bring confusion to the American colonies and neglect of the churches established there.

Although George Whitefield was a member of the Church of England when he came preaching with power in 1739, he was not welcomed by the colonial establishments of the Church of England. For one thing, he was preaching a strongly evangelical gospel, magnifying conversion and denouncing many in the ministry as "unconverted." Furthermore, he had been denied the use of churches in England and had gone to the fields for preaching. In addition, the enthusiasm and emotionalism of the Great Awakening were not to the liking of the orderly and staid episcopal adherents. In fact, Whitefield was called for trial before an episcopal ecclesiastical court in Charleston, South Carolina, and was convicted and suspended from the ministry by Commissary Alexander Garden for irregularities. Whitefield paid scant attention to the proceedings.

The Revolutionary War brought crisis to the Church of England in the colonies. She was a part of the English system and as such was distrusted by many and hated by some. Two thirds of her clergy were loyal to England during the war. In Virginia in particular there was much loss. Only fifteen of ninety-one clergymen could remain at their posts in that state, and much of their property was destroyed. The losses were not so great in Maryland, where out of forty-four parishes, each with a minister before the Revolution, almost two dozen of the clergy remained and the property loss was comparatively small. There was great opposition to the Anglican Church in New England, New York, New Jersey, and Pennsylvania, where organized efforts had been made prior to the Revolution to prevent the appointment of a bishop in America. At the very close of this period, steps were being taken to organize the Protestant Episcopal Church, a new body holding to doctrines of the Church of England but disentangling itself from English control.

Congregationalism.—By 1648 the Congregational churches in Massachusetts and Connecticut had developed a theocratic government. Right of franchise was limited to members of Congregational churches, and no new Congregational churches could be formed without permission from the old. A college (Harvard) was flourishing at Cambridge, Massachusetts, and the clergy was supported from tax funds. Dissenters like Baptists and Quakers were rigorously persecuted.

The work of the Westminster Assembly in England inspired New England Congregationalists to prepare a doctrinal statement, which was adopted at Cambridge, Massachusetts, in 1648. One of the important provisions was the requirement that any person admitted to the Lord's Supper must have made a public profession of faith (even though he had been baptized as a baby) and have given evidence of a Christian experience. Unless the parents of a child fulfilled these conditions, their child could not be baptized. Controversy began immediately. Unless one could relate a conversion experience and pursue an orderly walk, he could not partake of the Supper, he could not have his children baptized, he was disfranchised and disqualified for civil office, he knew the odium of religious ostracism; yet he must give money to support the Congregational ministry and churches. Finally, in 1662 the Half-Way Covenant was enacted, providing that children of moral and baptized persons might also be baptized, even though the parents could not qualify for admission to the Supper. This action increased controversy and practically eliminated any requirements for church membership.

In an effort to regularize and stabilize the practices of the various Congregational churches, a strengthening of external authority in the associations was attempted in Massachusetts, but the movement failed. A similar program in Connecticut, the Saybrook Platform in 1708, was successfully introduced there.

It can be recognized that a movement like the Great Awakening would agitate again the divisive question about a conversion experience. Jonathan Edwards was one of the outstanding figures of the revival. His deep piety, mingled with profound philosophical thought, made him one of the foremost American religious thinkers. His church at Northampton, Massachusetts, was the center of revival in 1734. Not all Congregationalists followed Edwards, however. In churches which did not favor the revival, some minority groups, insisting upon a conversion experience, withdrew and formed "New Light" churches or "Separate" churches. Some of these later adopted immersion and became Baptist churches.

The Congregationalists were strong patriots during the Revolutionary War period. They emerged from the war with considerable prestige because of their noble service for the new nation. Skepticism and infidelity played havoc with many of their churches, however. In addition, the lack of organization beyond the local level hindered larger denominational development and to some extent made it difficult to resist growing Unitarianism that was soon to rob New England Congregationalism of much of its church property. Despite these factors, as well as controversy and schism, the number of Congregationalist churches in New England—to which this denomination was generally confined—increased greatly during this period.

Calvinism.—Those following the teachings of Calvin came to America in various national groups during this period. The Dutch Reformed Church had been begun about 1628 in what became New York, and even after the colony fell to the English in 1664, the small Reformed group of Holland carried on their worship.

Scottish and Scotch-Irish Presbyterians had emigrated quite early to the New World. At the opening of this period, small Presbyterian churches could be found in many of the colonies along the coast. The important name in this early period of Presbyterian life was that of Francis Makemie, who came from Ireland in 1683. By his work American Presbyterianism organized the first presbytery in 1705 at Philadelphia with seven ministers. Eleven years later the first synod was formed, consisting of seventeen churches, three presbyteries, and nineteen ministers. Some French Reformed refugees (Huguenots) fled to America and settled principally in the South during the critical days after the Edict of Nantes was revoked in 1685.

The first German Reformed church was formed in 1719 at Germantown, Pennsylvania. Through the efforts of Michael Schlatter and the Dutch Reformed group, a synod was formed for the German Reformed Church in 1747, consisting of forty-seven congregations and but five ministers.

The Great Awakening brought dissension and schism among the Presbyterians. Gilbert Tennent, a young minister at New Brunswick, New Jersey, influenced by the pietistic spirit of Theodore Frelinghuysen, his neighboring preacher, delivered fiery evangelistic sermons. After 1728 revival occurred among the Presbyterians, and many were converted. In 1741 Tennent and his followers were ejected from the synod for unauthorized and censorious activities, causing an extensive schism which continued until 1758. Meanwhile, in 1745 the New York Synod established a college, which was to become Princeton University.

After internal peace was restored, Presbyterian growth, principally from immigration, was rapid until the Revolution. Almost without exception the Presbyterians were patriots and supported American independence. They aided greatly in the successful

struggle in Virginia for separation of church and state and religious liberty.

Lutheranism.—It has been seen that Lutheranism was first
planted in what became New York. While this colony was under
Dutch rule (1623–64), persecution of Lutheranism was carried
on, but after 1664 the English permitted relative liberty. The
Swedish Lutherans who settled in Delaware faced difficulties as
their colony was seized by the Dutch in 1655 and ceded to England in 1664, but a measure of religious liberty was permitted
under the rule of each. Lutheran growth was accelerated with the
coming of the Germans in the opening years of the eighteenth
century. William Penn had visited the war-torn and suffering
Germanic areas in 1681 and invited them to emigrate to his colony in America. The response came principally after 1708, and
large numbers of German Lutherans settled in New York, Pennsylvania, and the Carolinas. In 1734 many Lutherans from the
province of Salzburg in Austria, driven out by rigorous Roman
Catholic persecution, settled near Savannah, Georgia. The first
Lutheran synod was formed in 1735 in New Jersey, representing
sixteen congregations.

The patriarch of Lutheranism in America was Henry Melchior Mühlenberg, who was sent from Germany in 1742 to aid
the struggling American Lutheran churches. His wise and capable
leadership united and organized the early American Lutheran
movement.

The Great Awakening did not greatly affect American Lutherans. The Germans were somewhat responsive. Their rallying
around Mühlenberg and their active zeal probably stemmed in
part from the revival. The Swedish Lutherans, on the other hand,
did not enter into the movement. Lutherans almost to the man
supported the American Revolution, furnishing outstanding leadership and support. The two sons of H. M. Mühlenberg, Peter G.
and Frederick A. C., became eminent military and political leaders. Like all other denominations, the Lutherans suffered from
the loss of manpower and interest during the Revolutionary War,
but after its cessation rapidly recovered.

The Roman Catholic Church.—By 1648 the Roman Catholic Church had moved into America through the work of English, French, and Spanish immigrants. The English colony in Maryland in 1634 has already been described. French missionaries and explorers continued the work of Jacques Cartier (1534) and Samuel de Champlain (1613). La Salle (1676), Marquette and Joliet (1673), and many other lesser figures established missions and forts in the northern and central sections of the nation. The vast mission program of French Catholics, begun and continued under severe difficulties, was abandoned when defeat in the Seven Years' War (1756–63) brought cession of French claims in America. Spanish missionaries and monks were very active also in this period.

The Spanish missionary work in Florida in its early history was accompanied by coercion and the sword. By 1634 there were forty-four missions with thirty-five priests under the Bishop of Havana. In 1701, during the War of Spanish Succession, the English in the Carolinas and Georgia attacked Spanish Florida and burned St. Augustine in 1702. At the close of the war Florida was given to England, ending Spanish missions there.

Spanish priests striking northward from Mexico planted missions in New Mexico about 1598. By the opening of this period about sixty Franciscan monks were serving in this area. Internal bickering over authority, raids from wild Indians, and the recurrence of what a Roman Catholic author calls "cryptopaganism"—the reverting of the Indians to ancient pagan worship despite a claim of being Christian—brought problems. In 1680 the Pueblo Indians revolted and drove the Spanish from New Mexico for twelve years. Between 1692 and 1700 the area was reconquered, and missionaries were restored by force of arms, although the two principal tribes (the Moqui and the Zuni) refused to allow Catholic missionaries among them. At the close of the period the work was termed unsuccessful, partly because the missionaries refused to learn the language of the people.

A Spanish Jesuit monk toured Arizona about 1687, and in 1732 others arrived to begin missions in what is now Arizona. Jealousy between them and the Franciscans brought rivalry and strife, hindering effective results.

A Spanish missionary expedition was sent into Texas in 1689, and in 1716 work was begun; but Catholic historians call the work a failure, partly due to the large number of different tribes and dialects in the area.

Lower California had been explored and mission stations established in the late sixteenth century. Upper California had no mission work until 1769 when, doubtless to forestall the Russian advances down the coast, a Mexican military and missionary expedition entered that area. Junípero Serra led in the hard and perilous work of establishing Roman Catholic missions here. At the close of the period there were perhaps a dozen missions operating, although friction between the missionaries and the Mexican military leaders hindered the effectiveness of the work.

The Catholic colony in Maryland suffered from the political revolution in England in 1688. The overthrow of James II was the signal for the Protestants in Maryland to seize the government, and the Church of England was established under a new charter with Maryland as a royal colony (not proprietary) in 1692.

As might be expected, the Roman Catholic Church felt none of the impulses toward revival during the Great Awakening beginning about 1739. American Catholics played an honorable part in the Revolutionary War, although they were still comparatively few in number. At the close of this period it is estimated that there were approximately twenty thousand Catholics in the former English colonies of America.

It should be mentioned that Spain and Portugal had for a century been sending military forces and missionaries to almost every part of South America. Missions were established in the West Indies and Mexico, as well as Brazil, Peru, Chile, and Argentina. In this period the Roman Catholic missionaries touched almost all of Central and South America.

Baptists.—The handful of Baptists that organized Providence Plantations as a colony in 1638 increased slowly in this period. Congregations were formed throughout New England, the middle states, and the South before 1700. In 1707 Baptists around Philadelphia formed the first association in America—the Philadelphia Association. It stood alone until 1751, when the second was organized in South Carolina. Thereafter the growth of associations of Baptist churches was rapid.

Before the Great Awakening Baptist progress was slow. There were fewer than fifty Baptist churches in all America after one hundred years (by 1739). The Great Awakening multiplied American Baptists. At first New England Baptists were reluctant to have any part in the revival, partly because those engaged in it were their persecutors and partly because of the Arminian reaction against a movement among the Calvinists. However, the conversion to Baptist views of Isaac Backus, a Congregationalist New Light, began a movement that brought many New Lights into Baptist life. Between the revival and the Revolution, Baptist churches in New England increased from twenty-one to seventy-eight.

The middle and Southern colonies also felt the impact of the Great Awakening. Shubael Stearns and Daniel Marshall, converted under the preaching of George Whitefield, became Baptists and, aided by men like Colonel Samuel Harris, Elijah and Lewis Craig, and many others, led in the formation of new Baptist churches throughout Virginia, the Carolinas, and Georgia. Whereas there were only seven Baptist churches in the South before the Great Awakening, by the close of the Revolution Virginia had 151 churches, in addition to supplying Baptists for over forty churches in Kentucky; North Carolina had forty-two Baptist churches; South Carolina had twenty-seven; and Georgia, where Baptist work had begun in 1772, had six churches.

In addition, Baptists had a principal part in the struggle for religious liberty in Virginia and had established Brown University in Rhode Island in 1765 for the education of the ministry.

Baptists took a prominent part in the Revolution, several rising to important places in the chaplaincy and in the army. Hezekiah Smith, John Gano, and others were outstanding in New England and the middle colonies; in the South Richard Furman had a price

314

put on his head by the British as one of the outstanding patriots. At the close of the period Baptists were active and growing.

Concluding Summary

During most of this period France and England were rivals for control of the vast North American continent. England emerged victorious in 1763, but the American colonies won their independence in twenty years. A steady flow of immigrants came from England and the Continent. Their religious background had an important bearing on Christianity in the new nation. The First Great Awakening, beginning after 1726, profoundly influenced both religious and political life in the American colonies. The Revolution brought a rapid religious decline, accelerated by skeptical and rationalistic currents from England and the Continent. At the close of the period, Christianity in the United States was at a low ebb, and its prospects were dark.

BIBLIOGRAPHY

BETTENSON, HENRY (ed.). *Documents of the Christian Church.* New York: Oxford University Press, 1947.

GARRISON, W. E. *The March of Faith.* New York: Harper & Brothers, 1933.

LATOURETTE, K. S. *A History of Christianity.* New York: Harper & Brothers, 1953.

NEWMAN, A. H. *A Manual of Church History,* I. Philadelphia: American Baptist Publication Society, 1953.

NICHOLS, JAMES H. *History of Christianity 1650–1950.* New York: Ronald Press Co., 1956.

ROBINSON, JAMES HARVEY. *Readings in European History,* II. Boston: Ginn & Co., 1904.

SWEET, WILLIAM W. *The Story of Religion in America.* New York: Harper & Brothers, 1950.

VI. PERIOD OF GENERAL
SECULARIZATION (A.D. 1789 to present)

Introduction to the Period

This has been a period of revolution. The American nation was organized under a constitution in the opening year of this period, after throwing off the political yoke of England. France entered into her revolution at the very beginning of this period, also. The Congress of Vienna (1815) endeavored to restore traditional boundaries, but revolution had not yet ceased. New nations developed both in Europe and in the Americas.

There were revolutions in other areas also. Mechanical and industrial developments created a new sort of economic and social life. Scientific advance in the twentieth century has made almost every decade a startling and challenging era.

The modern mission movement helped to inaugurate this period. Its impact in the widespread enrichment of life and general humanitarianism can never be fully computed. Many extensive humanitarian movements in England and America sprang directly from missions and the revivals of religion of this period.

This has also been a period of extensive secularization of culture. By that is meant, as one writer expresses it, the development of the "religiously neutral civilization." This situation is not altogether good or completely bad, but is essentially true. To some extent this accounts for the extensive spread of denominational Christianity. The divorcing of church and state (one aspect of this secularization) has resulted in religion by conviction rather than by coercion. The second reformation in England during the first half of the seventeenth century developed numerous types of polity and doctrine. These were transplanted to America by immigration. The older movements on the Continent also moved toward America, but the tendency has been toward diversity in organization, even in those groups following a single system of theological thought. Calvinism, for example, was organized in America piecemeal by different groups. Scottish Calvinists not only did not join Calvinists from other nations but reproduced in America many other schisms which had taken place in Scotland. English, French, Dutch,

Swiss, German, and Scandinavian Calvinists retained their own separate types of organization, reflecting racial and language distinctions when they moved to America. As a result, the Christianity in colonial America was amazingly complex and has continued to develop new forms in the centuries that have followed. Doubtless a reaction against undue proliferation gave impetus toward the ecumenical and church union movements which came into considerable strength in the first half of the twentieth century.

In religious thought, this period has witnessed the high mark of rationalism, followed by a reaction in an attempt to retain elements of the older supernaturalism. There have been vigorous and numerous attacks on traditional supernaturalism during the first half of the twentieth century. The ultimate effect of the accelerated attacks must await description by a later pen.

Points of Special Interest

The student should notice the recurring cycles in religious thought. Generally the pendulum swings to one extreme, depending a great deal upon historical conditioning, and then away from it. Extreme views are basically self-destructive. This fact brings some comfort in periods of uninhibited speculation and corruption.

A related observation concerns the nature of man. As a self-conscious and spiritual being, man will never be satisfied with any religious system that appeals only to his intellect. Sterile scholasticism has no more vitality in the twentieth century than it had in the second. Ofttimes it will bring spiritual reaction and revival.

The secularization of culture and politics, which has occurred not only in the West but almost universally, is not an unmixed evil. A "neutral" state and culture will remove elements of harmful influence on Christianity, eliminate Christianity as a tool of low motivations, and minimize religious coercion. It should emphasize the spiritual nature and independent worth of true Christianity.

317

27

Continental European Christianity

A FULL DESCRIPTION of any aspect of this last period is manifestly impossible. Progress in technological development can hardly be believed or understood, not to speak of trying to describe it. Iron, steel, aluminum, and plastics successively brought great thrusts in the manufacture of basic commodities. Coal, steam (on both land and sea), electricity, petroleum, and atomic fission have provided power for transportation, communication, illumination, warfare, and many other uses. The industrial revolution mobilized and exploited these resources. Astounding research has been made in all the sciences from anthropology to zoology. The body, the mind, and the soul have been made the subject of intense study. Every part of man and his world has come under observation.

Strong intellectual currents have accompanied this physical progress. Charles Darwin (1809–82), after first making basic assumptions in an effort to explain change and progress in human history, developed a theory of evolution based on the survival of the fittest. The projection of this theory into the areas of religion and philosophy brought considerable controversy, which has not yet ended. Karl Marx (1818–83) propounded the belief in the necessity of the ultimate victory of a "scientific socialism"—the elimination of all economic classes and the final millennium of an equalitarian society. His communistic ideas are still being tested on a large scale. Representing just a cloud on the horizon at that time, Hegel (1770–1831) idealized the state and Nietzsche (1844–

1900) the "super race," laying the foundations for the twentieth-century totalitarian movements.

The political atmosphere of the world is reflected in the history of Christianity in Europe during this period. In general, it has been a period when national states have fought for their autonomy and demanded self-expression. The German empire was founded in 1870; Italy was unified and France became a republic in the same year; China, Japan, and the Orient were opened to Western culture; South American colonies became independent republics; and all across southeastern Europe new independent states sprang up. Popular government has almost universally dethroned hereditary sovereigns. Almost all the world has been explored, and improved communication and transportation have made it much smaller.

The principal Christian groups on the Continent in this period were the Roman Catholics, the Lutherans, and the Calvinists. These will be viewed briefly during the three chronological sections into which this period falls.

The French Revolution (1789–1815)

The history of Europe is bound up with the French Revolution during the first portion of this period. In the eighteenth century there came an increasing recognition by the common people across Europe that absolutism and oppression in state and church were largely responsible for their depressed economic and social condition. The corruption and luxury in high places in church and state contrasted greatly with the want and suffering of the lower classes.

This was particularly true in France. The Roman Church owned half the land of France and were as reprehensible as the secular state in their dealings with the people. There was general resentment against the various tithes imposed by the Church, against the rigorous repression of religious dissenters, and against the nonproductive monkish orders. The arbitrary national policies and the lavish personal habits of Kings Louis XIV, XV, and XVI (from 1643 to 1793) brought France to the verge of bankruptcy.

In order to levy additional taxes, the king was forced to call a meeting of the Estates General, a congress made up of the clergy, the nobility, and the commons. The representatives of the common people, known as the Third Estate, seized control and by their audacity and accurate representation of the temper of the times were successful in beginning a radical reform. On September 21, 1792, France was made a Republic, and four months later the king was executed.

In a reaction against the intense opposition of the Roman Church, the new republic was erected on atheistic lines at first but gradually relaxed to permit religious worship. Napoleon Bonaparte, a French general, was victorious in defeating a coalition of other powers attempting to put down the French Revolution. In 1798 Napoleon invaded Italy and dissolved the papal state, imprisoning Pope Pius VI in Paris, where he soon died. Napoleon was crowned emperor in 1804. His victories and diplomacy changed the map of Europe. However, he was finally defeated by a coalition of powers and exiled to St. Helena Island in 1815. The Congress of Vienna (1815) endeavored to restore the world which Napoleon had disarranged. It began a period of reactionary conservatism politically and romanticism in literature and religion.

The Roman Catholic Church.—In France itself the Revolution stripped the Roman church of her property, her establishment, her tithes and papal assessments, and her monastic system. The reorganization of religious life in France in 1790 by the National Assembly in effect ignored religious differences. In the Reign of Terror of the following two years, hundreds, perhaps thousands, of faithful Roman Catholic priests were slaughtered. In the reaction after 1795, however, Catholics and others were allowed privileges of worship. In 1795 Pope Pius VI joined with European leaders to put an army in the field against France. Napoleon Bonaparte defeated the coalition, captured Rome in 1798, and imprisoned the pope in France, where he died in 1799.

In 1801 the new pope, Pius VII (1800–20), secured an agreement with Napoleon to restore the Roman Church in France under radical limitations, but Napoleon abrogated most of this by his arbitrary interpretation. In 1809 he annexed the papal state to France. When the pope protested, imprisonment followed. In 1813 he coerced the pope into signing an agreement to allow annexation, but with his Russian debacle Napoleon lost his power to coerce. The pope repudiated his signature and in 1814 restored the Jesuit order. Although the suppression of this order in 1773 had theoretically meant total abolishment, it was found to be completely organized and at almost full strength to take up the battle. Cardinal Consalvi represented the papacy at the Congress of Vienna in 1815 and was able to secure the return of all that Napoleon had taken from the Roman Church.

Lutheranism.—The French Revolution greatly affected Lutherans in the German states. War and suffering revealed that skepticism and infidelity were not sufficient to meet the needs of the human spirit, and multitudes turned again to religious faith. The old Holy Roman Empire was dissolved in 1806, stimulating the strengthening of independent states like Austria, Prussia, and Bavaria. Later in the century this contributed to the unification of the German people under the leadership of Prussia.

Calvinism.—Calvinism in Europe also felt the shock of the French Revolution. Already skepticism had weakened this group in France, Switzerland, the German states, and the Low Countries. The unsettled political conditions that continued through the Congress of Vienna in 1815 brought disorganization and uncertainty to continental Calvinism.

Reaction and Continued Conflict (1815–70)

For a decade after the Congress of Vienna the reaction against revolution and democratic movements was apparent in the diplomacy and activity of the great powers. National feelings, however, could not long be suppressed. Twice more France set off explosive nationalistic movements in 1830 and 1848 in her search for a responsive and stable government. Holland (1815), Belgium (1830), and Greece (1832) established autonomous governments, and others began their journey toward statehood.

321

The German states provided the key to the momentous events in the latter part of this period. The Congress of Vienna had aided in the formation of a German union (*Bund*) composed of thirty-five states, and later a North German union headed by Prussia was organized. In 1870 Prussia declared war on France, and victory brought the organization of the modern German nation. Curiously enough, during the Franco-Prussian War, the French government took the step that led to the founding of a unified Italian state. French soldiers had been employed by the papal court to protect the papal state. When Paris was being threatened in 1870, France ordered these troops home, and the Italian patriots were able to overcome Rome and unify the several sections of the peninsula.

The Roman Catholic Church.—The reaction against the excesses of the French Revolution brought great prestige to the Roman Catholic Church as a conservative and stabilizing factor. Leo XII (1821–29) was able to negotiate favorable concordats, or agreements, with most of the important nations, including Protestant states. Catholics were given complete freedom in England in the year of Leo's death, and during the entire period accessions to the Roman church from the Church of England took place.

Another characteristic of this period was the continuance of anti-Protestant outbursts from the papacy. In 1816 Pius VII denounced Bible societies as fiendish instruments to undermine religion. In May, 1824, Leo XII published similar views and called their translations the "devil's gospel." In 1826 he announced that "everyone separated from the Roman Catholic Church, however unblamable in other respects his life may be, because of this sole offense, that he is sundered from the unity of Christ, has no part in eternal life; God's wrath hangs over him." Pius VIII (1829–30) also included liberty of conscience and Bible societies among other evils. Gregory XVI (1831–46) termed religious liberty as craziness or insanity. These utterances formed the background for the sweeping "Syllabus of Errors" of Pius IX, which will be considered shortly.

In this period, also, the movement known as "ultramontanism" reached its height. The word is a geographical reference to papal domination. The restoration of the Jesuits in 1814 was a large step in that direction. The conservative reaction after the Congress of Vienna favored it also. The movement came to its height during the pontificate of Pius IX (1846–78). Singularly enough, his doctrinal victories within the Roman Church and his political defeats from the outside paired up to exalt him and the papacy to heights heretofore unattainable. His strategy in his doctrinal victory was carefully planned and well executed. Pius became pope in 1846 during a very stormy political period. In 1849, taking advantage of the widespread Catholic veneration (and in some cases actual worship) of Mary, the mother of Jesus, Pius sent communications to all Roman Catholic bishops asking them if they desired the pope to set out an authoritative pronouncement with reference to Mary, showing his own opinions by saying, "Ye know full well, venerable brethren, that the whole ground of our confidence is placed in the most holy Virgin . . . God has vested in her the plenitude of all good, so that henceforth, if there be in us any hope, if there be any grace, if there be any salvation, we must receive it solely from her, according to the will of him who would have us possess all things through Mary."

After receiving the approval of the vast majority of the bishops, on December 8, 1854, Pius defined the official dogma. It will be recalled that a canon is a church law that may be changed subsequently if circumstances warrant, but a dogma is an official declaration of truth which cannot be changed or altered and which must be believed by all the faithful as a condition of salvation. This was the first time that a dogma had been promulgated by a pope without the authority of general council. Pius claimed that this dogma was revealed by God and must be believed firmly and constantly by all the faithful. It asserted "that the most blessed Virgin Mary, in the first instant of her conception, by a singular grace and privilege of Almighty God, by the intuitive perception of the human race, was kept immune from any contamination of original sin." Mariolatry was thus brought officially one step further. The Roman tradition had successively declared her a perpetual virgin, then freed her from sin after Christ's conception, then extended that freedom from sin to her own birth, and this dogma declared her without hereditary sin. It remained for the twentieth century to proclaim her bodily assumption to heaven at death.

In 1864 Pius IX issued his "Syllabus of Errors," which summed up encyclicals of immediately previous popes and brought the list up-to-date. In addition to condemning Bible societies, public schools, and freedom of conscience, he specifically denounced separation of church and state, insisted that the Roman pontiffs and ecumenical councils have never erred in defining faith and morals, and claimed the right to use force in carrying out papal policies. The succeeding pope (Leo XIII) declared that this syllabus denouncing these so-called errors was issued under conditions of infallibility.

In 1870 what may have been the last of the ecumenical councils of the Roman Catholic Church was held. Practically every detail was arranged by Pius IX before the council convened. Despite vigorous protests by a respectable minority of bishops who refused to be coerced, the council passed four decrees. The first asserted that Simon Peter was made by Christ to be the visible head of the Church, both in honor and jurisdiction. The second identified the Roman bishop as perpetual successor of Peter, endowed with all Peter's privileges. The third claimed that the Roman pontiff has immediate and full power over all the Church throughout the world. The last one asserted that when the pope speaks ex cathedra (from the throne) in defining a doctrine concerning faith and morals to be held by the universal church, he is infallible. The statement closed with the assertion that any such definition of the pope (without a council) is irreformable.

The strategy that had occupied the thinking of Pius IX for many years had been accomplished. By shrewd diplomacy he had declared a popular teaching to have dogmatic force, without the concurrence of an ecumenical council. It prepared the way for continuing papal domination. This infallibility declaration of 1870 rendered other ecumenical councils useless. All ex-cathedra definitions of faith and morals by the Roman pope now have the force of dogmas. The statement of this infallibility is quite ambiguous, which exactly suited the purpose of the Jesuit proponents of the action. When the succeeding "infallible" pope, Leo XIII, declared the "Syllabus of Errors" of 1864 to be ex-cathedra, however, he may have placed the Roman Church in such a position that there will be continual embarrassment, particularly to American Catholics who claim to accept the doctrine of separation of church and state and some who give lip service to liberty of conscience—basic American ideals.

All of this doctrinal development occurred during a period of political revolution. The papal state had separated the northern and southern sections of the Italian peninsula for over a thousand years. Italian patriots like Victor Emmanuel and Garibaldi fervently desired to unify the entire peninsula and make Rome the secular capital of the unified nation. The papacy vigorously resisted. However, popular revolution in the peninsula had already broken out when Pius IX came to the papal throne. In an effort to placate the people, Pius granted some reforms in the papal government, but nothing less than full surrender would satisfy the patriots in the south. Between 1859 and 1866, through diplomacy and war, Victor Emmanuel was able to secure four-fifths of the papal lands, leaving only Rome and its environs in papal hands. When France was forced to withdraw her troops from Rome to defend Paris, Emmanuel overcame the remaining resistance and captured Rome, making it the national capital of a united Italy.

The Italian patriots tried to placate Pius, but he was never reconciled to the loss of temporal administration and refused to leave the Vatican which, although a defeated combatant, he was permitted to retain. He plotted for the return of the papal state until his death in 1878. Succeeding popes maintained the pretense of being a prisoner in the Vatican until 1929.

In spite of the personal humiliation in this temporal loss, the papacy was greatly forwarded by it. Many friends of true religion had urged the papacy for five hundred years to get out of temporal competition with other nations in the interest of spiritual influence and well-being. Gifts now began to pour into the coffers of the pontiff, all the machinery of the Curia was turned toward ecclesiastical advancement rather than secular administration, and relations with the various national states were greatly improved in view of the diminishing secular power of an ambitious and coercive papacy.

One interesting result of the papal declaration of infallibility was the secession from the Roman Church of a large party who denied papal infallibility, including some very able scholars. The group took the name of the Old Catholic Church and reached a membership of perhaps a hundred thousand, but it has gradually decreased in size and has never gained the popular following that many supposed it would.

Lutheranism.—The history of European Lutheranism during the heart of the nineteenth century concerns principally the movement toward church union and philosophical developments.

The desire for unity by King Frederick William III of Prussia after the desolation caused by the French Revolution led him to listen sympathetically to suggestions by Schleiermacher and other leading clergymen that some sort of church union be attempted. Union of Lutherans and Calvinists in Prussia was decreed in 1817 and met with approval of the large majority of the Prussians. By 1827 many of the German states had followed this example. The University of Wittenberg and Halle united in one institution at Halle. A vocal minority protested against this general drift, particularly among the Lutherans. Klaus Harms led what was known as the Confessional School in opposition to union with the Reformed Church, and in 1841 a number of Lutherans seceded from the state church and organized the Evangelical Lutheran Church of Prussia. Lutheranism in other parts of Europe, particularly in the Scandinavian countries, continued to be infected with rationalism.

It will be recalled that rationalism had brought skepticism and atheism to the forefront during the last period in European Christianity (from 1648 to 1789). Immanuel Kant (1724–1804), although a product of the Illumination (as rationalism was called),

326

modified the crass intellectualism of Wolff by limiting the area of philosophical data to phenomena and by conceiving of man as more than a mind. Hegel (1770–1831) turned in other directions but, essentially, by his philosophical optimism and theory of development gave great impetus to a mediating position. F. E. D. Schleiermacher (1768–1834), early profoundly affected by German pietism, took a large step toward healing antagonism between rationalism and supernaturalism by making religion an inner experience—the consciousness of absolute dependence upon God. His system left much to be desired for those who believed in the objective reality of a personal, loving God but gave a certain respectability to the general tenets of Christianity. Soren Kierkegaard (1813–55), the "melancholy Dane," laid the foundations for a new theological formulation during this period, but he was not discovered for another century.

Calvinism.—The dire effects of rationalism are seen in the struggles of this period by the churches following the teachings of Calvin. In Geneva itself, the birthplace of Calvinism, the "venerable company" of the clergy refused to ordain candidates in 1817 if they believed the very things which Calvin emphasized—the deity of Christ, original sin, and predestination. The result was a schism, the conservatives organizing free and independent congregations. This movement spread throughout the remainder of Switzerland and beyond during the rest of this period. The leaders of this conservative movement in the Swiss cantons were Alexandre Vinet (1797–1847) and Frederic Godet (1812–1900).

French Calvinists had the same experience. Theological liberalism so prevailed in the French Reformed Church that the French Reformed Free Church was organized in 1849 by Frederic Monrod and Count Gasparin.

In the Netherlands a similar story may be told. Before 1834 nearly all the Reformed churches were included in the established church. Liberalism and religious skepticism reigned. Izaak da Costa (1798–1860), a convert from Judaism, became an evangel of orthodox Calvinism. From 1834 on, large numbers of churches left the established Reformed Church and joined with the con-

327

servative congregations, which were finally recognized in 1869 as the Christian Reformed Church. Many conservative Calvinists remained within the older establishment with the hope of leading it back. However, after half a century of struggle, these also separated from the established church and later united with the Christian Reformed group. Another party growing out of the rationalism of this period was known as the Groningen school, which placed emphasis upon love as central in religion. They were indifferent to orthodox Calvinistic doctrines.

The New Century (1870 to the present)

This final period has been marked by the rapid rise of Germany and Russia to the forefront as world powers. World War I (1914–18) grew directly from closely woven military alliances designed to maintain the balance of power. Hotheaded nationalism, ancient hatreds and rivalries, armament races, and irresponsible impulses completed the explosive picture in 1914. The spark came in a Balkan incident, and war began in the summer of 1914. Germany and her allies were finally defeated. After the war Germany became a republic for a decade. The manifest inequities of the peace treaty and the hard economic depression of the early 1930's encouraged the rise of Adolf Hitler and the national socialistic party in Germany. World War II began in September, 1939. The German coalition was defeated in 1945. The use of atomic bombs late in the war marked the beginning of a new era.

The Roman Catholic Church.—Despite the fact that World War I seriously crippled the strongest Roman Catholic continental powers, that church fared amazingly well in the conflict and appeared to be stronger in some respects after the war than before. The rise of the Nazi party under Hitler in 1933 marked the beginning of repression of the Catholics in Germany, which continued until the end of this period. At the same time, the threat of Russian communism came clearly into focus. At the very close of this period Russia enveloped many of the small Slavic border nations into her sphere of influence, in each case repressing the Roman Church in favor of the Eastern Orthodox Church.

Internally, the activity of the Roman Church may be summarized under three heads—struggle with modernism, strictures against Protestantism, and relations with secular states.

Leo XIII (1878–1903) succeeded Pius IX and was one of the ablest popes in this period. Although he is sometimes termed the "modern pope" because he displayed an interest in classical and scientific studies and permitted liberal clergymen to lead in social reform, a careful examination of his life and work shows that he continued the medieval dogmatism of his predecessors. In 1897 he set forth an encyclical censoring all books condemned before 1600, even though they might not have been included in later lists of prohibited books. Leo permitted only biblical and scientific studies that did not impugn the dogma of the Catholic Church.

Pius X (1903–14) was probably elected as a reaction to Leo. He had little appreciation of scholarship and higher education. Much of the work of Leo was virtually destroyed because of the personal and cultural hostility of Pius X. In 1907 he issued a new syllabus condemning modernism. His encyclical in the same year vigorously attacked modernism within the Roman Church. Pius advocated a return to scholastic philosophy and demanded the rejection of all who desired to study canon law except those with scholastic background. Any taint of modernism was sufficient for the rejection of a teacher in Catholic seminaries or universities and the expulsion of those already in these institutions. Bishops must attempt to prevent the publication of modernistic books and to eliminate them from the schools. All meetings of priests must be checked to see that modernism had no place. Benedict XV (1914–22) continued the fight against modernism, as have Pius XI (1922–39) and Pius XII (1939–1958).

This has been a period of continued attacks by the papacy against Protestantism. Leo XIII went out of his way to approve the Spanish Inquisition of the Medieval age, calling the flames "blessed." He praised the infamous Torquemada, the vicious leader of the Spanish Inquisition, for his "most prudent zeal and invincible virtue." In 1896 Leo denounced Anglican ordination and succession, condemning both the form and the intention. He set forth the typical Roman point of view relative to religious toleration, which asserts that when Protestants are in control of a nation, Catholics are to be tolerated according to the Protestants' general policy of religious toleration; on the other hand, when Catholics are in control, the Catholic policy of no toleration is to be followed. Pius X disapproved vigorously all Bible reading and study. His attack in 1910 on the Reformers and their followers as "enemies of the cause of Christ" aroused considerable antagonism. Benedict XV continued the papal fight against Protestantism.

Pope Leo XIII was quite successful in establishing friendly relations with some of the states. Through tactful diplomacy and laborious efforts by the Jesuits, the papacy made friends of Belgium, Spain, France, England, Russia, and the United States. His successors were not so fortunate. Under Pius X and Benedict XV severe blows were struck at Rome. In 1905 France enacted legislation separating church and state. Church property was confiscated, and all financial aid to religion was withdrawn. Revolutions in Portugal and Mexico further reduced the prestige of the pope. The blow was particularly radical in the Republic of Mexico. Their new constitution of 1917 separated church and state and confiscated church property. All Roman Catholic officials and priests were driven into exile.

It had been hoped that the Concordat of 1929 between Pius XI and the Italian government would bring peaceful relations between the parties. It will be recalled that in 1870 the Italian patriots seized Rome, the last of the papal territories outside of the few acres constituting the Vatican. Thereafter the popes refused to leave this area, calling themselves prisoners. In 1929 Mussolini agreed to pay the papacy an indemnity of $87,500,000, added a few acres to Vatican grounds, and recognized Vatican City as a free state. However, the bitterest controversy was carried on subsequently because each side was unwilling to keep the agreement. In 1946 the monarchy was overturned and a republican government was adopted. Theoretically, the Roman Church was no more favored than any other religious group, but in practice the Catholic background of the people gave the **Roman Church a** favorite place.

In Spain in 1931 a republic also replaced the monarchy, and the constitution provided for separation of church and state, giving hope that religious equality for all groups would be practiced. Civil war began in 1936, and in 1939 pro-Catholic General Franco became dictator. The Roman Catholic Church again became dominant as the established religion.

In France the Roman Catholic Church, the only religion of a large majority of the state, is ignored by most of its adherents and has little vitality.

Between the two wars, the Roman Church fought valiantly with the Nazis without much success.

Lutheranism.—Lutheranism in Europe has undergone severe trials in this period. Luther's reform was planted in an environment of farmers and peasants and had looked to the benevolent prince of a comparatively small state to maintain the purity and well-being of the Lutheran Church in his area. After 1870 radical changes came. The late unification of Germany into a single nation required considerable readjustment at the point of Lutheran organization and control. The rapid industrialization of Germany and the mechanical revolution also thrust upon European Lutheranism new social and economic patterns that demanded rapid, radical response. At the very time of this challenge militarism and war paralyzed or drafted Lutheran leadership. The Weimar Constitution adopted by the German Republic after World War I provided for separation of church and state, further adding to the woes of traditional Lutheranism. The vitality of Luther's movement slowly diminished in the first decades of the new century. It has been estimated that 75 per cent of the nominal Christians in Germany in the early twenties were indifferent to religion.

The rise of the Nazis in 1933 brought additional problems. Hitler's efforts to control both Lutheran and Reformed churches for the benefit of the state brought schism and conflict. Attempts were made to paganize Christianity in order to magnify racial and national factors. Hitler himself was willing to see a national church organized by a group called the Faith Movement of German Christians, but the opposition of men like Martin Niemöller, Berlin pastor, offered stiff resistance. A Confessional Synod opposing this Faith Movement was organized and included both Lutherans and Calvinists. World War II drastically curtailed all Christian work. In the Scandinavian countries Lutheranism has maintained itself as the religion of the majority.

Calvinism.—The turbulent years of two wars and an almost continuous ideological tussle in Europe added to the bitter modernist-confessional struggle within European Calvinism and sapped the vitality of the Reformed Churches on the Continent. It is true that Calvinism was better prepared by its general outlook to meet the industrial and mechanical revolutions of the new day than was Lutheranism. The disestablishment of the Roman Church in France in 1905 also aided Calvinism in its struggle. The same blows that shocked Lutheranism fell upon Calvinism. General disestablishment occurred in the cantons of Switzerland, partly because of Roman Catholic influx, mainly because of indifference.

From Switzerland, however, at the close of World War I came a strong protest against theological liberalism. Karl Barth (1886–   ), pastor of a small Reformed church in Switzerland, deeply moved by the violence of a world at war, formulated a theological system which has sometimes been called the theology of crisis because it interpreted contemporary problems and world convulsions as stemming from man's confidence in himself and consequent neglect of God's will; sometimes called dialectical theology, which refers to man's total inability to search out God and the necessity of allowing God through his sovereign grace to speak to man; and sometimes called neo-orthodoxy, which relates the movement to earlier Christian orthodoxy. Barth magnified God's sovereignty as transcendent and man's sin as overwhelming. Although Barth's system had elements unacceptable to many traditional supernaturalists, it was in marked contrast with the arrogant rationalism of a previous generation and has been greatly influential in contemporary theology.

Concluding Summary

The last period has been one of almost constant war and political revolution on the Continent. The Roman Catholic Church has been hit hard in what has been traditionally the area of its greatest strength. Indifference and secularism have been greater enemies of Rome than has modernism.

The tumultuous events of the period have rained heavy blows upon continental Protestantism. Internal decay because of widespread rationalism had more to do with the loss of vitality than have the frequent wars. Neo-orthodoxy, a reaction against humanistic optimism and aggressive theological rationalism, has provided the starting point for new theological formulations of various sorts.

28

English Christianity

THE NINETEENTH CENTURY belonged to England. Just as France became mistress of the Continent after the Thirty Years' War because of the severe losses of the other combatants, so England vaulted into leadership when France was overwhelmed in the backwash of her Revolution at the turn of the century. Queen Victoria (1837–1900), continuing a Hanoverian tradition for longevity, provided the setting for England's rise to world domination in the nineteenth century. No small part of this achievement was made possible because of the ability of England to profit from history.

The lessons of her own "Bloodless Revolution," the American Revolution (when one of her colonies secured political independence), and the French Revolution (when revolt against a nonrepresentative government occurred) were not wasted upon England. A program to bring increased responsiveness to the voice of the people was begun. In 1832 a sweeping Reform Bill was passed, one of the provisions of which was to increase greatly the number who could vote. The Second Reform Act of 1867 doubled the number of voters, while legislation in 1918 and 1928 brought almost total suffrage to the people. The policy of home rule for colonial possessions was established, Canada in 1867 receiving practically independent status in all domestic affairs; while other colonies moved in that direction. Exceptions to this liberal treatment were Ireland and India.

The twentieth century brought serious problems to the empire. The very areas not granted a measure of independence took matters into their own hands. India and adjacent colonies took large strides toward complete independence. Most of Ireland withdrew from the empire and by 1949 became completely separated. An imperial mercantile policy providing abundant and lush fruits was no longer feasible. Two expensive world wars brought heavy and varied burdens to the people and the nation.

Survey of Principal Religious Events

There were four extensive religious movements that affected England during this period.

Modern foreign mission movement.—The momentous victory of England over France in 1763 sent explorers scurrying to find new shores touched by the ocean now controlled by England—men like Commodore Bryon, Captain Wallis, and Captain Cook between 1764 and 1768. The field preaching of Wesley and Whitefield had to some extent divorced the gospel from buildings and had stirred the hearts of Christian people to compassion for those without salvation. Men like David Brainerd in America were seeking out the Indians for Christ. It remained for William Carey, a young Baptist cobbler, to inaugurate and exemplify the modern foreign mission movement. A Baptist society for foreign missions was formed in 1792. Carey and others were sent to India. Inspired by Carey, English independents and the Church of England organized foreign missionary societies. In the next two centuries almost every section of the inhabited world received missionaries from all parts of English Christianity.

Religious revival and humanitarian movements.—The fires of revival, diminished during the wars with the American colonies and with France, burned brightly for a brief time after the defeat of Napoleon in 1814. The ending of several exhausting wars with the peril of imminent invasion was marked by a genuine recognition of divine blessings. As was true a century before, a revival in the United States preceded the spiritual emphasis in Britain. As a matter of fact, the extent and effects of the revival in America in the opening years of the nineteenth century were far greater than were evident in England. Again after 1859 revival took place in all of Britain, receiving impetus with the preaching of Dwight L.

Moody more than a decade later and the influential ministry of Charles Haddon Spurgeon in London.

Along with this religious sensitiveness—perhaps occasioned by it—were a number of moral and humanitarian reforms. The large increase in the number of those in denominations other than the established Church of England, along with the general democratization of legislative processes in England and the enlargement of franchise, guaranteed that existing religious disabilities upon dissenters could not continue. By the 1860's the battle was almost entirely won, as one by one most of the radical discriminations were either eliminated or minimized. The unjust penal laws were slowly replaced, and the treatment and housing of prisoners were greatly improved. Slavery was abolished in 1833. Legislation curbed abuses in the factory system involving the long hours of women and children. The nation accepted additional responsibility for the education of its children and youth. A new sensitiveness to the public good brought legislation for various types of aid to the common welfare—police, cheap postage, public health, commerce and navigation, etc. The twentieth century brought the increasing consciousness of governmental responsibility for the citizens in the problems beyond the local level.

Skepticism and materialism.— The Wesleyan revival in the previous period turned the hearts of the masses from infidelity and skepticism, but a strong core of antisupernaturalism was never touched in this or later revivals. Several factors in the nineteenth century helped to swell the ranks of this group. One was the development of an articulate Socinian movement, appealing mainly to the intellectual classes and magnifying the Christian ethic as the principal contribution of the Christian Scriptures. Both in England and in America the development of organizational structure brought new adherents, particularly in the upper strata of society. Furthermore, in this period continental philosophers made radical attacks upon the Scriptures. The tendency to expurgate, negate, or modify Christian revelation, evident in the work of men like David Strauss (1808–74) and Julius Wellhausen (1844–1918), undercut the faith of some who had not been firmly moored.

Another factor inducing skepticism was the evolutionary hypothesis proposed by Charles Darwin (1809–82) in 1859. His ideas, ofttimes misinterpreted and misapplied, were enlarged from a theory based upon observation of biological phenomena to encompass social, ethical, and metaphysical pronouncements. Such projections of his theory were thought to undermine the possibility of a divine revelation (particularly one handed down from a less advanced state of society) and to minimize the need for divine creative activity and providential supervision.

Still another subversive factor could be termed "sciencism." Technological developments buttressed the older materialism and brought to many folk a blind sort of faith in the dynamic nature of human progress and ingenuity. The trying days of adjustment between wars, severe economic depression, the great human loss and physical destruction of war itself, the immediate social problems involved in wartime morality and displaced persons, and a thousand other stresses as well turned the thoughts of England away from spiritual things. There have been unmistakable evidences of religious decline in the present century. Financial support has decreased, church attendance has been quite poor, and except for the Roman Catholics, it has been difficult for the various religious denominations to find candidates for the ministry.

Ecumenicalism.—English Christianity as a whole has entered heartily into the ecumenical (universal) movement. To some extent, ecumenicalism rooted in the burst of enthusiasm for world missions that followed the inception of the modern mission movement by William Carey. The London Missionary Society of 1795 was made up of members from the Church of England, Scottish Presbyterians, Methodists, and independents. The British and Foreign Bible Society of 1804 was interdenominational; so were many other co-operative efforts in Britain, America, and on the mission fields during that century. Perhaps the principal antecedent of the movement was the formation of the World's Evangelical Alliance in London in 1846 after a preliminary meeting in 1845. The purpose of this body primarily was to promote unity rather than to carry on some immediate joint task. Subse-

337

quent conferences were held in Britain, on the Continent, and in the United States. In addition, interdenominational movements among young Christians increased the influence of the movement, including such organizations as the Young Men's Christian Association, begun in London in 1884, and other bodies both in Britain and in the United States.

The immediate antecedents of the modern movement were found in the interdenominational missionary conferences. Foreign missionaries, wrestling with mutual problems, met together in conference, sometimes official, sometimes unofficial. Well-known conferences were held in London in 1854, in Liverpool in 1860, and various parts of England intermittently until the turn of the century. Almost all denominations, other than the Roman Catholics, took some part in this movement.

A large forward step in the movement was the meeting in 1910 at Edinburgh, in which for the first time a conference composed of officially delegated representatives from mission boards and societies was held. The general motif was a united Christendom, and a Continuation Committee insured further conferences. Other conferences were held at Stockholm (1925), Amsterdam (1948), and Evanston (1954). The World Council of Churches was constituted at the 1948 meeting.

Survey of Principal Christian Bodies

The remainder of this chapter will be devoted to a brief survey of each of the principal Christian bodies in England during this period in the light of the general background.

The Church of England.—The Church of England in the modern period has been consistently missionary-minded. After the modern mission movement was begun by the Baptists, the London Missionary Society, formed in 1795, contained many Anglicans, while the Church Missionary Society in 1799 was made up solely of Anglicans. Anglicans also were a part of the Religious Tract Society of 1799 and the British and Foreign Bible Society in 1804.

It could be expected that the Anglican leadership, particularly

338

those who favored the sacramentalism inherited from the Roman Catholic Church, would look with disfavor upon the sweeping evangelical revivals of the eighteenth century and the increasing strength of evangelicals within the established church. The progressive growth of the dissenters and the removal of religious disabilities against them, together with the developing co-operation between evangelicals within the Anglican Church and the dissenters, was of grave concern to the older party. This general background, along with the skeptical intellectual currents sweeping across England in the nineteenth century, led to the development of three distinct parties within the Church of England.

One group of churchmen within the Church of England favored the doctrines of the Roman Catholic Church but allowed the English sovereign to be head of the Church instead of the pope at Rome. They were strict sacramentalists, desiring the retention of monks and nuns, emphasizing the vital nature of apostolic succession, and insisting upon the establishment of the Church within the English state. The success and increase of dissenters aroused them to feverish activity. They began in 1833 the publication of a series of *Tracts for the Times* covering church history and doctrine. The most important tract was the last one, written in 1841 by John Henry Newman (1801–90), attempting to show that the Thirty-nine Articles of the Church of England, heretofore considered as the most Protestant portion of the Anglican system, could actually be interpreted in a Roman Catholic sense.

Newman also favored other elements of the Roman Catholic system and in 1845 was received into the Roman Catholic Church. Many others of this party followed him. After his departure the leadership of the High Church party was assumed by E. B. Pusey (1800–82). In general, the High Church movement has Romanized many aspects of Anglican liturgical and devotional life. Monastic life for men and women has been encouraged. Auricular confession has been introduced. The High Church party received a blow in 1896 when the bishop of Rome declared that all Anglican episcopal succession was invalid. Nevertheless, the party has maintained a strong position in the Anglican Church.

The evangelicals in the Church of England have been termed the Low Church group. Many evangelicals left the Church of England with the Methodist movement, but the Gorham case proved that evangelicalism still may exist within the Anglican Church. In 1847 a High Church bishop refused to install G. C. Gorham, an evangelical in doctrine, because of Gorham's views. The case was taken to court, where the final decision favored Gorham, determining that evangelicalism had legal standing within the Anglican communion.

The Broad Church party favored the widest possible flexibility in the doctrinal and ecclesiastical standards of Anglicanism. This party has also secured legal standing in Anglicanism. In 1860 a collection of seven somewhat radical essays by liberal Anglican clergymen aroused the orthodox viewers, and two of the authors were tried for heresy in ecclesiastical courts. They were finally acquitted. The case revealed that the utmost freedom would be allowed in theological thinking and writing within the Anglican Church, outward conformity to the Thirty-nine Articles and the prayer book being the principal requirement.

The Church of England has been quite active in the ecumenical movement. It has looked upon itself as being the halfway station between Roman Catholicism and Protestantism and has felt that in such a position it would be the ideal place and pattern for reunion for all Christendom. The Lambeth Conferences—a world meeting of all bishops of the Anglican communion which has met in London about every ten years since 1867—explored the possibilities of union with others. In 1888 it approved four items which it considered minimal for union, as follows: the Old and New Testaments as the rule and standard of faith; the Apostles' Creed and the Nicene Creed as the doctrinal statements of faith; the observance of the two sacraments of baptism and the Lord's Supper; and the historic episcopate to preserve the continuing unity of the church. The Anglican Church has looked toward closer union with all Christian groups—Protestants, the Eastern Orthodox Church, and even the Roman Catholic Church. That the four items set out in 1888, known as the Lambeth Quadrilateral, were the very minimum is evident from the fact that when local groups attempted to establish union in South Africa in 1913, in Canada in 1925, and in South India in 1947, the Church of England stood aloof because the proper episcopal ordination was not uniformly secured.

The Church of England was greatly hurt by the two world wars that occurred in the first half of the twentieth century, accompanied as they were by a period of secularism and economic depression. There was a marked decrease in vitality and influence, the number of candidates for the ministry declined radically, church attendance and religious interest were curtailed sharply by war activities and weariness, and there was a continuation of skeptical literature and secular thinking.

In some measure this decline, along with the depleted resources of the nation and parliamentary disapproval of the revised prayer book in 1927 and 1928, brought demands both from within and without the Church of England that the church be disestablished. Those within felt that the vast endowments of the church, accumulated over four centuries, could probably provide for the financial needs of a disestablished church. However, others felt that disestablishment would soon be followed by disendowment. The High Church party, in particular, has opposed any plan for disestablishment.

In Wales the Church of England was established at the opening of this period, although a large majority of the people were dissenters. A series of revivals, particularly among the dissenting group but also entered into by the established churches of Wales, helped dissipate the lethargic and disinterested situation at the opening of the period. The Anglican establishment ended in Wales in 1920.

Until 1949 all of Ireland was a part of England. The parliament of Ireland had been dissolved in 1800, and representatives were given seats in the English body. The Church of England was established as the state church in Ireland for a small minority, despite protests by a large Roman Catholic majority and a vigorous Presbyterian minority in Ulster County. However, the Roman

Catholic Emancipation Act of 1829 removed many disabilities from the majority, and in 1868 the Anglican Church of Ireland was disestablished.

Australia was first colonized when Great Britain made it a penal colony in 1787. The outstanding name in the formative years was Samuel Marsden, chaplain of the Church of England from 1793 until his death in 1838. Through his efforts Christianity was forwarded not only in Australia but in New Zealand and the other Pacific islands as well. The large British immigration began in the first quarter of the nineteenth century, the majority being the Church of England adherents, while Irish Catholics, Scotch-Irish Presbyterians, and English Methodists formed most of the remainder.

New Zealand was about a decade behind Australia in colonization. Samuel Marsden took the lead here also in calling for an active missionary program. The English immigration came about 1840 and was principally Anglican.

Canada's history, predominantly French until 1763, then English, is reflected in her Christianity. That story will be briefly sketched in the chapter on American Christianity.

India and other colonies of England during this period were the recipients of much labor from the many missionary societies of Britain.

The Roman Catholic Church in England.—At the opening of this period there were severe disabilities against the Roman Catholics in England. They were unorganized on the higher level and not numerous. In 1829, however, the Roman Catholic Emancipation Act removed many of the civil disabilities. In 1850 the pope restored the hierarchy in England with the appointment of an archbishop of Westminster. This created quite a furor among those who feared the Roman Catholic movement.

The failure of the potato crop in Ireland shortly before the middle of the nineteenth century caused many of the Roman Catholic peasants of Ireland to emigrate to England, greatly swelling the number of that group there. Some joined the Roman Church from the Tractarian movement, while others emigrated from the Continent. As a result, the familiar institutions of Romanism soon appeared throughout England, Scotland, and Wales—churches, schools, monastic orders for both men and women. The large Irish Roman Catholic immigration provided an increasing number of that faith in England during the first half of the twentieth century, increasing the Roman Catholic population to about two and a half million. This group has grown more rapidly and withstood loss of vitality better than any other English denomination. The new nation of Eire, wrenched loose from the remainder of Ireland to become a republic in 1949, is predominantly Catholic.

English Calvinism.—Presbyterianism, so active in England during the Cromwellian period and shortly thereafter, practically disappeared after the Restoration, some falling into Unitarianism and others joining the Congregational movement. In the next century the only Presbyterians in England were the small congregations of Scottish Presbyterians who retained ties with their home base. These slowly increased during the nineteenth century and in 1876 organized the Presbyterian Church of England. By the first quarter of the twentieth century this group numbered almost 85,000.

Irish Presbyterians settled in northern Ireland in the opening years of the seventeenth century. When the Protestants William and Mary came to the English throne in 1688, the hard lot of the Presbyterian minority in Ireland was improved. By 1691, through subsidies provided by the English government, large numbers settled in Ulster County. Immigrants from these Scotch-Irish Presbyterians played a very important part in the rise of American Presbyterianism. In the opening years of this period Irish Presbyterians were struggling with the Unitarian views current in England at the time and finally triumphed. In 1860 the General Assembly of the Presbyterian Church in Ireland was formed. The disestablishment of the Anglican Church in 1868 gave impetus to the Presbyterians in Ireland, along with the fresh spiritual awakening about that time. Missions and education advanced, and the twentieth century found them numbering over one hundred thousand, although they suffered from the two wars and religious skepticism.

In the twentieth century efforts have been made to unite English Presbyterians with English Congregationalists.

Presbyterianism was the established church in Scotland at the beginning of the period. Scottish Presbyterians were not greatly influenced by the evangelical revival of the eighteenth century, perhaps a reaction against the Arminian doctrines of Wesley. A genuine spiritual awakening did occur, however, in the opening years of the nineteenth century, spearheaded by the Haldane brothers. This new spiritual life agitated an old problem, the question of secular control as seen in lay patronage. Do noble and wealthy patrons in a community have the right to name the minister of the church there? Doughty Scots had twice opposed this, bringing schisms in 1733 and 1760.

The nineteenth century movement was led by Thomas Chalmers (1780–1847). The General Assembly of the Church of Scotland took the side of the churches, declaring in 1834 that no pastor should be forced upon an unwilling congregation. In 1842 the matter reached the English House of Lords, who decided that a church must take a minister appointed by a patron, whether to their liking or not. In the following year, in an act of drama and sacrifice, nearly half the Presbyterians of Scotland left the salaries and buildings of the Church of Scotland in protest against lay patronage and formed the Free Church of Scotland. Most of these groups seceding over lay patronage came together by 1900 under the name United Free Church of Scotland, and in 1929 this body united with the established church again, the principle of lay patronage being eliminated.

Presbyterianism was carried to Australia and New Zealand in the wave of English immigration in the 1820's. Although fewer in number than the Anglicans and the Roman Catholics, they have considerable influence. The Canadian story will be told in connection with American Christianity.

English Congregationalism in this period was closely related to Presbyterianism, receiving many of its members and influencing the thinking of those who did not make the change. The Congregational movement was greatly blessed by the Wesleyan awakening in the eighteenth century, as well as by the modern mission movement and the brief revival after the Napoleonic wars. One evidence of the increased vitality in the early nineteenth century, in addition to growth in constituency and churches, was the development of a vigorous interchurch fellowship. First came the county unions, principally inspired by the challenge of home missions. In 1832 the Congregational Union of England and Wales was formed. By the present century English, Welsh, and Scottish Congregationalism, numbering perhaps half a million in 1928, carried on a vigorous program of education and other benevolences, although two wars and depression have taken their toll.

English Methodists.—English Methodism grew more rapidly than any other of the dissenting groups during this period, at the same time having considerable difficulty because of the great number of schisms. After the death of John Wesley in 1791, Methodism quickly separated from the Anglican Church. The rigid ecclesiastical organization and discipline of English Methodism brought a number of protests. The great leaders after Wesley were Thomas Coke (1747–1814), Jabez Bunting (1779–1858), and the contemporary John Scott Lidgett. The movement, of course, had an original divergence, one group becoming Calvinistic and the other Arminian. The latter became the dominant group. Among this group came schisms in 1797 over lay representation (the Methodist New Connection), in 1810 over camp meeting methods (Primitive Methodist Connection), in 1815 over zealous evangelism (the Bible Christians), and in 1828 over music (Wesleyan Protestant Methodists). By 1907, however, the organization of the United Methodist Church brought several of these together, and in 1932 most of England's Methodists, totaling over a million, united into one body. Methodists in New Zealand in the third decade of this century numbered near 30,000 and in Australia about 166,000. English Methodists also were dealt hard blows by two wars and the accompanying spiritual decline.

English Baptists.—This final period in church history is marked off in part by the English Baptists as they began the modern foreign mission movement. The Wesleyan revival brought new life into English Baptists. General Baptists benefited greatly by the work of Dan Taylor, founder of the New Connection of General Baptists. Particular Baptists were inspired to begin the modern mission movement. William Carey, a journeyman cobbler, became a Baptist in 1783. Unschooled, he became well educated through private application, mastering Hebrew, Greek, Latin, and Dutch in his spare hours. With the help of Andrew Fuller, John Sutcliffe, Samuel Pearce, and John Ryland, Jr., Carey organized a Baptist missionary society in London in 1792. In the following year Carey went to India as a missionary and with his companions translated the Bible into eighteen languages and published tracts in twenty tongues in nineteen years. In addition, more than seven hundred converts had been baptized and a dozen nationals had surrendered for the Christian ministry.

English Baptist work, both home and foreign, grew rapidly under the inspiration of this example. Schools were founded, and various social reforms were entered into in co-operation with other Christians. Preachers like Robert Hall (1764–1831), Charles Haddon Spurgeon (1834–92), Alexander Maclaren (1825–1910), John Clifford (1836–1923), and John H. Shakespeare (1857–1928) gave new respectability to the Baptist cause. In 1891 the division between General and Particular Baptists which had existed from the beginning of English Baptist life was healed, principally through the work of John Clifford. In 1953 there were 202,361 Baptists in England proper, about 100,000 in Wales, 20,000 in Scotland, and 5,000 in Ireland. Skepticism and two wars have slain their thousands among English Baptists in the twentieth century.

In the dominions, with the possible exception of Canada, Baptist work has been fed principally from England. Australian Baptists number over 30,000, New Zealand Baptists number about 11,000, while Canadian Baptists total almost 150,000.

Other Groups

There are many other smaller groups in England which cannot be discussed, although some of them have made vital and enduring contributions by their distinctive views.

Concluding Summary

In the opening years of this period, English Baptists inaugurated what has been termed the modern mission movement. During the nineteenth century practically all denominations in England carried on foreign mission programs in almost every part of the world. Skepticism and secularism have made large gains in England in the last two centuries, however, and the general picture is one of religious decline and lowered vitality. During the last century the ecumenical movement has gained favor with a large majority of English denominations. The Church of England has defined the four minimal points for church union, and it is apparent from developments in various parts of the world that each of these points is counted significant.

The churches and the Christian faith in England, along with the remainder of the nation, have suffered greatly from the two world wars in which England has been a principal combatant.

29

American Christianity

CHRISTIANITY IN THE United States during the modern period has had phenomenal growth. The tremendous expansion of
the country in extent and population partly accounts for this. In
1789 the territory of the United States was confined to the area of
what is now east of the Mississippi and north of Florida (which
included a strip of land across the Gulf coast to the Mississippi).
By means of purchase, annexation, and war the remainder of the
present nation was added—the vast area west of the Mississippi
known as Louisiana in 1803; Florida in 1819; Texas in 1847; the
Oregon-Washington area in 1848; California, Arizona, and New
Mexico by the Mexican Cession of 1848; Alaska in 1867; and in
1898 the several insular areas of the Philippine Islands, Guam,
Puerto Rico, Hawaiian Islands, Samoa Islands, and Wake Island.
The American population in 1790 was about four million, in 1880
about fifty million, about 1915 it neared one hundred million, and
by 1957 it reached almost a hundred and seventy million.

During this time the principal occupation of the nation changed
from agriculture to commerce and industry. Large cities and a
highly industrialized society have altered the complexion of daily
life. Unbelievable advance in technology and mass production
have brought wealth with its accompanying social and economic
problems. The organization of labor and extensive governmental
supervision have brought checks and balances to unlimited industrial empire. The impressive contributions of the United States to
World Wars I and II have brought her to a place of world leadership.

During these years as a nation the environment in America

has been peculiarly suited to the religious development of the people. A number of important factors mark the religious history from 1789 to the present. They are listed in approximately the chronological order in which they occurred.

Factors in American Religious History

Relation of church and state in the United States.—Some have judged that the greatest contribution of the United States to the science of government has been her development of the separation of church and state. It will be remembered that through the centuries the Roman Catholic Church maintained her strength and molded her system through the aid of the secular powers. It was only through the help of the state that Rome could enforce uniformity, repress heresy, and spread her system. Lutheranism, Calvinism, Zwinglianism, and Anglicanism were not averse to accepting aid from the state. In America it appeared that perhaps the government might find itself in the same dilemma of religious establishment. New Hampshire, Massachusetts, and Connecticut had Congregationalism established by law at the time of the American Revolution, while Maryland and Virginia had the Church of England so established.

The national pattern in relation to religion, however, followed none of these states but rather the system of Rhode Island—separation of church and state, much despised when first set up, but constantly winning adherents. For one thing, the American Revolution undercut the establishments of the Anglican Church on patriotic grounds, for it was not then known that the American followers of this system would set up an independent and national episcopal body. Furthermore, in the very area where this establishment was involved the strength of dissent was considerable, especially among the Baptists, Presbyterians, and Methodists. The democratic nature of the Great Awakening had deeply impressed the population, and these revivals were still occurring in Virginia and nearby states. The New World had been sought as a haven from religious persecution, and the spirit of democracy of the frontier and religious revivals resisted a national establishment.

In addition, at this very time the educated class was drinking deeply from cups of French philosophical and political liberalism. Democracy and liberty were large words. The dignity of the common man demanded respect and recognition. The unquestioned corruption and malignity of the Roman Catholic religion in France, which had fastened itself to the state and was slowly sapping its life, brought to American skeptical intellectuals in key political places additional reasons why there should be no religious establishment. The Revolution of 1776 itself was in the vanguard of religious liberty. The casting off of monarchy and the surge of democracy was the triumph of the theology of dissenters who in the revivals of the past generation had seen the spirit of God move freely among all people.

The victory of religious liberty began in Virginia. Here amidst stringent disabilities imposed by the established Church of England, the Baptists, strongly aided by the Presbyterians and the Methodists, began an active program to throw off the establishment. This was accomplished by 1787 through the political aid of James Madison. In addition, the new Constitution was approved by Virginians, with the understanding that there would be added immediately a bill of rights guaranteeing religious liberty. This promise was carried out, and the first of the rights protected the infant nation from the evils of an established church. It was, of course, a matter for the states to reflect this same spirit by eliminating establishments. The last of these, New Hampshire, Connecticut, and Massachusetts eliminated support of Congregationalism in 1817, 1818, and 1833 respectively, principally through the efforts of John Leland, a Baptist. To the present day there are still problems involved in the separation of church and state, but the continued stability of the American nation itself is wrapped up with the preservation of this principle.

Early infidelity and skepticism.—During the American Revolution and immediately thereafter, most of the colonies experienced a wave of infidelity. Part of the reason was the bitterness and cynicism that war always brings. Both the French and Indian War (1756–63) and the Revolutionary War (1775–83) had brought widespread suffering and moral decline. Close contact with English intellectual currents before the Revolutionary War and with France during that war had brought considerable amounts of their skepticism and infidelity to American shores. The anti-Christian writings of Voltaire (1694–1778) in France and Thomas Paine (1737–1809) in America were widely read and approved.

At the close of the Revolution it has been estimated that less than 10 per cent of the American population were professing Christians. The various "Christian" schools were filled with unbelievers and atheists. Only two of Princeton's student body professed to be Christians in 1782, and the other schools were quite as bad. Rationalistic and atheistic societies flourished. This was not so completely true in the lower South, where revivals of religion had continued from the days of the first Great Awakening (1739). The second Great Awakening in the opening years of the nineteenth century turned America again toward faith. Christians began to multiply much more rapidly than the population. While perhaps only about 275,000 out of 3,929,214 were Christians in 1790, over 83,000,000 were professed Christians out of a population of over 165,000,000 in 1956.

The second Great Awakening.—In New England, probably the area of greatest spiritual need, a second Great Awakening occurred in the opening years of the nineteenth century. It was quite different from the first Awakening of half a century before. There was less emotional excitement and less immediate controversy over methods of revival. Single outstanding leaders were fewer, and the power of the revival was channeled into benevolent objects. Because of it, practically all denominations were aroused to the importance of spreading the gospel, both at home and abroad. Increased efforts were made to Christianize the Indians, and plans were made for sending the gospel to the ever-receding frontier to the west. The Congregationalists organized the American Board of Commissioners in 1810 to carry on foreign mission work. Baptists developed the General Missionary Convention of the Baptist Denomination in the United States of America for Foreign Missions in 1814.

351

The American Bible Society was formed in 1816 on an inter-denominational basis, as were also the American Sunday School Union in 1824 and the American Home Mission Society in 1826. Baptists formed their Tract Society in 1824, one year before the interdenominational American Tract Society. Baptists also formed their Home Mission Society in 1832. The inspiration for the founding of these various benevolent societies doubtless sprang principally from the spiritual revival at the turn of the century. It is also true that the growing sentiment both in the North and in the South in favor of the abolition of slavery was accelerated by these revivals, especially those of Charles G. Finney.

Meanwhile, a revival of a different sort was experienced west of the Alleghenies in Tennessee and Kentucky about the same time. All denominations seem to have engaged in it, although the initial movement developed under the leadership of the Presbyterian, James McGready of Kentucky. In this revival the camp meeting became popular. Settlers drove from miles around to make camp in some central area. Ministers of different denominations preached at the same time at various parts of the campgrounds to crowds as large as their voices could reach. Great emotional and physical excitement were evident in the meetings. Shouting and weeping alternated with barking, shaking, running, crawling on all fours, and in some cases, the appearance of complete loss of consciousness. As a direct result of this revival, the Presbyterians refused to countenance the action of one of their presbyteries in ordaining new men for evangelistic work without the proper prerequisites, and a schism took place, resulting in the Cumberland Presbyterian Church. In general, the revival added great numbers to the churches in Kentucky and Tennessee, and practically all of the frontier denominations profited from renewed spiritual interest.

Flood of immigration.—One of the important factors in the religious history of the United States was the gigantic tide of immigration that flowed into the country. It brought repercussions in many directions. The religious characteristics of the immigrants gave color to American Christianity; the holding of these immigrants constituted a vast challenge to the religious denominations

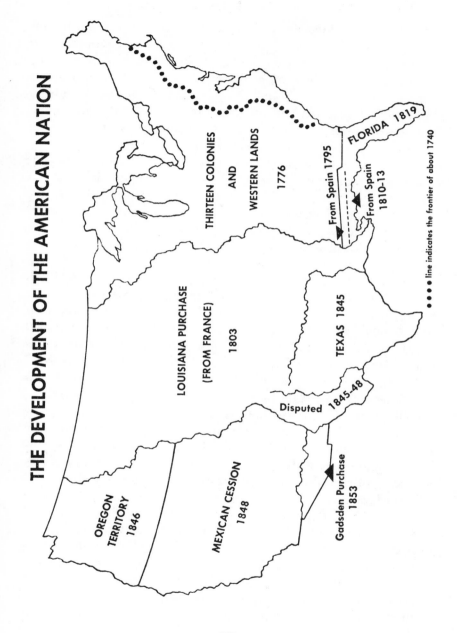

THE DEVELOPMENT OF THE AMERICAN NATION

THIRTEEN COLONIES
AND
WESTERN LANDS
1776

FLORIDA 1819

From Spain 1795

From Spain 1810-13

LOUISIANA PURCHASE
(FROM FRANCE)
1803

TEXAS 1845

Disputed 1845-48

OREGON
TERRITORY
1846

MEXICAN CESSION
1848

Gadsden Purchase
1853

● ● ● ● line indicates the frontier of about 1740

to which they belonged; large communities from a single nation greatly influenced others in the immediate area; the large accessions to those denominations in America to which the immigrants belonged brought them not only immediate problems but also a rapid increase in wealth and prestige; and when large numbers of immigrants landed and settled near the coast, the settlers in communities along the seaboard were influenced to move to the west where there was more room.

The number of immigrants was accelerated by many factors. The westward migration after the Louisiana Purchase in 1803 and the return of peace in 1815 brought immediate demands for laborers along the coast, especially for the extensive programs of building railroads, canals, and roads. Unrest, famine, and economic crises in various countries abroad served to drive many to American shores. The American Revolution and the War of 1812 discouraged immigration in the opening decades of the nineteenth century. By 1820, however, the immigrants began arriving at the rate of over 9,000 a year; between 1825 and 1835 they averaged over 30,000 a year; in the following ten years they averaged 70,000 a year; while between 1845 and 1885 almost 12,000,000 immigrants flooded the country, about 25,000 a month for forty years.

In the first half of the century the largest number of immigrants came from Ireland, where the failure of the potato crop in the 1840's brought virtual famine to millions. It is estimated that nearly two million of the Irish emigrated to America, practically all of them avid Roman Catholics. Not quite as many Germans made the journey, while a smaller number came from practically all the countries of southern Europe, also strongly Roman Catholic. This avalanche of immigrants greatly influenced the history of the several denominations in America.

Westward expansion and war.—The American frontier, an outgrowth of a great new continent of virgin land slowly becoming settled, had an unbelievably significant place in the religious life of the nation. It shaped the economy to one of plenty rather than of scarcity in the ownership of land. European land space had been exhausted or pre-empted for centuries, and land meant stability and wealth. In the virgin country the presence of a constantly expanding frontier gave every man a sense of financial independence and of worth. It provided a fluid society, for a person could move to the frontier for any reason or for no reason. It stimulated new immigration by pulling manpower, particularly the marginal laborer or unskilled worker, to the opportunities of the virgin country. It encouraged a democratic spirit inasmuch as every man must stand on his own worth in the harsh and rigorous areas of frontier life. It gave encouragement to those denominations of Christians which magnified democracy in church life—the Baptists, Methodists, and similar bodies. The rough, and many times immoral, frontier life challenged the Christian denominations in the older communities of the east to send missionaries to the frontier to encourage Christians and to win the lost. The camp meeting type of revival was developed for the preaching of the gospel to large numbers.

Another aspect of the importance of the frontier and the west concerned the political effect of newly settled states. The avalanche of westward emigration that brought a constant projection of the frontier line resulted in the settling of new states. One of the crushing problems of the new nation concerned Negro slavery, introduced in 1619 to the Virginia colony, impressed upon them by England against their protest, spread through the South by Northern importation and financing, and gradually embraced by the South through the devastating choice of a one-crop economic system. A climatic and geographic determinism limited Negro slavery almost wholly to the South in a feudal and anachronistic system. Without doubt the institution would have crumbled of its own weight, because it was economically unsound as well as morally wrong. It became a political issue, since those states denominated as "slave states" usually formed a united coalition. Had the older states remained as the sole members of the national union, the slave question would not have become politically explosive, but the question of state rights and sectional jealousies, combined with differences in the interpretation of the meaning of the Constitution, were sparked into conflict by the spread of slavery.

Many of the denominations divided over the slavery question. War came in 1861 and brought sorrow and loss to every part of the nation. The Union victory in 1865 assured the unity of the nation politically and sounded the death knell to American Negro slavery. Troops were stationed throughout the South until 1878, adding to the bitterness engendered by the war. The schisms caused by this issue in some of the denominations have not been healed to the present time.

New denominations.—It is not possible, of course, to sketch the entire story of American Christianity in a brief summary of this sort. The surge of freedom of choice in the area of religion brought a rich and uninhibited variety to denominations in America. Several of the more important are mentioned here.

Thomas Campbell and his son Alexander were a part of a widespread movement which desired to restore primitive Christianity by eliminating all creeds and denominational organization. Doubtless, the two received strong impressions in this direction by their contacts with Scottish Christianity, and especially with Greville Ewing, John Glas, and Robert Sandeman. Practically every distinctive doctrine of the movement was patterned after the Scottish practices. In America both of the Campbells left Presbyterian ranks and in 1812 joined the Baptist fellowship. About 1830 Alexander Campbell and his group left the Baptists, differing from them in several particulars, and took the name "Disciples of Christ." Campbell taught that baptism completes salvation, observed the Supper each week, and frowned upon any distinction between ministers and people, as seen in such titles as "clergy" and "laity." Walter Scott of Ohio and Barton W. Stone of Kentucky joined with Campbell in this "restoration" movement and greatly aided in its growth. Instead of eliminating denominational movements, Campbell began a new one, which slowly developed the characteristics of other denominations. Its total membership in 1956 was 1,897,736 in 7,951 churches. The conservative Church of Christ movement stems from Campbell also. In 1956 its membership was shown as 1,600,000 in 16,500 churches.

The Church of Jesus Christ of Latter-day Saints was founded in

1830 by Joseph Smith, who reported seeing celestial visions and receiving the *Book of Mormon* on gold plates. The westward trek in 1847 and the founding of Salt Lake City is a dramatic epic of American history. The portion of the movement which settled at Independence, Missouri, took the name of the Reorganized Church of the Latter-day Saints and now numbers 137,856 members in 808 churches. The Utah branch has spread and is quite active in propagating their tenets. Because of their belief in the continuation of prophetic gifts through their president and the sacred nature of the *Book of Mormon,* some have questioned whether Mormonism should be counted as a part of the Christian movement. They now report 1,230,021 communicants in 2,624 churches.

The Germans who settled in Pennsylvania and adjacent areas were influenced by strong personalities to form new denominational groups which combined the older traditions. Philip William Otterbein (1726–1813) and Martin Boehm (1725–1812), the one a Reformed minister and the other a Mennonite, joined in the holding of evangelistic meetings among the Germans in Pennsylvania and adjoining states during the Revolutionary War days. In 1800 they formed the United Brethren in Christ. This group united in 1946 with the Evangelical Church (organized by Jacob Albright on Methodist principles in 1816), and the combined body was called the Evangelical United Brethren Church. It now reports 737,489 members in 4,370 churches.

In 1831 William Miller (1782–1849), by carefully counting the symbolical numbers in the book of Daniel, concluded that Christ would return within the next few years and gathered a group known as the Adventists. Despite the failure of this principal prophecy, the denomination still perseveres, now numbering 277,-162 constituents in 2,858 churches.

A distorted type of apocalyptic speculation by Charles Russell in the late nineteenth century resulted in the International Bible Students' Association. It now claims 187,120 members in 3,484 churches. Mary Baker Eddy set forth a sort of modern Gnosticism and founded the Church of Christ, Scientist in 1879 in Boston, and her followers now operate 3,100 branches of the mother church.

The national churches of the East which broke fellowship with Rome in 1054 were slow in developing in the United States, but by immigration and birth the number has grown steadily. The various national groups formed their own churches, such as the Greek Orthodox, the Rumanian Orthodox, the Serbian Orthodox, and others. These have perhaps a million constituents in America at present.

Many other smaller, though important, Christian groups are found in the United States, but these cannot be discussed in a work like this one.

In addition, American Christianity has been characterized by many benevolent and semi-Christian movements, such as the Young Men's Christian Association, first organized in 1844 in London, and the Young Women's Christian Association, also organized in London in 1855. The English Salvation Army, founded by Methodist William Booth in 1878, has widely expanded in the United States, now numbering 249,641 adherents in 1,323 churches.

Resurging rationalism.—The older European systems of rationalism, illustrated by the philosophy of men like Christian Wolff in the seventeenth century, were confounded by Immanuel Kant, Schleiermacher, Ritschl, and others, who showed that man is not simply a thinking creature but is as well a moral, feeling, and choosing person. The last half of the nineteenth century, however, brought a rationalism of a newer sort. Physical science was added to philosophy, sociology, and psychology to raise doubts concerning the being of God or to oppose steadfastly the idea of a special revelation involving supernaturalism. The material world became very real. Even philosophy began to classify values in terms of whether they could successfully operate in a workaday world. Religion and spiritual matters were viewed in humanitarian terms and channeled into social betterment. In this milieu it is possible to mark off several attitudes in relation to traditional Christianity.

358

These are: (1) A definitely nontheistic or agnostic party. Despite the phenomenal advances of Christianity in America since the Revolution, a hard core of skepticism and unbelief was never touched. It denies the existence of God and scoffs at any idea of revelation. (2) A theistic party, but not distinctively Christian. This group is in the succession of English deism, which affirms that there is a God but that he has no special revelation. Hinduism thus is as valid a revelation as Christianity; every prophet in every religion has been inspired and adds something to the total revelation of God. (3) The nonsupernaturalistic Christian party. This group claims to follow the Christian tradition but denies many of the older beliefs. Revelation becomes meaningful only as it is reasonable. The Christian Scriptures in the main are historically unreliable and must be sifted carefully by human reason in order to find truth and significance. What is not reasonable in the human frame of reference is discarded. A substitutionary atonement is impossible because Christ was simply a good man. The immediate confrontation of God may be sensed by the human spirit and constitutes the only valid religious authority. For this group the principle value of religion comes in broad humanitarian channels. Perhaps the chief exponent of this party in America has been Harry Emerson Fosdick (1878–   ). (4) An American neo-orthodox party. This group, differing in some aspects from the thinking of Karl Barth but agreeing generally with him in basic approach, emphasizes the essential sinfulness of man. Like Barth, its followers are quite liberal with respect to many doctrines of traditional supernaturalism but cling to older orthodoxy at the point of man's sin and God's transcendent sovereignity. Perhaps the outstanding figure in this school is Reinhold Niebuhr (1892–·   ). (5) The party of traditional supernaturalism. This group endeavors to make the traditional Christian message relevant in a materialistic and scientific age, holding to the basic tenets of New Testament revelation and accepting the "unreasonable" supernaturalism of Christianity as exemplified in spiritual regeneration of the individual by the work of the divine Spirit.

Perhaps a sixth group should be included—what is commonly

known as fundamentalism, which in some cases goes to the other extreme from rationalism; that is, it completely eliminates the rational element from Christian revelation and religion in general.

Church union and ecumenicity.—For the most part, American Christianity has entered heartily into the movement toward church union and ecumenicity. The reasons are many and include: a basic desire for unity; the influence of English interdenominational movements, particularly in missions; the uniting of "family denominations"—those believing the same things and in the same tradition and needing union for strength and enlargement of work; the challenge of the foreign mission field, where there was need to place a united Christendom before a pagan world; the sweeping humanitarian movements, such as abolitionism, that crossed denominational lines; the cry for efficiency; the secular moves toward unity in the world, as seen in the United Nations; the need for a non-Catholic united front to match the organizational unity in the Roman Catholic Church; and the effect of liberal theology, where the toning down or denial of traditional Christian convictions makes lesser denominational distinctions seem relatively academic.

The specific antecedents of the modern ecumenical movement in America may be seen in the interdenominational missionary, tract, and Bible societies organized shortly after the turn of the nineteenth century. The American branch of the World's Evangelical Alliance, an interdenominational organization for the promotion of Christian unity, was organized in 1867 and for almost half a century promoted the cause of church union and ecumenicalism, although in the context of conservative evangelicalism. Other important organizations looking to the minimizing or eliminating of denominational lines were the Student Volunteer Movement (1886) and the World's Student Christian Federation (1895). The interdenominational missionary conferences, beginning in 1854 in New York, produced the Foreign Missions Conference of North America. The Federal Council of Churches of Christ in America (since 1950, the National Council) was organized in 1908. Most major American denominations, with the exception of

Southern Baptists and the Lutheran Missouri Synod, have participated freely in the world conferences at Edinburgh (1910), Stockholm (1925), Lausanne (1927), Jerusalem (1928), Oxford (1937), Edinburgh (1937), Madras (1938), Utrecht (1938), Amsterdam (1948), and Evanston (1954).

Two world wars.—The two global conflicts in the twentieth century in which America has participated have had significant effects. The aftermath of the first was a resurgence of liberal doctrine and an optimistic humanitarianism. Many believed that the last war had been fought and that there would soon come the millennium of universal peace and total prosperity. Man's capacity for achieving these things was hardly doubted. The cataclysmic financial depression and the bewildering rise to power of European dictators set the stage for a second world conflict. With it came a realization of man's need for God, and there is now widespread evidence of interest in spiritual things. Whether history will see this as the first religious revival of the atomic age, no one can know, but the adversities of mid-passage can be counted blessings if they deepen faith in God and encourage dependence upon him.

A Résumé of Older Denominations

Episcopalianism.—The American political revolution represented a religious revolution also for the members of the Church of England in America. There was no bishop in all America for this church, and the break with England politically left its status uncertain. After a period of indecision, a general convention was held in 1789 by representatives from all of the colonies, and the Protestant Episcopal Church in the United States of America was formed. It was based upon the doctrine, discipline, and worship formerly observed in the Church of England. Episcopal ordination for American bishops was received from Scotland and England between 1782 and 1790. The General Convention, consisting of a House of Bishops and a House of Clergy and Lay Deputies, was constituted as the governing body for the church.

Many factors combined to make the first four decades most disheartening for the new church. Its historical and doctrinal ties with England (again in a war with the United States in 1812) brought it unpopularity. Its formal type of worship was not effective on the frontier in America, so it was confined generally to the more inhabited areas. The shock of disestablishment, along with the lack of effective discipline and national leadership, brought many types of problems. The general skepticism and infidelity which pervaded the American colonies immediately after the Revolution greatly crippled this church also.

This lassitude was overcome, however. As a rule, the members of this church were of the educated and upper economic group. The several revival movements involving emotionalism and physical excitement were of no interest to them. Seminaries and missionary societies were organized in the second and third decades of the nineteenth century. After 1835 there was an increased zeal for converts, and under the leadership of men like William A. Mühlenberg a good growth was begun. Immigration from England brought many. As a matter of fact, the American Episcopal Church has been greatly influenced by trends in the Church of England. The High Church, Low Church, and Broad Church parties of England were reproduced in America. The effect of the Tractarian movement in England was also felt in America, when Bishop Ives of the Episcopal Church in North Carolina submitted to the Roman Catholic Church. There was actually no schism in this church during the Civil War. The Southern bishops were simply marked absent at the meeting of the General Convention in 1862, and after the war they were seated again.

The awakened rationalism that emerged in the last half of the nineteenth century affected the Protestant Episcopal Church. The first American Unitarian church came from their ranks. There was a rapid growth in the Broad Church party, which placed considerable emphasis upon social implications of the gospel and a liberal theological interpretation.

This church has been active in the ecumenical movement. Negotiations for church union have been carried on with the Russian and other Orthodox churches of the east, as well as the Old Catholics who left Rome after the promulgation of the infallibility decree, and others. In 1886 the General Convention suggested the plan for Christian reunion, which later became the Lambeth Quadrilateral.

At present this church has 2,757,944 constituents in 7,271 congregations in America and carries on a strong program of missions, theological education, and social service.

Congregationalism.—Congregationalism emerged from the Revolutionary War with bright prospects. Her leaders had supported enthusiastically the war for independence, and her American history was long and stable. The state support of her clergy in Massachusetts, Connecticut, and New Hampshire constituted a sore spot for those in other churches; however, particularly through the efforts of the Baptists (Isaac Backus and John Leland), by 1833 Massachusetts eliminated the last of American establishments.

The early skepticism probably affected Congregationalism more than any other denomination in America. Unitarianism (denying the essential deity of Christ) took large numbers from their churches. In some cases entire churches became Unitarian, including the first Congregational church in America—the Old Pilgrim Church of Plymouth. Through a legal technicality a minority of Unitarians were able to secure the church property in many cases from a Congregational majority. Harvard University became Unitarian in 1805. Within twenty years the Unitarian group organized and became vocal. At the present time the Unitarian Church reports 96,715 constituents in 378 churches.

Congregationalism was greatly blessed by the second Great Awakening at the opening of the nineteenth century. Many new churches were founded; schools and seminaries were begun; and societies for home and foreign missions, the publication of tracts, and the advancement of education were formed.

The westward movement challenged Congregationalists. Some thought that all of New England was moving to the west in the first half of the nineteenth century. However, Congregationalism lost many of their constituents who moved westward. A comity agreement was made with the Presbyterians in 1801, which planned co-operative efforts in founding new churches. The majority was to decide whether the church should be Presbyterian or Congregational, but in practice almost all of the Union churches became Presbyterian. Many hundreds of Congregational churches were probably lost to the Presbyterians before the plan was abandoned.

As a group Congregationalism strongly opposed slavery and aided the abolitionist movement, particularly in the early years of the movement. Civil war did not affect the fellowship of the churches, because this group did not have churches in the South. The renewed rationalism after the war profoundly affected Congregational leadership. Many became liberal theologically and magnified the social aspect of the gospel. Ecumenicalism and church union have been quite appealing. Congregationalism united with the Evangelical Protestant Church of North America in 1925 and the Christian Church in 1931 and now bears the name of Congregational Christian Churches. Their present constituency numbers 1,342,045 members in 5,561 churches.

Calvinism.—Calvin's religious system, altered in some ways by the various national groups of Europe who adopted it, is represented in America by the Presbyterians and the Reformed (and Evangelical) churches. In a sense, the Congregationalists belong to this family, but their independent background and type of church government differentiate them enough to discuss them under separate heading.

The Presbyterians acquitted themselves nobly on the patriotic side during the American Revolution. The physical damage and general disruption of war were more than offset by the heightened prestige after the founding of the new nation. In 1790 there were about eighteen thousand members, but several factors contributed to a rapid increase in constituency. They gained considerably from the sweeping revivals in Pennsylvania, Kentucky, and Tennessee in the opening years of the nineteenth century. Immigration added some. The completing of organizational structure doubtless gave impetus to growth also. At the very close of the previous period there came the organization of the General Assembly, which was the capstone of the local and territorial organizations. Thereafter

Presbyterian growth was accelerated. Another factor unintentionally worked to the growth of Presbyterians. The Plan of Union of 1801, seemingly fair enough for both sides, added many Presbyterian churches in the west at the expense of the Congregationalists.

Several schisms have divided American Presbyterians. In 1810 a small group in Kentucky withdrew over the question of prerequisites for ministerial ordination and organized the Cumberland Presbyterian Church. The schism lasted about a hundred years, although at the reunion in 1906 a minority refused to return. Doctrine and organizational forms brought separation in 1838 between the old and new school groups, while slavery also caused a schism which has not yet been healed.

Extensive benevolent work has characterized American Presbyterianism. Home and foreign mission societies were organized in the first half of the nineteenth century. Many schools and seminaries have been founded. At present there are about ten bodies of American Presbyterians, the largest of which are the Presbyterian Church in the United States of America with 2,645,745 members in 8,282 churches, and the Presbyterian Church in the United States (Southern Presbyterianism) with 810,917 constituents in 3,852 churches.

The opening years of the modern period saw the ending of schism among the Dutch Reformed and the adoption in 1792 of a constitution. Two years later the General Synod was organized. This denomination is similar to the Presbyterians in organization, for they have a common source in Zwingli and Calvin. The session they call a "consistory"; the presbytery they call "classis"; the synod they call a "particular synod"; and the General Assembly they call a "general synod." At present they have 804 churches with 205,323 members.

In 1934 the Reformed Church in the United States (German Reformed) united with the Evangelical Synod of North America as the Evangelical and Reformed Church. At present the number of this body includes 774,277 constituents in 2,732 churches.

Lutheranism.—The Lutherans were loyal to the colonies and active participants in the American Revolution. Although there were fewer than eighty ministers of this denomination in America at the close of the Revolution, the next several decades brought rapid growth, mostly by immigration. Both the growth itself and the type of growth brought problems of languages, organization, and doctrine. The strength of continental Lutheranism was in Germany and the Scandinavian areas. The semicongregational system of organization made it difficult to secure uniformity. Immigration from the Continent transplanted to America many of the divisive problems found in Europe. In the nineteenth century controversies arose over confessional and liberal points of view, as well as over differences in language, racial distinctions, and organizational forms.

In general, American Lutheranism has stressed the authority of each congregation, although some autonomy has been surrendered to the developing general organizations. The local church is governed by pastor and a church council. The larger organizational forms are the conference and the synod. Before 1820 American Lutheranism did not have a general body. In that year the General Synod was organized, although it did not receive widespread support for many years. Because of immigration and the development of general organization, American Lutherans by 1833 could count more than three hundred ministers serving 680 congregations with almost sixty thousand communicants.

The nineteenth century controversies have been succeeded in the present century by a spirit of increasing unity among Lutherans. The Synodical Conference was organized in 1872 for conservative or "strict" Lutherans, its largest constituent body being the Missouri Synod, which now numbers 2,006,110 members in 4,805 churches. The United Lutheran Church in America was organized in 1918 and now numbers 2,175,726 members in 4,050 churches. The American Lutheran Church was organized in 1930 and now has 836,485 members in 1,919 churches. An American Lutheran Conference was loosely organized in 1930 for fellowship and matters of common interest, but it was dissolved in 1954. American

Lutherans engage in all benevolent enterprises, including over three dozen theological seminaries and all levels of Christian education and an extensive missionary program. The latest statistics show that American Lutherans now total over seven million constituents in about twenty bodies.

Roman Catholicism.—At the beginning of the modern period the Roman Catholic Church had about twenty thousand constituents. Many of its members played valiant roles in the Revolution. The disorganized state of the new nation offered great opportunity for growth. The Great Awakening of 1800 had little influence upon this body, but immigration from Catholic countries of Europe provided unbelievable growth. In 1820 Roman Catholics in America were estimated at almost 250,000; in 1830, over 350,000; in 1840, 1,000,000; in 1860, 3,000,000; in 1890, over 10,000,000; and at present, 33,396,647 in 21,086 churches. Practically all of this growth has come from immigration and birth.

The Roman Catholic Church was quick to complete its organization in America, mainly because of the sagacity of John Carroll of Maryland, who became the first American bishop in 1790 and the first archbishop in 1808. For a brief season this church was plagued by a movement called "trusteeism," which in effect was the application of congregational authority. Language and racial issues also transplanted tension from the Old World. During the nineteenth century Catholicism was harassed by accusations of anti-Americanism. The present century has been comparatively free from such problems.

Two distinctive organizations have been developed on American soil. Elizabeth Ann Seton (1774–1821) began the parochial school system in the United States, which has become an outstanding institution for the Roman Church. The second influential organization founded by American Catholics was the fraternal society for Catholic men known as the Knights of Columbus, begun in 1882. This has become an aggressive and militant propagator of the Catholic faith.

The organization of the Roman Catholic Church in America is directly subordinate to Rome through an apostolic delegate at

Washington, D. C., as well as the offices of various cardinals and the regular organizational forms of parishes, dioceses, and more than a dozen archbishoprics.

Baptists.—American Baptists were wholeheartedly patriotic during the American Revolution, many of their ministers serving as chaplains in the army. This denomination took the lead in the movements in Virginia and New England that broke the shackles of state religious establishment, and it performed a similar service in securing the constitutional guarantees of religious liberty in the new nation.

Baptist organization and doctrine were peculiarly fitted for the extensive American frontier, and a large portion of the Baptist story deals with intrepid men who pioneered with their fellows during the day and preached to them at night and on the week end. The great revival along the frontier in the opening years of the nineteenth century added many to Baptist ranks. Simply the mention of the large numerical growth of American Baptists in the modern period gives evidence of their vitality and activity. They numbered less than 100,000 in 1789; at present they total over 18,000,000.

There may be several principal reasons for this tremendous increase. (1) The Baptists preached a simple gospel, minimizing theological formulations and emphasizing a life-changing experience. (2) As a rule, preachers sprang from among the common people. Problems of ordination, organization, and ecclesiastical authority were overshadowed by the necessity of trumpeting the story at the command of God. There was fire in the bones of the simple farmers and pioneers which transformed them into preachers. The fire spread. (3) The economic aspect of the ministry offered no difficulty. Most of these early preachers labored during the week along with their congregations and preached without remuneration at the end of the week. Whether by making tents or tilling the soil, the gospel was preached. (4) Each Baptist church was completely independent. This sort of principle appealed to frontier democracy. It gave opportunity for free expression of dissent as well as assent and stripped away the possibility of ministerial immunity when it came to consistent living and morality. (5) From the first, American Baptists have been missionary-minded. Both foreign (in Canada) and domestic mission work were done before the organization in 1814 of the first national foreign mission society and of the first national home mission society in 1832. A tract or publication society was organized in 1824 as a missionary aid.

Remembering the Baptist principle that each person is a priest of God through faith and regeneration and has the right to interpret the Scriptures for himself, it should not be startling to note that the American Baptist family has had some divisions. There have been controversies over organization, over the mission enterprise, over slavery and abolitionism, and over modernism. The last issue, in particular, has caused much controversy in the last half century.

Despite these problems, American Baptists have engaged in an active program of missions, education, and every other benevolence. Their growth in numbers and organization has been accompanied by an increasing sensitiveness to all the needs of their constituency and the world. The largest bodies in American Baptist life are the two national organizations of Negro Baptists now numbering 7,168,190 in 36,894 churches, the American Baptist Convention (Northern Baptists) with 1,513,692 members in 6,490 churches, and the Southern Baptist Convention with 8,467,743 members in 30,340 churches. The Baptist World Alliance was organized in 1905. Many Baptists in the North have been active in the ecumenical movement.

Methodism.—The close relationship of Methodism with English life, particularly during the lifetime of John Wesley (who died in 1791), and the fact that many Methodist ministers in the colonies were loyal to England during the American Revolution made the task of American Methodists quite difficult in the opening years of this period. Several factors soon altered this picture, however. The organization of the Methodist Episcopal Church in America in 1784 brought a new unity. The great leader of these early years was Francis Asbury (1745–1816), who introduced the office of bishop into Methodism. By his example as a tireless itinerant minister and his stern demand that his preachers follow this pattern, Asbury had a large part in the phenomenal growth of American Methodism. The simple type of organization and the singing, experiential salvation that was preached was ready-made for the extensive American frontier. The sweeping revivals in the west in the opening years of the nineteenth century brought Methodism a large ingathering.

There have been several schisms. Because it was a people's church, Methodism was among the first to feel the impact of the slavery-abolitionist controversy in the fourth decade of the nineteenth century, and schism came in 1844–45. Other important excisions from organizational unity came because of disagreement over church government and the doctrine of holiness. The new rationalism prevalent in the second half of the nineteenth century greatly affected Methodism and brought considerable controversy over the modernistic issue.

The schism over slavery ended in 1939 with the reuniting of the northern and southern divisions. American Methodism now numbers 9,292,046 constituents in 39,854 churches, most of whom are members of the new united body. This denomination has always been active in missions, education, and other benevolences and has taken an outstanding part in the ecumenical movement.

Canadian and Latin American Christianity

Canada.—In the opening years of this period Canadian Christianity was principally Roman Catholic of the French type. Following the Seven Years' War (1756–63) Canada was ceded to Great Britain by France, accompanied by an unusual religious settlement. By the Quebec Act of 1774 the Roman Catholic religion was guaranteed free exercise, and the Constitutional Act of 1791 practically gave Catholicism control of what became Lower Canada. As a result, Roman Catholicism is in a dominant position in Canadian religious life.

The considerable Protestant immigration to Canada from the United States and England during and after the Revolutionary

War gave the Church of England a foothold in Canada. After a period of trial and error with respect to state support and ecclesiastical organization, the Church of England in Canada was organized in 1861, although it was not supported or controlled by the government. In 1893 a general synod was formed to govern the Canadian Church of England.

In the twentieth century this denomination has not kept pace numerically with other groups, a dwindling immigration from England being part of the reason. Although favoring the establishment of an interdenominational church union in Canada, the Church of England refused to enter the United Church of Canada when that body was organized in 1925 by the Methodists, Presbyterians, and Congregationalists because the other parties refused to continue the historic episcopate.

Although one of the earliest groups to begin work in Canada, Congregationalism never really became a prominent part of Canadian Christianity. Baptists and Presbyterians profited by excisions from this denomination. Despite valiant work by a joint home missionary society organized by Congregationalists, Baptists, and Presbyterians in 1827, and the work of the Colonial Missionary Society formed in England in 1836, Canadian Congregationalists numbered but 12,586 when the United Church of Canada absorbed them in 1925.

Canadian Presbyterian life before 1875 was unbelievably complex, representing a melting pot of Calvinistic thought from various racial and doctrinal groups. Foreign quarrels and problems were transplanted from every part of the world. The formation of the Presbyterian Church in Canada in 1875, representing a merger of several bodies, brought increased vitality in all benevolences and education. In 1925 this denomination reported over 400,000 constituents at the time the majority entered the United Church of Canada. However, about 180,000 of these refused to participate in the union, continuing as the Presbyterian Church of Canada.

Canadian Methodists also had an almost infinite variety in organization and thought before 1884. In spite of gathering up all of the organizational, political, and doctrinal tensions of American

371

and English Methodists and adding some problems distinctly their own, Canadian Methodists made amazingly good progress despite diversity. When the Methodist Church of Canada was formed in 1884, its constituency numbered over 157,000. This denomination took the lead in working toward church union, and in 1925 when it became a part of the United Church of Canada, its membership numbered over 415,000.

Not long after the issuance of the Lambeth Quadrilateral (1888) interest was aroused in Canada over the possibility of church union. First efforts were not encouraging because only the Church of England desired to perpetuate the historic episcopate. At the turn of the century, however, Methodists, Congregationalists, and Presbyterians laid the groundwork for union. The Baptists declined an invitation to become a part of the movement. The final organization adopted elements of all three denominational types, and in 1925 the union was completed, bringing together 609,729 constituents from the three merging denominations. Growth since 1925 has been slow.

The Roman Catholic Church has made the greatest strides of all Canadian groups in the modern period. From constituting about 40 per cent of the population in 1911 and about the same in 1931, the Roman Church outstripped the population in the next decade and rose to about 44 per cent of the population in 1941; and because of the high birth rate among the predominantly French and rural members, the ratio doubtless has risen even higher in the last decade.

In addition to these principal groups in Canada, smaller denominations include the Baptists, Lutherans, Greek Catholics, Mennonites, and others.

Latin America.—At the opening of the period in 1789, Latin American Christianity—embracing principally Mexico, Central America, and South America—was almost wholly Roman Catholic, although the papacy had less control than the secular powers of Europe which claimed the different areas. This picture had been altered radically in the last century. It has been a century of revolution and change. French, Spanish, and Portuguese political control has been eliminated, and practically all of the Latin American states have become independent republics. Along with political revolution has come religious turmoil. Because the Roman Catholic Church was so closely related to the political powers, it suffered considerably from anticlericalism and from some patriotic movements.

In the second half of the nineteenth century, evangelicals (principally from the United States) began an active missionary program. Practically all American denominations have had a part in this missionary task, which has made great gains from the nominal Roman Catholic population. However, dominant Roman Catholicism still makes religious liberty an ideal rather than a reality.

Concluding Summary

Christianity in the United States was separated from the secular authority by the Constitution. After 1833 all state establishments were abolished. The revival in the opening years of the nineteenth century, known as the Second Great Awakening, greatly strengthened the Christian movement in the young nation. It established the dynamics for the extensive development of benevolent work. Societies for missions, publications, and Bible distribution sprang up quickly.

To a considerable extent the large immigration from abroad and the westward thrust of the frontier in the homeland shaped the characteristics of Christianity in the United States. Missionary zeal was forwarded, new denominations were founded, older denominations grew and in some cases divided, increasing financial stability provided support for churches in each community, and a distinctive type of Christianity in general took shape. The "grass roots" denominations grew most rapidly.

During this national period in the United States, Christianity has faced problems of industrialization, the rise of cities, extensive immigration, severe world wars, and both financial prosperity and depression. Perhaps none of these has been as serious as the inroads of rationalism and materialism.

The Contemporary Outlook

THE PRINCIPAL PORTION of this study has involved the dominant forms of Christianity in the geographical areas of their strength. This naturally means that many forms of Christianity in large portions of the world have been either completely neglected or sparsely treated. That is inevitable in a work of this kind. An effort will be made in this last chapter to survey briefly the course of Christianity in sections of the world other than Europe proper and North America. Many of these areas are looked upon as mission fields, although some of them have developed so far that they should be included in any history of Christianity. This rapid survey will be followed by several observations about some contemporary problems of Christianity.

The Near East and Africa

The birthplace of Christianity has been under Mohammedan control for over a thousand years. The Near East, including what was Palestine and contiguous areas, now consists of over a dozen small countries, the largest of which, populationwise, are Turkey, Egypt, and Iran. The story of the eclipse of Eastern Christianity by the westward push of the Saracens after A.D. 632 has already been told. This did not mean the utter destruction of Christianity. After the immediate shock of conquest the Moslem conquerors took a practical attitude toward the Christians. Although no Moslem could become a Christian, the Christians were permitted to remain true to their faith, inasmuch as the tribute of money—and sometimes of boys for military service—levied against them would have been diminished or eliminated if the Christians had been destroyed. For this reason no great effort was made to proselyte Christians to the faith of Islam.

It will be remembered that the Mohammedan invasion in the seventh century overwhelmed Alexandria, Jerusalem, and Antioch, disposing of them as episcopal rivals to the bishop of Rome. Constantinople, on the other hand, withstood the assaults of the Mohammedans and in some ways was strengthened as a rival to Rome. The schism between Rome in the West and Constantinople in the East in 1054 grew out of ceremonial, social, racial, political, and ecclesiastical differences, goaded by the burning ambition of the crafty patriarch of Constantinople.

The emperor at Constantinople meanwhile faced a new crisis. A civil war of terrible proportions had been draining the strength of the Eastern world for twenty-five years. The Seljuk Turks, a new revolutionary segment of the Mohammedans, were threatening to burst out of Asia into Europe. Their barbarous treatment of Western pilgrims desiring to visit the Christian relics at Jerusalem, along with the political and ecclesiastical developments in the West, prepared the way for the Crusades which, with the contemporary overwhelming of Russia and eastern Europe by Genghis Khan (1162–1227) and his successors, checked for three centuries the further advance westward by the Turks. Efforts were made to reunite Rome and Constantinople in religious matters in the hope that the West would drive the Turks away from the siege of Constantinople. Union of Greek and Roman Catholicism was twice proclaimed, once in 1274 and again in 1439, but in each case the East subsequently repudiated their representatives, apparently preferring the cruel Turks to Roman fellowship.

In 1453 Constantinople fell to the Moslems. The patriarch (archbishop) of Constantinople became a pawn of the Turkish sultan and has continued so to be until the present time. Eastern Christianity, loosely confederated in the Greek Orthodox Church, consists of many independent national or racial churches in eastern Europe, Asia, and Africa, including patriarchates in Constantinople (the first among equals), Alexandria, Antioch, Jerusalem, and Cyprus, and the abbotship of Sinai, along with the Russian church.

375

Meanwhile, the Moslems advanced up the Balkans in the fifteenth century but were defeated just before reaching Central Europe. Gradually they were pushed back into what was formerly called Asia Minor. After throwing off the yoke of the Turk, the various Balkan states generally adopted state churches affiliated with the Greek Orthodox movement.

The Moslems have been difficult to reach with the Christian gospel. As early as the fourteenth century Raymond Lull became a missionary martyr among them. Individuals worked among them in the sixteenth and seventeenth centuries, but organized work did not commence until early in the nineteenth century.

The large core of Mohammedan culture in the Near East at present makes the mission task more formidable. Iraq and Iran (Persia), as well as Arabia (the birthplace of Mohammedanism), have hardly been touched by Christian missions because of strong Moslem resistance. Strenuous missionary efforts have been made in Turkey, principally by American missionaries, despite many governmental restrictions. The Church of England has led in the Egyptian field, their efforts mainly looking toward the reactivating of Greek Orthodox Christianity in the areas where they work. Some important and significant schools have been planted in the Near East.

The majority of the people across the northern part of Africa, once possessing a thriving Christianity, are now fanatically Moslem. The same thing is true toward the south in Africa proper. From Alexandria to Capetown the threatening shadow of the Moslem crescent hangs over the country. The overwhelming Islamic infiltration from the north and east still continues. Mohammedanism now has ten times as many followers in Africa as all Protestant missions combined. The field has been actively worked by both Roman Catholic and Protestant missionaries, the former beginning in the late fifteenth century, principally from Portugal, and the latter mainly from America and England in the nineteenth century, in the inspiration of the Negro emancipation movement. Africa is bound to become a battleground between Mohammedanism, Christianity, and secularism in this her day of awakening and new awareness. The situation has been aggravated by the political events which brought the nation of Israel into existence. This has drawn the Moslem world closer together, and resentment toward outsiders, even missionaries, has been growing.

Russia

Sprawling over portions of both Europe and Asia is the extensive territory of the Russian giant. The beginnings of Christianity in Russia are shrouded among apocryphal tales and traditions. Perhaps the missionaries Cyril and Methodius planted the seed in the ninth century. The extreme illiteracy of the masses of the people for many centuries thereafter insured a sacramental and liturgical type of Christianity plagued with much superstition. The continuous internal warfare of the eleventh and twelfth centuries, followed almost immediately by the destructive invasion of Genghis Khan and his Mongolian hordes, inhibited Russian Christianity until the middle of the fifteenth century. After the fall of Constantinople in 1453 Russia became a stronghold of the Orthodox tradition, developing a Russian patriarchate in 1589. The Russian Church was completely subservient to the state. Peter the Great (1689–1725) abolished the patriarchate and established the Holy Synod under his control. Catherine II (1762–96) completed the humiliation of the Church by confiscating its extensive lands and serfs.

It should be said that the Church was doubtless as corrupt in every respect as it could possibly be. The serfs confiscated with the land, estimated to number over a million, probably received better treatment in secular hands than they had known from the ecclesiastical tyrants. The defeat of Russia by Japan in 1905 and the catastrophe of their fiasco in World War I contributed both to the Revolution of November, 1917, and the militaristic sensitiveness of the Bolshevik regime.

In January, 1918, not only were church and state separated, to the disparagement of the former, but after 1922 an effort was made to destroy Christianity, which had been identified for a thousand years with imperial cruelty and domination. The contemporary

377

policy of the Communist Party in Russia is to stamp out all Christian influence for the young but to let the older folk carry it with them to their graves.

Asia and Related Areas

The earliest mission field in the modern period was that of India, which now has more than 400,000,000 people living in an area of a little more than a million and a half square miles. The first missionary work was done by Pietistic Lutheran missionaries sent out by Denmark in 1705 to Tranquebar on the west coast of India. The Society for the Promotion of Christian Knowledge, organized in 1699 in England, also aided this work in the eighteenth century, as did the Moravian missionaries.

It was to India that William Carey went in 1793 to institute the modern mission movement. Since that time practically every major denomination has worked in India. Despite striking advances and sacrificial labors, the total of nominal Christians in India now does not exceed six and a half million, of whom less than half are Protestant. The nationalistic movement of the twentieth century which brought Mahatma Gandhi to the fore has, strangely enough, actually helped Christian missionary activities, because Gandhi made practical use of some of the principles of Jesus. There are more Moslems in India than anywhere else—almost one hundred million of them. About half of the entire population claim Hinduism.

China, with a population a little larger than that of India, became a Protestant mission field in 1807 when Robert Morrison entered Canton. Roman Catholics had worked in China since days of Francis Xavier in the sixteenth century. The Opium War of 1841 pried open five important port cities to foreign trade, and into these cities Christian missionaries poured. However, it took England two additional wars in the middle of the nineteenth century to convince the Chinese of their best interests. Most of the early mission stations dotted the coast. In 1866, however, J. Hudson Taylor and his China Inland Mission, operating through voluntary offerings on the faith principle, pushed into interior China.

Internal wars greatly disrupted missionary activity between 1900 and 1927. In 1931 the undeclared war with Japan was begun. World War II and the Communist regime in China have practically cut off all missionary work in continental China. Before the war there were about 750,000 Protestant adherents and over two million Roman Catholics. Ceylon, the island just off the southeastern edge of India, is strongly Buddhistic. Two-thirds of the population, numbering perhaps ten million, follow this religion. Roman Catholic missionaries began work there in the sixteenth century, while Protestants from England followed two centuries later. Before World War II Roman Catholics numbered about four hundred thousand and Protestants about fifty thousand.

Burma was entered by Christian missionaries from William Carey's Baptist mission at Serampore in 1807, but the first permanent work is credited to Adoniram Judson, American Baptist missionary, who arrived in 1813. Other denominations, principally the Anglicans and Methodists, have also opened missions here. It is estimated that there are about 175,000 Christians in Burma.

Christian missionaries are also working in Thailand; in Indochina, where French Roman Catholics almost pre-empted the field and claim about one and a half million adherents; in Malaya, where half of the population of over six million is Moslem; in Indonesia, where over two million adherents in a population of over 65,000,000 claim to be Christians, mainly Protestant, although the Moslem movement provides strong opposition; in Borneo; and in the Philippine Islands, where American missionaries claimed a following of about 330,000 before World War II.

Japan was first entered by Roman Catholic missionaries in the middle of the sixteenth century. For fifty years they worked with unusual success, but severe governmental persecution cut them short. Although Commodore Perry opened Japan to the outside world in 1853, missionary activity was retarded until 1873, after which scores of denominational bodies began work in Japan. The rising spirit of Japanese nationalism after 1900 created problems for Christian missionaries, as did the industrialization of the nation, which provided the background of Toyohiko Kagawa. Before World War II there were fewer than four hundred thousand Christians in Japan in a population of eighty-five million. After the war it appeared that many opportunities for Christianity beckoned from this island, but many of these doors are now closing.

The Dutch began mission work in Formosa in the first half of the seventeenth century, but with the overthrow of Dutch control this work stopped. Roman Catholic missionaries began their work two centuries later, as did Protestants. The number of missionaries has increased since the closing of China and the militarization of this island.

Korean Christianity, after a period of unusually rapid growth before 1910, felt the blighting effect of Japanese domination. Protestant communicants numbering a few less than 150,000 were reported before World War II.

Oceania

The various islands in the southern Pacific Ocean known as Oceania have also been the object of Christian missions. Adherents before World War II numbered almost half a million.

Some Concluding Observations

The Christian movement today faces major decisions and problems. Some of these will be discussed briefly to complete the story.

Supernaturalism amidst rationalism.—For over a thousand years Christian thinkers have wrestled with the problem of supernaturalism. Does it transcend man's rational powers? Is it complementary to logical thinking processes, or is there a basic antagonism between the two? Is it possible to hold to both rationalism and supernaturalism?

Eighteenth and nineteenth century Protestant continental philosophy and theology increasingly attacked belief in supernaturalism as being unnecessary and untenable. In the twentieth century a new approach has been made. This attempts to conserve the idea of a transcendental God and recognizes man as being a needy creature. However, the radical view of the person of Christ and the denial of the reality of a divine historical revelation which have characterized the liberal wing of this movement brings almost the same dilemma that faces continuing rationalism of the older sort —namely, does this world order know any historical, supernatural intervention of God? Many liberals are emphatically denying that the world does or can know such a supernatural intervention.

What is the logical conclusion to a denial of supernaturalism? It demands an acknowledged departure from the New Testament Scriptures and the historic Christian movement. To deny the supernatural resurrection of Christ from the dead is to refute a basic doctrine of Christianity (see 1 Cor. 15:13 ff.) . There can be no Christianity without a supernatural resurrection. The same thing is true with reference to a supernatural spiritual regeneration. When this point has been reached—the reduction of Christianity to a nonsupernatural account of the ethical teachings of a man who had delusions about his own relations with God and deceived others at this point—it seems only fair to deny that such a theological system should be called Christian. Many will term such conclusions as naive, but that cannot settle the problem. Undoubtedly this century will witness a bold effort to separate Christ from the Christian movement. An existential confrontation by a mysterious and unincarnated deity, who is prevented by either a limited sovereignty or a limited love from aiding the needy people in the temporal order of this world, would seem to be the general direction of contemporary liberal theology.

Missions amidst nationalism.—The extensive missionary program of the last two centuries has been among the heroic movements of human history. There is a serious question, however, whether the pattern that has been followed in these two centuries will be permitted to continue. The development of a strong nationalistic spirit among the newer nations of the world constitutes a challenge to the established order of missions. In some cases missions already are being viewed as an effort to supplant a native culture with a foreign one and are resented as such. Despite the sacrificial lives of previous missionaries, some still suspect that the missionary movement is a prelude to political and economic infiltration. In addition, the fact that America is giving extensive aid to all sections of the world has indirectly reacted against missions. American funds are now provided in many foreign countries for various services once carried on exclusively through missions. Governments that formerly allowed missionaries in their lands in order to reap the advantage of these services and institutions are now finding that they can provide their own services and institutions without permitting foreigners to work in their countries.

Faith amidst secularism.—The preoccupation of mankind with things has always been a deterrent to Christian progress. It has never been more of a threat than in this generation. Men have become increasingly indifferent to spiritual things. Even hostility toward Christianity has in many cases been replaced by a blithe ignoring of all religious values. This, basically, constitutes the subversive nature of Communist Russia. Her religious policy has stemmed principally from reactionary and political motivations. The indifferentism of Russia to spiritual things may in the long run be more harmful in the nations under her domination than the earlier policy of persecution.

One of the inviting elements to the areas of the world now awakening is crass secularism, whose gospel is simple and whose materialistic rewards are contemporary. America has been badly infected with this virus. How much it will sap the vitality of American Christianity in days ahead cannot be known, but without doubt it will contribute to crime and corruption through the elimination of spiritual support for moral and ethical values.

Denominationalism amidst ecumenicalism.—The ecumenical movement has made great strides during this century. Whether it will replace denominationalism is open to serious question. There is still considerable division among adherents of the movement as to whether federation or organic union is the ultimate goal. Organic union is not desired by many who are willing to federate or co-operate in areas where that is possible.

Minimal requisites for union cannot be compromised. The Lambeth Quadrilateral, for example, represents the very minimum requirements of the Church of England and Episcopalianism with reference to church union. Several historical examples in the past fifty years have shown that the omission of any one of the four items set forth in this statement renders union impossible. While other denominations have not specifically set out their minimal requirements for union, it is certain that there are doctrinal or ecclesiastical boundaries beyond which they will not go.

Many "family" denominations, split by historical agreements over matters not basically doctrinal or ecclesiastical, have been unable or unwilling to unite, despite the fact that the various groups involved pay lip service to the ecumenical movement generally.

The Roman Catholic Church has made it plain that they have no interest in church union, unless all other Christians desire to affiliate with them on their terms. This sounds a death knell to any ultimate goal of a united Christendom.

The wide gulf between sacramentalists and evangelicals in the basic interpretation of Christianity constitutes a major problem. In the area of life and work these groups can co-operate together and with many non-Christian bodies whose ethical and moral aims are similar. When the problem of Christian conviction is injected, however, as the Evanston meeting clearly showed, there must be freedom to follow that conviction in the spirit of love.

Concluding Summary

The twentieth century is fraught with more opportunities and more peril for Christianity than any century in a thousand years. Rapid communication and extensive enlightenment have put new burdens on the missionary; he is now forced to offer a Christianity to those who see it lived very imperfectly in the missionary's own land. Mohammedanism increasingly is challenging Christianity for the allegiance of mankind. The increasing influence of the Russian giant is a religious, as well as political, challenge.

BIBLIOGRAPHY

BETTENSON, HENRY (ed.). *Documents of the Christian Church.* New York: Oxford University Press, 1947.
CAREY, S. P. *William Carey.* London: Carey Press, 1934.

FERM, VIRGILIUS (ed.). *The American Church of the Protestant Heritage*. New York: Philosophical Library, Inc., 1953.

GARRISON, W. E. *The March of Faith*. New York: Harper & Brothers, 1933.

KIDD, B. J. *The Church of Eastern Christendom from* A.D. *451 to the Present Time*. London: Faith Press, Ltd., 1927.

LATOURETTE, K. S. *A History of Christianity*. New York: Harper & Brothers, 1953.

NEWMAN, A. H. *A Manual of Church History*, II. Philadelphia: American Baptist Publication Society, 1953.

NICHOLS, JAMES H. *History of Christianity 1650–1950*. New York: Ronald Press Co., 1956.

ROBINSON, JAMES HARVEY. *Readings in European History*, II. Boston: Ginn & Co., 1904.

SWEET, WILLIAM W. *The Story of Religion in America*. New York: Harper & Brothers, 1950.

Index

THE
LOST EMPIRE
OF ATLANTIS

By the same author:

1421: The Year China Discovered the World

*1434: The Year a Magnificent Chinese Fleet Sailed to Italy
and Ignited the Renaissance*

THE
LOST EMPIRE
OF ATLANTIS

|||||||||||||||||||||||||||||||||||||||

HISTORY'S GREATEST
MYSTERY REVEALED

GAVIN MENZIES

Swordfish

If you would like to contact Gavin Menzies and the research team,
please email them at: zhenghe@gavinmenzies.net
Our website www.gavinmenzies.net is a focal point for
ongoing research into pre-Columbian voyages to the New World.
Please get in touch and join us on this great adventure!

First published in Great Britain in 2011 by
Swordfish

1 3 5 7 9 10 8 6 4 2

© Gavin Menzies 2011

A CIP catalogue record for this book
is available from the British Library.

ISBN: 978 0 857 82005 1 (Hardback)
ISBN: 978 0 857 82006 8 (Export Paperback)

Typeset by Input Data Services Ltd, Bridgwater, Somerset

Printed and bound by CPI Group (UK) Ltd, Croydon, CR0 4YY

The Orion Publishing Group's policy is to use papers that
are natural, renewable and recyclable and made
from wood grown in sustainable forests. The logging
and manufacturing processes are expected to conform to
environmental regulations of the country of origin.

Swordfish

Orion Publishing Group Ltd
Orion House
5 Upper Saint Martin's Lane
London, WC2H 9EA

An Hachette UK Company

www.orionbooks.co.uk

This book is dedicated to my beloved wife Marcella,
who has travelled with me on the journeys
related in this book and through life.

Here is her name in Minoan Linear A script.

CONTENTS

BOOK III: JOURNEYS WEST

BOOK IV: EXAMINING THE HEAVENS

BOOK V: THE REACHES OF EMPIRE

BOOK VI: THE LEGACY

ACKNOWLEDGEMENTS

Encouragement to write this book

This book, like *1421* and *1434*, is a collective endeavour. Hundreds of people, by and large friends via my websites, have encouraged me by persuading me that multiple intercontinental voyages were undertaken thousands of years before Columbus: indeed, long before Admiral Zheng He's voyages. So I should start by thanking those people who have taken the trouble to send me emails.

All of my books rely heavily on my experiences as a submarine navigator or captain. I am indebted to the Royal Navy for investing in me, training me for over a decade to fulfil those duties. I am particularly grateful to Admiral Sir John Woodward G.B.E., K.C.B., who trained me to be a submarine captain and who taught me to think laterally – that is, to address problems by examining the evidence rather than by using preconceived notions.

There have been many authors, far more distinguished and knowledgeable than I, whose books have been an inspiration to me. In their book *Pre-Columbian Contact with the Americas Across the Oceans: An Annotated Bibliography*, Emeritus Professor John L. Sorenson and Martin Raish have produced a summary of over 5,000 books or articles describing transcontinental voyages across the oceans over the past 8,000 years. Emeritus Professor Carl L. Johannessen, in a series of books and articles, has published similar accounts of intercontinental voyages over many millennia. Sorenson and Johannessen have joined forces to publish *World Trade and Biological Exchanges Before 1492*, which I have used time and again to provide evidence to support my claims in this book. Recently Professor Sorenson has published 'A Complex of Ritual and Ideology Shared by Mesoamerica and The Ancient Near East', a paper in which he sets out descriptions of thousands of intercontinental sea voyages thousands of years before Columbus.

Emeritus Professor John Coghlan has provided intellectual backing these five years, in support of a non-scholar 'who marches to the beat of a different drum'. John has had to face virulent criticism for having done so and I am most grateful for his unwavering backing.

There are authors whose view of history differs from that of established historians – I thank Professors Octave Du Temple and Roy Drier, Emeritus Professor James Scherz, James L. Guthrie and David Hoffman for their work on the ancient copper mines of Lake Superior and the missing millions of pounds of copper from those mines, which apparently vanished into thin air.

My story is about the Minoan fleets that travelled the oceans of the world before the ghastly explosion on Thera in 1450 BC, which wiped out the Minoan civilisation. Professor Spyridon Marinatos alerted us all to this adventure in 1964 when he chose to excavate the town of Akrotiri on Thera (Santorini), which had been a major Minoan base in the 2nd millennium BC. By good luck and judgement he stumbled upon the house of an admiral, buried in 1450 BC but still with intact walls. This gave the world its first sight of the superb Minoan ships which had then plied the world.

Professor Marinatos' excavations mirrored those of Sir Arthur Evans in Crete, where Sir Arthur is a legend. Single-handedly, through decades of excavations and research, he revealed the fabulous Minoan civilisation which burst upon the world in 3000 BC. I have relied heavily on Sir Arthur's work, not least in the context of the inheritance of classical Greece and the debt Greece and Europe owe to the Minoan civilisation. Sir Arthur's mantle has fallen upon Professor Stylianos Alexiou, whose book launched our adventure, and latterly Dr Minas Tsikritsis, whose work is described later in the book.

Many authors have spent a lifetime describing intercontinental voyages across the oceans in the third and second millennia BC. I would particularly like to thank Dr Gunnar Thompson for his

accounts of the trade between America, Egypt and India, notably
the trade in maize; Charlotte Rees and Liu Gang for their works on
trade between America and China in the second and first millennia
BC; David Hoffman for his researches into prehistoric voyages for
copper between Europe and America, especially between the Great
Lakes and the Atlantic; Tim Severin for demonstrating to us all that
such voyages were possible; J. Lesley Fitton for knowledge of the
trade between the Atlantic, Europe and the eastern Mediterranean;
Professor Emeritus Bernard Knapp for his writings about the trade
between Crete, Africa and the Levant; Dr Joan Aruz for mounting
the superb exhibition 'Beyond Babylon' in the Metropolitan
Museum of Art, New York (I have extensively referred to the beautiful book she edited relating to that exhibition); Professor Emeritus
Manfred Bietak for his work on Minoan fleets in the Nile Delta;
Professor Rao for unearthing the Bronze Age Indian port of Lothal;
Professor Edward Keall of the Royal Ontario Museum for his team's
excavation of the Bronze Age hoard in the Yemen; Hans Peter
Duerr for his articles on Minoan trade with the Baltic in the 2nd
millennium BC; Professor Beatriz Comendador Rey for her research
and her team's excavations of Bronze Age seaborne voyages to
Spain; Tony Hammond for his information about Bronze Age mining
and trade in Britain; and Philip Coppens for his studies of the Great
Lakes copper trade in the 2nd millennium BC.

Minoan shipbuilding expertise, which led to the intercontinental
voyages without which there would have been no Atlantis civilisation, is at the heart of my story. Together with the rest of the
world, I am indebted to Mr Mehmet Cakir who found the Uluburun
wreck (c.1310 BC) and Professor Cemal Pulak who organised a very
skilful series of dives over eleven summers, which have resulted in
such a haul of evidence being taken from the seabed to the castle
that has been adapted to house these amazing treasures. Professor
Andreas Hauptmann and colleagues have analysed the chemical
composition of the copper ingots in the Uluburun wreck and a
number of other experts have carried out research into the goods,
flora and fauna found in the wreck, as evidence of the voyage of

the ship – notably Baltic amber; African ivory; shells from the Indian Ocean; and beads from India. Further thanks have been placed on my website.

Not only have I relied on the revolutionary research of those mentioned but I have equally depended upon the team without whom this book would never have been written. As in the past, Ian Hudson has co-ordinated the team with great skill and humour, integrating design work and Ms Moy's typing. Ms Moy of QED Secretarial Services has typed twenty-nine drafts speedily, accurately, economically and with good humour.

I owe a special tribute to Cedric Bell, who has supported my research in many ways for years. Originally a marine engineer, he has spent a lifetime in engineering. His roles have included those of surveyor, foundry engineer, works engineer and then production manager of Europe's largest lube oil plant. Following retirement he has spent fifteen years researching the Roman occupation of Britain on a full-time basis, finding many similarities between Chinese and Roman engineering. His contribution to this book has been enormous. Back in 2003 Cedric read *1421* shortly before visiting New Zealand. Several surveys then followed. These surveys proved that the Chinese had been mining and refining iron in New Zealand for 2,000 years. The evidence included harbours, wrecks, settlements and foundries. This led to a furore, followed by vitriolic attacks on Cedric by New Zealand 'historians'. I appointed a team of independent surveyors to check Cedric's finds by using ground-penetrating radar, sonics and the independent carbon dating of iron mortar and wood. The results are on my website. They show that Cedric's research was incredibly accurate.

As works maintenance engineer for Delta Metals in Birmingham, Cedric was responsible for a large non-ferrous foundry and extruders and an ore reclamation plant with ball mills, Wilfley tables and vacuum extraction flotation tanks. At the time, Delta produced 65 per cent of Britain's non-ferrous metals. Whenever I have come across a problem (there have been many) Cedric has either been able to answer me immediately or refer me to an expert who could.

He has also provided me with a stream of books, including the classic works on Bronze Age mining and smelting. Without his expert unfailing support, this book would not have been completed.

Luigi Bonomi, my literary agent, who has acted for me for the past ten years and has skilfully sold *1421* and *1434*, has been an inspiration. Luigi persuaded me to postpone my book dealing with Chinese voyages to the Americas in the 2nd millennium BC in favour of this one. Luigi has superb judgement on which I have relied throughout. Budding authors should beat a path to his door!

Luigi sold the world literary rights to this book to Orion – part of the Hachette Group, the world's largest publisher. Orion has been enormously supportive and enthusiastic. I should particularly like to thank Rowland White my publisher, his assistant Nicola Crossley and Susan Howe, foreign rights director and her team, as well as Helen Ewing and Georgie Widdrington.

Gaynor Aaltonen played a key role. She has skilfully turned my stilted prose into a readable book whilst at the same time incorporating an endless flood of new evidence, which has flowed on to our computers since Orion first took this book on. Without Gaynor's work there would not have been a book. I am indebted to her.

Finally Marcella, for without her unfailing kindness and support there would have been no *Lost Empire of Atlantis*. I and the book owe her everything. I am so happy the Minoan Linear A spelling of her name starts with the face of a cat!

Gavin Menzies
London
St Valentines Day 2011

LIST OF ILLUSTRATIONS
AND DIAGRAMS

The illustrations are inspired by the wonderful frescoes at Thera, Knossos and Tell el-Dab'a and drawn by Catherine Grant (www.catherinezoraida.com)

Book I: 'Minoan ladies in all their finery'
Book II: 'Lions pouncing on their prey at Tell el-Dab'a'
Book III: 'Minoan bull leaping – Knossos'
Book IV: 'The Prince of Lilies'
Book V: 'An ocean-going Minoan ship'
Book VI: 'The Phaestos Disc'

The following images from the frescoes are found throughout the book:

Swallow
Blue lion
Small boat from the 'flotilla' fresco
Fisherman
Antelope
Jumping deer
Partridges

LIST OF PLATES

Second plate section

The Hagia Triada sarcophagus © Nick Kaye

Sculpted stone sunflower juxtaposed with live sunflower, Halebid, Karnataka, India © Carl L. Johannessen

Wall sculpture from Hoysala Dynasty Halebid temple at Somnathpur, India, showing maize ears © Carl L. Johannessen

Stone carving at Pattadakal temple, India, shows a parrot perched on a sunflower © Carl L. Johannessen

Stone carving of a pineapple in a cave temple in Udaiguri, India © The American Institute of Indian Studies

Francisco José de Goya y Lucientes, The Agility and Audacity of Juanito Apiñani in the Ring at Madrid, plate 20 from the series La Tauromaquia, 1814–1816. Etching and aquatint. Meadows Museum, SMU, Dallas, Algur H. Meadows Collection, MM.67.07.20. Photography by Michael Bodycomb

Minoan bull leaper, British Museum, photograph by Mike Peel

Minoan bull leaper, Heraklion Museum, photograph by Jerzy Strzelecki.

Dover ship © Dover Museum and Bronze Age Boat Gallery

The Nebra disc, photograph by Rainer Zenz

Stonehenge, photograph by Stefan Kühn

A selection of photographs from the Wiltshire Heritage Museum, Devizes includes:

227: Upton Lovell G2 – Amber space-plate necklace with complex borings

599: Wilton, Bronze looped palstave

616: Rushall Down, Disc-headed bronze pin

340: Upton Lovell G1, Faience beads

159: Wilsford G56, Bronze dagger

266: Winterbourne Stoke G5, Bronze dagger

623: Found between Salisbury and Amesbury, Bronze bracelet

166: Wilsford G23, Bronze crutch-headed pin with hollow, open-ended head

237: Shrewton G27, Stone battle axe

All images © Wiltshire Heritage Museum, Devizes

Comparisons of Stonehenge, Uluburun and Great Lakes copper tools and implements:

Coiled snake effigy (Uluburun wreck and Great Lakes)

Animal weights at the British museum, the Uluburun wreck and the Great Lakes.

Conical points (Uluburun wreck and Great Lakes)

Triangulate spear head (Uluburun wreck and Great Lakes)

Gaff hooks (Uluburun wreck and Great Lakes)

Bronze knives (Uluburun wreck and Great Lakes)

To view photographs of Great Lakes copper tools and come to your own conclusions, please visit www.copperculture.zoomshare.com

The Amesbury archer, Salisbury Museum, photograph by Ian Hudson

Antikythera device, photograph by Marsyas

The Isopata ring, Heraklion Museum, Crete © Nick Kaye. All rights reserved

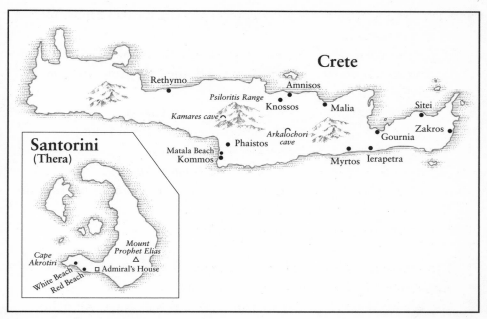

Minoan Crete and Santorini

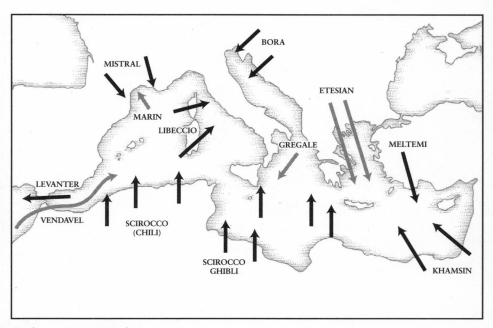

Mediterranean Winds

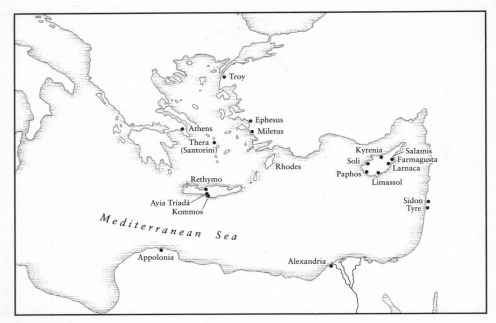

Minoan Trade Empire in the Mediterranean

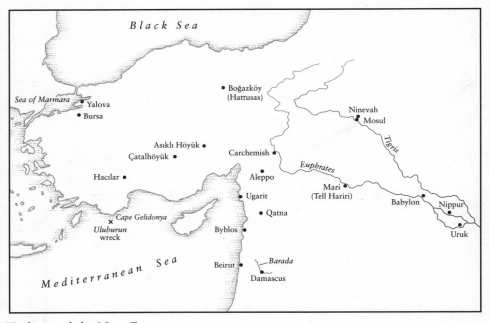

Turkey and the Near East

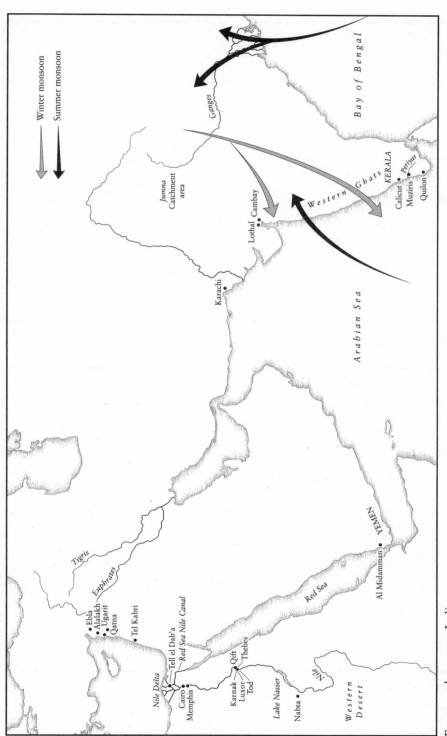

Egypt and route to India

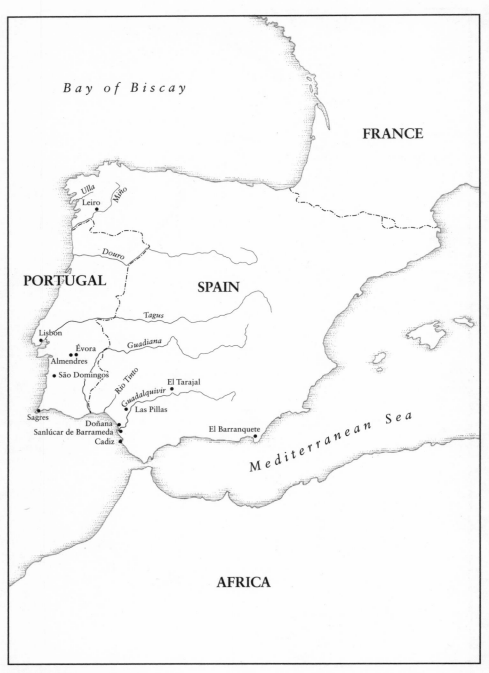

Spain and Portugal

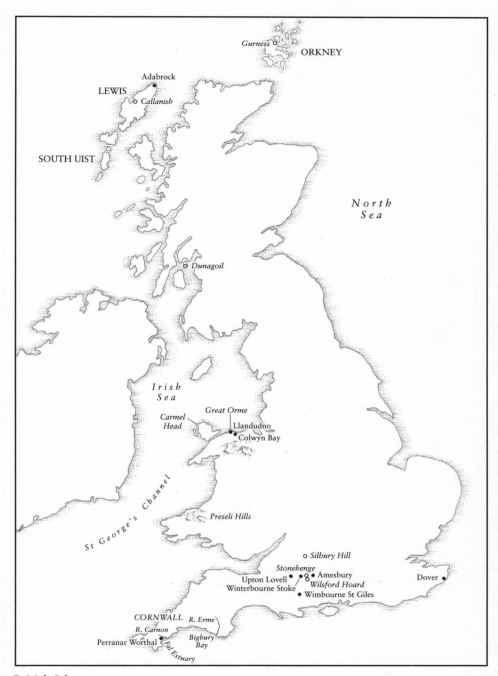

British Isles

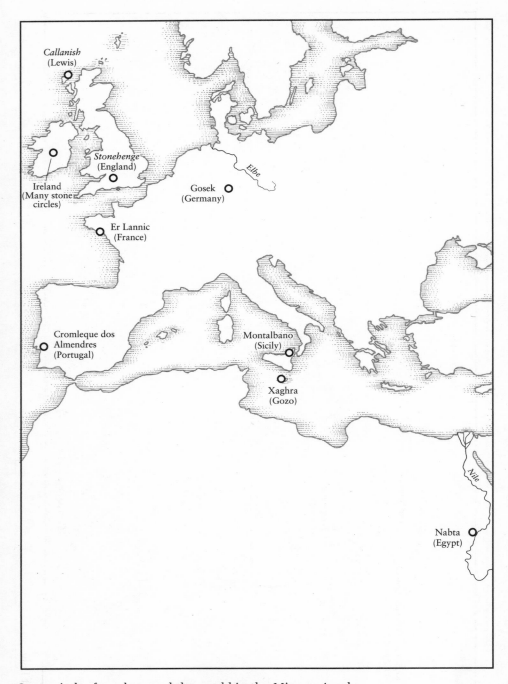

Stone circles found around the world in the Minoans' wake

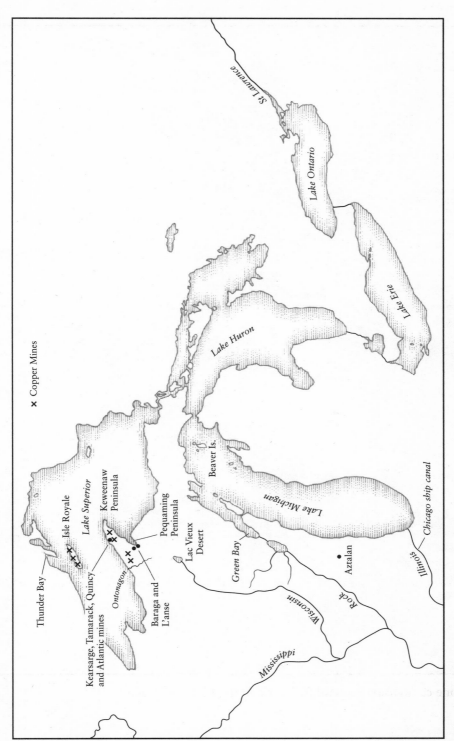

x Copper Mines

St Lawrence

Lake Ontario

Lake Erie

Lake Huron

Isle Royale

Lake Superior

Keweenaw
Peninsula

Pequaming
Peninsula

Beaver Is.

Lac Vieux
Desert

Lake Michigan

Chicago ship canal

Thunder Bay

Kearsarge, Tamarack, Quincy
and Atlantic mines

Ontonagon

Baraga and
L'anse

Green Bay

Aztalan

Illinois

Wisconsin

Rock

Mississippi

The Great Lakes

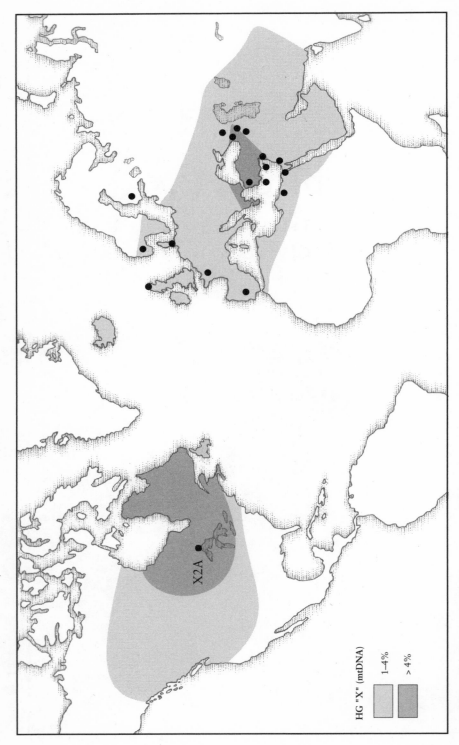

HG "X" (mtDNA)

1-4%

> 4%

X2A

Distribution of Haplotype X2

BOOK I

||||||||||||||||||||||||||||||||||

DISCOVERY

THE MINOAN
CIVILISATION

1

AN ADVENTURE ON CRETE

I was gazing north from the balcony of our hotel, the glowing lights of the town huddled at my feet. Far below, the Aegean stretched away through the night towards a lost horizon. Somewhere out there in the open sea lay the ancient, ruined island of Thera. What I did not know, as I turned and made my way back into the room, was that hidden beneath that island was a secret that was thousands of years old, a secret that would revolutionise my view of history. All of my ideas about history and world exploration were about to be turned upside down.

My wife Marcella and I had been looking forward to a quiet, contemplative Christmas, shut off from the world. After researching material for a new book I was dog-tired, so we decided to take a short break on the island of Crete. We would travel via Athens, one of our favourite places on earth. No more mobiles or email: we'd spend Christmas by candlelight in a former Byzantine monastery. Or so we thought. Our cosy dream of long walks through the classical ruins, followed by a week of Spartan simplicity in the mountains of Crete, was shattered when we arrived in Athens to find a mini riot in progress, right outside the hotel. In front of us protesting mobs of people milled around, shouting, waving placards and overturning cars. Police – bearing guns and wearing riot gear – stood menacingly in front of them.

So we took ourselves straight off to Crete, finding another spot, idyllic in its own way: a small hotel in the comfortable old Venetian port of Rethymno, in the north. Our first two days were marked by torrential downpours of rain. Then on Christmas Eve the rain lifted.

A few rays of sun turned into a soft mellow morning that beckoned us to explore beyond the snow-capped mountains we could see from our balcony. What we found that day put any thoughts of quiet, and of rest, out of the question: the discovery would set me on a determined hunt for knowledge around the globe.

We set out on a drive. In places, the narrow roads were more like fords, running with the past two days' rain. As we drove rather gingerly through a muddy series of pretty villages, we could see that grapes still hung on the vine. The roadsides were carpeted with yellow clover and the fig trees still had their deep green leaves, even at Christmas. Crete is an incredibly fertile island. As we left one rickety village, we saw two men drag a pig across the road and string it up between two ladders, ready for slaughter. After a journey along winding roads, often blocked by herds of black and white goats, their bells tinkling to ward off snakes, we pitched up at our destination, picked that morning at random: the ancient palace of Phaestos.

Myth has it that the city of Phaestos was founded by one of the sons of the legendary hero Hercules. It certainly looks majestic. The ruined palace complex unfolds like a great white plate on a deep green backcloth of pine forest to the south of the island. The ancient Greeks believed that this was one of the cities founded by the great King Minos, a mythological figure who reigned over Crete generations before the Trojan War. As we began to explore the ruins we quickly discovered that the symbol of Minos' royalty was the *labrys*, or double axe, a formidable ceremonial weapon shaped like a waxing and waning moon, set back to back. The other symbol of Minos' immense power was the terrifying image of a rampant bull.

We stepped out on to a ruin that was staggering. Phaestos is vast: bigger than the Holy Roman Emperor Charlemagne's royal palace at Aachen, and at least three times the size of London's Buckingham Palace. Its powerful but simple architecture is flawlessly constructed in elegant cut stone and it is laid out in what appears to be a harmonious plan. Wide, open staircases lead from the Theatre to the Bull Ring to the Royal Palace, and from there to smooth stone platforms that allow views of the ring of mountains beyond, the green plain sloping away to the distant sea. The overall effect was one of lightness and air. As the sun danced off the pools and courtyards, reflecting the azure sky, the whole site seemed like a mirage floating between heaven and earth. The serenity and scale of the place reminded us both instantly of the same thing: the monumental architecture of Egypt.

One other fact immediately gripped us. Like Knossos, its perhaps more famous sister complex further northeast of us, the palace at Phaestos is ancient, older by far than the magnificent Parthenon in Athens, built c.450 BC when classical Greece was at its height – the people of Phaestos had lived in luxury and comfort more than a millennium before that. The palace is as venerable as the Old Kingdom of the pharaohs of Egypt and as ancient as the great pyramids of Giza. The site had been inhabited, we discovered, since 4000 BC.

This came as a real surprise to me. How was it that I had heard so little of this extraordinary but relatively obscure palace, whose beauty rivalled that of India's Taj Mahal? What did I really know about the people who had built it: the people who are known as 'the Minoans'? As we walked across the baking hot palace court, we realised that while most Europeans were still living in primitive huts, the ancient Minoans were building palaces with paved streets, baths and functioning sewers. Unparalleled for its age, the Minoans' advanced engineering knowledge gave them a sophisticated lifestyle that put other contemporary 'civilisations' in the shade: they had intricate water-piping systems, water-tight drains, advanced air-flow management and even earthquake-resistant walls.

We climbed a huge ceremonial stair, the steps slightly slanted to allow rainwater to run off. At the end of a narrow corridor we suddenly found ourselves in an alabaster-lined room. Here, a light-well struck sunbeams off the silent walls. These rooms, once several storeys high, were known as the Queen's apartments, we were told. Phaestos' rulers enjoyed stunning marble walls in their palaces: the people lived healthy and refined lives in well-built stone houses. Secure granaries kept wheat and millet safe from rats and mice and

5

reservoirs held water all year round. The inhabitants enjoyed warm baths and showers – the men and women bathed separately – while their toilets had running water. Cut stone, expertly placed, lined the aqueducts that brought hot and cold water from the natural warm and cold springs which surrounded the palace. Terracotta pipes, built in interlocking sections, provided a constant supply of water, probably pumped via a system of hydraulics. All in all, what we saw before us was a more advanced way of living than in contemporary Old Kingdom Egypt, Vedic India or Shang China.

We duly bought Professor Stylianos Alexiou's book, *Minoan Civilization*, for seven euros. As we looked through the text it became evident that in ancient times, as now, Crete was an island of magnetic attraction, the sort of place storytellers and poets would speak of with awe. This reverence had inspired potent legends, both about the place and the people who lived there. The head of the gods, Zeus, was said to have been born and died on Crete and it was here that another god, Dionysus,  allegedly invented wine. In fact a large number of the ancient Greek myths I had learned at school had actually originated on Crete – their power so great that the tales have lasted for millennia. Epic sagas like those spun by the Greek poet Homer in the 8th century BC had been told at family firesides for centuries before that. In Book 19 of his *Odyssey*, Homer writes reverently about Knossos as a fabulous city lost in legend. After reading a little bit more about the Minoan civilisation, I realised that he was absolutely right.

This remarkable civilisation did not confine itself to Crete. Like the swallows we could see flying over our heads, the Minoans were seasoned summer travellers. In fact, the guide told us, Old Kingdom Egyptian frescoes showing diplomatic envoys from the Keftiu – as the ancient Egyptians called the peoples from Crete – decorate the tombs of dignitaries from the time of Thutmose III, in the 18th Dynasty. They were carrying ritual vases for pouring oils. That meant that from around 1425 BC there would have been Minoan travellers in Egypt: a pretty staggering idea. I wondered idly if these intrepid ancients had inspired some of the age-old Greek mythical epics: tales of Jason sailing the seas with the Argonauts, or of Odysseus' full decade of seafaring and dodging dangers before he returned home to his loyal wife Penelope.

I began my own Odyssey more than twenty years ago. It started with the discovery of a little-known Venetian map. Zuane Pizzigano's carefully drawn 15th-century chart showed both Europe and the supposedly undiscovered islands of Puerto Rico and Guadeloupe. Medieval history had become a consuming interest for me and that chance find eventually led me to believe that the history of the world – specifically the history of mankind's navigation of its seas – would have to be radically rewritten. Pizzigano's map was drawn in 1421 – and that's what I called my first book.

I found that the Portuguese who had embarked on Europe's restless voyages of discovery, uncovering the partly cloaked face of the globe, were themselves relying on much older maps. This begged an obvious enough question: who drew them? The trail of evidence led me to the other side of the world, to a people we have long admired for their ingenuity and wisdom. There was only one nation at the time, I realised, which had the material resources and, most crucially, the ships to embark on an adventure of such ambition: China. The Chinese had circumnavigated the globe a century before Magellan, I argued. They had discovered America – and had reached Australia 350 years before Britain's Captain Cook. To a former sea captain, Pizzigano's extraordinary chart held a hidden message, like a codex waiting to be uncovered. Although it was pure luck that I had found it at all, that first clue led me all over Europe and then beyond, to Asia, on a true voyage of discovery.

||||||||||||||||||||

Here I was again, this time in Crete, fascinated by a civilisation that appeared to have such depth, that must have been so important to the world, and yet was so little understood. In comparison to the impressive body of knowledge the world has accumulated about the lives of the ancient Egyptians, it seemed almost as if there was a giant conspiracy to keep the exotic, vibrant Minoan culture secret. On one level, I had already vaguely known about the remarkable archaeology of Crete. The brightness and brilliance of the culture that had produced it – of that I had simply no idea. The fact was that these fun-loving ancients – who lived so well, who went diving with porpoises and whose athletic young men leapt over bulls' backs – had also made some of the finest jewellery ever seen. And they had painted frescoes to rival the best the European Renaissance was to offer. All of this had completely escaped me. As if to rub in the irony of this yawning gap in my knowledge, I was not entirely new to Crete.

When I joined the Navy in the 1950s, Great Britain was still a world power. So in my early life as a sailor I had travelled with great fleets to sea bases all over the world – from the Americas to Australasia and China. In 1958, as a junior watch-keeping officer, I was on gun patrol around Crete's neighbour island of Cyprus; our mission was to prevent weapons being smuggled in by terrorists. The EOKA Greek Cypriot nationalists were fighting against British rule, and we were kept remorselessly busy. When HMS *Diamond* was given a week's leave on nearby Crete we anchored in Souda Bay and paid our respects to the fallen, at the magnificent Second World War memorial.

Crete, placed strategically between Europe, Africa and Asia, is a rectangular island that measures 155 miles (or 250 kilometres) from east to west and between 7 and 37 miles north to south. During the Second World War HMS *Orion*, a cruiser which my father later commanded, lost hundreds of men here to attacks from German fighter bombers. The island is a strategic prize and has been fought over for thousands of years. First of all the Mycenaeans, a people from what is now the Greek mainland, seem to have displaced the Minoans. Then the Greeks battled the Romans; the Byzantines fought the Venetians; the Venetians gave way to the Ottomans; and the Ottomans were ejected by the Cretans. Finally, the Germans and the Allies each fought desperately for Crete, both sides acting with exemplary courage and barbaric ferocity. Even today there is a NATO port and a joint Greek/US airbase at Souda Bay.

We marched up a disused railway track, which in spring was a carpet of glorious wild flowers. After the incessant rain of Cyprus the countryside made a vivid impression on us: the island's fertile plains are warmed by Mediterranean sunshine for nine months a year. That night fifty years ago a local farmer allowed us to camp in his field. He provided a lamb and a barrel of local Cretan wine; we built a fire and had a traditional sailor's sing-song. Cook Mifsud played the hurdy-gurdy; Chief Steward Vassalo recited poetry. Later, the farmer's charming daughter, Maria, took me on a walk. She wanted to show me a ruined stone city, which she said was close by. 'It is very old,' she told me. 'More than 2,000 years old – the other way in time.'

What she meant was that the site dated from 2,000 years *before Christ*.

That seemed extraordinary to me. I dimly remembered from my schoolboy studies that the heyday of ancient Greece had been some 1,500 years later than that, at around 500 BC. Much later on in life I worked out that Maria and I must have walked to Archanes, a village which may have been the summer retreat for those Minoans who lived sumptuously at Knossos. But as the next two months were a whirl of anchoring off remote islands, swimming with the local girls and absorbing as much of the local culture and the *dópio krasi*, or local Marisini wine, as we could find, I had soon forgotten about an abstract-sounding series of ancient dates.

Now here I was again, with our oak-coloured local guide insisting, as Maria had before him, that the civilisation behind his tiny island had been as important to the world as that of the Egyptians. What if they were both right?

It was a local businessman and amateur archaeologist, Minos Kalo-kairinos, a namesake of the fabled King Minos, who discovered the first and most famous of the ancient palaces of Crete – Knossos –

in 1878. Kalokairinos initially uncovered a large storeyard containing *pithoi* – huge, almost man-height vessels used to store olive oil. At a time when archaeology was in its infancy, Kalokairinos had brought up find after find, wonders that had been buried for centuries in the dark earth. Unfortunately for him, some local landowners stepped in and stopped his work. When the German archaeologist Heinrich Schliemann, the excavator of Troy and Mycenae, attempted to purchase the 'Kefala hill' he was put off by what he thought was an exorbitant price. Then in 1894 the pioneering British archaeologist Sir Arthur Evans heard about what was happening and applied for a licence, investing profits from his family's paper mill to win the right to excavate. The ruins Evans extracted from Crete's baked earth were those of a palace whose magnificence could scarcely be imagined.

Discoveries of other ancient palaces, towns and ports would follow that of Knossos over the course of the next century. Evans seemed to have uncovered an entire ancient civilisation; an entrancing race with an advanced and exotic culture. He dubbed them 'the Minoans'. Why had he opted for that name? Like others before him, Evans was seduced by the power of Greek myth.

Before 1900, when Evans began to uncover the spectacular palace, our only real knowledge of this ancient civilisation came from the extraordinary substratum of myth that surrounds the island, as well as the awed references to it by classical poets. By ancient Cretan tradition, the peak of Mount Juktas, which dominates the skyline looking south from Knossos, is said to hold the imprint of the upturned face of the mighty Zeus. It is as if he is buried there and supports the island with his slumbering body. Famously, the mythical home of the controlling ruler, King Minos, contained a vast underground labyrinth. The formidable Minos had been the patron of the great inventor, Daedalus – and, more alarmingly, according to legend, was the tyrant who exacted human tribute from the Athenian mainland. Within the labyrinth the King Minos of myth kept the terrifying Minotaur, a half-bull, half-man monster. Every year, Minos demanded youths from

Athens as tribute and imprisoned them in the labyrinth for the beast to feed upon.

As Evans was excavating at Knossos one of the workmen gave a terrified cry. The myth was surfacing from the dust. He had found a 'black devil', he shouted, shying away in horror from the object he had plucked out from the soil. In fact what he had uncovered was a remarkable, red-eyed bust of a bull's head – a sculpture of monumental power and menace, crowned by a huge set of horns. The sculpture was detailed, lifelike. It is said that when they pulled it from its ancient resting place, the bull's fierce eyes moved in their sockets. As they dug deeper, Evans and his team were amazed to discover that this beautiful hilltop palace did seem to have at its heart a genuine labyrinth – a maze of deep, underground tunnels – buried beneath it. Frescoes showing charging bulls added to the archaeologist's growing conviction: all of the evidence suggested that the people here had worshipped a bull god.

Thirty years earlier, Evans' fellow archaeologist Heinrich Schliemann had shocked the world when he had dramatically declared that he had 'gazed upon the face of Agamemnon'. He had been excavating at the citadel of Mycenae, while in search of the legendary heroes of the Trojan War. The claim that the German had found the actual body of the heroic figure of legend gave weight to a compelling idea – that the much loved ancient texts of Virgil's *Aeneid* and Homer's *Iliad*, if not literally true, had a strong basis in reality. A romantic, Arthur Evans was convinced that he had done the same thing for ancient Greek myth that Schliemann had done for Virgil and Homer's epics. He firmly believed that he had found the true home of the mythical King Minos and his evil Minotaur.

<hr />

Legend may have surrounded the island, but it was a very real people that Evans had plucked from the ancient shadows; a people who at their peak of prosperity around 2160 to 1500 BC had plainly commanded fabulous wealth and power. What was also intriguing was the society's high level of sophistication – almost modernity.

11

Men and women appear to have been equal. More than that, the Minoans seem to have worshipped a female goddess, as well as the bull.

Now here I was clutching a booklet that was making the astounding claim that Phaestos was as old as the oldest Egyptian pyramids: the palace was contemporary with the time of the Egyptian Old Kingdom (2686–2125 BC). It had been first built in the era of the pharaohs Khufu and Khafre and the Great Pyramid at Giza.

THE PALACES

Few civilisations have been so completely lost to history as that of the Minoans. This is partly because their remarkable palaces were destroyed not once, but twice. The principal palace of Knossos was first destroyed by fire around 1700 BC. The new palace built after that was more like an urban complex than a single palace, with parts of it five storeys high. It was not only a royal residence, but the heart of religious ceremony and political life on the island. It was also a manufacturing base for exports such as swords and pottery. It was a busy place: there were olive and wine presses and grain mills. The need for water was dealt with by an aqueduct that carried water from springs about 6 miles (10 kilometres) away, at Archanes.

The magnificent buildings and terraced gardens were grouped around a vast central courtyard, which was used for sacred nocturnal festivals, bull-jumping and torch-lit ecstatic dances, as the islanders worshipped their deities. The whole complex stretched out for 5 acres (2 hectares). An ingenious system of bays and light-wells brought cool, dappled light into the magnificent, colonnaded palace. They even had window panes, made of thin sheets of translucent alabaster. The buildings' columns were made from the trunks of cypress trees, which were painted red and then mounted on a plinth.

The double-headed axe, a symbol of the *minos*, or king, appears on many of its walls. The Greek term for the axe is a *labyros*, which gives the labyrinth its name. The palace, which contained 1,300 rooms, was so complex – such a mass of halls, corridors and chambers with vast underground storage chambers running beneath – that some speculate that the dark, oppressive labyrinth of fame and legend was in fact Knossos itself. The second destruction, which was originally thought to be by earthquake, happened around 1450 BC.

Life doesn't appear to have been too grim for the ordinary Minoan citizen. Heraklion Museum has a ceramic model that depicts delightful rows of cheerful houses in the town below, banded with bright colour. They played board games, such as a version of draughts, and barbecued food was prepared outdoors on charcoal braziers. In the countryside the better-off also had summer mansions.

The major palace complexes discovered on Crete to date are at Knossos, Phaestos, Malia and Kato Zakros. Zakros is a fifth of the size of Knossos. Most of the palaces seem to be oriented with the landscape. The immense age of the palaces poses a problem with dating them. One dating system is based on the architectural development of the palaces, dividing the Minoan period into the Prepalatial, Protopalatial, Neopalatial and Postpalatial periods.

There was more. Reading Professor Alexiou's book I discovered that the remarkable Egyptian sun king Akhenaten had owned many pieces of Minoan pottery and had installed them at his palace at Amarna. The implications of this idea halted me in my tracks. The professor, a highly distinguished figure in his field, was saying that the Minoans had not only travelled to ancient Egypt: they had even traded with the pharaohs. (See first colour plate section.)

> Fictional representations of Cretans, the famous Keftiu as the Egyptians called them, carrying zoomorphic rhyta (ritual vases for pouring) and other works of art typical of the Neo-Palatial period as gifts from Crete, decorate the tombs of dignitaries of the same dynasty. Finally fragments of Post-Palatial [Cretan] pottery [1400–1100 BC] found in the Palace of Amenophis IV or Akhenaten at Amarna (inhabited from 1375 BC) help to determine the beginning of the Post-Palatial era and also the date of the destruction of the palace [of Phaestos] since similar pottery was found on its floors.

Since starting research for my first book, *1421*, in 1988, nothing in those twenty years has surprised me more than Professor Alexiou's evidence of the long-standing maritime trade between Crete and Egypt from 1991 BC to 1400 BC. My own thesis had been that the Chinese had been the first navigators of the world, in the year 1421– AD!. But evidence of international trading many centuries and more *before* the birth of Christ put an entirely different perspective on my proposed book about Chinese voyages to the Americas. According to solidly researched and established archaeological evidence, the Minoans had travelled far beyond their native shores. What's more, said our guide proudly, the Minoans had achieved another significant 'first'. They had invented writing. This struck me as unlikely. Hadn't the Egyptians or the Sumerians got there before them?

When I challenged him, the guide pointed proudly to his hand-held notes, covered with slightly crumpled pictures. On his papers you could see a picture of a strange red ceramic plate, covered in clear, white markings. It was an enigma, like nothing else I'd ever seen. The symbols didn't go right to left, or even left to right, like Chinese script. The path of this language, if that's what it was, went round and round, in a labyrinthine circle.

'It's a mystery: it's something we cannot understand.' Our guide traced the symbols with his finger.

'What is it called?' I asked, truly intrigued.

'The Phaestos Disc,' he replied. He explained that these impenetrable ancient letters or words could be man's first linear writing: perhaps they could be better described as the first use of printing, given the fact that the symbols were stamped into the clay surface before it was fired, around 1700 BC. Here then was a hidden language; a secret history written in ceramic. The disc could be the key to understanding an entire, lost civilisation. But it was totally unintelligible, he said, even to the experts. Looking closely, I could see that the circular plate had 241 symbols imprinted on its surface. Some of the pictograms looked just like sticks, or maybe they were a form of basic counting. Others were strange, involved and full of what looked like symbolic meaning; images of fish, fruit and even human heads.

The disc was discovered in a small basement room in 1903, near the depositories of the 'archive chamber' in the northeast apartments of the Phaestos palace. A few inches away from it lay a tablet known as PH-1, which carried the first discovery of a mysterious Cretan written language. It is now known as 'Linear A'. Like the disc, it has so far completely eluded translation, although the script has since been found on many other objects and artefacts at various sites in Crete. Linear A's first known use was here at Phaestos, and some experts believe that Linear A and the strange pictographic language of the disc are closely related. How extraordinary: to hold the key to a lost civilisation right there in your hands, but to be unable to make sense of it. To view the Phaestos disc, please go to the first colour plate section.

Another overriding thought was troubling me: if the Minoans were so advanced – as educated and artistic as the ancient Egyptians, a civilisation which had invented both writing and printing, as well as employing an astonishing realism in art many centuries before classical Greece – why was it that the world knew so little about them? The next, inevitable question was: what happened to the Minoans?

Our guide's dramatic response to that question was to start me on my new quest. Phaestos, its sister palace-city of Knossos and the other Minoan cities were all 'destroyed in a massive earthquake', he told us. It seems that this captivating society had abruptly disappeared from view around 1450 BC. Ever since Knossos re-emerged from the fertile soil of Crete people have wondered what on earth could have happened to extinguish the life force of those exotic cities of long ago, each with a palace culture so powerful that it inspired the enduring myths of the ancient Greeks. Now I too was fired up to find out more.

'Are you sure it was an earthquake?' we asked the guide. 'Because it says in this book that the island of Santorini, or ancient Thera, about 90 miles away from here, was destroyed at the same time, by a huge volcano.' We had to follow the trail.

2

UNDER THE VOLCANO

Sixty-nine miles north of Crete lay an island in the Aegean Sea that might, we thought, yield the answers to the sudden disappearance of the Minoans. We were off to Santorini: known in ancient times as Thera.

We arrived late at night, exhausted, delayed by strong northerly winds. The Med, usually so calm and peaceful, can catch you out: within six hours of a 30-knot wind, the waves can reach 3 metres (10 feet) high. The Meltemi in particular is a violent wind which whips up in summer with little warning, often creating havoc with ships and ferries alike (see map). After that journey, even a short taxi ride felt like an expedition. Tired as we were, Marcella and I were excited as we approached our new destination: the Apanemo Hotel, built high on a rocky promontory. Although it was dark and we could hardly see a thing, we were finally here, safe, on an island that the world's first historian, Herodotus, called 'Kalliste' or 'The Most Fair'.

We awoke the next morning to a marvellous view overlooking the central lagoon, the so-called caldera or 'cooking pot', the volcano that had once been Santorini's molten heart. It sits on top of the most active volcanic centre in what is known as the South Aegean Volcanic Arc and we could see the effects of its violent geological past from our colourful Greek-style bedroom. The great crater blown out from its middle is spectacular: about 7.5 by 4.3 miles (12 by 7 kilometres) long and surrounded by steep cliffs 300 metres (980 feet) high on three sides. The water in the centre of the lagoon is nearly 400 metres (1,300 feet) deep, making it an extraordinarily safe harbour for all kinds of shipping. The islets of the upstart volcanic islands, Nea Kameni and Palae Kameni, lay right in front of us, the choppy narrow channel between them churned up by the northerly winds that had plagued us the day before. Far below us, two white cruise liners half the size of matchsticks were entering the deep blue of the caldera.

Today, the island's shape resembles a giant round black fruit cake with the centre gouged out, leaving a circular rim of inky volcanic soil surrounding the central lagoon. Like the icing sugar on a wedding cake, white villages tumble down in terraces and then cling for dear life to the caldera's circular rim and dramatic cliffs.

By chance I knew Thera reasonably well but only, as it were, from underneath. In the 1960s I was navigator of the submarine HMS *Narwhal*, attached for two months to the Greek navy, which had asked us to take periscope photographs in the caldera.

A submerged submarine is the same weight as that of the volume of water it displaces. The weight of this volume of water varies with temperature and salinity – the warmer the water, the lighter the submarine must become. To maintain neutral buoyancy the submarine's weight is altered by pumping out or flooding in water. Submarines are sensitive – 455 litres (100 gallons) of water was all that was required to achieve *Narwhal*'s correct weight when the submarine was moving slowly. (Though *Narwhal* displaced 3,000 tons when dived.)

There are to this day underground springs and volcanic fissures which spew hot water and magma into the base of Thera's lagoon. We did not know how these would affect the temperature and salinity of the lagoon and hence the amount of water we would need to pump out of the submarine as we travelled at periscope depth. Neither were we sure if we had enough pumping capacity to deal with the caldera.

The problem was accentuated because we would move over the hot volcanic springs as we navigated the caldera. That meant that the submarine's buoyancy could be continuously changing. The entrance channel to the lagoon was narrow – wide enough for us, but tight. The narrowest part of the deep entrance to the caldera was some 183 metres (600 feet) wide – about the length of a ferry sideways on. However, the channel here was nearly 305 metres (1,000 feet) deep – plenty of room to get underneath passing ferries, so we were reasonably relaxed.

After the reconnaissance, we set off back to Zakinthos for a rendezvous with some Greek girls on the beach at sunset. They were going to show us where turtles came ashore to mate and lay their eggs. Then we would dance in the moonlight. That wonderful evening, I have to say, was my most enduring memory of Thera. I'd forgotten about anything else for over forty years.

All of this was to change. Over a breakfast of honey and rich Greek yoghurt, the hotel owner told us about the extraordinary city that lies beneath modern-day Santorini. It was discovered through the determination of one man, the Greek archaeologist Professor Spyridon Marinatos. The professor already knew Crete very well; so well, in fact, that in the 1930s he had made one of the island's most significant finds there, at what is known as the Arkalochori cave. At that site, Marinatos found a priceless hoard of ancient bronze goods and weapons, as well as one of the most famous double axes ever discovered on Crete, the impressive bronze votive offering known as the Arkalochori axe. That intrigued me. Bronze weapons must have been highly valuable: why hoard them away?

For years, Marinatos had entertained a hunch that there would be an ancient town on Santorini, of a similar date to those on Crete. Marinatos was an inspired archaeologist, whose long and exciting career eventually included excavations at world-famous sites such as Marathon and Thermopylae. He also followed Schliemann and others by undertaking research at the Bronze Age city of Mycenae – but discovering Thera was arguably Marinatos' most inspired moment.

It was a chance observation that led to Marinatos' extraordinary discovery. Convention had it that it was an earthquake that had destroyed Crete's palaces and towns. Yet one day, when the professor was excavating a villa, he realised that the entire interior of the house was filled with volcanic pumice. No earthquake could have done that. He was digging at Amnisos, a Minoan port town due north of Knossos, which lies due south of ancient Thera and its volcano. Looking with new eyes, Marinatos could also see that blocks of stone had been dragged apart, as if by a huge body of water: the pumice, meanwhile, was mixed with beach sand, as if everything had been thrown up in the air together. The prevailing earthquake theory must, he thought, be flawed. Looking at the crumbling archaeological material in his hands, Marinatos saw a tale of violence and destruction, but not the sort caused by an earthquake. This kind of devastation, he thought, must have come from the sea.

It also seemed to him that the villa and the surrounding ancient Minoan town had both been destroyed in the course of a few minutes, suffering a sudden and catastrophic fate that was directly comparable with the disaster that had befallen the ancient city of Pompeii. The Roman city had been buried by Mount Vesuvius in AD 79, a volcano so powerful that when it erupts large areas of southern Europe are choked with suffocating layers of ash.

Aware that there had been an almighty volcanic eruption on Santorini/Thera c.1450 BC, the archaeologist's gut instinct told him that something significant – and something from the same era as Knossos – could be buried there. It took him decades, but finally he started a dig just outside the modern town of Akrotiri, where we were now staying. His patience was rewarded almost straight away when, helped by the advice of a local man who knew the fields, he struck archaeological gold.

Burrowing through many feet of volcanic pumice is a tricky job – and back-breaking work. But not for Marinatos, apparently. It was as if he were a man possessed. He chose the exact right spot, a place where the hardened layer of volcanic pumice thinned to about 5 metres. Like Schliemann at ancient Troy, his hunch had proven itself to be 100 per cent correct. He had discovered an abandoned city.

||||||||||||||||||||

After breakfast we sat on a sunny wall and read what the dig director, Professor Christos Doumas, had to say about the volcano and the island of Santorini. At one stage the island was called Strongili, 'The Round One', but volcanic eruptions have turned its former round, bun-like shape into a croissant. Much later in history, the conquering armies of ancient Sparta gave the crescent of islands the name Thera. According to Professor Doumas:

> ... In the last 400,000 years there have been more than 100 eruptions on this island, each adding a new layer of earth and rock, slowly making the island bigger. The last of these truly catastrophic eruptions came 3,600 years ago. ...

As we read on, we realised that there was a true miracle – and that Marinatos had found an entire lost city – right beneath our feet. It dated back to at least 1450 BC, the year it's thought that the volcano erupted. Logically, that ancient city, now buried under mounds of volcanic ash, must have existed at roughly the same time as the palace of Phaestos. This was astounding: two such urbane societies no more than 120 miles (195 kilometres) from one another and thriving during an age we had regarded as plain 'prehistoric'.

At this stage, we were strictly tourists – I had no plan to write about Crete, or for that matter Thera; our interest was the pure enjoyment of an ancient enigma. Sadly, today's crowds of eager tourists can't visit the ruins of the underground world that Marinatos saw. Less than a third of the archaeological site has been excavated and the site is still dangerous, given the risk of falls. But we knew from our hotel owner that some of the frescoes unearthed so far have been restored and are in the town museum. We sauntered in the next morning to see them. After that moment, all research for my current book would be abandoned, as fascination with this ancient puzzle grew and gripped me.

The frescoes that had been buried beneath the lava-drowned island of Thera are painted as if drawn from life. Brilliantly coloured, delicate and remarkably lifelike, they show a fertile island rich with plants and wildlife. There were people in this ancient painted paradise: beautiful people, who had lived a life of luxury. We had both assumed that 3,000 years ago life was a matter of pure survival, not of fun.

When you think of the Bronze Age you tend to imagine grunting 'prehistoric' men and women living in caves, wearing animal skins, clubbing one another and going generally unwashed. Yet here, at the very centre of the Mediterranean Sea, was a glittering and highly advanced society. There was nothing cave-man-like about it, even with the idea of bull worship. In fact it looked wonderful. The people in the frescoes were striking, to say the least. Women had tight uplifting bodices, slit to the waist to reveal their breasts, like those on the frescoes at Knossos. The men were athletic, long-limbed and handsome and both men and women wore jewellery – lots of it, from earrings and armbands to necklaces. As on Crete, living standards were precocious: the Therans had fountains, flush toilets and bathtubs. The red, white and black stone houses stacked neatly against the ancient hillsides seemed almost better built and certainly more finely decorated than our flimsy modern 'little boxes'.

Who were these ancient Therans, we wondered? And why did their frescoes remind us so much of the murals on Crete? Noticing a huge *pithos*, or storage jar, that looked just like those we'd seen at Phaestos, I began to realise that Thera must have had a strong connection to the Minoans. Thousands of shards of fine Cretan-style ceramics have been found here, of what experts call 'the highest palatial quality' – used, they think, in rituals.[1]

Was this civilisation, too, Minoan? Even to my untutored gaze, there were strong similarities in the culture, art and architecture of Thera and Crete. Just like the Minoans on Crete, the people of Thera had a taste for spectacle, for music, for festivals and for fun. There were both cultural and spiritual connections. Here, too, the bull was

Notes are at the end of Part 1 on page 70.

a creature of cult worship and their worship of female gods was as striking as that of the Minoans. The very word 'Crete', etymologists say, has links to today's Greek term, 'strong goddess'. It seems that at Knossos each king, or 'Minos', married the moon-priestess.[2] At Phaestos and Knossos, women were as athletic as men: in a famous painting of athletes somersaulting over a bull, two girls are holding the bull. Here, too, women were portrayed as important, possibly even ruling figures.

We moved on to the next series of frescoes. The prehistoric paintings on walls, floors and vases were stunning: flowing, filled with colour and life. What was more, the beautifully drawn,

lavishly coloured pictures were stylistically just like the highly realistic images we had seen on Crete: two young boys boxing; girls collecting saffron from flowers; a teenage boy carrying fish. The murals gave us an incredibly vivid picture of daily life: bulls chasing onlookers; swifts swooping through the sky; butterflies darting between fruit blossoms. We looked closer. There were more exotic images: lions leaping on deer; a herd of delicate oryx poised to flee. The wall paintings show animals foreign to Thera – African lions and monkeys, Arabian oryx. Where did these exotic influences come from? A tobacco beetle indigenous to America has even been found buried in pre-1450 BC volcanic ash.

As we moved on through the exhibition, we saw that it wasn't just the art on Thera that reminded us of ancient Crete. The link between the people of the two islands must have been remarkably close. Many of the ordinary domestic objects in the museum were exact copies of what we had found on Crete. Ah, you might say, a soup bowl is a soup bowl, in whatever country. Everyday objects are similar because they have the same function. But the experts specialising in both art and archaeology see a connection too: they even talk about the development of a 'kitchen kit' that became standard here – and on the other islands round about.[3]

While their artistic styles seemed remarkably similar, the resemblance between the societies' basic artefacts, such as fastenings and pins, was striking. To our eyes at least, the Therans' achievements in architecture and engineering were almost carbon copies of what we'd found on the larger island. As in Crete, some of the fine, ashlar-faced houses on Thera were three-storey mansions. Meanwhile, the scale and sophistication of the Bronze Age metals technology on Thera was, as on Crete, astounding.

At all three sites – Knossos, Phaestos and, as it now looked to my eyes, on ancient Thera – there had been marble-floored palaces of incredible luxury. Space, light, freedom: this was not what we normally regard as prehistoric living – this was hot and cold running heaven. The distinctive architectural features of ancient Crete – the light-wells, terraces, central courts, sunken baths and terraced and porticoed gardens – were here too. The open verandas and grand staircases must have made life on this already warm and welcoming island gracious and comfortable. They had fresh, running water, both hot and cold, and they even had a form of air conditioning.

According to one expert, Malcolm H. Wiener:

> When all of the categories of evidence are considered together in the context of Minoan power, wealth, population, trade networks and neopalatial expansion both within Crete and abroad, a major presence of Minoans and descendants of Minoans on Thera seems certain. They may have begun to arrive as individuals or an enclave in the protopalatial period, their number growing subsequently through further immigration and intermarriage.[4]

Still, I didn't have time fully to take in the startling implications of this idea. Because the most amazing fresco of all lay ahead of us. As we entered the room devoted to the West House, Room 5, Marcella and I could hardly believe the evidence of our eyes.

‖‖‖‖‖‖‖‖‖‖‖‖‖‖‖

A fleet of ships was just returning to harbour. Preserved for thousands of years beneath mounds of volcanic tufa, the images of the homecoming flotilla were largely intact and the colours as warm and glowing as if they'd been painted just a few days before.

Shouting to their friends, teenage boys rush through the town gate, along a narrow strip of land between the sea and the town walls. Women – perhaps mothers and wives, one lady with her young boy next to her – peek out of windows and balconies. Fishermen clamber up the slope from the beach, trying to reach the top of the hill and get the first view of the fleet already filling the harbour. The homecoming of the fleet is the climactic end of a story. What was the full story, I wondered? To view the magnificient Thera flotilla fresco please go to the first colour plate section.

Before us was what amounted to a stolen moment in time: a snapshot of an entire Bronze Age fleet, looking just as it did when it sailed into harbour 3,500 years ago. These must be by far the oldest images of European ships in existence, I thought.

Thinking about the ships took me straight back to Phaestos. Urgently, I scrabbled back through the guidebook. Minoan pottery – particularly the extraordinary black, cream and orange pots known as Kamares ware – has been found in various Egyptian excavation sites dated as early as Egypt's 12th Dynasty.

The Minoan pottery must have been transported to Egypt in ships like these, pictured right in front of us. These frescoes had been on the walls of an astonishing mansion found by Marinatos. The excavators thought the house had belonged to an admiral. If the Minoans had really possessed a well-developed naval command structure, to the extent of having ranks and leaders, then just how well travelled must they have been?

Could a Bronze Age people of 2700 to 1400 BC really have

THE FLEET FRESCO: POSITION OF THE SHIPS

These beautiful paintings, known as the 'Miniature Frescoes', show a spectacular procession of vessels moving between two harbour towns. The ships have figureheads at their prows: they look as if they are carved and painted as leopards and lions, but this could be the actual animal skins. There are garlands draped around these victorious ships, and the townsfolk are excited and jubilant. Every detail is so real and lifelike that I began to speculate that they *were* real; that they were a historical record, and that therefore, it could be possible to find the actual harbours they depict.

I spent 10 years as a navigator and then Captain of submarines, taking periscope photographs and making maps from them. I applied that knowledge to the area of coast west of Akrotiri (on Santorini).

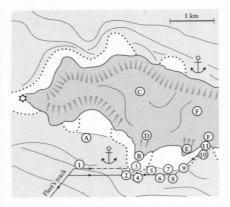

Linking the Fresco to the coast

The map based on Imray chart G33 has been marked, to show

A. Red Beach.

B. The protruding cape at the East of Red Beach.

C. The high hill behind Red Beach.

D. Two roads leading inland from Cape B.

E. Three roads leading inland to the Base (now being excavated).

F. The excavations at Akrotiri.

The map has been 'anchored' on the lighthouse at 36°21'30"N and 25°21'30"E.

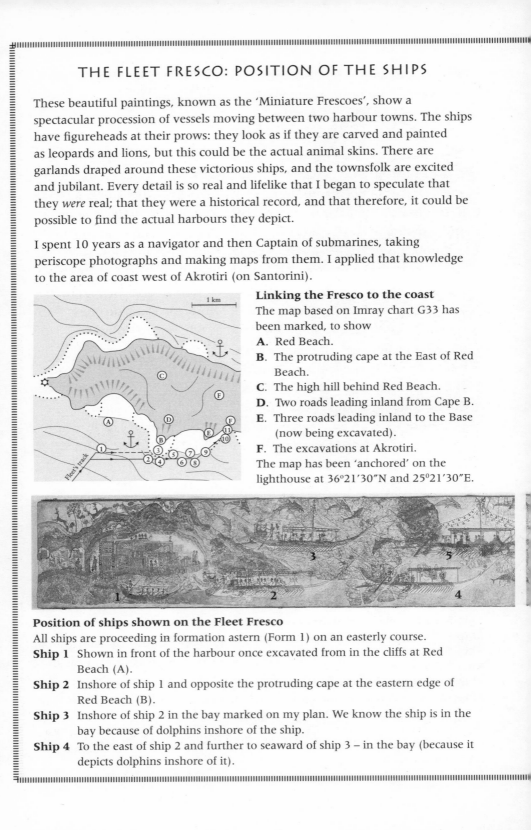

Position of ships shown on the Fleet Fresco

All ships are proceeding in formation astern (Form 1) on an easterly course.

Ship 1 Shown in front of the harbour once excavated from in the cliffs at Red Beach (A).

Ship 2 Inshore of ship 1 and opposite the protruding cape at the eastern edge of Red Beach (B).

Ship 3 Inshore of ship 2 in the bay marked on my plan. We know the ship is in the bay because of dolphins inshore of the ship.

Ship 4 To the east of ship 2 and further to seaward of ship 3 – in the bay (because it depicts dolphins inshore of it).

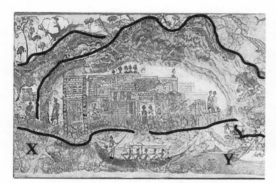

Tying the ships on the fresco to the coastline

The fresco is drawn in 3 tiers – tier 3 can be ignored as it is a river. The top tier shows the western part of the coast with ships 1–5. The middle tier shows ships 6–11 crossing the bay to reach harbour. The ships are numbered on the Imray chart.

Everything now becomes clear. The fleet sighted the high hill behind Red Beach (**C**) 30 miles out in the Mediterranean and steered towards it. When they reached shallow water they turned eastwards for home. Ships 10 and 11 are shown in harbour, ships 2 to 9 en route to home.

Note: the Anchorage signs are shown on the Imray chart. The harbour was presumably chosen (**F**) because deep water reaches there (7m³).

Ship 5 East of ship 3 and in the bay (dolphins).
Ship 6 Well to seaward. Still has sail rigging.
Ship 7 In the bay.
Ship 8 & 9 Just approaching Akrotiri i.e. the main base currently being excavated
Ship 10 & 11 Berthed in harbour.
Ship 12, 13, 14 Possibly berthed, but too indistinct on the fresco to be sure.
The positions of ships 10 and 11 coincide with the point where deep water reaches the shore. This area has yet to be excavated. I believe when excavated it will show a stone-lined channel leading to a quay in the area to the west of the steps leading to the Admiral's house.

constructed the world's first ocean-going vessels, loaded them with precious goods and started plying the world's first international trading routes? What if the centres of Knossos, Phaestos and Thera, island paradises separated only by a few short miles of sea, had been the central hubs of a much bigger sailing nation?

If the Minoans had mastered the supreme skill of shipbuilding they could have spread their growing influence by sailing these very same ships that were depicted in front of us now. The idea of a trading fleet or even a naval power made absolute sense: nothing less would fuel the sophistication and glamour of the Minoan culture, whose richness could still be seen on these walls. Nothing other than thriving international trade could have provided the extreme luxury and wealth which these people had obviously enjoyed.

||||||||||||||||||||

To my eyes, it certainly seemed possible: at least three of the eight vessels in the 'admiral's fresco' looked as if they could cross an ocean. There is so much realistic information on the frieze that you can even see the number of oars they had, work out the type and efficiency of the sails and estimate the sailing capacity of the ships. The size of one particular ship with a stern cabin suggests that it was the admiral's flagship – which explains its prominent position on the walls of his beautiful house.

Thousands of years ago, Room 5 was probably once a graceful reception room. Before disaster struck, it had had picture windows overlooking the sea and an impressive, wide staircase. I decided to rename Room 5 'the ballroom', as an *aide mémoire*. You can imagine the scene: men and women celebrating an arrival, a victory, or some very special occasion. The admiral's guests are admiring the fleet as shown on the fresco while they gather for drinks at dusk, before dinner. Perhaps they could see the real-life ships sitting at anchor in the bay below them, home after a long, adventurous voyage.

The superb fresco ran along the top of all four walls of the ballroom. Once in the room, guests would have been able to read the

28

story of a voyage to distant and exotic lands – moving anticlockwise, rather than our habitual left to right – and the sailors' victorious return to their home port, where the ships are joyfully greeted by the heroes' families and by the townspeople of Thera.

This was extraordinary, like diving through a porthole into a lost age. By pure chance I was on the trail of an untold and long-forgotten story. I began taking notes. The length, width and draught of the ships – and hence their seagoing capability – can be easily calculated, as well as the weight and volume of the cargo which could be carried. In short, the frescoes might even be able to tell us how far the ships could have sailed and in what weather.

To start analysing all this, I numbered each ship, starting with one on the far left and ending with 9, 10 and 11 – seen on the right-hand side of the picture, nearest to the admiral's house. The ships varied in size. Numbers 4, 5, 7 and 8 are the longest, and 5 and 8 have the largest number of oars: twenty-six a side. Number 6 has the most sophisticated sailing capability.

In fact, excavated Minoan seals[5] show that their ships had significant sophistication, including masts and sails, from at least 3000 BC. Inscribed clay roundels found at Chania, on the western coast of Crete, show the same symbolism for ships as the frescoes did – a hooked prow, a kind of cabin astern.

The small 'cabins' on numbers 1, 2, 3, 4, 5, 6 and 8 were in fact awnings, to shade passengers from the fierce sun beating down on them at sea. They look much like the decorated pavilions that knights in medieval Europe took to war. Amazingly, the remains of one of these cloth coverings had actually been found on the excavation – complete with the manorial arms and crests of a captain and an admiral. Yet more evidence of a highly controlled and well-planned naval infrastructure. The cabin was portable, as were the central square awnings. When they were at sail, the ships would have looked most like ship number 6 – which is dominated by a large, square-rigged sail on a central mast.

Ship number 6, I decided, was the most interesting. It had ten guy ropes controlling the sails: sailors call them sheets.

Using the sheets, a sailor could lower and hoist sails; reduce sail area (by furling); and alter the shape of the sail to get maximum forward thrust. The ropes were controlled using a brass adjuster at the masthead; I later found an early example of a similar system in a museum in Athens. This system of ten ropes allowed you to adjust the sail to maximise sail-power in any wind – full sail mounted crosswise when in light stern winds; lightly furled sail with the curvature narrowed when sailing into the wind; completely furled sail in a squall or in no wind, when the oarsmen could take over.

Each oarsman would need a space of at least 76 centimetres (2 feet 6 inches) in which to row, but 91 centimetres (3 feet) was comfortable and 107 centimetres (3 feet 6 inches) allowed for fast rowing. So twenty-six rowers needed a distance of 24 metres (78 feet) – ships 5 and 8. The oarsmen occupied half of the length of the ship, from the stern to the end of the prow, so this would make the ship 47.5 metres (156 feet) long, with a hull length of about 36.5 metres (120 feet). These were big seagoing ships, about the same size as the *Golden Hind* Sir Francis Drake sailed in Elizabethan times.

Thoroughly transfixed, I examined the fresco more closely. The vessels have several unique features, as far as I know. The first is the projection at the rear shown in ships 2, 3, 4, 5 and 8.

I thought the strange projections could only be hydroplanes, similar to submarine hydroplanes at the stern of a submarine. Stern hydroplanes are horizontal rudders. They adjust the position of the stern. The one on ship 8 would raise the stern and hence lower the bow, altering the configuration of the ship. In a stern sea, or following wind, it could be used in this position; in a head sea or wind it would be reversed, to lower the stern and raise the bow. You could probably shift the crew forward and aft to achieve the same result.

The ships shared another unique feature in this scene. You can see some 'lighter than air' objects floating above the bows of ships 2, 3, 4, 5 and 8. Close up, these objects must have put considerable upward force on the bows, because they are attached to the bowsprit by a thick piece of solid wood. It would seem that these vertical 'hoists' complemented the stern hydroplanes, giving additional lift when the hydroplanes helped to lower the stern (the hydroplanes are reversed from their position in ship 8). How these vertical hoists worked is a complete mystery to me – but I can think of no other explanation for them being there. Mere decorations would not have needed to be secured to the bowsprit with such thick wood.

As far as I know, these two features are unique to Minoan ships.

The third unique aspect of this fleet is aesthetic: the beautiful paintings on the sides of the hull. Ship 5 has lions and dragons; ship 6 sports doves. These extremely sophisticated ocean-going ships were capable of sailing in most weather conditions and were able to adjust both sail and hull configuration. What technology! And just like the airlines or train companies of today – such as BA or Virgin Atlantic – the Minoans branded their beautiful, world-beating ships with their own unique identity, born of their extraordinary talent in the fine arts.

3

THE SEARCH FOR THE
MINOAN NAVAL BASE

I needed to see for myself if Thera had once had a harbour deep enough for seagoing ships. Where would an 'Admiralty House' be built in relation to this harbour? Having visited naval houses all over the world, I know admirals often wish to live near their principal port, so they can greet ships when they return and entertain captains, officers and men. As a symbol of status, 'Admiralty House' is almost always built on a hill overlooking the port, like Mount Wise near Plymouth.

We needed to narrow the search. Any captain or admiral choosing a harbour would require shelter from the prevailing wind and sea. The prevailing wind on Thera is our old friend the Meltemi, known by the ancient Greeks as the Etesian winds. The system results from the high pressure system (>1025) frequently lying over Hungary and the Balkans and the relatively low pressure system (<1010) over Turkey.

This helped me pinpoint our search. The port would almost certainly have been built on a southern shore – either between Cape Agios Nikolaos and the foot of Mount Prophet Elias (see map), or on the south coast between Cape Akrotiri and Vlichada.

The ballroom frescoes show the land falling away to the sea, in a dramatic panorama of the coastline. My guidebook included reconstructions of maps of the coastline as it would have been in 1600 BC. The beach extended about 300 metres (980 feet) further to seaward than today, but the shape of the coastline remained broadly the same: though the admiral would have seen rather more of the coast and its anchorage than he could today.

32

Thanks to millennia of volcanic activity, Santorini must be one of the few places in the world that has beaches in three colours – with white, red and black sand. This headland has the strangest coastline I have ever seen. One of the beaches is called Kokkini, or Red Beach – and indeed everything is red, from the terracotta-coloured cliffs, the red sand and red pebbles to the sometimes red tourists, in places. But the water is deep, cool and crystal clear, shading from aquamarine through turquoise to cobalt and then black.

Thinking about it on a practical level, as a seaman, the most likely place for a port would be between Red Beach, 1,000 metres (3,300 feet) west of where the admiral's house was excavated, and White Beach, which is 2,000 metres (6,600 feet) further west.

Then it suddenly struck me – imagine if the admiral's guests were actually able to see the ships: not just on the fresco, but at sea? Supposing the painter of the frescoes was in fact painting the fleet just as it was – moored right in front of the admiral's house? It made perfect sense. Immediately we decided to sail out along the short stretch of coast that looked like the scene in the fresco. We racketed around the harbour until we found someone with a boat and then we set off, the wind in our faces and camera at the ready.

In 1600 BC there were a number of volcanoes affecting this island: La Thirasia, Megalo Vouno, and Mikros Prophet Elias, in the north. These would rule out a base on the sheltered north coast of the island. The port must have been on the south coast.

The sailors would want to be as far away from danger as possible – and all the evidence so far is that this strategy worked. No shipwrecks caused by the volcano have yet been found.

This was a trip to remember: the salt spray flying high as the cutter bounced and plunged its way along the spectacular coastline. The next major requirement of a port is for drinking water, from streams or rivers entering the sea, to stock ships before a voyage. On the south coast between White Beach and Vlichada, I counted thirteen streams. That would be why the merchants had chosen Akrotiri as the main port – to service the fleet's need for water.

We trained our telescopes and zoom lenses on the red cliffs behind the beach. As I framed the image in the lens, the link became unmistakable. Even today, the contours of the land match up with the fresco. The long-buried image Marinatos had uncovered wasn't just a pretty picture: it is in effect a map. You can see the three peaks of the island quite clearly. The only major difference is the shape of a central waterway, at the middle of the fresco.

On the right-hand side of the fresco were the houses now being excavated, not least the admiral's mansion. A broad stairway is shown leading up from the beach to the house. Then, proceeding westwards, tracking left across the painting, you can see a large building with triangular windows: it might have been a type of barracks, interesting to us as we look for evidence of a well-manned fleet, or, less helpfully, a prison. The site has yet to be excavated.

Tracing a line further west along the image of the fleet and the harbour we had in the guidebook, we came to the distinctive, pyramid-shaped hill behind Red Beach.

What we also saw from seaward, to our surprise, was a series of caves along the base of the red cliffs, one or two of them looking as if they were inhabited. We waded ashore to discover that this whole stretch of coast has a string of such caverns, carved out of the volcanic tephra. Later, at the hotel, Spiros the owner told us his grandfather still keeps his fishing boats in such a cave and that many people live in what's known as *skaptas*; long houses carved out of the tephra. They are easy enough to dig, but strong enough not to collapse. Many of them have been turned into restaurants. Starving, and with just a touch of sun and sea burn, we dined in 'Cave Nicholas' that evening, a cavernous room dug 12 metres (40 feet) into the cliffs, which yielded an excellent fish dinner.

Finding an entire lost city – many thousands of years old – was simply breathtaking. The drama of the story, along with the suddenness of ancient Thera's disappearance and its equally sudden discovery, has led many people to speculate that this was the long-lost civilisation of 'Atlantis'. I knew the tale well: it was a highly popular story when I was younger. A fabulous city had

been suddenly drowned underneath the sea. This was the gods' punishment, apparently, for its people's arrogance and hubris. I just dismissed this idea as nonsense. There was huge drama to Thera's destruction, true. It was terribly poignant that at the very height of its brilliance this civilisation's bright flame had been extinguished in a moment. Yet this wasn't a tragedy on the scale of Pompeii, it seemed. The archaeologists were convinced that most of Thera's citizens had escaped the ravages of the volcano. During Marinatos' excavations no actual bodies were found and there are many signs of preparation for the disaster: expressive details, such as food storage jars being left with a covering to protect against roof falls. Most valuables appear to have been removed, suggesting that the people of Thera had been given plenty of time in which to prepare for their escape from the volcano.

The idea of a lost civilisation is fascinating, but in the case of 'Atlantis' the whole concept has become the province of crackpots and charlatans. This puzzling story, and the enigma behind it, has inspired everything from poetry and science fiction to Hollywood films. Where was Atlantis? No one knew, but lots of people had an opinion. Everyone, from the 1920s occultist Rudolf Steiner to SS Reichsführer Heinrich Himmler, embroidered upon the myth. The Atlanteans have become all things to all men, accused of being anything from a race of Nordic supermen to intergalactic spacemen. Three thousand years ago ... it was astonishing to think of being plunged so far back in time that there were no books, no libraries, no contemporary written records – or at least ones that we could understand. As we read in one of our guidebooks, the only early record of Atlantis was a word of mouth account. It was later picked up and written down by a certain young Greek philosopher who was writing a theoretical 'dialogue', the details of which may or may not be true. It stretched my credulity that Plato's voice, reaching out over the wine-dark seas of time, could possibly hold any truth.

> In a single day and night of misfortune, all your warlike men in a body sank into the earth, and the island of Atlantis in like manner disappeared – into the depths of the sea.[6]

Plato's original texts, which had caused all the furore about the mysterious land of Atlantis, were in fact two 'dialogues' called *Timaeus* and *Critias*. Born 423/427 BC, Plato was the second among a great trio of ancient Greek philosophers, along with Socrates and Aristotle. *Timaeus* is concerned with the creation of the universe. *Critias* is incomplete, breaking off suddenly in the passage which concerns Atlantis.

Translations of the texts seemed to suggest that the ancient metropolis and the Royal City were separate entities, which I could see had a strong resemblance to the relationship between Crete and Thera. The main city, he said, lay on a circular island about 12 miles (19 kilometres) wide. The Royal City, meanwhile, was situated on a rectangular-shaped island. So Plato's Atlantis was certainly two islands and possibly more. There are plenty of islands to choose from in the Med. Yet given that Plato was writing a morality tale, it didn't necessarily follow that the details of his fable had to be true. His motive was not to tell future generations about Atlantis; his concern was to discuss philosophy and the failings of human nature. But his account was striking.

> Now in this island of Atlantis there existed a confederation of kings of great and marvellous power, who held sway over the island, and over many other islands also.[7]

I still dismissed the whole thing from my mind as nonsense.

As we observed in the *skapta* restaurant that evening, for the ancient Therans, murals must have been a kind of photography – a documentary as well as a decorative art form. The ships are shown proudly anchored in full view of the admiral's house, almost as if they were a memorial to him.

To my mind the harbour at Thera is actually far more impressive than those at either Amnisos or Kommos, the ports on Crete that served Knossos and Phaestos. One could imagine the Minoans from Crete first joining forces with Thera to face the enormous challenges posed by the Bronze Age. This large, deep-water port had the potential to be truly international.

The paintings tell the tale: of Egyptians in white robes, Africans with black curly hair and intriguing thin prisoners with red skins, who look northern European. They were documentary proof that there was a huge level of trade going on in the Aegean, before the beginning of recorded history.

In the Archaeological Museum of Heraklion there was plenty of supporting evidence: for instance, we'd found a staggering stone axe, skilfully sculpted in the unmistakable form of a panther (see first colour plate section). Panthers come from South America. Not the Mediterranean. One thing above all kept coming back into my thoughts: the tiny beetle that had been found in the volcanic ash. It came from a totally unexpected place: North America.

4

RETURN TO PHAESTOS

We returned to Crete with new eyes. Strolling through the market in Akrotiri, we'd seen that on this one remarkable island nature had provided almost everything that ancient man might have needed. It looked as if the Minoan Crete–Thera complex had been an international marketplace, exporting foodstuffs like olives and olive oil, figs and saffron, while importing other goods in return. Perhaps it was also one of the world's first true cosmopolitan societies? We counted 28 different varieties of fish in the market and sampled what may be the world's finest olives, plump as plums and twice as tasty.

Olives formed the basis of early commercial life on the island: the oil, say the experts, has been exported across the Mediterranean for millennia. As Dr J. Boardman wrote:

> Crete started to cultivate olives from the wild specimens early in the Bronze Age around 3000 BC. At Myrtos, a port on the south east coast of Crete, vats from this era for separating olive oil have been found. The early method was to crush the fruit, then plunge it into hot water which separated the oil before skimming it off. From olive stones found at this site it seems Crete may have been the first Mediterranean country to cultivate olives.[8]

The island certainly has the ideal geography and climate to do so. Olives are a hardy fruit, able to withstand the long, dry heat of a Cretan summer with its months of drought. A cold spell in winter usually plumps up the fruit for the principal harvest. The olive harvest comes conveniently after those of wheat and grapes, and before the sowing season – November to January. Life begins at 40 for the olive tree, after which farmers can hope for 50 kilograms of oil every second year. Provided they are tended and pruned to prevent them reverting to the wild, olive trees can live for centuries. Farmers plant for their grandchildren and those children plant for their own descendants, in a cycle that has gone on for thousands of years and is one of the first and best examples of sustainable agriculture.

One peculiarity is that heavy crops come in alternate years. This two-year cycle seems to be the same the world over. On Minoan Crete, the plentiful olive harvest every other year meant that Minoan palace bureaucracies had to come up with complicated arrangements that included extensive storage facilities and detailed planning to distribute the oil. In ancient Greece merchants booked olive presses two years in advance, just as farmers today book combine harvesters.[9] Dr Boardman cites evidence of huge quantities of olive oil being held in stock in the great storehouses and vats of the Cretan palaces – the West Magazine of Knossos Palace could store 16,000 gallons. Cretan Linear B tablets record details of the oil that was stored and distributed in the 14th and 13th centuries BC.[10]

Just how crucial this product was to the ancient world is demonstrated by the way in which the burning of olive trees eventually became a tactic of warfare, as evidenced in accounts of the wars between Athens and Sparta. Olive oil had numerous uses, quite apart from enhancing the flavour of food. It was used as an offering to the gods, as well as forming the basis of the Minoan cosmetic industry. Vases with a special shape (*pelike*) were used in the cosmetics trade and sales were carried out with special dippers and funnels. The palace of Knossos has records of hundreds of olive trees being used to create perfumed oil. The cycle of olive production, from harvest to distribution, is depicted on Athenian vases,[11] which show men beating the trees with long sticks to get the olives to fall, as they still do today. A statement on one such vase says: 'Oh, Father Zeus, may I get rich'.

Heading once again in the direction of Phaestos, this time we drove over the majestic Psiloritis mountain range, the highest point in Crete, where the olive trees vanished in favour of dark green pines, juniper and evergreen oak. Up until quite recently, the shepherds in these hills built beehive-shaped stone huts called *mitata*; seeing one, I could not help thinking of the prehistoric *tholos* tombs built by the warlike Mycenaeans, who were later arrivals on this island. The *mitata*'s traditional, stove-like shape transcends millennia.

We stopped at a mountain village for Greek coffee. The elderly innkeeper invited us to view the courtyard where there was a wood oven and we shared the space with a cluster of cats nestling for warmth. The enticing smell of roast meat and stuffed eggplants was coming from a large earthenware dish inside the oven. Naturally, we were unable to resist. This turned out to be the best kid I have ever eaten. It was first marinated in olive oil and lemons and then finished by cooking slowly with wine, basil, thyme and wild green vegetables – absolutely sumptuous. Crete's soil is so fertile that fennel, leeks and other wild leafy vegetables can simply be gathered at the side of the road. The island has the largest number of herbs growing wild in the world. Over the next few days I investigated the food that Cretans ate thousands of years ago, which has been analysed from remains found in their cooking pots. They ate kid cooked in just the same style as the dish we enjoyed. They also ate salads – of lettuce, onions, garlic and celery, again flavoured with olive oil and a variety of fruits and nuts; almonds and pistachios were popular. They drank Retsina (resinated wine) and beer brewed from barley. Like the superb Cretan olive oil, these products would soon become wildly popular abroad.

As the first view of the ancient palace emerged through the trees I decided to stop for a minute. We got out of the hire car and looked down on the velvet carpet of crops below us, stretching away like the Garden of Eden. We were at an altitude of about 120 metres (395 feet) above sea level. At this height, what were in fact the walls, pools and stairs of the palace looked like hieroglyphic markings. Rivers, we now realised, flowed all around the palace and then tumbled downhill towards the Minoan harbour. Phaestos, light and flawless under the azure sky, was at the centre of a landscape made for adventure.

As we drove off again we saw a sign pointing down a dusty track. I recognised the name. This was the remarkable Kamares cave I had read about; an extraordinarily deep shaft cave which archaeologists think had a sacred or cult religious role in the very early days of Crete.

The pottery told us loud and clearly that the Minoans had traded much more than foodstuffs and olive oil. The Kamares designs are dramatic, a modern-looking black and red, and the pottery was first excavated here in the early 1900s. I'd learned by now that it had been highly prized across the entire Mediterranean. It has been found across the Levant and Mesopotamia, from Hazor and Ashkelon in Israel to Beirut and Byblos in Lebanon and the ancient Canaanite city of Ugarit, near what is now the sea-town of Ras Shamra in modern-day Syria. Judging by the finds in Egyptian tombs and elsewhere across the region, the Minoan skill in art seems to have given the Minoans of ancient Crete a free pass to the glamour, science and civilisation of the two most advanced cultures of the Early Bronze Age: Mesopotamia and Egypt. Minoan creativity must have been a pearl beyond price. Minoan creative output was precious, perhaps almost holy, like the production of silk was to the Chinese.

We arrived at another one of those strange Cretan road signs that don't appear to refer to your real destination but end at a blank wall, or in this case a blind bend in the road. At first we shuffled about a bit, not knowing where to go in this remote spot. Then we realised that to get to the mouth of the cave – a steep, knee-taxing ascent – you had to turn off the road and climb on foot. You are rewarded at the top by breathtaking views through the trees to the plain of Messara and the Libyan Sea.

To visit the cave, you scramble through the gaping mouth of the entrance and down the giant, slippery boulder steps – built surely for monsters – scrabbling and sliding over the scree. The plunging path leads into a huge vaulted chamber, nearly 100 metres (330 feet) long. The atmosphere is intense and other-worldly; dark and alive with the spirit of an ancient age. The slope downwards is steep, some 40 metres down to a wide boulder-strewn floor, then it turns into a narrow, twisting passage. A second, much smaller inner chamber slopes down another 10 metres. You move in complete darkness until you reach an unmistakable, rather foetid smell: water. No wonder this evocative place remained embedded in folk memory. Deep in the bowels of the mountain, it is easy to see how a cave like this might have inspired the myth of the Minotaur's labyrinth. In myth, the young hero Theseus, blindfolded, had to try to find his way out of a place that you imagine to be as clammy and slippery as this: a labyrinth that was in truth a prison. There he would have had to confront the half-man, half-beast.

When the cave was excavated in 1913, hundreds of shards of Kamares pottery were found, together with animal bones, fragments of terracotta animal figurines and tools in both stone and bone, as well as six iron spearheads that were probably post-Minoan. Going by the differently dated finds, experts believe that the Minoans used the cave during the whole of the Bronze Age era (c.3000–1100 BC). The cavern is so huge, so daunting and so easy to defend that in later times it had a history of being used by whole villages to escape from danger. Yet the sheer amount of ancient Minoan Kamares pottery found inside it suggests that this wasn't simply a refuge: it had been used over the centuries for long-forgotten sacred rites. Caves seem to have been highly significant to the Minoans, in religious terms. Professor Marinatos found scores of precious bronze weapons hidden in the Arkalochori cave and hundreds of cult items have been found here at Kamares, from figurines to double-headed axes.

An extensive network of roads links the palaces at Palaikastro and Kato Zakros with the southeastern part of the island. I wondered if these ancient palaces had been among the earliest known city states, run like independent fiefdoms with dependent villages, much like medieval European towns. It seemed not. The engineers who built Crete's prehistoric roads had set up way stations and watch-towers, suggesting that lots of valuables had perhaps been moved along the roads. The Minoans had wanted to protect the goods travelling along them. Yet if each palace had been independent – and especially if those palaces were each other's rivals for political dominance – that degree of co-operation was unlikely. So in the Minoans we were talking about an amazingly sophisticated and developed people. It seemed they understood the value of an inter-connected society. They had cared for and looked out for each other; they had worked together for the common good.

We reached Phaestos, or Festos as the locals call it, in the heat of the noon, and waited in a tiny village café for the sun to lose its strength while I plunged back into my research. In the 14th century BC, said Professor Alexiou, the bounty of Crete – its skilled metal-work, olive oil, pottery, saffron and so on – was exchanged as gifts between eastern Mediterranean rulers. In return, the Egyptians sent exotica: gold, ivory, cloth and stone vessels containing perfumes.

The wealth of pottery, sculpture and jewellery that had been found on Crete was so old that no one could accurately date it, according to Professor Alexiou. So many ancient Minoan artefacts are in Egypt that experts are best able to date Cretan finds by comparing them to Egyptian ones, whose chronology is better understood. According to Professor Alexiou:

> The absolute date in years of the various Minoan periods is based on synchronism with ancient Egypt, where the chronology is adequately known thanks to the survival of inscriptions. Thus the [Cretan] Proto Palatial Period [2000–1700 BC] is thought to be roughly contemporary with the [Egyptian] XIIth dynasty [1991–1783 BC] because fragments of [Cretan] Kamares pottery attributed to Middle Minoan II [c.1800 BC] have been found at Kahun in Egypt in the habitation refuse of a settlement found in the occasion of the erection of the royal pyramids of this [XIIth: 1991–1783 BC] dynasty. One Kamares vase was also found in a contemporary tomb at Abydos [Egypt – Valley of the Kings]. The beginning of the Neo Palatial

period [Crete – 1700 BC] must coincide with the Hyksos epoch [1640–1550] since the lid of a stone vessel bearing the cartouche of the Hyksos Pharaoh Khyan was discovered in Middle Minoan III [c.1700–1600 BC] levels at Knossos [Crete]. Equally the subsequent Neo Palatial Cretan period [1700–1400 BC] falls within the chronological limits of the new kingdom with particular reference to the [Egyptian] XVIII dynasty [1550–1307 BC]: an alabaster amphora with the cartouche of Tuthmosis III [1479–1425 BC] was found in the final palatial period at Katsaba [Crete] ....[12]

Exploring the palace was not our mission today. We planned to walk south from the palace precincts to the prehistoric port of Kommos. What may even be the world's first paved road lay just a few hundred metres away from where we were sitting. Venturing out into Pitsidia village at about 3.00 p.m, we headed for the pretty, crescent-shaped beach of Matala. We would find the excavation of the port somewhere along here. Finally, we found a half-obscured sign on the right, next to a small supermarket. Tamarisk trees offered some pleasant shade along the way.

We marvelled at the road's perfectly fashioned stonework. The finely cut ashlar stone bed even has a slight camber: water would still drain off it easily after winter storms. The Minoan town was spread out over a low hilltop to the north and on the hillside south of it. Archaeologists say that Kommos' larger buildings were built c. 1450–1200 BC: that is, in the Minoan Neopalatial and Postpalatial periods.

It was remarkable to look over the low walls of the ancient town and think of how this quiet spot might once have felt, bustling with sailors making and mending their equipment, perhaps with vendors selling goods and refreshments on the quay.

The University of Toronto has been carrying out excavations here since the 1970s. Most – but not all – of the remains of Kommos consist of a single layer, or course, of cut stone. But the archaeological digs prove that this town had once been a major harbour, with large and imposing houses, grain storage, a central square and some monumental buildings. We could see raised paths and rows of steps, along with what looked like long, open, broad areas that would have been paved with stone, perfect for landing cargo. An enormous palace-like building, called for now J/T, had an extensive colonnade facing on to a court in its centre. It does not seem to have had the spaces for religious ceremony that you would expect in a palace.[13] Its back wall and much of its floor had been covered with vividly coloured and spiral frescoes.

The so-called 'Building P' was also fascinating. It might have been a storage yard for the Minoan fleet's sailing ships, when masts were lowered during the winter non-sailing months. Alternatively it was a vast storage shed, capable of warehousing large amounts of goods, ready for shipping. It had at least four 5.60 metres – (18 feet) – wide east–west galleries, which had no signs of closure at the west, where they face the sea. A broken Minoan limestone anchor was found in one of the long galleries, the kind used by large seagoing ships. Analyses have found that the stone for the anchor slab was quarried in Syria. It is pierced by three holes: one for the thick rope linking it to the ship and two smaller ones for the pointed wooden stakes that would hold the anchor to the sea floor. Having found huge storage jars here in the 1920s, Arthur Evans speculated that this could have been the 'Customs House' of Crete. He was not far wrong. According to the University of Toronto:

Our excavations have borne out Evans's suppositions regarding the commercial nature of the site and greatly surpassed our own expectations of what might be found at this beach-side spot. After 25 years of digging, Kommos is revealed as a major harbour, with monumental Minoan palatial buildings, massive stone storage complexes and a Minoan town (ca. 1800–1200 BC) ... The portable finds, which range from stone anchors to local and imported pottery and sculpture, speak of the seagoing interests and mercantile nature of the place. Vessels from Cyprus, Egypt, and Sardinia indicate the sphere of trade contacts enjoyed by the citizens of Bronze Age Kommos.[14]

As we walked around the sea port's perimeter we realised that its once sturdy houses and storerooms would have withstood the roughest gales. They would have had to. With the strong northwest trade winds in your face you could almost imagine this was a long-lost Cornish fishing village, lying semi-ruined in a welter of ancient weathered stone. Rolling in from the great width of open sea between Crete and North Africa, the waves are impressive and strong; totally unlike the usual soothing calm of the Mediterranean. What these ancient walls wouldn't have withstood was a tsunami. Kommos, facing the Libyan Sea, hadn't had to, which is why so much of it has survived.

Most experts now agree that a massive volcanic eruption had destroyed Thera c.1450 BC. The Theran explosion was one of the largest volcanic eruptions in about 20,000 years. And the titanic amount of lava pouring into the sea from the volcano, in turn, had triggered a gigantic tsunami. Racing across the sea between Thera and Crete, faster than an express train, the tidal wave had hit the bustling Minoan towns and palaces that for the most part hugged the ancient shore, reducing them to debris in an instant. Some evidence suggests that the wave may at points have been as high as 26 metres, over 85 feet.

The experts quarrelled angrily over the years, but the tsunami theory gradually gained ground. The force of the Santorini volcano, the Dutch geologist Professor van Bemmelen argued, was about 1,000 times that of the H-bomb that had split Bikini Island in half in 1954. And the H-bomb was itself equal to nearly 1,000 atomic bombs of the type that fell on Hiroshima. Many experts disagreed. To some, the disaster came about because of a pyroclastic surge, super-heated steam burning everything in its path. The most straightforward counter argument, though, was that it didn't make any difference that Crete was so near to Santorini/Thera. The damage the volcano caused was tiny.

If that were the case, then what had happened to the Minoans? It was simply a mystery. An unsolvable mystery. But the truly devastating power of a moving wall of water became clear to us all on Boxing Day (December 26) 2004, when Sumatra and the Indian Ocean were hit by a devastating tsunami. Two hundred and thirty thousand people were killed.

With the knowledge gained from the horrors seen at Aceh, Indonesia, on that day in 2004, scientists have since been able to analyse the tsunami phenomenon with the benefit of modern technology and techniques. At various sites on Crete, in residue deposited up to 7 metres (23 feet) higher than sea level, the remains of Minoan plaster, pottery and food were found pulverised together with tiny fossilised sea shells and microscopic marine fauna.

The geologist Professor Hendrik Bruins told the BBC that the shells and pebbles 'can only have been scooped up from the sea-bed by a powerful tsunami, dumping all these materials together in a destructive swoop'. (BBC Timewatch *The wave that destroyed Atlantis*) At one of the largest Minoan settlements, Palaikastro, on the eastern edge of the island, Canadian archaeologist Sandy Mac-Gillivray has found other tell-tale signs of giant waves. Town walls which face the sea are often destroyed, or missing altogether.

'Even though Palaikastro is a port, it stretched hundreds of metres into the hinterland,' he said, 'and it is, in places, at least 15 metres [50 feet] above sea level. This was a big wave.'

Those sea creatures referred to by Professor Bruins live only in really deep water. Today, many think Minoan Crete was hit by the biggest tsunami the world has ever seen. This giant wave must have hit the island at points as high as 30 metres (98 feet) above sea level. As sailors and traders, most of the Minoans' towns were built along the coast, making them especially vulnerable to this disaster.

To my surprise, the geophysical evidence tallied with Plato's account, which I'd read on Thera. Atlantis, he'd said, had been destroyed suddenly, 'In a single day and night'. It was a truly awful event that was followed by a terrible 'darkness'. Sickening plumes of gas and ash follow the eruption of a super-volcano. They would have created a vast black dust cloud that spread poisonously throughout the whole of the Med. The cloud's masking of the sun would, in turn, alter the climate, damaging crops. Today, the Belgian archaeologist Jan Driessen believes that the first wave of awesome seaborne destruction was followed sometime later by famine or epidemic. It was the tail end of a huge spiral of natural disasters.

|||||||||||||||||||

I looked at the ruined warehouses of Kommos, which had been built in stone cut with astounding precision. The fact that stone had been cut at all was the most telling point: it meant that the early Minoans must have had strong, sharp metal saws. And there was only one metal then available to do the job: bronze.

It was that ability to cut hard rock that freed humankind from the Stone Age. To cut cleanly through large blocks of stone, the pre-requisite is hard and sharp tools: bronze saws and chisels, adzes and other tools of the mason's trade. Once equipped with the marvellous implements made of the earth-changing metal alloy, bronze, a whole new world of technology opened up to the human race. It looked to me as if the Cretans had taken full advantage of that technology. They had done this long before mainland Greece and perhaps even before the Egyptians. The thing was, how to prove it.

I suddenly remembered a holiday in Egypt in 1977: our two girls were then still quite small. We'd been reading about the incredible significance of stone to the culture of Egypt. Until the appearance of the world's first known architect, Imhotep, even royal tombs were simply underground rooms topped with mud – they were known as *mastaba*s. Imhotep developed the lump-like *mastaba* into a much more impressive pyramid, built in hewn stone, for the powerful ruler Khafre. That first memorial tomb was simple, certainly by comparison with what was to come in architecturally ambitious Egypt. Nevertheless, it was encased in fine white lime-stone and rose in six steps to 60 metres (197 feet) high.

When we arrived at the Great Pyramid at Giza, our two daughters clamouring for a camel ride, we were amazed at this 146.5 metre tall – (480 feet) – miracle of construction. Napoleon was spellbound when he saw it, the oldest of the remaining ancient wonders of the world – and the only one still standing intact. Our guide had explained the sheer scale of the enterprise. Covering an area of 53,000 square metres (13 acres), the site of the Great Pyramid is large enough to contain the European cathedrals of St Peter's, Florence, Milan, Westminster Abbey and St Paul's together. Building it would have involved putting 800 tons of perfectly cut limestone and granite into place every day for 20 years. Each slab weighed between 2.5 and 50 tons. I'd asked, in admiration, how they had cut these huge blocks of stone with such accuracy. 'Saws,' our guide had said. 'Bronze saws.' Had Egypt imported its bronze tools from Crete?

Minoan Civilization even cited international correspondence with the Minoans, which was documented by the Egyptian pharoahs. All the evidence was that the Minoans' trading missions to Egypt were regular, not one-off events. To refer again to Professor Alexiou:

> There can be no doubt that the Cretan palace-sanctuary unit, with its huge store rooms, played the same central part in economic life, agricultural production and foreign trade as the Temple and Palaces of Egypt and the East. Conclusive evidence for the existence of workshops for stone masons, ivory carvers, makers of faience and seal cutters comes from Knossos and the great Cretan palaces ... Both agricultural produce such as olive oil, wine and saffron, and the accomplished Cretan metalwork pictured in the tombs of the 15th century Egyptian noblemen and described as 'gifts from the leaders of the Keftiu (Cretans) and the islands' were in all likelihood directly exported to Egypt from the Cretan palaces ... The Egyptians in return sent gold, ivory, cloth, stone vessels containing perfumes and chariots: besides monkeys for the [Cretan] palace gardens and Nubians for the royal guard.

We arrived at the beach, where it was very windy, if still sunny, to see the Stone Age cave houses, complete with passages, stone beds and fireplaces, snuggled into the cliffs.

I drove back towards the palace with mounting excitement. It was simply astounding to think of Phaestos guarded by Nubians: of monkeys gambolling about in this Cretan palace 4,000 years ago. Yet the evidence was gathering in front of our very eyes. Our experiences, both here and on Santorini, all added up to one thing. Unthinkable as it seemed at first glance, more and more evidence pointed to the Minoans as the world's earliest maritime traders. They had been consummate sailors and merchants; they had built and sailed some of the world's first seagoing cargo ships; and there were cosmopolitan, sometimes royal, travellers crossing the seas.

I could not let it go. I'd spent the best part of a decade establishing beyond my own doubt that the Chinese had been the world's first global travellers. Now my theory was being turned on its head. In some ways, I was almost galled to find that the Minoans seemed to have sailed to Egypt and perhaps beyond, when my book, *1421*, argued that the first voyages of world discovery were made in AD 1421, over a thousand years after the time of Christ.

We had set out to visit a simple Aegean island. What we'd found instead was the Paris, Hong Kong, New York and London of the ancient Bronze Age, rolled into one. We'd found not an island, but a trading empire.

5

THE ANCIENT SCHOLARS SPEAK

Racially, culturally and in terms of international trade there was no doubt about it: Crete was no ordinary island. Myth already had it that the king of the gods came from Crete: the poet Homer even calls King Minos the 'companion of mighty Zeus . . .'. Feverishly, we began to read more books and hunt through museums. Once you started looking, there were hints everywhere about the existence of a powerful island empire, long since lost to human memory. The ancient historian Thucydides wrote that 'King Minos' captured and colonised the Cyclades, driving out the Carians. And the 1st-century BC historian Diodorus Siculus claimed that five princes sailed from Crete to the Chersonnese peninsula opposite Rhodes, expelled the Carians and then founded five cities.

By now, I had collected lots of research material to read. I settled down on a worn wooden bench, peeled some books out of my rucksack and prepared for a breezy journey through some very ancient history.

A number of academics, I learned, were absolutely convinced that the Minoans ran a series of colonies and that their domination of the seas had led to a *Pax Minoica*, or 'Minoan Peace'. The island of Kea, which is much closer to mainland Greece than it is to Crete, was nevertheless a perfect example of a colonial culture that closely mirrored the Minoans.

The British Museum holds collections of Minoan pottery, jewellery and seals found in tombs and ruins spread all over the Mediterranean, in places such as the Gulf of Mirabello, Cyprus, Rhodes and Aigina. Interestingly, some of the jewellery in the

51

'Aigina Treasure', one of its most famous collections – which was largely made around 1850–1550 BC – proves that there was far-reaching trade abroad (see first colour plate section). The luminous amethysts that the goldsmiths had used could only have come from Egypt; there is also lapis lazuli which experts conclude must have come via trade routes from Afghanistan.

One of the books in my rucksack had been bought second-hand and some of the passages were already marked out for me in yellow marker. The book must have been well loved, because it was thumbed and worn, its pages now curling with the damp of the sea air. I noticed one passage in particular. It read:

> Minos was the first person to organise a navy. He controlled the greater part of what is now called the Hellenic Sea. He ruled over the Cyclades, in most of which he founded the first colonies.[15]

So did this great ruler, Minos, establish a sea-based empire, with colonies, or at least bases, over the whole Mediterranean? The aristocratic historian Thucydides, writing in Greek in the 5th century BC, certainly thought as much. Many modern scholars like Bernard Knapp agree:

> ... Minoan Thalassocracy [that is, control of the sea] during the Middle to late Bronze Age was well entrenched ... Minoan sea power [was maintained], through conquest, transplanted 'commercial colonies', and special trading relationships ... various sites in the Cyclades and Dodecanese and along the western coast of Anatolia [where the Uluburun wreck was found] formed part of a Minoan empire, and Knossos dominated the principal trade networks within the Aegean ... [16]

Moreover, Thucydides' text said: 'Agamemnon ... must have been the most powerful of the rulers of his day ...'.

I had a moment of recognition. The civilisation that took over on Crete, after the tsunami and the decimation of the Minoans' fleet, seems to have been its former colony at Mycenae. The Mycenaeans may well have inherited all that was left of the civilisation on Crete and Thera.

Thucydides went on: 'It was to this empire [of Mycenae] that Agamemnon succeeded, and at the same time he had a stronger navy than any other ruler.'[17]

So Thucydides was writing about the inheritance the Minoans had handed on to posterity: the skill to build ships and to sail them. Crucially, he was writing this nearly 130 years before Plato had written his *Timaeus*.

Suddenly, it all made sense. For many thousands of years the only practical way to travel with any speed was by water, certainly when you were talking about large distances. At the centre of the watery world of the Mediterranean was the island-filled Aegean. It must have been like Heathrow Airport is today; strategically placed between the time zones of east and west. The Aegean had been a transport hub: a vital carrier for settlers, merchants, and diplomats. To get to the more open waters of the west, captains had to navigate through the treacherous passage between the southern tip of the Peloponnese, Cape Malea, and the island of Crete, giving the Minoans of Crete and their satellite islands great power.

They appeared to have possessed remarkable technologies to shore up that power. There was one in particular that I was interested in exploring, because of its implications about trade: the creation of seals.

Vast numbers of ancient seals have been found on Crete. Tiny things, carved out of soft stones, ivory or bone. They speak volumes. Originally the idea of a seal might have been quite simple – to mark out personal property, or to seal jars and amphorae. But the point was, there were so many of them, each tiny piece giving a flash of insight into a vibrant prehistoric culture.

Over the years, archaeologists have found over 6,500 seals at Phaestos alone, stamped with more than 600 different designs. A system on this scale must have been about more than simply protecting private property – the seals had been used as tallies in the economically important business of trade.

According to Professor Alexiou, the doors to the palaces' many storerooms were found securely locked and sealed. If the Minoans were actually exporting[18] their extraordinary Kamares pottery, or their jewellery, or their olive oil, they would need to be organised. They would also need to deter theft. They had to keep lists of what was going where, and to whom. Were those seals needed to mark out goods in huge storerooms, ready to be shipped out across the Minoans' empire? More, did they go further afield, to a luxury, élite clientele?

As I peered through case after case in the island's museums, I was shocked to find some truly astounding designs on some of those ancient seals, particularly on the majestic seal-rings. The tiny, minutely inscribed discs seemed to me at least to be more than just badges of ownership. They were surely a status symbol: a route, perhaps, to sacred knowledge?

I marvelled at the sheer ingenuity of these truly exquisite things. How on earth did they make these tiny, minuscule engravings? The extraordinary answer is that the Minoans had already invented lenses: magnifying glasses, in modern terms. If you'd asked me beforehand, I'd have said that the Englishman Roger Bacon, a lecturer at the University of Oxford, had invented the magnifying glass in the mid 1200s. So much for that.

Such lenses weren't unknown to scholars of the distant past. The Roman Emperor Nero used a wafer-thin, lens-shaped sliver of emerald to correct his short sight. And during the siege of Syracuse in 214 BC the great inventor and mathematician Archimedes burned the attackers' ships using parabolic mirrors. Still, both these examples occurred much later in time. Had the original source of this technology actually been the Minoans?

One lens found on Crete can magnify up to seven times with perfect clarity. That particular lens has been dated to the 5th century BC, although looking at the miraculous level of detail that craftsmen managed to etch on to Minoan seals that are much older, the technology was definitely invented earlier. It seems that the seals – or perhaps the minute designs that had been inscribed on them –

were invested with a special spiritual significance. For instance, many of the lenses had been discovered hidden in a sacred cave, known as 'the Idaion cave'.

Mount Ida is on Crete's highest peak – slightly northwest of Kamares, above the barren plateau of Nida. This is where the mythological goddess Rhea is said to have hidden the infant god Zeus from his terrible father Cronos, who had jealously devoured all his other children. The story goes that to protect the baby Zeus from being eaten, special warriors, known as Kouretes, danced around him with shields and metal weapons, making such a clashing noise that his gluttonous father would not hear him cry. Is this another folk memory of the special power of bronze weapons?

This all adds to the powerful sense of mystery that emanates from the island. There are plenty of caves honeycombing the Psiloritis mountain range, including Sfendoni and Melidoni – along with one that is known to cavers and explorers as the Labyrinth. Much of this cave was used by the German forces to store armaments during the Second World War. They then blew them up during their forced retreat. Like Kamares, the Idaion cave was holy, but in this case it was more strongly associated with the mother goddess and with the deepest layers of pre-Greek myth.[19]

Crete, just as Plato describes Atlantis, was a metalworking civilisation with lush, fertile lands: a land of metal, milk and honey. All this is symbolised by a beautiful little bee brooch we later found in Heraklion's Museum of Antiquities. In Greek mythology, it was Melisseus (literally, the bee-man) who nursed Zeus as a baby. The jewel is a work of great delicacy and devotion; the ancient Atlanteans, or Minoans, were obviously as fond of harvesting honey as they were of making beautiful jewellery (see first colour plate section).

I was still sceptical about the 'Atlantis' theory, but I could quite see why enthusiasts might interpret the Minoan world as Plato's Atlantis. The implied skill with metals technology does, in fact, make 'Atlantis' sound like a Bronze Age culture. In his twin dialogues *Timaeus* and *Critias*, Plato describes his mythical island civilisation as having walls 'covered with brass'.

Just like the bees, the Minoans' wealth was founded on ingenuity and hard work. That incredible wealth, along with the extra-ordinarily creative skills of its people, must have given Crete a mythical aura, a status and standing that lived on well after the Minoans themselves.

What was certain was that the Cretans had possessed levels of technology we can hardly credit; after the loss of the Minoan civilisation, humanity had to wait for centuries to regain these skills and technologies, eventually rediscovering them in stages many hundreds of years after the birth of Christ. No wonder that, for the ancient Greeks, this magical land had reached the status of myth.

The key to understanding the Minoans seemed, at least on one level, to be the seals. What did they have written on them? Were they navigation instructions? Maps of the stars? Perhaps they were merely ownership details. However they had achieved it, both the skill and the knowledge of the Cretan goldsmiths were astounding. Some of the minutely inscribed seals seemed to show stellar con-stellations, like Orion. There was a growing conviction in my mind: the Minoans must have understood navigation and they must have used the stars to navigate. Whether or not they became successful world explorers would depend on just how well they could do it.[20]

Back at the hotel, I pored over images of the seal stones and then at the Phaestos Disc, back and front. I counted the pictographs on the disc and wondered if you could arrange the symbols into groups and categorise them. Did it show us something profound? Of course, I realised the disc could simply detail something prosaic – a list, perhaps. Why was the notion of the spiral – seen everywhere on Minoan pottery and jewellery and now here on the maze-like surface of the disc – so important?

In the last century scholars had managed to crack truly fiendish languages like Ugaritic. Even the language that followed Linear A on Crete, the so-called 'Linear B' adopted by the Mycenaeans, had been partly translated: but not this. The Phaestos Disc had eluded everyone who had ever tried to decipher it, while the seals told a story of a civilisation of unparalleled invention and technical ability.

I was fascinated, but my lack of expertise was frustrating.

Our modern world had unearthed ancient tokens like these seals and the Phaestos Disc, tools that could potentially unlock the mysteries of the ancient Minoan world. We held the keys to the puzzle; we just couldn't turn them in the locks.

6

THE MISSING LINK

The Bronze Age is named after a copper alloy. It was a miraculous material. Suddenly, metalworkers could change rock to metal, using the magic of fire. Today, world politics is dominated by areas rich in oil, uranium and knowledge. Many thousands of years ago, metal was as important for the development of wealth and power as energy supply and information are today.

It is not known quite when, or where, some unknown genius discovered that an amalgam of nine parts of copper to one part of tin would produce the metal we now call bronze. The discovery revolutionised the technology of the world. Bronze was sharp-edged, strong and durable. The texture and strength of this material makes it ideal for creating effective weapons and astoundingly flexible tools. This precious metal – for then, it truly was precious – totally transformed the world. It was essential to advancing technology and crucial to the development of civilisation. It gave man a modern material – an alloy – that could be moulded and beaten into any shape.

The new knowledge was a long time spreading. In countries where there were no native copper or tin mines, spears and swords could only be obtained through trade or conquest. They were of fabulous, untold value. The owners of bronze swords, bronze-tipped arrows and bronze shields would have seemed well-nigh invincible, a fact which must lie behind the many ancient legends and myths that concern magic swords and armour.

Suddenly, Bronze Age man possessed hard, corrosion-resistant metallic tools – shovels, axes, chisels and hammers. For the first time in the history of the world, with the free time bought by this helpful technology man was able to create products of pure luxury in large amounts, such as sumptuous jewellery. The Minoans excelled at jewellery production. They also had the sharp saws they could make from bronze to thank for their ability to build durable ships of carved hardwood. These true, all-weather ships could trade these new luxury goods with Egypt and across the Mediterranean.

And let's not forget weapons. While metals such as gold and silver could finance a war, the magical new metal of bronze could win one. The historian Herodotus talks about 'the men of bronze' who 'sold their fighting skills to the pharaohs of Egypt'.[21] We don't know who those 'men of bronze' were, but we know with certainty that until the destruction that so transformed life on Crete, a busy sword-manufacturing workshop was exporting its products throughout the Aegean, the Dodecanese area and on the Greek mainland.[22] Those bronzesmiths did some of their finest work when it came to weapons technology.

Modern bronze uses other metals like zinc and manganese as an alloy. In very early times bronzes were made using arsenic. Arsenic bronzes have an advantage over pure copper in that they require a lower firing temperature, although they do not cast as well. But dealing with a deadly poison has its drawbacks: in the early days of bronze, smiths could not have lived very long to forge another day. Hephaestus, the god of technology and metalworking, held so important a place in the Greek pantheon of gods that he was generally portrayed as the son of Zeus and Hera – king and queen, as it were, of the gods. Yet he is also ugly and lame, a grotesque figure in many ways, and this folk memory could well reflect the effect that working with arsenical copper would have had on an individual.

When the French Emperor Napoleon died on St Helena in 1821, it turned out that he had been poisoned. But his death was almost certainly not an act of murder, despite the former dictator's numerous enemies. It was totally accidental. The mystery of why the Corsican died was finally solved when it was worked out that arsenic had been used to 'fix' the vivid green colour of the wallpaper of his genteel island prison. Arsenic can cause multi-organ failure and necrotic destruction of the body cells. Arsenic poisoning leads to central nervous system dysfunction and eventually death.

So the bronze that set the age of metals alight is a combination of 10 per cent tin and 90 per cent copper. Tin holds no danger for the metalsmith. That is by no means the only advantage of tin bronze. A sword forged with a combination of copper and tin, like those we had found in Heraklion, is strong but not brittle. Bronze is also malleable. It can be cast into a myriad of shapes and is therefore streets ahead of stone or wood as an easily worked and dependable material.

Curiously, the ores of both metals were readily available in Britain, but not in Crete. The strangest thing about bronze is that its two basic ingredients are rarely found in the same place. There is no source of tin in the Aegean. Yet the Minoans used the material with lavish abandon. Arthur Evans found massive tin bronze two-man saws at Knossos; huge ceremonial swords and axes were unearthed by peasants in the 1910s in the sacred cave of Arkalochori, and sold as scrap metal in the markets; vast cauldrons were discovered at Tylissos and Zakros. Yet either trade or travel was essential to make it. The advantage of creating a secure chain of ports to support voyages to find tin would have been obvious to any ruling élite.

As one expert, M. H. Wiener, says, bronze was so crucial that it would have been the object of intense search, planning and investment. He wrote that:

> The security, economy and hierarchy of Crete depended significantly on bronze. It seems inconceivable that ... Minoan palace rulers would have waited passively, hoping for a new Eastern Merchant-man to arrive with copper and tin.

Mighty Egypt, then, had no tin and only limited copper in ancient times – her mines only produced around 5 tons of copper a year. Egypt could not possibly have made the huge numbers of bronze

saws required to build the pyramids unless either the raw materials
or the completed bronze saws were imported.

So how did the Egyptians actually get the raw materials? Because
this all predates widespread written records by many millennia,
deciphering the historical record is a painstaking task. Lead isotope
and archaeological evidence pins early sourcing of copper ore down
to the island of Kythnos; Siphnos played the same role for supplies of
silver and lead. Later in the Bronze Age, larger and more economical
copper deposits on the Greek mainland and Cyprus were used. After
doing some of my own digging and delving, I discovered that the
Troodos mountains in Cyprus held ancient copper mines. It is generally thought that Cyprus was known at the time as the kingdom
of Alashiya, which seems to have been a client state of the Hyksos
(15th-Dynasty Egyptian rulers). It may also have been difficult to
maintain a consistent supply of an ore which was in such high
demand.

Copper was also found in Anatolia (modern-day Turkey) and
Oman: at one point in prehistory there was also an important metals
market on the island of Bahrain. Early Bronze Age tin workings have
been found in Turkey's Taurus mountains, at Kultepe. However after
1784 BC there was no tin in the Mediterranean and not nearly
enough copper.

Tin was the strategic prize. Generally the metal was only found
far, far away from Crete – and there, I was sure, hung a tale. What
if a sailing nation had taken the helm of the new bronze revolution?
My research was all heading towards one conclusion: that the
Bronze Age couldn't have happened without the existence of world
trade. Who could have been behind that trade? The island of Thera
was, in the Bronze Age, a very important place, the equal of Phaestos, Alexandria, Tell el Dab'a, Tyre or Sidon: not many ports would
have had as many ships as can be seen on the admiral's frescoes.

Again, the evidence all pointed towards this one idea: to support
the thriving trade, a maritime network had existed across the
Aegean. The wonderful National Archaeological Museum in Athens
holds a wealth of foreign artefacts found in tombs on the Dodecanese

and Cyclades islands, notably on Thera and Samos, together with pictures of Bronze Age trading ships both painted and engraved on pottery.

That the Minoans had the ships, there was no doubt; but did their trading partners on the islands give them the scope to, in effect, rule the seas? How many Mediterranean Bronze Age ships were capable of following the Minoan ships to trade across the Mediterranean and beyond?

Historical sources – Homer's *Odyssey* and the later voyages of Pytheas the Greek – do suggest that maritime technology had been developing for many thousands of years before the Persians lost 300 ships in their famous first attempt to invade Greece (and 600 on their second attempt). Nearly 1,000 ships on both sides were involved in the second Persian assault. Although this was, of course, long after the Bronze Age, it does point to a long maritime tradition.

In order to try to make a reasoned estimate of the possible numbers of ships that had once plied the ancient seas, I started with the number of ports which existed in the Middle Bronze Age Mediterranean at around say, 1800–1500 BC, then I multiplied those ports by the number of ships each could have built. The Aegean has more than 1,400 islands and isles –'natural incubators for maritime technological development', according toWiener.

To give a couple of illustrations from these sources: Pytheas the Greek mentions Alexandria, Tyre, Sidon, Athens, Miletus, Apollonia, Odessus, Callatis, Olbia, Cumae, Nikala, Antipolis, Agde, Santa Pola and Carthage as established trading ports. We have Phoenician records for North African trade – at Ceuta, Melilla, Malaga, Algiers, Bizerte, Tunis, Tripoli and Sfax (to use later European names). The major Cretan palaces would probably each have had their own ships – Ayia Triadá, Phalasarum, Lisos, Souya, Prevéelli, Kommos, Lebèn, Myrtos, Iera Petra, Zakros, Sitei, Gournia, Malia, and Amnisos (Knossos' port). The Cypriot Bronze Age ports were Louni, Soli, Kyrenia, Peyia, Paphos, Corium, Limassol, Amathus, Larnaca, Agia Napia, Faralimni, Famagusta, Salamis and Trachinas. Adding these to the well-known Levantine and Black Sea ports suggests there were well in excess of seventy Mediterranean ports able to build and equip ships capable of sailing the Mediterranean and perhaps further (see maps).

How many ships would each port have built? This is almost impossible to answer. The Thera fresco shows ten ships, of which six appear to be ocean-going. For Thera to be able to have six ocean-going ships at sea at any one time, it is likely that she had at least another eighteen being built or repaired or under training – in short, a total of at least twenty-four Theran ships – let alone those docked at, or owned by, other Minoan ports.

As Homer describes Crete providing eighty ships from seven ports for the Trojan War, we may make a conservative estimate that each port built eight. There were seventy ports capable of shipbuilding. So we have around 560 – say 500 – ships capable of sailing the Mediterranean and beyond, able to carry the critical raw materials upon which the Bronze Age relied: copper and tin.

So the Minoans of ancient Crete had well-organised, well-planned cities; they had roads and ports; they had lighthouses; and they had ships. And those ships transported the goods they made – from honey to bronze tools, exquisite pottery and fine wine – which others wanted to buy. And on their fertile island heaven the Minoans happened to be very close to the rich markets of ancient Egypt and the Far East. Crete must have had fleets of ships sailing to Africa a full 4,000 years before Vasco da Gama and the 'Age of Discovery'.

Imagine a truly distant past. Crete is the magnificent crossroads linking three continents. On this strategically placed island the racial and cultural influences of Europe and Africa – and perhaps even Asia – all meet and mingle.

7

WHO WERE THE MINOANS?
THE DNA TRAIL

It was another newspaper report that prompted the next stage of my enquiry. 'Until now we only had the archaeological evidence [for Minoan genetic origins] – now we have genetic data too, and we can date the DNA.' I read this phrase on a Tuesday, over my morning coffee. By the Friday, I was on a plane to Istanbul.

Awoken at dawn by a deep-throated *muezzin*'s roar, I took a taxi to the hydrofoil in Istanbul's old Byzantine harbour. We skimmed across the Sea of Marmara (see map) to Yalova on Turkey's Asiatic Coast. At a spotless bus station with kiosks staffed by beautiful girls selling kebabs, tea and pastries, I discovered no fewer than 105 bays of buses, almost all of them huge and luxurious Mercedes vehicles. Grabbing one of them, I rode in air-conditioned comfort to the old Ottoman capital of Bursa, in western Anatolia.

There was at one time a theory that the Minoans' forebears were African. I knew that many experts disagreed: they believed that foreign settlers had arrived in Crete from southwest Anatolia, a people with a language related to that of the Hittites, further east.[23] There was a variety of evidence emerging from different fields of research. In 1961 Leonard Palmer noticed a link between Linear A and the Luvian language. In his book *Minoans*, Rodney Castleden argues that there may have been significant cultural contact between the Minoan and the Arzawa lands of southwestern Anatolia during the Second Temple period. The Hittite kingdoms at various points in history maintained strong contacts with Arzawa and Castleden mentions that the suffix '-me', which frequently crops up in Linear A associated with deity figures, in fact means 'lady' in the Luvian language. All of which would fit in with the Minoans' fervent goddess worship.

Now that scientists are able to test genetic theories with rigour, I was here because of the new study reported by *The Times*. New work by an international group of geneticists showed that a section of Crete's Neolithic population (i.e. pre-Bronze Age) did indeed go there by sea from Anatolia – modern-day Turkey. Professor Constantinos Triantafyllidis of Thessaloniki's Aristotle University had published the findings of a research group led by geneticists from Greece, the United States, Canada, Russia and Turkey. Professor Triantafyllidis said the analysis indicated that the arrival of these new peoples had coincided with a social and cultural upsurge that had led to the birth of the Minoan civilisation around 7000 BC. Specifically, the researchers connected the source population of ancient Crete to well-known Neolithic sites in Anatolia.

> The earliest Neolithic sites of Europe are located in Crete and main-land Greece. A debate persists concerning whether these farmers originated in neighbouring Anatolia and over the role of maritime colonisation. To address these issues 171 samples were collected from areas near three known early Neolithic settlement areas in Greece together with 193 samples from Crete. An analysis of Y-chromosome hectographs determined that the samples from the Greek Neolithic sites showed strong affinity to Balkan data, while Crete shows affinity with central/Mediterranean Anatolia. Haplo-group J2b–M12 was frequent in Thessaly and Greek Macedonia while haplogroup J2a–M410 was scarce. Alternatively, Crete, like Anatolia showed a high frequency of J2a-M410 and a low frequency of J2b-M12. This dichotomy parallels archaeobotanical evidence, specifically that white bread wheat (*Triticum aestivum*) is known from Neolithic Anatolia, Crete and southern Italy; [yet] it is absent from earliest Neolithic Greece.[24]

In the darkness before dawn we passed lines of pastry shops selling glacé fruit – oranges, black grapes, red cherries, auburn apricots. A charming city built on the slopes of Mount Olympus, Bursa is called

'The Emerald' with good reason. To her east lies the verdant and fertile Sakarya River valley, watered by streams from the mountains.

Forty-five minutes out of Bursa we began our ascent to the vast Anatolian plateau. The plain is lush and green with endless varieties of figs and a mass of apricots in the foothills. Flocks of black turkeys waddle beside the road. Here and there are plantations of poplars interspersed with oaks, pines and plane trees. Flocks of sheep and goats hold up the bus.

After two hours we reached the huge, rolling plateau of central Anatolia. Once the mass of apricots in the foothills had given way to poplars and plane trees, the trees disappeared to be replaced by long rolling wheat fields stretching to eternity, interspersed every 10 miles (15 kilometres) or so by giant sugar beet factories. Lines of greenery marching away to the distant mountains told of the track of watercourses. The houses in this area are huge – far bigger than in rural Greece or Romania to the north. Clearly Anatolia could feed tens of millions of people: it had so many natural advantages – rich soil, abundant water, plentiful sunshine.

For hour after hour we roared across this great plateau, heading for Boğazköy, 125 miles (200 kilometres) east of Ankara, which thousands of years ago had been the centre of the Hittite civilisation. I knew that name from the Bible: some of King David's most valued soldiers had been Hittites, although I'd never before troubled to find out exactly what that meant. In Boğazköy's museum I found seals with merchants' signatures, dating from 4000 BC. Arrows, axe heads and jewellery fill the rest of the museum.

Boğazköy is a higgledy-piggledy town with red pantile roofs and an antiquated *dolmus* bus that won't leave the square until it is totally full. This is where some of the very first Minoans may have come from. But then, you'd need a scorecard to keep track of all the peoples and cultures that have passed this way. The estimate is that the people whose arrival so transformed Neolithic Crete would have left this region around 100,000 BC.

The former Hittite capital of Hattuşa rises rather accusingly from the top of a huge crag, high above the present-day village. A hot walk up a tarmac road reveals an imposing lion gate but little else other than the rubble and footings of a ruined acropolis. The lions look strangely like puppies; obviously sculpted by someone who had never had the opportunity to study the beasts at first hand.

At its peak c.1344–1322 BC, this great palace was protected by 4 miles (6 kilometres) of stone walls. Now it looks about ready to turn back into dust.

To my right, as I walked through the ruins, was the outline of the oldest-known library ever to have existed. It is now nothing more than a few dents in the ground. I scrolled my toe through the dust and earth. Archaeologists tell us that all those years ago the cuneiform tablets stood on end in rows, like modern books on a shelf. There were even indexes, also marked out in the baked clay, telling you what was inside each stack of 'books': for instance, a label saying 'Thirty-two tablets concerning the Purulli festival of the city of Nerik'.

I wondered what it would have been like to go to a Purulli festival. Purulli was a storm god so I thought of the British music festivals, so often plagued by rain. Quite some way off from Glaston-bury, I suppose, but maybe not radically different – all that mud and all those brollies.

I was glad, then, that I'd gulped down my coffee and headed for the airport. A whole new way of investigating the Minoans' past had now opened up to me: through DNA.

The Hittites must have been a formidable people. They signed peace treaties with Egyptian pharaohs and Assyrian kings. They also conquered Babylon and were a well-ordered society, worshipping many deities, including, I noticed, a female god – Hepatu, the sun goddess. I didn't know for certain whether that was a direct link to the powerful goddesses of Knossos, but it felt right. Just to the south of here, on the Konya plain, is Çatalhöyük, known as the world's first major human settlement, of c. 7500 BC to 5700 BC.

Turkey not only straddles two continents, it seems. It straddles time itself.

||||||||||||||||||

What was the link to ancient Crete and to the Minoan civilisation that once flourished there? Very early settlers to Crete introduced cattle, sheep, goats, pigs and dogs, as well as vegetables and cereals. The earliest communities grew up around the coast on the eastern and southern parts of the island. Yet something appears to have happened to Crete and its culture after 7000 BC – something momentous. People suddenly learned advanced practices in agriculture. They developed pot-making, and metalwork. Next, quite suddenly, came an incredible period of palace development. How did such amazing sophistication appear so suddenly?

Boning up on the research I'd first read about in the newspaper report, I discovered that the DNA haplogroups J2a1h-M319 (8.8 per cent) and J2a1b1-M92 (2.6 per cent) linked the Minoans to a Late Neolithic/Early Bronze Age migration to Crete no later than 100,000 BC. Specifically, genetic researchers connected the source population of ancient Crete to the well-known Neolithic sites of ancient Anatolia, not too far away from my present location – such as Asýklý Höyük, Çatalhöyük, and Hacýlar. That made the blood surge a little faster. If researchers could find and track an ancient DNA link to Crete from the region I was now visiting, then perhaps I could follow the Minoans – via their DNA – to some of the other places I suspected they'd been. And in so doing reinforce my notion that they'd been the most important international trading culture of their age. And as such a key defining force in global history.

All human beings carry DNA (deoxyribonucleic acid) in every single cell of their bodies. Each cell contains 46 chromosomes, which cluster in pairs: half derive from your mother and half from your father. Chromosomes contain tightly coiled DNA, divided into sections known as genes. Genes tell the cells what proteins to make. The proteins, in turn, control everything that happens in your body when it comes to identity and growth: for example, one protein might make your eye pigment, others might decide the size and shape of your teeth.

The paired DNA strands wrap around one another to make a double helix. Each person has their own unique genetic fingerprint. It is unlike the DNA of anyone else, but there is a useful rider to that. While women have two X chromosomes, men have one X and one Y. The Y chromosome is always passed down the male line from father to son. That unique factor makes the Y-line virtually like a surname: it is transmitted, almost intact, down the male line from generation to generation.

The Y chromosome is altered only by rare spontaneous mutations. These mutations can be used to identify sequences of the Y chromosome, known as haplogroups. Being no expert in DNA, I had to do a bit of reading up here. The word 'haplogroup' comes from the Greek and means single, or simple. Haplogroups reveal deep ancestral origins dating back thousands of years. Males with the same haplogroup must have shared a common male ancestor in the past. This was intriguing, because according to what I was now learning other great peoples, such as the Etruscans, seemed to share some common ancestry with the Hittites of Anatolia. Haplogroups also incorporate smaller Y-DNA sequences know as haplotypes – groups of genes that share a common ancestor. Thanks to the work of the Human Genome Project, many of these have been identified and given codenames, e.g. J2a-M410.

It was Professor Constantinos Triantafyllidis of Thessaloniki's Aristotle University who had released details of the research and it was his comment that had launched me from my lukewarm morning coffee to a blasting hot plain in central Turkey. According to his initial findings, today's Cretan population was genetically intermingled with yesterday's people of Anatolia. Professor Triantafyllidis believes the arrival of these people had coincided with a social and cultural upsurge. It led, around 7000 BC, to the birth of Europe's first advanced civilisation.

I remembered very clearly one surprising image imprinted on the Phaestos Disc. It was of a man wearing a striking feather headdress. My trip to Turkey had confirmed my suspicion: during the Bronze Age, such warlike headgear was worn by the Lycians of Anatolia.

Notes to Book I

1. Marthari personal communication; S. Marinatos 1974, 31 and Pl. 67b and d; C. Doumas. C., in *Thera and the Ancient World*, 1983, p. 43
2. Rodney Castleden, *Minoans: Life in Bronze Age Crete*, Taylor and Francis, 2007
3. M. H. Wiener, *Thera and the Aegean World III*, vol. 1, *Archaeology*, Proceedings of the Third International Congress, Santorini, Greece, 3–9 September 1989, p. 128
4. Ibid
5. Papapostolou, L, Godart and J. P. Olivier, pp. 146–7, *Roundels among Minoan seals* (2009)
6. Plato, *Timaeus*, trans. Robin Waterfield. Oxford World Classics, 2008
7. Ibid
8. J. Boardman & colleagues, 'The Olive in the Mediterranean: Its Culture and Use', Royal Society Publishing, vol. 275, No.936, JSTOR
9. Ibid
10. Ventris and Chadwick, *The Decipherment of Linear B*, Cambridge University Press, 1958
11. Shaw, B. D., *The Cambridge Ancient History*, Cambridge University Press, 1984
12. Stylianos, Alexiou, *Minoan Civilisation*, Spyros Alexiou Sons; First Edition (1969)
13. Bruins, MacGillivray, Synolakis, Benjamini, Keller, Kisch, Klugel, and van der Plicht, 'Geoarchaeological tsunami deposits at Palaikastro (Crete) and the Late Minoan IA eruption of Santorini', Journal of Archaeological Science 2008, 35, pp. 191–212
14. Joseph Shaw (www.fineart.utoronto.ca/kommos/kommosintroduction)
15. Thucydides 1.41. trans. Benjamin Jowett. Oxford, 1900
16. Bernard Knapp, 'Thalassocracies in Bronze Age Eastern Mediterranean Trade: making and breaking a myth', in *World Archaeology*, vol. 24, No.3, Ancient Trade: New Perspectives, 1993
17. Thucydides 1.9.1,3
18. Stylianos Alexiou, *Minoan Civilization*, trans. C. Ridley. Heraklion Museum, 1969
19. Robert Graves, *The Greek Myths: Complete Edition*, Penguin, 1993
20. Stylianos Alexiou, *Minoan Civilization*
21. Herodotus, *Histories*. trans. George Rawlinson, Penguin Classics, 1858
22. Sandars 1963, p. 117; Popham et al. 1974, p. 252; Driessen and Macdonald 1984, pp. 49–74, 152 in "*The Isles of Crete? The Minoan Thalassocracy Revisited*, The Thera Foundation (www.therafoundation.org)
23. Sinclair Hood, in *Archaeology: the Minoans of America*, vol. 74, 1972
24. Constantinos Triantafyllidis, Aristotle University, Thessaloniki

BOOK II

|||||||||||||||||||||||||||||||

EXPLORATION

VOYAGES TO THE
NEAR EAST

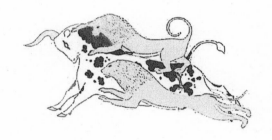

8

THE LOST WRECK AND THE
BURIED TREASURE TROVE

By now I was becoming convinced the Minoans were the forebears of the mythic heroes who sailed to Troy: Agamemnon, Achilles, Odysseus et al. But without any actual physical evidence of the kinds of ships they would have sailed, I feared that the trail had run out. Then one night I heard about a wreck dating from c.1305 BC that had been found on the seabed of the nearby Turkish coast – a discovery which, to a former sailor like me, counts as one of the greatest archaeological finds ever made.

In sea terms Uluburun, a promontory off the coast south of Bodrum, is quite close to Thera. Significantly for me, it is in exactly the zone – western Anatolia – that Bernard Knapp had described as being under the control of the Minoan empire. In Turkish the term 'Uluburun' simply means a rocky plinth of land; but the reef below it, like all reefs, is treacherous in bad weather.

I arrived at nearby Bodrum early in the morning, having spent an uncomfortable night chugging along the Aegean on yet another ferry. To get here, we puffed in the opposite direction from the beautiful Sea of Marmara and the teeming, anarchic sights of Istanbul. A litter of rocky islands stood in our way; as we puttered forward, I thought you'd have had to be a pretty good navigator just to travel north–south across the Aegean Sea.

We awoke to a fresh wind and the unmistakable bustle of a boat nearing port. I rushed out on deck in the sharp air of the early morning to catch my first glimpse of coastal Turkey for more than twenty years. Purple hills, deep grey-green olive groves, the azure sea and the romance of the deep past: I breathed it all in.

Excitement made my skin prickle. I could be on the threshold of a real breakthrough in my quest to uncover the truth behind the explorers and the seafarers of the ancient world – today at the town museum I'd get my first view of the oldest-known shipwreck in the world.

Bodrum is more or less the home of history; at least, it was home to the world's first superstar historian, Herodotus. The town's ancient name was Halicarnassus and its walls once encircled a mausoleum that was one of the famed seven wonders of the ancient world. It was such a pleasure to be here and breathe it all in; you can still trace the ancient walls that once embraced nearly the entire town. Bodrum Castle, now the Museum of Underwater Archaeology, was built by the Knights of St John in the 15th century. I felt instantly connected to the castle: its five major towers include the English, or Lion, Tower. Colourful rows of huge amphorae are mounted on the entrance wall.

The Uluburun wreck is the kind of heart-stopping find that archaeologists dream about; one of those discoveries that helps rewrite history. Quite why the boat came to grief – near what is today the pretty little fishing village of Kaş – no one will ever know for sure. The ship foundered a hundred years or so after Thera's frescoes were painted. Yet this is hardly a blink in time: in the interim, shipbuilding technology would not have changed much at all.

Poignantly, the wreck held one of ancient history's most extraordinary finds: the earliest 'captain's logbook'. But the captain remains mute, his words – written in soft wax – obliterated by time.

||||||||||||||||||||

For centuries the wreck lay quiet, in total obscurity, protected from looters by 45 deep blue metres (150 feet) of silent sea. Then in 1982, thousands of years after its last journey, a sponge diver found it by total accident. We must thank the stars for Mehmet Cakir's decency and honesty. If it were not for him, some of the world's greatest treasures could have gone via the black market to unscrupulous dealers. For what Cakir found was a hoard worthy of an Aladdin's cave – mound upon mound of sunken treasure.

The ship's extraordinary cargo could have come from a modern French luxury goods house – except that these opulent objects were much more exotic than even the highest quality champagne. The treasure, found scattered over 250 square metres (300 square yards) of the jagged, rocky seabed, came from as many as ten different Bronze Age nations. The Uluburun ship carried exquisitely wrought gold and silver jewellery and a cornucopia of rich fruits and spices, as well as huge amphorae from the Lebanon; terebinth resin, used to create perfumes; ebony, which had come all the way from Egypt; and all manner of exotic goods like elephant tusks, hippopotamus teeth and ostrich and tortoise shells (see first colour plate section).

Before you see the ship, the museum guides you through the finds from its hold. The material found in shipwrecks can only be rescued with a huge amount of hard work. Firstly, artefacts are put in vats of water, where they will remain for approximately six to eight years. It takes a minimum of five years, and sometimes up to ten years, just to remove the salt from porous substances. The water is changed every fifteen days, depending on what the gauges indicate. After the salt is removed, the objects are placed in a vat containing polyglycol for a period of four to five years. Every possible care has been taken to save these precious things. It was not difficult to see why.

The greatest treasure, a prize find worthy of a king, lay at the stern. It was an extraordinary chalice of pure gold. Homer describes the legendary war hero Achilles drinking from a golden goblet just like it:

> Achilles strode back to his shelter now
> and opened the lid of the princely inlaid sea chest
> that glistening-footed Thetis stowed in his ship to carry,
> filled to the brim with war-shirts, windproof cloaks
> and heavy fleecy rugs. And there it rested . . .
> his handsome, well-wrought cup.[1]

Achilles' golden chalice was found nestling on the seabed next to an exotic pendant in the form of a golden falcon, which was clutching a giant cobra in its talons. In the hold was yet more treasure, including a gold scarab bearing the name of the celebrated Egyptian beauty Nefertiti, queen and wife to Akhenaten, the all-powerful pharaoh of Egypt.

But in many ways I was less interested in all this exotica than in the 'everyday' story this traveller could tell us. The ship was a time capsule, speeding us back to the daily life of the Bronze Age: for me, it would be almost as if I were stepping into Doctor Who's Tardis.

As I travelled along the solemn line of glass cases, I could see knives and weighing scales – practical tools that had been used by ordinary sailors thousands of years ago. There were many animal-shaped lumps of bronze: deer, cattle. They stood out because they looked like toys, but in the catalogue they were described as weights. The weights used for scales were particularly eye-catching, even charming. There were stone mortars for grinding food and fish hooks to catch it. There was a barbed trident: it made you think of the Roman *retiarii*, or net and trident fighters – introduced to a much later Roman empire by Emperor Augustus.

The *retiarius* was modelled on a fisherman: the edges of the net he used like a lasso were weighted with lead. Right in front of me were the Bronze Age predecessors of that military innovation; hundreds of net sinkers, the weights that the crew used on the edges of their casting nets. There was also a harpoon – and a set of knucklebones, for playing a game of chance on those long nights at sea, a night's entertainment lit by the comforting yellow glow of oil lamps. Weapons, too – arms that had been wielded by wizened and ancient hands more than 3,000 years ago.

Then I reached the last display case. Its contents, for me, were far more valuable than all of the silver and gold, however beautiful. I took a sudden deep breath.

I was right. What was the wreck's main cargo? The raw materials for making bronze. They were even in the right proportions: 10 tons of copper and 1 ton of tin.

This was truly a Bronze Age vessel, made with bronze tools and carrying enough copper and tin to make weapons for an army. There were 121 copper 'bun' ingots, together with enough fragments to make another 9, and 354 copper 'oxhide' ingots, with an average weight of 23 kilos. Each copper oxhide ingot was about a metre long, with sharp corners. They are called oxhide ingots because their distinctive shape is a bit like the hide of an ox when it has been flayed and stretched. At one time it was thought that they may have represented the value of an ox; now archaeologists think the shape is simply easy to handle.

IIIIIIIIIIIIIIIIII

I slowed down as I approached the next room. Ahead of me was what I had been looking for: part of the oldest ship I had ever seen. About 15 metres (50 feet) long, her charred timbers were spindly and frail. She may have been ravaged by centuries of seawater, but there was a strength and grace to this boat's design that made you forget about her current dishevelled state. Here was a ship that could sail like the wind; nimble, responsive and manoeuvrable. There were quite a few other visitors in the room, but the atmosphere was hushed and thoughtful: after all, on this vessel people had struggled for their lives. And lost.

It took an astonishing eleven years and 22,000 dives to excavate the Uluburun. The ship had come to rest listing 15 degrees to starboard, facing east–west. A large piece of the hull had lain intact on the seabed for almost 3,500 years. It seemed incredible to me that it had survived at all.

The ship was built of cedar in the ancient hull-first tradition, with pegged tenon joints securing planks to each other and then to the keel. To build her, a team of men would have cut down a tall cypress tree, stripped its bark and carved the length into a keel.[2] Crete was covered with cypress forests in the Early Bronze Age: the wood is ideal for shipbuilding because it expands in water, making the seals between joints waterproof.

The shipwrights then 'edge-joined' a long cleanly sawn plank of cypress to each side of the huge keel. Chiselling out deep rectangular matching mortises every 25 centimetres (10 inches), they worked along the length of the keel. They cut flat rectangular pieces of wood (tenons) to fit snugly into the matching mortise slots. Then they fitted another plank to the tenons that were sticking out of the slots on the keel.

Methodically, the shipwrights added plank after plank to both sides of the keel, to build up a sturdy hull. The boat needed very little caulking given the edge-joined planking, although they did waterproof the seams with a resin mixture. The shipwright who worked for the mythological hero Jason, Argus, had cut his timber on Mount Pelion: but according to Thucydides, the search for wood for battle fleets meant that the plentiful forests of Greece were stripped bare as early as the 5th century BC. The Uluburun's sturdy oak mast was about 16 metres (52 feet) tall and secured with rigging made of strong hemp ropes. As someone who had spent many years at sea, I was sure that boats like these were fully capable of surviving long and hazardous ocean voyages, despite this individual vessel's fate.

But could I prove it? Were the exploits of ancient adventurers simply the stuff of legend, or could they be close to the facts? Luckily, I had an ancient myth and a modern real-life explorer's vessel to compare it with. Scholars say the legendary 1,500-mile voyage of Jason and the Argonauts, to win the Golden Fleece, happened during the Bronze Age, if it ever really took place. In the 1980s Tim Severin became obsessed with recreating a boat that could test the reality behind the myth.

The myth itself is a sort of ancient Greek *Mission Impossible*. The hero's kingdom is under threat from a usurper, his uncle, King Pelias. The gods command Jason to find a magical ram's fleece before he can reclaim his father's kingdom of Iolkos. So Jason has to embark on a treacherous sea voyage into an unknown land.

To test whether the tale could ever have held any truth, Severin reconstructed an ancient galley with documentary precision. With oars as well as sails, a galley is the logical choice for a vessel that might have to fight its way through hostile waters. I seemed to remember that Severin had managed it as far as the Black Sea without sinking – although there had been some pretty tricky moments.

The Uluburun ship would have fared even better. She was an altogether bigger and more seaworthy affair. The ship's cargo alone told us that her owners felt she could travel far and fast. It included Baltic amber from the north; ebony wood, hippopotamus teeth and elephant tusks from equatorial Africa; and goods from both the eastern and the western Mediterranean. The voyage itself almost certainly included stops in Cyprus for copper, Egypt for gold and Syria for ostrich eggs and pomegranates. That involved steering to all parts of the compass. If Tim Severin could make it, then so could the ship I had in front of me in Bodrum. The Uluburun wreck may have gone down like the *Titanic*, but that was because the captain was negotiating a dangerous promontory, perhaps braving the greater dangers of sailing in winter. In normal conditions, she was definitely able to weather even high sea states.

Archaeologists agree that the discovery of the Uluburun has pushed back the history of seafaring by centuries. I say that the evidence of the frescoes on Thera pushes that history back much, much further. Given the dating of the frescoes, which show ships of the exact same construction, there must have been a long trad-ition of sailing – and the know-how was alive and in use by the time the artists put paint to plaster. Shipbuilding technology changes, but it does so only slowly – or did, until the breakthroughs that came with the Industrial Revolution: steel and steam. Had he been alive, the expert mariner Sir Francis Drake – whose famous *Golden Hind* was a round-bellied Tudor ship – would still have been able to make a good fist of sailing Admiral Lord Nelson's much larger and slimmer HMS *Victory* at Trafalgar in 1805, some two hundred years later.

The Uluburun's mast had a single boom about 10 metres (33

feet) long to hold the top of the sail. The centre of the boom was connected to the mast by a thick strong ring of rope, loosely wrapped around the shaft of the mast (see also Thera ship 6). This meant the boom could pivot freely about the mast in the wind. It could be easily raised or lowered with ropes running through a bronze fixture on the masthead. The orientation of the boom and the sail in the wind could be controlled from the deck with ropes, allowing the ship to tack quite well into a head wind.

Thinking back to the frescoes, the evidence here in Bodrum confirmed what I had already noticed. Each of the long ships was a masterpiece: I was overwhelmed. All of the evidence told me that shipwrights were definitely capable of building ships fit for ocean travel as early as c.1450 BC. The sailors had sophisticated methods of hoisting, lowering and adjusting sails, not least the bronze fixture on the masthead. There is other evidence of this impressive development in technology: the mechanical principle is shown by two separate examples in the Egyptian Gallery in the National Archaeological Museum in Athens. Those fixings show that many centuries ago ships were confidently expected to sail into the wind as well as before it: the men knew they could lower sail very quickly in the event of an unexpected squall. By comparison with the Uluburun's hold, I estimated that the cargo capacity of the admiral's ship at Thera would have been about 50 metric tons.

Using bronze tools, particularly the large two-handled saws that were almost 2 metres (6 feet 6 inches) long and a third of a metre (13 inches) wide, these ancient craftsmen had achieved levels of shipbuilding expertise that Renaissance Europe had taken centuries to rediscover. This was a Bronze Age civilisation. But making the most of Bronze Age technology, it seemed, was not exactly making the best of a bad job.

The museum held another surprise. The Minoans have always been characterised by archaeologists as a wholly peaceful people. If so, their level of weaponry is highly surprising. Arthur Evans had bitter experience of violence, witnessing massacres in Crete as the *Manchester Guardian*'s war correspondent during the 1897 Greco-

Turkish war. After discovering Knossos, Evans declared that by contrast his beloved Minoan civilisation had been totally peaceable. As Cambridge University research scholar Cathy Gere describes it:

> Evans had reported with fairly even-handed revulsion the terrible Muslim/Christian massacres on Crete. Keen to represent the past as a site of healing and reconciliation, Evans resurrected Bronze Age Crete as an unfortified idyll, internally peaceful under the benign reign of Knossos, and protected from its enemies without by the legendary seafaring skills of King Minos' navy.[3]

Since then, most academics have followed his lead and depicted Crete as a peaceful society, mainly because its cities didn't have fortified walls. The Minoans lived a harmonious life in lush, civilised surroundings, they say, calmly governed in a democratic way. They didn't need city walls. Their kingdoms resembled peaceful heavens on earth.

Yet as I moved through the closeted dark of the exhibition rooms, I came upon case after case of weapons recovered from the wreck. Bronze weapons, manufactured in large quantities. Green and corroded as they were from centuries on the deep seabed, I could clearly see that this prehistoric ship had carried everything a troop of warriors would need – arrowheads, double-headed axes, spears, swords and daggers as well as the adzes, saw screws and razors that had more peaceable uses.

Crete's largest archaeological museum, at Heraklion, also has cases full of ordinary soldiers' bronze weapons – from spears to daggers and nasty-looking rapiers. Some of them are obviously ceremonial – like the extraordinary dagger found at the town of Malia, its hilt decorated with gold leaf; but towards the end of the period it was plain that swords had been made for only one purpose: fighting. Short blades had been adapted for cutting, as well as thrusting strokes. They were made for warriors.

Without doubt, the Minoans' military strength came from their fleet. Coupled with the sophisticated design of their ships, it seemed to me that far from being entirely peaceable, the Minoans had possessed formidable military might. The warlike Mycenaeans on the mainland of Greece would later wage war against the Trojans, as described in the *Iliad* and the *Odyssey*. Yet the Minoans seemed to live at peace with them. In fact, much of the archaeological record points to the idea that the mainlanders were either a Minoan colony or a compliant ally of the Minoans – until the point at which Crete was fatally weakened by the devastating loss of its wooden fleet in the tsunami.

Of course the Minoans may have preferred not to use force: who knows? They were certainly as interested in trade as they were in weapons. Yet it was noticeable that their fast, sturdy ships were the type that could be mobilised speedily, carrying soldiers armed to the teeth with a lethal array of bronze weapons of war.

Like most British citizens of my age, whose parents had been through a war, I understood the strategic value of being 'an island nation'. The sailors of Atlantis were already the world's top naval power. With ships that were far in advance of any others in Europe or the Near East, the result must have been that the Minoans feared no one. Their remarkable cities had few defensive walls precisely because they had the sea instead. Leaving them wide open to the biggest tidal wave the world had ever seen.

At least one of Thera's marvellous frescoes shows soldiers in battle helmets getting ready for war, along with an admiral commanding a sea battle. And winning it. They'd evidently had the might to control the entire Mediterranean. Maybe they'd used it.

And that's what I was determined to find out next.

||||||||||||||||||

In construction, the Uluburun wreck had been almost identical to ship 5 on the fresco in the West House. That meant one thing was certain: the Minoans had similar, deep-sea trading ships – at least a hundred years before the ship that had gone down off the coast of Turkey. I left the calm and quiet gloom of the museum with the blood spinning in my head. Ostrich eggs from Syria; gold from Egypt; precious amber from the Baltic; hippopotamus teeth from equatorial Africa . . . all of the riches of the world. All here.

Here in Bodrum I felt I was looking at positive proof that the Minoans, these highly creative, ingenious and artistic people, were also the world's first explorers.

9

SAILING FROM BYZANTIUM

I'd left Turkey and the Uluburun wreck with a sense of sadness. The captain's book, that simple writing tablet in folding wood, dominated my thoughts. The captain had loaded all of the riches of the world on to that boat – from tortoise shells for making musical instruments, and the much prized blue cobalt glass, to the smelly murex shells that were collected in their millions on Crete, and which produce the world's most brilliant purple dye. But nothing could protect either him or his passengers and crew from the perils of the sea. Even those with the most extraordinary sailing skills must wrestle with the elements, and rocky reefs, from time to time. And sometimes they will lose the fight.

The world's oldest book was made of two boxwood leaves, joined by a three-piece cylindrical hinge in ivory. The cavity was inlaid with wax. But again, like the Phaestos Disc, the words themselves escaped me. The captain was mute, his writing scoured away by the seas that had killed him. I could tell nothing whatever about his journey, or the skills he had as a sailor. The very fact that he had set out, though, was proof paramount that Bronze Age sailors had considered themselves capable of ambitious and wide-ranging journeys at sea.

The book must have held instructions from the ship's owner, or even from the ruler, I thought, about the cargo and where it was headed. It would read something like this: 'The captain is to proceed to Byblos from Thera and unload the cargo. This special cargo is the property of X, and consists of 340 ingots of copper, and 60 of tin . . .'. Then would follow a detailed list, written with a bronze stylus, of all the valuable articles on board, as well as weights, measures and destinations. I fell to thinking: if a thief had wanted to steal that captain's cargo, or if the captain himself had been dishonest, then wax is not exactly the ideal recording medium. A heated spatula would easily smooth it out, making the figures easy to alter.

The log – for that's what it must have been – was tied closed. It would also have been sealed with the owner's personal seal. And so that the system was foolproof, the owner and the captain used a common system of weights. On that fateful day the weights and at least three sets of balances were on the ship, suggesting that there were a number of different merchants taking passage on the journey. Already, in the Bronze Age, a single mass standard was used across the Mediterranean, based on a unit weight of 9.3 to 9.4 grams.

Sceptics may think that, surely, this skill with sailing could not have come suddenly, from nowhere, as if by magic. True enough: long-distance sailing is demanding. It takes great skill, intimate knowledge of the seas and constant vigilance, not forgetting bravery, perseverance and a certain amount of luck. When Tim Severin set out on the trail of the Golden Fleece, pessimists calculated that unless they had favourable winds to help them, the crew would have to row more than a million oar strokes each to reach Georgia. A testing mission.

This scepticism would be misplaced. When we 'discover' a new city, a new monument, or a new wreck, we don't manage to do it in neat, chronological order. To early archaeologists and explorers the ancient Egyptians must have seemed to have had almost pre-ternatural abilities. To many of us, they still do. Yet their technology wasn't sent down to earth by aliens, as some have claimed. The truth is that those achievements look surprisingly sudden to us because we are missing the various stages of development in between. In the case of the Egyptians, many sites dating from before Old Kingdom Egypt simply hadn't been dug up – or recognised for what they really were – until relatively recently.

Just like the hidden passages and chambers in the great Valley of the Kings tombs of the Egyptians, the Minoans' seafaring skills didn't come from thin air. This resourceful culture had built up a body of knowledge over the centuries, as I'd found when tracing their DNA trail back to the Hittites. Just as in Egypt, the longer we wait, the more evidence of early Cretan seafaring we will find.

I had to know more about Minoan sail-power.

Ships were essential to move the raw materials on which Minoan civilisation was based. They had to shift their finished works for export and they also needed to transport the raw materials for their products: whether that meant copper from Cyprus, elephant and hippopotamus ivory from India and Africa, gold from Upper Egypt, gypsum and glass from the Levant or the mysterious substance amber from the Baltic. They therefore needed ships that could travel hundreds of miles across the Mediterranean and, in the case of the precious amber, to the Baltic. Could they possibly have done that?

So I turned my thoughts back towards the actual task of sailing and to Tim Severin.

VOYAGE TO THE BLACK SEA BY REPLICA SHIP

A Harkness Fellow at the universities of California, Minnesota and Harvard, Tim Severin has written many books on exploration, from *Tracking Marco Polo* to *Vanishing Primitive Man* and, most importantly for me, *The Jason Voyage*.[4]

When Homer wrote the *Odyssey*, around the 8th century BC, he said that Jason and the Argonauts' brave and epic voyage in search of the Golden Fleece was already 'a tale on all men's lips'. This would have been a generation before the Trojan War. Critics have been sceptical. The voyage couldn't have had any basis in reality, they argued, because this was too far back in time; the technology simply wasn't in existence. Severin's aim had been to find out if Jason could have really sailed to the Baltic in 1300 BC. To quote him:

> ... we hoped to track them [the Argonauts] in reality. So we rowed aboard the replica of a galley of Jason's day, a twenty oared vessel of 3,000 year old design, in order to seek our own golden fleece ...

He based his reconstructed ship upon drawings on Bronze Age pots and frescoes, as well as carvings on armour, jewellery and seals. For reasons of cost it was a half-scale model, 16.5 metres (54 feet) long 'from the tip of her curious snout-like ram in the bows to the graceful sweep of her tail'. Later pictures of ships dating from the 7th to the 4th centuries BC gave Severin further technical details to follow, such as the way the sails were rigged and controlled.

In Homer's writings, Greek ships are measured by the number of oars. They came in three sets of twenty, thirty and fifty oars. To save money, Severin chose the smallest.

Severin was going against the currents all the way, with no help from the prevailing wind. The ship he would sail would be some two centuries younger than those shown on Thera's frescoes. It was a difficult task: although his ship was just half the length and breadth of ships 5 and 8 at Thera, with half the number of oars, its volume would be just one eighth of that of the Thera ships. This placed a considerable strain on cargo capacity, water and food – and on the crew. Because of the lack of space, sleeping was hard and the crew were permanently exhausted as a result.

Along with naval architect Colin Mudie, Severin examined every aspect of ships built in the area more than 3,000 years ago and how to sail them – not least in relation to the crew. The physique of man in the Bronze Age was smaller than today. Cretans were also small – they were perhaps 165 centimetres (5 feet 5 inches) tall and about a stone lighter than today. The pair searched for a boatbuilder who specialised in building traditional Aegean sailing ships, one who would work in the same wood that was used thousands of years ago. Vasilis Delimitros was reputed to be the best shipwright on Spetses, which is now a picturesque, car-free island and a splendid holiday haven. In Jason's time it would have been a Mycenaean stronghold. The galley was built using the same bronze adzes and saws which were in use in the Bronze Age. Delimitros followed Colin Mudie's drawings closely, not least when constructing the hull, where the planks were joined edge to edge as in the Uluburun wreck. Grooves were chiselled out of the plank, a tongue of oak was inserted, a matching tongue was cut out of the plank to be joined, the two were hammered flush together, then a hole was drilled for a locking peg through the matching tongues. To Vasilis it was no problem. He built one complete side of the ship by eye, then the next. The planks were slotted together as quickly and smoothly as if he had been doing the job all his life.

When the hull was ready they carved the mast from a tall, straight cypress tree, as well as two 3.5-metre (12-foot) high steering oars. The rigging was similar to ship 6 in the Thera fresco – hemp woven and stitched to make stays, sheets, and halyards. The pulleys were copied from the oldest-known shipwrecks, with wooden sheaves fixed around wooden pins. Finally the fierce and brave *Argo* was ready – and was even painted in the livery of red, white and blue found both in Mycenaean ships and on the Theran wall frescoes.

What now follow are my own impressions. At times they may appear critical: that is not the intention. I have unqualified admiration for what Severin achieved with a largely amateur crew on a journey of 1,500 miles (2,400 kilometres) across open sea. The personal toll was extreme. For instance, Severin describes an occasion when a gnawing storm brewed up in the Black Sea, and the heavy downpour turned the hands of the rowers a horrible, pulpy white. As he describes it: 'Their hard-won blisters looked like dead flesh.'

The incident itself clearly shows the dangers that Bronze Age sailors would have had to face routinely. Severin was attempting to reach a calm cove, against the pressure of great round-shouldered waves, through a narrow cut in the cliffs:

We were getting dangerously near the rocks, and the crew were falling quieter as the constant slog began to sap their energy ... I turned *Argo* at right-angles to the entrance and drove her hard at the gap. She rose on the back of a wave, heaved forward, fell back and was picked up a second time. The crew rowed flat out to keep her moving through the water so that I had enough speed to steer her and to keep the boat from wavering off-course or broaching to the waves. In a spectacular roller-coaster ride the galley went tearing through the gap, her fierce eyes staring straight ahead, and we entered the haven.[5]

There were plenty of disasters, but in the event many things went better than planned. Firstly, the bow ram proved a convenient place for the crew to sit to relieve themselves. A line of pegs doubled as a ladder to climb back on board. The sailors could wash themselves and their clothes when becalmed – as well as fish from the ram.

Secondly, the twin steering oars (which were worked in opposite directions), turned the ship easily. Then in flat calm seas without wind, twelve oarsmen (out of the twenty) could push the ship along at 3 to 3.5 knots, even faster if the centre of gravity was adjusted by shifting the resting oarsmen and cargo aft. Severin writes:

> *Argo* spent all that day skimming over the waves in Jason's wake like a ship out of a dream. Under full sail she behaved superbly. The hull cleaved through the blue sea and with the merest touch on the two steering oars, *Argo* responded like a well-schooled thoroughbred. She turned as deftly as one could wish, and a second touch on the tillers to bring them level brought her back on course, running sweetly forward. One could feel the ship quiver as she sped downwind, her keel and planks thrumming as she rolled over to the following seas while her ram threw aside a cresting bow wave ... For hour after hour *Argo* ploughed along at 5–6 knots leaving a clean wake behind her, while the crew relaxed on the benches ...

Finally, *Argo* had very good sea-keeping qualities in a gale. Although she was wallowing and lurching, and was seemingly threatened by wave after wave, she did not take on much water. The crew – although they got seasick – just sat and waited for the gale to pass. *Argo*'s natural position was to lie broadside on to the waves, rising and falling to their advance and giving a lurching sideways heave as each crest passed under her keel.

Now for the bad news. Rowing had been a nightmare. Continuously soaked, chafed and wet, the crew suffered multiple salt-water sores – their hands a mass of blisters. Even when they'd replaced mutton fat with olive oil as a lubricant, rowing was only practical in a flat calm. The slightest wind was a nightmare – ' . . . a scarcely perceptible breeze blowing against the prow of the boat cut down her speed alarmingly. It was not just like walking uphill, but like walking uphill through shifting sand'.

In any sort of sea the oars got banged about and rowers were thumped in the back. The steering oars were not strong enough and broke frequently. Neither were the rowlocks, which snapped. The cotton sail became mildewed with damp (I think using a cotton sail was a mistake: Minoans used woven sheep's wool impregnated with fat).

After only five months' sailing the hull of the ship was covered in barnacles, reducing speed by one knot (the Thera frescoes show that the Minoans sheathed the hull in canvas, which would have eliminated most barnacles). Despite all of this the *Argo* covered 1,500 miles (2,400 kilometres) in three months – against the wind and current – with a constantly changing, inexperienced crew. It was an astonishing achievement.

||||||||||||||||||||

Severin and his crew had shown that boats like the *Argo* could have successfully plied the Mediterranean in the Bronze Age. By this evidence, they could even have got as far as the Baltic. Yet there were still major questions that needed answering, as far as I was concerned. I particularly wanted to discover whether it was specifically the Minoans who had developed the art of seafaring? Did they have a far-reaching tradition that made them better sailors than, say, the peoples from mainland Greece?

In spring 2010, I once again picked up my *Times* newspaper, and found, by luck, another piece of the puzzle.

Quartz tools at least 130,000 years old, such as hand axes, cleavers and scrapers, had just been found in an area of southwest Crete from Plakias to Ayios Pavlos, including the famous Preveli Gorge. They dated from the Lower Palaeolithic period. The fact that Crete has been isolated from the mainland by the Mediterranean Sea for five million years told the archaeological team that these early settlers must have arrived by boat. The team, headed by Dr Thomas Strasser of Providence College Rhode Island and Dr Eleni Panagopoulou of the Greek Ministry of Culture, had surveyed caves and rock shelters near the mouths of freshwater streams, the sorts of sites where Palaeolithic man is likely to have lived. Professor Curtis Runnels of the Plakias survey team told the newspaper: '[They] reached the island using craft capable of open-sea navigation and multiple journeys – a finding that pushes the history of seafaring in the Mediterranean back by more than 100,000 years.'

All in all the team recovered more than 2,000 stone artefacts from 28 sites. The quartz rocks from which the tools were fashioned were sufficiently abundant for tools to be discarded when blunted. At five of the sites the geological context had helped the team arrive at an approximate age for the stone tools. Professor Runnels estimated that they were at least 130,000 years old and could be much older.

In the report Dr Runnels suggested that they could be at least twice as old as the geologic layers (i.e. 260,000 years old). Dr Strasser went further – they could be at least 700,000 years old. Dr Strasser, who has conducted excavations in Crete for the past twenty years, bases his estimate on similar double-bladed hand axes fashioned in Africa 800,000 years ago. He believes that the large sets of hand axes found on the island suggest a substantial population, who must have made multiple sea crossings, all landing at the same place. In order to achieve that, Palaeolithic man must have had seaworthy vessels more than 100,000 years ago. He must also have had a system of navigation which allowed later arrivals to find Crete and the landing stages reached by earlier voyagers. The newer settlers must have heard about the previous voyages in detail – this at a time before the invention of writing as we know it.

Before these extraordinary finds were made, it was thought seafarers had not reached Crete until around 6000 BC. But it is now generally accepted that by 4000 BC at the latest Cretan people had sufficient food, shelter and clothing to have surplus time on their hands – and at this point life ceased to be purely a battle for survival.

The Plakias survey team believed that this was the earliest evidence of Lower Palaeolithic seafaring so far found in the Mediterranean. Crete's very first inhabitants had arrived at the island by ship. Who knows what archaeologists will find next? We don't know in what sort of craft, but it seems that people were navigating Homer's 'wine-dark sea' tens of millennia earlier than anybody has ever dared to think.

10

LIFE IN THE LIBRARY

My task now, if I was going to get any further with my quest, was to find out more about the Minoans' need to sail. What exactly were they trading and how far did they have to travel to get it? The Uluburun wreck had told a fascinating story and I needed to unravel it. Dauntingly, I had to bridge the more than 3,000-year gap between the wreck and our own age.

Luckily it was not that difficult to stroll from my home in north London to the British Library. I spent three long weeks researching the Uluburun wreck and the objects found in its hold, going back and forth to the library's enormous new red-brick building on the Euston Road, breathing in the calm and scholarly atmosphere with real enjoyment. It is somehow rather comforting to sit inside a building with so much knowledge propping it up from all sides. It feels like a cocoon against the world, a time shuttle carrying everything in its red-brick hold, from beautiful historic maps to rare manuscripts. I like to think of all those books and papers mouldering away in basements underneath but the reality, as a diligent and helpful librarian explained to me, is that they are kept in vast climatically controlled racks underground, often in off-site storage facilities as far away from London as Boston Spa.

Now I was able to check up on the Uluburun's cargo in detail. Only a few months ago, the ancient world had been simply darkness, as far as I was concerned. Gradually, flashes of bright colour were piercing through that shadow and murk. I was beginning to get a feel for the real lives of a fast-developing people who had been inhabiting an extraordinary, active, bustling world that a few months before I had scarcely known existed. I also wanted to discover more about the Egyptians' political and strategic alliances. It seemed to me that the Minoans must have developed a long-standing relationship with Egypt, if they'd traded so many goods from Africa and the Middle East.

Fairly quickly, I learned that Minoan Crete had been renowned for its sophisticated perfumes, which it exported across the Mediterranean. Terebinth, with its hyacinth-shaped candles of bright red flowers, still grows on Crete – and is often used to lace the local brandy. To people in ancient cultures scent was of great value. They burned many kinds of resins and woods in their religious rituals, as well as adorning themselves. I already knew from past travels to Egypt and the west bank of the Nile that Queen Hatshepsut had led whole expeditions in search of another intense scent, incense: the results were recorded on the walls of the mortuary temple created in her honour at Deir el-Bahri, near the entrance to the Valley of the Kings. In the Uluburun wreck's hold the spirit of 'waste not, want not' was evident – the stalks and leaves of the terebinth bush itself had also been used on the ship as a springy packing material, protecting delicate items on the journey.

One look at a botanical tome, and unwittingly the humble terebinth plant had helped me to find what I had not quite known I was looking for. The resin only comes after the early winter frosts. This small fact, along with the fact that the ship was also carrying ripe pomegranates in the hold, stopped me in my tracks. Surely, this meant that the ship was on a winter voyage? This would imply that by the time the Uluburun sank, and maybe long before that, voyages were no longer confined to high summer. Bronze Age sailors were sailing in all seasons, and into the wind.

These early research successes aside, I soon realised that the task I had set myself was not as straightforward as it might have seemed. There was a geographical anomaly in the Uluburun's hold, and it was staring me in the face.

There was a rare ceremonial sceptre-mace on board. The expert analysis was that it came from either Bulgaria or Romania – from halfway up the Black Sea. Also in the hold was a large quantity of amber, the fossil produced by pine resin, which actually came from the Baltic. I thought at once of Severin's voyage – the parallel with Jason's voyage and the tale of the Golden Fleece – and then brushed it from my mind. This was real life we were talking about, not myth. Tim Severin had got as far as the Black Sea. The Baltic was an altogether more dangerous proposition. Had the Minoans truly obtained Baltic amber all the way from the north? Today polished amber is highly prized, treated like a jewel and bartered like one. But then?

A quick look at the work of the great classicist Robert Graves[6] and some science journals yielded a further series of supporting clues: apparently, wine is quite possibly a Cretan invention and not just in myth. The linguistic evidence comes with the fact that the very word is from Crete. The vines used to make it are thought to have first come from the area around the Black Sea, where they originated in the wild.

My research also confirmed that amber had been both valued and used since the Stone Age. The Greek name for amber is *electron*; the origin of our own word electricity. Rub amber with a cloth and it will become electrified and even attract paper.[7] It must have induced a real sense of mystery and wonder. It was certainly used in sympathetic magic. Worn as a charm, the belief was that amber protected against sore throats, toothache and stomach upsets. It was also seen as a remedy for snake bite and newborn babies were given amber necklaces to protect against infection. In much later times, even the prophet Muhammad valued it: he said that a true believer's prayer beads should be made of amber.

So amber was a true treasure; a great prize. To obtain it our ancient mariners would have needed to sail through the Kattegat and Skagerrack. Even those great sailors of latter times, the Vikings, had occasionally come to grief doing that.

I cast my mind back to Jason and the Argonauts and thought how dangerous travel in rocky seas would have been. Yet the Baltic amber that had evidently been found in many ancient gravesites in mainland Greece, as well as on the Uluburun wreck, must have got there somehow. Neither did it feel like a coincidence that Crete had such a reputation for wine, if its sailors had been the first to discover vines, and grapes, because of their adventurous travels.

I could see that to piece all of the strands of evidence together I needed to learn much, much more about the fascinating process of world trade from all that time ago. I decided to concentrate on four significant categories of the traded goods and see if I could discover more about the process. Taking a notebook, I began what for me was several days' work, but it is summarised here as just five sections.

AMBER

Infrared spectroscopy proves that most of the amber found in ancient sites in the Mediterranean came from the Baltic, as did that in the Uluburun wreck. The earliest Baltic amber found in the Mediterranean was found at Mycenae (shaft grave O) and is dated to c.1725–1675 BC. A vast amount of the jewellery found at Mycenae was originally Minoan.

A total of 1,560 pieces using amber were found at Mycenae, 1,290 from shaft grave IV alone. It is intriguing that these earliest consignments show a remarkable similarity (in the design of their spacer plates) to amber necklaces of the same period found in Britain. Which also originated in the Baltic. So it appears possible that Crete's expanding empire was already trading in amber by 1725 BC.

I soon discovered that there are others apart from myself who believe that the Minoans were behind the ancient amber trade. In 1995 Hans Peter Duerr, who was then a director of the German scientific research organisation the Max Planck Institute, decided to take his family on holiday to the North Sea islands, near Hamburg. Duerr was interested in the lost city of Rungholt, which in the Middle Ages sank beneath the waves in a tempest.

Medieval Rungholt, then a part of the nation of Nordfriesland, had a population of some 1,500 people and a reputation as an astoundingly wealthy port. It became victim to the first *'Grote Man-draenke'*, a Low Saxon term for 'A Great Drowning of Men' – a vicious North Sea storm tide that swept over England, Denmark, Saxony and the Netherlands in 1362, smashing island groups apart and killing an estimated 25,000 people.

Duerr's most exciting findings, he told the German magazine *GEO*, lay underneath the late medieval Rungholt – beneath, and therefore older than, a Bronze Age layer of peat dated to 1200 BC. They were just ordinary, everyday items; items that sailors, who were there for far more valuable goods, had left behind at a port.

> We came across remains of Levantine and especially Minoan cer-amics, the daily kind used to transport goods. They were dated 13th and 14th century BC. Amongst these were shards of two tripod cooking pots from Crete. That's why we believe ships were sailing in 1400 BC from Crete to the coast of Northern Frisia.[8]

There is a possibility that these pots could have been antiquities which were being carried much later by a more modern ship. Duerr doesn't believe that, because the items themselves were so ordinary. The cooking vessels were scarcely 'antiques'.

> The pots we found were not trade goods being carried by merchants. The ceramics were of practical daily use – belonging, with great certainty, to equipment on a ship.

The finds did include lance tips and incense, but mainly what they found were containers for drinking and eating. Most crucially, Duerr discovered a seal that he claims had a Linear A inscription on it.

What could have tempted the Minoans from Crete to the North Sea in the 14th century BC?

Their interest was first prompted, Duerr believes, by: 'Tin from Cornwall. The finds point to a shipwreck.' He went on:

> I can now add it was not far from Britain to Frisia, where amber came from, beloved by the people of Mycenae. It was possible for the Minoans to navigate the North Sea 3,300 years ago . . . .

Tin from Cornwall: navigation of the highly dangerous North Sea . . . For now, I was going to put those astonishing assertions aside and continue investigating the Uluburun's hold.

ELEPHANT TUSKS

A length of elephant tusk, cleanly sawn at both ends. Heavily stained by the copper ingots in the wreck, it was found at the stern of the ship. Ivories were regularly traded as luxury goods. I vividly remembered seeing the charred ends of an elephant tusk in Heraklion's museum; it had been found in a 15th-century BC tomb at Zakros in Crete. Elephants are, of course, found in both Africa and India, but the tusks discovered in the Uluburun wreck have not yet been classified. However, we know Indian elephant tusks did reach the wider Mediterranean in the Bronze Age. Five tusks from Indian elephants have been found in the ruins of a Middle Bronze Age palace at Alalakh in southern Turkey and more at Megiddo, in northern Israel's Jezreel valley.

HIPPO TEETH

I have a soft spot for the hippopotamus and its teeth. In 1959 I had the misfortune to be serving on HMS *Newfoundland*, a cruiser returning from Singapore to the UK to decommission. *Newfoundland* was an old Second World War ship, useless in the age of strike aircraft and nuclear submarines. She had a complement of fifty-eight officers, when eight would have been enough. For most of the time we had nothing to do, so we drank heavily to pass the time.

We berthed at Lourenço Marques in southern Mozambique and spent the first night at a seedy Portuguese night club. One of my favourite singers, Maria de Lourdes Machado, was singing *fados*, the sad Portuguese songs of lost love and betrayal. I think we must have all over-indulged . . . It was a beautiful dawn and we decided to go on a hippopotamus shoot in the delta of the Limpopo River, to the north. We took one of the ship's motor boats, a crate of rum and some limes and set off.

We found plenty of hippos snorting in the shallows and we started shooting at their flat backs. The hippos didn't like this at all. In fact, they rammed the boat. I remember seeing the boat in the air, cartwheeling upside down, with the propellers still turning. An angry hippo with red, bloodshot eyes and huge teeth was staring at me from a few feet away, eyeing me up for breakfast. Too drunk to care, I vomited green bile, which spread in an oily slick across the muddy Limpopo water towards him. In disgust, he dived under me and disappeared.

So I had had a good enough close-up of hippopotamus teeth. More to the point, their teeth have been worked into ivory jewellery for a very long time. A fragment of a hippopotamus lower canine was found at Knossos in the ruin of an early Minoan (3rd millennium BC) palace. So there was trade between Africa and Crete long ago.

SHELLS

It's extraordinary to think that objects as delicate as ostrich eggs managed to survive the wreck of the Uluburun, but some of them did. At least five tortoise carapaces were also on the ship; the bowl-like shells were used for making lyres.

But I was interested in two types of shell in particular. The first sort came in their thousands: those of *murex opercula* sea snails. Crete was the world centre of the trade in the prized purple dye that was extracted from these incredibly smelly molluscs. It took thousands of murex to make enough dye for the hem of a cloak and the Minoans had farmed them in great numbers for this lucrative trade. The presence of so many of them on the wreck supports the idea that the ship was Minoan.

I was also intrigued by twenty-eight rings from an unidentified, large shell. The rings were found cut into shape and ground down. Their size implies that they were not from the Mediterranean, but from the Indo-Pacific region. They had already attracted the attention of experts:

> ... The Uluburun rings provide evidence for trade between the Persian Gulf and the Levantine coast during the 14th century BC. Shells were either imported into Mesopotamia as finished rings, as may have been the case at Usiyeh, or made into rings there and probably also embellished with inlays affixed with Mesopotamian bitumen, before being exported to the Levant.[9]

So here we have a hint of the trade between the Minoans in the Mediterranean and the Indian Ocean.

THE COPPER INGOTS

When he discovered the Uluburun wreck Mehmet Cakir was looking for sponges. What he found, instead, he said, were biscuits – 'biscuits with ears'. What looked to him like biscuits turned out to be copper and tin ingots, lying near the keel. Many of the tin ingots had corroded into sludge, but the copper ones remain in remarkable condition even after their 3,500 long years under water.

The total weight of the ingots was some 11 tons – 10 of copper and one of tin. There were 354 copper ingots in the shape of an oxhide, 121 smaller bun-shaped copper ingots and fragments forming another nine. No moulds have been found to show how the molten metal was formed into these shapes, but it seems that there were two pours of molten metal into one mould, in rapid succession – evidenced by cracking during cooling as the metal contracted. Most of the ingots were incised with marks when cold – probably at the trading place where they were collected and sold.

The origins of this copper are heatedly debated: this is also true of the tin. If we knew its sources, it could explain how the Mediterranean exploited such enormous quantities of bronze, when there appeared to be insufficient numbers of mines to satisfy the demand.

A thorough analysis of the copper ingots has been carried out by Professors Andreas Hauptmann, Robert Maddin and Michael Prange. It is described in their paper 'On the structure and composition of copper and tin ingots excavated from the shipwreck of Uluburun'.[10] They write:

> The ship carried ten tons of copper and one ton of tin. The cargo thus represented the 'world market' bulk metal in the Mediterranean ... Cores drilled from a number of ingots show an extraordinarily high porosity of the copper. Inclusions of slag, cuprite and copper sulphides suggest the ingots were produced from raw copper smelted in a furnace and in a second step re-melted in a crucible. Internal cooling rims point to a multiple pouring. We doubt that the entity of an ingot was made of one batch of metal tapped from a late Bronze Age smelting furnace. The quality of the copper is poor [viz. the smelting process] and needed further purification before casting, even if the chemical composition [i.e. the raw copper] shows that it is rather pure. The copper was not refined. The tin ingots in most case are heavily corroded. The metal is low in trace elements, except for lead.

The authors were studying the smelting process. Yet in examining that procedure, they also had to analyse the raw material. And the results intrigued me. They continued:

> From the chemical point of view, the purity of this copper is extraordinary in comparison with other sorts of copper distributed in the late Bronze Age Old World. For instance copper from the Wadi Arabah is much higher in lead (up to several per cent) ... copper from the Caucasus area is extraordinarily high in arsenic (up to several per cent) ... copper from Oman usually contains arsenic and nickel in the percentage area.

The authors don't believe that this extraordinary purity could have been the result of smelting

> ... the concentrations, for instance, of lead, arsenic, antimony, nickel or silver do not change very much during smelting ... We therefore

conclude that the ingots reflect the composition of 'pure' copper ores that were smelted to produce the metal.

Detailed results, including a table for the composition of each ingot, showing the staggering purity of the copper, are contained on our website.

I was more than surprised. There is only one type of copper with that level of purity, the copper that comes from Lake Superior on the Canadian–American border. I only knew about it because many North American readers of my earlier books about Chinese discovery, *1421* and *1434*, had written to me on the subject. The Keweenaw Peninsula in Michigan still boasts some of the purest copper ever found: a metal so pure you scarcely had to refine it to make your burnished copper cooking pots. Millions of pounds of copper from North America – mined in the 2nd millennium BC – appeared to have been exported somewhere, no one knew where. Readers had been wondering if it had been taken back home to China, in Chinese ships.

How could ten of the bun-shaped copper ingots found in the Uluburun wreck be made up of Lake Superior copper? But then, how could a tiny American tobacco beetle have turned up in a ruined merchant's house on Thera, in the middle of the Mediterranean?

In an Annex on our website there is, firstly, Professor Hauptmann and colleagues' report on the chemical analysis of the Uluburun wreck copper ingots. Secondly, there are extracts of thirteen reports on Lake Superior copper. As may be seen, all thirteen copper samples from Lake Superior and ten ingots from the wreck have purity of at least 99 per cent – purity unique to both Uluburun ingots and Lake Superior copper.

The great pyramid of Khufu, Egypt.

An image, painted circa 1479–1425 BC in the tomb of Menkheperraseneb, clearly shows a 'Keftiou' (Cretan) bearing a gift of a bullhead rhyton.

A view of the magnificent Palace of Knossos, Crete.

The archaeologist Arthur Evans, who first unearthed the palace of Knossos and named the 'Minoans' after King Minos.

The bullhead rhyton unearthed at Knossos.

The enigmatic Phaestos disc. Experts have struggled for over a century to decipher both it and the mysterious Minoan language, Linear A.

A view of the great Palace of Phaestos, Crete.

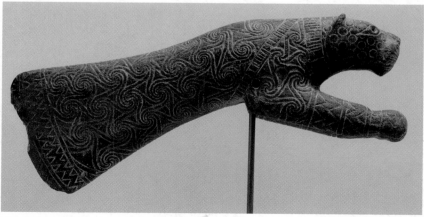

A beautiful carved axe in the form of a panther – Heraklion Museum, Crete.

A beautiful Minoan fresco at the Palace of Knossos.

The throne room at Knossos.

Pithoi storage jars, as seen at Knossos, have been found at various sites around the Mediterranean and beyond.

Jewellery in the 'Aigina Treasure' – the Master of Animals at the British Museum.

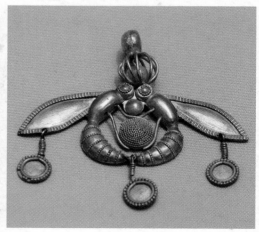

A golden bee pendant and a Minoan bee brooch at the Heraklion Museum, Crete.

The flotilla fresco at Akrotiri,
unearthed by Dr. Spyridon Marinatos in 1967.

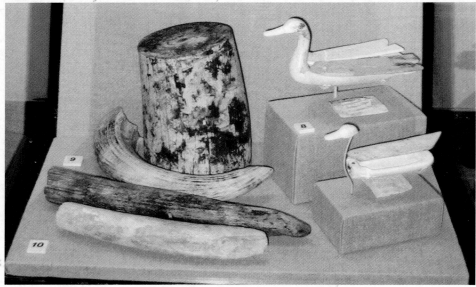

Items from the Uluburun shipwreck treasure trove include copper ingots, hippo teeth and elephant tusks.

Bronze tools and implements from the Yemeni Al-Midamman bronze hoard.

That evening, unable to put the subject or myself to bed, I read up on the investigating chief archaeologist's account of the find. Dr Cemal Pulak is director of research at, and vice-president of, the Institute of Nautical Archaeology in Turkey.

Because of the enormous value of the goods in the Uluburun's hold, Dr Pulak believes that when it came to grief the wreck had been carrying a royal or élite shipment. Even some of the 'everyday' objects on board bear this theory out. For instance, both the Minoans and their successors the Mycenaeans preferred to be clean-shaven. Dr Pulak believes that at least two Mycenaeans were aboard, escorting the goods. His theory was partly based on the evidence of five typically Mycenaean bronze razors found on board.

Dr Pulak's thesis is that the ship's home port may have been in Canaan, in what's now the north Carmel Coast of Israel, mainly because of the characteristic Canaanite design of twenty-four stone anchors found with the wreck. However the typically Minoan construction of the ship leads me to think that its origin was on either Thera or Crete, during the Mycenaean era.

The ship's carrying capacity was at least 20 tons, the archaeological team calculated, a figure they had worked out by tallying the recovered objects, including the 10 tons of copper and tin. I had estimated the admiral's larger vessel's carrying capacity at 50 metric tons.

IIIIIIIIIIIIIIIIII

It was from Dr Pulak's work that I learned, with great curiosity, of the existence of the so-called 'Amarna Letters'. The name Amarna had cropped up before, when we were on Crete. I now knew it as the alternative capital city founded by the Egyptian pharaoh Akhenaten of the late 18th Dynasty – husband to Nefertiti – and that the new capital had been abandoned shortly afterwards. The letters prove that during Akhenaten's reign there was a sophisticated and developed system of trade going on between Egypt and a number of nations. They also show just how crucial it was to Egypt's power base to keep up a continuous supply of bronze.

Akhenaten (c.1353–1336 BC) is now remembered mostly as father to Tutankhamun, the famous boy king. Statues show Akhenaten to have been fleshily handsome: his long face bears large, well-defined features and has a high forehead. In fact, you might even say he looks headstrong. Akhenaten was a radical, so much so that he broke with the worship of traditional Egyptian gods. He built his new capital Amarna in an extraordinary new style. Thousands of years later, in 1887, a Bedouin woman was working in what appeared to be just a field when she discovered a cache of cuneiform (the ancient Mesopotamian lettering system) stone tablets.

Dating of the 382 tablets is difficult, except to say that most of them would have been written well before Amarna was abandoned, shortly after Akhenaten's reign.

As the translator and Assyriologist William Moran confirms: 'The chronology of the Amarna letters, both relative and absolute, presents many problems, some of bewildering complexity, that still elude definitive solution.'[11]

What these tablets and fragments do tell us is about the established and elaborate trading etiquette that existed between kings. For example, the king of Alashiya wrote that he was late on delivery because much of his workforce had been 'slain' by the god of pestilence:

> As to the fact that I am sending you only 500 [shekels of] copper, I send it as a greeting gift to my brother. My brother, do not be concerned that the amount is so small. In my country all the men have been slain by the hand of Nergal, and there is nobody left to produce copper ... send me silver in quantity, and I will send you whatever you request ... [12]

Experts think this was a negotiating tactic: if the king can send copper later, then it's unlikely that the men he would have relied on to produce it had genuinely died. In effect what the king is doing is buying time and testing out his potential client: he is sending a sample and asking Akhenaten for silver in return.

This world was beginning to form more and more complex

dimensions; a multi-faceted but elusive jewel, the colours drifting slowly into place. To me, it looked increasingly as if the Minoans had sailed to all parts of the compass. It also looked like I was going to have to follow them.

11

A PLACE OF MANY NAMES
AND MANY NATIONS

Today's destination: Tell el Dab'a, a Middle Kingdom palace on a hill in the Nile Delta. Our goal is an ancient port beside the modern city, a place that was named Avaris during the Egyptian 13th Dynasty, when it was a crucial trading port dominated by the commercial traders known as the Hyksos.

A group of friends had agreed to get involved with the first stage of my quest: an expedition to Tell el Dab'a and then on to the Nile Delta, following the old Red Sea–Nile canal north of Cairo to Zagazig, to test what I thought must have been Minoan trade routes. *En route* we visited Bubastis, the old capital city of the 'Cat Pharaoh', Bastet, simply for fun, but my true aim was to track Minoan influence and involvement though ancient Egypt.

I'd decided that I would have to explore the routes the Minoans had taken, using the sources of the Uluburun wreck's treasures as my guide. Doing so would be a £100,000 gamble of a trip starting in Beirut, then on via Damascus and Aleppo to Babylon, the beating heart of the Bronze Age world. All were important trade hubs during the Bronze Age. But first, I was going to take my time travelling through one of my first loves, the sacred land of Egypt, hunting down the truth behind this statement, written by Bernard Knapp:

> ... Egyptian Keftiu documents clearly indicate the leadership of Crete ... The recently uncovered 'Minoan style' frescos at the site of Tell el-Dab'a in Egypt's eastern Delta and the Minoan style painted plaster floors at Tel Kabri in Israel open up the likelihood of diverse social or political contacts.[13]

It can be much harder to locate and investigate the remains of Bronze Age Egypt here in the fertile flat lands of the Delta north of Cairo than it would be in the dry south of the Nile valley. For millennia the Delta has bestowed plenty upon Egypt. These are some of the richest agricultural lands in the world: Egyptian farmers simply plant their crops and wait for the annual Nile floods to fertilise and water their land. Naturally, this fertility has meant that the land has been ploughed up mercilessly. But the wetter atmosphere has also made the old cities of the Delta crumble, while the great works of art of the old civilisation have long since disappeared back into the soil. Ashes to ashes.

To begin with, we simply munched croissants and sipped strong Egyptian coffee, watching farmers set off to work on their donkeys. Skeins of geese migrate in the sky high above us. Each house has its dovecote. Now and then an old railway train chugs across the flat land, belching black smoke over the people hanging from its roof.

It was market day and the village was full of women in black burkas carrying their shopping on their heads. Their baskets look like a cover for one of Claudia Roden's beautiful Middle Eastern cookbooks: loaded down with beans, cucumbers, lentils, chickpeas, dates, olives and cabbages.

But personally I've been drawn here not by the delicious food, but by a geographical survey by the Austrian Archaeological Institute. The survey revealed the existence of a buried harbour basin about 450 metres square (540 square yards), with a canal connected to the Pelusiac branch of the Nile.

This region is where the biblical Jacob is said to have brought his family. All that's left to see today are a few flattened, dusty ruins in the farming villages round about. The rest, like much archaeology, stays firmly hidden underneath the modern town. But in c.1783–1550 BC this whole area must have been a hive of commercial activity. Radar imaging by the team of Austrian archaeologists shows that in the Bronze Age not only were there two islands and a tributary of the Nile running through Avaris, but a second harbour once sat alongside Palace F/II of the Middle Hyksos period. Historians have always thought that Egypt was no sailing nation. If this is true, then why the harbours? A third harbour or dry dock lies north of Avaris, at the Nile branch itself.

Bronze Age Egyptians are probably best known for their remarkable building achievements and their elaborate cult of the dead, especially the art of mummification. Until very recently, it was assumed that the Egyptians knew little of boatbuilding, despite the obvious importance of the Nile. Yet after the Hyksos period, Avaris became a famous naval base. It was built primarily by Thutmose III and Amenhotep II and was at times called Peru-nefer.

Timing is difficult to establish, for certain, and it involves a degree of analysis of the complex knots of peoples, races and historical figures who have passed through this ancient land. The Hyksos probably arrived in the late 12th Dynasty (Middle Kingdom) period. They may have come originally as shipbuilders, sailors, soldiers and craftsmen. It's not difficult to imagine Avaris as the Dubai of its day, with a vast building workforce drafted in from overseas. The pharaohs settled them here deliberately in the late 12th Dynasty, to create a harbour town and perhaps even build the ships. But at a later time of political weakness the workmen established their own small but independent kingdom and had to be swatted back. Hyksos artefacts have been found in the Knossos labyrinth.[14]

Thutmose III, also known as Thuthmosis, was the warlike stepson of the bearded lady ruler Hatshepsut. He created the biggest empire Egypt had ever seen, an empire that ran from Nubia to Syria. At Luxor, on the heavily decorated walls of the tomb of Thutmose's valued vizier, Rekhmire, is a famous fresco. It shows a procession of men whose looks and dress are definitely Minoan (see first colour plate section). They come, as they say, bearing gifts. The painting is surmounted by a line of hieroglyphs. The translation reads: 'The coming in peace by Keftiou chiefs and the chiefs of the islands of the sea, humbly, bowing their heads down because of His Majesty's might, the king Thuthmosis III.'[15]

Whatever this city's name was – through time it has been Avaris, Piramesse or Peru-nefer – it was certainly a major port, bustling over the summer trading season and humming with the activity of many ships. And as I was about to find out, the Minoans, or Keftiu, were here in force.

Avaris/Peru-nefer became a crucial military stronghold. The city was the starting point for the overland route to Canaan, the famous 'Horus Road'. Known in the Bible as the 'Way of the Philistines' (Exodus 13:17), the road was used for military expeditions as well as for commercial traffic. The site appears to have been abandoned for a time, after the Hyksos were driven out. However, by the end of the 18th Dynasty, when the Egyptians were back in control, Avaris boasted three large palaces ringed by an enclosure wall. The whole complex was about 5.5 hectares (13 acres) in size. At least two of the palaces excavated here, Palace F and Palace G, held some truly extraordinary finds.

When the Austrian archaeologist Professor Manfred Bietak first worked here in the 1960s, he was amazed to come across thousands of fragments of exotic wall paintings. They did not look remotely Egyptian. As he pieced them together, a somehow familiar work of art gradually unfolded before his eyes. It had a beautiful blue background. As he worked he realised that there were some human figures: one was jumping. He was leaping over a bull. The archaeologist was astounded. He had definitely seen that image before. But where?

In fact Bietak's boy – seen jumping over bulls on a blue background – was exactly the same image as that on a fresco unearthed by Arthur Evans, almost a century before. At Knossos. The electrifying discovery that Minoan artists had worked at foreign courts has had the art and museum worlds transfixed ever since. And now me.

A number of different scenes showing bull hunts and acrobatics were discovered here, painted on the hard lime plaster favoured by the Minoans of Crete, rather than Thera. Some of them are set against a maze pattern. Hunting scenes, life-size male figures with staffs and heraldic griffins have been pieced together from the tiny fragments of plaster scattered across the site. The griffin is a typically Minoan motif and the Avaris griffins were as large as the ones painted at Knossos. There is also an intriguing painted figure of a woman, shown in a flowing white skirt similar to those of the priestesses of Knossos. Although it is impossible to establish with absolute certainty whether the patrons and the painters were from Crete, this is what the experts now believe. It looks strongly as if this was a Minoan trading outpost, a wing of the widespread empire I now suspected existed.

If we think about today's modern, multi-billion international trade in art, the thought prompts images of high fashion, of status, of rich people striving to create an ultra-sophisticated world that will impress those around them. The Minoans' great artistic skills would have been in great demand, because they were of the highest order and were very rare in the Bronze Age world. Yet the colourful frescoes of Avaris are unlikely to have just been items of fashionable interior decor. On Crete, artists' use of the bull-leaping scenes and the half-rosette symbols were tightly controlled. Many of the Tell el Dab'a scenes show motifs which the experts believe are specifically royal: they may also have had spiritual significance. The images were restricted to formal buildings, particularly at Knossos, indicating the city's power. This outpost, therefore, must have had the same command and control-type role.

It's more than possible that a political encounter on the highest level took place between the courts of Knossos and Egypt.

In Harold Evans' rather old-fashioned, Edwardian take on the world, the throne room at Knossos was created for the male ruler, Minos. Now, after nearly a century of new finds and new palace digs, archaeologists think that the throne was made not for a king but for a queen. The Minoans' gods were female. As in Egypt, the ruler was the gods' representative on earth. At Knossos, that queen sat on her throne between two seated griffins – an allusion to her role as the Great Goddess, Mistress of Animals. Those griffins are exactly like the pair uncovered at Avaris, in Palace F.

Could it be that the Minoan presence in Egypt was formalised in the time-honoured way, by marriage? Having this base would mean that the Minoans could not only trade *en route*, but provision themselves for a long voyage. They could load their ships with dates, fresh vegetables and salt fish for expeditions to the East.

Digs at the surrounding settlement, dated by pottery and scarabs, place the palaces in the late reign of Thutmose III and that of his son, Amenhotep II. This fits in with the scenes on Thutmose's vizier's tomb. It all made perfect sense. A formalised pact with the Minoans would have provided a pathway for Egyptian traders to the southern Greek mainland and Greater Anatolia. It would also have given the Egyptians what we would now call in our modern-day terminology 'knowledge transfer' – access to the Minoans' tremendous seafaring and shipbuilding abilities.

Perhaps there was more besides. I'd arrived armed with the knowledge that the art world, at least, was convinced that even

before the birth of Christ the art market was fully international. Gradually, I was forming a picture of the Minoans as trendsetters as well as globetrotters: the Damien Hirsts of their time, skilled practitioners who possessed ingenuity beyond price. After all, at Thera they had painted graceful and lifelike scenes of monkeys, antelope and lions: paintings so accurate that they had to have been copied from life. Minoan artists were not just skilled. They were celebrated.

So in a sense it was no surprise for me later to find that their work appears on ancient palace walls not just here in Egypt but in a huge, south-sweeping arc through the eastern Mediterranean – at Mari in modern-day Syria, at Ebla about 34 miles (55 kilometres) away, at the ancient royal town of Qatna, which is currently being excavated by a German/Syrian alliance, at Alalakh in southern Turkey and at Tel Kabri in Israel. The ancient city-state of Alalakh is near Lake Antioch, in the Orontes River valley. Sir Leonard Woolley, who led the excavations in the 1930s and 1940s, uncovered royal palaces, temples, houses and town ramparts here. The discovery of what we would now interpret as Minoan frescoes came slightly later. At that time, archaeologists hadn't built up an understanding of the Minoans' cosmopolitan adventures, or of the no doubt complex relationship of Crete with Anatolia. The discovery of the frescoes came more or less out of the blue and threw the art world into consternation. The revelation caused archaeologists to speculate that Crete's magnificent murals were in fact Asian. Woolley argued that:

> There can be no doubt but that Crete owes the best of ... its frescoes to the Asiatic mainland. We are bound to believe that trained experts, members of the ... Painters' Guilds were invited to travel overseas from Asia, to ... decorate the palaces of the Cretan rulers.[16]

Yet the evidence that these were Minoan artists of great skill, exporting their talents in an arc reaching all the way to Babylon, has mounted inexorably with each new dig in the region. The excavators of Tel Kabri discovered fragments of a fresco that looked almost exactly like a reproduction of the beautiful miniature fresco in the West House on Thera.[17]

Written archives found at the ancient Sumerian city of Mari show that King Zimri-Lim, who lived between 1775 and 1761 BC, prized his Minoan pieces so highly that he gave them as prestige gifts to other rulers. The poetry of Ugarit, an important city of the time that is today known as Ras Shamra, suggests that the Minoans didn't just decorate foreign palace walls. They were architects of international renown, who built their clients' buildings too.

|||||||||||||||||||||

Before I'd left for Egypt, the Metropolitan Museum of New York had mounted an exhibition named 'Beyond Babylon'. The fascinating catalogue was written by a series of specialists, their expertise drawn together specially for the exhibition.[18]

The experts believe that the discoveries at Tell el Dab'a testify to an Egyptian special relationship with Crete. As Joan Aruz wrote in the catalogue:

> The stunning discoveries of unquestionably Aegean-looking frescos around the Mediterranean littoral have dramatically enhanced our picture of cultural exchange during the 2nd millennium BC ... the presence of Minoan artists at foreign courts has transformed our view of cultural interaction in the eastern Mediterranean world.

'Beyond Babylon' also cites 'Papyrus BM 10056', a document in the British Museum that mentions Cretan ships being docked in an Egyptian harbour. The document refers to a place named 'Per-unefer'. The palace complex at Avaris/Peru-nefer had evidently had quite a history: Tell el Dab'a may well at one point have been home to the biblical figure Moses, as well as being the summer residence of the pharaohs. In short, prior to the Exodus of around 1446 BC, it was one of the most exciting places in the world; a totally cosmo-politan melting pot and a meeting place for world leaders. David O'Connor, Professor of Egyptian art and archaeology at New York University, wrote the following in the catalogue:

> The usual interpretation is that these ships, which are mentioned only during the reign of Thutmose III, were of Cretan type, or were sailing to Crete. However, it would be more logical to assume that Minoan ships were actually moored, and were repaired at Perunefer. If one can identify Tell el-Dab'a, with its palatial Minoan wall paintings as Perunefer, then it is conceivable that Egypt

fostered its special connections with the Minoan Thalassocracy in order to build up its navy for military enterprises in the Near East.

If Palace F was indeed a Minoan political base placed right within the beating heart of Pharaonic Egypt, the most powerful nation on earth, my case for a Minoan super-trading empire – beginning with this truly special strategic relationship – was getting stronger all the time. Avaris, with its repair facilities, food and water, in effect provided an ideal forward base for onward voyages. So – exactly how far across the world did the Minoans get?

12

A SHIP IN THE DESERT

My friends' flight home was in a few days: I was due to go on to Mari. In the meantime, while I was still in Egypt I got a call from Marcella, already dutifully back at her work desk in London.

By a stroke of luck, she had come across a report in *USA Today* that shed more light on my quest. It was a piece by Dan Vergano, the magazine's science reporter, about a new discovery in the desert. She read the report out to me:

> Archaeologists generally downplay the *Indiana Jones* side of their discipline, full of derring-do and unexpected discoveries. But every once in a while, an amazing find surprises even the most experienced researchers ... That's just what happened when Boston University's Kathryn Bard reached into a hole in the sand at the edge of the Egyptian desert ... Her research team of Italians and Americans now knows those caves hold the most ancient ship stores ever discovered; perfectly preserved timbers, ropes and other fittings perhaps 4,000 years old.[19]

Braving high temperatures and the poisonous vipers that are rife in the desert, in December 2005 Bard had found a hidden chamber in an area named Wadi Gawasis, along the Red Sea coast. Exploring the back of a cave, Bard's fingers had met with thin air; making the team realise that there was a hidden chamber of some kind, waiting to be found. Later, her Italian colleague Chiara Zazzaro cleared some fallen rock – and exposed the back of a second cave. The cave had been expressly cut, by hand, from the rock. Here, on this dried-up ancient watercourse, the team had found a hidden, secret shipyard.

Indiana Jones associations aside, this was genuinely an extraordinary moment. Finding an industrial site, one that tells us where everyday Egyptians worked, rather than a carefully preserved ceremonial one, is unusual enough. But finding a site like this, with many working materials still intact and untouched after perhaps 4,000 years, is absolutely unprecedented in Egypt. The amazed team opened up cave after cave and found ancient coils of rope, ship parts, jugs, trenchers and everyday linens; all deeply practical items which drew a lively real-life picture of Egypt's ancient seafaring past. To date, the team have uncovered a complex of eight caves, a network of rooms filled with relics over 4,000 years old that proved that the Egyptians had mastered advanced ship technology. In the complex were dozens of nautical artefacts: limestone anchors, eighty coils of knotted rope, ship timbers and two curved cedar planks that seemed to be the steering oars from a 21-metre-long (70 feet) ship.

Bard and her colleagues now believe, from studying satellite images at the Wadi, that there may be another ancient structure needing investigation, in the form of a slipway or dock below what was the Pharaonic harbour.

When they created this harbour, the Egyptians were almost certainly aiming to exploit the wealth of the famous Land of Punt. The actual location of this fabled place is a mystery, although Bard thinks it may have been in today's Sudan. The pharaohs were organised, methodical and they thought for the long term. Although such expeditions were probably a rarity, they must have been occasions of great prestige. Sometimes Punt is referred to in Egyptian records as *Ta netjer*, the 'land of the gods': they must have prized it highly. All we really know is that the mysterious Land of Punt, or Pwnt, was fabled for its prized luxury goods such as wild animals, perfumes, African blackwood, ebony, ivory, slaves and gold. It may have been in today's Somalia or around the hook of Africa in Ethiopia: but wherever it was, it was an entry point to the tremendous and exotic natural wealth of wider Africa.

We know that the most famous ancient Egyptian expedition that sailed to Punt was made personally by the remarkable Egyptian queen, Hatshepsut. She is not the only female ruler in Egypt's illustrious past, but she was certainly the only one regularly depicted wearing a beard. Hatshepsut built a Red Sea fleet to bring mortuary goods back to Karnak in exchange for Nubian gold. Details of her five-ship voyage to Punt are narrated on reliefs adorning her mortuary temple at Deir el-Bahri, mentioned in chapter 10. A voyage of this kind would have been a huge logistical undertaking, requiring scribes, quartermasters, pack animals, workmen and shipwrights, as well as sailors. This may have been the preparation point for one leg of her journey. Still, the new Wadi Gawasis find shows that enterprising Hatshepsut was by no means the first Egyptian ruler to target the riches of the land of the gods.

The archaeologists suspect that the port at Wadi Gawasis was used by the Egyptians for centuries; perhaps from as early as the time of the Old Kingdom (2686 –2125 BC) and lasting until around 1500 BC. They discovered limestone stelae in niches bordering one of the cave entrances. Many were indecipherable, but one clear-as-day inscription mentioned at least two early expeditions, one to Punt and one to Bia-Punt. They were commissioned by Amenemhat III (12th Dynasty), who reigned about 1860–1814 BC. The expedition was led by two brothers, one named Nebsu and the other Amenhotep. Another inscription found there romantically describes the sea the brothers set out to conquer as 'The Great Green'.

The craft appear to have been up to 21 metres (70 feet) long, powered by rowers and sail. The cedar timbers used to build the ships were, as you would expect, cut and aged in Lebanon, then shipped to Egypt. It looks likely that they were built into boats on the Nile, at a port site near modern Qift, then disassembled and trekked on donkeys across the desert for ten days and reassembled at Wadi Gawasis, which was then the site of a lagoon, long since silted up. Now the Institute of Maritime Research and Discovery is supporting the visit of several nautical specialists to the Mersa/Wadi Gawasis expedition.

It must have been an extraordinary moment when the archaeologists opened up this mysterious cave to find rope neatly coiled and knotted, stored exactly as some meticulous sailor left it, over 3,800 years ago. The team found forty large empty wooden boxes in the storage rooms – these were cargo boxes waiting to be packed up with exotic wares. Two of them were labelled with a painted inscription, like an advertising slogan. It read: 'The Wonders of Punt'.

13

NEW WORLDS FOR OLD

So: it was extraordinary to think of it, but I now had proof positive. Far from the Bronze Age being a dark and obscure time, with little going on except hunting, trapping and some farming, I had discovered an international jet-setting scene; a glittering art world and a sophisticated world market for metals and luxury goods. Avaris had been a revelation to me. The convention of history was wrong: the Egyptians had definitely ventured off their own shores, voyaging on ships that their honoured Cretan guests might have captained or crewed, like a modern lease. The Minoans and their sailing skills were so highly regarded by the Egyptians that they had been given special dispensation to set up an outpost there. With their skills in art, design and metallurgy, the glamorous 'Keftiu' sat at the very centre of this cosmopolitan world.

There was just one last enigma I had to solve to my own satisfaction, while I was still in Egypt. It was a small detail that took me back to the walls of Thera and to one tiny little American tobacco beetle that had been worrying me ever since.

In 1992 a well-respected pathologist, Dr Svetlana Balabanova, decided on an experiment. She took samples of hair, bone and soft tissue from nine Egyptian mummies and in a one-page article in the German publication *Naturwissenschaften* reported her astonishing findings of cocaine and hashish usage in all of the mummies. A further eight showed the use of nicotine.

Her findings were immediately attacked, on the grounds that two of the substances found – inside a mummy nearly 3,000 years old – were derived from indigenous American plants; cocaine from

Erythroxylon coca and nicotine from *Nicotiana tabacum*. Tobacco, which contains nicotine, is an American plant. The idea that there could have been any transatlantic contact between America and Egypt – not just before Columbus, but even before the birth of Christ – was obviously so ridiculous that the experts felt that actual scientific enquiry could be ignored.

Balabanova's team stuck to their guns. As she said, '. . . the results open up an entirely new field of research which unravels aspects of past human lifestyle far beyond basic biological reconstruction . . .'.

Since 1992 Dr Balabanova has tested a number of mummies from ancient Egypt. Nicotine showed up everywhere – for instance in three samples from Manchester Museum's collection and fourteen samples taken directly from an archaeological dig near Cairo.

The pathologist's results show that American tobacco was taken by ancient Egyptians as a matter of course. So who brought it to them?

I well remember one particular tomb on Crete. It's known as the Hagia Triada sarcophagus, a small limestone coffin of the Late Bronze Age (see second colour plate section). It is unlike most Cretan sarcophagi, in that it tells its own story. The tomb is decorated with a fascinating narrative scene, done on plaster. The painted frieze shows a sacred ceremony: a rite. It is intriguing that no similar painted sarcophagi have been found in excavations elsewhere on Crete. The joyful, pleasure-loving Minoans usually seem to have reserved fresco painting for the pleasure of the living, not of the dead. This may therefore be the tomb of someone who had travelled and was aware of customs elsewhere – especially in Egypt, with its tradition of painting tombs.

The puzzle is one that teases art historians greatly. The tomb shows, quite clearly, a man being carried off to his grave. As he is carried off, he is shown smoking a complicated pipe. (Some have interpreted it as a musical instrument, but I think this is unlikely.) It is clear to me at least that he has been either smoking tobacco or taking drugs, perhaps as part of a ritual, or more probably to dull the pain of whatever it was that ailed him.

I felt this was an enjoyable little coda to my revealing exploration of Egypt. Dr Svetlana Balabanova had proved that high-born Egyptians were fond of American tobacco; the tobacco beetle found in the ruins of Thera's buried city strongly suggests that the Minoans were the ones to provide it. In turn, they were given special status in Egypt. Perhaps some of them lived out most of their lives in a foreign land, adopting local customs, wearing local dress and generally 'going native'. Perhaps for the man on the Hagia Triada sarcophagus, this even meant adopting the Egyptians' special habit of drug-taking, before returning home to Crete to die.

The Hagia Triada sarcophagus has recently been redated to around 1370–1320 BC – to the time around the end of Egypt's 18th Dynasty.

14

RICH, EXOTIC LANDS

I am on my way to Mari, a hugely important former trading city on the western bank of the Euphrates. I am touring the eastern Mediterranean in search of the evidence – trade goods, vases, or even, should needs be, drugs – that will tell me more about the Minoans' influence in this region. Today this is an ordinary enough town on the Syrian border, named Tell Hariri. Once it was the site of King Zimri-Lim's exotic capital, an ancient Sumerian city finally destroyed by the powerful Hammurabi, king of the city-state of Babylon.

Mari was rich. Its position between Babylon, Ebla and Aleppo gave it control of key trade routes between the East and the West. The city collected taxes on all of the goods that travelled along the River Euphrates between Syria and Mesopotamia. The Old Assyrian traders paid taxes to the local rulers to try and protect their donkey caravans. In return, the rulers had to ensure that they would not be robbed along the way; if they failed they would give the merchants some recompense for the loss. Mari was also a key point on the land route that crossed the desert from northern Mesopotamia to southern Syria.

When Hammurabi attacked, Zimri-Lim disappeared from the record: we assume that he must have been killed. Over the centuries Mari itself was totally forgotten about and Zimri-Lim's rich and tremendous palaces were razed to the ground.

Nevertheless, at the beginning of the 2nd millennium BC Mari's magnificence was renowned throughout Mesopotamia. I am here to see a painting that shows the throne room at Mari, a scene which has remarkable parallels with the frescoes of Crete, including one in which a priest leads a bull to be sacrificed.

Mesopotamia's lost city was finally rediscovered when a large, headless statue was unearthed at Tell Hariri, on the west bank of the River Euphrates. The initial excavator of Mari, a French archaeologist named André Parrot, began by unearthing a large number of alabaster statues. He was convinced that what he was unearthing from the ground had strong connections to Crete. He particularly compared the painted stone imitations he'd found to those painted on dados from Knossos: perhaps the world's first examples of the technique of *trompe l'oeil*.[20] While a lot of the original frescoes are now in Paris at the Louvre, the whole southern façade of the 'Court of the Palms' of Zimri-Lim's 2.5-hectare (6-acre) palace, with its 260 rooms, has been reconstructed at the Deir ez-Zor Museum in Syria and is fascinating to see.[21]

Letters from the Mari archives give us countless examples of international intrigue and diplomacy: of diplomats, agents and spies who travelled extensively through the Bronze Age.

For now, I had decided to follow in King Zimri-Lim's footsteps and take a royal diplomat's view of the age. He had put a great emphasis on diplomacy, marrying off as many of his eight daughters as he could to regional rulers, in order to secure his networks of influence. Mari's official records, found in the 1930s and translated by French archaeologists, also give us the only detailed historical account in the world of a Middle Eastern diplomatic mission – or at least one that took place in the Bronze Age.

The records of Zimri-Lim's remarkable journey show how vital a role trade played in promoting the art and science of the time. Taking with him an enormous retinue of more than 4,000 men and coffers of gifts and tin ingots, the likable bon viveur travelled for six months. The records show that the king was an avid collector of Minoan art and pottery. Three months after setting forth, Zimri-Lim reached Ugarit on the Mediterranean coast, a scene of Minoan influence, where he stopped for a month, striking up a friendship with a local *danseuse* – not so different to today's Saudi princes in Beirut!

I will be following his trail and also tracking down many of the finds from Mari, which have ended up in the museums at Aleppo and Damascus.

Zimri-Lim's journey started at the beginning of the twelfth month of the Mari calendar, probably in mid April. As the king progressed north up the Euphrates he distributed gifts to the local rulers. Tin was the most sought-after commodity.

My own journey will last just a week but I expect to see some of the same sights (excluding the dancers ...) as in Zimri-Lim's day, nearly 4,000 years ago. On the way, I re-read Jack M. Sasson's account of that Bronze Age world:[22]

> The terms 'global' and 'multicultural' are often applied to contemporary society, which has just stepped out of the 2nd millennium AD. Remarkably, such concepts were relevant as well to the 2nd millennium BC, when building upon the momentous developments of prior millennia – the origin of cities and the invention of writing. An expanding social elite required bronze and demanded exotic luxury goods from distant lands. These needs fostered the creation of an era of intense foreign contacts, with new technological breakthroughs such as the invention of glass and a revolution in travel.

This global culture was astounding. Sasson's research reveals a world in which kings exchanged gifts of extraordinary beauty and elaboration; salt cellars in the shape of lions and calves; drinking bottles in the shape of a horse, inlaid with gold eagles and lapis lazuli; even, as in the Uluburun wreck, a golden chalice fit for a hero.

Mari's official records show just how full and sophisticated a trader's life could be. As well as trading in basic goods – livestock, grain, oil and wine and raw materials such as wool, leather, wood, reeds, semi-precious stones and metal – they dealt in exotics – models of Cretan ships, desert truffles, rare wild animals including bears, elephants and wild cats. Of equal importance to the development of civilisation, countries of the eastern Mediterranean and Mesopotamia exchanged intellectual ideas: concepts in philosophy, science and religion.

In this cultured environment, anyone who had a valued, specialist skill could move freely from place to place – astronomers, physicians, translators, gymnasts, cooks and seamstresses. Travelling artists were especially prized. Musicians came from Qatna, Aleppo and Carchemish.

Cowries from the Maldives were used for currency. How did these cowries get to Mari when the Maldives are deep in the Indian Ocean? Jewellery was made from lapis lazuli from Afghanistan and turquoise, jadeite, cornelian and quartz from India. By 2680 BC cedar was imported from the Lebanon and glass beads in their thousands from Indian rivers. Perhaps the best-known treasures from Mari are the proud bronze lions, now in the Louvre.

Most of all, the Minoans drove the process of international development – they had the ships and they brought the essential raw materials upon which the crack pace of Bronze Age civilisation relied – copper and tin.

Travel across Mesopotamia was for the most part by river. The River Euphrates Zimri-Lim would have known teemed with boats, barges and rafts, perhaps even more than it does today. Levantine cities put on concerts with varied and colourful programmes – men belched fire and swallowed swords; jugglers, wrestlers, and acrobats performed for the public; as did actors and actresses in masques and plays. New ideas and inventions travelled up and down this vital causeway. I settled back to enjoy the ride.

Next stop, Beirut. Before the civil war of the 1970s and 1980s, the Beirut I knew was an enchanting city, with its backdrop of cedar-clad mountains. It used to be a haven for Saudi businessmen. Here they could escape the pressure of commercial life in Saudi Arabia: they could gamble in lush casinos, eat pigeon *libanaise* in the glitzy restaurants which lined the corniche and have their pick of the local dancing girls for a night. You could ski on the placid seas and on the mountain snow on one and the same day.

Today's Beirut, sadly, remains partly ruined. Happy memories have gone. I cannot get out of the city fast enough, so I haggle with minibus drivers to take me across the mountains to Damascus. The price is usually halved by evening. That way the driver can return with a van load of vegetables from the Bekaa valley, in time to sell at dawn in Beirut's markets.

Like the Lebanese, the Minoans were master traders. I thought about that principle – if you travel one way carrying human cargo, when you return you maximise your assets by bringing something else back with you. Perhaps the Minoans did the same.

At the Syrian border, Ahmad, our driver, plonked our passports in front of the Syrian customs officer. Fat, agitated and energetic, Ahmad ate continuously. His side pocket bulged with seeds, which he nibbled.

There was something odd about this minibus. Perhaps that explained why the customs officer is not being obliging enough. Ahmad pulls out a wodge of Syrian pound notes which the customs officer pockets without a trace of emotion, or thanks or receipt; now we can set off again. Once in no man's land Ahmad stops to collect eight full black plastic bags which he hides in the spare tyre bay. I hope these are not drugs. If not, we should have a clear run.

Damascus claims to be the oldest city in the world – a title also fought over by Samarkand, Bukhara, Aleppo and Cairo, among others. From late November to early March, the River Barada carries rainwater down to the plain, creating a large, rich oasis named 'the Ghouta'. The city not only has a beautiful climate, rich soil and abundant water but was at the crossroads of ancient trade routes (see map). One route led north from Egypt up the fertile crescent through Damascus and on to Mesopotamia. Coming from the opposite direction, a merchant from the East landing from India in the Euphrates estuary could travel upriver through Mesopotamia then turn south through fertile land, by-passing the mountains all the way to Egypt. I intended to explore the museums, to get a snapshot of the trade and civilisation of 5,000 years ago.

For thousands of years Damascus has been famed for her craftsmen, masters of inlay on wood – pearl inlaid on rose, walnut or apricot – her women and her precious damasks. Yet Damascus Museum – possessing probably the finest collection of sumptuous Mesopotamian art in the world, stretching back over five millennia – is still a disappointment, with little information to be had and still less scope for research. The few guidebooks are sycophantic to the point of hilarity. One introduction reads: 'To President Al Assad, whose march of correctionism is an inspiration and a stimulus'!

Although I had found plenty to interest me, I hoped to find more accurate information about Bronze Age artefacts at Aleppo. At the bus station, a stunning Syrian girl seems to be expecting me. 'Sit down – I will get you a ticket.' She takes my money and touts around the buses to find one which will take me for 200 Syrian pounds, then pockets the change. Soon we are rolling northeast in a comfortable Mercedes 403. The road is on a dividing line. To the west the mountains and the sea, to the east a lush plain watered by the Barada River.

Seven hours out of Damascus the bus pulls up in central Aleppo opposite Baron Street. There are four hours of daylight left – just enough to visit the souk. I dump my bags in Baron's Hotel and hurry to the marketplace, a vast space that still, today, eventually leads to a copper market. What an amazing experience – little has changed for 5,000 years. It is covered by great stone archways for some 18 miles (30 kilometres). The first line of stalls is for butchers who sell sheep's testicles (at a cost of 90p each) and nothing else. They are huge, each the size of a squashed orange. The butchers, I notice, all specialise in different parts of the animal: the first in the pancreas, then the liver ... a group of the next few stalls are selling hooves and tails. I have walked for a mile and have only seen bits of sheep! I explored the place solidly for four hours: there must have been 50 miles (80 kilometres) of vaults and stalls. The organised commercial districts are known as Khans. At Khan al Nahasin (the Khan of the coppersmiths) is Aleppo's oldest continuously inhabited house, which has been kept almost exactly as it was four centuries ago. It was once lived in by a man called Adolphe Poche, whose parentage was both Venetian and Belgian. Poche was born in this house and yet became Belgian consul to Syria in 1937. Appropriate for Aleppo, I suppose: for thousands of years it's been one of the most important trading cities in the world. Only a few hundred kilometres away from the Mediterranean, this ancient city is the meeting point of the two oldest land trade routes known to man.

Baron's Hotel was founded in 1909 as a lodge for Mr Baron to relax in after duck shooting. Little has been altered since then; perhaps not even the bedclothes. It is a delight to be here. Slightly foxed posters in the rather *louche* bar – a mix of 1970s high stools and what looks like 1940s everything else – advertise the inaugural Orient Express train journey to Aleppo. Mounted above the bar is Lawrence of Arabia's bill – extravagantly high, at £72.09. A young female French archaeologist and I are the only guests.

The crime writer Agatha Christie and her archaeologist husband Professor Mallowan stayed here for months. Professor Mallowan had left the hotel a hand-drawn map. Stretching away in an arc to the east of Aleppo, it showed the mass of extraordinary archaeological sites of the middle and upper Euphrates. There are between fifty and a hundred sites, going back 5,000 years. In the very early dawning of the Bronze Age this area was the most heavily populated in the world.

Breakfast is at dawn. The French archaeologist, a dark young woman with a pinched face, offers me her boiled egg and cheese provided I do not talk to her.

Then we set off into the rising sun in Ahmad's battered minivan. The land is flat as a pancake; the horizon flirts with infinity. On the outskirts of Aleppo the figs and apricots are ripening. Further out come poplar plantations, then the endless vista of rich, cultivated land. Red earth under plough, bilious green rice, thin winter barley and dark ochre stubble where the last of the cotton has been harvested.

Cotton stalks are piled high beside the farmhouses for winter kindling. Flocks of fat-tailed sheep and slim black turkeys scavenge the fields. Each house has its own pigeon loft. Skeins of duck, high in the sky, migrate south. No one is shooting them now. I suspect that there is much more to discover about Aleppo, but I am happy with what I found in the museum, including some cuneiform slates about Mari that were originally discovered by Max Mallowan. Mounds of quinces and watermelons lie beside the road.

15

PROUD NINEVEH

Nineveh, at the centre of what was Babylonia, is less than a day's travel and my final destination before I return to Beirut. I was here, again following in the wake of the Minoans, because this great city was once the epicentre of world knowledge. It was here that the Minoans could have pursued their understanding of the heavens to sacred levels. This time, I was on the trail of some sacred omens; omens written down by trusted Babylonian priests during the Old Babylonian period (1950–1651 BC). This would have been hard-won information, collected for generations and then written on clay.

The ancient mounds and ruins lie at the crossing of the Tigris and the Khosr rivers, near the modern-day Iraqi town of Mosul. The 'exceeding great city', as it is called in the biblical Book of Jonah, lay on the eastern bank of the Tigris in what was ancient Assyria. It is now one immense area of mounds and broken walls, overlaid in parts by rackety modern suburbs.

In its calm and quiet, Nineveh's atmosphere must have once been like what we would today call a university town, like Oxford, Salamanca or Bologna. And yet here, in what's now the Iraqi desert, all that remains are humps of rubble and mounds of bare earth. I was reminded of the biblical prophecy against 'proud Nineveh': 'And He will stretch out His hand against the north and destroy Assyria, And He will make Nineveh a desolation, Parched like the wilderness.'[23] That's pretty much what seems to have happened.

But it was here that the great Assyrian king Ashurbanipal, or Aššurbanipal, had his palace and a library of world renown. Under his rule the Assyrian kingdom stretched as far as the Gaza Strip to the west, Armenia to the north (towards the Black Sea), east towards the Caspian Sea and the Persian Gulf to the south.

Aššurbanipal reigned much later than the Minoans' time, in the 7th century BC. Assyria's genius had been built on the foundations of extreme military might, the imposition of ruthless discipline on its people and the exercise of extreme brutality over those it conquered. The Assyrians seized Babylon in the 8th century BC. Yet this contact at least seems to have been a civilising one, inspiring the Assyrians to educate themselves. Aššurbanipal was the ruler who finally managed the impossible: uniting the two traditions of Mesopotamia – war and words – within one culture. His significance for me was that, far-sightedly, he had put together a collection of much older astronomical and scientific texts. This was sacred knowledge, all of which he had ordered to be collected together from all over Mesopotamia, not least from the already ancient cities of Babylon, Uruk, and Nippur. His collection began with the work of the Sumerians, to whom we owe so much of our own modern-day culture, including the division of time into twelve- and six-hour blocks. Aššurbanipal's library was still in use when Alexander the Great defeated the Achaemenid King Darius III and conquered Mesopotamia.

When it was unearthed the library painted a vivid picture of a violent past; it also held a version of the biblical story of the great flood. Aššurbanipal's collection also proves that as far back in history as you can look, humanity has been obsessed with the heavens. The seasons ruled people's lives. Farmers calculated what work they had to do, and when, according to which constellations were rising and setting at dawn. At that time of mystery and wonder, celestial movements in the sky must have seemed like the jousting of the gods. The constellations were seen as miraculous things; they still inspire wonder today, thousands of years after Homer's hero Odysseus made his slow way home by the stars:

> Sleep did not fall upon his eyelids
> as he watched the constellations – the Pleiades,
> the late-setting Boötes, and the Great Bear,

which men call the Wain, always turning in one place,
keeping watch over Orion – the only star
that never takes a bath in Ocean. Calypso,
the lovely goddess, had told him to keep this star
on his left as he moved across the sea.[24]

I was here because I had a problem. My theory that Minoan ships could cross the Atlantic depended on one thing: navigation.

It is relatively easy to find latitude at sea. One way is to calculate the angle of the sun in relation to the horizon, at dead noon. It can be done using a very basic quadrant. With three pieces of wood and a little luck (no cloud or rain!) you can calculate your latitude to a fair degree of accuracy. You can also use the night sky and you can even use the simplest equipment of all, your own arms, to do it. In the northern hemisphere, all you need to do is point to the North Star, Polaris, and extend your other arm to the horizon. If the angle is 30 degrees, you are at 30 degrees north. At the equator – zero degrees latitude – Polaris appears to be on the horizon line.

Longitude is a very different matter. It is much, much harder to calculate. It was the greatest problem for navigators in Europe up until the 18th century. Yet from my initial investigations into ancient records I had a strong feeling that the Babylonians had found a way of establishing longitude as far back as 1300 BC. And that their Minoan trading partners shared that knowledge.

Could the Minoans truly have navigated well enough to be the world traders I thought they'd been? If so, how had they done it?

||||||||||||||||||||

In the West, we think it was Copernicus who first realised that the earth and the planets orbited around the sun. The truth, I'd discovered, could hardly be more different. It is clear that the Babylonians had realised this. How had they come upon such remarkable levels of knowledge?

The answer lies in their extraordinary dedication to stargazing. To begin with, this was nothing to do with navigation. They believed that the gods had created the movements of the planets to help people on earth tell the future. The stars were used like a horoscope, to predict future happenings – and to try to avert catastrophes. One such prediction ran:

> When in the month of Ajaru, during the evening watch, the moon eclipses, the king will die. The sons of the king will vie for the throne of their father, but will not sit on it.[25]

Apparently, just before a disaster like this was predicted to happen, the king would temporarily abdicate his throne. A substitute then took the crown. If the prediction was death, the unfortunate replacement would be killed. What's known as a self-fulfilling prophecy . . . or having your cake and not eating it.

So the Enuma Anu Enlil tablets, preserved for posterity by Aššur-banipal at Nineveh, are full of astronomical events that successions of Babylonian peoples and their kings had been charting, documenting and collecting for many generations. Astronomers worked for centuries, detailing exactly which stars rose on a particular day, the angle they rose at, at what time – and the distance between the stars. For instance, they knew that a different star rose on the eastern horizon each sunset over a time span of four years and they realised that after that the cycle repeated itself.

Some of the tablets are missing and some are difficult to decipher. Yet many describe clearly the timings of moonrise and moonset, the rising and setting of the planets and the patterns of both solar and lunar eclipses. Tablets 1 to 22 (dating from around 1646 BC) describe the moon's movements; tablets 23–36 the sun's eclipses, coronas and parhelia; tablets 50–70 the planetary positions; and tablet 63 shows the movement of Venus.

By the time of the final, mathematical phase of Babylonian astronomy, so much data had been collected that scribes were able to calculate what was about to happen in both the day and the night sky simply by looking back in their records. Ephemeris tables (using both the sun and the stars) and sidereal tables (solely the stars) are essential to navigation. They show the day-by-day positions by sign and degree of the sun, the moon, Mercury, Venus, Mars, Jupiter and Saturn. The *Oxford English Dictionary* defines them as 'a table showing the predicted (or, rarely, the observed) positions of a heavenly body for every day during a given period'. In short, an almanac.

Supposing the Minoans had relied on their trusted trading partners for reliable astronomical tables that would help them with their astronavigation, especially for determining latitude at sea with accuracy. Perhaps they'd taken that precious knowledge and worked out ways to produce their own star charts, for nearer home. I had to find out.

I read and read: as a submarine navigator I'd spent many years of my life calculating both latitude and longitude, sometimes by using meridian passages of the moon. So I could anticipate some of the practical problems that the Bronze Age navigator must have faced. There are two essentials: having a fixed point, or observatory, as your reference point, and – and this is the killer – knowing the exact time of day.

In navigation, time translates as distance. Most sailors know the adage: 'Longitude west, Greenwich time best. Longitude east, Greenwich time least.' In other words, travel east and you are ahead of Greenwich Mean Time. Go west, and you are behind it – or in other words, later than GMT. Thus, if you live near Greenwich, London, never ring a friend in Greenwich, New York State at nine in the morning. The chances are you'll get someone with a bear for a head.

Unfortunately, when navigating, you cannot get this wrong. While miscalculating a minute of latitude could put you out by a negligible 1.15 miles (2 kilometres), degrees of longitude vary in size, getting smaller towards the poles, where the meridians converge. If you guessed the time when trying to find your longitude at sea, you could easily be 'out' by 1,000 miles (1,600 kilometres) without knowing it.

Nowadays, it only takes a few seconds to download pre-calculated ephemeris tables on to your computer. However, the moon is nothing if not changeable. Calculating these lunar ephemerides is so complex that in the 18th century – all knowledge of Babylon's tables having been wiped out by history – vast riches lay in the path of those who could find a new method of doing so. If my understanding of tables 20 and 21 of the Enuma Anu Enlil was correct, the extraordinary Babylonians were able to predict eclipses of the moon over its entire, 18.61-year cycle. Whether or not this enabled them to calculate longitude I was not sure. It is beyond strange to think that man already had this sacred knowledge 1,500 years before the ancient Greeks and more than three millennia before Copernicus or Galileo.

16

THE KEY TO INDIA?

Having arrived back in Beirut, I kept thinking back to Mari, on the middle Euphrates, to the northeast of Damascus. Diplomatic missions crossed frontiers and the Minoans traded here extensively. Intriguingly, by 2680 BC Indian glass beads in their thousands and cowries from the Maldives were used for currency.

Where were the Minoans leading me now? So many of the items found at Mari and now housed in Aleppo's museum seemed to have had their origins in India. How did all those cowries and beads I'd seen in the museums get to Mari – when the Maldives are deep in the Indian Ocean? From their base in Tell el Dab'a, could the Minoans have got to India? It took some stretch of the imagination to dare to think that. I had travelled all this way: it had taken me weeks and months of planning to do so. Imagine the challenges for a traveller during the Bronze Age.

My mind turned back to the Indian elephant tusk I'd seen at Heraklion on Crete: excavators had found it in the ancient town of Zakros. There was also a similar one found packed into the hold in the Uluburun wreck. From the Yemen to India is some four weeks' sailing on the southwest monsoon, which starts in June. Let us push on to India, in the wake of the ghosts of the Minoan fleet. Perhaps there is evidence that they did in fact reach the subcontinent somehow, travelling via the land mass of Egypt, just as the Egyptians had evidently reached the fabled Land of Punt?

To my astonishment I discovered that a considerable number of hoards of bronze goods, deliberately hidden underground, have been found over much of northern India. There have been 129 of them to date, most frequently found near the Ganges – in the Jumna catchment area. Most of these sites have been discovered by local farmers ploughing their land rather than by controlled excavation, so it has not been easy to date them. However on a number of sites a distinctive ochre-coloured pottery has been found which has been much easier to date – to the 2nd millennium BC, once again, which according to all the evidence was the primary era of Cretan ascendancy and contemporaneous with the Minoan palace at Tell el Dab'a.

Typically these Indian Bronze Age hoards consist of harpoons, swords, rings, chisels and axes, including double axes similar to those of Minoan Crete. The hoards have several noteworthy features. Firstly, they rarely include the implements and tools used by Indian village people – such as the knives, digging tools and arrowheads that you imagine would have been useful in the daily life of Indians as it was in the 2nd or 3rd millennium BC.

Secondly the blades or cutting edges of the tools are seldom worn or chipped – they do not appear to have been actually used. They are more like samples, or stores, carried for sale.

Who were these travelling salesmen of the Bronze Age? A possible answer is Minoan traders in fleets operating from their base in Egypt. It could, of course, be a series of coincidences that the Indian copper hoards are of the same era (the 2nd millennium BC). It could be another coincidence that they contain unused double-headed axes, of exactly the same design as the distinctive Minoan ones and that these implements were foreign to India (in the sense that they were not used by the local people as tools).

The possibility of coincidence would be greatly reduced if there was evidence of trade between India, Egypt, and the Minoans in the 2nd millennium BC. I was going to have to go back to my research sources: there was a lot I had yet to understand. The bit was firmly between my teeth.

THE SEARCH FOR THE RED SEA–NILE CANAL

... And if they did reach India, then how? The key lies in that rich strategic relationship that Crete had with Egypt. Using Tell el Dab'a as a base meant the Minoans could load their ships with dates, fresh vegetables and salt fish ready for expeditions to India and the East. Queen Hatshepsut's well-documented expedition to Punt in the summer of 1493 BC was prepared for in exactly this way. She had sent a fleet of five ships with thirty rowers each from Kosseir, on the Red Sea. Where would the Minoans go from Tell el Dab'a? The answer, I suspected, would be found near the Red Sea–Nile canal.

In 1998 a group of stone megaliths was found at the coastal plain of Tihamah, Yemen (see map). The site was investigated by the Royal Ontario Museum, Canada and the Yemen Government. Beneath the standing stones they found a hoard of copper and bronze artefacts and tools, dated between 2400 BC and 1800 BC. As Edward Keall of the Royal Ontario Museum said at the time:

> We didn't know what was keeping people in this terribly marginal desert area ... Was it a natural resource or a strategic position that prompted these people to invest such effort in creating these remarkable monuments? (www.archaeology.org)

Why else, I thought to myself, than because of the Red Sea–Nile canal? 'King Scorpion' is said to have been the very first Egyptian canal builder. His superb macehead is now in Oxford's Ashmolean Museum, like many fascinating artefacts from the Bronze Age, including the controversial fresco fragments from Alalakh. After an extraordinary refit the museum has emerged, blinking, as it were, into the new light. It was once something of a labyrinth of its own, where it was hard to find all but its most famous curiosities, such as Lawrence of Arabia's cloak. The Minoan collections are fascinating: they include a six-tentacled octopus storage jar of around 1400 BC, a large decorated *pithos* from the storerooms of Knossos and weapons from the so-called 'warrior graves'.

Once I discovered that Arthur Evans had worked there, I soon began to explore the museum for inspiration as well as information. In Evans' archive is a photograph of a pillar being excavated in the east pillar crypt at Knossos. The symbol of the *labrys* – the double axe – is marked on every surface.

Meanwhile 'King Scorpion's' huge pear-shaped macehead shows a threatening scorpion hovering in the air. Wearing the tall white crown of Upper Egypt, the king stands on the bank of the Red Sea–Nile canal, with a digging implement in his hands. Down below, the king's workmen are seen putting the final touches to the canal banks. The limestone mace dates from the 4th millennium BC.

We know little about this pharaoh save that he conquered part of the Delta. The first king after 'Scorpion' whom we can date with reasonable accuracy is King Menes, who lived around 3000 BC in his palace at Memphis. According to Herodotus he dammed the Nile some 12 miles (19 kilometres) south of Memphis and directed the waters to form a new lake linked to the Nile by a canal. In the 6th Dynasty (c.2300–2180 BC) Pepi I planned a canal through the first cataract – to tame it. The canal was cut by Uni, the governor of Upper Egypt. Sometime during the Middle Kingdom (2040–1640) a canal was dug between the Red Sea and the eastern branch of the Nile at the Delta.[26] Using captured enemies as slave labour, Egypt set off on an orgy of water-channel-making, so much so that the face of the nation was completely changed.

> ... All Egypt is level; yet from this time onwards it has been unfit for horse or wheeled traffic because of the innumerable canals running in all directions, cutting the country into small segments. It was the King's desire to supply waters to the towns which lay inland at some distance from the River, for previously when the level of the Nile fell, the people went short and drank brackish water from the wells. It was this King also who divided the land into lots and gave everyone a square piece of equal size and from the produce extracted an annual tax ... Perhaps this was the way in which geometry was invented ... [27]

Herodotus says Egyptian priests informed him that at one time the Red Sea and the Mediterranean were connected. Thousands of years later, Napoleon carried out a cadastral (land boundaries) survey after his conquest of Egypt in 1798. His maps of the Delta and the Red Sea–Nile canal may be viewed in the Louvre. The Red Sea–Nile canal is also shown on a British cadastral survey of 1882. By comparing this 1882 map with Napoleon's maps and Google Earth, even today one can see the route of the ancient waterway. After heavy rain in particular, you can trace its course on satellite photos as it passes under Ramses II Street, emerges in northeast Cairo and then heads toward Zagazig, in the eastern part of the Nile Delta. You can follow its faint outline all the way to the Red Sea.

\|\|\|\|\|\|\|\|\|\|\|\|\|\|\|\|\|\|\|\|

Assuming for the moment that the Minoans did use the Red Sea–Nile canal, quite possibly in company with Egyptian sailors or ships, they would have entered the northern Red Sea – the adventurer's route to the heady lands of Punt and India. If the Minoans had used the canal frequently, I reasoned, there could still be some concrete evidence left. I wondered if I could uncover any of the traces left behind, in the form of Bronze Age ports or buildings on the land which borders the Red Sea – either in Egypt, Arabia or the Yemen.

The hoards of bronze near the stone megaliths of Tihamah speak of trade. A photograph of axe heads in the hoard is shown in the first colour plate section. Not only that, but the megaliths themselves also tell their own story, a story I shall return to later on in this book.

The important thing is this. From the Yemen, reputedly the Land of Punt, to India is some four weeks' sailing on the southwest monsoon, which starts in June.

17

INDIAN OCEAN TRADE
IN THE BRONZE AGE

Sailing in the Indian Ocean is determined by the monsoon wind, which is caused by the difference in temperature between the massive Himalayan Plateau and the sea (see map). In summer the Asian land mass becomes hotter than the ocean, sucking winds and water vapour off the sea. In April the southwest monsoon is heralded by westerly winds in the Indian Ocean. By May the southwest monsoon hits Indochina, to reach its peak and constancy in July, by which time winds reach 30 knots in the South China Sea. By then, India is inundated with monsoon rain. During September the temperature drops and by November, when the Himalayas have become bitterly cold, air is drawn off the mountains by the warmer seas.

The northeast monsoon starts in late December, after which the wind gradually abates until April, when the cycle begins again. Sailing ships voyaging between Egypt, Africa, India and China would have had to take advantage of the monsoons in order to sail before the wind, returning on the next monsoon to their respective countries. They awaited the change in a sheltered harbour. Hence the need for capacious ports around the Indian Ocean, where goods could be stored from one monsoon season to the next.

Monsoons are so predictable – and so important – that they were later incorporated into calendars, which illustrated the highly synchronised system of regular shipping between Egypt, East Africa, India and the Gulf. For example one such calendar has this for day 68 (March 16): 'End of sailing of Indian ships from India to Aden: no one sets sail after this day' and 'on day 100 (April 15) the last fleet from India was scheduled to arrive in Aden . . . on Aug 14 (day 220) the last ship from Egypt arrived in Aden. Six days later ships from Sri Lanka and Coromandel set out on their voyage home.'[28] The last departure from Aden, powered by the monsoon, was on day 250 (September 13).

In short, ships sailing from Egypt for India would be carried by the southwest monsoon which ends in September. They could then trade in India until it was time for the northeast monsoon starting in December, which would carry them back home to Egypt and, via the Red Sea–Nile canal, to the Mediterranean. They had a free ride each way. The west coast of India has many great rivers carrying melted snow down from the mountains. Their estuaries provide the opportunity: wonderful ports could be built in the shelter of most of them, from which to export the riches of India. Marcella and I decided to take advantage of an invitation to speak at a naval academy event. The coasts of India beckoned: and who were we to gainsay that?

I reasoned that there should be Bronze Age ports from Karachi in the north of India all the way down the coast to Kerala, in the south. As I began my research, I realised that three ports – Lothal, Cambay and Muziris – were important in the Bronze Age, specialising in exports.

LOTHAL – AN INDIAN BRONZE AGE PORT

In a series of articles published between 1955 and1962, Professor S. R. Rao, an Indian marine archaeologist, describes his excavation of a port at Lothal, inland from the Gulf of Cambay in northwest India. Lothal was then much closer to the sea than today (see map).

In those seven years, Professor Rao and his team unearthed channels and locks leading from the river to a large rectangular port area. The dockyard itself was lined with well-made bricks and was designed to control the flow of water through a sluice from the river into the dockyard. Lothal had the world's first lock system.

The town that surrounded the dockyard was built between 2500

BC and 1900 BC. The dockyard itself provided sheltered mooring in an enclosed harbour measuring 214 × 36 metres (702 by 118 feet) – absolutely enormous for 4,500 years ago. The entire settlement was divided into two parts: a citadel or acropolis for the ruler and wealthy merchants and a lower town for the workers. Acropolis houses were built on 3-metre-high (10 foot) brick platforms and were provided with running hot and cold water, a well for drinking water and a sewage system that was designed for flushing out and for solid waste to be removed. A large warehouse which was situated at the southwest corner of the Acropolis was again raised on 3-metre stands. Goods were protected from flood or theft by being raised from the ground, by wooden walls on four sides and by a wooden roof.

The surrounding land was well watered and produced fine Indian cotton and plentiful rice. The sea coast provided shellfish and the river had beads in profusion.

Thus, with an abundance of fresh water and with a river leading to the sea, Lothal became the most important port in India – and from the point of view of archaeological finds one of the richest sites in the subcontinent. These finds are now exhibited at Lothal in a modern archaeological museum that was established in 1976. To summarise the official description:

> The museum has three galleries. In the front gallery, a canvas depicts an artist's impression of how the town was laid out. There are also introductory maps and descriptions to explain the importance of Lothal. The left hand gallery displays showcases with beads, terra-cotta ornaments, seals, shells, ivory, copper and bronze objects, bronze tools and pottery. The right hand gallery has games, and human figurines, weights, painted pottery, burial and ritual objects and a scale model of the whole site. (www.indianetzone.com)

The famous Indian beads found in local rivers are of cornelian, agate, amethyst, onyx, semi- precious stones and faience. Tiny micro beads can be seen through magnifying glasses.

The seals are engraved on steatite with Indian writing and animal figurines on the face. Shells are made up into bangles, necklaces, games and musical instruments.

Copper ingots of 99.8 per cent purity were imported, as was tin. These were smelted to make a wide array of weapons, tools and cooking implements. Pottery, including huge *pithoi* for storage, came in all shapes and sizes. There were games made of bone, shell and ivory as well as clay figurines representing subjects such as a gorilla, or humans. The gold work was extremely fine, with minute golden balls that require a microscope to view them properly. The people who had made the artefacts had a standardised weight system, using weights made of cornelian, jasper, agate and ivory.

The similarities between these archaeological artefacts excavated from Lothal and those found in Minoan sites or Minoan wrecks are striking – even astounding. The same can be said for the layout and construction of the town.

A comparison between forty-six artefacts excavated at Lothal with those at Minoan sites or in Minoan wrecks of the same era – the 3rd and 2nd millennia BC – discloses that all forty-six are very similar, or identical. Could these artefacts have developed independently? Did the Minoan and Indian civilisations develop at the same time, needing the same goods? I believe this argument breaks down for three principal reasons. Firstly, Lothal imported copper and bronze. For reasons which will be considered in more detail later, the copper ingot found at Lothal was of over 99.8 per cent purity. The only mines which produced copper of that purity in 2500 BC were the mines of Isle Royale and Lake Superior. Ships must have brought that copper, crossing the Atlantic to do so. Minoans had ships capable of such journeys. Secondly, items unique to India – elephant tusks and Indian beads found in Indian rivers – have been found in Minoan palaces and wrecked ships (Uluburun). So, I would argue that Minoan ships must have sailed to India to collect those items. Thirdly, it's worth noting the scale of the coincidence – if there were a dozen excavated artefacts one could just about attribute it to chance, but 46 ?! You can make up your own mind by visiting the gallery pages on our website.

What is I think possible, even likely, is that there was a substantial exchange of goods and ideas. Minoan ships took copper and tin to India and returned with ivory and cotton and perhaps many Indian ideas about town planning, civic engineering and astronomy. Sooner or later, Indian shipowners would have wanted their vessels to accompany Minoan ships across the world, to collect valuable goods for themselves.

It is time to leave Lothal and travel southwards once more down India's beautiful seaboard. We had intended to visit Cambay, north of Bombay, knowing Cambay had been a great international port in the Bronze Age. However we learned that the town is now beneath the sea, due to a shift in the continental plates. So we must push on further south knowing little of the ports of southern India.

How can we narrow our search to find ports which flourished in the 2nd millennium BC? I've prepared a plan, which involves starting with the accounts of those celebrated authors who had described trade in prehistoric times. Professor A. Sreedhara Menon, in *A Survey of Kerala History*, has provided a very useful summary. He describes classical writers giving vivid accounts of the thriving spice trade between the Kerala coast and the Roman Empire through the ports of Muziris (South India), Tyndis and Barace – the classical writers being the Greek ambassador Megasthenes (4th century BC), the anonymous author of *The Periplus of the Erythraean Sea* (1st century AD) and Ptolemy (2nd century AD). And the Peutingerian Table, a set of maps dating from about AD 226 that is reputed to have been copied from fresco paintings in Rome, is said to show a temple of Augustus near Muziris and a Roman army being stationed in Muziris for the protection of the Roman spice trade with India. The location of Muziris will be discussed later.

To match these Roman and Greek accounts, Professor Menon cites Sanskrit works. The *Mahabharata* mentions the king of Kerala providing provisions; the 4th century BC *Arthashastra* mentions the River Periyar as one of the rivers of Kerala where pearls can be found. The *Puranas* also mention Kerala. Apart from Sanskrit (language of North India), Tamil writings in the language of South

THE LOST EMPIRE OF ATLANTIS

India are also important sources of information: ancient Tamil literature is replete with references to the land of Kerala, its rulers and its people and its well-developed civilisation. The *Patittupattu* (Ten Decads) is an anthology of 100 poems which reconstruct the history of ancient Kerala and her trade.

To these classical, Tamil and Sanskrit accounts, we can add those of the Chinese: Hiuen Tsang in the 7th century AD; Wang da Yuan in *Descriptions of the Barbarians of the Isles* (1330–49); and Ma Huan, who accompanied Admiral Zheng and describes Cochin and Calicut with great verve.

Arab writers al-Idrisi (AD 1154) and Yaqut al-Hamawi (1189–1229) give descriptions of Kerala's coastal towns and their trade, Al-Kazwini (1236–1275) provides information about Quilon and Dimishqi (AD 1325) writes about the Malabar coast. Also, the accounts of Ibn Battuta describe his six visits to Calicut and the pepper trade operating out of the port of Quilon, where there were huge Chinese junks.

Finally we have the early European travellers who describe a very old spice trade between Kerala and the Arab, Mediterranean and Chinese worlds – Friar Odoric of Pordenone who reached Quilon in 1322 *en route* for China; Friar Jordanus of Severic who came to Quilon in 1324; the papal legate John de Marignolli of Florence who lived in Quilon for a year; and Nicolò da Conti (1420s–30s) with his description of the ginger, pepper and cinnamon trade of Quilon and the jack fruit and mango trees along the coast. The Persian ambassador Abdul al-Razzak (1442) testifies to the rich Malabar trade with the Arab world, as does the Russian Athanasius Nikitin in 1468–74.

In short, accounts from many sources stretching back thousands of years testify to the fact that the Malabar coast of Kerala and her ports of Calicut, Cochin, Quilon and Muziris traded valuable spices with the Arab world, the Mediterranean, Africa and China.

LOCATING MUZIRIS

The port whose name crops up time and again is Muziris. Muziris was an important spice port long before Roman times. We therefore intended to locate Muziris and, having done so, to see whether there is evidence that Minoan ships traded there.

Muziris is likely to have been a natural harbour near where the most valuable spices, that is pepper and cardamom, grew. We can narrow our search by locating the best growing areas for pepper and cardamom.

Southern India has a peculiar geography. It is near the equator and therefore will have an equatorial climate, but this is modified by a range of mountains called the Western Ghats, which run north–south, parallel to the coast for some 995 miles (1,600 kilometres). Their average height is 900 metres (2,950 feet). The Ghats are punctuated by a number of wide valleys which allow monsoon winds to funnel through. The result is that there are three seasons: summer, rainy season and winter. The coast is hot and wet but it is cool and pleasant in the hills with light sea breezes in the foothills. Pre-monsoon rains called 'mango showers' are beneficial to coffee and mangoes. The southwest monsoon arrives at the end of May with 2 to 4 metres (6.5 to 13 feet) of rain all along the coast. This high rainfall, high humidity and a long wet season has given rise to dense, evergreen luxuriant vegetation ideal for palm trees – Kerala means *kera* (palm) and *la* (land). The cool, moist hill slopes of the Ghats provide ideal conditions for tea, coffee and spices. Kerala is the world's largest producer of cardamom, the most valuable spice, today costing four times as much as black pepper. The coast of Kerala, from Calicut in the north to Quilon in the south, is characterised by a number of lagoons called backwaters, providing a series of internal waterways – canals protected from the sea by sandbanks, resulting in wonderful natural harbours. Moreover, into those protected harbours flow no less than forty-four rivers, which rise in the Western Ghats. In short, along this stretch of coast, named 'The Malabar Coast' by the British Raj, are endless fine protected harbours. Rivers lead explorers quickly to the foothills of the Western Ghats, where pepper and cardamom flourish. The elusive Muziris, confusingly known by a number of ancient names including Shinkli, is therefore likely to have been situated along this 620 mile (1,000 kilometres) stretch of coast (see map). This preliminary conclusion appears to be borne out by a huge hoard of Roman coins found inland near Palghat in central Kerala.

THE LOCATION OF MUZIRIS

In 2006 the Kerala Council for Historical Research (KCHR) found a prehistoric Bronze Age site at Pattanam, 25 miles (40 kilometres) north of Kochi (Cochin), near the estuary of Kerala's largest river, the Periyar. The research team, headed by its director, Dr P.J. Cherian, started excavations near to the position of previous finds of Roman amphorae. An earlier team had found Roman coins, a bead chain and Roman artefacts nearby. To quote extracts from KCHR:

> ... The third season (2009) archaeological excavations at Pattanam reiterates the assumptions that Pattanam might be the oldest port site with extensive evidence for Roman contacts on the Indian Ocean rim or beyond ...

> ... The initial inference from the field is that the majority of the samples [of pottery] are of the campanian type of south Italian origin with volcanic elements. Greek sources such Kos and Rhodes and Egyptian and Mesopotamian amphora sherds were also found.

> ... This time small finds abound and include a variety of non-local (foreign) ceramics, a large number of semi-precious stones and glass beads (over 3,000), copper coins, most of them in a corroded condition, iron, copper, gold and tin artefacts, cameo blanks, spindle whorls, terracotta lamps and so on.

> Pattanam, located 5.5 miles (9 km) south of Kodungallur, is said to

have been first occupied around 1000 BC and continued till the 10th century AD.

... The evidence points to the possibility that the site had the benefit of the services of a large number of artisans and technicians but not necessarily residents on the site. The plethora of artefacts and structures indicate that this site could not have been provisioned without a skilled workforce.

... The workforce comprised blacksmiths (large quantity of iron objects such as nails, tools etc.), coppersmiths (copper objects), goldsmiths (gold ornaments), potters (huge quantity of domestic vessels, lamps, oven and other terracotta objects), brick makers, roofers (large quantity of bricks and triple grooved roof tiles), stone bead makers, lapidaries (as indicated by a variety of semi-precious stone beads, cameo blanks and stone debitage) and weavers (signified by spindle whorls).

So here we have a site dating back to 1000 BC – well before the heydays of classical Greece and Rome – which contains central Mediterranean artefacts. Moreover some of these items, such as the gold ornaments, terracotta objects and lamps and stone beads, appear to be remarkably similar to those found in the Uluburun wreck; this will be considered in more detail later.

As the Vice-Chancellor of Tamil University, Mr M. Rajendran, said in a KCHR press release:

I am personally surprised to see the huge quantity of glass and semi-precious stone beads at Pattanam which goes well with those at the Kodumanal site, excavated by the Tamil University. The evidence unearthed at Pattanam definitely points to connections of the region with the Mediterranean world, South-East Asia and Sri Lanka.

I should add at this point that teak provisionally dated to the 2nd millennium BC and originating in Kerala has been found in the foundations of the Mesopotamian city of Ur.

VISIT TO COCHIN (KOCHI)

We selected Cochin as our base for a research expedition as it is on the backwaters of central Kerala, at the mouth of an estuary of the Periyar River. It is also near Pattanam, which is thought to be the site of ancient Muziris. From here we could explore both the coast and the interior by travelling up the Periyar.

Never will I forget arriving in Cochin at the Old Harbour Hotel at dusk on a warm tropical day. The hotel was once the Portuguese viceroy's palace. It has been superbly converted; the bedrooms have the original teak floors, with planks over 10 metres (33 feet) long and 1 metre (3 feet) wide.

Our bedroom overlooks the old harbour, which is framed by Chinese fishing nets perched along the length of the coast. These resemble great spiders whose front legs lean forward into the sand when the net (beneath the spider's belly) is lowered into the sea. There it rests for some five minutes before a counter-weight is lowered between the spider's rear legs. This raises the front legs and the net – now full of fish. We rush down and buy a big pomfret and a fresh snapper, which the hotel cook grills for our supper.

We eat in the central courtyard, which is centred around a large pool on which float purple water lilies. The air is redolent with frangipani. A sitar and an Indian flute play in the background. The courtyard is shaded by a huge rain tree from which enormous bats flit across the sky. A mango tree sprouts pink orchids; bamboos sway in the sea breeze; jasmine, jack fruit, spider lilies and heliconia surround us as we drink our chota pegs. Later the honk of ships passing downriver to distant lands lulls us to sleep – life could not come better than this; we are so incredibly lucky to experience such a day.

On our second night we ask to move temporarily next door to experience life in the Koder House. It was built by the Koders, prominent Jews, whose forebears traded in Kerala long ago. Our bedroom is 20 metres (65 feet) long, with the same enormous teak floorboards as in the Old Harbour Hotel. The family patriarch,

Samuel Koder, built the house on top of a former Portuguese palace. His house hosted various presidents, prime ministers, viceroys and ambassadors. Sam Koder's 'open house' every Friday was a focal point of the Raj establishment weekly social round. Kay Hyde, an 81-year-old from that era, describes Friday Open House:

> I met so many bigwigs there. Because of the Koders I met Benjamin Britten the famous composer; Peter Pears the singer; Princess Margaret of Hesse, sister of the Duke of Edinburgh; and Maharani Gayatri Devi. In those days Jew town at Cochin was full of Jews – almost all emigrated with the creation of Israel of 1948.

Lord Curzon, the British Viceroy of India, wrote an open letter of greeting to the Jewish community:

> Cochin and its people owe much to you. The memory of your early association with this country has always been pleasant. It is recorded by historians that your people began to visit this coast as early as the days of King Solomon [10th century BC] and they formed one of the earliest links binding East and West, fast with each other.

What I had picked up was an intriguing detail, in the form of the Jewish name for their home town. The Jews called their old settlement 'Shingly', an echo of the ancient name for Muziris. The fame of this settlement, ruled by a Jewish king, spread far and wide. To quote Rabbi Nissim, a 14th-century poet:

> I travelled from Spain,
> I had heard of The City of Shingly
> I longed to see an Israel King
> Him, I saw with my own eyes

Shingly became a haven for the Jews; their attachment was so strong that until relatively recently the Jewish custom worldwide was to put a handful of Shingly sand into any coffin, together with a handful of earth from the Holy Land.

THE BACKWATERS

By now Marcella and I have a reasonable feel for Cochin. Before our journey into the interior to find the fabled spices of the foothills of the Western Ghats, we decide to investigate the backwaters around the estuary of the Periyar River. This is the area where Muziris and other prehistoric ports emerged. We take a punt arranged by the Cochin Tourist Board. Our first impression is one of monotony – in whichever direction one looks there are coconut palms of the same shape and height for mile after mile. A navigator approaching the coast on the monsoon winds would find identifying the port area a very difficult task – he would have to know the precise latitude of the place or risk missing it altogether.

The excited foreign mariner arriving off the Periyar estuary would find a string of sandbanks sheltering lagoons from the sea on which to anchor, fresh water from the streams emptying into the back-waters, fish and fruit of every description as well as wild ducks, pheasants and quail.

JOURNEY INTO THE INTERIOR

We shall travel to the foothills of the Western Ghats up the Periyar River. These days it has channels which enter the Indian Ocean at Cochin and Pattanam (Muziris). Over the centuries the river has changed direction at its estuary, on account of the silt continuously brought downriver by the monsoon rains. Today the big estuary is at Cochin, 2,000 years ago it was at Pattanam. As the river changes course so do the ports where sea meets river. Up until Alwaye the river is as wide as the Thames at London or the Hudson at New York. Pattanam/Muziris is at the northern end of Vypin Island, which can easily be reached from Cochin by the ferry opposite the Old Harbour Hotel – cost three rupees (approximately four cents). Above Alwaye the river runs in a remarkably straight course, fringed by palm trees – just like the river in the frescoes of Thera (described in chapter 2).

For the first two hours we travel beside the river. There are still wild elephants in the forests here as well as tigers and leopards in the Periyar Nature Reserve. The land is rich in fruit – mangoes, bananas, papayas, pomegranates, tree tomatoes, passion fruit and chikoos. The river, according to Roman accounts, is rich in pearls. The woods were famous for jungle fowl, francolins (a type of

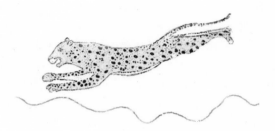

partridge), peafowl and wild deer – once again plenty of food for seafarers travelling upriver.

We have come at the tail end of the monsoon in mid-October to the festival of lights – Diwali. By the time we reach the foothills of the Western Ghats it is raining, or rather there is a thick wet mist dripping off the trees and shrubs. Josey, our splendid driver, suddenly stops and we get out. He shows us a tree surrounded by a climbing vine, with bunches of small green berries – pepper! Within a 5-square-yard (4 square metres) stretch of forest are wild coffee, cocoa, pepper and cardamom bushes or trees. It is the first time I had seen cardamom growing in the wild – cardamom grows on little stalks at the base of the shrub whose shape resembles a bamboo but with thicker leaves. Josey tells us that these foothills of the Western Ghats have perfect conditions for pepper and cardamom: just the right amount of shade and moisture, the right altitude – 600 to 1,500 metres (2,000 to 5,000 feet) – ideal soil conditions and a suitable all-year-round temperature.

The *Rough Guide to Kerala* has a very good summary that illustrates the lure Kerala would have had for any enterprising foreign trader:

Aromatic spices have been used to flavour food, as medicines, and in religious rituals for many thousands of years in Kerala. Traders from Sumeria first sailed across the Arabian Sea in the 3rd millennium BC in search of cinnamon and cardamom – centuries before the Romans mastered the monsoon winds and used them to reach the Malabar pepper, the 'black gold' prized in Europe as a taste enhancer and preservative . . . few aspects of life in Kerala have not been shaped by spices in some way. Eaten by every Kerallen every day, they're still a source of export dollars and a defining feature of the interior hills, where they are grown in sprawling plantations.

The mariner approaching Kerala 4,000 years ago would have arrived at a coast rich in fish, fruit, game, water and building materials. Sailing up the Periyar River would have brought him into contact with elephants, falcons, leopards and pearls. Travelling further on foot he had the world's richest spices at his feet – pepper and cardamom, literally worth their weight in gold. All he had to do was to pick them or buy them dirt cheap. They were easy to ship and could be sold in the spice bazaars of Cairo or Mesopotamia for fifty times what he had paid in Kerala. Prodigious wealth was there for the taking. No wonder mariners have crossed the Indian Ocean for millennia with the trade winds to reach fabled Muziris and her black gold.

Arriving at the clubhouse of the High Range Club, a hill station above Munnar Town, is like entering a 1920s time warp. The walls of the formerly 'Men Only' bar are covered with photographs of man-eating tigers shot by members and of members who have played 'a hole in one' on the golf course. Marcella and I unwind over a chota peg while playing billiards. The golf course is flooded, so we opt for squash. We are the only visitors, spoilt by being surrounded by old-fashioned retainers in the livery of clubs of long ago. Tiffin has to be ordered an hour in advance and we are given strict instructions about dress – ties and dinner jackets on Saturday night. Drivers are not allowed to park on the gravel. All *ayas* have to leave by six p.m. and are not allowed in guest bedrooms before ten a.m. The setting is superb; we are surrounded by mountains covered in tea bushes, all clipped so even that the slopes resemble a vast sloping billiard table. By nightfall the temperature drops to near freezing and we fall asleep to the sound of distant macaques.

MINOANS IN KERALA?

The Uluburun wreck contained a number of items which could have come from India, including cowrie shells that the 'Beyond Babylon' exhibition had identified as from the Indian ocean. The elephant tusks in the Uluburun wreck could also be from Africa rather than India, but some animals shown in the frescoes at the Minoan home base of Thera are of certain Indian origin.

Admittedly, the leopards seen on the Thera frescoes could have been from Africa as well as India. The straight, palm-fringed river on the miniature fresco could be the Nile just as well as the Periyar. However prehistoric tusks found beneath Middle Minoan II tombs in Crete have been positively identified as being from Indian elephants.

Certain botanical specimens found in Mesopotamia and the Mediterranean in the 2nd millennium BC are uniquely Indian and can only have been carried from India to the Middle East by ship. Foremost among these is teak. As we have seen in our journey up the Periyar River into the interior, Kerala's cool rainforest on the foothills of the Ghats provides ideal conditions for both teak and sandalwood trees. The trade in teak between Kerala and the Middle East is proven by finds at both the prehistoric Egyptian port of Berenice and in excavations at the Mesopotamian city of Ur.

Archaeologists from UCLA (University of California, Los Angeles) and the University of Delaware excavating at Berenice have found extensive evidence of sea trade between the Far East, India and Egypt. They reported:

Among the buried ruins of buildings that date to Roman rule, the team discovered vast quantities of teak, a wood indigenous to India and today's Myanmar but not capable of growing in Egypt, Africa or Europe.

... The largest amount of wood we found at Berenice was teak ...

The archaeologists uncovered the largest amount of Indian goods ever found along the Red Sea, including the largest cache of black pepper from antiquity: 7 kilos (16 pounds).

Peppercorns of the same vintage have been excavated as far away as Germany. The team also found Indian coconuts and batik cloth, sapphires and glass beads which appear to have come from Sri Lanka and beads which appear to have originated in Java, Vietnam or Thailand. Even more curious, the remains of cereals and animals indigenous to sub-Saharan Africa were found, pointing to a three-way Indian Ocean trade – southern Africa to India, India to Egypt, Egypt to southern Africa. Roman texts that address the costs of different shipping methods describe land transport as being at least twenty times more expensive than sea trade.

This international trade evidenced at Berenice is mirrored by that of Muziris/Pattanam, where the earliest dating (charcoal fragments trench II) is 1693 BC to 509 BC. This trade between the Mediterranean and the Indian port of Muziris in described in Tamil Sangam poems:

... Where the splendid ships of the Yavanas bring gold and return with pepper beating the foam on the Periyar ...

Ptolemy in *The Periplus of the Erythrean Sea*, and the Greek historian Strabo, have written numerous descriptions of trade between the Malabar coast and the Western world.

Professor Cherian and colleagues state:[29]

The excavation findings suggest that Pattanam had a key role in the early historic Indian Ocean trade. The archaeological evidence vouches for its cultural linkages with the Mediterranean, Red Sea, west Asia, Ganga Delta, Coromandel Coast and South East Asian regions ...

... An interesting possibility emerging out of the present study could be the possibility of tracing back the antiquity of external contacts to the pre-Roman period. The presence of non-European especially Nabatean (?) and West Asian variety of pottery could be another indication for maritime activities at Pattanam in the pre-Roman era.

Professor Cherian's work is corroborated by Emeritus Professor John Sorenson and Emeritus Professor Carl Johannessen's painstaking putting-together of the evidence for extensive maritime activity between India and Egypt, India and America (trading cotton) and America and India (trading corn) dating back four millennia. Their research shows that sea trade – pioneered by the Minoans and later adopted by the Phoenicians and Romans – between America and India was commonplace a full 3,000 years before Columbus.

By now I was convinced of the Minoan presence in Kerala during the Middle Bronze Age. I looked about for their 'signatures' – beyond those of the bronze weapons I already knew were found buried in the area of the Junma catchment of the Ganges. Could I find any 'signature' Kamares pottery, distinctive or amber jewellery, frescoes, or particularly unusual customs, such as the practice of bull-leaping?

The pottery excavated so far comes in shards and to my unpractised eye does not conclusively 'shout' Kamares ware. There was some interesting evidence of bull-leaping in the annual celebrations of 'Jellikata', a ceremony during which youths lead the bull to 'encearos' then attempt to somersault on to its back. I was struck by the Spanish-sounding terminology, but I am no linguist and certainly not when it comes to Indian dialects. This strange custom is still practised and young people get gored, just as they do in Spain today (as described later). However, though bull-leaping appears an odd and unlikely custom, this in itself could be a coincidence. It seems less so when you consider that this is a Hindu society, where cattle are considered holy, objects of veneration. This custom has clear similarities to those ancient Crete.

I felt confident that Minoans used to travel upstream on the

Periyar River for pepper, cardamom, teak and perhaps occasionally exotica such as leopards and monkeys. It was hard, though, to keep tabs on information from India, so once we'd returned to England I retained an agency to search English-speaking Hindi and Malay-alam newspapers for relevant leads.

We did not have long to wait although the lead, when it came, was from a totally unexpected direction. On 10 June 2009 *The Hindu*, India's national newspaper, ran this headline in its online edition: 'Prehistoric Cemetery discovered in Kerala.'

> Triruvananthapuram: Archaeologists have discovered a pre-historic necropolis (cemetery) with megalithic cairn circles dating back 2,500 years ... a woodhenge-like ritual monument and a site of primitive astronomical intelligence at Anakkara, near Kuttippuram in Mal-appuram District [about 93 miles (150 kilometres) north of the Periyar River estuary].

According to the press report, interred objects suggested that the find was around 2,500 years old.

> We could also trace some broken pieces of an unidentified copper object. These artefacts could be indicative of the earliest trade con-tacts of the region ...

It continued:

> ... Similar posthole finds at certain necropolis sites of Anatolia, Syria, Greece, London and so on have been reported in connection with the Neolithic as well as Bronze Age cultures of secondary burial practices. Nevertheless, our traces of erecting posts in their holes using insights of experimental archaeology, have turned out to be quite interesting and revealing. The posthole alignment looks exactly like that at Woodhenge, in England. The holes of uneven sizes, big and small interspersed, in a strikingly wide open site ideal for star watching probably indicate patterns of heavenly bodies and are suggestive of primitive astronomical intelligence.

This was totally unnerving. The dates seemed to match, closely following the time that the Minoans would have been at their most active. How strange that a European-style prehistoric ceremonial circle should have been found in Kerala and that it should be so close to the river that I was sure the Minoans had traversed.

The newspaper's assertion that the Keralan wooden circle was for star-watching is what held my particular attention. Wherever they were, the Minoans would have needed to navigate their way back. And, like Homer's hero Odysseus, they would have had to do that via the stars. Perhaps they had relied on observatories. Perhaps the Minoans had even built those observatories.

18

THE TRUTH IS IN THE TRADE...

I have long been convinced that world travel has had a much more complex history than historians allow. And as I was researching the products and produce that the Minoans brought through Egypt and into India – and back again – I was uncovering so much unexpected information I hardly knew where to begin to unravel all the leads.

In India, I'd discovered that beautiful rock art carvings and paintings of American bison have been found on the borders of Kerala and Tamil Nadu, near the point where the Periyar River rises. They were dated to the 2nd millennium BC. I had to ask myself how Keralan artists of 4,000 years ago had any knowledge of American bison.

The answer seemed to be that the connecting tissue between all these strong, growth- and wealth-hungry cultures was the enterprising and dauntless Minoans. To take this any further, I needed to find whatever proof I could that there had been transatlantic contact millennia ago. Back at my desk, I struck gold when I turned once again to Emeritus Professors John Sorenson and Carl Johannessen. Both academics have documented a considerable amount of intercontinental trade before Columbus, as has Dr Gunnar Thompson. Researching their carefully documented material over painstaking decades, they have produced a huge amount of detailed information on the 2nd millennium BC, which has been contested by those who seem unable to ditch the paralysing historical convention that only Christopher Columbus could have discovered America.

From their work I found that there were largely six categories of goods for which there is substantial proof of trade. That exchange was between India, Egypt, the Minoan lands and North America, in the era of Hatshepsut's expeditions to the East: that is, during the 3rd and 2nd millennia BC. They have documented: (1) maize transported from the Americas to Egypt and India; (2) descriptions of the origins of this maize given by Indian and African peoples; (3) cotton taken from India to the Americas; (4) tobacco and drugs transported from the Americas to Egypt via Thera; (5) squashes and fruit shipped from America to India; (6) gourds exported from India to America. This will, of course, only be relevant if it can be demonstrated that it was Minoan ships in particular that traded with the Americas as well as with Egypt and India.

To concentrate on a few specifics that clearly illustrate local Indian knowledge of 'exotic' produce: in a highly detailed work of scholarship, Professors Carl L. Johannessen and Professor Anne Z. Parker contend that stone carvings of maize exist in at least three pre-Columbian Hoysala stone temples near Mysore (see second colour plate section). Professor Johannessen has also found the sunflower, another New World crop, in pre-Columbian Indian temple sculptures.[30]

Their conclusions are supported by a separate research project undertaken by the Indian botanist Professor Shakti M. Gupta,[31] of Delhi University, who agrees:

> Different varieties of the corn cob (Zea Mays Linn) are extensively sculpted on the Hindu and Jain temples of Karnataka. Various deities are shown as carrying a corn cob in their hands, as on the Chenna Kesava Temple, Belur.

Professor Gupta continues:

> The straight rows of the corn grains can be easily identified. In the Lakshmi Narasimha temple, Nuggehalli, the eight-armed dancing Vishnu in his female form of Mohini is holding a corn cob in his left hand and the other hand holds the usual emblems of Vishnu .... a 12th century sculpture of Ambika Kushmandini sitting on a lotus seat under a canopy of mangoes holds in his left hand a corn cob ....

The number of instances is overwhelming. Professor Gupta identifies sunflowers, pineapples, cashews, custard apples and monstera – all of them New World species – in the pre-Columbian art of India. Carvings depicting the sunflower, a native of Central and South America, are found for example in the Rani Gumpha cave, Udayagiri (2nd century BC). As Professor Gupta reports, a pineapple is clearly depicted (see second colour plate section) in the Udayagiri core temple, Madhya Pradesh (5th century AD); a cashew in the Bharhut stupa (2nd century BC) and monstera – a climber native to Central America – in Hindu and Jain temples in Gujarat and Rajasthan (11–13th centuries BC).

As for dating the era when maize first appeared, Professor Gupta implies that it may have been in existence long before it appeared in the carvings described above:

> . . . it is quite conceivable that maize was present in the subcontinent [India] for many centuries before the Hoysala dynasty [described by Professor Johannessen], and that distinctively Asian varieties were developed early on.

Indian and African people believed maize was first brought to their countries 'from Mecca' in the case of Indians and 'from Egypt' in the case of Africans. These descriptions would make sense if my suspicion that the Minoans had known exactly how to get to America was true. Perhaps now was the moment to investigate the little *Lasioderma serricorne* beetle in more detail.

THE TOBACCO BEETLE

If, as it appears, the Minoans carried tobacco from the Americas to Egypt, then there should be evidence of American tobacco in Crete itself or on Thera, the principal Minoan base. Finding such evidence may be complicated by the destruction visited on both islands by the volcanic eruption.

There is, nevertheless, such evidence – in the form of the tobacco beetle, which I suspected would also be found in ancient Egypt. The first specimen I had encountered was buried beneath the 1450 BC volcanic ash of a merchant's house in the Minoan town of Thera, modern-day Akrotiri.

Lasioderma serricorne was indigenous to the Americas. Yet, as Sir Walter Raleigh, who brought tobacco to 16th-century England as a prize for his queen and sponsor Elizabeth I, would have testified, the plant is not indigenous to Europe. Nor did it grow there in 1450 BC.

The life-cycle of this little beetle, averaging forty to ninety days, is highly dependent on temperature and food source. Females lay ten to a hundred eggs in the tobacco and the larvae emerge in six to ten days. The larvae cannot hatch below seventeen degrees Celsius and they die when the temperature falls to four degrees Celsius. In short, the beetles can only breed in warm conditions. In the right season, Minoan ships would have had a warm hold, with sailors sleeping in it off watch.

After a period of further desk research, I knew that this tobacco beetle had also been found in the tombs of pharaohs who had clearly smoked the weed – Anastase Alfieri reported finding them in King Tutankhamun's tomb (1931 and 1976) and J.R. Steffan (1982) in the visceral cavity of Ramses II. Alfieri (1976, 1982) reported specimens from Alexandria, Cairo, the Nile Delta and the Fayum and Luxor regions – all places visited by the Minoan fleet. So I believe that the carriage of tobacco and the tobacco beetle is another 'signature card' of Minoan voyages to the Americas and back; as well as to Egypt and the Mediterranean. It is a card just as distinctive as the Minoans' cult of the bull. It also dates at least some of their travels to the specific era between Tutankhamun and Ramses II. The date range would have been 1336 BC (Tutankhamun) to 1260 BC (Ramses II at the age of about 38), and in Thera to before 1450 BC (the possible date of the volcanic eruption) – a 200-year spread.

Yet there was another obstacle in the way of this theory. It came very literally, in the shape of Africa. From Crete's position in the Mediterranean; from the Egypt of the pharaohs; from India, it was all the same. The vast looming land mass of Africa is dominant on any modern map. From both Egypt and India, the so-called 'Dark Continent' is right in the way of anyone attempting to get to the Americas. It appeared to me that there was only one way that North American produce could ever have reached India. The Minoans can only have gone west, not east. They must have braved the perils of the North Atlantic ocean and breached the Straits of Gibraltar, passing the landmark that the ancient Greeks, believing that the two magnificent peaks were the gates to the end of the world, called 'The Pillars of Hercules'. The pillars beyond which, according to Plato, lay the lost realm of Atlantis.

Notes to Book II

1. Homer, *Iliad* 16.221–30; 23.196, 219, trans. Robert Eagles. Penguin Classics, 1998

2. G. F. Bass, 'Cargo From the Age of Bronze', in *Beneath the Seven Seas*, Thames & Hudson, 2005

3. Cathy Gere, *The Tomb of Agamemnon*, Profile Books, 2006

4. Tim Severin, *The Jason Voyage*, Hutchinson, 1985

5. Ibid. p. 161

6. Robert Graves, *The Greek Myths*

7. D. Grimaldi, 'Pushing Back Amber Production' in *Science*, 2009 p 51–52

8. Hans Peter Duerr, *GEO Magazin*, no. 12/05. Dienekes 8/2008

9. Joan Aruz, *Beyond Babylon: Art, Trade and Diplomacy in the Second Millennium BC*, Barnes & Noble, 2008

10. A. Hauptmann, R. Maddin, M. Prange, 'On the Structure and Composition of Copper and Tin Ingots Excavated from the Shipwreck of Uluburun' in *Bulletin of the American Schools of Oriental Research*, no. 328, pp. 1–30

11. William L. Moran, *The Amarna Letters*, John Hopkins University Press, 1992

12. Joan Aruz, *Beyond Babylon*, p. 167

13. Bernard Knapp, 'Thalassocracies in Bronze Age Eastern Mediterranean Trade: Making and Breaking a Myth', in *World Archaeology*, vol. 24, No.3, Ancient Trade: New Perspectives, 1993

14. Rodney Castleden, *Minoans*, p. 32

15. D. Panagiotopoulos, 'Keftiu in context: Theban tomb-paintings as a historical source', *Oxford Journal of Archaeology* 20, 2001, pp. 263–4

16. Leonard Woolley, *A Forgotten Kingdom*, Penguin, 1953, pp. 74–75

17. The Thera Foundation 2006, Heaton 1910; 1911; Forbes 1955, pp. 241–242; Cameron, Jones and Philippakes 1977; Hood 1978, p. 83; Immerwahr 1990a, pp. 14–15. *Aegean Frescoes in Syria-Palestine*

18. Joan Aruz, *Beyond Babylon: Art, Trade and Diplomacy in the Second Millennium BC*, Barnes & Noble, 2008

19. From USA Today, 5th March, © 2006 USA Today. All rights reserved. Used by permission and protected by the copyright laws of the United States. The printing, copying, redistribution or retransmission of this content without express written permission is prohibited

20. André Parrot, 1958a, 165 n.2, *Samaria: the Capital of the Kingdom of Israel*, SCM Press, 1958

21. The Teaching Company User Community Forum Index, Alexis Q. Castor. 'Between the Rivers: The History of Ancient Mesopotamia,' Teaching Co. Virginia, USA

22. Jack M. Sasson, in *Beyond Babylon: Art, Trade and Diplomacy in the Second Millenium B.C.* Yale University Press, 2008

23. Zephaniah 2:13 (Destruction of Syria and Nineveh)

24. Homer, *Odyssey*, trans. Samuel Butler, Longmans, 1900

25. Enuma Anu Enlil 17.2

26. The Canal Builders, Payn, Robert, MacMillan, New York, 1959

27. Herodotus, *Histories*, trans. George Rawlinson, Penguin Classics, 1858. p. 109

28. Paul Lunde, *The Navigator Ahmed Ibn Majid*, Saudi Aramco, 2004

29. Professor Cherian and colleagues, 'Chronology of Pattanam: a multi-cultural port site on the Malabar coast'

30. 'Maize Ears Sculptured in 12th and 13th Century A.D. India as Indicators of Pre-Columbian Diffusion', *Economic Botany*, 43

31. Shakti M. Gupta, *Plants in Indian Temple Art*, B.R. Publishing, 1996

BOOK III

JOURNEYS WEST

19

NEC PLUS ULTRA:
ENTERING THE ATLANTIC

Helen of Troy's face is said to have launched 1,000 ships. Plato, meanwhile, claimed that the kings of his fabled Atlantis had 1,200 ships.

Even by the time of the Trojan War, Homer was still able to describe ancient Crete as the provider of eighty ships for the joint campaign to avenge Paris' abduction of fair Helen. We've established that the Minoans were a mighty sea power until the volcano struck. Thera alone, at the time of the admiral's fresco, seems to have had at least ten ships, and possibly more. Minoan power and reach expanded steadily as the Bronze Age developed.

I was now searching for the answers to two major questions. The tobacco beetle *Lasioderma serricorne* must have been brought to Thera somehow: exactly how? I also suspected that at least some of the near-pure copper found in the Uluburun wreck originated at Lake Superior. How could two so very different items from America have surfaced so far away, in the exotic island culture of the ancient Mediterranean? Geography dictated that it was almost impossible that anything from North America could have reached Minoan Crete via Egypt, or even through India. There was no other answer: sailors, not necessarily the Minoans themselves, must have crossed the Atlantic – and to meet up with them, the Minoans must have made their way west as well.

Yet to brave the unknown, voyaging through the Pillars of Hercules, which the ancient Greeks believed held up the very sky, would have taken real courage. There is much dispute about the location of the pillars – and indeed, about what exactly they were.

Although some scholars believe that the mythic hero Hercules performed his labours in the Greek Peloponnese, and dispute that the pillars lay between Spain and Morocco, there is an overwhelming amount of evidence in favour of the Straits of Gibraltar.

What would have tempted the Minoans to sail westwards in the first instance? Surely the answer has to be something to do with finding, or producing, the substance that ignited the whole age – bronze? The Uluburun wreck, much smaller than the ships shown in the Thera frescoes, carried 10 tons of copper in its hold: a vast amount.

Crete, the birthplace of Minoan civilisation and the lynchpin of the Bronze Age, had no copper in usable amounts. The island had some small amounts of surface copper, but not enough to fuel the huge amount being smelted and worked on a grand scale in Minoan Crete, not least in the palaces themselves. Intriguingly, at Chrysokamino on the northeast coast of Crete there is evidence of smelting activity stretching as far back as c.4500 BC. Crete had no tin. It had to be imported by sea.[1] The surrounding, colonised islands were also engaged in smelting: after all, the magical metal of bronze was the crude oil of its day, as valuable as the gold that made Croesus rich. So where did the raw materials that fuelled the Minoan brilliance in bronze actually come from?

Copper, and later on in time the finished bronze, must have been imported by sea.[2] The nearest copper mines were at Lavrion in mainland Greece and on the island of Kythnos in the Cyclades.

||||||||||||||||||||||||

Bronze, to recap, ideally contains around 90 per cent copper. The other 10 per cent is made up of tin or arsenic. Mediterranean traders could definitely find arsenic-alloyed copper, but no tin. Almost all copper ores contain some level of arsenic. Arsenic ores are more common than tin ores and are generally found in mines in western Asia. And, in fact, since 3000 BC, Cretan and western Mediterranean bronzes had been made with arsenical copper. So there was no real need for tin – or so it might appear on the face of things. The deadly drawback in working with arsenical bronze, however, is a major one: the risk of death by poisoning. Perhaps it was partly as a result of this danger that bronze-making carried with it a strange allure.

All of the evidence suggests that in the Bronze Age the actual bronze-maker, or master, was respected – lionised, almost – as if he were a magician. In some cultures, the actual bronze-making process was top secret: given the alloy's huge value, the knowledge may also have been regarded as sacred, and could even have been restricted in some societies to kings or shamans. Yet king or not, the unfortunate Bronze Age coppersmith's lot would have been an unhealthy one. For all his status, he could not have avoided breathing in the fumes of arsenic as he heated, cast and hammered the hot arsenical bronze.

The smiths' illnesses have come down to us through legend – both the Greek god Hephaestus and his Roman counterpart Vulcan were crippled. So this must be at least one reason why tin bronze had become the Minoans' metal of choice by about 2600 BC. When it comes to making desirable objects such as swords, tin bronze also has the technical edge; while arsenical copper melts at 1,084 degrees Celsius, tin bronze melts at 950 degrees Celsius, making it much less prone to cracking in the mould.

There were some sources of base metals in established trade areas near to Crete. Göltepe in the Taurus mountains, in what is now Turkey, had tin mines producing substantial quantities of ore from 3290 BC until 1840 BC, when the town was sacked and tin production ceased.[3] So from 2600 BC up until 1840 BC there was theoretically a tin source readily available in the Mediterranean. Yet the records of King Sargon of Akkad say that Minoan ships had been sailing to the Atlantic to obtain Iberian and English tin since 2350 BC. Once again, why bother to look westwards in the five centuries *before* Göltepe ceased tin production?

The answer, I think, lies in the third material required to make bronze – wood. To produce just 1 kilogram (2 pounds) takes around 300 kilograms (660 pounds) of charcoal, smelting 30 kilograms (66 pounds) of ore. The Bronze Age may have opened up almost limitless opportunities for civilisations to grow and develop, but like the Minotaur it was a ravenous beast to feed, devouring acres and acres of trees. The evidence is in the *Epic of Gilgamesh*.

Archaeology owes a lot to a Victorian Londoner with the unassuming name of George Smith. Only a few months before, in my journey to the Near East, I'd sought to the great city of Nineveh to track down Aššurbanipal's library. Where I had found only mounds of earth and ruptured walls, however, George Smith had found real words, real stories and real history – and in translating them, told us much of what we now know about ancient Mesopotamia and the Middle East, and the region's lost legions of precious trees.

Nineveh was first rediscovered by the French Consul General at Mosul, Paul-Émile Botta, in the 1840s. By the time the British adventurer Sir Henry Austen Layard had later uncovered the fabled library, Nineveh was still less of a city than an ancient conundrum, shrouded in mystery. With archaeology still in its infancy, academics were at a loss. They could not interpret what had been found – although they knew they had at least one source of information: the Bible. Nineveh is first mentioned in the Old Testament, in Genesis 10.11. By the time we get to the Book of Jonah, though, things have gone very badly wrong for its citizens; God has brought down destruction upon a corrupt society. Rigorous historical knowledge about the city, however, was almost completely lacking. Smith is the rather unexpected figure who let us in through the Assyrian city's gates by translating the cryptic cuneiform inscriptions – and the stories – left us by the ancients. The translator was from a poor family, so he had received little education: and he certainly had no background as a linguist. Even so, he was both determined and dedicated. In 1876, Smith became ill and died while he was searching for more missing tablets around Nineveh. But not before translating the first written poem in history – the stone tablets that together form the *Epic of Gilgamesh*.

The epic tells us that in antiquity vast forests grew in the Middle East. That can be hard to believe today, when what we so often see, particularly on the news or in documentaries about the Middle East, is an unrelentingly barren and unforgiving landscape of hard earth, baked dry by the sun. Yet in the early part of the 3rd millennium BC, the mountain slopes of the region were covered with massive cedar forests. In the resource-hungry millennium before Christ's birth those millions of trees, including many of the much prized cedars of Lebanon, essential for building ships, were to disappear totally.

The real-life Gilgamesh was a Sumerian king of Uruk, living around 2700–2500 BC, who after a series of victories in war ruled the whole of southern Mesopotamia. The middle stories of the Gilgamesh epic warn about the perils of deforestation.[4] Approximately 4,700 years ago in Uruk, a city-kingdom in southern Mesopotamia, the king and his companion set off to Lebanon to cut down her famous cedars. They incur the wrath of the forest god Humbaba, who in his turn punishes Gilgamesh. The story illustrates the fact that Mesopotamia did not have enough wood to support its flourishing Bronze Age civilisation. As Mesopotamia constructed thousands of roads, cities, canals and palaces using bronze, the forests were felled to fuel the furnaces. These new cities needed public buildings, palaces and cisterns in which to store water in the dry summer months. For these they also needed cement, plaster, brick and terracotta – all of which required fuel for their manufacture.

It's intriguing that Plato also talks about an environmental crisis. In his dialogues he describes the consequences of deforestation on the Acropolis:

> The land was the best in the world ... in those days the country was fair as now, and yielded far more abundant produce ... there remained only the bones of the wasted body, as they may be called, as in the case of the small islands. All the richer and softer parts of the soil having fallen away, and the mere skeleton of the land being left ... there was [long ago] abundance of wood ... the traces still remain.

The problem of deforestation became so serious that around 1750 BC King Hammurabi of Mesopotamia set up laws against unauthorised tree-felling.⁵ So I was beginning to suspect that war may not have been the only reason why tin mining did not start again in Göltepe after it had been sacked – perhaps it had used up its wood supply.

The difficulties involved in replacing and replanting timber are much more acute in dry Mediterranean countries than in wet northern Europe, where trees grow relatively quickly. In the Mediterranean, rain is restricted to winter and tends to be sudden and violent. The irony is that without trees to anchor it, the soil itself gets depleted – just, in fact, as Plato had described.

> ... winter rains on steep deforested slopes quickly degrade the soil by washing it downhill. Seedlings have difficulty in re-establishing the forest, especially after clean cutting, and the soil quickly degrades to the point that pine forest cannot recover ... The tremendous tonnage of ancient copper slag on Cyprus suggests that the Cypriot copper industry collapsed around 300 AD, simply because the island ran out of cheap fuel. The slagheaps suggest a total production of perhaps 200,000 tonnes of copper – and that in turn suggests that fuel equivalent to 200 million pine trees were cut to supply the copper industry, forests 16 times the total area of the island.⁶

The problem would have been exacerbated by the conditions in the dry eastern Mediterranean, because the coastal cities and nearby Mesopotamia and the Levant were all developing rapidly and doing so in parallel with each other.

If Mari's glorious 5-acre palace is anything to go by, then the Bronze Age was nothing if not architecturally ambitious. Meanwhile Egypt needed incalculable amounts of bronze to make the tools for its astonishing, relentless programme of pyramid and temple construction. Not that much later in time, the Mycenaeans would construct entire roads leading into magnificent edifices that blazed with gleaming copper and bronze.

Later on in history, the problem becomes still more acute. The Athenian fleet that defeated the Persians at Salamis was built from timber that came from the Balkans and southern Italy, rather than Greece, because Athens had so depleted her own forests. T.A Wertime estimates that the Laurion silver mines near Athens consumed an awe-inspiring 1 million tons of charcoal and 2.5 million acres (1 million hectares) of forest.[7] The mines perhaps did not stop production because of a shortage of ore, but because imported fuel costs had risen so much that they were no longer economic.

Seen in that light, developing trade with the western Mediterranean and possibly even further – to the wet, Atlantic shores of Europe – made absolute sense. Not only were there abundant supplies of copper and tin in Iberia – but timber was plentiful. There was a lot of evidence on the museum shelves at Thera that suggested, at the least, mutually profitable trade. The Minoans would export their finished goods in return for the natural resources of wider Europe: much like Europe's relationship with Africa today. Bronze pins, for example, of the same type are found across Iberia, France and Britain. I'd seen the exact same design in the museum at Akrotiri. Were they exported from Thera?

In this scenario, Minoan shipbuilding expertise now becomes even more valuable. They did not have the metal ores on Crete. Paradoxically, this negative situation eventually turned out to be a strength for the Minoans; it meant that, latterly, large-scale smelting did not have to take place on Crete. If that had been the case they would still have had the wood to build their ships – and with that ability to travel came the opportunity to smelt plentiful ores *in situ*, where both the ore and the wood were readily available. They could have controlled the entire supply of bronze to the eastern Mediterranean. The Holy Grail was theirs.

At first, it seemed almost fanciful to think that the Minoans would roam that far across the globe. But bronze was the most powerful metal yet known to man. I knew there had been plentiful supplies of Cornish tin and Welsh copper in the British Isles. Now I discovered that experts believe that during the Bronze Age about half of the 'wildwood' or native forest disappeared from Britain: suggesting the possibility of smelting on an industrial scale.[8]

To achieve their goal the Minoans would have had to pass right through the Straits of Gibraltar, into the unknown. I thought of that eerie phrase, which ancient accounts say was once written in stone on the Pillars of Hercules:

Nec plus ultra (venture thus far, but no further).

Many hundreds of years later than the Minoans, the Greeks and the Romans were so scared of the Straits that there were dire admonitions not to go there. There were terrifying stories of petrifying monsters of the deep in the unknown ocean beyond. Perhaps the Minoans, whose rich and artistic culture was passed on to the Greeks, had also had their own fears?

Yet, drawing on my own knowledge of seafaring, I was beginning to piece together a picture of the ancient Minoan mariners as the greatest sailors the world has ever known. We tend to think of 'progress' as if humankind is in perpetual forward motion; as if knowledge, technology and culture always advance relentlessly, hand-in-hand.

Studying the Bronze Age gave the lie to that proposition: under the microscope of history I could see great civilisations rise and fall like waves breaking over a ship's prow. I was learning that knowledge, even advanced knowledge, is as slippery as the deck of a clipper; and it can be lost a lot more easily than it can be gained.

|||||||||||||||||||||

The breezes in a Mediterranean summer often blow in the evening, because of the difference in temperature between the land and the sea. At dusk, the desert cools surprisingly quickly and the wind blows offshore to the warmer sea. Thus, I calculated, hugging the Mediterranean coast from Crete to the Straits of Gibraltar – setting sail after dusk and sailing for a few hours each night – should allow a galley with a decent sail to reach the Straits of Gibraltar in fits and starts even without the use of oars (see map showing Mediterranean winds).

Based on the three months that Severin's *Argo* took to run the 1,500 miles (2,400 kilometres) from Spetses to Georgia, against wind and current, I thought the voyage from Thera to the Straits would perhaps have taken a third longer – four months.

There is solid evidence that the Minoans travelled westwards across the Mediterranean. A tale told by an intriguing name: a settlement called Minoa. According to Rodney Castleden:

> There was a port called Minoa on the south-west coast of Sicily, which may have been a Crete-controlled trading station. Quite what the Minoans wanted from the West is unknown ... the Minoans needed tin to make bronze, and the sources of their raw materials are unknown. The tin may have come from Etruria, Bohemia, Spain, or even Britain ... A gold-mounted disc of amber found at Knossos may have come from the Wessex culture of southern England.[9]

Over the half-century since Spyridon Marinatos' astonishing discoveries on Thera, the documented evidence of Minoan settlements has grown and grown and the movement seems to have been westwards. Some of those settlements may have had the suffix 'Minoa' added to their names. Those client islands, or colonies as they may have been, are identifiable by features shared with Bronze Age Crete: such as an irregular street plan in the towns; the distinctive Minoan style of architecture; Minoan burial customs; and the introduction of Minoan pottery shapes and styles – including wares that were not imported from Crete, but show the local inhabitants adopting Minoan designs for themselves. Sometimes, there is also evidence of the introduction of Minoan religious rituals, such as ritual cups or figurines.[10]

There seems to have been a rapid growth in the Minoan trading empire between 1700 and 1500 BC. The settlement at Kastri on Kythera, which began in early Minoan times, is an early and small move westwards; by contrast, Minoa's presence in Sicily shows the Minoans venturing far into the central Mediterranean, moving ever closer to the Balearic Islands and Spain.

So this left me with a question. Could the Minoans have set up further foreign bases, just as they had done at Avaris (Tell el Dab'a) in ancient Egypt? If I was correct, and copper of the purity found on the Uluburun wreck could only have come from America, ships setting out across the Atlantic would need a base for repairs, provision and preparation for the serious journey ahead. They would need storage facilities and possibly labour. Could there have been permanent forward bases established in southwest Spain or Portugal?

If the Minoans had got as far as the Straits, I reasoned, it would have been logical for them to explore the lands they had discovered there. I'd read various books that hinted at Minoan interest in Britain. Logically, they would have traded with Spain well before they even got to the British Isles. By chance, I also happened to know something about the wealth of minerals in what was once known as Iberia. Later in history, the Romans had been eager to conquer the peninsula for that very reason. Today's Spanish term for a stream, 'arroyo', comes from the Latin 'arrugius' – meaning a gold mine. Both Spain and its neighbour Portugal would have held great riches for eager traders in search of bronze. Could I too strike gold? I decided that Spain would have to be my next stop in the journey.

20

A FOLK MEMORY OF HOME?

Once the Minoans had succeeded in sailing the Mediterranean, it was surely only a matter of time before they discovered Iberia, one of the most heavily mineralised places on earth. Beyond the Straits are two majestic rivers, both of which would have led the Minoans straight to all of the glittering prizes of this land – not only copper, but gold and silver.

I will never forget entering the Guadalquivir in HMS *Diamond*, when I was officer of the watch. The Atlantic coasts of Spain and Portugal are always memorable to seafarers; not least because of the smell of hay as you pass Cape St Vincent *en route* to the magic East; on the way home, turning north on passing Sagres, you savour the scent of pines.

It was 1958. Like the Rio Tinto, the Guadalquivir debouches into the Atlantic Ocean at the very southern tip of Spain and would have been readily visible to Minoan mariners had they dared to broach the Straits. The river is one of the longest in Spain. It flows west for 408 miles (657 kilometres), emptying into the Atlantic at Sanlúcar de Barrameda on the Gulf of Cádiz. We had been ordered to pay a goodwill visit to Seville, some 70 miles (112 kilometres) upriver. The Guadalquivir is so shallow that a ship of the *Diamond*'s size could only pass over the bar at Sanlúcar de Barrameda at high spring tide. Which happened to be exactly the same time that every year a sheer wall of water, a 'bore', surges up the river. We had to time our entrance to the minute.

There was a huge judder underneath us. Then good old HMS *Diamond* had to mount the bore and travel on its crest which, since it races along at more than 20 knots, is a hair-raising experience. It was like skiing on stilts. What's more, a big ship travelling at this kind of speed causes a vast wave of its own. In vain we flashed our lights and blasted our fog horn to warn the farmers who were pootling their way to market along the riverbanks. Time after time the wave caught them – fortunately with no casualties, bar the odd half-drowned, furiously braying donkey.

So I had a special fondness for the Guadalquivir and paid attention when I noticed magazine reports which said that a Bronze Age settlement had recently been discovered on its estuary. In the process of creating a beautiful national park, the Doñana, the excavators had uncovered an ancient human settlement. They had also found the wrecked timber carcasses of what could well be Bronze Age ships, in the swamps the Spanish know as 'Las Marismas'. It would be a long time before all of the archaeologists' detailed studies were complete, but initial carbon dating estimates from the French excavating team suggested that the remains dated from 2000 BC.

I also knew the large modern port of Huelva, about 50 miles (80 kilometres) north, which is fed by the Rio Tinto. I'd visited it in the 1950s, but now I saw a completely different side to what I'd always thought of as just a 17th-century port town. The town's origins were definitely ancient and there were still a number of Roman remains, I read. Yet what was most intriguing here was that a specialist in human prehistory, Martín Almagro Basch, had investigated a hoard of bronze artefacts found hidden in the area. Other archaeologically significant hoards had also been found in the region, notably the Leiro hoard, which was discovered by a fisherman in 1976 in the estuary waters of the Ulla River, near Leiro in Galicia.

The River, or Rio, Tinto is named 'the red' for a good reason: as it trickles past the ancient fortified walls of Spanish medieval towns it runs a symbolic blood-red. Copper. Copper ore everywhere. The sheer wealth of the minerals in this landscape of other-worldly greens, yellows and reds gave the area a fabled status in times of yore: these were, according to legend, King Solomon's mines.

IIIIIIIIIIIIIIIIIIIII

I began to research, again using the British Library – and this time, the Web.

If the Minoans did come here, then initially at least they could have simply sifted the incredibly rich alluvial sediments for metallic ore. Was there any evidence that they had done so? Much later than the Minoans, ancient Greek and Roman writers such as Strabo (63 BC–AD 23) wrote that northwest Iberia was by then well known as a rich source of tin, as did Ptolemy.

Starting a survey of Spain from the north, I looked for as much evidence as I could. Professor Beatriz Comendador Rey of the University of Vigo believes that northwest Iberia could also have a rich archaeological heritage of metallic finds, but that the wet climate of this part of Spain makes dating and scientific evaluation problematic. I was interested in this area, as I had already come across a lot of evidence to suggest that the Minoans had reached the Baltic. If they had, they would have had to follow the coastline, and from here at the chilly tip of Vigo move north through the markedly colder English Channel.

Professor Comendador Rey links similar finds by Almeida with Bronze Age awls found on the nearby islet of Guidor Aredso. She also refers to the artefacts recovered from the River Ulla, mostly swords and spearheads dating from the Middle/Late Bronze Age. Taking all of these finds together, it seems beyond argument that they came from shipwrecks of the Middle/Late Bronze Age.

Moving south, the vast Rio Tinto copper, silver and gold mines were first worked during the third millennium BC.[11] Mark A. Hunt Ortiz dates the mines' initial period of use to around 2900 BC.[12]

It is worth pausing at this point: continuing up the Guadiana River (see map) would bring us to Évora. Ten miles (16 kilometres) west of Évora is the Bronze Age stone circle of Almendres Cromlech. I looked at some pictures I found of the circle on a website. 'How strange,' I thought. 'That picture shows a carving on one of the menhirs.' An enthusiastic amateur photographer had somehow got a shot that was at exactly the right angle to show something carved into the rock. To my eye, it looked like an axe. Thinking back to the newly discovered stone circle by the Red Sea and also to the 'woodhenge' of Kerala, I made a mental note to return to Évora, both in body and in thought.

Sailing northwestwards along the coast for another 30 miles (48 kilometres), from the Rio Tinto estuary, would have brought the Minoans to the Rio Guadiana, and what we would now call Portugal. Its waters were most likely just as red as the Rio Tinto, for just 40 miles (65 kilometres) upstream are the copper mines of São Domingos (see map). To this day the water is still contaminated by copper, a threat to the health of both people and wildlife in the region. Archaeological digs at the mine have found prehistoric tools, showing that the ores here were exploited more than 4,000 years ago.

The Rio Guadiana is navigable upriver for over 100 miles (160 kilometres) into the interior after Évora: the river continues past Badajoz to Cuidad Real and the romantic, gaunt and beautiful land of La Mancha.

During the past thirty-five years, the work of Spanish archaeologists in La Mancha has revealed what is probably the highest density of Bronze Age settlements in Europe. There are many massive stone complexes of large, permanent, fortified Bronze Age settlements. Their extent only became apparent after excavations had been carried out by the University of Granada in 1973. Survey work in Albacete has documented no fewer than 43 Bronze Age settlements and another 300 Bronze Age occupation sites. According to Dr Concepcion Martin:

> The concentration of surviving early 2nd millennium Bronze Age settlements in La Mancha has few parallels elsewhere in western Europe.

> Almost all our knowledge of the Bronze Age of La Mancha comes from recent excavations ... It is clear that La Mancha is a region

where many of the most important questions in European Bronze Age studies can be addressed.[13]

The La Mancha Bronze Age settlements date from about 2250 to 1500 BC – which fits in with the pattern of Minoan trading – with the Rio Tinto mines being worked for several hundred years, the miners later moving upriver and starting to farm on the Meseta, dotting the area with heavily fortified sites. As Dr Martin explains, the settlers in La Mancha coped with climatic uncertainties by practising relatively intensive agriculture.

The spectrographic analysis of bronzes from La Mancha sites show that they almost all consist of unalloyed copper of 96.9 per cent purity, with an arsenic content averaging 1.81 per cent. There is hardly any tin bronze. This arsenic content would have caused serious lung problems for the smelters.

Key to this argument is that ivory – which must have been sourced from Africa or India – has been found in excavation sites in the south of La Mancha. About 400 grams (14 ounces) of the material has emerged, mostly from buttons and bracelets: both raw, semi-worked up and as finished jewellery. It appears that ivory was worked up in La Mancha workshops – evidence of regular long-distance commerce. The well-defended, massively constructed settlements were also associated with new levels of intensive agriculture, of a more modern, Mediterranean character.

|||||||||||||||||||||||

The early Iberian settlements with either mining operations or the structures to defend them were at Los Millares – copper; Almizaraque – silver; El Barranquete – gold; El Tarajal – both gold and silver; and Las Pillas – gold (see map). At that stage the work was primitive, the copper pure.

One particular mining culture, the 'Los Millares' people, caught my eye, thanks to the research of W. Sheppard Baird. Their name is derived from a major copper mining settlement of perhaps 1,000 people, on a site that had been discovered in the 1890s as the authorities were building a railway at Almería. Little is known about the Millares culture, but it seems to have spread across the southeast of Spain and it possibly reached as far west as the red-limbed Rio Tinto. As W. Sheppard Baird states:

> ... When they [the Minoans] surveyed the river basins of Almería in south eastern Spain they found everything they were looking for. For several centuries they probably would have been satisfied to sift the alluvial sediments for metals and established settlements in the river basin areas. Eventually they would have moved up to the inland sources of the alluvial metals to form permanent mining settlements, and that's exactly what they did. By 3200 BC many of the towns of the Aegean Minoan colony (Los Millares culture) had been founded.[14]

The intriguing thing from my point of view was that a wholly new influence penetrated the Iberian culture around 1800 BC. The Millares people suddenly took a giant leap forward in copper metallurgy. They began smelting arsenical copper: I would infer that the Millares learned so quickly at this early stage as a direct result of early contact with the Minoans.

Then, in turn, a mysterious new people, the El Argar, quite suddenly took over from the Millares. Excitingly, the El Argar influence began early, around 1800 BC, but it then developed: in 1500 BC the El Argar people entered their so-called Phase B, at which point a detectable Aegean presence infiltrated the culture. New introductions included huge *pithoi* – vases like the ones I'd first seen on Crete and Thera.

Crucially, from my perspective, the El Argar were people who had substantial links to the outside world. I am convinced that the El Argar were in truth the Minoans and that the vast expanse of southern and central Spain and its rich mining territory became one of their many colonies.

There are many clues to a history of Minoan colonisation at Los Millares – and to a later Mycenaean influence. For instance, its cemeteries have *tholos* (beehive) tombs identical to the Minoan beehive tombs that are found on both southern Crete and on the central Mesara plain. The remains of pottery, ivory and ostrich eggshells also hint at a culture that had substantial contact – at the very least – with our Mediterranean traders.

Ivory, bronze and ostrich eggs – suddenly, they all connected in my mind. Lisbon is possibly my favourite port in the world and I had been there many times. Had I not also heard tell of similar treasures, found in the ancient fortress of São Pedro at the estuary of the Tagus?

|||||||||||||||||||||

Entering the Tagus estuary is an experience no sailor ever forgets – it's a truly magnificent natural harbour. The Tagus itself is a majestic river that knows no national boundaries. It strikes right through the heart of both Spain and Portugal, passing the magnificent, solitary splendour of Toledo, south of Madrid.

Vila Nova de São Pedro was a great Bronze Age fortress; built, archaeologists think, in a concentric style. It sat overlooking the Tagus estuary and was first excavated by the anthropologists H.N. Savory and Colonel do Paço.

To my delight, I discovered that there was a match, of a kind: São Pedro is completely contemporary with Los Millares. In his research papers, Savory draws parallels with the metalworking culture of the Los Millares late phase: 2430 BC. São Pedro's tombs did in fact contain exotic goods like ivory, alabaster and ostrich eggs – the classic signs of Minoan trading and influence. My memory had served me well. There was also evidence of a religious cult involving a female goddess – a deciding factor in Minoan religion.

Savory memorably describes the way in which c.2500 BC Vila Nova de São Pedro II had its own concentric fortifications. He makes analogies with Chalandria on Syros, another Minoan base in the Mediterranean, and his instinct seems to have been that the Early Bronze Age colonisation here came from the Mediterranean.

|||||||||||||||||||||

I was hatching a plan. At some point I was due to give a lecture at Salamanca University. Marcella and I should take advantage of the trip and investigate the Tagus and its path through Spain.

The Guadiana River (see map) would take us to Évora. Just west of there, close to the copper mines at São Domingos, was my target, the Bronze Age astronomical site of Almendres Cromlech. A sister site of Stonehenge in England, Almendres was fascinating to me partly because it is not exactly unique. The devil, as ever, is in the detail.

Almendres is interesting in the context of this quest primarily because of one thing: it was built at the precise latitude where the moon's maximum meridian altitude is the same as the latitude of the site – 38 degrees 33 minutes north. This means that when the moon is at its highest, its orb is directly above the observer on the ground.

The only other latitudes where this happens are at Stonehenge and Callanish, on the west coast of the isle of Lewis in the Outer Hebrides.

Scholars already agree that the stones of Almendres, like those of Stonehenge, mark where the sun rises and sets at the equinox. The first excavator to investigate Almendres was the archaeologist Luis Siret. The evidence he saw convinced him that the new 'El Argar' settlers in Iberia were civilised seagoing traders who sought ores and kept the natives in the dark when it came to the huge value of the substances they traded. In his early reports Siret also mentions that the settlers traded in and manufactured oriental painted vases in red, black and green pigments. As we know, the Minoans' absolute speciality was colourful pottery. Black and green are colours derived from copper. The settlers also brought objects such as alabaster and marble cups, as well as Egyptian-type flasks, amber from the Baltic and jet from Britain.

So: we have strong evidence of a new culture arriving in Iberia, a people who were interested in the raw resources of gold, tin, copper and silver, and there is a gathering weight of evidence that these people were the Minoans.

This was the crucial link. The Minoans needed to read the stars: without that, they couldn't navigate. Astronomical stone circles could have been used to determine latitude and longitude and the dates of the equinoxes and to predict the positions of the sun and the moon and their eclipses way into the future. What if the Minoans who'd worked or supervised the copper mines at São Domingos and perhaps elsewhere in Spain had also – somehow – been involved with the astronomical stone circles at Almendres?

||||||||||||||||||||

For now, though, there were plans to make. We flew to Madrid, with the aim of heading through Ávila and Zamora to Lisbon. *En route* we would try to find evidence of Minoan visits following the course of the Tagus, either in museums or at archaeological sites. I rang one of the professors at Salamanca for advice and was advised to take a look at Almendres. I was also given an intriguing fact: that the La Mancha Bronze Age had ended abruptly. The well-defended, massively constructed settlements came to a relatively sharp end about 1500 BC – at the time when Minoan Crete was also abruptly crushed by the Theran tsunami.

The Morra, Motilla and Castillejo settlements of La Mancha were suddenly abandoned – virtually all of the radiocarbon dated sites withered within a century of one another. I would later find out that Bronze Age mining ceased equally suddenly in Britain, Ireland and America at around the same time:1500 BC.

21

SPAIN AND LA TAUROMAQUIA

But we still had some time to spare in Madrid. I asked the professor: what should we do?

'Oh, go to the Prado. It's unmissable.'

Unmissable it certainly was. The Museo del Prado has one of Europe's most extraordinary collections of art. The collection once belonged to the Spanish royal family. We went through gallery after gallery of the most exquisite work – from *The Garden of Earthly Delights* by Hieronymus Bosch to Rubens' *The Three Graces* – very robustly fat, as he chose to show them. We thought what we'd seen could scarcely be bettered until, with sore feet and a desperate need for something wet to keep the energy up, we stopped for a cup of tea.

Marcella had a teacake and a fresh injection of blood sugar. While I sat, still stupefied by the weight of my aching feet and the sheer enormity of the Spanish kings' echoing palace, she began diligently researching what remained to be seen.

'I'm not convinced I can take any more culture,' I grumbled.

Marcella firmly piloted me towards a quiet but large room, where a number of silent students, charcoal in hand, were absorbed in sketching. The gallery had a hushed and reverent atmosphere and I soon understood why. The room houses an electrifying series of sketches by the romantic Spanish genius Francisco José de Goya y Lucientes.

Goya's 19th-century series of etchings, 'La Tauromaquia', is a mesmerising sequence of images that document the bullfighting stunts and techniques used in his time. In his pictures, matadors stand on tables, or even chairs. Dogs are used to bait the bull. You see *'encierros'*, where the bulls are let loose to run through the town. In one picture the matador is standing firm . . . while in another, he is pole-vaulting over the bull.

Sketch No. 90 is called: *The Agility and Audacity of Juanito Apiñani in [the ring] at Madrid*. The bold Apiñani is in the act of somersaulting backwards between the bull's horns, with the aid of a pole. The matador leaps over the bull's back, to land triumphantly behind its rear legs (see second colour plate section).

What was so familiar about this astonishing spectacle? It suddenly hit me where I'd seen it before – at the Minoan palace of Knossos. The fact that the image itself originally came from a miraculously long-lived fresco created sometime between the 17th and 15th centuries BC only made this all the more astonishing.

Was this a coincidence?

I thought not. Long ago in Medina, on the night before the Feast of the Assumption, I'd witnessed the extraordinary spectator sport of bull-leaping. Lately, I'd seen evidence of it again in Crete, southern India and Kerala. What I'd been witnessing – had I stopped to think about it – was a calling card. It had been sitting out the centuries, but it was there, written in the colourful script of the Minoans. This practice, I was sure, was a signature that the Minoans had left for us to read: those same Minoans who had probably first emerged from Çatalhöyük in southern Anatolia – possibly the world's first city and a place that the Minoans had perhaps first built. The evidence from Çatalhöyük shows that its people worshipped the bull; logic tells us that when they then reappeared in Crete the bull became central to their sacred festivals.

I'd found images showing the practice of bull-vaulting wherever I'd since speculated the Minoans had been; starting at Crete's palace of Knossos and voyaging all over the Near East to the Egyptian Nile Delta, then Syria, across the Aegean and all the way down to the south coast of Kerala in South India. The practice had also survived here in Spain, a popular inheritance that has lasted from the 3rd or early 2nd millennium BC to the present day.

189

The spreading cult of the bull was also backed up by a growing number of archaeological artefacts. Thanks to the 'Beyond Babylon' exhibition at the Metropolitan Museum of Art, I'd seen figures leaping the bull in Babylon, the image stamped clearly on a clay seal. In Athens' National Archaeological Museum is a bronze ring that shows a clean-shaven bull-leaper wearing a Minoan-style loincloth somersaulting on to the bull's back. His long hair flows in the air. Again, at Kahun in Egypt an image on a wooden box shows the leaper's epic dance against death. At Çorum in Turkey, a vase from an old Hittite settlement is decorated with thirteen figures gathered around the bull while once again the bull dancer plays out the dangerous game. In Antakya you will find a similar scene in a simple black and white drawing.

A distinct spring had come back into my step; all tiredness forgotten. What was not forgotten was an image that was still alive in my head. It was from the Archaeological Museum on Crete and to me it almost proved everything about my theory. Tiny, but telling: it was a Minoan medallion, about 6 centimetres (2.5 inches) wide, that I'd noticed in a cabinet towards the end of the rows of exhibits. It depicts a bull being led on to a ship.

'I've got gallery knees,' I announced, as we emerged into the wide avenues and blasting heat of Madrid. 'And museum legs.' But I wouldn't have missed the drawings I'd just seen for the world.

22

BLAZING THE TRAIL TO DOVER

Southern England: the 20th century AD. It was 1992 and workmen in Dover, England's busy passenger port, were digging an underpass to link with that wonder of modern transport technology, the Channel Tunnel.

As they dug down below what had been the debris of the medieval town – and then went even deeper, past the Roman layer – the men struck the perfectly preserved remains of a prehistoric ship. Downing tools, they stared in amazement. They knew, because of the depth at which they were working, that they were looking at something extraordinary. Gleaming in the narrow beams of their tungsten lights were the gnarled, blackened remains of a wooden ship.

Archaeologists mounted a rescue operation to record and salvage the timbers, cutting the boat into thirty-two pieces after carefully photographing and recording each piece. They were concerned that the ship, which had been preserved in the wet clay for thousands of years, would disintegrate into a puff of smoke once it reached dry air. So as they lifted the thirty-two sections by crane they placed them in a special container filled with preservative chemicals, itemising them meticulously so that they could be sure to replace the pieces according to the order in which they had been found.

This amazing rescue took just twenty-two days, a great tribute to all involved. Today the consensus is that the Dover Boat deserved all of its reverential treatment. The oaks that had made it had been cut down around 1500 BC. This boat was sailing long before Tutankhamun ruled in Egypt and at a time when ancient Britons were still using Stonehenge. Yet it is not just its great age that makes this ship remarkable. As one of the few pieces of complex technology from the Bronze Age that has survived almost intact, it tells us a great deal about the era; and Britain itself.

The boat is one of the oldest found in the world. What strikes the visitor instantly is the vessel's brute strength. Her timbers, although black with age, are perfectly preserved, glinting with what looks like a veneer of jet. The planks which form the hull were carved, rather than sawn, from whole tree trunks. It's what's called a 'sewn' boat; thongs bind the planks together, which were caulked with moss and beeswax.

The train from Victoria was running late that day and I could feel the anxiety of the other travellers as they thought about their delayed meetings, or missed connections at the port. Luckily, I didn't have any such time pressures. Looking at the soft-focus mist that was beginning to descend, I tried to project my thoughts back to the morning of 26 August 55 BC, when Julius Caesar arrived with his Roman invasion fleet. He came, he saw, but he didn't conquer. Nevertheless, by the 3rd century AD, when Dover's so-called 'Painted House' was built (alternatively known as the brothel), the town was a fully fledged Roman settlement. Even the ancient grass trackway, which became known as Watling Street, was paved over on its way to Canterbury.

So I paid the £2 ticket price for a round-trip bus ride and settled down to see 'Dubris', the town the Romans founded on the River Dour to defend their British interests. It was amazing to think how much must still be lying undiscovered underneath the ground, forever locked up by the mass of modern, Georgian or even medieval buildings that have been stuffed on top of Dover's Roman layer. No one had even known how much of it was here until the 1980s, when the town council dug up a car park and found a Roman fort. Up on the hill, Dover Castle looked down haughtily as I struggled to see the *Pharos*, or Roman lighthouse, through the gathering mist.

We got to the market square and I ambled off to see the boat itself, wondering what I would find. What I saw was, in some ways, a shock.

I thought back to the light-as-air ships of Thera's frescoes, greeted by diving swallows swooping around them; the crowds massing to see them as they arrived safe home from a major sea voyage. And then there was the steeplechaser that was the Uluburun. By comparison the British boat is an arthritic old carthorse. The Dover Boat had no rudder, mast or sails – all of the power came from rowers or paddlers. She also looked extremely heavy – more suited to the calm of a meandering river than the open sea. To view the Dover Boat please go to the second colour plate section.

And yet, says the ancient ship expert Peter Clark:

> We have archaeological evidence that contact [with Europe] took place by the early Bronze Age, so that it is generally accepted that there must have existed a capability for cross channel voyages and coastwise travel along the Atlantic seaboard, extending from Iberia, round Brittany to western England ... the scene changes from the early Bronze Age onwards, with the discovery of the examples of plank-built boats found to be widely distributed round the British coasts. Some of these might reasonably be believed to have had the ability to travel coastwise, or when conditions were favourable to make short sea crossings.[15]

According to English Heritage, the boat's conservers:

> ... The Langdon Bay hoard of bronze implements, largely of French origin, found by divers just east of Dover harbour – clearly lost in the wreck of a sea-going vessel and of middle Bronze Age date – is good enough evidence that there was routine traffic between Britain and mainland Europe at this period. The Dover boat provides convincing evidence of an actual vessel with appropriate capability.

Of course I don't doubt for a minute that cross-Channel trade took place in the Bronze Age. Dover to Boulogne is the shortest stretch of the English Channel; and many historical sources mention various forms of commerce crossing the seas. Pytheas the Greek describes the Cornish tin trade in some detail. The first person to realise that the tides were caused by the moon, Pytheas made his journey to Britain in the 4th century BC – but judging by the way he discusses the trade, it is clear that it had already been in existence for centuries. Cornish tin would have been a valuable prize: it is cassiterite tin, which is harder than other forms and twice as shiny. Cassiterite still prompts wars in the Congo, where it is now found. Ancient Britain had so much of it that the Phoenicians named the country 'the Cassiterides'. [16]

There is much more evidence of the roaring trade in tin. Bronze Age specialist Professor Barry Cunliffe describes divers recovering forty tin ingots from a wreck found at the mouth of the River Erme as it enters Bigbury Bay. Found within 26 metres (85 feet) of each other, all of the tin ingots were quite clearly cargo from a vessel which had foundered – perhaps near Portland Bill, well known as the Cape Horn of the English Channel. Several pieces of ancient timber were recovered in the same area and were carbon dated to more than 4000 BC – 'far too early for the tin trade', according to Cunliffe. But is 4000 BC really far too early? The dates when we assume international maritime trade was taking place are continuously being pushed back.

Whether the Bronze Age came to Britain in 4000 BC or in 2300 BC – the generally accepted date – we can say for sure that boats like this could have been carrying tin from Britain to Europe by 1500 BC, the date of the Dover Boat. But this boat had nowhere near the sophistication, strength or resilience of the Mediterranean ships shown on the Thera frescoes. The Dover ship's weight and inflexibility also meant she could carry far less cargo than the Uluburun or Theran ships and so she must have been far less suited to ocean-going trade.

The English Channel tides are strong, which, coupled with the funnelling effect of the French coast, means that in any wind short steep waves form – they are maybe as high as 2 to 2.5 metres (6 to 8 feet). This is known as the 'Channel Chop', and I can't imagine that the Dover Boat would have fared well against it.

A few short calculations gave me a picture. I imagined the Dover ship being paddled by sixteen strong sailors for five hours at 2 knots across the English Channel, with 3 tons of copper or tin on board – while four men furiously bailed out. With that amount of physical blood, sweat and tears, they could only have rowed for five hours a day. A ship like the Uluburun could have kept going for days on end, with more than four times the cargo capacity on a like for like basis: and without leaking.

The Uluburun sailors would also have lowered the ship's centre of gravity and increased stability by placing copper and tin ingots as ballast at the bottom of the hold, beside the keel. This would have reduced roll, pitch and sagging. Placing ingots low in the hull of the Dover ship would not have had the same effect. The weight of the planks higher up her hull would have made her comparatively top-heavy.

When it came to trading, the Bronze Age Brits faced world-beating competition. Had the Minoans seized that opportunity by the horns of their deity, the bull?

|||||||||||||||||||||

I settled down to delicious bacon and eggs in a handy 'greasy spoon' cafe, nose in book. It felt good to be reading the work of a Roman naval commander and author in a Roman city like Dover. I was beginning to catch up with my neglected classical education, and I was having to do that fast. There is a well-known but apparently much disputed passage in Pliny the Elder's writings, that concerns the history of the British:

> Next to be considered are the characteristics of lead, which is of two kinds, black and white. The most valuable is the white; the Greeks call it 'Cassiteros' and there is a fabulous story of its being searched for and carried from *the Islands of Atlantis* [my italics] in barks covered with lead ...

> Certainly it is obtained in Lusitania [Iberia] and Gallaecia [Brittany] on the surface of the earth, from black coloured sand. It is discovered

by its great weight, and it is mixed with small pebbles in the dried bed of torrents. The miners wash those sands and that which settles out, they heat in the furnace.[17]

So: 'Atlantis' again, but this time the connection is being made by a Roman, not the Greeks. By the early years of the 1st century AD, Pliny seemed to have identified 'Atlantis' as both the past and the present source of the tin being shipped into the Mediterranean.

Minoan seafarers in search of those precious Bronze Age metals would have had to turn north towards Britain and cross the notorious Bay of Biscay in their markedly superior boats. One long 310-mile (500-kilometre) lee shore, the Bay stretches along the northern coast of Spain and around the western coast of France. The crews of the sailing ships of old had a great fear of being driven ashore here – or worse, wrecked – by a westerly gale. Biscay is notoriously stormy. Many mariners have run before the Atlantic's driving currents and ferocious gales, only to founder when they struck the Bay's vicious reefs and its shallower coastal shelf. June and July are the best months to cross: it is important for our seafarers to sail before the middle of August, to avoid the first autumn storms.

Even when sailing the relatively placid Mediterranean, it would have been foolhardy to travel before the beginning of May, after which the Mediterranean winter gales should have ceased. That should mean reaching the Straits around late August. Over-wintering in Sanlúcar, the Minoans could have repaired any broken steering oars and sails and careened the ship to remove barnacles from the hull.

Let's imagine a sophisticated band of travellers, the Minoan seafarers. A hardy bunch of persuasive, charming and determined people, they are wily and well travelled. From what we'd seen on the frescoes, they are also lively company and extremely good-looking into the bargain. Their metallurgical know-how is unrivalled, in a society that values metals, and magic, above all things.

They have one goal in mind: riches. They need to find precious metals, make successful trade deals, and return to Phaestos, Knossos or Thera as rich men, bearing the raw materials that drove the most advanced technology of the entire age: copper and tin.

Each member of the crew is a hero. He has seen the wonders of the world, and will return to his people bearing the future in his hands – or within the hold of his ship.

23

THE LAND OF RUNNING SILVER

The early Greek historian Diodorus Siculus called Britain 'the bright country'. And indeed, Cornwall, the first part of Britain any seafarer striking from Portugal through France is likely to hit, does have a remarkable quality of light. But I think Diodorus' description is more likely to have been inspired by the sparkling richness of the country's metals. This was an island where the sun set in a blaze of tin, copper and gold.

After I'd gone to see the Dover Boat, and satisfied myself that foreign traders had little to fear from native competition, Marcella and I decided to make a week of it. We hired a cottage on the Cornish coast near St Mawes. From here we could explore the Carnon River, which in the Bronze Age almost ran with sparkling, silver-coloured tin ore.

For once we found that the subject was not controversial. English people in general, and Cornishmen in particular, readily accept that in the Bronze Age foreign sailors came from the eastern Mediterranean to mine tin. The usual date being given was around 2000 BC.

In fact, all sorts of folk memories have grown up around the export of the ore. The brasswork in King Solomon's Temple is said to have been made from Cornish tin, and an old legend has it that Christ himself visited Cornwall with his merchant uncle Joseph of Arimathea, who came to buy precious ores.

Much of Cornwall's bedrock is granite. As this cooled many millions of years ago, fissures and cracks opened up when the granite was still molten and hot rock from the earth's core bubbled up through the cracks. As these new rocks crystallised, they formed mineral lodes – tin, copper, zinc, lead and iron, with a little silver. Because the ore-bearing rocks came from vertical cracks, they had to be mined vertically – straight down into the earth.

Streams often ran across the tin deposits and sometimes sliced through them. Tin, being so heavy, was often left on the stream bed. In this part of Cornwall evidence of Bronze Age mining is everywhere, even to the body of a poor Bronze Age miner found at Perranarworthal.

The richest area of all in those days was the Fal Estuary (see map) and particularly the rivers to the west of it; notably the Carnon River, which was navigable throughout the Bronze Age, upstream as far as Twelveheads.

Another crucial factor that would have made Britain highly attractive to the Minoans was its incredible woodlands – as well as the type of wood that grew. From the air, Britain would have looked almost as the Amazon jungle does today: a mass of vital, living green, punctuated with the chattering rivers that shone with glittering grains of tin ore.

The mighty hornbeams, feathery oaks and majestic beeches and willows of Britain all respond well to pollarding and coppicing (cutting off young tree stems close to the ground). Much like a good haircut, cutting the wood short does two things. Firstly, it makes the tree healthier, so it lives longer. Secondly, it makes it grow more branches and produce more wood, a substance that is vital, as we already know, for the smelting process. Wood, as the *Epic of Gilgamesh* implies, was already becoming a scarce resource in the wider Mediterranean.

Why should we believe it was the Minoans, rather than the Phoenicians of a later time, who reached Britain and began to exploit its resources? Partly because of the great Akkadian Emperor Sargon I, 'the Magnificent', who lived around 2333–2279 BC. He commissioned a 'road-tablet', which recorded the mileage and geography of the roads through his vast Mesopotamian empire. A copy of it, made by an official scribe in 8 BC, was found at the Assyrian capital of Assur.

The tablet details 'The land of Gutium' and 'tin-land country, which lies beyond the upper sea (or Mediterranean) ... '.[18]

This latter reference was translated slightly differently by a former Oxford professor of Assyrian studies, Professor Sayce. His version reads: 'To the tin-land (Kuga-Ki) and Kaptara (Caphtor, Crete), countries beyond the upper sea (the Mediterranean).' In other words, his translation links the 'tin land' and ancient Crete together.[19]

There's another link in the evidence we should bear in mind. Why was there a sudden switch in Britain from copper axes to bronze ones between 2800 and 2500 BC? And why, around 2200 BC, did the tin content of British axes suddenly leap from virtually zero to 10 or 11 per cent? This date coincides neatly with the height of the Minoan trading empire, which I now propose was well under way. As Professor Cyrus Gordon wrote: 'The existence of an ancient formidable commercial network of which the Mediterranean Sea was the epicentre is being revealed.'[20] The Minoans had the technology: fast, sail-driven, ocean-going ships and the knowledge to navigate them. They also had the all-important know-how, when it came to smelting and processing their finds, and the advanced technical and design skills necessary to forge beautiful objects in metal. They had an insatiable thirst for bronze, the wondrous material that was helping their culture become the world's most advanced, in the process turning the Minoans of the ancient Mediterranean into some of the wealthiest and most powerful citizens of the known world.

The Minoans would have been drawn to Britain by the lure of rivers running with tin. They would have been unlikely to meet with much local competition. Imagine their jubilation when they discovered that another great prize was also here: copper.

24

A LABYRINTH IN DRAGON COUNTRY

Any ship sailing north from Cornwall's tin mines up the St George's Channel would have noticed a handsome group of mountain peaks near what we now call Caernarvon (Caernarfon), in northwest Wales. The curious mariner might then have turned eastwards into Colwyn Bay on reaching Carmel Head (see map), to investigate. This is what I believe happened in the Middle Bronze Age around 2500 BC, when the first Minoan explorers, having gathered a load of Cornish tin, pushed north to explore further.

Before the age of the dinosaurs this rocky foreshore was a tropical seabed. The huge carboniferous limestone headland of today began forming about 300 million years ago. Stone Age man would almost certainly have shared the Orme with mammoth, lions and the woolly rhinoceros, but archaeologists don't know for certain when *Homo sapiens* first arrived on the headland.

Many thousands of years later, two mining enthusiasts were investigating 19th-century mine workings. Wales is famous for mineral exploitation on an industrial scale in that century. But what Andy Lewis and Eric Roberts came across instead was a spectacular warren of copper mines that didn't conform to either 18th- or 19th-century mining practices.

Worried about exploring too far underground without taking safety precautions, they managed to get the local council to agree to do a survey. What that survey found shocked everyone, including themselves. A labyrinth.

Beneath their feet was a maze of prehistoric mine workings that extended into a dense warren of shafts, tunnels and side-chambers.

The dark, buried passages and chambers were immeasurably old, not at all like the shallow-cast pre-Victorian mining the Welshmen had been expecting. Quite by accident, Lewis and Roberts had unearthed the enormous Great Orme Bronze Age copper mine.

The Great Orme Exploration Society meets every Thursday night in the King's Head in Llandudno. So today you can visit them and drink a fine pint of bitter to Lewis and Roberts and those ancient pioneers who opened up the land, and the world, to a shining past: a technological age we had scarcely dreamed of.

I visited the site in late spring. It is an easy journey from London: first flat out to Warrington and then taking a leisurely local train westwards along the beautiful Flint and Denbigh coasts for another hour and a half. To the south lay the intriguing snow-capped peaks our Minoan mariners would have sighted; to the north a succession of shallow bays where they could have beached their craft. Today the coastline is a mixture of caravan sites, oil refineries and field upon field of Wales' ubiquitous sheep.

The terminus for my journey was the genteel yachting town of Llandudno. The Great Orme mine is halfway up Llandudno's 'peak', which is reached by a cable car and a tram that connects the town to the summit. It would be a spectacular and healthy walk up to the very top, where the Telegraph Inn was once the vital communications link between Holyhead and the busy global trading port of Liverpool, advising of the imminent arrival of sailing ships laden with valuable cargo. Still, I cheat and take the charming, stubby little blue-painted tram, which drops me off at an unassuming group of low, white-walled buildings – and puddles of grit and mud.

Inside the Great Orme mine one's first reaction is incredulity. If you were to draw a cut-through diagram of this place, its tunnels would look like the branches of a vast spreading oak tree, stretching right through the entire hill. The complex is different to anything I have ever seen – it's almost as if you are entering a huge subterranean sponge or ants' nest, where humans would have crawled down into the tunnels, crevices and fissures, steep shafts and side chambers. Some of the tunnels are so narrow that it seems that all those thousands of years ago only children could have excavated them. What a Herculean task it must have been.

Judging by the archaeological evidence, the first miners used antlers and shoulder blades to scoop out the ore before it was hauled to the surface by a system of ladders and windings. Once above ground, the copper ore was pulverised with stones. They were the shape and size of ostrich eggs. Usually coloured a rich cobalt blue, the ore was smashed out and then heated in a heaped crucible, using a pair of bellows surmounted by a pile of charcoal.

The liquid copper could then simply be poured into the mould as required – the process was as easy as that. When cooled, the copper could be worked in its own right, or it could be mixed with molten Cornish tin to create the all-important alloy of hard bronze. The end product – whether axe, knife or sword – was either hand-beaten or shaped by clay moulds. Sharp weapons and tools could be made stronger and more flexible by beating them after the initial moulding.

So here in north Wales we have the first industrial process in Britain, which started 4,500 years ago – a date determined by the carbon found in the charcoal residue here. Could this operation possibly have reached this level of sophistication so fast without the input of outsiders?

The origin of the word 'Orme' is lost to history, although we do know that many centuries later the Norsemen often used the term to refer to dragons, or 'worms'. From the sea, the great headland could indeed have looked like a sea serpent as it stretched its neck out into the waters. Perhaps the idea reflected exactly how much treasure lay guarded in the bowels of the earth.

For this was a hoard indeed. Mining engineers have calculated that 1,700 tons of copper must have been extracted from these ancient mines. That is enough to make more than ten million axes – three for each man, woman and child who then lived in Great Britain.

Alternatively, look at it this way. The copper could have supplied enough bronze for three million saws. Enough for the pyramid builders, 2,000 miles (3,210 kilometres) away in Saqqara, ancient Egypt.

TECHNIQUES WITH BRONZE AND COPPER

Professor R.F. Tylecote of Durham University describes the process of pouring copper or bronze into moulds to make bronze tools and weapons. He begins with the basic problems of casting. First, when metals are heated in solid fuel furnaces they absorb gases from the fuel – wood, in the case of the Bronze Age. Of these gases, by far the most troublesome is water vapour, which dissolves in contact with the metal into copper oxide and hydrogen. The hydrogen enters the liquid metal and stays dissolved until the metal cools and begins to solidify, when it emerges as gas bubbles which spoil the casting.

This problem can be alleviated by giving the gas plenty of time to rise to the top of the molten metal – that is by cooling the liquid metal slowly. That is easier if you are making a large amount of alloyed metal at one time.

Another problem is shrinkage, which occurs as the metal cools and contracts, causing cracks and cavities in the casting. These cracks can be filled by pouring in more liquid metal from the feeder. In a thin section like a sword or a socketed axe, a washer was removed and the sides of the casting mould were moved slightly together as the metal cooled. The majority of Bronze Age castings were of this type. The density of the cast object can be increased, and cracks reduced, by hammering the metal after the casting – this was done in the case of flat copper axes, principally to harden their cutting edges.

The better the mould, the sharper the axe. By the early Bronze Age, stone moulds were used. There was little variation in this type of manufacture. Moulds were cut from blocks of stone, with cavities for two or more axes, the moulds being closed together with a flat removable washer or gasket between the two. That would be withdrawn as the metal started to cool. In the early Bronze Age, most of the stone for the moulds came from the Pennines, a mountain chain in the north of England.[21]

The whole experience resonates in my mind as I return to the hotel for a quick wash and brush-up, followed by a snifter at the bar. A fascinating picture of prehistoric Britain is coming to life in my mind: a society with a level of industrialisation and organisation that is astounding. This is not anything like how we tend to think of ancient Britain: perhaps we need to think again.

The copper ore is mined in Wales, the tin in Cornwall. The axes are made in north Wales from smelted metal, using local charcoal. Casting is done with hard limestone from the north of England. The large numbers of new bronze-workers eat locally farmed Welsh cattle and lamb; clothiers and shoemakers use the hides. All of these workers need bread and the best corn lands are in the dry, sunny east of England. Woods and forests there are cut down, using brand new Welsh axes. The grain is then transported by ships constructed from crude planks made from the swaying trees of eastern England – which are taller and thicker than wind-blown Welsh trees.

At the mine itself, the dendrochronology (tree-ring dating) of the charcoal shows that the miners used standard-sized, pollarded branches. So we now have yet more groups of workers at Great Orme – not just miners, but foresters, charcoal-makers and a host of other tradespeople; huge numbers must have been involved. The miners used antlers and bones for their digging – these animals had to be hunted. Their skins were stretched and dried to make leather clothes and shoes – which means leather-workers, clothiers and shoesmiths. More and more men kept their hair tidy and shaved with bronze razors; they also used copper eyelets to tie up their clothes and button their shoes. Copper from the mine then began to be hammered into decorative ornaments and jewellery, as locals became more wealthy.

For the Minoans and their budding empire, Britain would have been like a treasure trove. It was a treasure trove, moreover, that gave them a jumping-off point for the whole of northern Europe. Perhaps even further.

That tell-tale prickling of excitement was in my veins again. I was going to track my Bronze Age pioneers even further, if I could. Another sea voyage of my own beckoned.

25

STRANGE BEASTS AND ASTROLABES

The dead of night: Saxony-Anhalt, northern Germany: 1999. Two hundred miles (322 kilometres) away from here, at the amber-trading city of Rungholt, is the very place where Hans Peter Duerr had found his Bronze Age Minoan cooking pots and had concluded that the Minoans had been sailing here – routinely.

Three black-clad figures were combing through a deep forest at Nebra, with illicit metal detectors.

After several cold, dark hours of scanning the forest floor, the men found themselves in a small clearing near a hill. Suddenly their detectors came alive. That high-pitched whine meant metal – lots of it. They tore into the earth with pickaxes. After a brief struggle that earth gave way – and yielded up a treasure it had kept safe for more than 3,000 years.

Carefully, one of the men picked a strange, flat object out of the hole and delicately brushed it free of the clinging forest loam. What was it? Pocked and covered with a green-bronze sheen, in his hands lay something that looked strange, almost magical.

A bronze disc 30 centimetres across; its surface inlaid with gold. Even in the moonlight, the men could see that they had found something special; something that drew an incredibly vivid image of the heavens. You can view the disc in the second colour plate section.

The sun – or possibly a full moon – faces a crescent moon. The two images are divided by what seem to be stars. The surface of both the sun and the moon are pockmarked with metal corrosion, making them look eerily realistic as if their real, crater-ridden counterparts had been studied through a telescope. A boat navigates the sea beneath. To a traveller the boat design seems similar to the barge of the Egyptian sun god, Ra.

This object is unique. Nothing like it has ever been seen before. We now know it as the 'Nebra Sky Disk'.

A few years later, the Nebra Disk was rumoured to be circulating the black market with a price-tag of a quarter of a million pounds. Unauthorised digging of archaeological finds is a crime in Germany. In an elaborate sting operation dreamt up by Harald Meller, who had just been appointed head archaeologist at the nearby museum of Halle, the looters were caught in a hotel – and the Disk was rescued.

Meller was the hero of the hour. He had won the Disk for posterity – and for his museum. When he finally got his find back to the calm and quiet of his office, he must have smiled in relief, and then thought: 'After that huge struggle to get hold of it – now what?'

What exactly had they won? Was it an astronomical device? The surface of the mysterious Disk was a mass of symbols. Were these just random images, or did they mean something more? The astronomer Professor Wolfhard Schlosser, of the University of the Ruhr, was called in to try to verify if these symbols might in fact represent heavenly bodies – the constellations.

Could northern Europeans have been advanced enough in the Bronze Age to have mapped out the stars? If not, the Disk's existence supported my theory that the Minoans had been here – and that they had had access to knowledge at least the equal of that of the Babylonians. Professor Schlosser's first move was to isolate the largest group of 'stars'.

The 'star' marks were spread out in a pattern across the object's surface. The professor ran them against a recognised computer programme to see if they would match with the stars in the night sky, first in the northern hemisphere and then in the southern. But there were no matches. These dots, it seemed, were just decoration.

Then the professor looked at the small cluster of seven stars in the middle of the Disk, right between the circles that might represent the sun and the moon. They seemed to form a distinct pattern. Could that be a constellation?

Professor Schlosser quickly realised that the cluster resembled one above all others: the Pleiades. The ancients thought there were only seven stars in the cluster. To them it was one of the most beautiful in the night sky. Significantly, in the mythology of the ancient world, where the greats literally became stars, it was celebrated for being made up of the seven daughters of one of the great Titans. His name was Atlas.

Today we know that the Pleiades is made up of eleven main stars, but only some of them are easily visible to the naked eye. So Schlosser turned to the oldest images of the Pleiades that he could find: tablets and scrolls from the East. And there he saw a wonder: the Pleiades, drawn with just seven stars. An image just like that on the Disk.[22]

The Nebra Disk had been found buried with a trove of bronze artefacts: two bronze swords, two hatchets, a chisel and fragments of twisted metal bracelets. Although the swords themselves look to be of German design, their metal content is not. Analysis found that the gold was from the Carnon River, where Marcella and I had been staying in Cornwall. The tin content of the bronze was also from Cornwall. If the swords were in fact made at the same time, they dated the Disk to c.1600 BC.

Two golden arcs run along the sides of the Nebra Disk: they appear to have been added later. Those mysterious arcs tell another story, but to relate it we need to travel a few miles further, to the Saale valley.

High on a plateau overlooking the valley, just 15 miles (25 kilometres) away from where the Nebra Disk was first found, is the tiny hamlet of Goseck. Here is another hidden treasure, one which was only discovered by chance in 1991, by aerial reconnaissance. A large, double concentric ring of post holes, pierced by gates and surrounded by a circular ditch. Again, as a specialist in astro-archaeology, Wolfhard Schlosser was called in to investigate.

The first clue as to the function of this new discovery was the fact that the gate leading into the Goseck circle's wooden palisade is precisely aligned with north. The site was positioned to observe the movements of the sun, the moon and the stars and for keeping track of time. The southern gates marked the sunrise and sunset of the winter and summer solstices.

Schlosser believes that the Nebra Disk and the circle are connected and that the constellation patterns on the Disk were based on previous astrological observations, possibly made over a period of time at Goseck. The two golden arcs that were added to the Disk, he reasoned, must also mark the winter and summer solstices. Spanning an angle of 82 degrees, the arcs mark the same angle that occurs between the positions of sunset at the summer and winter solstice at the latitude of this area, Mittelberg (51.3 degrees north).

I think that the Nebra Disk is a device that links the sun's movement with that of the moon. What use would the people here in Saxony – whoever they were, whether locals or visiting travellers – have put that knowledge to? Well, the very name 'the Pleiades' is from the same root as the Greek word *pleio*: 'to sail'. We now know that in ancient times, the Pleiades' heliacal rising was used to predict the time that ships could set sail from the Mediterranean: from early May to early November.[23]

Needless to say, I believe that the device must have been brought here by the only people who had this sophisticated understanding of the skies, the Minoans. Hans Peter Duerr's experience is proof of the Bronze Age Minoans' journeys to this area. The only people who had the reason to be here – in this case probably bartering their precious bronze for the sumptuous prize of Baltic amber – were the Minoans.

What reason could they have had to create the Nebra Disk? Why, for example, would it have been found so close to an ancient wooden circle aligned with the stars? I am convinced that this is no accident. This beautiful little object, like the extraordinarily intricate gold seals found on Crete, has in fact a highly practical purpose.

I am sure the Disk was used, perhaps in ceremonial fashion, as an aid in navigation.

There was now a huge, and to tell the truth somewhat overwhelming, question hovering in my mind. Almendres; the circle here at Goseck; the one near the Red Sea; the one in Kerala; and even Stonehenge. Why did stone and wood henges keep cropping up on my trail? I could no longer avoid the moment. It was now imperative for me to explore one of the world's most ancient mysteries: the ceremonial stone circle.

Notes to Book III

1. Philip P. Betancourt, *The Chrysokamino Metallurgy Workshop and its Territory*, A.S.C.S.A, 2006
2. Gerald Cadogan, *Palaces of Minoan Crete*, Routledge, 1991
3. K. Aslihan Yener. 'An Early Bronze Age Age Tin Production Site at Goltepe, Turkey', The Oriental Institute and the Department of Near Eastern Languages and Civilizations, University of Chicago, 2007
4. Richard Cowen, UC Davis
5. C. H. W. Johns, *Babylonian and Assyrian Laws, Contracts and Letters*, 1904. Project Gutenberg (www.gutenberg.org/ebooks/28674)
6. Richard Cowen, UC Davis
7. Theodore A. Wertime. 'Man's First Encounters with Metallurgy' in *Science* 25, December 1964, vol. 146, no. 3652, p. 1664
8. Oliver Rackham, *The Illustrated History of the Countryside*, J. M. Dent, 1996
9. Rodney Castleden, *Minoans*
10. The Thera Foundation (www. therafoundation.org)
11. F. Nocete, 'The smelting quarter of Valencia de la Concepción (Seville, Spain): the specialised copper industry in a political centre of the Guadalquivir Valley during the Third millenium B.C. (2750–2500 B.C.)', *Journal of Archaeological Science*, 35:3
12. Mark A., Hunt Ortiz, *Prehistoric Mining and Metallurgy in South West Iberian Peninsula*, Archaeopress, 2003
13. Concepcion Martin et al. 'The Bronze Age of La Mancha' JSTOR
14. W. Sheppard Baird, 2007 (www.minoanatlantis.com)
15. Edward Wright, in *The Dover Boat*, ed. Peter Clarke, English Heritage, 2004, p. 261

16. Barry Cunliffe, *The Extraordinary Voyage of Pytheas the Greek – The Man Who Discovered Britain*, Walker & Company, 2002
17. Pliny XXXIV, 47, Harvard Classics
18. In *Keilschrifttexte aus Assur verschiedenen inhalts* 1920, no. 92, trans. Professor Waddell
19. A. Sayce, *The Religions of Ancient Egypt and Babylon*, 1902, p. 3. Project Gutenberg (www.gutenberg.org/ebooks/35856)
20. Cyrus Gordon, *Before Columbus; Links Between the Old World and Ancient America*, Crown Publishers, 1971, p. 81
21. R.F. Tylecote, *The Prehistory of Metallurgy in the British Isles*, Institute of Metals, 1986
22. Schlosser, W. (2002), 'Sur astronomischen Deutung der Himmelsschiebe von Nebra', *Archäologic in Saschsen-Anhalt* 1/02: 21–30.//E. and C-H Pernicka, 'Naturwissenschaftliche Untersuchungen an den Funden von Nebra', *Archäologic in Saschsen-Anhalt* 1/02: 24–29
23. Theophrastus of Eresus, *On Weather Signs*, Brill, 2006 pp. 29, 43

BOOK IV

|||||||||||||||||||||||||||||||||||||

EXAMINING THE HEAVENS

26

SEEING THE SKIES IN STONE ...

A visit once again to Egypt: the majestic and formidable Minoan ally, and a cultural lynchpin of the era. Egypt was my next logical step in following the trail of ancient knowledge around the world. This is because the oldest stone circle on the globe lies on the Upper Nile.

The stone circle at Nabta was begun in the 5th millennium BC. I sensed that as privileged guests in Egypt, the Minoans might well have been able to study the Nabta site. I knew little about Europe's oldest astronomical observatory at Gosek, 200 miles (322 kilometres) up the Elbe, and the Nebra Disk found so close to it. Neither could I rely on written research, or much in the way of expert help: Gosek has been little studied. But Gosek and the Nebra Disk seemed to be pushing me towards a solution that was obvious enough to be staring me in the face.

A pattern was emerging. Wherever the Minoans had travelled, a stone or wooden circle seems to have appeared. Was this idea too improbable? I decided to follow my instincts and research the oldest stone circle in the world, to uncover the truth.

|||||||||||||||||||

I am convinced that the Minoans' drive to travel was supported by their astounding grasp of navigation. But to navigate you need reliable calculations about the stars – and that information needs to relate to your precise location on the globe. How did they obtain such information? Like many others, I strongly suspected that stone circles were built for astronomical as well as ceremonial purposes and that they were used for far more than predicting the seasons. I was convinced that the Minoans needed to build on the astronomical and navigational knowledge they had already gained from Babylon. The only way they could do that was to create their own observatories by building, or perhaps adapting, suitable structures. Stone circles.

At the edge of the Western Desert, 500 miles (800 kilometres) south of Cairo, near the border between modern Egypt and Sudan, lies the flat, arid bed of an ancient dried-up lake. It is a desolate spot between the desert springs of Bir Kiseiba and the shores of Lake Nasser, and about as far away from civilisation as you will ever find. Dust is everywhere: in summer the wind roars over the nearby sandy ridge. Once this place was green and lush, a seasonal lake filled by the summer rains. Now the land is a barren sea of sand, and the heat is crushing.

A millennium before the beginning of the Egyptian 1st Dynasty, nomadic tribespeople – cattle herders who normally roamed wide over the Sahara with their livestock – would congregate here with the arrival of those all-important rains. They slaughtered some of their precious cattle as a sacrifice of thanks.

Nabta Playa, as it is now known, has forced Egyptologists to rethink their theories about Egypt's origins. It was an enigma: a totally unexpected stone circle set in one of the world's most isolated spots, until a trunk road was put in to allow construction traffic to reach Egypt's New Valley Project. About 62 miles (100 kilometres) west of here are the colossal Nubian rock monuments of Abu Simbel, imposing huge sculpted figures that are now part of a World Heritage Site. The impressive statues were relocated by the authorities in the 1960s, to accommodate a new dam on the Nile.

Nabta, on the other hand, has remained exactly where it stands today. It seems as old as the sky. As Toby Wilkinson writes, all the signs are that the first peoples who lived here c.7000–6000 BC were much more sophisticated than their contemporaries in the Nile valley. They built both above and below ground, they had planned settlements and they may even have imported their livestock from southeast Asia.[1] Greater Egypt would of course later catch them up.

Scattered through the moon-like landscape at Nabta are carefully placed stone megaliths: sentinels standing guard on the horizon. An oval ring of strange, humpback stones surrounds a group of uprights, mostly at differing heights. At the centre, two pairs of stones point north–south. Another pair is also pointing towards the midsummer sunrise. Why are the stones here? The answer is unavoidable, once you look at a map. The stone circle, built in the 5th millennium BC, is positioned exactly on the Tropic of Cancer.

The Tropic of Cancer is a latitude line that circles the earth. On this latitude, every year at the time of the midsummer solstice, the noon sun at its zenith hangs directly overhead. In other words, this is a very special place on the planet, a fact that the ancient Egyptians must have understood perfectly well. As at the far more rudimentary Goseck, the only logical conclusion is that Nabta must have been an astronomical observatory, that every June was used to prepare for the rains and watch the stars – perhaps even use them as a guide for global voyages.

Nabta's stone circle is far smaller than later observatories like Stonehenge. The first phase of development here began around 4800 BC. Later, between 4500 to 3600 BC, megaliths were dragged into new places – and aligned with Sirius, Arcturus, Alpha Centauri and the Belt of Orion. As the skies changed, more stelae were rearranged to align with the brightest stars like Kochab, in the constellation known as Ursa Minor: the Little Bear.

The 12-foot circle of stone holds four pairs of taller stones aligned opposite one another. As the sun rose on the summer solstice, when it was at its furthest apparent northerly position, the great burning orb would appear like a sudden omen through the two sets of standing sentinel stones. In other words, the stones are a window into time, marking the passage of the seasons. There were two sets of alignments – cardinal (north–south) and solar. This was all that was needed to mark the passage of the year in Bronze Age Egypt.

Because the circle is set exactly on the Tropic of Cancer, there would be no shadow cast by the stones at midday on the summer solstice. Moreover, this would happen at a time when day and night were the same length: twelve hours. The astronomers at Nabta must have realised that this phenomenon was caused by the earth rotating on its axis once every twenty-four hours, and on a repeating annual cycle. They would also have noticed that at sunset each day after the midsummer solstice, a different star to that of the day before rose on the eastern horizon.

In short, using this observatory you could work out that the sun, the earth and the stars were governed by different rules – the earth rotated once every twenty-four hours, while the stars moved independently of the earth and the sun.

Observers watching the stones' shadows would have noted the change as those shadows grew longer and longer throughout the six months that preceded midwinter. Then they started to shorten again until midsummer, when they disappeared. As the shadows lengthened, the sun grew cooler – because it was further away. Yet at sunset, different stars still appeared in the east each day. This would have led to the realisation that the earth and the sun were nearest to each other at midsummer and furthest away at midwinter. The observers would have worked out that midsummer appeared after 366 sunrises and the earth rotated every twenty-four hours, and would have deduced that either the earth circled the sun or the sun circled the earth.

This scientific examination of the heavens told the people the correct times to sow crops – when the Nile flood was nearly due – and when to harvest, when the floods should have peaked and passed. The Egyptian farmer, the *fellahin*, could merely plant and wait. Surely this shows that in 4500 BC Egyptian astronomy was among the world's most advanced? The Egyptians knew they could establish true north by examining a star within the Little Bear constellation, Ursa Minor. It was called Kochab, and it was then the pole star. We know they understood this because the Giza pyramids were also aligned with Kochab.

The astrophysicist Thomas G. Brophy suggests that the prehistoric stargazers who built the Nabta stone circle must have known a great deal more about the heavens than we assume. One of the stone 'doorways', he points out, is aligned north–south – this seems reasonable, because it aligns with Kochab's position. Brophy further suggests that the six central stones inside the circle represent the three stars of Orion's belt (the southerly line), while the northerly line of three stones stands for the three stars that defined the shoulders and head of Orion, as they then appeared in the night sky. These correspondences were for two dates, c.4800 BC and at precessional opposition.

In short, if Brophy is correct, the Egyptians must have worked out the long-term precessional 26,000-year pattern caused by the wobble in the earth's axis by 4800 BC. This change is what makes the night skies look different over time – and is the reason why we don't see the exact same patterns in the stars as the ancients saw. (It is also why all astrology, which fails to take account of precession, is bunk.)

Over vast periods of time – 26,000 years, to be precise – the night skies transform themselves into bewitching new patterns. This happens because the earth is slightly fatter at the equator: as it rotates it acts like a spinning top, changing posture in its ever-so-slow ellipse around the sun. The dance takes 13,000 years to complete and as our own position changes, so does the position of the stars we see. Today, true north is determined by the star Polaris. In another 13,000 years this inevitable process will bring a new star into the position of true north. Then it will be the bright little Vega, in the constellation Lyra. In 26,000 years' time, the cycle will be over and Polaris will once again be the North Star. It's a humbling realisation. This ancient site in the Nubian desert tells the story of a 'primitive' people who knew far more about the earth than the average university student does today.

Nabta's sacred landscape is also dotted with peculiar mounds, marked out with round, flat stones. Under one of them, in an underground chamber, a huge sandstone monolith was found. It is possibly the first monumental sculpture ever made in Egypt. The stone is carefully shaped and dressed to look like a wild beast: the unmistakable figure of a bull. I can't help but make a mental connection with the Minoans.

Their status as privileged guests in Egypt – as we know from the royal palace at Tell el Dab'a – would have meant that if they did not already have this astrological knowledge they would have been privy to the Egyptians' knowledge of the heavens. Moreover the Egyptians were in their debt, because they were reliant on the Minoans for their bronze and their tools.

By the time the Minoans reached the Upper Nile in King Amenemhat II's reign (1919–1885 BC) they could also have acquired much Babylonian astronomical knowledge, and might have been in a position to trade bronze finished goods with the Egyptians in return for that knowledge.

IIIIIIIIIIIIIIIIIIIII

I was beginning to suspect that the Minoans used their understanding of Nabta to alter and improve upon other rudimentary stone circles they found on their voyages. These already existed, but had probably been built for different purposes.

There is an unmistakable pattern of observatories being found near mineral mines around both the Mediterranean and the Atlantic coastlines (see map). All were built between 4000 BC and 2500 BC:

- *Malta*
- *Sicily*
- *Portugal*
- *Brittany*
- *Ireland*
- *Britain*
- *Hebrides*
- *Orkney Islands*

All of these stone observatories were based on the same principles – and were built using the same system of measurements. They also had the same goals: to record astronomical events such as sunrise and sunset at equinoxes or solstices, the moon's meridian passage, solar and lunar eclipses and occasionally the rising and setting of Venus.

In order to reach Nabta, the world's very first stone observatory, the Minoans would have had to sail up the Nile: a round trip of nearly 1,000 miles (1,600 kilometres). Would this have been feasible? We know from Egyptian records that the pharaohs of the Middle Kingdom built locks to tame the cataracts and rapids of Aswan, so the journey to Nabta by river could have been possible. We can say for sure that the Minoans reached the Valley of the Kings, which lies three-quarters of the way to Nabta.

We know this because there are numerous Egyptian records describing Cretans bringing gifts to the pharaohs, whose court was then in the Valley of the Kings. Further evidence that the Minoans had travelled as far as Luxor, ancient Thebes, had come in the form of my old friend the American tobacco beetle, which has also been found at Luxor.

So Marcella and I put the idea to the test by hiring a felucca, and sailing upstream. Egyptian murals suggest that the basic rig of this traditional wooden sailing boat has been in use for thousands of years. The Nile was placid, running northwards towards the Mediterranean at a speed of about half a knot. A pleasant wind blew over from the Mediterranean, carrying us upstream at about 3 knots against the current. At that rate I reckoned the journey to Abu Simbel would have taken about six weeks, sailing eight hours per day.

There is some tantalising evidence that the seafarers had gone even further. Millennia before us, the Minoans seem to have broken their journey: at Tod. Here, underneath a temple dedicated to the hawk-faced god of war, Montu, French archaeologists had made a fascinating discovery. A treasure trove (see map).

This find fleshed out the bones of my theory, that the Minoans had travelled far into Egypt's vast interior. Tod was a huge surprise to me. The temple's stubbiness came as quite a jolt: unlike Egypt's more famous temples and pyramids it is a workaday building, much less monumental than I'd expected. There is a chapel there they call the 'birth house', dedicated to the female gods.

On the western side of the site is a well-preserved quay with paved flooring. It led to what was once an avenue of sphinxes and the main part of the temple. Was I treading on the very paths the Minoan explorers had once followed?

I was certain they had once travelled in this region. What the French archaeologist Fernand Bisson de la Roque unearthed in the form of the extraordinary Tod treasure goes a long way to prove it. Buried here at Tod beneath the floor of the temple of Sesostris I (c.1934–1898 BC) were four copper chests. They bear the cartouche of Amenemhat II (1919–1885 BC) of the 12th Dynasty – a pharaoh who lived at the height of Minoan trading power and influence.

The exotic hoard of treasure found in the chests may well have been a sacred offering to Montu, the god who is said to have slain the sun's enemies from the prow of a boat. It is really intriguing that an offering of Minoan precious gifts was made to Montu, since at this point in history the god was portrayed as having a bull's head.

Now divided between the Louvre in Paris and the Cairo Museum, the treasure had with it pieces of silver and gold ware that were clearly not Egyptian. The smaller chests contained silver cups with a design similar to ceramics from the Protopalatial period – c.1900–1700 BC – at Knossos.[2] The handle of one silver cup is the same as that on Minoan vases from the Middle Minoan period.

Other objects in the hoard seem to be mainly from the Levant and Anatolia – places that I now knew were regularly visited by Minoan traders. The necklaces are distinctly Minoan in style. In summary: if the Minoans had managed to reach the Valley of the Kings by the Middle Bronze Age, Nabta would have been an obvious next step. The Minoans took knowledge just as much as they took precious lapis lazuli and silver. By the same token, they sought it.

Sure that I was getting ever closer in the hunt for the truth, I took leave of Egypt and Nabta's eye-opening standing stones. The lead I needed to chase down now was something much, much closer to home: that is, Britain. My next stop would be the stone circles of Europe.

Yet my trip to Egypt had yielded another avenue of enquiry. If we take a leap of faith and assume for a minute that, as in Egypt, Minoan traders brought with them hoards of bronze then we should also be able to trace their progress as they moved north into Spain, then into northwest France and Britain. I needed to look at what they had left behind them – hidden underground.

27

MEDITERRANEAN AND ATLANTIC MEGALITHS

As the far-sighted physicist Sir Isaac Newton once said, no great discovery was ever made without first taking a bold guess. Many academics have taken this to heart in examining the stone circles of Europe and beyond. They wanted to see if there was any common factor that explained why they were all such similar structures. My guess is that it was because they all share a great secret: the influence of the Minoans.

As the Minoans expanded their trading empire across the Mediterranean from Crete, first to the copper and tin mines of Iberia and then on to northwest France, Britain and Ireland, I believe they built – or more probably modified – circular observatories based on the Nabta blueprint they had studied in Egypt. A quick summary of these stone circles includes:

MALTA

Like Crete, Malta has a superb strategic position midway between the toe of Italy and Africa to the south. It also happens to lie midway between the copper and tin mines of Iberia in the west and the rich market for bronze to the east. Malta has been fought over by Arabs and Christians, the French and the British and finally the British and the Germans in the Second World War. The island finally won independence in 1964.

The archaeological record reveals unequivocally that around 2500 BC a new people carrying an entirely different culture arrived on the island. The new inhabitants disposed of their dead by cremation and made use of bronze tools and weapons. Both factors reveal their kinship with the warlike Bronze Age cultures occupying Greece, southern Italy and Sicily at around the same time. This is a strong reminder of Plato's story of Atlas and his brothers – brothers who were given kingdoms of their own.

A substantial stone circle appeared at Xaghra, a village on the smaller of Malta's two islands, with a megalithic structure inside it. It is uncertain whether there was one structure here or two, but it was here. And the timescale fits in with the pattern of Minoan bronze-bringing – and the Minoans' voyages of discovery.

SICILY – MEGALITHS OF MONTALBANO ELICONA

During my trip to Malta I was told Sicily had identical stone circles. We took a ferry from Valletta to Syracuse, where I had a serious disagreement with a taxi driver, who charged the equivalent of 70 US dollars for a two-minute ride from the ferry to the hotel. The taxi driver had powerful friends, so I ended up in prison for failing to pay more than a reasonable fare and languished there for the night. I was released at dawn and we set off.

The huge stones in the wild, romantic landscape at Montalbano Elicona are now interspersed with wild flowers and wind-bent yew trees. They were reputedly erected by 3000 BC and the stones aligned to the summer solstice. Some work has been done towards checking the alignments of these stones with other stars in the heavens, but, as at Malta, Sicily's famous site would reward more archaeological study. In form, Montalbano Elicona resembles a much smaller Stonehenge: a prototype, if you will.

CROMELEQUE DOS ALMENDRES, PORTUGAL

The Almendres stone circle we have met before. It was built on top of a hill 10 miles (16 kilometres) west of the Bronze Age copper mines of São Domingos (chapter 20) in around 4000 BC. The site consists of two circles, built in sequence. The result is an oval of ninety-two upright stones measuring 30 metres by 60 metres (98 by 197 feet). Some of the stones have decorative cut marks, spirals and circles, and there are stones that point to sunrise and sunset at the equinoxes. More interesting is the latitude of the site: 38 degrees 33 minutes north.

At this precise latitude, the moon's maximum altitude at its meridian passage is directly overhead. If you looked into a well, you would notice that your head was directly in the shadow of the moon. This is because the moon's orbit around the earth is in a different plane to the earth's orbit around the sun. As I've already mentioned, the only other latitudes where this occurs are at 51 degrees 10 minutes north, the latitude of Stonehenge in southern England and Callanish in the Outer Hebrides. This cannot be a coincidence – these three sites in particular must have been built by people who had the same astronomical knowledge. I would speculate that this interest in the meridian passage of the moon may have been for religious reasons.

Luis Siret's finds at Almendres, especially the ceramic wares, bear the distinctive imprint of Minoan pioneers: how involved had they been here in Portugal?

BRITTANY

On the islet of Er Lannic in the Gulf of Morbihan in northwest France are two half-submerged stone circles. Both circles contain sixty stones, although only the northern one is still visible. The site was excavated in the 1920s by Zacharie Le Rouzic, who calculated Er Lannic had been erected c.3000 BC. Le Rouzic found that the lines of the stone circle pointed to the cardinal points of north, south, east and west. The site is conveniently near prehistoric tin and gold mines.

IRELAND

Irish stone circles of the Early Bronze Age are much smaller than their British counterparts such as Stonehenge, Avebury or Callanish, but nevertheless have stones which point to sunrise at the summer solstice and sunset at the winter solstice. Because Ireland has so many stone circles it was thought they were built for religious reasons. Recently, expert opinion has shifted, with many agreeing that they must have been created to study the skies.

NORTH GERMANY

I have already referred to the Goseck observatory on the River Elbe and the Nebra 'Sky Disk' that was found nearby. Goseck's draw for the Minoans would have been the amber trade, which will be described in some detail later.

OUTER HEBRIDES – CALLANISH

This observatory is one of the most interesting (see Almendres, above). It too will be analysed in more detail in another chapter.

This is also an opportunity to examine the claim of L. Augustine Waddell, that the people who built the circular stone observatories across the western world were the same people who mined copper and tin; and in particular that these stone observatories were built in places where the Minoans traded extensively. The Minoans seem to have adapted existing circles, but to have used stones in place of wood. They were able to do this because after 2200 BC they had the technology needed – bronze axes and saws sharp enough to trim stone.

||||||||||||||||||||||

The circles I am interested in are in different parts of the western world and may even lead ever further west again – to North America. Those I have so far mentioned may have varied in shape and size, but they had many important things in common. They were often accompanied by *cursi*, ceremonial pathways marked out by megaliths, that led the way into the stone circle. Built using a common measurement, the megalithic foot, they were constructed to record the same astronomical events – usually the rising or setting of the sun at equinoxes or solstices; the moonrise; moonset and the moon's eclipse; and occasionally the rising and setting of Venus. Because of the different latitudes of these stone circles, different layouts were adopted to record astronomical events.

There is another common factor. All building on European stone circles ceased by 1450 BC, when Thera's volcano erupted, destroying the Minoan civilisation.

28

STONEHENGE: THE MASTER WORK

In the previous chapter I mentioned Sir Isaac Newton's thesis that new ideas can only develop following an initial leap of faith. Newton also said that nothing made his head ache so much as accounting for the motions of the moon.

Stonehenge is the perfect place, on a clear midsummer night, to develop an obsession not just with the moon but with the amazing sweep of the whole night sky. Stand on any nearby hilltop, the breeze in your face, and let your gaze sweep the landscape. Drink in the ceremony and drama of the henge itself; its solidity, its permanence. Look harder and if it's still light enough you can see grand, ancient ceremonial avenues, *cursi* and hundreds of burial barrows. Stonehenge is magnificent, sacred and sublime, the bare bones of Britain's prehistory.

People have been worshipping here, it's thought, since 7200 BC. Stonehenge itself – the name probably comes from the Saxon *stân* meaning 'stone', and *hencg* meaning 'hinge', or 'hanging' – was built in three main phases. The first probably dates from 3000 BC to 2920 BC, when people dug out a roughly circular enclosure about 100 metres (330 feet) in diameter, surrounded by a ditch or inner bank, which was built of the earth from the ditch. There were two entry points to this initial enclosure, from the northeast and the south-west.

The ditch was crudely made. In the 1920s Colonel William Hawley, one of the pioneering archaeologists at Stonehenge, likened it to 'a string of badly-made sausages'. It was dug using picks made from the antlers of red deer and spades made from their broad shoulder blades – the same implements that had been used to dig the Great Orme Mine. The site has been carbon dated from these bones. It seems that the original purpose of this first site was cere-monial – as a gathering place to celebrate the arrival of spring, and possibly as a cemetery for the dead.

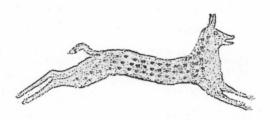

The next phases changed Stonehenge's character completely, because the builders used stones. Vast stones. For reasons we don't fully understand, around 2500 BC these huge lumps of rock were brought to the site, probably from the Marlborough Downs 23 miles (37 kilometres) away. Known as sarsens, they were cut from dense, durable silicified sandstone. Each stone erected in the outer ring was about 4.1 metres (13 feet) high and weighed around 25-tons. The large stones in the inner ring – ten uprights and five lintels – weigh up to 50 tons each and are linked to each other using complex jointing techniques. Stonehenge's builders set up the massive sarsen uprights to tolerances of just a few centimetres. It makes you marvel: how was all of this done?

An even greater mystery is how the smaller stones, collectively known as blue stones, were brought here. Although there is a theory that glacial action brought them near to the site, this seems highly unlikely. The 2- and 4-ton stones seem to have come from the Preseli Hills of south Wales – a full 150 miles (240 kilometres) to the west of Stonehenge (see map). Intriguingly, as the crow flies Preseli is about 100 miles (160 kilometres) south of the Great Orme mine, which was in full swing by this time. One new theory, supported by radiocarbon dating, has it that the stone construction at the henge began between 2400 and 2200 BC. The change of date intrigues me.

This new survey by Professor Tim Darvill and Geoffrey Wainwright contends that the smaller stones were arranged in two concentric circles within an older wooden enclosure. The big sarsen stones were now carefully trimmed with bronze axes, adzes and saws to produce sharply defined rectangular blocks with mortise and tenon and tongue and groove joints to lock the stones together. The final arrangement of the stones was almost certainly completed sometime between 2280 and 1930 BC.[3]

The scenes here at the summer solstices of the 21st century AD – with hippies banging drums and the Wiltshire police force's new aerial drone sweeping back and forth, lights flashing, filming the crowds from a hundred or so metres (a few hundred feet) in the air – may seem worlds away from what would have happened in the era before Christ. Yet perhaps it is not all that different in spirit. The crowds all come for the consuming drama of one moment – when the sun rises from behind the magnificent Heel Stone. Somehow, for a magical few minutes, it feels as if the sun has stopped dead in its tracks and hangs suspended in time.

The structure that was completed sometime between 2280 and 1930 BC was sophisticated. For example, the horizontal stones that were locked in place on top of the upright ones were not perfectly rectangular. The stones are gently and deliberately curved on both inner and outer faces. As a result the stones appear as a perfect ring, suspended high above Salisbury Plain. This effect, playing with the perspective supplied by the human eye, may well be a technique imported from the Mediterranean. The Minoans certainly used it and they handed it down to the Greeks, whose word for it is *entasis*.

From a navigator's point of view, the circle of horizontal stones provided a perfect artificial horizon. That would have enabled astronomers to note precisely when the moon rose, or which was the first star to rise in the east after sunset. It would also allow them to time both solar and lunar eclipses accurately and determine the exact times of sunrise and sunset.

The Minoans had arrived in Britain by 2300 BC to collect tin and their technological influence can be seen in bronze implements dated 2200–2000 BC, when the percentage of tin content in those implements leaps to 11 per cent.[4] At some stage (it is hard to prove definitively when) five huge stones were repositioned at the centre of Stonehenge, in a very similar way to the central stones at Nabta. So we have builders who could transport massive stones hundreds of miles, then prepare them with bronze tools for astronomical purposes, using a similar layout to the one found at Nabta.

Could the Minoans have been behind that change? It's their appetite for luxury that gives them away. I am here at Stonehenge armed with the knowledge that oriental cowries and jewellery, including blue-glazed and glass beads very similar to those produced on ancient Crete, have been excavated from a number of Bronze Age graves at Stonehenge. They are, according to Professor L. Augustine Waddell, 'of the identical kind common in Ancient Egypt within the restricted period of between about 1450 BC to 1250 BC'. The Uluburun wreck's cargo included almost identical examples of blue glass, cowries and amber.

Was this idea too incredible? Could I realistically expect to challenge the official version of history, especially when it came to one of Britain's most loved, most written about, most iconic monuments? The fact is that the more one peers into the mists of Stonehenge, the more the evidence of Minoan influence appears from the murk.

The most exciting initial discovery? During a casual Internet search, I chanced across an old Australian blog. The blogger gave an account of his tour of Stonehenge in the 1950s. You could still walk among the stones at that time, and he described a particular beam of light that had allowed him to see a carving of a double-

headed axe . . . etched along the stones. I immediately thought back
to Almendres and another tourist's hastily shot photograph showing
what looked to me like a carving of a *labrys*, a Minoan double axe,
its shape eroded over the many centuries that have passed. I'd
scarcely paid any attention to it. Then it clicked. I remembered
Knossos, and what archaeologists call the 'mason's marks' engraved
on its stones – again in the form of Minoan double-headed axes.

Here is the remarkable truth. As soon as I realised that there was
an exciting lead to track down, I began looking for answers. Within
just hours, thanks to the wonders of the Web, I'd discovered that
there is not just one such 'axe' carving on the megaliths of Stonehenge: there are many. They were created nearly 4,000 years ago.
Some have interpreted these weathered, axe-shaped marks – a
'stalk', as it were, supporting a horizontal line – as mushroom
shapes. However when archaeologist Richard J. C. Atkinson drew
them in 1953, he realised that one of these centuries-old carvings
was probably a dagger, the other a double-headed axe. What is also
remarkable is the fact that these carvings were rediscovered in the
last century – and yet fifty years on, they had still not been studied
and were scarcely even recorded.

With the British weather fast eroding their outlines the marks
are rarely seen today, if only because no one is allowed close
enough to the monument to photograph them – except during
the chaotic celebrations that annually mark the summer solstice.
What with the impact of wind and rain, time was, in a sense,
running out.

In 2002 Wessex Archaeology contacted Archaeoptics Ltd of
Glasgow, which is a specialist company at the leading edge of applying pioneering new techniques to archaeology. The year before, the
company had laser-scanned the timbers of Seahenge, the intriguing
Bronze Age circle of waterlogged wooden posts exposed by the sea
on a remote beach in Norfolk. The results had been high-resolution,
digital 3-dimensional (3D) models – most helpful for analysis.

Wessex Archaeology decided to investigate the potential of laser-scanning the Stonehenge carvings. Specialists Alistair Carty and Dave Vickers travelled to Wessex Archaeology's Old Sarum head-quarters near Salisbury with an impressive array of equipment, including a Minolta VIVID-900 scanner, capable of capturing millions of points in 3D and taking measurements just microns apart. The team included Wessex Archaeology's Thomas Goskar, also a specialist in digital techniques.

The surfaces were photographed and scanned at a resolution of 0.5 mm, creating hundreds of thousands of individual 3D measurements known as a point cloud, which could then be animated into a 3D solid model.

This is Goskar's description of the images scanned on 'Stone 53', one of the famous sarsen trilithons:

> The first carving is 15 by 15.3 cm [5.9 by 6 inches], with a broad upturned blade, and a form of 'rib' a third of the way down the length. Although further analysis is needed, this shape could represent two axes, one carved over another. The second carving, 10.6 by 8.6 cm [4.2 by 3.4 inches], is very faint indeed, but seems to be a normal flanged axe, as we find elsewhere on the stone ...

> There was something poetic about the juxtaposition of the most advanced Early Bronze Age technology, with the most advanced 21st century archaeological recording methods. What was intended as an investigation into how well the carvings would be recorded by a laser scanner, turned into a major discovery.

> We must remember that while the sarsens are thought to have been erected around 2300 BC, metal axes were not in common circulation for generations after this. Whatever the carvings mean, accurate recording is vital to our understanding of the monument as a whole.[5]

EARLY RESEARCH

During the early dawn of the British archaeological profession in the 18th century, the antiquarian William Stukeley discovered what local people had probably always known. That at midsummer sunrise the first of the sun's rays shine into the centre of the rings of stone, meeting between the open arms of a horseshoe of stones. In fact, in the early 20th century Sir Norman Lockyer argued that there was a ritualistic connection between Stonehenge and sun worship. The precision of the alignment of these ancient megaliths with the sun could not be an accident.

Then Dr Gerald Hawkins, a well-known astronomer from America, burst upon the scene. Hawkins was Professor of Physics and Astronomy at Boston University in Massachusetts. In 1962 he and his assistants filmed sunrise at the summer solstice at Stonehenge. They plotted every stone and pit on the site and fed their co-ordinates into an IBM 704 computer, then the world's most powerful – computers being in their infancy. The journal *Nature* published Hawkins' first results in 1963.

Hawkins argued that the computer results proved that Stonehenge was a giant observatory for predicting eclipses of both the sun and the moon. His claims generated huge publicity. Professional archaeologists were furious. Here was an astronomer, and an American to boot, trampling over their patch and using new-fangled, unproven computer methods to uncover the secrets of 'their' beloved Stonehenge. Richard Atkinson described Hawkins' argument as 'tendentious, arrogant, slipshod and unconvincing' – to Atkinson, the builders of Stonehenge were 'howling barbarians'.

The archaeologists had overplayed their hand. It was obvious that Hawkins knew his subject – Stonehenge was his sixty-first published paper. Then again Hawkins was not, in fact, an American, but came from Suffolk. His degrees were in physics and pure maths and his PhD in radio astronomy was obtained at Manchester

University. Hawkins had forever changed the way we think of Stonehenge.

Next into the fray was Sir Fred Hoyle, the most highly respected British astronomer of the day. He examined Professor Hawkins' research and went even further. To him, Stonehenge was a model of the solar system. Hoyle selected three stones representing the sun, the moon and the moon's orbit. These stones were then rotated around the holes of the Aubrey Hole ring relative to one another.

Hoyle could show that when the three marker stones lay either close to each other or opposite each other, eclipses would take place. The eclipse would occur when the moon stone was closest to the sun stone or was precisely opposite to it on the other side of the Aubrey Hole ring. Hoyle's method is more accurate than Hawkins', because Hoyle's system could predict the actual day of lunar eclipse nineteen years into the future. Hoyle also identified many other astronomical alignments at Stonehenge. Hoyle and Hawkins had to take a leap of faith, based on the evidence before them: they did not have all the detailed proof we now have about the sophistication of Babylonian, Minoan and Egyptian astronomy, a body of knowledge that already existed during the latter stages of the building of Stonehenge. Neither did they have proof that the Bronze Age world was as elaborate and sophisticated as we are only just now beginning to understand – nor that there was long-standing contact between the civilisations of the Minoans, the Egyptians and the Babylonians.

From the Egyptian astronomers at Nabta, the Minoans could have known of the sun's daily maximum elevation and dec-lination. From the astronomers at Giza we know that the Egyptians also knew about the earth's precession – from the apparent precession of Kochab. The Minoan mariners may have learned much more from the Mesopotamian astronomers, not least the precise times of the moon's rising – something that, if Hoyle was right, could also be measured at Stonehenge. Had they had a good clock they could have calculated accurate longitude from the moon's eclipse. From the altitude of the sun, taken each day at its maximum elevation, they could have deduced declination to determine latitude.

29

FROM THE MED TO THE MEGALITH

Supposing for a moment that the builders of Stonehenge did complete phase III of the circle around 1750 BC. If there really had been that much Minoan influence on the extraordinary monument, then logic would suggest that the travellers would have left evidence from the eastern Mediterranean: goods, perhaps, or traces of trade or even physical habitation.

To quote Professor Hawkins again:

> Archaeologists are traditionally conservative and ungiven to theorising, but the indications of a Mediterranean origin for Stonehenge [phase III] are so strong that they allow themselves to wonder if some master designer might not have come all the way from that pre-Homeric but eternally wine dark southern sea [the Mediterranean] ...

R.J.C. Atkinson inclines seriously to this theory, making much of the evidence of dagger and axe carvings and Mediterranean artefacts in the burials of Stonehenge.[6] Atkinson's views are supported by a number of distinguished historians. For instance, according to Professor W.J. Perry:

> Megaliths [stone circles] all over the world are located in the immediate neighbourhood of ancient mine workings for tin, copper, lead and gold or in the area of the pearl and amber trade.

As Herodotus wrote: ' ... it is nevertheless certain that both our tin and our amber are brought from the extremely remote regions in the western extremes of Europe'.[7]

Had the Minoans left any distinctive 'calling cards' on the rolling plains of Wiltshire? I set out for Stonehenge on a fair September day and enjoyed the sight of the stones as they leapt majestically into view from the much despised A303 road.

It's fair to say that until recently the wider landscape around Stonehenge, which is mainly rolling farmland, has been pretty much ignored. The long and bitter public dispute about burying the road, which roars past the stones on its way to the West Country, has dominated the Stonehenge debate to the detriment of other things. Yet it is obvious now that this special area was a vast, interconnected sacred landscape. The largest prehistoric mound in Europe, Silbury Hill stands just one mile (1.5 kilometres) to the south of the monument, flanked by the West Kennet Long Barrow. Avebury's stone circles are just 15 miles (24 kilometres) to the north. There is a lot more yet to discover.

Kings and important figures were buried in round mounds called barrows and many of them overlook the stones. Of late the archaeological pace has been increasing, with some spectacular finds of Bronze Age tombs. The so-called 'Amesbury Archer' was only discovered in 2002, when a new housing development was begun at a nearby village. The press dubbed him the 'King of Stonehenge', because the goods found buried with him were so rich in quality.

Twenty-nine groups of exhibits came from the barrow group of Winterbourne Stoke. The earliest is a Neolithic long barrow. More than a thousand years later, it was followed by a line of large bowl and bell barrows. The barrows are a mile southwest of Stonehenge, lying in a NE–SW line. Access is easy; there is a lay-by on the A303.

Almost all of the barrows were excavated in the early 19th century, though some were investigated in the 1960s. The most spectacular finds were the remains of two wooden coffins, many decorated pottery vessels and spearheads and daggers of bronze.

I arrived after a brisk five-minute walk through the woods to see pairs of disc, bell and pond barrows and nineteen bowl barrows. Each of the round barrows held one body – presumably a chief living at Stonehenge. The excavations yielded daggers, knives, awls, tweezers, cups, amber, dress pins, faience beads, food containers and urns.

For me, standing beside this line of barrows was a moment of *déjà vu*. I'd seen burial tombs just like them near the palace of Phaestos in southern Crete, where our adventure began. They lie on the foothills of the Cretan mountains, inland from Phaestos, on the Mesara plain. The tombs of Mesara are constructed of local stone bound together with mud, the roof supported by a type of corbel construction. They are the same height and circumference as the barrows at Winterbourne Stoke.

This could of course be coincidental. To be more certain of a cultural link I needed to go and see the actual grave goods that had been found in the barrows. They included armour, weapons, farming equipment, woodworking tools, jewellery and household and domestic utensils: many are on display in local museums. The two key museums are the Wiltshire Heritage Museum at Devizes and the Salisbury & South Wiltshire Museum, opposite England's loveliest cathedral.

These marvellous museums have thousands of Bronze Age artefacts, especially from the hoards buried at Wilsford (see map), Upton Lovell, Winterbourne Stoke, Amesbury and Wimborne St Giles. The extremely helpful director of the Salisbury Museum, Adrian Green, and the equally helpful director of the Wiltshire Heritage Museum, David Dawson, kindly let me photograph the exhibits.

I separated the Early, Middle and Late Bronze Age artefacts buried in the barrow mounds into twenty categories. The main ones were axes; adzes; jewellery; personal hygiene; woodworking tools (chisels, hammers, etc.); farming implements; dress and couture; hunting equipment; weapons offensive and defensive; votive offerings; ceremonial items (mace, Minoan double-headed axe); games and pastimes;

trade goods (balance weights); and kitchen and cooking equipment. These twenty principal categories were then further broken down – kitchen equipment into pots and pans, cups, knives, spoons and so on.

I then placed photographs of artefacts in these twenty categories beside similar items found in the Uluburun and Gelidonya wrecks. (I established that the objects found in the wrecks were in fact Minoan in the manner described in chapter 37.) The results may be seen on our website.

The results speak for themselves (see second colour plate section). The people buried at Stonehenge in the Bronze Age used the same bronze weapons as their Minoan counterparts – tanged and riveted knives, swords, lances and arrows, the blades often with the same ornaments. The simplest explanation is that the objects were in fact Minoan.

The presence of Minoan-type artefacts at Stonehenge does not mean that both civilisations had reached the same stage of development and that these items were made by Britons. Anyone who has visited the magnificent palaces of Knossos and Phaestos becomes conscious of the huge gap between ancient British and Minoan culture. The building technology alone reinforces this point: were there any similar Bronze Age palaces in Britain? The answer is a resounding no.

Amber has been found in twenty-nine graves in the area, not least in the form of some exceptionally valuable necklaces. This jewellery is often Minoan in character. Archaeologists have had some of the amber scientifically examined – and I was not surprised to find it comes from the Baltic. Between the amber pieces in many of the Stonehenge burials are amber spacers and faience beads made of crystal or glass. Archaeologists already accept that at least some of these came from the eastern Mediterranean. Faience beads of the same shape and colour were found in the Uluburun wreck. The ceremonial mace at Stonehenge had its counterpart at Mycenae, and so on. The plot was beginning to thicken.

Seen in that light the close similarity of awls, knapping tools, bracelets, armbands, scales, knives, twisted bow drills, triangulated socket points, spades, daggers, necklaces, earrings, bangles, torcs, rings, brooches, earlobe adornments, cups, plates, lance heads, chisels, spearheads, gaff hooks, weights, pins, buttons, fasteners, cleavers, hammers, saws, bradawls, drills – thirty-two separate types of artefacts – cannot be a coincidence. The most exciting of all these ancient things? Two Minoan double-headed axes in the local museum. Just like the famous *labrys* of King Minos, found at Knossos.

Was Stonehenge a holy site for the Minoans? Perhaps even a place of pilgrimage? Had they, as part of the long-term trading agreements they held with the local Britons, begun to settle here?

30

THE LAND THAT TIME FORGOT

It was at Callanish on the lonely Isle of Lewis that I suddenly had a breakthrough. I realised that, in a manner of speaking, I'd been barking up the wrong tree. The hoard I was here to see, one of the finest Bronze Age hoards ever found in Scotland, contained Irish bronze tools and beads of Irish gold. But it was the trees, not the hoarded bronze and gold that I began thinking about. More precisely, it was the lack of them. It was then I realised that my thinking about Minoan journeys to the west had been, in effect, the wrong way round.

Today, Lewis has large areas of peatland and bog. But reading my guidebook, I discovered that until about 1500 BC the island had been warmer, more fertile and much less wet. I suddenly realised that it was deforestation as well as climate change that had denuded the land. Deforestation. The kind that happens after shipbuilding and repair; the kind that happens after large, industrial-scale smelting operations . . .

At first sight, it seems highly unlikely that Minoan ships from sunny Crete would have ever ventured to the stormy, wet wilds of the Hebrides. But there were many more of these mysterious Bronze Age stashes hoarded in this general area – at Gurness on the Orkneys, for instance and at Dunagoil on Bute. Why, here, on this wild and windy series of islands? What did these sites have in common? One fact was immediately obvious: they had all been built before widespread local deforestation. Was that purely happenstance?

Had this remote island had a population large enough to carry out an elaborate build, such as the Callanish stone circle? It seemed unlikely. Or had the islanders had help when creating the stone ring – in the form of either hostile invaders or very persuasive outsiders? Was there a lack of trees because large-scale smelting had taken place on these islands?

There was one stunning new piece of evidence: DNA. Examining the DNA of the island's current population, I discovered that Lewis had a high frequency of haplogroup X2; and one of the few other places that had a similar high incidence of haplogroup X2 was – Crete.[8] (DNA is described in more detail in chapter 38.)

I was seeing a repeating pattern of activity. Could this idea be true? The connections seemed to be there. Besides the Irish wares, the hoard at Adabrock on Lewis also contained the Minoans' characteristic calling cards of amber from the Baltic and glass from the Mediterranean. That was all well and good. But the inevitable question arose: what had been the Minoans' real interest in the windswept Atlantic island of Lewis?

The true scale of the Minoans' trading ambitions was beginning to dawn on me. I was standing at the epicentre of what had been a network: I was unveiling a true trading empire, with bases and ports set up along the entire route. This empire hadn't simply straddled the eastern Mediterranean. The people of Crete had been the East India Company of their day, a maritime enterprise whose size and ambition took your breath away. Where those trading colonies or bases would be was defined by a number of factors – the frenetic trade in bronze, and the desperate need for exploration, to keep that river of bronze going.

I had been hoping that later at night I would watch the moon skim the stones, setting them aglow. Although I was unlikely to see the phenomenon that Diodorus Siculus had described, 'the god' of the moon 'visiting the island'. Sadly, I was here at the wrong point in the lunar cycle: I would need to wait until 2034 to observe that almost magical event.

It kept niggling at me as I walked. Why here? Why would the Minoans come all this way, up to the northern tip of the Outer

Hebrides? It was then that it struck me. What if they hadn't been coming to Lewis, like tourists? What if they'd actually been *en route* to somewhere else? The idea struck me like a blow to the head. What had I been thinking all this time? I'd been looking at things the wrong way round. When they reached Callanish, our ancient travellers had been *returning home* from a much longer journey – one they had made on the wings of the Gulf Stream. Forget Christopher Columbus. It was the Minoans who had first discovered America.

IIIIIIIIIIIIIIIIII

THE JOURNEY TO AMERICA AND BACK

If Callanish had been the landfall for the Minoan traders returning from America, where did they start from? If the sailors overwintered in Spain, ships intending to make an Atlantic crossing in the favourable season of May–August could begin their voyage from an Atlantic port such as Cádiz or San Lúcar de Barrameda, where Bronze Age ports have in fact been found. Put another way, ships from Thera could winter somewhere like San Lúcar before starting an Atlantic crossing the following year. Overwintering in San Lúcar they could have repaired any broken steering oars and sails and careened the ship to remove barnacles from the hull. In May, past the hurricane season, they could use sail, rather than oar power, and the massive force of the ocean currents to take them to new-found lands.

Then, loaded with copper and following the huge circle of the Gulf Stream, they could speed their way *back* to Britain from America. On the return journey, reaching landfall at Lewis would have meant being halfway for the Minoans. The Gulf Stream is a massive force to be reckoned with. This colossal current of moving water is caused by the earth's rotation. The great stream flows clockwise all the year round in the North Atlantic, bringing the warmth and fertility of orange-growing Florida northwards with it. It's part of a whole network of currents; the Spanish used their sublime force and power to reach the Caribbean, in their treasure-hungry galleons.

In Britain we have the Gulf Stream to thank for our relatively warm weather. When the American statesman Benjamin Franklin analysed its properties in the 1760s, he managed to knock weeks off the standard sailing time between America and Britain by refining the routes ships would take, employing the forces of nature rather than struggling against them. When the Minoans discovered the Gulf Stream, they must have realised that it gave them an express train ride, for free.

In 1970, as captain of the submarine HMS *Rorqual*, returning from America to Scotland, I requested permission to vary my sailing orders so that I could pass through the Denmark Strait and then through the Faroes Gap and on to northeast Scotland. I wanted to travel with the Gulf Stream and see when it petered out.

A submarine is the ideal vehicle with which to measure the power of this mighty river of warm water as it carves its way across the Atlantic. A submerged submarine needs to equal the weight of the water it displaces. In hot water, the submarine must lighten its weight. If the water then gets colder, the submarine needs to flood in seawater. So when the warm Gulf Stream water disappears – if, say, the submarine is below it at 152 metres (500 feet) – this will become apparent from the submarine's weight. We discovered that in terms of volume the Iceland–Faroe flow is the strongest of the three current branches flowing from the Atlantic Ocean into the Nordic seas, across the Greenland–Scotland Ridge.

By the time they got to Lewis, on the extreme western edge of Europe, laden with copper from America but desperate for food and water, the Minoan crews would have needed to rest up, repair their ships and restock.

The islands would have become a pivotal point in a powerful Minoan trading empire that spanned the entire Atlantic. From here, these enterprising explorers would have been able to launch further lucrative trading missions to Denmark, Greenland and beyond. These were consummate businessmen: they would maximise their reach to maximise their profit.

The Hagia
Triada
sarcophagus,
Crete.

Clockwise from top left: Sculpted stone sunflower juxtaposed with live sunflower, Halebid, Karnataka, India; Stone carving at Pattadakal temple, India, shows a parrot perched on a sunflower; Stone carving of a pineapple in a cave temple in Udaiguri, India; Wall sculpture from Hoysala Dynasty Halebid temple at Somnathpur, India, showing maize ears.

Clear similarities in the custom of bull leaping, which transcends cultures and countries. *Top:* Engraving by Goya, 'The Agility and Audacity of Juanito Apiñani in the Ring at Madrid'. *Middle:* Minoan bull leaper, British Museum. *Bottom:* Minoan bull leaper, Heraklion Museum.

The Dover Boat at the Dover Museum and Bronze Age Boat Gallery.

The mysterious Nebra disc, found in Germany, 1999.

England's most celebrated stone circle, Stonehenge, Wiltshire.

An amber necklace from the Upton Lovell Bronze Age hoard, Wiltshire Heritage Museum, Devizes.

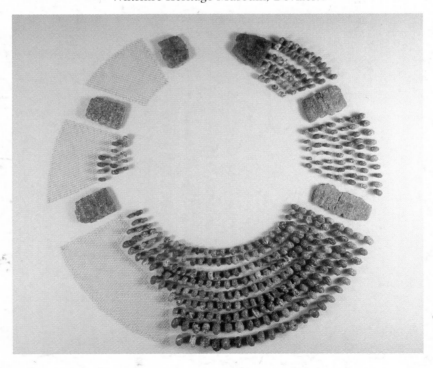

A selection of artefacts found near Stonehenge and in the surrounding area,
courtesy of the Wiltshire Heritage Museum, Devizes.

Comparisons of copper tools and implements found in the Mediterranean and at the Great Lakes, USA:

Coiled snake effigy (Uluburun wreck and Great Lakes).

Animal weights at the British Museum.

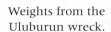

Weights from the Uluburun wreck.

Weights found in the Great Lakes area of the USA.

Conical points (Uluburun wreck and Great Lakes).

Triangulate spear heads (Uluburun wreck and Great Lakes).

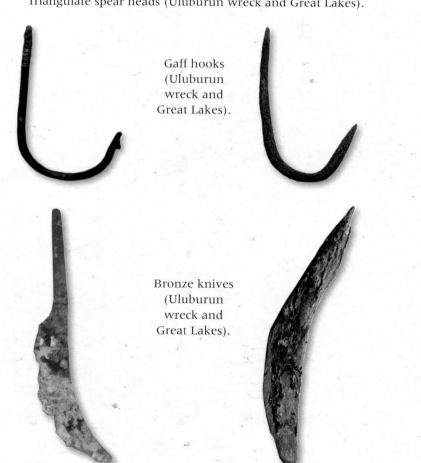

Gaff hooks
(Uluburun
wreck and
Great Lakes).

Bronze knives
(Uluburun
wreck and
Great Lakes).

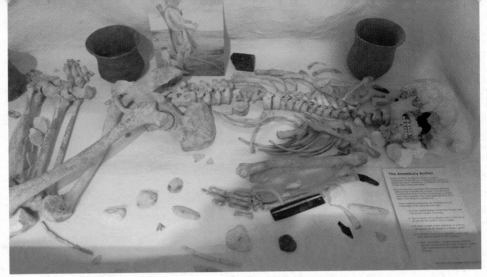

Skeleton known as the 'Amesbury Archer', now in Salisbury and South Wiltshire Museum.

The Antikythera device, National Archaeological Museum of Athens, Greece.

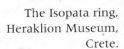

The Isopata ring, Heraklion Museum, Crete.

As Plato had said: 'This power came forth out of the ocean.'

It was as I had suspected: the Minoans' tremendous seafaring capability had given them control of a vast trading empire; an empire far larger than simply the Mediterranean. It was one that took full advantage of the vast mineral wealth of the west, of America, 'an island larger than Libya and Asia together'.

|||||||||||||||||||||

The Minoans probably did not set out to colonise the Outer Hebrides or the Orkneys, but arrived there while heading for home, ships filled with pure American copper (see chapter 33). With that in mind we can look at what they left behind them: starting with voles.

There is clear evidence of the human introduction of three types of vole in northern Europe: the field vole to the Outer Hebrides, the bank vole to Ireland and the sibling vole to Svalbard. None of these voles are found on the mainland of the British Isles.

Which group of humans brought these voles, and when? Radio carbon dates of $3,590 \pm 80$ (i.e. c.1500 BC) and 4800 ± 120 (i.e. c.2700 BC) are from two bone samples of voles excavated in the Orkneys.[9] DNA comparisons made by York University show the closest match to the Orkney vole are those of southern France and Spain. So it seems seafarers came from southern France or Spain to the Orkneys between 2700 BC and 1500 BC. Rodent stowaways in Minoan ships would have been commonplace – the Uluburun wreck had a Syrian mouse! An alternative explanation is that the voles reached the Orkneys first, then southern France and Spain.

The common vole is the only vole on Orkney. It inhabits eight Orkney Islands: Burray, Eday, Mainland, Rousay, Sanday, South Ronaldsay, Stronsay and Westray. The vole cannot swim, so it must have been brought by humans. It is most likely that they were in the hay or straw which seafarers took along for animals. This vole is not found on the adjacent Shetland Islands, nor on mainland Scotland or in England. It is at least arguable that the voles link the Orkneys with southern France and Spain.

CONCLUSION

Because of their physical location at the end of the Gulf Stream, the Outer Hebrides and the Orkneys became trading hubs for Minoan ships bringing copper from the Great Lakes to Europe. Perhaps burials in the Orkneys would tell us more?

A BBC television programme contained this report by David Keys:

> According to sensational archaeological discoveries currently being made in Scotland, Bronze Age Britons were practising the art of mummification at the same time as 'mummy culture' was in full swing in Pharaonic Egypt. It appears that ancient Britons invented this skill for themselves . . . [10]

A team of archaeologists, led by Dr Mike Parker Pearson of Sheffield University, had made an astounding discovery on the Hebridean island of South Uist. Two mummified bodies were buried under the floor of a prehistoric house in an area called Cladh Hallan. The house was part of a unique Bronze Age complex. The report said that the complex was made up of seven houses arranged as a terrace, and 'is as mysterious as the preserved corpses that were buried there'. The report went on:

> To the astonishment of the archaeologists, they saw that one individual, a male, had died in around 1600 BC – but had been buried a full six centuries later, in around 1000 BC. What is more, a second individual (a female) had died in around 1300 BC – and had to wait 300 years before being interred . . .

The report speculated that the bodies could have been members of some ritual élite, potentially priests or shamans. It is just as possible that they were new arrivals or settlers. I suggest the people were Minoan leaders. The Minoans knew of mummification from the Egyptians, notably from their extended stay at Tell el Dab'a. It's worth mentioning that when he was excavating at Mycenae,

Heinrich Schliemann noted that one of the bodies he uncovered had been mummified.

The extraordinary thing was that the more I looked, the more there was to find. We will seek to have the DNA of the South Uist mummies tested to see whether the haplogroup X2 is in their genes. The intriguing fact about haplogroup X2 is that it has been found not just in the Orkneys and not just where the Minoans originated (see chapter 38) but in the Americas of the Great Lakes. Nowhere else is this haplogroup so prevalent and so highly marked in local populations of today. As Professor Theodore Schurr states, 'A genetic marker appropriately called Lineage X suggests a definite – if ancient – link between Eurasians and Native Americans.'[11] So the scientific evidence backs up the high incidence of shared DNA between Orcadians and Cretans: both have a very high incidence of haplogroup X2 (7.2 per cent) in their genes.

31

THE BRONZE BOY

Now, I realised, the Minoans ran a vast Bronze Age 'Common Market', stretching from the Orkneys right through to India. They took English copper and tin all the way to ancient Egypt to make the Saqqara Pyramid's bronze saws. However, as time went on, the copper and tin became scarce. But if the Minoans fuelled the entire global trade in the raw materials and finished products of the Bronze Age, then where else could it have been sourced? I already had an idea. But before we leave Britain's shores to brave the Atlantic, there is one last thing I would like to do: like a million or more others, I am going to return to Stonehenge.

Only last year, in 2010, came a rather stunning discovery. Scientists from the British Geological Survey had conducted tests on the body of a fifteen-year old boy – a body found in 2006 at Amesbury, quite near to the henge. The boy had been placed in a simple grave just a mile from the stone circle, an amber necklace of huge wealth – with ninety beads – by his side. The tests prove that he died of infection, rather than from any violence. More to the point, a broad range of scientific studies prove the teenager was from the Mediterranean.

The discovery adds further meat to my overall thesis. The Mediterranean boy was buried here in around 1550 BC, a date that has significance. He could have been here as an apprentice, to pick up and capitalise on the Minoans' lucrative system of established trade routes. Alternatively, he could have been a Minoan fleeing the Mycenaeans' invading armies.

I'm convinced that Stonehenge was a prehistoric international landmark. In the words of project archaeologist Andrew Fitzpatrick:

> We think that the wealthiest people may have made these long-distance journeys to source rare and exotic materials, like amber. By doing these journeys, they probably also acquired great kudos.[12]

The most spectacular spiritual sanctuary in the world, Stonehenge would have been famous beyond measure, because reading the heavens and learning how to travel the world was tantamount to reading the will of the gods. It was a religious rite.

Other people who had visited Stonehenge from afar include individuals found in a collective Bronze Age grave, the 'Boscombe Bowmen', who were almost certainly from Wales.

Crowds came here initially for the religious ceremony and observation of the stars. But where better for the bringers of bronze to conduct trade than at a place where thousands gathered in prayer? Bronze Age wealth transformed the entire plain into a major centre of commerce and exchange.

At that other mystical stone circle, Callanish, I had already made the connection between the Minoans and copper-prospecting in the Americas. Now here, at Stonehenge, I was beginning to think there could be much more evidence of transatlantic trade. This grave and the body of this teenager weren't found until the 21st century: how much more, then, is left to find out?

In May 2002, Wessex Archaeology was doing a routine excavation in an area that was due to become a housing scheme at Amesbury, a few miles from Stonehenge. It was simply standard procedure in an area like this to look, before the whole thing became covered in concrete. If they found anything at all, the Wessex team were expecting to come across Roman remains. But it wasn't long before the archaeologists found something that turned their whole view of this place on its head. What they'd uncovered was a grave. No ordinary burial, this outwardly unassuming site was filled with pottery dating back at least 2,500 years before the Romans arrived in Britain.

By mid-afternoon the team had literally struck gold: gold

jewellery. A bank holiday was due that weekend and there was a danger that the grave would be robbed or disturbed if it was left unattended. The archaeologists knew they couldn't leave this find, so the diggers worked on through the night, with just their car headlamps for lighting. By dawn they had unearthed the entire skeleton of a man. His was the richest Bronze Age grave ever found in Britain.

The body of the man, also known as the 'Amesbury Archer', has since been dated to around 2300 BC, the early Bronze Age, almost a thousand years earlier than the burial of the Mediterranean 'Boy with the Amber Necklace'. This was around the time that the first metals were brought into Britain. His mourners had laid the 'Archer' on his left-hand side, with his face to the north. Buried alongside him were the weapons of a hunter, including three copper daggers. Bound to his wrist was a slate guard, to protect him from the snap recoil of a bowstring.

Clearly, this was a man of high status. Only the non-organic objects he was buried with survive, so we don't know what he was wearing, but with him were two beautifully worked earrings in gold and two golden hair ornaments.

The archaeologists' dating places him here at the exact same time that the massive stones were being erected at Stonehenge. And as he was buried less than 3 miles (5 kilometres) away, there is specu-lation that this man of special status had had a hand in the planning of the monument.

Later, another grave was found close by. Curled up in a foetal position and lying against the pockmarked chalk of his grave, this younger man was almost certainly related to the first. Both skeletons had the same highly unusual bone structure in their feet – the heel bone had a joint with one of the upper tarsal bones in the foot. It is possible that they were father and son.

When he died the 'King' was thirty-five to forty-five years old. He was buried with objects useful to him in the next world, including arrowheads and copper knives. His cushion stone, for working metal, lay right next to him. He may have been one of the first people in Britain to have been able to work gold: hence the richness of his grave.

His teeth were examined by oxygen isotope analysis, which can help identify where a person lived when he or she was young. Stronger than bone, tooth enamel is the hardest and the most mineralised substance in the human body – one of the reasons why human teeth can survive for centuries after a person has died. It envelops the teeth in a protective layer that shields the underlying dentin from decay. The enamel grows quickly until puberty and holds a chemical record of a child's environment, even stretching to the climate and local geology.

The enamel's chemical components are mainly calcium, phosphorus and oxygen, with trace amounts of strontium and lead. Of these it is the isotopes of oxygen and strontium that are the strongest indications of the climate where a person grew up. The ratio of heavy to light oxygen isotopes depends on the water you drink when you are young. Drinking water in a warm climate results in more heavy isotopes, while cold water produces a lighter chemical signature.

An analysis of the oxygen isotopes within the dental enamel of the two skeletons showed that the older man came from a colder climate than was then found in Britain. The wisdom teeth of the younger man, who was between twenty-five and thirty years old when he died, revealed that he spent his youth in southern England, but then moved to the Midlands or northeast Scotland in his late teens. Because the 'King' came from a colder climate, archaeologists think he may have come from the Alps, or possibly northern Germany. I would argue that he could just as well have come from Lake Superior. Assuming he was the 'King's' son, the boy could have been left in England rather than brave the Atlantic as a child, but might have been taken to the Minoan trading posts in the Hebrides or the Orkneys as a teenager. DNA tests should determine more about the ancestry of the two men.

A famous skeleton has been found on Lake Superior in the United States, which is approximately the same age (c.2300 BC) as the 'King' of Stonehenge. The 'Rock Lake' skeleton was buried with a copper axe similar to those found at Stonehenge. We are hoping to have his DNA compared with that of the 'King of Stonehenge', to see if both are those of Minoans with the rare haplogroup X2. A number of locally found skeletons – now in Milwaukee Public Museum – have peculiar bone deformities to their feet.

ıııııııııııııııı

There were other, independent reasons I thought I should look westwards to the Americas. I knew from enthusiastic letters and emails sent to my website that the Americas had significant amounts of copper ore. Bronze Age tools found at the copper mines of Lake Superior are remarkably similar to contemporary artefacts discovered in Britain. What's more, experts say that many of the copper artefacts found in ancient American mounds were actually produced by molten casting, a technique that was developed in the Mediterranean and was otherwise unknown in America at that time.

Tests by both the US National Bureau of Standards and the New York Testing Laboratory confirm that many artefacts found in American mounds were made using Old World casting technology. Dr Gunnar Thompson is sure that this is clear evidence of overseas contact:

> Recent assays record that some of the copper artefacts found in North American burial mounds were made from zinc–copper alloys used in the Mediterranean. Ancient metal crafters added zinc to harden copper into a bronze alloy. The shapes of the copper tools found in American archaeological sites are identical to those of the ancient Mediterranean – including chisels, dagger blades, wedges, hoes, scythes, axes and spear points. These tools often have specific modifications including the use of rivets, spines and sockets. All of which were characteristic of Mediterranean tools. The fact that most of the tools were cast from molten metal implies that foreign craftsmen participated in their manufacture.[13]

If it is true that indigenous American peoples did not cast copper or make bronze, then the masses of specialist mining tools found at Lake Superior must have been made by foreigners. The foreigners can only have come by sea. If these seagoing people who sailed to America were not the Minoans, then who were they?

Notes to Book IV

1. Toby Wilkinson, *The Rise and Fall of Ancient Egypt*, Bloomsbury, 2010
2. *Complete Temples*: Wilkins on RH, 2000
3. BBC *Timewatch*, Professors Tim Darvill of the University of Bournemouth and Geoffrey Wainwright, President of the Society of Antiquaries
4. Needham, S. L. et al. 'Developments in the early Bronze Age Metallurgy of Southern Britain', *World Archaeology*, vol. 20, no.23
5. Thomas Goskar, *British Archaeology* 73
6. R. J. C. Atkinson, *Stonehenge*, Pelican, 1960
7. Herodotus 3, 115, trans. Basil Gildersleeve, in *Syntax of Classical Greece*
8. *The American Journal of Human Genetics* (AM J Hum Genet) 2003, November, 73 (5) 1178–1190–X2 of Orkney inhabitants is 7.2 (research of Helgason et al. 2001) – the second highest after Druze
9. Hedges, R. E. M., Housley, R. A., Law, I. A., Perry, C. and Gowlett, J. A. J., 'Radiocarbon Dates from the Oxford AMS System: Archaeometry Datelist 6', *Archaeometry* 29 (2), 1987, 289–306
10. *The Mummies of Cladh Hallan* BBC, 18 March 2003
11. T. G. Schurr, 'Mitochondrial DNA and the Peopling of the New World', *American Scientist*, 18 (2000)
12. Andrew Fitzpatrick, *National Geographic Magazine*, 13 October 2010
13. Dr Gunnar Thompson, *American Discovery*, Misty Isles Press, Seattle, 999

BOOK V

|||||||||||||||||||||||||||||||||

THE REACHES
OF EMPIRE

32

THE SEEKERS SET SAIL

It may have taken thirty days or more to reach landfall. The passing days would have turned into weeks and the crew would be getting anxious. Just how anxious is illustrated by the first nail-biting voyage made across the Atlantic by the explorer Christopher Columbus. When he supposedly 'discovered' America in 1492, a continent which he thought was Asia, Columbus kept two logs. One showed the true distance the ship had sailed on a given day. The other one he faked, to make the distance they'd travelled look greater. As the days turned into weeks, the falsified log was the only one he dared show his increasingly terrified crew.

Could Minoan ships have dealt with the rigours of an Atlantic crossing? Well, with very similar rigging the Vikings managed the same feat. Minoan sailing gear was planned for the best efficiency. Columbus' ship, the *Santa Maria* – also known as the *'Marigalante'*, or 'gallant Maria' – was fitted out with two square sails on the foremast and mainmast. She had a single lateen (a triangular, Roman-style sail) at the stern. The log details that one of the smaller ships accompanying the *Santa Maria*, the *Niña*, left Spain with lateen sails on all masts. By the time they got to the Canary Islands, Columbus had ordered her to be refitted with square sails, like the *Santa Maria*, to take advantage of the winds. The Thera frescoes show us quite clearly that the Minoans already sailed square-rigged, in the 2nd millennium before Christ's birth.

The central reaches of the Atlantic have always worried sailors, even in more modern times. Its sinister-looking masses of moving sargassum (floating seaweed); the fact that you can travel for weeks and still not reach land – all of this is deeply unsettling. In the days of sail, ships would also get hopelessly becalmed in the so-called 'Horse Latitudes', at which point the crew had to confront the very real risk of dying from thirst. You can imagine the sailors thinking: 'Is this, in fact, the edge of the world? Is this where our ship is finally going to fall off?' Truly, if 'there be monsters', they'd be here in the Sargasso Sea.

Assuming they didn't make the mistake of sailing into the Sargasso, helped by the current, the Minoans would loop up past the Antilles and on into the Gulf of Mexico. It is a monumental journey. As Columbus said of the currents of the Caribbean:

> When I left the Dragon's Mouth, I found the sea ran so strangely to the westward that between the hour of Mass, when I weighed anchor, and the hour of Complines, I made sixty-five leagues.

Strangely enough, when it comes to navigation, we can take an initial steer from the ancient palaces of Crete. We know the Minoans could calculate bearings with accuracy, not least because the alignment of all of the Minoan palaces is the same, to within just a few degrees: NNE–SSW from a datum line, or 8 degrees east of north.

The palace builders used a standard unit of measurement – the Minoan foot – as they did at their global observatory sites. J. Walter Graham, in a fascinating paper I'd searched out, studied in detail the Cretan palaces of Phaestos, Knossos and Malia and the small, Late Minoan palace of Gournia, and then put that measurement at between 203 and 204 millimetres (approx. 8 inches).[1] This alone implies that using their common unit, the Minoans had a way of calculating complex numbers and therefore distance.

I would venture further. The knowledge and sophistication of the Minoans was such that they were expert mathematicians. The late American professor and cryptologist Cyrus Gordon certainly believed this, often pointing out that in Linear A script, a small circle seemed to represent the number 100.[2] Only very recently, the Oxford University archaeologist Anthony Johnson proposed that the builders of Stonehenge were actually using Pythagorean geometry. This was a good 2,000 years before Pythagoras.[3]

Now we have certain proof. In 2010 Dr Minas Tsikritsis, a Greek mathematician, published a book about Minoan astronomy, in which he presented convincing new evidence that the Minoans had developed a solar calendar of 365.3 days. His certainty that they did so comes from his study of seal stones, rings and other ancient Minoan artefacts. Put together, the dating of those artefacts suggests that the Minoans had already developed their calendar by 2200 BC. This is around 1,700 years earlier than the Babylonian astronomer Nabu-rimanni is said to have invented the solar calendar. He did so at some point between the Persian (539 BC) and the Macedonian (331 BC) conquests of Babylon. If this is true, then it strongly indicates that the Minoans could calculate longitude – and they could do it independently of Babylon.

Here is how the Minoans calculated numbers. They had two basic forms to construct their digits: symbols which to us look like a straight line and a circle. A vertical straight line signified the number one [|], while a horizontal straight line [–] was ten. A circle [O] denoted one hundred, while a circle with four equally spaced projections [◇] denoted a thousand. Ten thousand was represented by adding the symbol for ten to the unit for a thousand.

So a large number such as 14,266 would have looked like this:

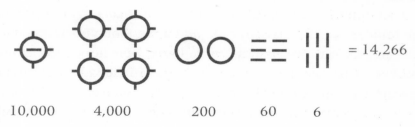

| 10,000 | 4,000 | 200 | 60 | 6 |

Thanks to Dr Tsikritsis' years of painstaking research we now know for certain that our ancient adventurers from Crete could count the number of units they reckoned they had travelled in a day – what we now call sea miles. They could record the number of days they had sailed by logging the number of sunsets since leaving Crete. So they could keep a log showing how far and in what direction they had travelled.

Now to refine our ideas about Minoan ocean navigation. They started their voyages in spring, say a month after the spring equinox (which they calculated from their stone circles). This month is described in Linear B archives by the name 'po-ro-wi-to'. The name meant 'the month of voyages'.

There are no signposts in the open ocean. The Minoan navigators, as we've already explored, must have used a virtual reference grid – their own equivalents of latitude and possibly even longitude lines – to work their way across the world. They noted the height of the pole star and hence the latitude of their home port in Crete or Thera. This is the latitude they must reach to return.

We now know from the positioning of the stone circles at Stonehenge, Almendres and Callanish that the Minoans could determine latitude to within a mile – and they would have had to do so to avoid getting lost. Latitude is relatively easy to determine because there is a star at the extension of the North Pole billions of miles away in space. If you stood at the North Pole in 1450 BC and looked vertically above, at 90 degrees you would see the star Kochab. Because Kochab is so far away, at the equator it appears on the horizon at zero degrees; so by measuring the height of Kochab in the sky you could calculate your latitude.

Assuming this is not their very first voyage to America, our explorers know that they have to sail due west for, say, twenty days to reach the African coast at Tunis. Then they hug that coast for another fifteen days to reach the Pillars of Hercules (Straits of Gibraltar) whose latitude they know. They set off steering west by noting the position of sunrise and sunset, dividing this angle in half to find south, and checking that bearing at midday when the sun is at its highest – they then continue to steer west, at right angles to south.

At night they steer by the stars. At sunset they note the star on the western horizon nearest west and steer towards it. When that sets they pick another star on the horizon nearest to where the sun set and so on until morning, when they revert to using the sun. They duly hit the coast at Tunis, fill up with fresh water, fruit and food and sail on. When they think they are near the Pillars of Hercules they adjust their latitude to that of the Pillars by using the pole star. So far so good: they know their latitude, and they are in the Atlantic.

During this period, steering due west on the same latitude, they would have been able to check the height of the sun each midday at the same latitude – they could cross-check their latitude with Kochab. They would have noticed that the sun rose higher in the sky each midday towards summer, reaching its maximum height on midsummer's day. They would have noted that a simple correction (declination) could be applied each day to the sun's maximum measured height at midday (meridian altitude) to give latitude using this equation: Latitude = 90 ± Declination.

They could also have learned how to make these calculations at Nabta, or other stone observatories. After they had recorded the daily declination, they would have been able to use the sun to calculate latitude each day if Kochab was not visible – i.e. south of the equator. They probably ran a sweepstake; a friendly bet on how far they would travel each day.

When in the Atlantic, they turn southwest for the Canaries, where the 'conveyor belt' of the elliptical Atlantic current takes over, carrying them first southwestwards to the Cape Verde Islands, then westwards to the Caribbean. It is worth noting that cotton with chromosomes unique to North America has been found in the Cape Verde Islands. The Minoans record the time the voyage has taken so far. After resting and provisioning, the current carries them on their way northwest through the Caribbean into the Gulf of Mexico. All the time, the pole star is becoming higher in the sky. As soon as it reaches the latitude of the south tip of Florida they know they must head due west to reach the Mississippi.

They then use 'signposts' set up in earlier voyages to guide them to the rich ores of Lake Superior. They steer north up the Mississippi or west up the St Lawrence River, using these dolmen stone sign-posts.

On the return journey they again use the 'conveyor belt'. This time it takes them across the Atlantic to the Outer Hebrides (Lewis) and the Orkney Islands, where their compatriots have erected 'observatories' of stone circles, as at Stonehenge. They then follow what are now known as the English, French and Spanish coasts, with the current. Now the pole star is sinking lower in the heavens. When it reaches the latitude of the Pillars of Hercules, they know they must head due east, which they do. On entering the Mediterranean they retrace their journey to Crete, reversing their outward bound passage until they reach their joyous point of return.

Using latitude only would not have told them how far – in other words, for how many days – they needed to travel. For this they needed to be able to calculate longitude. As Charles II and the first British astronomer royal, the Revd John Flamsteed, knew, navigation is an art as much as it is a science. That art was so elusive that it became an international obsession in 18th-century Europe. In England, the struggle to perfect navigation became a long-standing joke: to be 'discovering the longitude' meant basically attempting the impossible.[4]

MINOAN CALCULATION OF LONGITUDE

Any heavenly event such as (i) an eclipse of the sun or the moon (ii) the rising and setting times of the planets (iii) the times when planets pass in front of the stars, sun or moon or (iv) the stars' rising and setting times, can be used to determine longitude, provided the observers have accurate star tables and an accurate clock. This method is described in my book *1421* at Appendix 2 pages 598–607 and in *1434* at pages 24–38.

The first requirement is for an accurate clock. Professors J. Fermor, J.M. Steele and F.R. Stephenson have summarised the inaccuracy of water clocks used by the Babylonians.[5, 6, 7] There is no way they could in practice have used them to determine longitude. However Professor Steele, in a review of N.M. Swerdlow's book, *The Babylonian Theory of the Planets*,[8] writes:

> We know that Babylonian astronomers were capable of measuring longitudes if they wished; the existence of a fragmenting star catalogue proves this. Furthermore he [Swerdlow] notes that the preserved diaries do not contain as many reports of the distance of a rising or setting planet to a normal star (from which the longitude could be obtained using something like the star catalogue mentioned above) as one would need to derive the planetary parameters. However this does not necessarily imply that such measurements were not available, or could not have been made by the astronomers who formulated the planetary theories.[9]

So how are these apparently contradictory positions reconciled? The answer I think is to do away with the water clock and rely instead on star tables, which show the rising of stars on the eastern horizon at sunset each evening for four years. At this point the cycle would repeat. In short the navigators would use the slip between sidereal and solar time, as explained in *1434*.

For example on, say, day sixty-eight the star tables published in Babylon state that Aldebaran rose simultaneously with the top tip of the sun disappearing below the western horizon. Out in the Atlantic on day sixty-eight, a second observer notes Betelgeuse not Aldebaran rose at sunset. The angular difference between Aldebaran and Betelgeuse was six hours, one quarter of twenty-four hours. Thus the Atlantic observer would know that his longitude was 90 degrees west, one quarter of 360 degrees. This eliminates the need for a clock. However, it only works if the observers are on the same latitude and if the Minoans had copies of Babylonian star tables – or had produced their own device, capable of both measuring geometrical angles and operating as a calendar.

The fact is that such a device does exist. It was discovered in a shipwreck at Antikythera in 1900; then it was locked away – and simply forgotten about.

THE ANTIKYTHERA MECHANISM

Antikythera is a tiny island just a few miles northwest of Crete.

This is how the magazine *Nature* put it:

> Two thousand years ago a Greek mechanic set out to build a machine that would model the workings of the known universe. The result was a complex clockwork mechanism that displayed the motions of the sun, moon and planets on precisely marked dials. By turning a handle the creator could watch his tiny celestial bodies trace their undulating paths through the sky . . .
>
> . . . Since a reconstruction of the device hit the headlines in 2006, it has revolutionised ideas about the technology of the ancient world and has captured the public imagination as the apparent pinnacle of Greek scientific achievement.
>
> Now, however, scientists delving into the astronomical theories encoded in this quintessentially Greek device have concluded that they are not Greek at all, but Babylonian – an empire predating this [ancient Greek] era by centuries.[10]

The importance of the Antikythera device is that it could provide planetary information – not least the position of the planets at sunset. Provided the observer at sea had the same set of tables as the observer in Babylon, the angular distance between the planets at sunset would give the difference in longitude. The Antikythera device could in fact be used as a longitude calculator – a vivid example of the brilliance of early astronomers. You can view the device in the second colour plate section.

Hoyle believed that a highly sophisticated mathematical and astronomical civilisation was behind the creation of Stonehenge. He said:

> It is not until we come to Hipparchus and Ptolemy that anything of comparable stature can be found in the ancient world, and not until we move forward to Copernicus in the modern world. To paraphrase Brahms in his reference to Beethoven, we hear the tramp of the giant behind.

Stan Lusby has actually tracked those giants' footsteps. A sea surveyor and a specialist in ancient navigational techniques, Lusby
used a computer programme, as he put it, to 'navigate its way
through myth'. He took Homer's description of Odysseus returning
home guided by the stars literally, to see whether it would have
been possible to cross the Atlantic:

> The late-setting Boötes and The Bear, which we also call the Wain,
> which ever circles where it is and watches Orion, and alone has no
> part in the baths of the ocean. For this star Calypso, the beautiful
> goddess, had bidden him to keep on his left hand as he sailed over
> the sea. For seventeen days then he sailed over the sea and on the
> eighteenth appeared the shadowy mountains of the land of the
> Phaeacians.[11]

Lusby set up his 'Skymap' computer programme so that the night
sky would appear as it would have done on 22 November 1350 BC,
at latitude 23 degrees north and longitude 22 degrees 50 minutes
west. The night sky would have been very similar to the period
during which I believe the Minoans were exploring the Atlantic.
The position Lusby chose to study, the point between the Canary
and the Cape Verde Islands during the mid 14th century BC, is the
very same course the Minoans would have steered *en route* to
America. The 'Skymap' shows the perfect symmetry of the night
sky at that date, with Libra and Aries on opposing horizons. Lusby
argues that the ancients used 'star maps' to achieve certain latitudes
then steered along that latitude – for example when voyaging south
down the coast of western Europe the explorers would arrive at a
latitude where Aldebaran could be seen to be vertically above
Alnilam in Orion's Belt. Then they would have time to turn west
into the ocean to pick up the 'conveyor belt' which would carry
them to North America.

To quote part of Stan Lusby's paper, 'Odysseus, James Cook of
the Atlantic':

The landfalls detected are too numerous to be confined to chance and they reveal the existence of a chart-in-the-sky for the North Atlantic that had a degree of orthomorphism [readability in terms of its good shape] part way between a modern Admiralty chart and a metro or underground schematic. It, together with Homer's writings, indicates the safest, most efficient way to cross the Atlantic to take advantage of prevailing winds and currents . . .

Even if they could not determine longitude, Lusby has illustrated that after an initial exploratory mission the Minoans would have been able to find their way to the sources of copper in Lake Superior and then navigate their way home by using latitude only.

|||||||||||||||||||||

There is another reason why I feel that the Minoans were slightly more comfortable in calculating latitude than longitude and it has to do with a recent re-interpretation of the evidence on a tiny golden coin. After the collapse of Minoan power, the Phoenicians inherited the remains of their Mediterranean trading empire. There are many indications that the Phoenicians travelled to Iberia, Britain, Ireland, India, Africa and possibly even America. Did they inherit Minoan maps, I wondered, and if so could these maps be found? I searched for a long time with no success, then via our website a friend referred me to the work of Mark A. McMenamin, Professor of Geology at Mount Holyoke College, Massachusetts. A palaeontologist, geologist and celebrated fossil hunter, he is nevertheless a much published authority on the Phoenicians, their language, coins and maps – a very rare combination indeed.

Professor McMenamin has studied a number of coins minted in Carthage, the Phoenician western capital, between 350 and 320 BC. The provenance and authenticity of these coins has not been challenged. Of relevance to this story is a particular golden coin, on which a horse stands proudly on top of a number of symbols.

Scholars originally surmised that these symbols were letters in Phoenician script, a theory that was discounted in the 1960s. Following 3D imaging analysis of the coin, McMenamin has interpreted the design as a representation of the Mediterranean, surrounded by the land masses of Europe and Africa with, at the upper left, the British Isles. If he is right the Professor has shed a radical new light on the 'discovery' of the New World.

To the left of the Mediterranean, under the horse's left rear hoof, is what he believes is a depiction of the Americas. So McMenamin postulates that the Phoenicians reached America – which I am quite sure they did.

Latitudes on the McMenamin 'Phoenician' map are pretty good. The longitude of the Atlantic and of America, by contrast, is drastically foreshortened. This would be accounted for by the navigator determining longitude by dead reckoning – he would not have appreciated how far west he had travelled with the help of the current. The map would thus not show the true width of the Atlantic. Where I respectfully differ from Professor McMenamin is that I believe that the initial provenance of the map on the coin is Minoan.

My reasoning is prompted first of all by the locations displayed on the map. It details all of the places which Minoan fleets visited, including the British Isles, the Baltic and the Indian Ocean. In short, Professor McMenamin's map coin shows the Minoan trading empire. More importantly, there are some particularly Minoan aspects to the map – for instance the importance (from their size) of the representations of Crete and Cyprus. Most crucially, the Mississippi, which the Minoans followed to reach Lake Superior, appears on the coin's representation of America.

It seems to me that the initial information to compile this map came from Minoan sources: perhaps other maps which have since been lost.

In the light of all this new evidence, I think the Minoans may have had the capacity to use dead reckoning to draw up simple world maps. I believe an original Minoan map will one day be found and authenticated. It will show all of the places the Minoans visited – from the relatively straightforward seas of the Mediterranean, Crete,

Cyprus, the Middle East and Iberia, to the quite simply audacious: Ireland, Britain and the Baltic. Not to mention North America, Africa and India – destinations that took extraordinary levels of bravery and daring to reach.

My belief is based upon the very exact geophysical locations of the observatories that, in my opinion, the Minoans either built or adapted. These sites in Kerala (South India); Malta; Stonehenge; northwest France; Ireland; and the Orkneys – and on the Elbe and the banks of Lake Superior – span nearly half the world in longitude from South India (77 degrees east) to the Great Lakes (89 degrees west) – a total of 166 degrees. Moreover, the latitudes allow for the cross-checking of results – Babylon (32 degrees north); Malta (35 degrees north); Brest, northwest France and Lake Superior (both 48 degrees north). To have done all of this required planning; a sense of overview. In other words, it required maps.

IIIIIIIIIIIIIIIIIIII

By comparing lunar eclipses on the same day (achieved by counting sunrises) the Minoans could trace the moon's passage across the sky and its position relative to a fixed star. This would help them create ephemeris tables (records of the co-ordinates of celestial bodies at specific times) of the moon for Kerala, Babylon, Malta, Stonehenge, probably northwest France and, as I was soon to find out, Lake Superior. Having an observatory in America would make a lot of sense, because it is such a long way west of our Bronze Age meridian of zero degrees longitude – the magical datum line I believe the brilliant Minoan navigators set at Stonehenge. They did this so they could cross-check and refine results and extrapolate them to make ever more accurate ephemeris tables, in the same way that declination tables could be made for each day, to enable latitude to be determined by using the sun. In short, they could make world star maps for the northern hemisphere from India to Lake Superior.

I asked the former Royal Navy Admiral Sir John Forster 'Sandy' Woodward for his view on my theory. Could the ancients really have achieved all of this? His thoughts were:

The whole business of going trans-ocean would have been very rough – enough to get you there but not all that much more. In fact, rather like my cross-channel voyages in a 21ft sail boat – I didn't bother much with accurate navigation. I headed well to one side of my destination [the uptide/upwind side] and turned downtide/downwind when I reached the coast until I reached the place I'd intended. OK, so a compass, the tide tables, etc., made my DR [dead reckoning] pretty good, but as I was keen to show with 'pool navigation', approximate navigation is usually entirely adequate. [Pool of Error navigation is discussed on my website.]

In a ship, you can never forget about obstacles: reefs and rocks, even icebergs. Even the ultra-modern *Titanic* was lost to an iceberg, four days into the ship's maiden voyage. The cruel seas took 1,517 lives.

This would have been a dangerous business, especially if the Minoans met with conditions of low or zero visibility, heavy rainfall or snow; mists and fogs. Yet copper and tin were the most valuable substances in the known world. Wouldn't the Minoans have risked life and limb to find them?

33

A METALLURGICAL MYSTERY

Over the past seven years, since we set up our website, we've had hundreds of emails from North American readers of *1421* and *1434*. They all tell a tale of a mysterious conundrum. To this day the perplexing story of America's missing copper is taught in American and Canadian schools. The story began with Professor Roy Drier, who in the early part of the 20th century was Professor of Metallurgy at the Michigan College of Mining and Technology. The mystery itself, however, dated from the Bronze Age.

In the 2nd millennium BC millions of pounds of copper were mined out of mineral-rich Lake Superior, in North America. Yet where are the Bronze Age artefacts to show for it? While Bronze Age relics do exist, there is a significant mismatch between the number of finds and the evidence left by the miners. The copper, and the bronze it helped create, appears to have vanished into thin air. Could the Chinese explorers I wrote about in *1421* have taken the copper ore back home to China, my correspondents asked?

I didn't have the answers, but I knew enough to start digging. I was also reminded by Dr Gunnar Thompson (see chapter 31) that some of the copper artefacts that are found in American burial mounds show evidence of foreign influence.

Immense wealth – in the form of gold, silver and amethysts – lies just beneath the surface of the vast body of water that is Lake Superior. What's more, Lake Superior's mines were the richest source of copper on earth. Over a billion years ago, copper crystallised in the lava bed that lay deep under the waters of the largest and most northerly of the Great Lakes of America. Glacial action

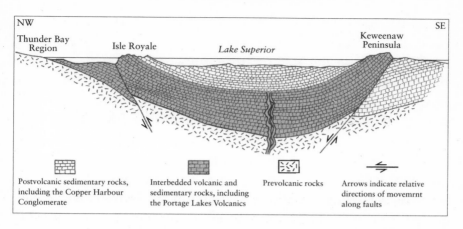

NW   SE

Thunder Bay Region   Isle Royale   *Lake Superior*   Keweenaw Peninsula

Postvolcanic sedimentary rocks, including the Copper Harbour Conglomerate

Interbedded volcanic and sedimentary rocks, including the Portage Lakes Volcanics

Prevolcanic rocks

Arrows indicate relative directions of movemrnt along faults

L a k e   S u p e r i o r

Keweenaw Bay

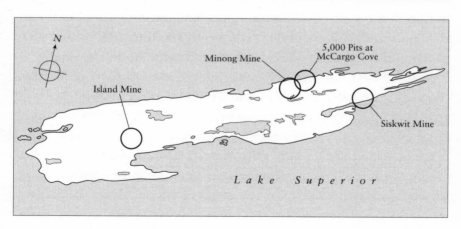

N

Island Mine

Minong Mine

5,000 Pits at McCargo Cove

Siskwit Mine

L a k e   S u p e r i o r

exposed some of those mineral riches, in some cases leaving vast rocks of 'float copper' in river beds, on lake shores and glinting out of rocks. On Isle Royale, a particularly copper-rich island in the northwest of Lake Superior, and on the Keweenaw Peninsula, a further site on the lake's southern shore, Drier found over 5,000 mines. Those workings were not from our time: they dated from between 3000 and 1200 BC...

Drier wondered if the missing copper had been made into goods that were no longer in North America. In other words, he wondered if the resource had actually been exploited by outsiders and not by the native peoples of America. In the 1920s, so soon after the loss of the *Titanic*, this was an almost unthinkable proposition. Could seafarers from the Old World have achieved such a crossing? The mystery remained unsolved.

⁙⁙⁙⁙⁙⁙⁙⁙⁙⁙⁙

The Menomonie Indians of north Wisconsin have a perplexing legend that speaks of an ancient network of mines. The stories describe the mines as being worked by 'light-skinned men', who were somehow able to identify the right place to dig by throwing magical stones on to the ground. When they struck, the instruments made the copper ores ring, like a bell. It's possible that the legend conflates the start of the mining process – finding the ores – with the end results of it; in other words, with creating a metal. A similar practice was used to find tin in Europe during the Bronze Age.

S.A. Barnett, the first archaeologist to study Aztalan, an archaeological site near the Menomonie Indians' native lands, believed that the miners of ancient times originated from Europe. His conclusion was largely based on the type of tools that had been found there, tools which he said were not used by the local people. But where was the workforce and where were the villages, the rubbish tips, the burials? The answer: nowhere. Only their tools remained.

The two world experts on this mystery, Octave Du Temple and Professor Drier, staged a number of expeditions to Isle Royale, hard on the Canadian border, in the 1950s. Their research gradually convinced them that an ancient civilisation far beyond North America had in fact mined and taken away the copper. At first they considered the Egypt of the pharaohs as a possibility, but they eliminated that line of research when they could find no evidence of Egyptian ships having reached North America.

They did, however, manage to fix dates for when the copper was mined. Charcoal found in the bottom of two pits on Isle Royale in Lake Superior confirmed that they had been worked from at least 2500 to 2000 BC.

A huge copper nugget found 5 metres (16.5 feet) down in the Minong mine on Isle Royale weighed 2,390 kilograms (5,270 pounds). There is an old black and white photograph of it in the Detroit Public Library. The copper had been hauled out of the ground on stretchers, or 'cribs'. In another pit, a crib of solid oak had somehow survived without rotting, because of the anaerobic conditions. It had been crafted out of the original oak tree over 3,000 years ago. Mining had certainly been going on here for many centuries before the birth of Christ – efficient mining, conducted on a huge scale.

The ancient miners built large bonfires on top of the copper-bearing veins. Once the rock was glowing with heat they split it by pouring cold lake water over it. Solid copper of extraordinary purity was taken from the veins and smashed with stone hammers. But there seemed to be no trace of these people. They left behind no carvings, writings or paintings. And they left no dead – or so it appeared. Their tools remained in the American mines, just as if the miners expected to return on the following day. They never did. They disappeared – into thin air, it seemed – around 1250 BC.

These ancient miners were clearly very highly skilled. Every major seam opened in the area had already been worked in pre-historic times. Carbon dating of the wood timbers left in the pits puts the first mines at 2450 BC, and the abrupt end of the mining at 1200 BC. The idea of the 'singing' device used by the miners to find the copper was strange, but there was no doubt: these people had been expert miners.

Even today, it is difficult to source original metal ore; in our own times, the price of copper is an economic bellwether, because it is used in so many things, from washing machines to houses. The estimates of the amount of copper ore excavated in the Lake Superior region thousands of years ago are staggering, although they vary hugely. One claim is that as much as 230 million kilograms (500 million pounds) of extremely pure copper was mined here. Another estimate is far more conservative, putting the total at 1.4 million kilograms (3 million pounds).

Yet whatever the precise figures, you would still expect to find large numbers of Bronze Age artefacts here in the New World, either as pure copper or as alloyed bronze. Not so. That copper – tons of it – has disappeared from the archaeological record. The estimate is that if all of the historic copper artefacts of the right date ever found in North America were added together, they would still account for less than 1 per cent of the copper mined from Lake Superior.

⠀⠀⠀⠀⠀⠀⠀⠀⠀⠀⠀⠀⠀⠀⠀⠀⠀⠀⠀⠀⠀‖‖‖‖‖‖‖‖‖‖‖‖‖

We'd chosen the former French fur trading outpost of Thunder Bay as our base and had reserved seats on the port side of the connecting plane. On the beautiful, bright afternoon of our flight, we could see the island stretched out to the southwest, clear as crystal.

Although Isle Royale is technically in the United States, Thunder Bay is right on the border, on the western arm of Lake Superior. Isle Royale itself has been turned into a nature park and is now about as remote a wilderness as you can get.

We were up at dawn, eagerly reporting for duty outside a stout Edwardian classical revival building, the Brodie Resource Library, a minute before opening. Apparently, this part of Ontario holds the world record for wind chill factor: luckily, a helpful librarian let us in out of the cold.

Her name, as it turned out, was Wendy Woolsey and she gave us the quick five-minute tour, explaining that when the library opened in 1885 the Carnegie Foundation had wanted 'to promote a desire for good wholesome literature'. Along the way, the owners had made sure that readers could also get cleaned up: in the original building, the smoking and recreation room had contained a bath. It was good old, paternalistic stuff; during staff picnics, games were to be played and 'steps taken for the safety of women and children'. I noted that this effectively meant 'no liquor'.

The library staff, Wendy, Karen Craib and Michelle Paziuk, were extraordinarily helpful, and kindly agreed to trawl through the library archives looking for:

1. DNA reports on prehistoric miners' skeletons and the dating of these skeletons.
2. Prehistoric miners' skulls, especially those which had been carbon dated, with reports on their heritage – whether European or Native American.
3. Reports on the prehistoric mines, not least methods of mining and the tools left behind.
4. Rock art – particularly any pictures of prehistoric ships.
5. Descriptions of artefacts found by the first Europeans to reach Lake Superior – not least by the Jesuits.
6. Legends and folklore of the indigenous Native American peoples. In particular whether they had mined or assisted in mining in prehistoric times.
7. Chemical analyses of Lake Superior copper and in particular Isle Royale copper. Was it really 99 per cent pure? Were there any corroborative chemical analyses?

The five of us had an amazing day. Marcella and I discovered that even today Thunder Bay is a major port, with extensive grain storage facilities. Isle Royale is 15 miles (24 kilometres) from here. The huge poking finger of the Keweenaw Peninsula, another major site known for ancient mining, is a further 40 miles (64 kilometres) south of us, across the water on the Michigan side of the vast Lake Superior. An official 'water trail' has been mapped out for those who want to visit what was once called 'Copper Island', but it would take a full five to ten days to complete, depending on weather conditions.

Meanwhile, our three helpers were unstoppable. A list of the reports they helped us dig up is on the website.

While Karen dredged up reports on mining, Michelle tracked down skeletal remains and local myths and Wendy looked up local art finds. She also guided us through textbooks and papers that contained chemical analyses of the local ores.

The mining methods Karen's reports described are identical to those used at the Great Orme in north Wales. The Bronze Age metal hunters smashed out the ore with copper axes, adzes and awls which were almost straight duplicates of those at the Great Orme, and they bashed the excavated ore with stone 'eggs', just as they had done in Wales. Perhaps this was the device behind the folklore, behind the Menomonie Indians' myth? The 'eggs' were once again identical in shape, size and weight to those in the Welsh mine.

Thirteen chemical analyses of Great Lakes copper since 1894 at: the Kearsarge and Tamarack mines; Isle Royale; the Phoenix Mine; the Quincy Mine (Keller); the Quincy Mine (Ledoux); the Atlantic Mine; the Osceola and Franklin Mines; Lake Superior (Carpenter 1914); Lake Superior (US Bureau of Standards 1925); Keweenaw (Phillips 1925); and Lake Superior (Voce 1948), show trace elements in the copper of 0.09 per cent or less. That is, the copper is 99 per cent or more pure. The ten copper ingots found in the Uluburun wreck (out of over 300) as analysed by Professor Hauptmann and colleagues can only be Lake Superior copper, because of this extraordinary purity.

Karen also found page after page of detailed descriptions of prehistoric pottery and tools from thousands of prehistoric mines. We looked at old mine workings; mauls and hammers; skeletons and skulls; copper spears and arrows; knives; chisels; punches; awls; needles; harpoons and fish hooks; necklaces; spatulas. There was even a 'Minoan-style' double-headed axe.

The excavation was in 1924 and was known at the time as the 'Milwaukee Expedition'. Over 10,000 Bronze Age artefacts taken from the mines are now in the Milwaukee Public Museum. Experts like Professor N.H. Winchell later argued that the indigenous peoples had no knowledge of refined metalworking. He also had intriguing evidence that the prehistoric miners had had a distinctive genetic characteristic: a remarkable flattening of the shinbone.[12] That took me aback a second – didn't the 'Amesbury Archer', or 'King of Stonehenge', and his 'son' both have a marked bone peculiarity?

Michelle had so far had no luck with ancient skeletons. She did, though, find us some highly interesting information on the changes in the water levels of the Great Lakes over the past five millennia. The fact that the water levels had changed radically since the Bronze Age would later become a crucial piece of evidence in my search for the truth.[13]

The first modern-day mining operations began near the Ontonagon River on the Keweenaw Peninsula. Wendy had dug out details of a strange, so-called 'perched' rock at Pequaming which is carved with a prehistoric Caucasoid human face. The rock is aligned with a dolmen that sits on top of Huron Mountain – and is in line with sunrise at the winter solstice. Could it have been used by the Minoans as a kind of signpost? Like a child in a sweet shop, I hardly knew which morsel of information to chew on first.

34

ADVENTURES BY WATER

The imposing scale of Lake Superior comes as a surprise, rather like the sight of the Grand Canyon for the first time. The colours of the shoreline are vivid and varied: red and grey granite, white quartzite, black basalt and golden beaches. The hills behind the shoreline soar to a height of 305 metres (1,000 feet). This is the southern end of the Canadian Shield, a 4-billion-year-old almost soil-free area of the earth's crust, with its edges clawed but barely diminished by the grumbling glaciers.

And to the west, nothing. No land, no ships, no sails, no people. Just water.

Isle Royale was turned into a national park in the 1950s and today it certainly qualifies as a wilderness – 22 miles (35 kilometres) from Grand Portage, Minnesota; 56 miles (90 kilometres) from Copper Harbor, Michigan; 73 miles (117 kilometres) from Houghton, where the boat service starts. Six and a half hours by boat and then a long hike from the camp site through wild country.

The largest island on the largest freshwater lake in the world, Isle Royale has no modern infrastructure to speak of – no bridges, causeways, or even roads. A deserted, marshy island in the middle of nowhere and populated, I'd been told, mainly by moose. Oh, and wolves.

This is the middle of mining country. You can see on maps that the lake's silting-up has changed the settlement's position relative to the water. On a satellite image I could just make out the outline of a likely area, huge and flat, through sun-dappled shadows in the trees.

Why did these miners leave their tools so suddenly, as though they were planning to come back again the next day? Could there have been an epidemic? Could the whole community have fallen sick and died? Or was it connected with matters at home – the Thera eruption? I suppose that is something we will never be able to work out for sure ...

||||||||||||||||||||

Another day; another island. This time on Lake Michigan, the mid-section of the great butterfly shape drawn by the Great Lakes on the face of America. Beaver Island – 45 degrees 39 minutes north/ 85 degrees 33 minutes west – is also known as 'the Emerald Isle'. It's a fertile gem of a place, set among the best fishing fields of the lake. Fourteen miles (22 kilometres) long, it is a thirty minute ferry ride from the city of Charlevoix.

Tracking the Minoans across the lakes was one of the most thrilling moments of my discovery. A treasure trail of clues had already been leading me towards this island, whose geographical position is key to its importance. A large number of storage pits that still hold traces of corroded copper lead from the Keweenaw Peninsula to Beaver Island.

That was as nothing to the news I had read of a stone circle on the island. Apparently, the native Americans call it a 'sun circle'.

A native American elder had told Professor James Scherz that a mystical series of stone circles lay submerged in the northern reaches of Lake Michigan. The elder told Scherz that these stone structures were all linked by what he called 'Thunderbird lines'. They all led to a large stone circle on Beaver Island.

In the 1950s Scherz made a study of the ring, which is made up of 39 stones and is 121 metres (397 feet) in diameter. He concluded that it was built for astrological purposes.

As my time in Canada drew to an end, evidence of a Minoan presence here was pouring in. North of L'Anse, on the Pequaming Peninsula in Keweenaw Bay, we'd found raised stone cairns that were probably used as beacon markers to guide in the ships. Archaeologists have found the remains of prehistoric cemeteries, created for the mine workers of old, near Green Bay opposite Beaver Island. Sea shells from the Gulf of Mexico and the North Atlantic lie beside the fragments of bone – in some cases, alongside copper jewellery. These copper artefacts appear to be identical in style to those found in the Uluburun wreck.

Hundreds of large, cast copper axe heads had been found – a hoard, just like in Europe – by an archaeologist named Warren K. Moorehead. Near Copper Harbor, above what would have been a beach 3,000 years ago after the retreat of the last glacial ice age, a petroglyph (rock engraving) of an ancient sailing ship. The design, roughly drawn, shows a ship that looks just like the graceful Minoan ships of Thera.

Most excitingly, a second stone circle has now been found nearby, near Traverse City: the only problem being that the site is now under water. Mark Holley, Professor of Underwater Archaeology at Northwestern Michigan College, discovered the series of stones 12 metres (40 feet) below the surface of Lake Michigan.

By his account, amidst the watery gloom Holley thought he could see that one of the stones appeared to have been carved. The markings are about 1 metre high and 1.5 metres long (3 feet by 5 feet). They are worn and the pictures Holley brought back were inconclusive: people speculate that the stone carries a pictogram of a mastodon (elephant-like mammal). Yet mastodon, say archaeologists, were not common this far north, and by this time the huge, tusked mammals were dying out.

The Minoans, I was learning, left little to chance. I admired their strategic choice of location. Beaver Island is about halfway between the southern shore of the narrow part of Michigan's Upper Peninsula and the entrance to Grand Traverse Bay. In other words, it is easy to get to with ships under your command and it's in a great strategic position. It would also be easy to defend – a great site for a trading centre.

Here, at the heart of America, there appears to be a Minoan star observatory, a mini-Stonehenge. Far from leaving without trace, the ancient mariners had left behind something infinitely more precious, to me at least: a mass of copper tools and artefacts. I felt closer than ever to these fearless seafarers, the sailors who had tamed the Atlantic Ocean to become the men of Atlantis.

35

A HEAVY LOAD INDEED

There was, however, a problem to resolve. How would the Minoans have transported the copper? There are only two possible routes: the first is east, through the Great Lakes. You would have to work your way laboriously across Lake Erie and Lake Ontario to the St Lawrence and then head for Newfoundland. As a sailing challenge this is very, very hard to do. The advantage would be that you would be on the right latitude to cross the North Atlantic quickly, to reach bases in Britain. The problem is, it's highly dangerous.

No one is sure whether Giovanni Caboto (John Cabot), the first European since the Vikings to reach the eastern coast of Canada, landed at Newfoundland or Cape Breton Island in 1497. Aided by strong west winds and the Gulf Stream, he took only a triumphant fifteen days to get back. However, it almost goes without saying that the North Atlantic is never to be trusted. In 1498 Cabot tried to do it again, but he never made it. He and his five ships, commissioned by the ambitious English King Henry VII to find 'the Indes', were lost at sea.

The other, safer, route could be via the mighty Mississippi, the largest river system in North America. It is less than a mile from some parts of the southwestern shore of Lake Michigan to rivers that are part of the Mississippi watershed. There are also a number of places in Wisconsin, south Michigan and north Indiana where you could carry boats (in a process known as 'portage') from the Lake Michigan watershed to the Mississippi watershed. Looking at the map, I could see that such an approach would take the Minoans south via evocatively named places like Poverty Point and Cahokia.

Would journeying this far south have made sense?

Yet again, Wendy and her colleagues were being wonderful, supplying me with a lot of papers. It looked to me as if, due to geographic change, this route south had been navigable in the Bronze Age in a way it isn't today. I've made a note of which reference sources were the most useful in the search later in this chapter, but I am starting here with Professor James Scherz, the first man to examine Beaver Island's stone circle. He had also made a special study of ancient trade routes.[14]

Professor Scherz writes:

Immediately after the glaciers melted, water levels of the Great Lakes were much lower than today with the main outlet through North Bay [i.e. into the St Lawrence]. But as the land rose under the melted glacier, the river at North Bay also rose. So did lake levels behind it, until the waters of Lakes Huron, Michigan and Superior combined into a giant body of water called 'Lake Nipissing' ... but the water could continue rising only so long, and finally a southern outlet opened into the Illinois River over the present Chicago Ship Canal [at the southern end of Lake Michigan. 'CSC'].

Another book showed me pictographs of very old sailing ships – beside Lake Superior. Of course. When Lake Superior and Lake Michigan were one, there was no water level difference at Sault Sainte Marie. So there I had my answer: the Minoans would have been able to ship their precious copper out of America by sailing the grandest river of them all. The Mississippi.

I was still unsure. How on earth, I kept thinking, did they get upriver against the current? And then I realised. I'd got it wrong: the bones were all there, but I'd assembled the skeleton wrongly. Of course, they didn't; they waited for a favourable wind to be able to sail against the current. Large vessels from the Mississippi could then have sailed directly into Lake Nipissing, and then on to Keweenaw and Isle Royale. And coming back, they would have used the current – the current on the Mighty Miss can be very strong in high water periods and the speeds range from 1 to almost

6 knots. If they caught the tide right, travel was dead easy.

If copper was floated south, then there should be evidence of that downriver: evidence of smelting going on, for instance. Finding that would be my next task. It would have been relatively easy to float the copper south on rafts – as indeed logs, cattle and corn were transported south in the early days of European settlement.

The Mississippi would have connected the Great Lakes with the Gulf of Mexico and thence the Atlantic. The river is a series of wide streams – for the most part a steady, fairly even water flow. Sailing north against this flow is tedious, but it is possible in high summer, when the prevailing wind is from the southwest. Mark Twain describes sailing on the Mississippi against the current and some Spanish explorers also used the river to travel north, as did the French Jesuits. The Minoans also had experience of sailing upstream on the Nile – a river which is just as long as the Mississippi.

A bit of further reading and I had calculated that it would take around eight weeks to get from the Gulf of Mexico to the Great Lakes, sailing and rowing against the current. Floating south, on the other hand, was simple, using the current as the method of propulsion.

HOW WAS IT DONE?

The mining areas are shown on the map 'The Great Lakes' map at the front of this book. Various mines are marked with crosses – please also refer to the diagram showing the Geology of Michigan copper in Chapter 33, and James Scherz's 'Ancient Trade Routes' in America's Copper Country' (*Ancient American*, issue 35). At the time those mines were operated (2400–1200 BC) the ice sheets had retreated, to leave Lake Superior ice-free in summer. Mining would take place during the summer months and the ore was carried by ship or raft across the Great Lakes, which were then distinct, but connected, sheets of water. Come winter it would only be possible to move the copper across the lakes by sledge or raft. Mining would not have been possible, given the severe cold.

TRANSPORTATION – LAKE AND RIVER SYSTEMS

The most northerly river, the Ontonagon, flows north through the copper mines into Lake Superior, while the others – the Wisconsin and Rock Rivers – flow south into the Mississippi. As a consequence copper from all of the principal mines could be shipped downstream to Lake Superior using the Ontonagon River or the rivers on Isle Royale which connect the mining area to Lake Superior. This explains the loading harbours found on the northern part of the Keweenaw Peninsula (Pequaming, Anse and Baraga) and around Lake Superior (Otterhead harbour and on Isle Royale). So using natural resources Minoan miners could collect copper and then ship it to Lake Superior without going against the current or negotiating rapids.

LIVING QUARTERS

Come autumn, Lake Superior, the surrounding rivers and the land would have frozen over. In summer, miners would need living quarters within reach of the mines. The map of the Great Lakes shows the areas in which towns fortified sites have been found.

THE VOYAGE SOUTH

I drew my finger southwards down the map, trying to take in the names of the many places at which the Minoans may have rested. It is a long way to what is now Louisiana: they must have stopped to trade what they could for food, and they may well have stopped to process the copper.

'Are there any major prehistoric sites you know of that could have acted as a trading centre?' I asked Wendy, who was fast becoming a near-expert on the Bronze Age.

She knew of several, but the most interesting was a major early native Indian settlement at the mouth of the Mississippi. It was a name I had noticed before on the map: Poverty Point. There had even been claims that in times past this very site was Atlantis: might that be a folk memory of the people who had once come here to trade?

Whether or not it had a link to the real Atlantis, this intriguing ancient site had definitely been a major trading point. It had been built over a long period, between 1650 and 700 BC – eight centuries after the building of the Great Pyramid. The dates worked. So did the fact that huge firing ovens have been found near there – as had copper from the Great Lakes.

FOOD

One would have imagined maize would not have grown this far north in 2000 BC, but surprisingly the crop has been found in human graves at Baraga on Lake Superior. It may have been brought up the Mississippi – as I will describe later. Fish and game would have been abundant. Lack of vitamins would have otherwise been a severe problem in winter as would have been lack of potable water; perhaps deep wells were in use and these were not frozen.

A CAMP TO TRADE NEAR POVERTY POINT

On the Pearl River mouth of the Mississippi, near where it debouches into the Gulf of Mexico, we find one of the most revealing bits of evidence. The Claiborne and Cedarland Rings, very near to the trading centre of Poverty Point – and contemporaneous with it – sat on high ground above the marsh created as the Mississippi debouches into the Gulf of Mexico. Excavated by James Bruseth of Louisiana State University in the 1970s, the sites had unfortunately been quite extensively damaged by relic-seekers.

Bruseth was called in just before the bulldozers arrived: a new harbour facility was being built, which was how the site had been uncovered. Along with large concentrations of charcoal, the archaeologist found 'an enormous hearth, as long as a football field: 6 foot [1.8 metres] deep and 300 feet [91 metres] long'. The huge 91-

metre hearth was on a level with a number of smaller hearths, between 50 and 60 centimetres (20 and 26 inches) wide. He put a radiocarbon date of 1425–1400 BC on his finds. He also found large numbers of clay moulds: presumably the remains of the moulds used to cast the copper into ingots.

In the middens, or rubbish pits, Bruseth found hundreds of bits of broken clay which he thought must have been thrown away because they had been broken during the firing process. The fact that they were broken tells us quite the opposite. These were clay moulds, broken when the Minoans hammered them apart to get at the precious cast metal inside. Ingots of pure copper.

How did the Minoans get to Poverty Point?

36

INTO THE DEEP UNKNOWN

This is what I think happened. Early Minoan explorers crossed the Atlantic with the Equatorial Current, the 'free ride' that would be relatively easy in summer before the hurricane season. They visited Meso-America; the proof that they traded cotton, fruit and vegetables is discussed by Professor Sorenson, who has tracked these exchanges.[15]

After visiting Yucatán, the current would have carried them north to the Mississippi Delta, where they discovered that today's 'land of opportunity' was even then a land of unimaginable riches. They saw float copper (copper lying loose in the soil) being used by the people of Poverty Point, who were international traders. At Poverty Point they were told of the original source of the copper in the Great Lakes: particularly at Lake Superior. On reaching the Great Lakes they saw huge nuggets of pure copper simply lying on the ground. They built a stone observatory on Beaver Island to fix the latitude and longitude of this incredible treasure and drew up a map. Then they set up an entire system to bring the riches back to Europe – creating protected townships for the miners in summer at Lac Vieux Desert, and winter quarters at Aztalan and perhaps Rock Lake.

Lac Vieux Desert is part of the drainage shore of the Mississippi today. Sometime between 1300 and 1200 BC the Aztalan settlement was abandoned, for reasons that remain unknown to this day. During the Bronze Age both the Lac Vieux Desert site and Aztalan were fortified, as well as being protected by water – in the middle of a lake (Vieux Desert) or by the Rock River (Aztalan). Recently, walls and substantial pyramid structures have been found submerged in Rock Lake. Both sites are protected by double embankments. The miners clearly feared attacks – by humans or bears.

I assume Lac Vieux Desert was the summer camp, from which mines could be reached downstream via the Ontonagon River. Aztalan, further south and therefore warmer, was the winter quarters, reached via the Rock River from Lake Michigan.

They built shipyards on Isle Royale, at Otterhead Island and at the northern end of the Keweenaw Peninsula at Pequaming, Baraga and L'Anse. Later they had the sad duty of constructing burial mounds for those workers who died at Aztalan, Rock Lake and Green Bay.

The copper was loaded on to pallets, which were extended to form rafts. These rafts were floated down the Mississippi via Lake Michigan to Poverty Point in the south. Here the vast kilns awaited them. The rafts were broken up to be used for charcoal: the copper was turned into ingots before they'd even left, and stored to await collection by Minoan ships which crossed the Atlantic.

On the return leg, the ancient traders pitched up just north of the Mississippi Delta – and waited for Nature's largesse. Who knows? Perhaps it was Nature herself who taught them how to get home. We know that 19th-century whalers understood about the currents, because we have records of them watching the great humpback whales hitch a free ride north, and then following them. Our intrepid Minoans may well have followed the loggerhead turtles, fabulous creatures born under a million stars on the beaches in Crete, as they began their epic journey home to breed.

On the return journey they again found a free ride on the Gulf Stream. Warmed by the sun in the shallow waters of the Gulf of Mexico, water rushes east through its only point of escape, the narrow Straits of Florida. Thirty million cubic metres (39 million cubic yards) per second of water drain out of the Florida Straits, pumping our Minoan ships north.

It's difficult fully to grasp the immensity of this great ocean river. To carry just the sea salt that flies through the Straits every hour would take more ships than exist in the entire world today. A billion cubic feet of water streams past Miami every second of the day.

The push through the straits, only 50 miles (80 kilometres) wide and 2,500 feet (760 metres) deep in places, increases the speed and force of the Florida current. Deflected to the north by the Bahamas, the Florida Current then joins with the Antilles Current. The Gulf Stream System, as it has just become, then triples in volume and pushes north.

The Minoans may have whiled the hours away watching the whales, as the huge mammals fed off the plankton-rich waters along the current's edge. Or they could have seen the blue sharks that use the current to reach their pupping grounds off southern Ireland, west Wales, Spain and Portugal. The total round trip made by these amazing predators is 9,500 miles (15,300 kilometres).

The current flows north along the southeastern United States, slowing as it runs toward Cape Hatteras, and then turns towards the east. Off the Grand Banks of Newfoundland, the Gulf Stream and the Labrador currents collide, creating fogs and storms famous for their treacherous nature. The ocean water temperature changes are often dramatic: as much as 20 degrees of change as you cross from one current to the other.

The huge wheel of the North Atlantic continues to turn. As they pass Nova Scotia the water flow increases to 150 million cubic metres (195 million cubic yards) per second, pushing them on to the Outer Hebrides (Lewis) and the Orkney Islands. Here at their bases their compatriots have erected 'observatories' – stone circles as at Stonehenge – where they can compare and update their star charts. They then follow what would later become the English, French and Spanish coasts as they set out for home.

Now the pole star is sinking lower in the heavens. When it reaches the latitude of the Pillars of Hercules, they know they must head due east – and prepare for a joyous return to Crete.

I could rest now, happy that I had solved my conundrum. The solution to the mystery of the missing copper, I now realised, had been staring me in the face at the beautiful, autumnal Lake Superior: in the form of Mother Nature.

Nature provided everything – from the copper sitting right on the surface, ready to be collected, to the wood for the rafts and the water to carry them. Mother Nature was behind the significant change in water levels over three millennia. And in riding the Gulf Stream back to Britain, the Minoans used what came perfectly naturally to them – the power of the seas.

37

SO: THE PROOF

I decided to look in detail at the prehistoric mining tools and copper implements found on the Keweenaw Peninsula and on Isle Royale, starting with the stone hammers.

The fact that Great Orme and Isle Royale copper miners used identical mining tools could, of course, be a coincidence. It could simply be put down to the designer's favourite adage: form follows function.

What about the other copper implements left by the miners for other purposes? To ascertain the full extent of the similarities we built up a file of prehistoric Lake Superior copper implements.

We also took photographs at a number of American museums and obtained others from an excellent website called *The Great Lakes Copper Culture*. Thousands of different copper and bronze tools have been found around Lake Superior: projectiles with flat, conical and rat-tail points and square and ornate sockets; harpoons with flat and round tangs; knives of every shape and function – with crescent-shaped, straight and curved blades; all manner of fish hooks; scrapers and spatulas; axes, adzes, palstaves; punching instruments in the form of awls, needles, gorges, mandrils, finger drills; fasteners in the shape of staples, clasps and rivets; personal adornments – bracelets, rings, beads, gorgets, tinkling earrings. There were literally hundreds of varieties of copper and bronze implements, running into thousands of individual items.

Then it struck me. If, as I had been contending, it was the Minoans who had mined the copper of the Great Lakes, then we should compare artefacts like for like with artefacts found in Crete, on Thera and in the Uluburun wreck. So I re-examined the museum catalogues. These, time and again, showed photographs of bronze utensils identical to their Lake Superior counterparts of the same age. You can view a selection of compansons in the colour plate section and on our website.

||||||||||||||||||||||

DETERMINING THE SOURCE OF COPPER ARTEFACTS THROUGH TRACE ELEMENT PATTERNS AND X-RAY SPECTROMETRY

A number of American geologists agree that Great Lakes copper was of extraordinary purity. Professor James B. Griffin of the University of Michigan puts the total trace elements in the material at 0.1 per cent or less: i.e. the copper is of 99 per cent purity or more.

It should be possible to use non-invasive X-ray spectrometry to measure the trace elements in copper artefacts from Lake Superior and the Uluburun wreck and then use the results to discover if the Great Lakes were the original source of the copper.

As far as I know, two attempts to use this method have been made, in studies thirty years apart. The first one was made by Edward J. Olsen[16] and the second by Georg (Rip) Rapp, James Allert, Vanda Vitali, Zhichun Jing and Eiler Henrickson.[17]

I found both easy to read. Essentially they both reached the same conclusions. There are so many variables that any conclusion reached has to be on a 'balance of possibility' basis (my wording) and treated with great caution. It may one day be possible to be certain, but much more work is required. George Rapp and colleagues state that their purpose was to (1) indicate the extent to which sources of natural copper can be chemically distinguished; (2) present a methodology for trace-element sourcing; (3) publish a small database; (4) provide another means by which archaeologists can approach complexities in trade and exchange networks. There is a final caution concerning finding a 'reasonable' geographic source area. (As soon as the word 'reasonable' appears, it seems to me that the possible area of the source becomes too wide to draw definite conclusions.)

Edward J. Olsen lays out the problems one after another. He explains lucidly how the method works. Each trace element in the copper sample is energised by X-rays and then emits a signal. The intensity of the signal denotes the strength of the trace element. The method can be used for trace element 22 (titanium) upwards. However the accuracy depends on:

1. Size of sample and whether it is an aggregation or one single mass.
2. The particular trace element and its relationship with copper: i.e. zinc's trace element 'peak' is so close to copper's 'peak' that it can be masked; another example, silicon, increases the apparent intensity of aluminium. Then the efficiency of the X-ray tube depends on the trace element being sought and how this differs from trace element to trace element.

He summarises:

> Thus, in order to determine the chemical characteristics of copper [artefacts] from a given locality one must be aware that trace elements are exceedingly unreliable.

Bearing these two reports in mind, I wanted to double-check my contention that Bronze Age copper of 99 per cent purity was only found in the mines of Lake Superior. Unfortunately, the distinguished Professor Hauptmann believes it is impossible to be this precise. As he wrote to me: 'you cannot prove [10 Uluburun ingots] came from Lake Superior'.

Despite this I maintain my assertion – firstly because the reports assembled by Professor Griffin are not dealing with artefacts but with mined copper. Secondly, there is an almost complete lack of trace elements in the reports Griffin has assembled – which record the analysis of Lake Superior copper. We are not considering minute differences between one trace element and another but the virtual absence of all of the trace elements. The argument is about statistics, factorial probability, and not about the accuracy of the X-ray method deployed.

As to the actual artefacts themselves, I undertook an extensive study of my own. My first job was to separate out the different implements on the Uluburun wreck, then combine those objects with those found on the Seytan Deresi (16th century BC) and Cape Gelidonya (late 13th century BC) wrecks; the aim being to show exactly what was in use in the Mediterranean between 1600 and 1200 BC. All three wrecks were discovered off the coast of Turkey.

Then I decided to combine the implements from these shipwrecks with similar Bronze Age implements, tools and artefacts found at Minoan sites of the same age. These sites were in Crete, Santorini (Thera), some of the Cyclades islands and Mycenae. Marcella and I had already visited the principal museums in those places – the Heraklion and Knossos museums in Crete, the Archaeological Museum of ancient Thera; the National Archaeological Museum in Athens and museums in Mycenae and Tiryns.

The purpose of this exercise was to see whether any items found in the wrecks were different from those that could have been found in Minoan bases near and around Crete. As far as we could see there were none. The style of tools, weapons and implements found in the Uluburun and Cape Gelidonya wrecks were also found in Crete, Thera and Mycenae. In other words this was a check and balance to confirm that it was Minoan bronze artefacts, as opposed to various imports, that filled the wrecks. Images of the artefacts – separated out into those found in the two wrecks and four museums – are shown on our website.

COMPARISON BETWEEN MINOAN BRONZE AGE ARTE-FACTS FOUND IN CRETE, THERA AND THE BRONZE AGE WRECKS WITH THOSE FOUND IN LAKE SUPERIOR

We trawled through the Bronze Age bronze, copper and tin artefacts left by the miners who mined the copper from Lake Superior, in particular those from the Keweenaw Peninsula and Isle Royale. We separated these Bronze Age artefacts into the same categories as those from the Old World, as described in this chapter. As far as I can see, every item found in Lake Superior has its near-counterpart in Minoan artefacts of the time. Lake Superior's ancient miners had the same array of implements, weapons, tools and domestic equipment as the people who lived on Bronze Age Crete, Thera and Mycenae.

This could, of course, be simply the phenomenon known as parallel development. The Isle Royale miners needed bronze weapons to defend themselves, to hunt and to eat the food they caught. So they designed implements whose form would 'follow function', as a modern-day designer would put it. The logical result of that process, of refining a design until it reaches an optimum point, could end in tools that are highly similar to their Old World, Minoan counterparts. This argument will have its supporters, naturally. Yet how can it be coincidence that the measuring weights used so many thousands of years ago take the form of animals? (See second colour plate section.)

It is also intriguing that even local Native American myth appears to support the idea that it was outsiders who were mining the area's islands and peninsulas. This has a bearing on the other potent argument for the involvement of outsiders in Lake Superior's mining heritage: namely, the industrial scale on which the copper was mined and processed. This area was so rich in minerals that local people didn't need to mine: they could use the abundant float copper found on the surface. Those who mined the copper were clearly not indigenous Americans. I suggest the best explanation is that the miners were the same people as those who so efficiently controlled the bronze trade in the Old World.

The stone astronomical structures were so like those in Britain. Grave barrows, astronomical alignments, avenues and *cursi*: the elements were the same. One could just about argue that these basic structures, particularly those based on fundamental geometrical elements like the circle, could have been arrived at by different cultures acting independently of each other. Yet combine that with the discovery that the tools are of the same design and I felt that the evidence for a common culture was building. I knew that it could be a long haul to prove my case definitively, but it was getting there ...

It does not of course follow that after a certain period in prehistory the Minoans used Lake Superior copper exclusively. But it is an inescapable fact that certain ingots in the Uluburun wreck do not match any known European source.

If I am right, we have another fixed date to work with: the Minoans were sailing to Lake Superior before the Uluburun was wrecked in 1310 BC.

Notes to Book V

1. J. Walter Graham, 'The Minoan Unit of Length and Minoan Palace Planning', *American Journal of Archaeology*, 64 (1960)
2. Cyrus Gordon, *Forgotten Scripts*, Basic Books, 1982
3. Anthony Johnson, *Solving Stonehenge: The New Key to an Ancient Enigma*, Thames & Hudson, 2008
4. Dava Sobel, *Longitude*, Fourth Estate, 1998
5. J. Fermor and J. M. Steele, 'The Design of Babylonian Waterclocks: Astronomical and Experimental Analysis', *Centaurus*, 42, 2000 pp. 210–222
6. J. M. Steele and F. R. Stephenson, 'Lunar eclipse times predicted by the Babylonians', *Journal for the History of Astronomy*, 28 (1997)
7. J. M. Steele, 'The Accuracy of Eclipse Times Measured by the Babylonians', *Journal for the History of Astronomy*, 28 (1997)
8. N. M. Swerdlow, *The Babylonian Theory of the Planets*, Princeton University Press, 1998

9. J. M. Steele, *Journal of the American Oriental Society* 119 (1991), p. 696

10. *Nature*, vol. 468, (2010) pp. 496–498

11. Homer, *Odyssey*, trans. Samuel Butler, 1998

12. N. H. Winchell, 'Ancient Copper Mines of Isle Royale', *Popular Science Monthly*, vol. 19, 1881

13. James B. Griffin (ed.), *Lake Superior Copper and the Indians – Miscellaneous Studies of Great Lakes Prehistory*, University of Michigan, 1961

14. Based on a number of research papers published in *The Ancient American – Archaeology of the Americas Before Columbus*, and by researchers from the Ancient Artefact Preservation Society, notably an article by Emeritus Professor James Scherz titled 'Ancient Trade Routes in America's Copper Country' (*Ancient American*, issue 35)

15. Professor Sorenson (Refer to select bibliography in this book)

16. Edward J. Olsen, 'Copper Artefact Analysis with the X-ray Spectrometer, *American Antiquity*, vol. 28, no. 2 (October, 1962)

17. George Rapp et al., 'Determining Geological Sources of Artefact Copper: Source Characterisation using Trace Element Patterns', *American Antiquity*, vol. 68, no. 2 (April 2003)

BOOK VI

|||||||||||||||||||||||||||||||||

THE LEGACY

38

THE SPOTS MARKED 'X'

By now, I was running to catch up. I'd got solid proof that the Minoans had travelled throughout most of Europe and that they had explored a large part of North America. Now I needed to find out if there were any studies that showed a common thread. Tracking down DNA evidence would be my next line of enquiry.

'X' usually marks the spot in any treasure hunt. By pure coincidence, the same was true of my own hunt for gold – in the form of information. There is a widespread, but much contested theory that the first Amerindians originally came from East Asia. However, an intriguing DNA haplogroup has recently been found in several Native American populations – haplogroup X. The X group is the only Amerindian haplogroup that does not show a strong connection to East Asia.

What is interesting is that although haplogroup X is itself rare, it has a perplexingly wide geographic range: despite its relative scarcity the group is found throughout Europe and the Middle East.

In North America this haplogroup is found particularly among Native Americans, especially tribes living in and around the Great Lakes, while in Scandinavia, for instance, it is found in only 0.9 per cent of the population.

Haplogroup X2 is a rare subgroup of X that appears to have expanded quite widely in the Mediterranean and the Caucasus around 21,000 years ago. It's now more concentrated in the Mediterranean, particularly in Greece, along with Georgia, the Orkney Islands and the Druze community in Israel. I looked for a summary. Here is the best I found, written by Jeff Lindsay. As he points out, some geneticists believe that 'Lineage X' suggests a 'definite' – if ancient – link between Eurasians and Native Americans.

ENTER HAPLOGROUP X

The team, led by Emory Researchers Michael Brown and Douglas Wallace, were searching for the source population of a puzzling marker known as X. This marker is found at low frequencies throughout modern Native Americans and has also turned up in the remains of ancient Americans. Identified as a unique suite of genetic variations, X is found on the DNA in the cellular organelle called the mitochondrion, which is inherited only from the mother . . .

. . . Haplogroup X was different. It was spotted in a small number of European populations. So the Emory group set out to explore the marker's source. They analysed blood samples from Native American, European and Asian populations and reviewed published studies.

'We fully expected to find it in Asia, like the other four Native American markers [A, B, C and D],' says Brown.

To our surprise, haplogroup X was only confirmed in a smattering of living people in Europe and Asia Minor including Indians, Finns and certain Israelis. The team's review of published MtDNA sequences suggested it may also be in Turks, Bulgarians and Spaniards. But Brown's search has yet to find haplogroup X in any Asian population.

'It's not in Tibet, Mongolia, South East Asia or Northeast Asia,' [Theodore] Schurr told the meeting. 'The only time you pick it up is when you move west into Eurasia.'

Haplogroup X is found in several places outside of Asia, including among the Finns for example (Finnila et al. 2001), who are often thought to be an earlier group in Europe in the light of Y chromosome studies but nevertheless appear to share many MtDNA lineages with other Europeans. Detailed information about the mutations separating the X haplogroup from the Cambridge Reference and other European haplogroups are provided by Finnila et al. (2001): especially see their Figure 2.[1]

In chapter 7, I'd discovered that the Minoans most likely arrived in Crete from central and eastern Anatolia. One would therefore expect to find a high incidence of X2 from that area. In fact, the statistics live up to expectations. The figures in brackets are percentages.

Turks (4.4); Iranians (3.0); Nogays (4.2); Adygeis (2.5); Abazins (6.3); Kumyks (3.6); South Caucasians (4.3); Georgians (7.6); Armenians (2.6); Azeris (4.2).

Here is where X2 has been found in significant amounts:

Belgium (FTDNA 3)
Crete (Reidla et al)
Egypt (Kujanova)
Finland (Mishmar and Moilanen)
France (FTDNA 4)
Israel/Lebanon (Shlush)
Morocco (Maca Meyer)
Navajo (Mishmar)
Ojibwa/Chippewa – Great Lakes (Fagundes, Achilli, Pirego)
Orkneys (Hartmann)
Portugal (Pereira)
Sardinia (Fraumene)
Tunisia (Costa)

The geographical spread of X2 was most helpfully summarised by Finnila and colleagues.[2] It is replicated on our website.

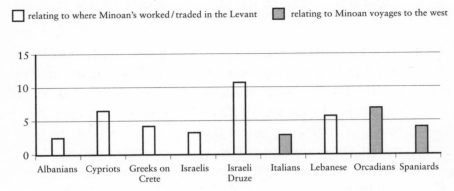

☐ relating to where Minoan's worked / traded in the Levant   ▨ relating to Minoan voyages to the west

The American inheritors of X2 (Ojibwa/Chippewa, around the Great Lakes) have their own sub-divisions of X2: X2a1; X2a2; X2aib; X2a1a; X2g.

From the higher percentages involved, it seems that X2 originated in the Near East, and particularly eastern Anatolia, just as the Minoans had done. There is much controversy over the dating of the DNA, i.e. when the mutations which resulted in the sub-haplogroups occurred. It would be difficult to say with certainty when the European carriers of X2 reached America. At present there are two possible dates for the arrival of X2: 9,200–9,400 years ago or 2,300–3,800 years ago. I would summarise the research in this way:

1. The implications are that the X2 populations in North America could have been caused by Y-DNA mutations from European X2 ancestors (c.1800 BC) or from a much earlier migration by Europeans to North America 9,420 years ago.

2. The people with one of the highest incidences of X2, the Ojibwa, live mainly around Lake Superior in Michigan, Wisconsin, Minnesota, North Dakota and Ontario (Canada) – i.e. near the copper mines described in chapters 33–37.

3. No fewer than sixteen European and Mediterranean countries in which significant levels of X2 DNA have been found were visited by the Minoans, as described in chapters 1–15.

4. DNA X2 has thus been found on both sides of the Atlantic and throughout the Minoan trading empire. Taking all of the evidence in the round, it appears that the Minoans could well have been the carriers of X2: it has been found where the Minoans originated, where they settled and where they traded. Other unknown European travellers appear to have reached America 6,000 years before them in substantial numbers.

5. X2 is not found outside the areas I have already identified as probable trading outposts of the Minoan trading empire.

Bearing in mind that X2 is also found where Minoan Linear A script is found, it seems to me that we can learn lessons from the DNA reports, not least:

(i) The Minoans originated from northeast rather than central Anatolia – because of the high incidence of X2 in that area and in neighbouring Georgia, Armenia, Iran and Azerbaijan (Finnila).

(ii) The mutation from X2 to X2a in the Ojibwa/Chippewa probably took place between 1800 and 1200 BC.

(iii) There seems to have been little sexual contact between the Minoans and the English (0.9) or the French (0.8) compared to that which took place between the Minoans and the Orcadians (7.2) or the Spanish (4.2).

(iv) The Minoans did not get to central, southeast or East Asia nor to West or southern Africa, but did apparently reach the Gulf States (Oman 1.3), Saudi Arabia (1.5) and Kuwait (2.0).

(v) The Minoan presence in what are now Israel, Syria, Lebanon and Jordan was even more pronounced, as evidenced by X2 in populations of Israeli Druze (11.1), Israelis (3.4) and Lebanese (5.8).

39

A NEW BEGINNING

In some ways this book was ending as it had begun. I had been working flat out, starting at 05:00 a.m. and working through for twelve hours each day. My right wrist was locked with arthritis and once again I was dog-tired. Still, my team and friends, especially Cedric Bell and Ian Hudson, had also been working hard, collating a stream of evidence from the well-wishers contributing to our website. I owed it to them to finish the manuscript and get the book published.

Nonetheless, the prospect of describing the end of the Minoan civilisation filled me with foreboding. For the Minoans, the end of empire was a slow and painful death, not a sudden execution. I could hardly bear to think of it. All that brilliance, all that invention – and all their cultural and technological expertise lost.

Thera's volcano had given several weeks' notice of its anger, so it must have seemed as if disaster had been averted. The island was thoroughly evacuated: the absence of carbonated corpses, as found at Pompeii, tells us that. The real tragedy was yet to come.

For safety's sake, everybody on Thera most likely sailed to the mother island, Crete. How could they know what would happen next? For days there would have been grumblings, maybe even the flash of an odd explosion, coming from the direction of Thera. Then it happened for real. An almighty thunder clap seemed to split the horizon. Next came a sinister rush of sound, as ash and gases blasted up from the volcano's heart.

After the staggering eruption, the heavy sky must have felt leaden and threatening. A spreading stain of purple on the northern horizon heralded the sulphurous clouds to come. I imagine a terrible moment of calm; a charged silence as, inexplicably, the sea reared back from the shore, leaving a mass of gasping and struggling sea creatures in its wake. Then came a low and distant roar. A gathering wall of water raced across the sea towards the mother island, its sheer force pulverizing everything in its path.

A hundred-foot wall of water hit Mochlos, the harbour town on eastern Crete. The tsunami probably destroyed the entire Minoan fleet, as it lay tied up in the various ports. If the first surge didn't pull them apart, the next one would have seen to that. The evacuees recently arrived from Thera were all sheltering in the coastal towns, so the disaster may have taken many lives. A superheated pyroclastic surge of gas, light ash and pumice may have followed. At Mochlos, it probably killed everyone. Plato's words came back to me:

> In a single day and night of misfortune, all your warlike men in a body sank into the earth, and the island of Atlantis in like manner disappeared – into the depths of the sea.

In Crete the human casualties, the destruction of houses and temples and, above all, the total annihilation of the shipping on which the island's prosperity relied must have been crippling. After the volcano came days, possibly weeks of toxic gas and lethal ash falling thick upon the ground, suffocating people and plants and poisoning the water supplies. The catastrophe appeared to be coming from the very skies the Minoans had studied for so long. They must have thought the gods had abandoned them. There may still have been plenty of people left alive. But the towering wall of water – and the smothering ash – had destroyed everything of the Cretan harvest's famous bounty.

Then came famine.

⁂

A telephone call. Would I be interviewed by Greek national TV about the new book I was thinking of doing? It was a great excuse to get away. Marcella and I decided, as we had done on a previous Christmas, to revive morale with a special trip.

We drove to Venice and from there we boarded a magnificent car ferry, which at noon sails splendidly past St Mark's Square and into the Adriatic, *en route* to Greece. Forty-three years ago we sailed this same route, sleeping on the upper deck. Now, in old age, we can afford a cabin. As night falls we dine on rabbit cooked in white wine, gazing at the gathering darkness over a calm sea.

Six hundred years ago it was Venice that controlled the seaways of the Mediterranean. Her fleets were based at the (Croatian) island of Hvar in summer and further south at Corfu in winter. Pirates were ruthlessly crushed, free trade made safe. Three thousand years earlier, the Minoan fleets had performed the same role.

Marcella and I were sailing in the wake of history.

Once Minoan control of the seas collapsed, the pirates that King Minos had suppressed would have had free rein. The Adriatic is peppered with hundreds of small islands, perfect for camouflage and shelter. There are many more such in the Aegean.

The Minoans' extraordinary trade network did not immediately waste into nothing. For two hundred years or so, from around 1400 to 1200 BC, it seems that Mycenae took over the controlling role of the seas. The great city-state also assumed power over Crete. We don't know for certain whether this was the action of an ally helpfully stepping in to fill a power vacuum, or whether this was a hostile takeover by an aggressive force. When Mycenae's influence eventually waned, the era of safe seas ended – and so did the glories of an age.

Quite suddenly, between 1225 and 1175 BC, the Bronze Age ended in the eastern Mediterranean. So did the voyages to northern Europe and the Americas. The Keweenaw and Isle Royale mines on and around Lake Superior stopped production at least as early as 1200 BC. English tin mining stopped at the same time, as did work at the Great Orme copper mine. Bronze Age settlements in La Mancha, southeast Spain, were all abandoned too.

Many reasons have been advanced for the sudden collapse of the

311

Bronze Age – a crisis in civilisation that some have put down to comets, climate change, earthquakes, sunspots, or plagues. A great disaster had befallen the sophisticated world of the eastern Mediterranean. Some scholars call it simply 'the Catastrophe'.

Most scholars now agree that the Catastrophe was caused by a mysterious new military force. They were a people who left few traces behind them, save fifty years'-worth of widespread destruction. Their ferocious armies fought with new-fangled weapons such as javelins and wore defensive armour such as greaves and corselets. Their small, round shields suggest that they may have evolved radical new battle techniques, using infantry soldiers to great effect. The Egyptians called them 'the Sea Peoples': to this day no one knows who they were, or where they came from.

Between 1225 and 1175 BC the raiders overran the great civilisations of Crete, Mycenae, Anatolia and Upper Mesopotamia. Many of the cities and fortified palaces along the eastern coast of the Mediterranean, from proud Mycenae through Troy to the ancient Anatolian kingdoms of Kode and Hatti, were sacked. The Sea Peoples swept through the Amorite city-state of Emar and the city of Ugarit – both were in what is today known as Syria – and may even have reached as far inland as Hazor, north of the Sea of Galilee. As Robert Drews writes:

> The catastrophe peaked in the 1180s BC and ended about 1179 BC, during the reign of Ramesses III in Egypt, virtually the last of the great Pharaohs. The regimes in the region had been stable, palace-centred, wealthy and relatively peaceful. What followed, at least in Greece, was a Dark Age.[3]

Two hundred and fifty years after the Minoan civilisation on Crete had collapsed, the Hittite and Mycenaean empires fell. All in all, forty-four cities were lost to the Sea Peoples – until finally Ramesses III managed to defeat the marauders. Lower Mesopotamia and Egypt escaped the wholesale destruction. Yet both were fatally weakened, and a two-decade famine in Egypt all but destroyed that remarkable empire.

The explosion on Thera was the first mortal wound to the Bronze Age cultures of the eastern Mediterranean. Then the Sea Peoples came along and delivered the *coup de grâce*. The very thought depressed me. What would have happened to the world had its first great sea power, the ancient Mediterranean's brightest jewel, not been destroyed?

40

A RETURN TO CRETE

I had to keep my appointment with Greek national television. The interview itself passed off without incident. Following me in the studio discussion, although I didn't know it, was a charming and unassuming man from Crete. I have relied on his inspired research more than once: his name cropped up when discussing Minoan mathematics (chapter 32). Dr Minas Tsikritsis was on the programme to talk about his ground-breaking research into Linear A, one of the world's greatest linguistic conundrums.

The next day, Marcella checked our emails. 'You've got a new message. From a Dr Minas Tsikritsis.' Marcella and I were still treating our stay in Athens as a bit of a vacation, but holidays were soon to be off the agenda. I looked at the message, first curiously, then in shock.

Dr Tsikritsis had been studying my old friend, the Phaestos Disc. Not only that, but he felt that we would have a lot to talk about in terms of Minoan astronomy. Apologising for his use of English, the professor said he wanted to talk to me about his specially written computer programme. It had helped him to decipher some key aspects of Linear A – would I like to know more?

Dr Tsikritsis was excited. But not as excited as me. I read on. His new translation of Linear A, he said, allowed him to identify Minoan text and inscriptions wherever they could be found. He had identified inscriptions in Linear A written on ancient stone markers found by explorers in hundreds of different locations, which proved that the Minoans had visited India, the Baltic, northern Europe and Greenland.

Many of the ancient Minoan writings he'd decrypted tallied with the archaeologists' current view, that the entire Aegean had been under Minoan sway. The empire was, in effect, a confederacy of twenty-two cities. But, he said, that was not all: the Linear A evidence had convinced him that the Minoans had founded further colonies, in (here I copy his email direct):

1. Sicily
2. Syria, Palestine
3. The Bosphorus
4. Bavaria and Baltic Sea. [They travel for obtaining amber.]
5. Greenland for obtaining pewter [tin and lead]
6. Nordisland
7. India (a colony called 'Asteroysia')
8. Arabian Gulf. [There are findings of writing in caves in a Minoan colony in Paghaia Island.]

'I have evidence (photos, bibliographic references in Greek literature) for the above findings.'

His research matched my own findings – despite being arrived at through an entirely different process. Giddily, I did a quick calculation. With nine locations involved, the chance of this being a coincidence was factorial 9,360,000 to one.

||||||||||||||||||

Lovely though Athens was, this lead was more important. Marcella and I hurried to get back to Crete. This time, we were headed for the very centre of the island, atop a precipitous hill at Skalani, outside the lovely restored village of Archanes.

Dr Tsikritsis, his wife Chryssoula and his son Dimitris greeted us with the kind, warm hospitality that Cretans are famed for. He is a thoughtful man with strong features and even stronger opinions.

The family took us into the garden and showed us their organic olive trees, their wood oven and the tomatoes growing underneath the vines; an organic way of keeping the pests away. Tsikritsis gave me a bottle of his lemon-infused home-pressed olive oil, made to a traditional recipe that his father, also an ancient history enthusiast, had rediscovered and handed down to him.

'You are the only one to count the oars,' he said to me, rather unexpectedly, referring to the Thera frescoes. 'This is twenty-eight oars each side, a big, big ship . . .'.

Then we entered a light, airy drawing room, built on two levels. In one corner was Dr Tsikritsis' study, a small, book-lined cubby hole with a telescope and a traditional Cretan wooden trestle stool. We hunkered down for a long talk.

As he began to explain his methods – with Chryssoula and Dimitris occasionally translating – it became clear to me that this was Dr Tsikritsis' life's work. He initially learned ancient Greek from his father, an expert in ancient scripts. Later, he developed his own specialist skills with degrees in mathematics and physics. He also has a master's degree in the methodology of religion and a doctorate in content analysis from the Aristotle University of Thessaloniki.

Few linguistic experts have a similarly broad skill base. For twenty years Dr Tsikritsis had devoted every moment of his spare time to understanding Minoan culture and deciphering Linear A.

Tsikritsis explained that to help him break the hieroglyphic code behind Linear A, he'd used the technique of consonantal comparison. It was crucial that he was already familiar with ancient Greek, Cypro-Minoan and the Mycenaean script Linear B, as well as with Cretan hieroglyphs. However, it was his more modern skills – in computing and mathematics – that had made the crucial difference. The breakthroughs started to happen when he tried statistical cryptographic techniques. He used many different Minoan texts as the basis for the work. Unfortunately for scholars, to translate a language with absolute statistical certainty you need at least fifty-six symbols. The Phaestos Disc has only forty-eight. He has been busily finding other tablets and artefacts to help him go further with the translation and it's this breadth of knowledge that seems to have been key. He told me what had inspired him.

'I think my first inspiration was when looking at a spiral design on a ring. The Minoans used spiral designs all the time, just as on the Phaestos Disc. This ring, I suddenly realised, could be read backwards, as well as forwards.

'... Another breakthrough was realising that there were fifteen symbols that were identical to Linear B.

'... Then I realised that a symbol's meaning could be changed by the word you put it next to.'

This was where the contextual analysis came in.

This is all complex stuff, but as Dr Tsikritsis showed me chart after chart of comparisons I saw it all unfold as a rational system: a beautiful, flowing language. It was simply astounding, the amount of evidence: again and again, on tablets and discs several millennia old, Dr Tsikritsis' systematic solution to the ancient mystery of Linear A seemed rational, consistent and clear.

His translations, time and again, involve that most magical substance: bronze. The Minoans accorded the alloy a special significance; almost a reverence. The translations show the Minoan society's huge prosperity and document the vast amounts of grain, pottery, olive oil and other goods that they shipped across the world. Dr Tsikritsis has even unearthed documents that show that this extraordinary society distributed food and goods to each according to their need. He also showed me the photographs of the ancient inscriptions he had mentioned in his email, which he would identify as being written in Minoan Linear A. They are found from Norway to the Arabian Gulf.

One of his most astounding discoveries is about the Minoans' in-depth understanding of mathematics, which helped them develop their knowledge of the stars.

'In mathematics it's always thought that the Babylonians and the Egyptians were far more advanced than the Minoans,' he said. 'But in 1965, Mario Pope found something unique – a proper fraction. It was written on a wall in Hagia Triada.'

Hagia Triada, just 2.5 miles (4 kilometres) west of Phaestos, was

317

a town with a royal villa at its centre. The inscription, which reads 1:1½: 2¼: 3⅜, shows each number progressing by one and a half times the previous one. The calculation may have been drawn casually upon the wall for working out interest payments. What's striking, said Dr Tsikritsis, is that we know that the Egyptians also studied mathematical progression. They, on the other hand, only used integers. This formula was mathematically far more sophisticated.

Once he first began to suspect that the Minoans' grasp of mathematics was as inventive as that of the Babylonians, Dr Tsikritsis made it his business to discover other formulae that the Minoans had left behind. He discovered that they could count; in tens of thousands if they needed to. They could add, divide and subtract. What was interesting was their need for large numbers: the large amounts of goods and grain they were trading demanded that they developed this skill.

Showing me many diagrams, he convinced me that the Minoan use of geometry was unrivalled. For instance, to construct their signature spiral designs, they had to understand the use of tangents and cosines. It is Archimedes who is famed for defining the spiral in *On Spirals*; yet Archimedes' account didn't emerge until around 225 BC.

One of Dr Tsikritsis' more electrifying ideas could be really highly controversial. He is convinced that almost every single Minoan ceremonial object or building conforms to the 'golden mean' of φ, or 'Phi'. One of the most talked about, disputed and revered aspects of practical mathematics used in the arts and architecture, Phi is also known as 'The Golden Section,' or 'The Golden Ratio'.

This is a most significant claim. You can express Phi, the golden ratio of divine proportion, through this equation:

$$\varphi = \frac{1+\sqrt{5}}{2} \approx 1.6180339887\ldots$$

Dr Tsikritsis has found this specific proportion of 1.61 in literally hundreds of Minoan objects and buildings he has measured and he does not think this can possibly be a coincidence. Today the Greeks usually attribute the discovery of Phi to Pythagoras, who lived c. 570–495 BC.

One ancient Minoan object in particular illustrates his point about Phi and the art of proportion, on two levels. It is an exquisite stone vase, found at the lesser-known palace of Zakros, that has what appear to be mysterious fire scorch marks on it. The Heraklion Museum dates it to 1500–1450 BC, although Professor Tsikritsis believes it may be older.

It is a libation vase, also known as a *rhyton*, which was used for ceremonial drinking. On it, you can see a design – a shrine or a temple, shown in a mountain landscape. Now brown with age and smoke, this precious thing was originally much prized. It is decorated with gold leaf. Both the proportions of the vase itself and the design inscribed on it conform to 'the golden ratio'. Draw a rectangle over the vase as a whole or the image of the shrine and then measure it: you will find that the proportions conform to Phi, says Dr Tsikritsis. In other words, both the form of the vase itself and the imagery upon it are composed using a mathematical ratio that we have always attributed to the ancient Greeks – and not to the Minoans. These are the very proportions that Iktinos and Kallikrates later used to build that greatest of world temples, the Parthenon, creating an unrivalled sense of harmony and serenity. 'This,' Dr Tsikritsis said, warming to his theme, 'is all about beauty.'

All of his studies show that the Minoans believed that Phi's beauty and harmony was sanctified. A vase constructed according to the Golden Mean would, they believed, be holy. Its very perfection would purify the water: a bit like the idea of Feng Shui today.

But it was when it came to describing the Minoans' love of the stars that these new revelations really came alive for me. Here I felt I knew these fascinating people. Dr Tsikritsis' theory is that for the Minoans the constellations were not merely stars. They felt they were gods, who lived and moved in the sky. Not only that, but, much like the Chinese believed until very recently, the ancient Minoans were convinced that their ancestors had joined those gods in the skies. They had become celestial bodies.

One of the absolute masterpieces of Minoan gold work, the Isopata ring, illustrates Dr Tsikritsis' ideas perfectly. The entire ring is only 2 centimetres (three-quarters of an inch) across and the skill it must have taken to cut it is extraordinary. It was found in a tomb at Isopata, near Knossos. (See second colour plate section.)

Four women seem to be enjoying an ecstatic ritual dance; their heads, though, are not human. They have the nodding heads of wheat or corn. In the background you can see the symbols of an eye and a snake. A smaller figure drifts downwards into the picture, as if she is from far away: she may be a goddess descending from the heavens. Dr Tsikritsis' theory is that the snake, which pops up time and again from object to object, is a Minoan symbol for the constellation of the Corona Borealis. In English, we call it the Blaze Star, but it is also known as the 'Northern Crown'. The crown, he believes, was given to King Minos' daughter Ariadne at her wedding ... the Corona *is* Ariadne, forever guiding her people out of the maze.

This ring, Dr Tsikritsis believes, is a type of sacred calendar. It shows a way of counting down towards the rainy season, using the position of the stars ... and the symbolic know-how of Ariadne. The stars didn't just guide the Minoans and inform them about the changing seasons – the Minoans thought that their ancestors were now their guiding stars: celestial bodies.

||||||||||||||||||

Dr Tsikritsis and I agreed that this complex and detailed subject was definitely meat and drink for another book. In the meantime, we all needed lunch. We'd walked through the village, reached the stone-built restaurant and ordered our food, but still we couldn't stop swapping notes. There was so much to talk about.

'What about the Phaestos Disc?' I asked.

'I haven't translated it all,' Dr Tsikritsis was keen to stress. 'I think that at least one side is a ... Τραγούδι.' I must have looked blank. He turned to Chryssoula. They had a quick discussion about the translation.

'A *tragoudi*,' said Chryssoula, leaving me none the wiser.

'. . . A sailor's song,' said Dimitris.

'. . . A sea-shanty,' I murmured.

I could scarcely believe it. Sitting in this warm and cloistered room, with the age-old aroma of slow-roasting lamb drifting into our nostrils, all of us seemed suddenly closer to the ancient world than to the modern one. I remembered the happy scenes of the frescoes, those sailors arriving back in Thera, the people thronging to the shore to greet them. The Phaestos Disc, a fire-hardened clay roundel found in the charred remains of a ruined palace, was what had started me out on my quest. Why had the mysterious object struck me quite so strongly? It seemed so appropriate, somehow. The disc that had fascinated me so much records a departing sailor's sea-shanty.

41

THE LEGACY OF HOPE

After this adventure Marcella and I returned to Athens with a lot more energy. Before meeting Dr Minas Tsikritsis, I had pretty much decided that most of the Minoans' fantastic cultural legacy had been entirely lost. The idea had filled me with gloom. Now I could see that was simply not true. The Minoans may have suffered terribly, but their work, their invention and even their sense of fairness had lived on.

In the fading sun we wandered at the foot of the Acropolis, admiring the play of light and shade along the Parthenon's soaring columns. The temple, designed to meet the ultimate standard of perfection, the Golden Section, points proudly towards the Bay of Salamis. Here Themistocles' fleet destroyed the invading Persians' mighty navy. The Parthenon is still to me the most beautiful building in the world: now I understand why.

> In this island there existed a confederation of kings of great and marvellous power, who held sway over the island, and over many other islands also.[4]

Plato's words echoed in my mind. The Minoans had achieved exactly this. Like ancient Crete with its mysterious Linear A, Plato's Atlantis was a literate state; we know this because he describes the god Poseidon giving out rules, which the first prince 'inscribed on a pillar of orichalcum'. What was 'orichalcum'? It was a copper alloy. Plato describes such a substance lining the walls that entered the city of Atlantis, which gradually became more and more lavish as you approached the main temple.

322

... And they covered with brass, as though with a plaster, all the circumference of the wall which surrounded the outermost circle; and all that of the inner one they covered with tin; and that which encompassing the acropolis itself with orichalcum, which sparkled like fire ... [5]

and a little later:

... All the exterior of the temple they covered with silver, save only the pinnacles and these they covered with gold. As to the exterior, they made the roof all of ivory, variegated with gold and silver and orichalcum.[6]

The Minoans were master smiths in metal and, of course, they were fabulously wealthy: it was certainly conceivable that they could line their city walls with decorative panels of bronze, copper, silver and gold. I realised now that everywhere that I had been, Plato's majestic concept of Atlantis had dogged my every footstep.

As I'd realised in chapter 3, Plato's text suggests that the ancient metropolis and the Royal City were separate entities. This bears a strong resemblance to the relationship between Crete and Thera. The main city, he said, lay on a circular island about 12 miles (19 kilometres) wide. The Royal City, meanwhile, lay on a rectangular-shaped island. So Plato's Atlantis was certainly two islands and possibly more. There are plenty of islands to choose from within the *Pax Minoica*. Plato claimed that the kings of his fabled Atlantis had 1,200 ships; as I've explored in chapters 6 and 19, Crete had certainly had ships – in their many hundreds. Plato believed that Atlantis had suffered an environmental crisis and that the soil had become depleted. This is exactly what I'd found out had applied to the whole region of the eastern Mediterranean. Not only that, but he'd said that the people of Atlantis had been brave enough to breach the Pillars of Hercules. All of these things the Minoans had done, and more.

As Plato says, in those far-off days the ocean was navigable; since there was in front of the strait which I've heard you say your countrymen call 'the pillars of Heracles'. This island was bigger than both Libya and Asia combined; and travellers in those days used it to cross to the other islands, from where they had access to the whole mainland on the other side which surrounds that genuine sea.[7]

The sea that we have here, lying within the mouth just mentioned, is evidently a basin with a narrow entrance; what lies beyond is a real ocean, and the land surrounding it may rightly be called, in the fullest and truest sense, a continent.[8]

This, with thanks to a new translation by Rodney Castleden, can only be America, across the Atlantic. Plato writes about Poseidon:

Poseidon ... named all his sons. To the eldest, the king, he gave the name from which the names of the whole island and of the ocean are derived – that is, the ocean was called the Atlantic, because the name of the first king was Atlas.[9]

Most crucially, Poseidon and Cleito were the parents of five sets of twin brothers and they divided the island equally between them. Those brothers and their descendants had founded not an island, but an entire empire. I could see it now. What I was confronting was not a 'lost island', but the Lost Empire of Atlantis.

Clearly the great classical tradition hadn't all begun here, in ancient Athens. Iktinos and Kallikrates' great temple was built on a great legacy. The golden era of classical Greece had evolved from a heroic tradition of enterprise and adventure. It was the fortunate heir to a much, much older civilisation. With new eyes I could now trace a clear evolution from the purity and grace I'd seen in Minoan architecture – a delicacy of form that came about due to the Minoans' love of spiritual and mathematical perfection – to the eloquent classical ideal of the Golden Number. From there on, the genius of Greek architecture had flourished. It went on through revival after revival, affecting everything from Renaissance Rome to 18th-century Washington. The Minoans' remarkable influence did not simply stop dead in its tracks.

There were also the 'inventions' that we have always attributed to the glory that was classical Greece: coinage; a system of standard weights; music, architecture and art; theatre; even the very idea of spectacle. As Arthur Evans had pointed out, the long-robed Cretan priests of Ayia Triadá were playing the seven-stringed lyre a full ten centuries before it was supposed to have been invented on the island of Lesbos.

Perhaps the greatest legacy is the idea of art for art's sake – and the pursuit of knowledge for its own sake. The Minoans gave the world exquisite painting, ceramics and jewellery and an appreciation of the finer things in life. Their building technology was superb, their ideals were glittering. They did have rulers, but they believed in share and share alike: out of this generous impulse, revolutionary ideals such as democracy would eventually take shape.

This legacy also applied to war. When the Greeks won the crucial battle of Salamis against the invading Persians they had behind them the inspiration given them by a long-standing tradition of shipbuilding technology: it was a baton that had been handed them by the Minoans.

ATHENIAN TRIREMES

The Athenian ships deployed at Salamis were called triremes. They were on average about 5.5 metres wide and 39.5 metres long (18 feet by 130 feet), approximately the same size as the Minoan ships before 1450 BC. Like the Minoan ships they were dual-purpose vessels, with a large square sail on a horizontal yard when in trading configuration and with the mast stepped and powered by oars when in military mode.

The Athenians had modified the Minoan ships in such a way that two banks of oarsmen, one on top of the other, were used when fighting. These newer ships carried 150 men rather than the Minoan ships' 120, so they could be rowed faster than the Minoan ships, to reach a speed of 10 knots. Their principal weapon was a ram in the bows, to pierce the enemy's hull. However, they were inferior to the Minoan ships when they were underway, with a higher centre of gravity that made them much more likely to capsize in a gale in the open sea.

Just as the Athenian ships were developments of the Minoan ones, so was Athenian weaponry and armour. The Athenians' helmets and shields were made of bronze, as was their body armour – one can see the similarities in the bronze Minoan armour that has been found in Crete itself and in Mycenaean graves.

At first sight the idea of militarism fits badly with the Minoans' reputation as a carefree society which did not need the protection of soldiers and fleets – after all, Crete's palaces were not guarded. Yet recent research by Stuart Manning has shown that although Crete itself was not protected from invasion, having no defensive walls to speak of, the wider empire was. The further away from Crete, the greater the level of protection. At the height of Minoan power and influence in the Aegean, there were no fortifications on the 'Minoanised' islands closest to Crete – that is Kythera, Thera and Rhodes. However the more distant sites, such as Ayia Irini on Keos and Kolonna on Aegina, were fortified. Mycenae's great defensive walls are explained by the fact that it was on the mainland, and less easily defended.

The Minoan lead in art, science and astronomy was inherited by a Greek civilisation that went on to produce ageless works of art and literature; the Greeks invented theatre, devised calendars, became skilled engineers. Cherished ideals such as citizenship and democracy and disciplines such as philosophy and science followed.

Most astonishing of all is that the Minoans achieved all of this 2,000 years before the birth of Christ, 1,500 years before Buddha or Confucius and 2,500 years before Muhammad. Beauty had been this people's watchword. They had shown the world that a peaceful existence was a profitable one. They had rid the oceans of pirates and then with luck, daring and great maritime skill they had voyaged on adventures beyond imagination. The Minoans hadn't just been the bringers of bronze: they breathed the Bronze Age into life.

To me, the story of the Minoans – and as I now realised, that of the people of Atlantis – is truly one of wonder. But it is not one of fantasy. This was no underwater daydream. Yes, this was a society lost to history. But it was not a lost race of miraculous beings with fantastical powers. It was a real place of real achievement, where lived a people whose brilliance and resourcefulness resounds through the centuries. Atlantis was not one place, but an empire of many places – an empire that reached out across the world, bringing a magical new technology with it.

This is a tale that tells us one thing: that the history of this world is far more fascinating, complex and indeed more beautiful than we could ever imagine. Most important of all – what do you think?

Gavin Menzies
London
St Swithun's Day 2010

Notes to Book VI

1. *Science*, 1998, vol. 280, p. 520
2. Pubmed Central Table 1, *American Journal of Human Genetics*, 2003; November 73(5) 1178–1190 as Table 1
3. Robert Drews, *The End of the Bronze Age*, Princeton University Press, 1995.
4. Plato, *Timaeus*, 25a, trans. Robin Waterfield, Oxford World Classics, 2008
5. Plato, *Critias*, 116b, trans. Robin Waterfield, Oxford World Classics, 2008
6. Plato, *Critias*, 116d, op. cit.
7. Plato, *Timaeus*, 24e, op. cit.
8. Plato, *Timaeaus*, 25a, trans. Rodney Castleden in *Atlantis Destroyed*
9. Plato, *Critias*

TIMELINE

B.C. 300,000
◇ Indo Europeans settle in central Anatolia.

B.C. 100,000–B.C. 5000
◇ Emigraton of these people to Greece and Crete, via Rhodes.

B.C. 4500
◇ First copper smelted in Crete.
◇ Almendres stone megalith observatory started (Portugal).

3200
◇ Minoans from Crete arrive in South East (Mediterranean).
◇ Spain found mining colonies (Millaren culture).

3000
◇ Millaren culture peaks c.2600 B.C.
◇ Minoan seals show ships with masts and sails.

2900
◇ Minoan seals and Egyptian scarabs of that date found in Crete.
◇ Tinto copper mine starts production SW Spain (Ortiz).

2800
◇ Minoan trading contracts with Syrian – Palestine coasts, Byblos, Ugarit, Mari flourish.

2650
◇ Saqqua Pyramid completed.
◇ Mari producing exquisite jewellery.

2570
◇ Khufu Pyramid completed.
◇ Huge demand for copper and tin.

2500
◇ Great Orme Copper Mine (U.K.) starts production.
◇ Copper axes found in U.K.
◇ Stonehenge Phase II (Sarsens) started.
◇ Avebury man.
◇ Malta invaded by sea peoples.
◇ Megalith observatories started at Villa Nova de San Pedro.
◇ Fortress built in estuary of Tagus (Portugal).

2450
◇ Indian port of Lothal in operation – visited by Harappan Traders (Rao) and Minoans.
◇ Stele showing Sumerian soldiers with copper armour, copper helmets and copper weapons.

2340
◇ Sargon I Emperor of Akkad – huge demand for bronze.
◇ Minoans in Britain for tin (Waddell and Rawlinson) Sargon attacks Crete? (3 times – Sargon autobiography).

c.2280–1930
◇ Stonehenge phase III completed.

2200
◇ Bronze axes appear in Britain (Needham).

2100
◇ Egyptian scarabs common in Crete.

2000
◇ (1950) 'Palace' trade between Crete and western group of Islands – Thera/Melos, Kea. Protopalatial Cretan pottery at Akrotiri (Thera); Phylakopi (Melos);

Ayiarini (Kea) Cretan palaces are prime movers in long distance trade.

◇ Large quantities of Minoan pottery at Fayun Egypt, Kamares pottery at Byblos, Ugarit, Beirut, Qatna and Hazor. Laurion silver exported via Crete.

2030
◇ Ferriby ship (planks) built in Britain.

2040–1640
◇ Red Sea Nile Canal built.

◇ Cretan textiles to Egypt in substantial quantities (Buck). Portraits of Cretans in Egypt bringing gifts. (Buck).

◇ No evidence of direct trade between Levant and Egypt nor Cyclades and Egypt/Levant – Trade in Cretan ships (Buck).

2000
◇ Bronze age hoards found in estuary of Rio Minho (Portugal).

◇ Flat copper axes in use in Ireland.

1900
◇ Tod treasure found below temple near Luxor, contains Mesopotamian materials and silver cups from Crete, labelled with Amenemhet I (1922–1878) cartouche.

◇ Goods from Crete appear in Mari. King of Mari sends Cretan gifts to Hammurabi of Babylon. 'After the foundation of the Palaces, Crete became an international player as never before . . . a major presence on eastern Mediterranean stage'. (Fitton).

◇ 'Protopalatial period represented first great flowering of Minoan culture' (Fitton).

2400–1800
◇ Yemeni bronze hoard.

1800
◇ Trade between Crete and Keos, Delos, Thera, Naxos, Aegina, Kythera, Paros and Amorgos (Buck/Scholes). Minoan settlement in Aegina (Buck). No evidence of direct trade between Middle Helladic Greece and Egypt (Buck) – Goods carried in Cretan ships.

1783
◇ Tell el Dab'a founded.

◇ Minoan decorated palace. Minoan ships use harbour.

1785
◇ Indian cotton appears in American middens (Sorenson).

1700
◇ In MM III (1700–1600) Minoans engage in large construction projects to repair earthquake damages.

◇ 'In the period of the second palaces [1700–1400] the island of Crete was home to a remarkable civilisation. Characterised by flourishing palaces, urbanisation on a scale not seen elsewhere . . . era widely seen as apogee of Minoan civilisation' (Fitton).

1600
◇ Volos ship.

◇ Dover Bronze Age Boat.

1500
◇ c.1492–1458 Hatshepsut expeditions to Punt (Somalia).

1450
◇ Thera explodes. End of Minoan Civilisation.

1400
◇ Rekmires Tomb (Thebes) shows American corn (Thompson).

◇ Indian temples show American plants (Gupta).

EPILOGUE
PLATO AND ATLANTIS, THE LOST PARADISE

Listen then, Socrates, to a tale which, though passing strange, is yet wholly true, as Solon ... once upon a time declared.

This is Critias, a lone voice introducing a tale about a lost paradise, a magical Garden of Eden which was struck down by the awesome force of nature. This beautiful island was the cradle of civilisation, but was destroyed by the gods because of the arrogance, the hubris, of its people.

PLATO'S TALE OF 'ATLANTIS'

Long ago there existed an island, populated by a noble and powerful race. This beautiful place was the domain of Poseidon, god of the sea, who had fallen in love with a mortal woman, Cleito. He created a magnificent palace for her in the centre of the island. The people of this land possessed great wealth thanks to the abundant natural resources of the island, which was also a centre for trade and commerce. The rulers held sway not just over their own people but over the Mediterranean, Europe and North Africa.

For generations the people of the island(s) led a noble and unselfish life. They prospered from their skill in using copper and precious metals. But slowly, corrupted by avarice and greed, they changed. They decided to use their powerful navy to invade Greece and Egypt. Zeus noticed their immorality. He sent a huge wave. This drowned Atlantis, which vanished forever in a sea of mud. Greece was saved.

333

This is a brief summary of the tale related by Plato around 360 BC, in his dialogues *Timaeus* and *Critias*. These two accounts are the only known descriptions of Atlantis and have promoted controversy and debate for over 2,000 years. Many believe the stories are morality tales and fables, works of Plato's wonderful imagination. Others think that Plato may have been describing a lost civilisation, one that really existed, that he called 'Atlantis'.

FINDING THE TRUTH

It is extraordinary to think it, but the story of the Minoans is so incredibly ancient that even the ancient Greeks had forgotten it. History got lost in the mists of time. The tale was finally retold by Plato, but it is only because of this one sole author, and two texts, one of which is unfinished, that we know anything about ancient 'Atlantis' at all. So why, then, would we think it could possibly be true?

Here I have to acknowledge my debt to A.G. Galanopoulos, whose book *Atlantis: the Truth Behind the Legend*, was written with Edward Bacon in 1969. Together they mounted the first serious challenge to the orthodox academic view of the time – that Atlantis was total invention. It was Galanopoulos who first told the world the truth about the sheer scale of the 'Theran event', as the vast volcanic eruption is known. He was also the first to speculate that the tsunami that then hit Crete would have been of huge, destructive force.

It was also Galanopoulos who pointed out, quite rightly, the sheer number of times that Plato insisted that, although he was no historian, his account was based on truth. In Plato's two dialogues it is not just Critias who insists that the story is true: Socrates ends Critias' tale by saying:

> And the fact that it is not invented fable but a genuine history is all-important.

Plato makes the point that this is not 'a story', but historical fact not once, but four times. As Galanopoulos points out, Plato isn't creating a fictional world, the details of which were in his control. He actually seems worried about the inconsistencies in his account. For instance, he questions whether or not a trench as deep as he states it is could even be built. If this was indeed fiction, then why would he worry?

It seems fitting that these major breakthroughs should have been made by the top seismologist of his day. The climax of the story of Atlantis is also the story of one of the biggest geophysical events the world has ever seen. And with irreproachable scientific logic, Galanopoulos also worked out the solution to another of the great mysteries behind the Atlantis 'myth'.

Plato's account throws a few rotten eggs our way. He says that the date Atlantis was eaten up and buried under the sea was 9,000 years before the information was passed on by an Egyptian priest. Plato also greatly exaggerated the size of Crete, doubling its actual size. He gives the dimensions of the plain of the Royal City as 3,000 by 2,000 stades. Both figures have confused the picture. Scholars have triumphantly held them up to demolish the arguments in favour of Minoan Crete being Atlantis. It was Galanopoulos who pointed out the obvious.

'The solution of this riddle,' he said, 'is as simple as the mistake which created it.'

It was simply an error in the maths. Plato's Atlantis (Crete) is given as 3,000 stades, twice the length of Crete. Either Plato, or more likely the Egyptian priests who passed this information on, simply mis-translated the numbers.

As Bacon and Professor Galanopoulos pointed out, the parallels between Crete, Santorini/Thera and Atlantis are unavoidable. Minoan Crete was densely populated, as was Plato's Atlantis. Atlantis was divided into settlements each with a separate leader, but all subject to the Royal City. On Minoan Crete the king appears to have been the overall leader, with (let's call them) nobles governing other centres across the island in the king's name. The bull is crucial to

Minoan life and art; in the *Critias* (119c-120d) we find that this is the case in Atlantis, too:

> In the sacred precincts of Poseidon there were bulls at large; and the ten princes being alone by themselves, after praying to the God that they might capture a victim well-pleasing unto him, hunted after the bulls with staves and nooses, but no weapons of iron.

Plato is known to have visited Crete in person. What is not certain is whether he himself made the connection between 'Atlantis' and Crete. Here I have put together a commentary on some of the things Plato says, and how it is possible to interpret them, once you know something of Crete, Santorini, and their eventful pasts.

PLATO'S DESCRIPTION OF MINOAN CIVILISATION

Plato writes that the civilisation of Atlantis employed highly organised methods of agriculture. To cite *Critias*:

> ... It produced and brought to perfection all those sweet-scented stuffs which the earth produces now, whether made of roots or herbs or trees or of liquid gums derived from flowers or fruits ...

GM: Here Plato is referring to Crete's perfume industry in the Bronze Age, based on olive oil with terebinth resin as a fixative and perfumes of fruit and flowers (see chapters 8 and 10). Plato continues his description:

> ... The cultivated fruit also [vines] and the dry [corn] which serves us for our meals – the various species of which are comprehended under the name of 'vegetables' – and all the produce of trees which contains liquid and solid food and unguents and the fruit of the orchard tree so hard to store, which is grown for the sake of amusement and pleasure, and all the after-dinner fruits which we serve up as welcome remedies for the sufferer from repletion – all these that hallowed island [of Atlantis] as it lay beneath the sun produced in marvellous beauty and endless abundance ... [1]

GM: The 'hallowed island' of Crete provides everything Plato describes. Moreover Plato writes that the island is rectangular and that the island has heavy rainfall in winter, both true of Crete. Plato's island has mountains and plains in the same position as Crete's.

Plato states in *Critias* that the civilisation of Atlantis was a place of conscious amenity, leisure and public service:

> ... The springs they made use of, one kind being of cold, another of warm water were of abundant volume, and each kind was wonderfully well adapted for use because of its natural taste and these they surrounded with buildings and with plantations of trees such as suited the waters; and moreover they set reservoirs round about some under the open sky; and others under cover to supply hot baths in the winter; they put separate baths for the king, and for the private citizens, besides other women ...

GM: Phaestos and other Cretan palaces had all of these amenities (as described in chapter 1). By contrast, other great civilisations of the time in Egypt, the Levant and Mesopotamia had the amenities but were not islands.

Plato describes Atlantis as a literate state.

> ... The relations between her ten kings were governed by the precepts of Poseidon as handed down to them by the law and the records *inscribed* [my italics] by the first prince on a pillar of orichalcum which was placed within the temple of Poseidon in the centre of the island ...

GM: The Minoans had the Linear A and later the Linear B scripts and a numbering system. No other island at that time had writing. Plato says Atlantis was a metalworking state based on copper. Orichalcum, described above, is a copper alloy. Two further passages in the *Critias*:

> ... And they covered with brass, as though with a plaster, all the circumference of the wall which surrounded the outermost circle;

337

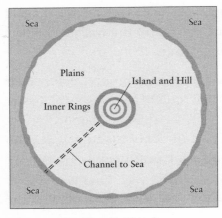

Diagram 1 – Plato's island.

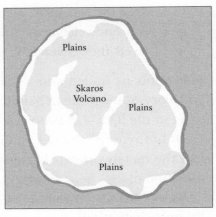

Diagram 4 – Santorini before first eruption c. 15,000 BC.

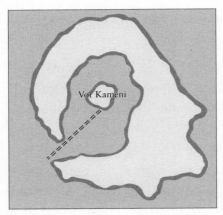

Diagram 5 – 'Minoan' island before 1450 BC eruption showing canal.

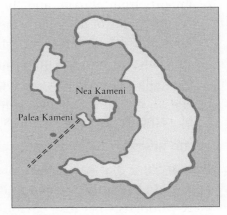

Diagram 6 – Island today – after 1450 BC eruption.

and all that of the inner one they covered with tin; and that which encompassing the acropolis itself with orichalcum which sparkled like fire ... [2]

and a little later:

... All the exterior of the temple they covered with silver, save only the pinnacles and these they covered with gold. As to the exterior, they made the roof all of ivory in appearance variegated with gold and silver and orichalcum and all the rest of the walls and pillars and flowers they covered with orichalcum ...

GM: Minoans traded and worked copper, tin, bronze, gold, silver and ivory. Some Minoan buildings had roofs of translucent alabaster to let in the light – as Plato describes it, 'ivory in appearance'.

Only Crete fits the description and the only island people who had the metalworking skills in the period described by Plato were the Minoans.

Plato expands on the metal-making and trading capacity of the Atlantis civilisation:

... For because of their headship they had a large supply of imports from abroad, and the island itself furnished most of the requirements of daily life – metals to begin with, both of the hard kind and the fusible kind which is now known only by name [orichalcum] but was more than a name then, there being mines of it in many places of the island. It brought forth also in abundance all the timbers that a forest provides for the labours of carpenters and of animals it produced a sufficiency, both of tame and wild [elephants] ... [3]

Plato's claim that Atlanteans 'produced a sufficiency, both of tame and wild elephants' seemed to demolish my claim that Atlanteans were Minoans – because obviously, there are no tame elephants to be found on the Mediterranean islands which were part of the Minoan trading empire.

However, I found to my amazement that pygmy elephants were found on Cyprus, Rhodes, the Dodecanese islands, the Cyclades islands, and on Crete, Malta, Sicily and Sardinia in the late Bronze Age (Masseti; Johnson.) their bones have been dated to 2900 BC– 1700 BC. Elephants could not swim to Cyprus. They must have been taken by ship and thus must have been tame.

THE VOLCANIC ERUPTIONS.

> Looking towards the sea, but in the centre of the whole island, there was a plain which is said to have been the fairest of all plains and very fertile.

GM: This is the plain on Thera, shown in Diagram 4, before the first major eruption (Diagram 5). When (Plato says 9,000 BC) the island was egg-shaped with a central plain, and almost the same size as Plato describes. The plain was rich in phosphates and nitrates from previous volcanic eruptions and hence very fertile:

> Near the plain again, and also in the centre of the island at a distance of about 50 stadia [10,000 yards; 9,000 metres] there was a mountain not very high on any side. In this mountain there dwelt one of the earth-born primeval men of that country whose name was Evenor, and he had a wife named Leucippe, and they had an only daughter who was called Cleito.

GM: This mountain was Skaros volcano, shown on Diagram 4, which was approximately in the centre of the island and 9,000 metres from the east coast. It was not very high compared to the plain – less than 200 metres (220 yards).

> The maiden [Cleito] had already reached womanhood, when her father and mother died; Poseidon fell in love with her and had intercourse with her, and breaking the ground enclosed the hill in which she dwelt all around, making alternate zones of sea and land larger and smaller, encircling one another ... so that no man could get to the island for ships and voyages were not as yet ...

GM: Poseidon 'breaking the ground' to seal off the central island, thereby enclosing 'the hill' was in reality the first major volcanic explosion, which would have been passed down in folk memory and would have turned Thera from the island shaped as in Diagram 4 to that shown in Diagram 5. Skaros volcano (4) has become Vor-Kameni island (5). 'For ships and voyages were not as yet.' This signifies that this major explosion was before 6000 BC – when Cretans had ships (they arrived in Crete in 7000 BC).

> He himself, being a god, found no difficulty in making special arrangements for the centre island, bringing up two springs of water from beneath the earth, one of warm water and the other of cold . . .

GM: These are the hot and cold springs in which tourists visiting the central islands of Nea Kameni and Palae Kameni bathe today (Diagram 6). So Plato's description accords with the appearance of Thera both before the central lagoon was flooded and then again, after that point. Plato describes this eruption:

> But at a later time [viz. after Poseidon had surrounded the central island of Nea Kameni with water] there occurred portentous earthquakes and floods and one grievous day, night befell them . . .

GM: The night is the darkness caused by the explosion of Thera's volcano – the debris would have blotted out the sun, causing crop failures.

> . . . when the whole body of your warriors was swallowed up by the earth and the island of Atlantis was swallowed up by the sea and vanished; wherefore also the ocean at that spot has now become impassable being blocked up by the shoal mud which the island created as it settled down . . .

GM: Plato is here describing the last catastrophic eruption, which changed Thera from what is shown in Diagram 5 to that shown in 6 – more huge chunks of the island have been blown away. A large part of the town now buried beneath modern-day Akrotiri would have gone, as would have some of the settlements on the western part of the main island. Doubtless the shallower parts of the central caldera became a shoal of mud. The sea would have been covered with volcanic tephra, making it appear as mud.

For beginning at the sea, they bored a channel right through the outermost circle which was three plethora in breadth, one hundred feet [30 metres] in depth and 50 stades in length, and thus they made the entrance to it from the sea like that to a harbour by opening up a mouth large enough for the greater ships to sail through.[4]

GM: The route of this channel is shown on Diagrams 5 and 6 from the sea south of Aspro Island, northeast to the central island. Today there is a passage of 30 metres (100 feet) or more in depth and over 6,400 metres (7,000 yards) in length from the sea to Nea Kameni. Plato is probably using some poetic licence; this channel was created by the first major volcanic eruption (compare Diagrams 4 and 5 which let the sea into central Thera) rather than by man – just as the circle of water surrounding the central island was the result of a volcanic eruption, rather than being manmade as Plato claims.

The docks were full of Triremes and naval stores, and all things were quite ready for use.

GM: The busy docks are shown in the Thera fresco as are the triremes and their stores, not least cattle being driven to be loaded on to the ships.

The entire area was densely crowded with habitations; and the canal and the largest of the harbours were full of vessels and merchants coming from all parts who from their numbers, kept up a multitudinous sound of human voices and din and clatter of all sorts, night and day.

GM: Merchants of different nationalities (from their clothes and the colour of their skins) are shown in the frescoes – Libyans, Africans, Minoans, and passengers in the ships with their white gowns.

All of this [dockyard] including the zones and the bridge, they surrounded by a stone wall on every side, placing towers and gates on the bridges where the sea passed in.

GM: The towers and bridges and the surrounding stone wall encircling the dockyard are clearly shown on the Minoan fresco.

> The stone which was used in the work they quarried from underneath the central island, and from underneath the zones, on the outer as well as the inner side. One kind was white, another black and a third red, and as they quarried, they at the same time hollowed out double docks, having roofs carved out of the native rock. Some of these buildings were simple, but in others they put together different stones, varying the colour to please the eye, and to be a natural source of delight.

GM: The white, black and red stones which Plato described appear in the frescoes and are still seen on the cliff faces of Thera today. The coloured stones are also shown in the buildings on the frescoes, as is the subterranean double dock with the roof hollowed out of native rock. This was carved out of the cliff at Red Beach. Just as subterranean docks (for fishing boats) are carved on Santorini today and subterranean houses and restaurants are still being used today.

MYTH, MAGIC AND FINDING AMERICA

Visiting Mycenae on mainland Greece made a big impression on me, not least because it was clear that Heinrich Schliemann had followed Homer to the letter in finding both Troy and Mycenae. Homer had been extraordinarily accurate. This fitted with my own experience, firstly with *1421* and then with *1434*, when it became apparent that the legends of indigenous peoples concerning their ancestors were almost always based on fact. This was especially true in the Americas, where the Indian peoples living on the thousands of miles of Pacific coast that stretch from the Arctic down to South America all maintained that their ancestors came by sea. The same story was later repeated on the North Atlantic coast.

Applying that principle to the history of the Mediterranean, it gradually seemed to me that Plato could have been telling the truth.

I also thought that Greek or Roman historians must have recorded histories of the great Minoan trading empire.

In 1954, at the Naval Training College, Dartmouth, we had been taught Greek and Roman history. So I was in a position to investigate whether Herodotus, Homer or Plato had in fact described Minoan voyages to the Americas. I quickly discovered that authors much more learned than I considered that Homer's *Odyssey* did indeed describe a European Bronze Age fleet circumnavigating the world. I studied some of these histories, notably those of the American ancient history expert Henriette Mertz and several French historians. The problem was that their accounts, which could well be true, were not specific enough – the descriptions could be of America, but they could equally be of the Mediterranean. So reluctantly I discarded them. Then, Marcella found *Atlantis: the Truth Behind the Legend*, by A.G. Galanopoulos and Edward Bacon, the landmark book which opened my eyes.

Over the past forty years, since Professor Galanopoulos and Edward Bacon's book was published, there has been an avalanche of new evidence about the Minoans and their fabulous civilisation. Galanopoulos and Bacon did not have an analysis of the Uluburun wreck and its cargo to go by nor, most important, knowledge of the copper ingots in its hold and their chemical analysis. Nor did they know of the millions of pounds of high-quality copper which disappeared from the mines of Lake Superior in the 3rd millennium BC, apparently into thin air. And they did not have the opportunity to compare the hull of the Uluburun wreck with the Thera frescoes, so as to be in a position to appreciate the magnificent seagoing qualities of Minoan ships. The results of the excavations of Iberian rivers, notably the Bronze Age hoards and Bronze Age ports, were not available to them. The full extent of the Minoan empire, notably the base at Tell el Dab'a in Egypt, was not known to them. As to Stonehenge, the discoveries of Minoan artefacts and skeletons of people who had originally lived in the Mediterranean is very recent. The Minoan pottery in north Germany has only just come to light.

Galanopoulos and Bacon did not know of recent discoveries of Minoan artefacts in copper mines across the world. Neither had they the benefit of the monumental works since published by the Emeritus Professors Sorenson and Johannessen, in which they described enormous levels of transcontinental trade in the Bronze Age. Thanks to new evidence provided by a great many people far more knowledgeable than I, it has been possible to build on Galanopoulos and Bacon's ideas to advance an explanation of Plato's Atlantis which is at once simple and all-embracing.

With the benefits of the enormous amount of recent research we can critically examine Plato's descriptions that concern America:

> ... For the ocean that was at that time navigable; for in front of the mouth which you Greeks call, as you say, 'the Pillars of Heracles' [Straits of Gibraltar] there lay an island which was larger than Libya and Asia together; and it was possible for the travellers of that time to cross from it to the other islands and from the islands to the whole of the continent over against them which encompasses the veritable ocean ... [5]

Here we have Plato describing the Atlantic and America; and stating that the Atlantic is navigable via islands (Canaries and Cape Verde outward bound; Hebrides and Orkneys inward bound).

Plato describes the Minoans' elegant civilisation and says that their empire stretched from across the Atlantic to Europe and embraced the Mediterranean. America lay to the west of the Atlantic '... encompass[ing] the veritable ocean ...', which was navigable in those days.

The huge island in the western Atlantic 'encompassing the ocean' can only refer to America; the fleet returning from America across the Atlantic to attack Athens refers to Minoan ships returning from their voyages with Lake Superior copper.

Such has been the interest in the Atlantis story that a huge amount of investigation and research has been devoted to Thera by professors and experts in all sorts of disciplines – volcanologists, archaeologists, oceanographers, art historians, geographers, meteorologists. It is all fascinating stuff. A selected bibliography of their research is on our website.

THE CONCLUSION THAT'S HARD TO AVOID

The simplest explanation for all these similarities is that Plato was indeed describing the Minoan civilisation. However Plato's story is a conflation of three realities – first, that the Atlantis metropolis was really Santorini; secondly that the island in the Atlantic as big as Libya and Egypt was in fact America; thirdly that Atlantis' manufacturing base and bread basket was Crete. Atlantis was not a single place, but an empire, now lost. Today a visitor taking a colour photograph of the frescoes with him or her can board a boat and sail past Red Beach and in doing so is viewing Plato's Atlantis almost as it was 4,000 years ago.

Truth is indeed stranger than fiction.

Notes to Epilogue

1. Plato, *Critias* 115b
2. Ibid. 116d
3. Ibid. 115e
4. Ibid. 115d
5. Plato, *Timaeus* 25A
6. Masseti and Johnson DL, JSTOR Journal of Biography, vol 7 (1980) p383–398
7. Ibid.

Full details of diagrams on page 338 are contained on ourwebsite. This includes acknowledgements to the German vulcanologists whose plans I have copied.

SELECT BIBLIOGRAPHY

(Full bibliography on website)

Book I: Discovery
The Minoan Civilisation

Alexiou, Stylianos, *Minoan Civilization*, Heraklion, Spyros Alexiou, 1973

Aristotle, *Politics*, 'The olive harvest', 1259a, Cambridge University Press, 1988

Boardman, J., Kenyon, K.M., Moynahan, E.J. and Evans, J.D., 'The Olive in the Mediterranean: Its Culture and Use (and Discussion)', in *Philosophical Transactions of the Royal Society of London, Series B, Biological Sciences*, vol. 275, no. 936, 'The Early History of Agriculture' (27 July 1976), pp. 187–196

Castleden, R., *Minoans: Life in Bronze Age Crete*, London, Routledge, 1992

Crete–Egypt, 3 Millennia of Cultural Interactions, Heraklion Archaeological Museum, 1999

Graves, Robert, *The Greek Myths*, QPD, 1991

Greece, Insight Guides, 1987 and 2008, APA Publications Pte Ltd

Greek Islands, The, Dorling Kindersley, Eye Witness Travel Guide, 1998 and 2007

Hadzi-Vallianou, Despina, *Phaistos*, Athens, Archaeological Receipts Fund, 1989

'Heraklion Archaeological Museum, temporary exhibition', Ministry of Culture, 2007

Knapp, A. Bernard, 'Thalassocracies in Bronze Age Eastern Mediterranean Trade: Making and Breaking a Myth', in *World Archaeology* (Ancient Trade: New Perspectives), Taylor & Francis, vol. 24, no. 3, pp. 332–47, 1993

Michailidou, A., *Knossos – A Complete Guide to the Palace of Minos*, Athens, Ekdotike Athenon S.A., 2006

Museum of Ancient Agora of Athens, Athens, Hellenic Ministry of Culture and Tourism, 1990

National Archaeological Museum – Athens, Athens, Archaeological Receipts Fund, 2009

Sakellarakis, J.A., *Heraklion Museum: Illustrated Guide*, Athens, Ekdotike Athenon S.A., 2006

Tsikritsis, M. (see separate section at the end of the bibliography)

University of Toronto, 'Kommos Excavation Crete'

www.fineart.utoronto.ca/kommos/kommosIntroduction.html

Wave that Destroyed Atlantis, The, BBC,

www.news.bbc.co.uk/1/hi/6568053.stm

Maps and Charts

Plans in the Southern Kikladhes, Admiralty Chart 1541

Santorini, 1–35,000, Road Editions

Southern Cyclades, 1–190,000, Imray, 2008

Book II: Exploration
Voyages to the Near East

Aruz, Joan, excerpts by, in *Beyond Babylon: Art, Trade and Diplomacy in the Second Millennium* BC, The Metropolitan Museum of Art, New York. Copyright © 2008. Reprinted by permission.

Bard, K., '2006–7 Excavations at Mersa/Wadi Gawasis', paper presented at the 58th annual meeting of the American Research Center in Egypt

Bass, G.F., 'A Bronze Age Shipwreck at Uluburun', in *American Journal of Archaeology*, 1986

Bass, G.F., 'Cape Gelidonya and Bronze Age Maritime Trade', in H.A. Hoffner (ed.), *Orient and Occident*, Alter Orient und Altes Testament, Neukirchener Verlag, 1973

Bass, G.F., 'Cargo From The Age of Bronze: Cape Gelidonya Turkey', in *Beneath the Seven Seas*, London, Thames & Hudson, 2005

Bass, G.F., 'The Construction of a Seagoing Vessel of the late Bronze Age', in H.F. Tzalas (ed.), *Proceedings of the 1st International Symposium on Ship Construction in Antiquity*, Piraeus, 1989

Bass, G.F., 'Evidence of Trade from Bronze Age Shipwrecks', in N.H. Gale (ed.), *Bronze Age Trade in the Mediterranean*, Göteborg, Paul Åströms Förlag, 1991

Bietak, M., 'Avaris and Piramesse: archaeological exploration in the eastern Nile Delta', in *Proceedings of the British Academy 65*, 1979

Bietak, M., 'Some News about Trade and Trade Warfare in Egypt and the Ancient Near East', in *Marhaba*, 3/83

Bietak, M. and Marinatos, N., 'Avaris and the Minoan World', in A. Karetsou (ed.), *Krete-Aigyptos: Politismikoi desmoi trion chilietion*, Athens, 2000

Casson, L., 'Bronze Age Ships. The Evidence of The Theran Wall Paintings', *IJNA*, 4, 1975

Crete–Egypt: Three Thousand Years of Cultural Links, exhibition catalogue, Heraklion and Cairo: Hellenic Ministry of Culture, 2000

Dienekes' Anthropology Blog, 'Minoans in Germany'
http://dienekes.blogspot.com/2008/08/minoans-in-germany.html

Doumas, C. (ed.), *The Wall Paintings of Thera*, Athens, The Thera Foundation, 1992

Duerr, H.P., interviewed in *GEO* magazine
http://www.geo.de/GEO/kultur/geschichte/4669.html

Duerr, H.P., *Rungholt: Die Suche nach einer versunkenen Stadt*, Frankfurt, Insel Verlag, 2005

Gale, N.H., 'Bronze Age Trade in the Mediterranean', in *Studies in Mediterranean Archaeology*, vol. 90, 1991

Gale, N.H., Stos-Gale, Zofia and Maliotis, G., 'Copper Ox-hide Ingots and the Mediterranean Metals Trade', Congress of Cyprus Studies, 2000

Gere, Cathy, *The Tomb of Agamemnon*, London, Profile, 2006

Gimbutas, M., 'East Baltic Amber in the Fourth and Third Millennia', in *Journal of Baltic Studies*, 16, 1985

Gray, D., 'Seewesen', Archeologia Homerica – Lieferungsausgahe, Göttingen, 1974

Grimaldi, D., 'Pushing Back Amber Production', in *Science*, vol. 326, no. 5949, p. 51

Haldane, C., 'Direct Evidence for Organic Cargoes in the Late Bronze Age', in *World Archaeology*, Taylor & Francis, vol. 24, 1993

Hauptmann, Andreas, Maddin, Robert and Prange, Michael, 'On the structure and composition of copper and tin ingots excavated from the shipwreck of Uluburun', in *Bulletin of the American Schools of Oriental Research*, no. 328 (November 2002), pp. 1–30

Hood, Sinclair, *The Minoans; The Story of Bronze Age Crete*, New York, Praeger, 1971

'Mersa/Wadi Gawasis: A Pharaonic Harbor on the Red Sea', exhibition at the Egyptian Museum, Cairo, 2011

Muhly, J.D., 'Sources of Tin and the Beginnings of Bronze Metallurgy', in *American Journal of Archaeology*, vol. 89

Muhly, J.D., Maddin, R., and Stech, T., 'Cyprus, Crete and Sardinia Copper Oxhide Ingots and the Bronze Age Metals Trade', in *Report of the Department of Antiquities*, Cyprus, 1988

Nomikos, P.M., *Sea Voyages: The Fleet Fresco from Thera, and the Punt Reliefs from Egypt*, Piraeus, The Thera Foundation, 2000

Pulak, C., 'Discovering a Royal Ship From The Age of King Tut: Uluburun Turkey', in *Beneath the Seven Seas*, London, Thames & Hudson, 2005

Pulak, C., 'Evidence for Long-distance Trade from the Late Bronze Age Shipwreck at Uluburun', Johannes Gutenberg University, Mainz, 2001

Pulak, C., 'A Hull Construction of the Late Bronze Age Shipwreck at Uluburun', in *INA Quarterly*, 2000

Pulak, C., 'Paired Mortise and Tenon Joints of Bronze Age Seagoing Hulls', in *Boats Ships and Shipyards: Proceedings of the Ninth International Symposium on Ship Construction in Antiquity*, Oxford, Oxbow, 2003

Raban, A., 'The Thera Ships: Another Interpretation', in *American Journal of Archaeology*, vol. 88, 1984

Severin, Tim, *The Jason Voyage*, London, Hutchinson, 1985

Tod, J.M., 'Baltic Amber in the Ancient Near East', in *Journal of Baltic Studies*, 16, 1985

Vergano, Dan, 'In Egyptian desert, a surprising nautical find', *USA Today* www.usatoday.com/tech/science/columnist/vergano/2006–03–05-egyptian-ship – x.htm

Wiener, M.H., 'The Isles of Crete? The Minoan Thalassocracy revisited', in D.A. Hardy, C.G. Doumas, J.A. Sakellarakis and P.M. Warren (eds), *Thera and the Aegean World III*, vol. 1, *Archaeology*, pp. 128–161, London, The Thera Foundation, 1990

Yener, Aslihan K., 'An Early Bronze Age Tin Production Site at Göltepe, Turkey', Oriental Institute, University of Chicago, 1994

India

Abram, D., *The Rough Guide to Kerala*, Rough Guides, London, 2007

Chaudhuri, S.B., *Trade and Civilisation in the Indian Ocean*, Cambridge, Cambridge University Press, 1985

Cherian, P.J. and colleagues, 'Chronology of Pattanam: a multi-cultural port site on the Malabar coast', in *Current Science*, 2009

Frampton, P., *Hidden Kerala: The Travel Guide*, London, MHi Publications, 1997

Frater, A., *Chasing the Monsoon*, London, Penguin, 1991

Hall, R., *Empires of the Monsoon*, London, Harper Collins, 1999

Hindu, The (India's national newspaper), 10 June 2009, 'Prehistoric Cemetery discovered in Kerala'

Kerala Council for Historical Research (KCHR) www.keralahistory.ac.in/

Lothal Guide – http://www.indianetzone.com/6/lothal.htm

Rao, S.R., *Lothal and the Indus Civilisation*, Bombay, Asia Publishing House, 1973

Sreedhara Menon, A., *Kerala History and its Makers*, Madhaven Nayer Foundation, Madras, 1989

Book III: Journeys West

Agricola, G., *De Re Metallica*, New York, Dover, 1950

Baird, W. Sheppard, 'The Early Minoan Colonization of Spain' www.minoanatlantis.com/Minoan–Spain.php

Burl, A., *The Stone Circles of the British Isles*, New Haven, Yale UP, 1976

Cadogan, Gerald, *Palaces of Minoan Crete*, London, Barrie & Jenkins, 1976

Clark, Peter (ed.), *The Dover Bronze Age Boat*, © English Heritage, 2004

Comendador Rey, B., 'Early Bronze Age Technology at Land's End, North Western Iberia', presented at the International Symposium on Science and Technology in Homeric Epics, Olympia, Greece, 2006

Comendador Rey, B., 'The Leiro Hoard (Galicia, Spain): the lonely find?', in *Gold und kult der Bronzezeit*, Germanisches National Museum, Nuremburg, 2003

Comendador Rey, B. and Mèndez, J.L., 'A patina over time: ancient metals conservation in North-Western Iberia', presented at the symposium 'Looking Forward For The Past: Science and Heritage', Tate Modern, London, 2006

Cowen, Richard, University of California, Davis
http://mygeologypage.ucdavis.edu/cowen/~gel115/115ch4.html

Cuncliffe, B., *Facing the Ocean: The Atlantic and Its Peoples 8000 BC–AD 1500*, Oxford, Oxford University Press, 2001

Drews, R., *The End of the Bronze Age: Changes in Warfare and the Catastrophe ca. 1200 BC*, Princeton, Princeton University Press, 1995

Goya, Francisco, *La Tauromaquia (1815)*, Prado, Madrid

Henderson, J.C., *The Atlantic Iron Age*, London, Routledge, 2007

Herodotus 3, 115, 'Tin in Europe's extreme west', trans. G. Rawlinson The History of Herodorus, Kessinger Publishing (September 2010)

Hunt Ortiz, M., *Prehistoric Mining and Metallurgy in South West Iberian Peninsula*, Oxford, Archaeopress, 2003

James, D., 'Prehistoric Copper Mining on the Great Ormes Head', *Early Mining in British Isles*, PlasTan-y-Bwich occasional paper No 1, p1–4

Maddin, R., Wheeler, T.S. and Muhly, J.D., 'Tin in the Ancient Near East: Old Questions and New Finds', in *Expedition*, 19.2, 1977

Martin, C., Fernandez-Miranda, M., Fernandez-Posse, D. and Gilman, A., 'The Bronze Age of La Mancha', Universidad Complutense de Madrid, 1993

Muhly, J.D., 'Copper and Tin: the Distribution of Mineral Resources and the Nature of the Metals Trade in the Bronze Age', in *Transactions of the Connecticut Academy of Arts and Sciences*, vol. 43, article 4, 1973

Needham, S., 'The Extent of Foreign Influence on Early Bronze Age axe development in Southern Britain', in Ryan (ed.), *The origins of metallurgy in Atlantic Europe*, Dublin Stationery Office, 1979

Needham, S. et al., *Networks of Contact, Exchange and Meaning: the Beginning of the Channel Bronze Age*, London, British Museum, 2006

O'Brien, W., *Ross Island and the origins of the Irish-British Metallurgy*, publication for 'Ireland in the Bronze Age', Dublin Castle Conference, 1995

Rackham, Oliver, *The Illustrated History of the Countryside*, London, Weidenfeld & Nicolson, 2003

Roberts, E.R.D., *The Great Orme Guide: The Copper Mine, The Prehistoric Period*, 1993

Tylecote, R.F., *The Early History of Metallurgy in Europe*, London, Longman, 1987

Tylecote, R.F., *A History of Metallurgy*, London, The Metals Society, 1976

Tylecote, R.F., *Metallurgy in Archaeology – A Prehistory of Metallurgy in the British Isles*, London, Edward Arnold, 1962

Wertime, T.A. and Muhly, J.D., *Coming of the Age of Iron*, New Haven, Yale UP, 1980

Book IV: Exploring the Heavens
Stonehenge

Atkinson, R.J.C., *Stonehenge*, London, Pelican, 1960

Goskar, Thomas, *British Archaeology*
www.britarch.ac.uk/ba/ba73/feat1.shtml

Hawkins, G., *Beyond Stonehenge*, New York, Harper & Row, 1973

Hawkins, G., *Stonehenge Decoded*, London, Souvenir Press, 1967

Hoyle, F., *On Stonehenge*, San Francisco, Freeman, 1977

Johnson, Anthony, *Solving Stonehenge – The New Key to an Ancient Enigma*, London, Thames & Hudson, 2008

Needham, S. (in course of preparation), *The Archer's Metal Equipment*

Pearson, Parker et al., 'The Age of Stonehenge', in *Antiquity*, vol. 81, 2007

Needham, S., Leese, M.N., Hook, D.R. and Hughes, M.J., 'Developments in the early Bronze Age Metallurgy of southern Britain', in *World Archaeology*, Taylor & Francis, vol. 20, no. 23

Timewatch, BBC, Professors Tim Darvill of the University of Bournemouth and Geoffrey Wainwright, president of the Society of Antiquaries

Book V: The Reaches of Empire
Astronomy and the Calculation of Longitude

Aveni, A., *Stairways to the Stars*, New York, John Wiley, 1997

Brack-Bernsen, Lis, 'Predictions of Phenomena in Babylonian Astronomy', in J.M. Steele & A. Imhausen (eds), *Under One Sky: Astronomy and Mathematics in the Ancient Near East*, Alter Orient und Altes Testament, Muenster, Ugarit-Verlag, 2008

Brack-Bernsen, Lis, 'Some Investigations on the Ephemerides of the Babylonian Moon Texts, System A', in *Centaurus: International Magazine of the History of Science and Medicine*, vol. 24, 1980

Fermor, J. and Steele, J.M., 'The Design of Babylonian Waterclocks', in *International Journal of the History of Mathematics*, vol. 42, issue 3, 2000

Marchant, Jo, *Decoding the Heavens*, Windmill, UK 2009

McKinstry, E. Richard, The Ephemera Society of America, 'So, Just What is Ephemera?' http://www.ephemerasociety.org/news/news-oed.html

Neugebauer, O., *A History of Ancient Mathematical Astronomy*, Berlin, Springer-Verlag, 1975

Neugebauer, O., 'Studies in Ancient Astronomy. VIII. The Water Clock in Babylon', in *Isis*, vol. 37, 1947, reprinted 1983

Oxford English Dictionary (online edition): 'A table showing the predicted (rarely the observed) positions of a heavenly body for every day during a given period.'

Rochberg, F., *The Heavenly Writing*, Cambridge, Cambridge University Press, 2004

Steele, J.M., *A Brief Introduction to Astronomy in the Middle East*, London, SAQI, 2008

Steele, J.M., *Calendars and Years: Astronomy and Time in the Ancient Near East*, Oxford, Oxbow, 2007

Steele, J.M., 'A Commentary on Enuma Anu Enlil 14', in *From the Banks of the Euphrates: Studies in Honor of Alice Louise Slotsky*, Eisenbrauns, Indiana, USA, 2008

Steele, J.M., 'Eclipse Prediction in Mesopotamia', in *Archive For History Of Exact Sciences*, vol. 54, 2000

Steele, J.M., 'Observation, Theory and Practice in Late Babylonian Astronomy: Some Preliminary Observations', in *Astronomy of Ancient Civilizations*, Moscow, Nauka, 2002

Steele, J.M. and Imhausen, A. (eds), *Under One Sky: Astronomy and Mathematics in the Ancient Near East*, Alter Orient und Altes Testament, Muenster, Ugarit-Verlag, 2001

Swerdlow, N.M., 'The Babylonian Theory of the Planets', in *Journal of the American Oriental Society*, vol. 119, 1999. Review by J.M. Steele.

Van der Waerden, B.L., 'Babylonian Astronomy: The Earliest Astronomical Computations', in *Jaarbericht Ex Oriente Lux*, 10, 1948 and *Journal of Near Eastern Studies* 10, 1951

Lunar Eclipses for the 7th Year of Cambyses

(16 July 523 BC and 10 Jan 522 BC)
Steele, J.M., 'Babylonian Predictions of Lunar and Solar Eclipses Times', in *Bulletin of the American Astronomical Society*, vol. 28, 1996
Steele, J.M. and Stephenson, F.R., 'Lunar Eclipse Times Predicted by the Babylonians', in *Journal for the History of Astronomy*, vol. 28, part 2, pp. 119–31

Trans-oceanic Trade

Alfieri, Anastase, 'Les insects de la Tombe de Tutankhamon', in *Bulletin de la Société entomologique d'Egypte*, vol. 24, 1931
Balabanova, S., 'Drugs in Cranial Hair of Pre-Columbian Peruvian Mummies', in *Baessler Archiv NF*, 1992
Balabanova, S., 'First Identification of Drugs in Egyptian Mummies', in *Naturwissenschaften*, 79, 1992
Balabanova S. et al., 'Nicotine and Cotinine in Prehistoric and Recent Bones from Africa and Europe and the Origin of these Alkaloids', in *Homo*, vol. 48, 1997
Carter, G.F., 'Plant Evidence for Early Contacts with America', in *Southwestern Journal of Anthropology*, vol. 6, 1950
Conway, T. and J., *Spirits on Stone – The Agawa Pictographs*, San Luis, Heritage Discoveries, 1990
Coppens, P., 'Copper: A World Trade in 3000 BC?'
http://www.philipcoppens.com/copper.html
Dewdney, S. and Kidd, K.E., *Indian Rock Paintings of The Great Lakes*, University of Toronto Press 1962
Drier, Roy W., 'Prehistoric Mining in the Copper Country', in Drier and Du Temple (eds), *Prehistoric Mining in the Lake Superior Region: A Collection of Reference Articles*, privately published
Drier, Roy W. and Du Temple, O., *Prehistoric Mining in the Lake Superior Region: A Collection of Reference Articles*, privately published

Du Temple, O., 'Prehistory's Greatest Mystery: Copper Mines of Ancient Michigan', in *Ancient American*, vol. 5/35

Fonseca, Olympio da, 'Parasitismo e migrações humanas pré-históricas: contribuições da parasitologia paro o conhecimento das origens do homem americano', Brazil, University of São Paulo, 1970

Griffin, James B. (ed.), *Lake Superior Copper and the Indians – Miscellaneous Studies of Great Lakes Prehistory*, Ann Arbor, University of Michigan, 1961

Gupta, Shakti M., *Plants in Indian Temple Art*, Delhi, B.R. Publishing, 1996

Heine-Geldern, R.V., 'The Problem of Transpacific Influences in Meso America', in *Handbook of Middle American Indians*, vol. 4, Austin, University of Texas Press

Heine-Geldern, R.V., 'Traces of Indian and Southeast Asiatic Hindu-Buddhist Influences in Mesoamerica', *Proceedings of the 35th International Congress of Americanists*, Mexico, 1962. (Large four-masted Indian ships in prehistoric times were perfectly capable of sailing to the Americas. Wheeled animals show a likely link between India and America from the 3rd millennium BC.)

Heyerdahl, J., *Early Man and the Ocean*, London, George Allen & Unwin, 1978

Hoffman, D., 'Missing: Half-a-billion Pounds of Ancient Copper', in *Ancient American*, vol. 5/35

Jeffreys, M.D.W., 'Pre-Columbian Maize in the Old World: an examination of Portuguese sources', in M.L. Arnott, *Gastronomy: the anthropology of food and food habits*, The Hague, Netherlands, Mouton, 1975, pp 23–66

Johannessen, Carl L., 'Distribution of Pre-Columbian Maize and Modern Maize Names', in Shue Tuck Worg, ed., *Person, Place and Thing: Interpretative and Empincal Essays in Cultural Geography*, volume 31 of *Geoscience and Man*, Geoscience Publications, Louisiana State University, Department of Geography and Anthropology, Baton Rouge, 1992

Johannessen, Carl L., 'Maize Diffused to India Before Columbus came to America', in *Across Before Columbus*, NEARA, 1998

Johannessen, Carl L., 'Pre-Columbian American Sunflower Maize Images in Indian Temples', in *NEARA Journal*, vol. 32, 1998

Johannessen, Carl L. and Parker, Ann Z., 'American Crop Plants in Asia prior to European Contact', in *Proceedings of Conference of Latin Americanist Geographers*, 1989

Leon, Fideas E. et al., 'HLA TransPacific Contacts and Retrovirus', in *Human Immunology*, vol. 42, 1995, p. 349

Meggers, Betty J., 'Yes if by land, no if by sea: the double standard in interpreting cultural similarities', in *American Anthropologist*, 78, 1976

Muhly, J.D., 'An Introduction to Minoan Archaeometallurgy', in *Proceedings of International Symposium*, Crete, 2004

Olsen, Edward J., 'Copper Artefact Analysis with the X-ray Spectrometer', in *American Antiquity*, vol. 28, no. 2, 1962

Riley, Caroll L. et al., *Man Across the Sea: Problems of Pre-Columbian Contacts*, Austin, University of Texas Press, 1971, pp. 219–41

Scherz, J.P., 'Ancient Trade Routes in America's Copper Country', in *Ancient American*, vol. 5/35

Silow, R.A., 'The Problem of Trans-Pacific Migration involved in the origin of the cultivated cottons of the New World', in *Proceedings of Seventh Pacific Science Congress*, vol. 5, New Zealand, 1949

Sorenson, John L., 'The Significance of an Apparent Relationship Between the Ancient Near East and Mesoamerica', in Carroll L. Riley et al.

Sorenson, John L. and Johannessen, Carl L., *World Trade and Biological Exchanges Before 1492*, New York, iUniverse, 2009

Sorenson, John L. and Raish, Martin H., *Pre-Columbian Contact with the Americas across the Oceans: an annotated bibliography*, 2 vols, Utah, Research Press, 1996

Thompson, Gunnar, *American Discovery: Our Multicultural Heritage*, Seattle, Sasquatch, 1999

Thompson, Gunnar, *Secret Voyages to the New World*, Seattle, Misty Isles Press, 2006

Winchell, N.H., 'Ancient Copper Mines of Isle Royale', in *Engineering and Mining Journal*, 32, 1881

Wuthenau, A. von, *Unexpected Faces in Ancient America, 1500 BC–AD 1500: THE HISTORICAL TESTIMONY OF PRE-COLUMBIAN ARTISTS*, New York, Outlet, 1975. (The Babylonian god Humbaba shows up in faces in Veracruz, Chiapas, Columbia and Ecuador. This extraordinary work has been carefully ignored by conventional archaeologists.)

Book VI: The Legacy

Brown, M.D. et al., 'MtDNA Haplogroup X: An Ancient Link Between Europe/Western Asia and North America?', in *American Journal of Human Genetics*, vol. 63, 1998

Cook, R.M., *The Greeks Till Alexander*, London, Thames & Hudson, 1961

Evans, A.J., 'Minoan and Mycenaean Element in Hellenic Life', in *Journal of Hellenic Studies*, 32, 1912

Fitton, J.L., *Minoans*, London, British Museum Press, 2002

Finila, American Journal of human genetics, 2003, November 73 (5), pp 1178–1190, Pub. Med table.

See also Sutton Theory and 'Coming into America: Tracing the Genes', PBS 2004, and 'Stone Age Columbus', BBC 2002, and 'Ice Age Columbus', Discovery 2005, and 'Diffusion of Mf DNA Haplogroup X', American Journal of Human Genetics, 2003.

Galanopoulos, A.G. and Bacon, Edward, *Atlantis: the Truth Behind the Legend*, London, Thomas Nelson, 1969

Graham, J.W., 'The Minoan Unit of Length and Minoan Palace Planning', in *American Journal of Archaeology*, 64, 1960

King, R.J. et al., 'Differential Y-chromosome Anatolian influences on the Greek and Cretan Neolithic', in *Annals of Human Genetics*, vol. 72 (2), 2008, pp. 205–14

Lindsay, Jeff, *Enter Haplogroup X*, www.jefflindsay.com/LDSFAQ/DNA.shtml#x

Morell, Virginia, 'Genes May Link Ancient Eura Sians, Native Americans', Science 24 April 1998: Volume 280, no 5363, p. 520

Reidla, Maere et al., 'Origin and Diffusion of MtDNA Haplogroup X', in *American Journal of Human Genetics*, vol. 73, 2003

Schurr, T.G., 'Mitochondrial DNA and the Peopling of the New World', in *American Scientist*, vol. 18, 2000

Shlush, I. et al., 'The Druze: A Population Genetic Refugium of the Near East', in *Plos One 3*, 2009

Taylour, W., *The Mycenaeans*, London, Thames & Hudson, 1964

Torroni, A. et al., 'Mitochondrial DNA "clock" for the Amerinds and its implications for timing their entry into North America', in *Proceedings of the National Academy of Sciences* (USA), 9, 1994

Triantafyllidis, C. of Thessaloniki's Aristotle University talks about DNA and Minoan genetic origins: http://www.ekathimerini.com

Works of Dr Minas Tsikritsis

(Read after *The Lost Empire of Atlantis* was written)

Calendar Almanac of Cretan-Mycenaean Civilisation, Lawyer's Association of Heraklion, December 2005

Cretan Scripts and the Disc of Phaistos, Secondary Education Office of Heraklion, December 2006

'Egyptian Healing (treatment) Spells in the Language of Keftiu', *Patris* newspaper, 19 April 2005, p. 22

'The Mathematics of the Minoans, Fractions and Decimal System, Geometric Regression', *Eleutherotypia* newspaper, 9 December 2006, p.59

'Medicine in the Bronze Age', *Ichor* magazine, vol. 80, September 2007, pp. 65–6

'Minoans, the Rulers of the Mediterranean', *To Vima* newspaper (science section), 12 August 2007, pp. 27–9

'The Origin of Olympic and Ancient Minoan Games', Prefecture of Heraklion, April 2004

Linear A to the Mountain of Giouktas

'The Disc of Phaistos, A Guide for its Decipherment'

'Linear A – Contributing to the Understanding of an Aegean Script', Vikelea Municipal Library, Heraklion, 2001

'Minoans: The First Cartographers in the World', *Eleutherotypia* newspaper, 24 January 2009

'Plato, Crete, Atlantis and the Holy Mountain of Giouktas', Heraklion, 2008

INDEX